NOW SHOON THE ROMANO GILLIE

NOW SHOON
THE ROMANO GILLIE

Traditional Verse in the High and Low
Speech of the Gypsies of Britain

TIM COUGHLAN

UNIVERSITY OF WALES PRESS
CARDIFF
2001

British Library Cataloguing-in-Publication Data.
A catalogue record for this book is available from the British Library.

ISBN 0–7083–1498–8

Typeset at University of Wales Press, Cardiff
Printed in Great Britain by Bookcraft, Midsomer Norton, Avon

Contents

This book is for you, Jo. Thank you for everything.

Foreword

by

SIR ANGUS FRASER

It is some twenty years since I first heard of Tim Coughlan as a man who took a deep interest in every aspect of the language and history of the Gypsies. At that time we were both civil servants working in London, and I made contact with him at his parent Department – Education and Science as it then was. We fell into the agreeable habit of meeting from time to time in a nearby pub to talk about our shared interest. I quickly found that Tim, blind though he was, seemed to know all the books and to carry most of them in his head. On certain topics, the wise course of action was to stay quiet and listen to what he had to say. This was especially so if the conversation turned to Gypsy song, for then he would compare a range of different versions, speculate on their authenticity, draw parallels with, perhaps, an Irish song or two, and analyse the strengths and weaknesses of the various collectors.

When he and his wife eventually decided to move to Ceredigion, it became possible for him to devote time to analysing systematically the traditional verse of Gypsies and other Travellers in the British Isles, alongside more laboured productions of Victorian gypsylorists. He set himself the task of bringing together, from a vast diversity of sources, the song repertoire as it had emerged in print over the past 150 years or so. It has required great tenacity to assemble this treasury of song texts and then assess them within a commodious framework of linguistic, ethnic and socio-historical comparison. The result is a wide-ranging survey of considerable originality that will be of value to a variety of disciplines. And already, Tim Coughlan is at work on a companion piece, a history and analysis of the Canting tongue and its corpus of literary and demotic verse.

Acknowledgements

If I have seen further, it is by standing on the shoulders of giants.
(Sir Isaac Newton, 1675)

In introducing a work of this kind it is customary to begin by thanking all those who have been of assistance in its preparation. This is particularly appropriate in the present case as, without the help so freely given by Daisy Blackaby, Peggy Moger, Bríd Kelly, Mabel Foster and Jo and Betty Coughlan, it would have been quite impossible for me to have even contemplated making a start. Between them, they have read aloud to me almost every item of source material, be it in Romani, English or any other language. On a number of occasions this has also meant spelling out entire texts letter by letter and without omitting a single cedilla or semicolon. Their patience and generosity are all the more remarkable in that, as I soon came to realize, none of them share my obsessive interest in the subject with which they consented to live for so long. I can only hope that any pleasure the reader may take in these pages may go some way towards making good any shortfall in my own inadequately expressed gratitude. At the same time, I should like to make it perfectly clear that I take full responsibility for any errors which may have crept into the printed text.

A special word of thanks is also due to Dennis Binns, HMI Arthur Ivatts and Sir Angus Fraser, both for their encouragement and support generally and for underwriting my request for partial funding of the project by the Leverhulme Trust. In thanking the Trust for their help in this matter I am in no doubt as to the part played in their decision by the letters of support provided by my three referees.

Despite my best endeavours I have been unable to contact all those whose consent I would like to have obtained before making use of their work. I can only apologize for this and assure all concerned that I have been entirely punctilious in my ascription of all the various works cited in this book. Whilst singling out for special mention Peter Kennedy, Mike Yates, John Brune and Thomas Acton, my thanks are also due to all those other collectors and commentators, past and present, without whose patience and dedication the raw material for this book might well have been lost. It would, I fear, be impracticable to list them all here, but I trust that my bibliography, together with the many passing references in the text itself, will stand as adequate testimony to their work and my gratitude to them. If I have contributed anything in the way of original thought, this has only been possible in the light of their shared knowledge. In this connection, I should also like to say a special word of thanks to Christine Mason of the Bodleian Library and Bob Scoales of the Ealing Public Library Service for all their help in tracking down the various works consulted, and to Arthur Ivatts for allowing me the run of his own private collection.

I am only too well aware of the fact that many Travellers are less than happy at the idea of outsiders poring over their language and culture. I am also conscious of a growing unease within myself at subjecting a living culture to the sort of critical scrutiny more appropriate to the consciously contrived productions of art or science. If I have offended any, I am truly sorry. All I can say in my own defence is that my only motive has been an abiding interest in and respect for my subject, and if this book should in any way help to penetrate the fog of prejudice and misunderstanding which has for so long clouded our perception of the Travelling People, then I may perhaps be said to have gone some way towards honouring my debt to those most deserving of my thanks, the Gypsies themselves.

Ferwig, December 1995

The Romani Rai he wels akai
To dik the Romani-Chels,
To shun the lavs that lenghi pens
And chiv 'em adré his lils

(Lias Robinson, 1891)

Introduction

It is true that the words of most old Gypsy songs are not verse in the accepted sense of the word. This is perhaps the reason for their almost total omission from folk song books.

(Brune, 1975)

Although it is now a little over a hundred years since W. F. Prideaux first argued for the systematic collection of those songs and ballads still current among the English Gypsies (*NQ* 7 Ser. (1887), 288), it is only since the Second World War that any serious attempt has been made to answer his call. Even today, however, despite the extensive work undertaken by such contemporary collectors as Yates, Kennedy, MacColl and Seeger, those few anthologies which have so far been published have, for the most part, concentrated on Traveller songs sung in English rather than on songs composed and sung by the Gypsies in their own language. Indeed, whilst Gypsy music elsewhere – such as the Gypsy Jazz of the French and German Sinte and Manouche and the Flamenco of Spain – has, over recent years, won for itself an international audience, the singing tradition of native British Travellers continues to be largely ignored by all but a handful of devout enthusiasts.

When the Gypsies first arrived in Britain, some time during the second half of the fifteenth century, it may safely be assumed that they brought with them a body of orally transmitted song in their own language. By the early years of the nineteenth century, however, this original repertoire had, at least in England, been almost entirely replaced by a mass of new material, either composed by the Gypsies themselves or borrowed from other sources and sung either in English or Romani English. This is apparently true even of those northern Travellers, Boswells and Hernes, among whom the older inflected language seems to have survived far longer than in the south.

In Scotland, too, although Simson tells us that, in his youth, his father often heard the Gypsies singing songs 'in their own language' (Simson

1

1865, 306), it seems clear from elsewhere in the text that what he meant was not the old inflected speech but 'the Gypsy language intermingled with English words'.

Only in Wales, where the old language continued in use into the second half of the twentieth century, have any examples of 'deep' Romani song been recovered in these islands, though the fact that they are associated with tunes drawn from the native British repertoire would seem to suggest that they are of a relatively late date.

Yet, whilst British Gypsy song undoubtedly underwent something of a sea change as the language and culture of the first settlers came under increasing pressure from those of the indigenous population, enough of its former character remains to set it apart from what, for convenience, may be termed 'mainstream song'. In form and outlook alike it is still essentially Romani and, as such, offers an intriguing insight into the habits of mind of a people whose way of life has proved a constant source of fascination for scholars and laymen alike for upwards of five hundred years.

The fact remains, however, that, apart from a few isolated outliers, it was not until the middle years of the nineteenth century that the first genuine examples of English Romani song found their way into print and even then they were to be greatly outnumbered by the largely spurious productions of the *Romané Raiá*, the gentlemen amateurs of Victorian Gypsiography. Even the most serious students of Gypsy language and lore seem not to have grasped the true significance of this aspect of their subject. Smart and Crofton, whose study of the older inflected dialect (Smart and Crofton 1875) remains the most important statement on the subject, include only four sacred verses composed by their principal informant, Sylvester Boswell, whilst Groome, the first *Gaujo* scholar to master and comment upon the importance of Welsh Romani, appears to have believed that the Gypsies of Britain no longer possessed a body of folk song of their own devising. Sampson, it is true, did go some way towards redressing the balance in his 'English Gypsy Songs and Rhymes' of 1891, but it is indicative of the way in which the subject has otherwise been neglected that, even today, with only eighteen sets, it remains the single largest collection of published texts in broken Romani. In his otherwise comprehensive survey of the language of the Gypsies of Wales, however, whilst including a list of upwards of twenty song titles, he gives only a half-dozen sets, of which the longest amounts to no more than four lines.

Yet, despite the apparent indifference of Gypsiographers and folk-song collectors alike, enough material has survived from this early period to justify the conclusion that, whilst English Romani song may have known better days, it was by no means a dead letter as Groome supposed. The purpose of the present work is to offer as complete a picture as possible of the Welsh Romani and Romani English repertoire as it has emerged in print over the past 150 years, and in so doing to seek to identify and explain both its principal characteristics and its underlying mode of thought. Also included, for purposes of comparison, are a handful of texts in Scottish and Irish Travellers' Cant and a number of examples of songs composed by *Gaujos*, non-Gypsies, in both high and low Romani. The inclusion of these latter is justified on the grounds that they serve to illustrate the high regard in which the language was held by even the most outspoken critics of native Gypsy composition and because there is a certain amount of evidence to suggest a degree of interaction between such material and the oral tradition.

Although we are here concerned with Gypsy texts alone – rather than with the airs to which they were set – it must be remembered that they were originally intended to be sung, and for this reason may rightly be described as (folk) songs. The term 'folk song' is a relatively recent coining, being an extension of the earlier 'folk lore', first used by the English antiquarian, J. W. Thoms, in 1846 to describe the traditional beliefs and customs of the unlettered classes. Exactly what is meant by 'folk song' is, however, still subject to debate. Broadly speaking, there are two opposing theories. The first holds that it is nothing more than art music which has been modified and, more often than not, debased as a result of its repeated iteration by successive carriers of an essentially oral tradition. This view may be discounted, however, if for no other reason than that art music, like art itself, is clearly the product of a long and complex process of evolution whose origins lie in those altogether more primitive forms forged in the collective consciousness of emerging man.

Whilst not precluding the possibility that any given example, or its underlying idea, may have commenced life in the mind of a particular individual, the second theory holds that the folk song is, first and foremost, a communal composition invested with the peculiar characteristics of the culture within which it has evolved. This definition, with its emphasis on the link between folk song and the surrounding culture, is altogether more satisfactory, although it does seem to ignore the possibility that other forms, originated under entirely different circumstances, may be absorbed by and become indistinguishable from material generated within the oral tradition.

A more useful definition for present purposes is that adopted by the International Folk Music Council in 1955, even if, as with any compromise, it is unlikely to find favour with purists on both sides of the argument:

> Folk music is music that has been submitted to the process of oral transmission. It is the product of evolution and is dependent on the circumstances of continuity, variation and selection.

... The term can therefore be applied to music that has been evolved from rudimentary beginnings by a community uninfluenced by art music; and it can also be applied to music which has originated with an individual composer and has subsequently been absorbed into the unwritten, living tradition of a community. But the term does not cover a song, dance, or tune that has been taken over ready-made and remains unchanged. It is the fashioning and re-fashioning of the music (or song) by the community that gives it its folk character.

In the course of this book, a number of different terms have been used to describe the form of language employed in those texts forming the core of the collection. In referring to the language spoken by the first Gypsy settlers, prior to their westward migration into Wales, I have opted for the blanket term 'British Romani', differentiating thereafter between the *Puri Chib*, the older inflected speech preserved by the more conservative English families, and its altogether purer analogue, Welsh Romani. When referring to the language in its Anglicized form, a number of essentially inter-changeable and self-explanatory terms have been used, including the *Poggadi Chib*, or broken speech, *Romanés* and *Posh 'n' Posh*, half and half. What is meant by 'the high and low speech of the Gypsies of Britain' is Welsh Romani as compared with the heavily Anglicized *Poggadi Chib*.

Two further terms, however, require a word or two of explanation. In recent years, opinion has been divided as to whether the ethnic speech of contemporary English Travellers ought properly to be regarded as a dialect of Romani or an albeit highly specialized register of English. Using the terms coined by Professor Ian Hancock and Dr Donald Kenrick, the two models are here referred to respectively as 'Angloromani' and 'Romani English'. The term 'Anglo-Romani', as used by such nineteenth-century writers as Groome and Smith, has no significance in this context.

Although, in recent years, the term 'Traveller' has been appropriated by various individuals and groups adopting a nomadic way of life for a variety of reasons, both economic and ideological, it is here used only to refer to Travellers of Gypsy origin or to their traditional socio-economic counter-parts of Scotland and Ireland, commonly known as 'Tinkers'. In referring to the ethnic speech of Scottish and Irish Travellers, a number of different terms have also been used. Although commonly referred to by both groups as 'Cant', among Irish Travellers it is also known as 'Gammon', a term derived by some scholars from old Irish Ogam. In reality, the form of language heard in the Anglo-Scottish border country might more accurately be described as a form of northern English Romani, although here, too, the preferred term among those who use it is Cant. Both Scottish and Irish Cant, which themselves may be further subdivided along broadly regional lines, make use, in varying degrees, of a range of extraneous lexical material, which may also include Romani. The older core-element, itself of uncertain origin, is generally referred to in the literature as *Shelta*, a term no longer in common use among Travellers themselves (see notes accompanying texts 28–9 and 58).

With one or two stated exceptions, the texts included in the body of this work are reproduced in the form in which they first appeared in print, and no attempt has been made to impose a uniform system of orthography. Where possible, however, all those Gypsy words occurring in the texts are referred in the vocabulary to the form in which they appear in Smart and Crofton (1875) and Kenrick and Wilson (1985). Readers should bear in mind, however, that Romani is an essentially oral language with no fixed standards and may, therefore, vary not only between groups but between individual families.

The reader, I hope, will not find repeated references to the vocabulary too much of a chore. For me to have translated every song would, I fear, have added intolerably to the length of the book and, for this reason, I have had to confine myself to those in inflected Romani or which, on a purely subjective reading, seemed likely to pose a particular problem for the reader. In one or two other cases, the author/collector's own translation has also been included where this was thought to shed further light on their understanding of the material under consideration.

I have tried to keep notes to a minimum. Points arising in the songs themselves are marked with an asterisk and are dealt with at the end of the relevant text.

1

The High and Low Speech of the Gypsies of Britain: British Romani and the Poggadi Chib

Our language is the reflection of ourselves.

(Mahatma Gandhi, 1916)

When the Gypsies first arrived in these islands, probably some time during the second half of the fifteenth century, they brought with them their own language, influenced, it is true, by centuries of exposure to a multiplicity of other tongues, but complete in itself and capable of articulating the full range of their experience, intellectual, spiritual, emotional and practical. Today, however, the everyday speech of the Gypsies of England is that of the surrounding population – English – supplemented by a special lexis of between one hundred and a thousand words, predominantly of Romani origin, which may be substituted for their English equivalents as and when the need arises (Acton 1974, 56; Kenrick 1979, 114).

Unlike the old language, Romani in its reduced form has only a limited range of functions, including trade, identification (of self and others), in songs, oaths and terms of endearment, and as a means of private communication in the presence of outsiders. With few exceptions, the words comprising this lexis are acquired, not in infancy, but in early adolescence from other older members of the group (Kenrick 1979, 114–19; 1985, *passim*).

In recent years, opinion has been divided as to how and when this change took place and whether what remains of the Romani tongue in England ought properly to be regarded as a dialect of Romani or as merely a dialect or register of English. In a debate at the National Gypsy Education Council Conference in Oxford (Acton 1971a), Professor Ian Hancock took the view that what he calls 'Angloromani' was formed in fairly rapid order and by a conscious process akin to creolization at the time of the first language contact between the Gypsies and the native British rogues (criminal itinerants) some time during the sixteenth century.

Against this, Dr Donald Kenrick argued that what he prefers to call 'Romani English' is the product of a much longer process of deterioration and that what remains might more accurately be described as a dialect or register of English, analogous to, for example, Jewish English or army slang. This, too, Kenrick suggests, may be regarded as a form of creolization but of a different order from the emergence of a contact language created for a specific purpose by two or more speech communities seeking a common medium of exchange. The opposing arguments are set out in some detail in Acton and Kenrick 1985.

In broad terms, a pidgin may be described as

> a system of communication which has grown up among people who do not share a common language, but who wish to talk to each other, for trading or other reasons . . . They have a limited vocabulary, a reduced grammatical structure, and a much narrower range of functions compared to the languages which gave rise to them. They are the native language of no one but they are nevertheless the main means of communication for millions of people . . .
>
> A pidgin is not a language which has broken down; nor is it the result of baby talk, laziness, corruption, primitive thought processes or mental deficiency. On the contrary, pidgins are demonstrably creative adaptations of natural languages, with a structure and rules of their own . . .
>
> They are evidence of a fundamental process of linguistic change as languages come into contact with each other, producing new varieties, whose structures and uses contract and expand. They provide the clearest evidence of language being created and shaped by society for its own ends as people adapt to new social circumstances . . . (Crystal 1992, 334)

Although some pidgins have proved so useful that they have assumed a more formal long-term role, functioning as auxiliary or even official languages within the communities they serve, they tend, for the most part, to be short-lived, falling into disuse either because the specific purpose for which they were created has ceased to exist or because the two communities have moved apart, or members of one community have learned the native speech of the other. When this happens, rather than simply 'ceasing upon the midnight', they may gradually lose their distinctive features, approximating more and more nearly to one or other of their source languages until they become no more than a social or regional dialect of that language.

Alternatively, in those cases where an increasing number of speakers begin to use a pidgin as their main means of communication and, as a consequence, their children hear it spoken more than any other language, it may, within a generation or two, assume the status of a mother tongue in its own right. In such cases, the result is known as a creole.

7

Once established, however, a creole may, in its turn, be subject to attack by one of those languages which it has displaced but with which it may have continued to coexist. One consequence of this may be the emergence of several varieties of creole at varying degrees of distance from the standard form of the displaced language – the so-called 'post-creole continuum'; another may be an aggressive reaction on the part of speakers anxious to assert the independence or even the superiority of their new vernacular.

It is against this background that Professor Hancock's proposition falls to be considered – that is, that 'there are sufficient references from the 16th and early 17th centuries to a contact language used between Gypsies and non-Gypsies, for it to be possible that Angloromani became distinct from Romanes during that period' (Acton and Kenrick 1985, 97). It is not my intention to quarrel with his proposition that 'in terms of an historical continuum, the core of direct retention for the former may be shown to be Romanes' (ibid., 96); nor do I entirely reject the notion that what he calls Angloromani may have come into existence by a process akin to pidginization. What I hope to demonstrate, however, is that this process was confined to the Romani speech community, and that, as a result of certain changes in the way in which the language is transmitted and used, it may no longer be appropriate to regard it as a creolized dialect of the original inflected tongue.

On p.89 of *Romani Rokkeripen To-Divvus* (1985), Hancock begins by offering the following summary of his position:

> . . . the earliest and *most significant* statements about the language appeared in the mid sixteenth century. The hypothesis presented here is that Angloromani developed as a specifically reduced contact language within the first half-century after the arrival of Gypsies in Britain, between English and Gypsy outlaws . . . Because of the isolated situation of the British Isles, and because Gypsies arrived there during the earlier European diaspora, and have not had contact with any other non-British languages (including other dialects of Romanes, the original inflected, non-reduced language of the Gypsies) since, the contact variety has gradually supplanted the once more widely spoken inflected sourceform. This has happened to the extent that today, only a tiny minority of Gypsies in Britain are acquainted with it. (emphasis added)

He then goes on to say (ibid., 90):

> The first reference to Angloromani as a newly-devised speech, distinct from the above, is found in Harman's Caveat (1566 or 1567):

As far as I can learne or understand by the examination of a number of them, their language – which they terme peddelar's French or canting – began but within these XXX yeeres or lyttle above.

'The argument supported in this discussion', he continues, 'is based upon an interpretation of Harman's statement by John Camden Hotten in his *Slang Dictionary* (1864 edn) at pp.5–12, which introduces the idea that Angloromani developed as a "compromise" language':

Harman, in 1566, wrote a singular, not to say droll book . . . wherein the history and various descriptions of rogues and vagabonds are given, together with their canting tongue. This book, the earliest of its kind, gives the singular fact that within a dozen years after the landing of the Gipsies, companies of English vagrants were formed, places of meeting appointed, districts for plunder and begging operations marked out, and rules agreed to for their common management. In some cases, Gipsies joined the English gangs; in others, English vagrants joined the Gipsies. The fellowship was found convenient and profitable, as both parties were aliens to the laws and customs of the country, living in a great measure in the open air, apart from the lawful public, and often meeting each other on the same by-path, or in some retired valley, but seldom intermarrying, or entirely adopting each other's habits. The common people, too, soon began to consider them as of one family, all rogues, and from Egypt. The secret language spoken by the Gipsies, principally Hindoo, and extremely barbarous to English ears, was found incomprehensible and very difficult to learn. The Gipsies, also, found the same difficulty with the English language. *A rude, rough, and most singular compromise was made* and a mixture of Gipsy, Old English, newly coined words and cribbings from any foreign, and therefore secret, language, mixed and jumbled together, formed what has ever since been known as the Canting Language or Pedlar's French; or, during the past century, St. Giles' Greek. (emphasis added by Hancock)

By what process of deduction or inspiration Hotten arrives at his understanding of Harman's remarks it is quite impossible to say. Even the most superficial reading of the original text is sufficient to show that Harman makes only one reference to the Gypsies, saying nothing of their language or the time of their arrival, and making it quite clear that he was under the impression that they had been forced to abandon the country as a result of punitive legislation:

I hope their [the rogues'] sin is now at the highest; and that as short and as speedy a redress will be for these as hath been of late years for the wretched, wily, wandering vagabonds calling and naming themselves Egyptians, deeply dissembling and long-hiding and covering their deep, deceitful practices, feeding the rude common people, wholly addicted and given to novelties, toys and new inventions; delighting them with the strangeness of the attire of their heads, and practising palmistry to such as would know their fortunes; and, to be short, all thieves and whores, as I may well write, as some have had true experience, a number can well witness, and a great sort hath well felt it. And now, thanks be to God, through wholesome laws, and the due execution thereof, all be dispersed, banished, and the memory of them clean extinguished; That when they be once named hereafter our children will much marvel what kind of people they were. And so, I trust, shall shortly happen of these.

He is equally unequivocal regarding the nature and pedigree of the true subject of his treatise, calling them 'Cursetors' – a term signifying 'runners or rangers about the country, derived from this Latin word *curro*' – and identifying them with those 'lewd loiterers' known in earlier times as '*Faitours, Roberdsmen, Draw-Latches* and *Valiant Beggars*'.

In doing so, he is at particular pains to explain that his principal object is to avoid any confusion on the part of his readers:

> If I should have used such words, or in the same order of writing as this realm used in King Henry the Third or Edward the First's time – oh, what a gross barbarous fellow we have here! . . . But according to my plain order, I have set forth this work, simply and truly with such usual words and terms as is among us well known and frequented.

Against this background, there can be no doubt that Harman intended his remarks to be taken at face value and that had he intended to imply any form of collusion or confusion, linguistic or otherwise, between the Gypsies and native English outlaws, he would have said so. He does not.

As regards the form of language employed by these same 'Cursetors', Harman, although including a brief vocabulary and exemplary dialogue, offers only the following general remarks, none of which can be construed as in any way referring to Romani in either its high or low form. Indeed, on each occasion he specifically states that the language in question is 'Pedlar's French' or 'Canting', adding, significantly, that it was known only to the beggars themselves.

> 1. And as far as I can learn or understand by the examination of a number of them, their language – which they term Pedlar's French or Canting – began but within these XXX years, little above; and that the first inventor thereof was hanged, all save the head; and that is the final end of them all, or else to die of some filthy and horrible disease.

2. Also, I have placed in the end thereof their lewd language, calling the same Pedlar's French or Canting.

3. Here is set before the good reader the lewd, lousy language of these loitering lusks and lazy lorels, wherewith they buy and sell the common people as they pass through the country; which language they term Pedlar's French, *an unknown tongue only but to these bold, beastly, bawdy beggars and vain vagabonds,* being half mingled with English when it is familiarly talked. (emphasis added)

4. By this little ye may wholly and fully understand their untoward talk and pelting speech, mingled without measure. And as they have begun of late to devise some new terms for certain things, so will they in time alter this, and devise as evil or worse. This language now being known and spread, yet one thing more will I add unto, not meaning to English the same, because I learned the same of a shameless doxie. But for the phrase of speech I set it forth only:

> There was a proud patrico and a nosegent. He took his jockam in his famble and a wapping he went. He docked the dell; he prig to prance. He binged awaste into the darkmans. He filched the cove without any filchman.

Hancock's analysis of Harman's 'Caveat' is, he says, based on an earlier interpretation advanced by John Camden Hotten (originally John William), the nineteenth-century author and publisher whose *Dictionary of Modern Slang* first appeared in print in 1859, shortly after his return from the United States. In fact, Hotten's conclusions are somewhat less clear-cut than his earlier remarks might have led one to expect. Although he believed that 'Marsden . . . when he declared . . . that the cant of English thieves and beggars had nothing to do with the language spoken by the despised Gipseys, was in error', he also upbraids Tom Moore for 'magnifying the importance of the alliance', when he suggests in *Tom Crib's Memorial to Congress* of 1819 that 'the Gipsey language, with the exception of such terms as relate to their own peculiar customs, differs but little from the regular Flash or Cant language'. Moore, he says, knew little or nothing of Romani, 'appealing to the glossary of Cant for so-called "Gipsey" words at the end of the *Life of Bamfylde Moore Carew*' – 'hence his confounding Cant with Gipsey speech' (Hotten 1864 edn, 13).

Yet there is no doubt that Hotten's estimate both of the Gypsy content of English slang generally, and of the degree of influence exercised by Romani on old English Cant in particular, was greatly exaggerated (indeed, it is noticeable that of the numerous examples adduced, both by Hotten, and in the wider literature, of actual or supposed borrowings from Romani, no more than four or five may be traced back to contemporary

Tudor or Jacobean sources). Thus Groome (1880, 251), speaking of ' . . . the entire absence of Cant words from Romanes, and the almost entire absence of Romany words from Cant',[1] goes on to say: 'In Hotten's *Slang Dictionary*, many of the words marked "Gypsy" are as little Romanes as they are Iroquois, e.g. *bamboozle, bloke, cheese, gad, lunan, moke, mort, rig, slang* and *snack.*'

'Of terms of indubitably Romani origin', he continues,

> the following is the sum total: – *bosh*, fiddle (*bóshoméngrí*); *cosh* life-preserver (*kosht* stick); *couter* sovereign (*kótor* piece, guinea); *dicking* watching (*dikáva* I see); *dookin* fortune telling (*dúkeráva* I tell fortunes); *drum* road (*drom*); *gorger* swell (*górgio* gentile); *jib* tongue (*chib*); *lob* word (*lav*); *lil* pocket book (*lil* book); *loaver* money (*lóvo*); *munging* whining, begging (*mongáva* I beg or pray); *nark* to 'nose' or suspect (*nok* a nose); *pal* friend (*pal* brother); *parney* rain (*páni* water); *posh* halfpenny (*posh-hórri*); *pukering* talking privately (*púkeráva* I tell); *raclan* married woman (*rákli* girl); *stir* prison (*stáriben*); *vardo* wagon (*várdo*); and *voker* talk (*rókeráva* I speak).

To these, Groome also adds two further examples of rather more doubtful etymology: *dust*, money (Rom. *dósta*, plenty) and *conc*, nose (possibly a back-formation of *knock* = Rom. *nok*). Apart from these, we may also mention *minche*, vagina; *nash*, to flee; and *vonger*, money (properly 'coal'; see notes accompanying text 126). According to Borrow, *belúna*, queen)[2] and *canihen*, jail-fever/plague (*kani naflipen*, stinking sickness) may also be derived from Romani originals, and further examples are to be found scattered throughout the literature, as in the following extract from 'A Budg and Snudg Song' ('A Warning to Housekeepers . . . by one who was in Newgate', 1676):

> But if the cully nap us,
> And the lurries from us take,
> O then they rub us to the whitt
> And it is hardly worth a make.

So, too, in John Harper's 'Frisky Moll's Song' (Thurmond 1724) we find the Romani *chiv*, to cut:

> He broke thro' all rubbs [restraints] in the whitt [Newgate],
> And chiv'd his darbies [fetters] in twain . . .

But perhaps the earliest example of a Gypsy word occurring in a Cant text is to be found in Robert Copland's 'Hye-way to the Spyttel-hous' of *c.*1535 (itself the earliest surviving reference to Pedlars' French), where we find *jere* = turd – arguably a transferred epithet from the Romani *jeer*, rump (Turk. Rom. *ghür*, groin). Cf. Scotto-Romani *jir*, 'to ease nature' (M'Cormick 1906, ix–xxiv). Leland's suggestion that Copland's *peck*, to eat, is also from the Romani *pekker*, to roast, may, however, be discounted (Barrère and Leland 1889–90, x).

Before leaving this aspect of our subject, it is perhaps only fair to say that Hotten was not alone among his contemporaries in believing Romani to have had a far more profound effect on the underworld slang of his day than was actually the case. Thus, the Revd J. W. Horsley, who served as chaplain to HM Prison, Clerkenwell, during the years 1876–86, tells us in his *Jottings from Jail* of 1887 that prison slang

> is yet mainly derived from Romany or Gypsy talk, and thereby contains a large eastern element, in which old Sanskrit roots may readily be traced. Many of these words would be unintelligible to ordinary folk, but some have passed into common speech. For instance, the words *bamboozle*, *daddy*, *pal* (companion or friend), *mull* (to make a *mull* or mess of a thing), *bosh* (from the Persian), are pure Gypsy words, but have found some lodging, if not a home, in our vernacular.

It may be observed, however, that, in a piece entitled 'The Autobiography of a Thief in Thieves' Language', which appeared under Horsley's name in *Macmillan's Magazine* for October 1879, there is only one word of Romani origin: *chiv*, knife.

But, to return to Hotten: whilst his reading of Harman may be grossly in error, he does not actually go so far as to equate the new speech form adopted by the rogues and their supposed new-found allies, the Gypsies, with a newly reduced form of Romani. Indeed, he makes it quite clear that what he had in mind was Thieves' Cant of the conventional kind. Rather, it is Hancock himself who seems to have made this somewhat startling equation.

I do not wish to suggest here that Hancock is under any misapprehension regarding the difference between what he calls Angloromani and Thieves' Cant as they came to be represented in the later literature. This is clearly not the case, although one is forced to ask why he should suppose it to have been necessary for the Gypsies and the native English outlaws to have developed two lingua francas – Angloromani and Cant – for the one purpose. Nor, indeed, as I hope to show at a later stage, do I wish to suggest that at no time in its development would it have been appropriate to refer to Romani English as a compromise language or creole. Rather, the point at issue here is whether or not there is a *prima facie* case, supported by contemporary evidence, for the emergence of broken Romani as a contact language between the English rogues and the Gypsies in the period immediately following their first arrival in these islands. The view advanced here is that there is not and, moreover, that broken Romani has never served as a contact language of any kind but, throughout its history, has only ever been used by the Gypsies themselves.

Hancock next calls in evidence an extract from Harison's 'Description of England' which precedes the 1578 printing of Holinshed's *Chronicles*. Harison, he says (Acton and Kenrick 1985, 90), also noted that the Gypsies and the British outlaws

> have devised a language among themselves which they name Canting but others Pedler's French, a speeche compact thirty years since of English and a great number of od words of their own devising, without all order or reason; and yet such is it as none but themselves are able to understand; the first deviser thereof was hanged by the neck, a just reward no doubt for his desartes . . .

Once again, Hancock's use of this early source material is somewhat misleading, the more so as he opens his reference in mid-sentence. What Harison actually says is:

> Into this nest is another sort to be referred, more sturdie than the rest, which hauing sound and perfect lims, doo yet notwithstanding sometime counterfeit the possession of all sort of diseases. Diuerse times in their apparell also they will be like seruing men or laborers: oftentimes they can plaie the mariners, and séeke for ships which they neuer lost. But in fine, are all théeues and caterpillers in the common-wealth, and by the word of God not permitted to eat sith they doo but licke the sweat from the true laborers browes, & beereue the godly poore of that which is due vnto them, to mainteine their excesse, consuming the charitie of well disposed people bestowed vpon them, after a most wicked & detestable manner.
>
> It is not yet full thréescore yeares since this trade began: but how it hath prospered since that time, it is easie to iudge, for they are now supposed of one sex and another, to amount vnto aboue 10000 persons; as I haue heard reported. Moreouer, *counterfeiting the Egyptian roges they haue deuised a language among themselues, which they name Pedlers French*, a speach compact thirtie yeares since of English, and a great number of od words of their owne deuising, without all order or reason: *and yet such is it as none butt themselues are able to vnderstand.* The first deuiser thereof was hanged by the necke, a iust reward no doubt for his deserts, and a common end to all of that profession. *A gentleman also of late hath taken great paines to search out the secret practises of this ungracious rabble. And among other things he setteth downe and describeth thrée & twentie sorts of them, whose names it*

14

shall not be amisse to remember, wherby ech one may take occasion to read and know as also by his industrie what wicked people they are, and what villainie remaineth in them. (emphasis added)

The first point to be made here is that Harison does not say, as Hancock suggests, that 'the Gypsies and the British outlaws . . . have devised a language among themselves . . . ' What he actually says is that 'counterfeiting the Egyptian rogues', the subjects of his treatise, 'have devised a language among themselves . . . '

That he is not referring to the Gypsies is also apparent both from the text, taken as a whole, and from his obvious indebtedness to, and acknowledgement of, Harman's earlier work on the subject. That Harman was, indeed, the 'gentleman' referred to seems clear when one compares Harison's list of 'The seueral disorders and degrees amongst our idle vagabonds' with the various headings in Harman's *Caveat*, a work predicated upon the assumption that the Gypsies had already been forced to quit the kingdom. Harison, it is true, omits 'counterfeit cranks' and introduces 'mortes' as a separate type, but in every other respect retains both Harman's original categories and order of precedence.

As regards the language devised by Harison's rogues, we may make the following points:

(a) it was devised among the rogues themselves and in imitation of the Gypsies not in association with them;

(b) it was known as 'Canting' or 'Pedlars' French', a well-documented form, owing virtually nothing to Romani;

(c) it was composed of 'English and a great number of odd words of their own devising'. Nowhere does Harison suggest that it included elements borrowed from the Gypsies. If he had read Boorde, as seems likely, he would have known that the Egyptians had their own language and, if he was at all familiar with Harman, as he almost certainly was, he could not have failed to recognize the fact that it was quite different to the Cant. In suggesting that the latter consisted of nothing more than a mixture of English and a number of terms of the rogues' own devising, we may, therefore, assume that he knew exactly what he was saying and intended no hidden extras;

(d) no one but themselves (and, therefore, not the Gypsies) was able to understand it – a contention supported by Dekker some thirty years later: 'They have a tongue of their own which they call Pedler's French or the Canting Tongue . . . a speech none but themselves should understand.'

Hancock's 'next important quotation' is from Samuel Rowlands's *Runnagate's Race* of 1610, in which the author speaks of a meeting supposedly held between the leader of the English rogues, Cock Lorrel, and the Gypsy chief, Giles Hathor, 'a little over a century earlier',

> to parle and intreete of matters that might tend to the establishment of this their newfound gouernment; and first of all they think it fit to deuise a certaine kinde of Language; to the end that their cousenings, knaueries, and villanies might not be so easily perceiued and knowne in places where they come.

'This statement', says Hancock, 'agrees with the findings of Harman who, as already indicated, believed this distinct form of the language to have developed separately from the original inflected variety initially brought into Britain, and not to have existed earlier than about 1535' (Acton and Kenrick 1985, 91).

In fact, nothing could be further from the truth. Harman, as shown above, says nothing of the Gypsy language and little enough of the Gypsies themselves, believing them to have been driven out of the kingdom by the grace of God and the due execution of wholesome laws. As regards Rowlands's remarks, whilst it is true that, of the four texts cited by Hancock, his is the only one in which the author seems explicitly to refer to the creation of a form of language specifically designed to serve as a medium of exchange between the Gypsies and native-born vagrants, nowhere does he suggest that the result was a form of Romani, and it is difficult to see what grounds there are for assuming this to have been his intention. Indeed, as with the extract taken from Harrison, Hancock, by failing to quote his authority in full, succeeds in conveying entirely the wrong impression. What Rowlands actually says is:

> and first of all they think it fit to deuise a certaine kinde of Language; to the end that their cousenings, knaueries, and villanies might not be so easily perceiued and knowne in places where they come, *and this their language they spunne out of three other tongues, viz. Latine, English, and Dutch: these three especially, notwithstanding some few words they borrowed of the Spanish and French*. They also gaue names to such persons of their company according to the kind of life that he undertooke: as for example, A common begger or rogue, they termed a Clapper-dudgeon, one that counterfeited the falling sickness, they termed him a counterfeit Cranke, for Cranke in their language is the falling sickness, and so Counterfeit Cranke is the false falling sickness: and so of the rest. (emphasis added)

Could anything be clearer? Two groups of rogues, one of them calling themselves Egyptians and perhaps to be equated with the Gypsies (although this is by no means certain), met together in order to discuss matters of mutual interest; devised a form of secret language using items borrowed from Latin, English, Dutch, Spanish and French (examples of all of which are to be found in early Cant vocabularies); and gave good Canting names to the various orders of rogues – clapperdudgeon, counterfeit crank etc. In what sense could this be said to refer to the creation of Angloromani or Romani English? Even if we accept that Hather and his followers were genuine Gypsies, and that, together with their new allies, they had worked up a new jargon, the better to prosecute their common aims, we are no further forward. Both here and elsewhere in his treatise, Rowlands makes it perfectly clear that this newly contrived speech was nothing other than conventional Cant and we are, therefore, left wondering why, if Hancock is broadly correct in his overall analysis, it should also have been found necessary to develop a second compromise language, the original of contemporary 'Angloromani'.

An altogether more plausible assessment of the outcome of any such early contact between the Gypsies and the native English rogues – and one which finds support in the passage quoted above from Harison – is offered by Turner in his *History of Vagrants and Vagrancy* (Ribton-Turner 1887, 467). 'It is probable', he says,

> that after the arrival of the Gypsies in England, about the year 1505, the example of their language, which was perfect in itself, stimulated English vagabonds to polish and improve their Cant so as to make it a current medium of speech; no single individual has ever yet invented a spoken language, and cant words must have existed long before the time of Henry VIII.

Indeed, rightly or wrongly, Turner goes so far as to number among these early Cant speakers the *Gwestwyr*, itinerants of largely Welsh or Irish stock whose activities had given rise to considerable public concern in the early years of the fourteenth century.

Hancock's final exhibit consists of the following statement from Samuel Rid's *Art of Jugling* of 1612 which 'is significant since it may be argued that so few items actually (or possibly) traceable to Romanes occur in the early vocabularies of rogues' slang . . . that the 16th and 17th century writers may have been referring to Cant rather than to Angloromani' (Acton and Kenrick 1985, 91): '. . . many of our English loyterers joyned with them, and in time learned their crafte and cosening. The speeche which they used was the right Egyptian language, with whom our English men conversing at last learned their language.'

Once again, it is difficult to see how Hancock is able to deduce from Rid's remarks evidence for the more or less deliberate formation of a reduced variety of Romani suited to the needs of the new arrivals in their dealings with native British rogues. If Rid's observations are taken at face value, they do not appear to admit of any other interpretation than that those native lawbreakers who wished to join with the Gypsies had to learn the old inflected Romani – 'the *right* Egyptian language' – and that this inevitably took some little time – '. . . with whom our English men conversing *at last* learned their language'. Indeed, this interpretation would seem to be wholly consistent with, if not actually supported by, Crofton's suggestion that the earliest examples of the inflected language now extant may have been obtained from a British *Gaujo* rather than a native speaker (Crofton 1907, 164).

Even if one accepts that the 'right Egyptian' was nothing more than a reduced variety of the language, it is quite clear from Rid's remarks that it was the Gypsies' own language, formulated by themselves rather than developed as a compromise between the two groups, and that it had, there-fore, to be learned by any English outsiders wishing to associate with them.

'Thus', wrote Hancock in an earlier essay on the same theme based solely on a consideration of Hotten's interpretation of Harman's *Caveat*,

> we have documentation of the 'incomprehensible' and 'difficult' language of the Romanichals coming into contact with the equally difficult English, resulting in a third compromise language used only when each group was together. At this stage the Romanichals would have continued to employ their own Romanes among themselves although doubtless using English words for concepts unfamiliar to them. In turn, however, the Romanes–English pidgin gained greater currency over the original Romanes, giving rise to the now creolized Anglo-Romanes dialect. (Hancock 1970, 43–4)

That the old language continued in use alongside the reduced variety at least until the middle decades of the nineteenth century is self-evident. That the former remained the Gypsies' sole property whilst the latter was used wholly or partly as a contact language is, however, open to serious question on a number of counts, not least because there is no evidence whatsoever, contemporary or otherwise, to suggest that this was ever the case.

~

> We find in western Europe the nomad Kalderash and other groups speaking ten or more languages for trading purposes, while there is no sign of their developing a 'pidgin' for communication with the local population.
>
> (Kenrick 1985)

In the course of their long westward migration, the Gypsies were to en-counter a wide variety of peoples, each of whom spoke their own language or dialect and with whom, in order to survive economically, it would have been necessary to establish a viable means of communication at relatively short notice. That this was achieved by means of a series of linguistic compromises or pidgins, as Hancock suggests was the case in England, seems most unlikely as, in order for a pidgin to develop, it must surely be seen to be to the advantage of all parties to the transaction. Thus, as Hancock himself has pointed out, the majority of those English-derived pidgins found in West Africa and the Far East may be said to have had their origin in a mutual desire to trade, whilst the fact that certain varieties were perpetuated owes much to the continuing communication needs of slaves drawn from a multiplicity of different tribes, each with its own language or dialect (Hancock 1970, 43).

In the case of the Gypsies and the settled population, however, it is difficult to see exactly what benefit the latter would have derived from the process. As 'pilgrims', the Gypsies' contribution to the local economy would have been a wholly negative one whilst, other than as purveyors of magic and other novelties to the poor, they possessed little or nothing in the way of craft skills or trade goods which were not already available from other sources. Given the well-documented reluctance of the settled community to accommodate this race of disruptive dark-skinned strangers, it is also almost certainly the case that the Gypsies would have found it expedient to flatter any potential customers by dealing with them in their own language. Thus, it is noticeable that whilst the Gypsy words for stealing, fortune-telling, cozening, begging and drug/medicine are Indian in origin, and the word for luck Persian, the words for tongs, file, solder/lead, kettle, knife-edge, horseshoe, nail and certain of the common metals and some of the numerals, are drawn from Greek – a fact which would suggest that, whilst a little bit of eastern mystery may well have served the purpose when practising the magic arts (see notes on Jaques's song on page 83), the Gypsies, as honest smiths, clearly found it more expedient to acquire elements of the relevant specialist vocabulary in the language of their first major European contacts. Had such words simply formed part of a Graeco-Romani commercial pidgin rather than being taken into the language proper, one would have expected them to have fallen out of use as the Gypsies moved on, being replaced by fresh items more appropriate to their changing communication needs. Modified Greek words would, after all, have been no more useful than deep Romani when trading with Poles, Swedes or Welshmen. In the event, what actually seems to have happened is that, despite its unsuitability as a trade/commercial register anywhere out-side the Greek-speaking territories, this vocabulary was to be thoroughly absorbed by and remain an integral part of the language for the next 700 years.

The notion that the Gypsies, rather than trading through a series of pidgins, found it more expedient to learn a little of each language with which they came in contact, is wholly consistent with Krantzius's statement to the effect that, having no homeland of their own, they spoke many tongues (Krantzius 1580, lib. xi, cap. 2, 285–6). It also chimes well with various references in early Spanish legislation to a 'people who pretend they are Egyptians and speak all languages' (Bercovici 1929, 172), and with the current situation where the wandering Kalderash and other nomadic groups are able to do business in ten or more different languages whilst showing no signs of developing any form of trade pidgin for the purpose (Kenrick 1985, 81).

That the Gypsies had acquired a degree of familiarity with a variety of different languages at a relatively early date is further suggested by the number of loan-words in Welsh Romani which cannot be explained by more recent contact with other dialects. In the language as recorded by Sampson, only 60 per cent of its vocabulary is of Indian origin, the remainder deriving, *inter alia*, from Persian, Arabic, Afghan, Kurdish, Byzantine and modern Greek (both directly and indirectly), the Slavonic group, German and French (Sampson 1926, 411–19). The dialect also contains a significant number of borrowings from English and Welsh but these were clearly acquired at a somewhat later date.

The nature of this loan-lexis would also suggest that such borrowings went far beyond what might have been required simply in order to trade, a fact which would suggest that the core language itself was already showing signs of a fatal susceptibility to external influence long before the Gypsies' first arrival in Britain.

It is true that Hancock does not suggest that his Romano-English pidgin had its origins in legitimate trade but in the illegal commerce which had sprung up between the Gypsies and the native British underclass. But were this the case, one might have expected such common Gypsy words as *mang*, *chore*, *hokki*, *plastramengro*, *nash* (signifying 'to hang'), *pi*, *lubni*, *suv* and *kari*, to have found their way into Cant or that they themselves would have been replaced by their Cant equivalents. After all, as Harman, Hancock's principal witness, tells us, the essential purpose of this 'lewd, lousy language . . . which . . . they term Pedlars' French' was to 'buy and sell the common people as they pass through the country'.

Again, even if, despite all the evidence, Hancock is right, one is still bound to ask why a similar pattern of development is not apparent in all those other areas occupied by the Gypsies.[3] One answer might be that, as pidgins are essentially ephemeral in character, all evidence of their existence elsewhere among the Gypsies has long since been lost. Yet even if this were so, we are still left with the task of explaining why a Romani-derived pidgin should have survived in a creolized form in England and not, say, among the Vlasika Roma of eastern Europe or the Woods of Bala. Of significance here may be the fact that the only other areas in which the language does seem to have developed along broadly similar lines – Scandinavia and the Iberian peninsula – are, like Britain, located at the very margins of the European Romani diaspora. Denied the reinforcement which would otherwise have been forthcoming from regular contact with the Romani heartlands of eastern and central Europe, and forced to compete with a single dominant language rather than a variety of conflicting tongues, it is quite possible that the Romani spoken in these outlying areas would have been much more susceptible to extensive linguistic penetration leading to its eventual collapse.

In broad terms, the argument advanced in the following pages holds that, whilst Romani English may well be the result of a compromise between English and British Romani, the point of contact between the two languages lay not in the linguistic no man's land between the Gypsies and elements of the native population (a circumstance for which there is no evidence whatsoever), but in the collective consciousness of the Gypsies themselves. In other words, Romani English today is the result of a prolonged period of attrition involving the linguistic penetration of a weaker language, Romani, by a stronger, English – a process whose origins lie in the Gypsies' unilateral and unsupported adoption of bilingualism in order to meet their continuing communication needs. At the same time, it will be argued that, having more or less entirely displaced the older inflected form of the language – acquiring in the process the characteristics of a register of English rather than a dialect of Romani – the *Poggadi Chib* then underwent a further significant change involving its redefinition as a functionally specific Cant as opposed to a mother tongue.

Although in its early stages, this process may well have had certain features in common with pidginization, the result might perhaps be more accurately described as 'language shift' or, depending on one's understanding of the term, 'language death'.[4] For Fasold (1984, 213), 'language shift simply means that a community gives up a language completely in favour of another one. The members of the community, when the shift has taken place, have collectively chosen a new language where an old one used to be used.'

Although societal bilingualism may not always result in 'language shift', in those cases where shift does occur it would seem to constitute a necessary precondition. Where shift is in progress, it would also certainly be apparent in a far higher proportion of older speakers making use of the declining language – a point to which we shall return later. Yet whilst almost all cases of shift involve intergenerational switching (Lieberson

21

1972), the majority in any given speech community seldom abandon one language for another in the space of one lifetime. Indeed, as would seem to be the case with the transition from Scottish Gaelic to English (Dorian 1981), the process may well be extremely protracted, involving the gradual erosion of the weaker language by the stronger.

~

. . . among the English Gypsies we can trace the steady degeneration of a language with its own system of grammar and vocabulary into a creolised dialect with Gypsy terms and an extremely sub-standard English. Finally, among the great majority of English and American Romani, the language has become an English approaching more and more nearly the standard type with an ever-diminishing number of Gypsy terms, many of those which survive serving chiefly as cant to prevent non-Gypsies from understanding what is being said.

(Gray 1939)

As indicated above, the principal alternative to the contact language theory holds that *Romanés* today is the product of a more or less prolonged period of attrition, involving both the loss of its own distinctive syntax, phonology and morphology and much of its original vocabulary. Indeed, so little now remains of the language spoken by the first Gypsies to settle in these islands, that, for proponents of this view, what is left might best be described as a register of English which, 'apart from the lexis . . . does not differ from the language spoken by Gajo (non-Gypsy) people of similar class and education' (Kenrick 1985, 80).

Although the absence of any significant linguistic data for the period in which British Romani may be supposed to have suffered maximum damage means that the attrition theory, too, remains no more than a working hypothesis, the internal reduction of one language by another more powerful neighbour without creating a third creolized form common to both sets of speakers is not without parallel elsewhere and, if only by analogy, may be called in evidence here. As early as 1690, for example, William Sacheverell, governor of the Isle of Man, noted that 'in the northern part of the island they speak a deeper Manx, as they call it, than in the south' (Jenner 1876, 180), suggesting that the language had become more or less bastardized in those areas closer to the centre of English power and influence.

Although deep Manx was to linger on as a mother tongue until the latter part of the twentieth century, the terminal point of this parallel process of attrition may be observed in the following verse noted in Arbory by William Cubbon, a former curator of the Manx Museum. It is a variant of the song known variously as 'Arrane Yn Sheeaghyn Troailtagh' (Song of

22

the Travelling Fairies) and 'Arrane y Cleanlhannoo' (Cradle Song), of which the full Manx version given below was first published by Mona Douglas in 1930.

> In the *glion* [glen] of Ball Comish,
> The *lhondhoo* [blackbird] will build her nest.
> Sleep thee, my baby;
> Sleep thee, my *graihagh* [loving] baby;
> Sleep thee, my baby,
> And thou'll get the birdie.

The deep original runs as follows:

> V'ad oie ayns y Glion dy Ballacomish,
> Jannoo yn lhondhoo ayns shen e hedd.
> Chaddil oo, lhiannoo, hig sheeaghyn troailtagh orrin;
> Bee dty host nish, ta mee g'eamagh er'n ushag.

The way in which the Manx words are substituted for their English equivalents in the first of the foregoing stanzas is by no means dissimilar to the way in which the *Poggadi Chib* itself is formed. Compare, for example, Cubbon's verse with the following lines from Carolyne Hughes, in which a number of other Romani words might well have been used had she so wished:

> Now I'll take my week's wages,
> And to an' ale-house I'll jel;
> Oh, an' there I'll set drinking
> 'Til my vongar's all gone.
> (Folktracks 60–043)

For present purposes, however, a more useful example of the way in which a living language may be infiltrated by another more powerful neighbour, and one which may offer a possible clue as to the likely condition of British Romani at a relatively early stage in the reductive process, is provided by the penetration of north Pembrokeshire Welsh by the English spoken in the south of the county – a process which, exacerbated by intermarriage, trade and labour links and official neglect, had its origins long before the introduction of radio and television and the massive inward migration of recent years. As Charles has pointed out in his essay on the dialect (1971),

Over a long period before it began to degenerate into an adulterated patois under twentieth century conditions, the dialect had been exposed to English influence. The Anglo-Norman conquest of south Pembrokeshire in mediaeval times and the settlement there of a large colony of English immigrants from the west country ousted the language from the area and replaced it with English.

Here, the most obvious example of English influence lies in the whole-sale importation of English words, of all classes, for most of which there also exist wholly satisfactory native Welsh equivalents: e.g. *iwso*, *off*, *lot*, *neis*, *bil lectric* etc. Even the numerals, when used in combination as in a telephone number, are not infrequently given in English. Compare modern Welsh Romani: *melino*, yellow (Welsh: *melyn*); *skabora*, barn (Welsh: *sgubor*); *efo*, with (Welsh: *efo*); *ger*, near (Welsh: *ger*); *fino*, fine; *vlija*, village (Tipler 1957, *passim*).

Although many English loan-words are now used consistently by many Welsh-speakers in the area, others occur less frequently, depending perhaps on the nature of the exchange or the perceived status of the individual addressed. Thus, speakers who regularly make use of a wide range of English words and forms when talking with family or friends may, when addressing their children's teacher or some other professional, make a conscious effort to employ purer native forms. As with *Romanés*, speakers may also switch from Welsh to English and back again in the course of the one exchange. It is also not unknown for two native Welsh-speakers to speak only in English when addressing each other whilst reverting to Welsh when in three-handed conversation with a third party.

As well as the wanton use of English words, almost any English idiom may be literally translated whether or not there exists a suitable Welsh alternative: e.g. *tyn dy fys maes*, get a move on (lit. pull your finger out); *rhedeg i lawr*, to detract (lit. to run down); *torri lawr*, to break down. Cf. Welsh Romani: *madiben/madimen bakrī*, wart (Welsh: *dafaden wyllt*); *sǻla 'rē tō šērō*, he is laughing at you (Welsh: *mae fe'n chwerthin ar dy ben*) (Tipler 1957, 65, 112); and the common expletive, *ratvalo*, bloody.

This not only has the unfortunate effect of robbing the spoken language of much of its original and unique flavour but, more importantly, en-courages the wholly inappropriate use of English grammatical forms: e.g. *tyn dy ddillad off*, take your clothes off; *beth wyt ti'n chwilio am*, what are you looking for; *mae'r tegell dist a berwi*, the kettle's just boiling; *rydw i eisiau*, I want: cf. Welsh Romani: *šomas uštilō 'dova bār*, I was lifting that stone; wedi *lō mulō*, after he was dead (Welsh: *wedi iddo farw*) and the tendency to place the adjective after the noun in imitation of Welsh (Tipler 1957, 5, 94 and *passim*).

Although, both in west Wales and elsewhere, the spoken language may have parted company with the literary norm so far as its morphology is concerned, north Pembrokeshire Welsh shows few signs of interference from English. With the exception of a number of plural forms, nouns and adjectives in Welsh have not been declined for upwards of 1,500 years. In so far as any change may be required, however, loan-words, though not without exception, tend to follow the Welsh pattern: e.g. toiled*au*, toilets; gutter*au*, gutters. Loan-verbs, too, are conjugated as in Welsh: e.g. ffon*ia'i chi*, I will phone you; *fe f*ild*odd e*, he built it. Compare Welsh Romani: tiz*alo*, teased; mínas*ela*, he means (Tipler 1957, 14, 96); and the following sentences, in which *griga* (Welsh: *grug*) appears in the instrumental case, and *halikon*, a singular form derived from the Welsh plural *helgwn*, in the nominative plural: *taseren o bov grigasa*, they heat the oven with heather; *prasten o halikuna kedives*, the greyhounds are running today (Sampson 1926, 112, 115).

In both Romani in its more debased form and in north Pembrokeshire Welsh, one also occasionally meets with examples of the unnecessary retention of the original English inflection in tandem with its Romani or Welsh equivalent. Compare, for example, *he's nash'dedo with a vasavi grasni*, he's gone with an evil mare (text 130), where *nash* is inflected both English- and Romani-fashion, and *mae'r hen gerins bach bron a sythu*, the poor little dears are nearly frozen, where *caran* has been pluralized Welsh-fashion by internal vowel change and English-fashion by the addition of a final 's' (Charles 1971, 110).

It may also be observed, however, that in Tipler's sample of modern Welsh Romani, which appears to have decayed to a point somewhere between north Pembrokeshire Welsh and the *Poggadi Chib*, the conjugation of verbs also shows signs of imminent collapse: for example, in the use of the auxiliary verb in conjunction with the main verb, in imitation of the Welsh, and in the past tense where his informants seem to have lost the first person plural in '-om', replacing it with the singular '-am'.

There is more to be said on the subject of Tipler's Romani at a later stage in the argument. For the moment, it is sufficient to note that, although regrettably small, his sample shows clear signs of interference from *both* English and Welsh, and, this being so, it is difficult to see how it could ever have served as a linguistic bridge between either Romani and English or Romani and Welsh.

What is also noticeable both in Romani and north Pembrokeshire Welsh is that, in the process of adoption, loan-words generally acquire the characteristics of the receiving language. In the latter case this is achieved either by substituting Welsh sounds for English ones (Parry-Williams 1923) or by the addition of Welsh suffixes – *-a*, *-ach*, *-an*, *-en*, *-es*, *-yn*, in the case

25

of singular nouns; *-edig, -gar, -(l)lyd, -us,* in the case of adjectives; and *-an, -ha, -i, -ial, -ian, -io, -o, -u,* in the case of verbs (Charles 1971, 104).

In the same way, loan-words drafted into Romani acquire the characteristics of their new milieu – *kariavola,* mountain ash (Welsh: *criafolen*); *paburna,* rush (Welsh: *pabwyren*); *bita,* little (French: *petit*); and *sketana,* girl (Sampson 1926, 258 and Tipler 1957, 9, 66). The last of these is of particular interest as it appears to derive from the Caernarfon dialect form *scertan,* itself from English, skirt.

As regards their phonology generally, both 'Broken Romani' and north Pembrokeshire Welsh show clear signs of simplification making them more accessible to non-native speakers. In the latter, for example, the common diphthong 'ae' is regularly flattened out into a long 'a', whilst initial 'chw' is more often heard as a faintly guttural 'wh'. Cf. Romani English, where the medial 'a' of older continental forms has been broadened out into an 'o', whilst the uvular fricative 'x' is now generally heard as 'k' or 'h'.

Although the process of deterioration is clearly more advanced in the former, the following examples will be sufficient to illustrate the similarity between 'Broken Romani' and north Pembrokeshire Welsh in its most debased form:

NP Welsh: Desid*odd yr* head *i ala'r crwt gartre* 'cos *o'dd e'n* sik.
The Head decided to send the boy home because he was sick. (example of poor Welsh from school textbook)

Mae fe wedi improvo *fy* knowledge *o Gymraeg* one hundred per cent.
It has improved my knowledge of Welsh one hundred per cent. (overheard)

Dim point *i fi* b*led*io not guilty.
No point in me pleading not guilty. (radio drama)

Rom.: *Toóti* can't *jal adré* the *bengésko-tan,* 'cos *odói* there's *rovaben* and *dand*ing o'*danyaw.*
You can't go to hell, because there's wailing and gnashing of teeth there. (Smart and Crofton 1875)

I'd sooner *shoon* his *rokrapen* than *shoon* Lally *gil* a *gillie.*
I'd sooner hear him speak than hear Lally sing. (Borrow 1874)

From the foregoing brief sketch, it will be readily apparent that, at no time during its long history, could north Pembrokeshire Welsh have functioned as a linguistic bridge between monoglot Welsh- and English-speakers. The proposition advanced here, however, is that the gradual Anglicization of the dialect may well offer both a pattern for the slow descent of British Romani into the *Poggadi Chib* and an indication of its likely condition at a relatively early stage in its formation. Why it should have proved so much more susceptible to attack is a point to which we shall return at a later stage in the argument.

A further clue to the likely condition of the language at least 100, and possibly 200, years after the Gypsies first arrived in Britain is provided by the Welsh Romani encountered by Sampson during the last decade of the nineteenth century. In a paper delivered before the Liverpool Welsh National Society in January 1901, he states that English and Welsh Romani were originally one and the same, any differences then existing between them being due 'not to the separate origin of the Welsh Gypsies from a later arriving Continental stock, but to the accidental preservation among the hills and fastnesses of Wales of a form of the tongue which was once common to the Gypsy population of Britain'. This, he suggests, may be inferred both from the relatively large number of English loan-words – 160, as compared with eighty from Byzantine and modern Greek (the second most prolific source) and only thirty-six from Welsh – and from a small number of items common to English and Welsh Romani but found in no other continental dialect (see pp. 411–19 of Sampson's *Dialect of the Gypsies of Wales*, a work significantly subtitled *The Older Form of the British Romani Preserved in the Speech of the Clan of Abram Wood* (Sampson 1926)).

If Sampson was right, then it may be safely assumed that, at the point at which the Gypsies first entered Wales, English, or rather British, Romani was, in some areas, at least as well preserved as its late nineteenth-century Welsh derivative. The question is, however, at what point did this westward migration take place?

Although earlier legislation (such as the Vagrancy Acts of 1530 and 1562) was clearly intended to apply to both England and Wales, perhaps the earliest substantive reference to the Gypsies in the Principality occurs in an official communication described in the Acts of the Privy Council for 10 January 1579, as

A letter to the President and Councell in the Marches of Wales signifieng that where their Lordships do understande by a letter written unto Mr. Comptroller from the Sheriffe of the Countie of Radnor that he hath of late apprehended the number of XLtie vagrant persons themselfes Egiptiens, who according to the Statute of the Vth yeare of her Majesties raigne are to be arraigned as fellons; Forasmuch as the Sheriffe desirethe for the avoyding of charges that may growe by the feeding of so greate a number in prison till the next Assises there might be a Commission graunted for the trying of them according to the said Statute, their Lordships have therefore thought good (they having a Commission for that purpose remayning with them) to require them fourthwith to appointe a convenient number of Commissioners who maie immediatelie proceade to the triall of the Egiptiens within the countye where they were apprehended.

Although this points to a fairly significant incursion some time during the 1570s, there is no surviving record of any subsequent legal action and it is, therefore, quite possible that it was merely an isolated incident and that the prompt incarceration of those involved was sufficient to discourage any follow-up. This apart, the earliest documentary evidence for the involvement of Gypsies in criminal proceedings in Wales is contained in the Montgomery Great Sessions gaol records for 1715 (2 Geo. 1 Wales 4/172/3) and concerns an assault and robbery upon the person of Mary Smith at Borth and the subsequent search for those responsible. This being so, one is bound to ask how likely it is that a significant number of Gypsies could have passed the entire seventeenth century in the Principality without becoming involved in any form of legal action (for a full account of the Borth affair see Jarman and Jarman 1991, 47).

That the 1578–9 incursion was nothing more than an isolated incident is further suggested by the fact that the only other references to the Gypsies in Wales which might be supposed to relate to the period prior to 1600 are, first and foremost, literary anecdotes, the earliest source for which would seem to be an eighteenth-century manuscript held in Jesus College, Oxford – Jesus Coll. 18 (see J. Gwenogfryn Evans, *Reports on Welsh Manuscripts,* ii, 86). Although he offers no evidence for this, Sampson, in his lecture to the Liverpool Welsh National Society, dates this manuscript no later than 1630.

Of these, only the first, which takes as its subject the poet Siôn Tudur (*c*.1530–1602), is of interest here:

A great Gibbsie of an Alehouse in St. Asaph, who when or where shee met him [sc. Siôn Tudur], would (because he was a bigge lustie man) crie Bwbach or Bugge [thou squitter, thou great bogey-man] and soe run from him as faste as shee could; but one time coming to the alehouse he met her full in the face; she presently perceaved that it was hee returned with open mouth crying – y bibbach, y bwbach mam – whereupon he presently said:

> Bwbach a wnelo it bibo, buten;
> Dy boten a chwyddo;
> Dy 'menydd oll a gollo,
> Dy gont a ddyco dy go'.
> (Jesus Coll. 18, (= lxxxviii) 33 (*JGLS* 9 (1930), 65)

Tudur's riposte, reproduced here according to the rules of contemporary Welsh orthography (Jarman and Jarman 1991, 34), has been translated as follows by J. Glyn Davies:

> May a bogey make thee squit, thou whore;
> May your paunch swell out;
> May thy brains vanish,
> And may thy c..t run away with thy reason.

The foregoing is of particular interest in that, if accurately reported, the Gypsy woman mentioned in the piece was apparently sufficiently well established in the country to have picked up enough Welsh not only to have addressed the poet in his own language but, presumably, to have understood his reply. In this connection, it is worth noting that, in his autobiography, the nineteenth-century clergyman, Robert Roberts (1834–85), includes the following reminiscence of his great-grandmother which would seem to suggest that, even as late as the second half of the eighteenth century, by no means all those Gypsies then resident in the Principality had been there long enough to acquire a knowledge of the language. The old lady was aged about ninety in 1840 (Roberts 1991, 31):

> When we were living at Tynyfownog, and when I was a young lass unmarried, the family of Abram Wood first came into the country. Who they were and where they came from, no one knew. They said that they came from Flintshire, somewhere about Clawdd Offa; however, though they called themselves Welsh, they knew no Welsh, and looked more like Gipsiwns.

That the woman in the Tudur tale was, in fact, a Gypsy, is by no means certain. Gypsy women were seldom if ever known to engage in prostitution, and it would, in any case, have been most unusual to find a lone female Traveller established in an alehouse and acting in so profligate a manner. *Gibbsie*, here, may simply have been a term of abuse, as in Morris Cyffin's *cywydd* on the burgesses of Holt in the districts of Maelor and Iâl (see W. Prichard Williams (ed.), *Y Deffyniad Ffydd Eglwys Loegr* (1908), p. 276). Some time during his lifetime (*c.*1555–98), Crown tenants in the area had found themselves in dispute with the Crown assessors who had sought to raise their rents and, in the course of a satirical diatribe on the subject, Kyffin describes them as *siapsach a gweflau Sipsiwn* (scabs with Gypsy lips). In contemporary Welsh, *Sipsi mochyn* may still be heard as a non-racially-specific term of abuse.

Apart from the foregoing, the earliest Welsh references to the Gypsies are to be found in the *Gweledigaethau y Bardd Cwsg* (Visions of the Sleeping Bard) of Ellis Wynne (1703), an allegorical prose narrative in the style of Quevedo's *Visions*. These, too, however, are also literary rather than documentary in character and, indeed, in language and content are clearly reminiscent of other early British quasi-documentary accounts. It is, for example, noticeable that the colours favoured by the 'Gypsies', red and blue, are those of the livery of hell as depicted in the tale of Collen's subjection of Gwyn ap Nudd. In the first, Wynne tells how he encountered a group of gaily clad figures disporting themselves on a 'dancing knoll' and, believing them to be Gypsies, was reluctant to approach them lest they should determine to eat him, saltless, for their supper.

Wynne's second passage describes the reception of a group of Gypsies in hell, where, in consigning them to outer darkness, Lucifer enjoins his henchmen to throw them a frog every one thousand years if they will only spare him the sound of their 'barbarous chatter'.

Unsatisfactory as it may be, the original of the phrase 'barbarous chatter', *gibris dyglibir dyglabar* (Eng. gibberish + glibber-glabber), is the earliest reference we have to the language of the Gypsies of Wales. Like Kyffin, however, Wynne is known to have spent some time in England and one cannot, therefore, say for certain in which of the two countries he may have encountered the language if, indeed, he ever did. Again, whilst it may be inferred from his chosen phrase that any Romani he may have heard sounded entirely foreign to him and must, therefore, have been relatively pure, even this cannot be assumed with any degree of certainty. As already mentioned, for a number of early collectors, unfamiliar with the spoken language, the *Poggadi Chib*, even when well diluted, had a wholly alien ring.

The earliest substantive examples we have of Romani in Wales are included as an annexe to a letter published in the Welsh-language periodical *Seren Gomer* for February 1823, in which the anonymous author asks: 'What would you say to Hindustani, one of the languages of the East Indies, being spoken by a tribe of people who have lived in our country for ages? And those who speak it are the despised people who are today called the *Shipswnt* and, in English, the Gypsies.' Although we cannot be sure that the author had not gathered his material elsewhere in Britain, there can be little doubt that the list was compiled by a native Welsh-speaker rather than simply copied from materials gathered by an English collector. This is apparent from the frequent use of the Welsh vowel 'w' and the 'f' in *defus* which, in Welsh, would be sounded as an English 'v'. The full list, together with the author's own 'Hindustani' and Welsh equivalents, is printed below. An English column has been added, referring in each case to the Welsh. Where this would seem to conflict with the original Romani, an alternative rendering is given in brackets.

Shipswnaeg	Hindustani	Cymraeg	English
ec	ek	un	one
dws	dw	dau	two
trin	trin	tri	three
star	tshar	pedwar	four
pantsh	panj	pump	five
tshow	tsho	chwech	six
efta	hefta	saith	seven
ochto	aute	wyth	eight
henia	enia	naw	nine
desh	des	deg	ten
cam	cam	haul	sun
shan	tshand	lloer	moon
defus	dewus	dydd	day
ratti	rat	nos	night
tuttw	tutta	gwres	heat, warmth (hot)
sonnia	swna	aur	gold
rwp	rwpa	arian	silver
dad	dada	tad	father
dai	da'i	mam	mother
bibi	bibi	modryb	aunt
ria	raie	arglwydd	lord
riana	ra'eni	arglwyddes	lady
pani	pani	dwfr	water
bwropani	bwrapani	y môr	the sea
mutshi	mutshi	pysgod	fishes
gur	ghur	tŷ	house
rwc	rwclo	pren	tree
mul	mwl	gwîn	wine
lwn	lwn	halen	salt
mas	mas	bwyd	food (meat)
tshar	tshar	lleidr	thief
bul	bal	gwallt	hair
aoc	awk	llygad	eye
nac	nac	trwyn	nose
shing	sin	corn	horn
can	can	clust	ear
caliban	calaburn	du	black (blackness)
bwlsi	buholsi	mawr	big
tshater	tshater	pabell	tent

The Welsh Gypsies themselves, as reported by Sampson, believed themselves to be 'the descendants of an eponymous ancestor, Abram Wood . . .
who was born before the close of the seventeenth century' (Sampson 1926,

vii). Exactly when this was, however, is far from clear. He is first mentioned in the parish register of Selattyn as 'king of the Gypsies' in connection with the baptism of his son, Bohemia, on 25 October 1715, but he must surely have been a very young man at the time as his funeral is recorded as having taken place in Llangelynin on 12 November 1799 (*JGLS* 11 (1932), 62). Oddly enough, the same man, if so he was, is also described in the parish records of Llangernyw for 1760 as no more than 'Abraham Wood . . . a vagrant' (*JGLS* 11 (1932), 63) and, at the time of his burial, as 'Abram Woods a traveling Egyptian'. It is possible, however, that this apparent loss of status simply reflects a growing disenchantment with the Gypsies in general; cf. the altogether more dramatic decline in the fortunes of the Scottish Faas during the latter part of the sixteenth century.

The exact date of his arrival in Wales is equally difficult to determine with any degree of accuracy. According to John Roberts, as reported in the *Wrexham Advertiser* for September 1876, 'About two hundred years ago came an old man of the name of Abraham Wood, his wife, three sons and a daughter . . .' Four years later, however, the same informant suggests (Groome 1880, 197) that Wood in fact 'came up into Wales about one hundred and fifty years ago or thereabouts', which would place the event some time around 1730, fifteen years after the baptism of Bohemia Wood at Selattyn.

Another tradition, mentioned by Lockwood, was that those Welsh Romani-speakers whose language he describes ' . . . remembered that their forebears had come from Somerset in the eighteenth century' (Lockwood 1975, 243). Analysis of the various non-standard items in the list of English etymons appended to Sampson's Welsh–Romani lexicon would, however, seem to suggest that the ancestors of his informants may have lingered longest a little further north. Although many of these dialect items have a fairly wide distribution – tending perhaps towards the northern half of the country – a significant proportion are associated with the western counties of Gloucester, Warwick, Worcester and, more particularly, Shropshire. Indeed, two (*swedle* and *crawn*) would seem to have been peculiar to the last-named, whilst a third (*bunnell*) was apparently confined to Shropshire and west Worcestershire (compare Sampson 1926, 418–19; and Wright 1896–1905, *passim*). It may also be observed that the earliest accounts of the Gypsies in the Principality refer to mid- and north Wales which would suggest that they entered the country from the midland or northern counties of England rather than from the south-west.

The Abram Wood referred to by John Roberts should almost certainly not be confused with his altogether less illustrious namesake mentioned in Robert Roberts's autobiography (Roberts 1991), even though both were apparently resident in the vicinity of Llangernyw at about the same time –

the former's youngest son, Solomon, was baptized there on 9 January 1760 (*JGLS* 11 (1932), 63) .

By Robert Roberts, the family is described as wild and reckless, heedless of the Sabbath and much given to poaching and sheep stealing. In his account, too, Wood's wife is named Nelly and his five children, Phil, Jake, Tom, Robin and Esther. Sampson's subject, on the other hand, is credited with a wife, Sarah, and five children – Bohemia, Valentine, William, Solomon and Damaris – whose subsequent history (with the exception of Bohemia) is described by John Roberts in the *Wrexham Advertiser* article already mentioned.

There are, moreover, certain folkloric elements in Robert Roberts's account which suggest that it may, in part at least, be apocryphal. The family home, for example, is given the name Llety'r Gŵr Drwg (The Devil's Lodging-House), whilst Abraham himself is said to have owned a black dog of supernatural power who was eventually reclaimed by the devil while his master was out hunting on the Sabbath.

More importantly in the present context, Robert Roberts's grandfather (Roberts 1991, 37), in describing an abortive attempt to retrieve two stolen wethers from the Woods' new home on Mwdwl Eithin, mentions that the family spoke English mixed with a kind of thieves' gibberish. By contrast, the Abram Wood of Welsh Gypsy tradition must surely have spoken good 'deep' Romani, given the quality of the language still in use among his descendants some one hundred years after his death.

In all probability, the source of this confusion lies in the fact that, by the end of the eighteenth century, so well had the original Abram Wood established himself in the popular consciousness that his name, or rather that of his family – *Teulu Abram Wd* – was applied without distinction to all Gypsies then resident in the Principality (cf. the use of the family name Faa as a cognomen for all Scottish Gypsies). If the family mentioned by Robert Roberts's grandfather and great-grandmother were as heedless of the law as we are led to believe, they may well have chosen to hide their true identity by making use of this fact.

If, on the basis of the foregoing, we accept the proposition that, apart from a few earlier minor incursions, the Gypsies had probably begun to establish themselves in Wales some time during the latter part of the seventeenth or the early part of the eighteenth century, and that the language they carried with them was more or less representative of that still spoken by or known to a significant portion of the English Gypsy population, it follows that British Romani must then have been at least as well preserved as its late nineteenth-century Welsh derivative. This being so, we are bound to ask why if, as suggested by Hancock, the *Poggadi Chib* began life as a politically/commercially expedient contact language in the years immediately following the Gypsies' first arrival in Britain, it had apparently failed to find favour among the ancestors of the modern Welsh Romani. After all, the relatively high proportion of English loan-words in the Welsh dialect would suggest that they had been resident in England for some time prior to their removal into the Principality and would, therefore, presumably have been subject to the same pressures and influence which, we are told, led to the early emergence of the *Poggadi Chib*. By the same token, we may also ask why, following their entry into Welsh-speaking Wales, it was not found necessary to develop in quick order a form of language analogous to 'Broken Romani' but based on Welsh rather than English. Even as late as the 1950s, whilst there is evidence of growing interference from Welsh, this is hardly sufficient to suggest that Welsh Romani could ever have served as a linguistic bridge between the Gypsies and any section of the settled population. A comparison of Tipler's Romani (1957) and the material gathered by Sampson around the turn of the century would, moreover, suggest that both Welsh and English had made their most significant inroads during the first half of the twentieth century rather than at an earlier stage in the development of the dialect.

This is not to say, of course, that 'Broken Romani' could not have been in existence in England at the time of the Gypsies' first migration into Wales. What it does suggest is that it was by no means as widespread as it was to become, and that its adoption by the mass of the Gypsy population must, therefore, have been the result of a relatively slow process of attrition – a supposition lent additional support by the fact that significant elements of the old inflected language were to linger on in parts of England until the middle years of the nineteenth century.

~

First-hand linguistic data for the period prior to the publication of Marsden and Bryant's Gypsy word-lists of 1785 are, unfortunately, extremely scarce. Apart from a handful of personal names which would seem to contain elements of Gypsy origin (MacRitchie 1894, 33, 37), the earliest example of British Romani now extant consists of thirteen sentences published by Andrew Boorde in his *Fyrste Boke of the Introduction of Knowledge* of *c.*1547–8, and first recognized as such by Zupitza in 1874 (Furnivall 1874, 100). Of these, at least two – the sixth and the tenth – show signs of interference from English:

6. *hyste len pee* (= *besh telé* (a)'n'(d) *pí*)
    Sit down and drink

10. *Achae*, a wordey *tusse* (= *atch*, *chai*, a word *tusa*)
    Stay, maid, a word with you.

34

Whether we accept Smart and Crofton's assertion (1873, 289) that 'it may safely be assumed that Boorde obtained his examples from English Gypsies' or Crofton's revised position (1907, 164) that it 'seems probable that his informant was a British *Gajo*, who consorted with Gypsies, and whose knowledge of Romanes was imperfect', it would seem reasonable to conclude that the language had not yet been reduced to the point where it could usefully serve as a linguistic bridge but, as Rid tells us, would have had to be learned by any outsider wishing to associate with the Gypsies on their own terms.

It is also worth noting here that, among the personal names mentioned by MacRitchie, are *Hatseygow* and *Grasta Neyn* which, if he is right in his analysis, would suggest that the original informants were sufficiently confident in both Romani and English to engage in a little gentle word-play. The first, he suggests, equals '*hatch* I go', where *hatch* in fact means the exact opposite. The second, he equates with '*grasta* (horse) neighing'. MacRitchie also suggests that two further names may contain elements of German – Geleyr (Germ. *gelehrt*, learned) and Beige (Germ. *bihge*, a fiddle bow). If this is so, it would certainly seem to be consistent with the various contemporary references to the Gypsies' ability to speak many languages.

When next we encounter the language – in the second half of the eighteenth century – it is possible to draw two significant if tentative inferences regarding its nature and status. The first, based on the altogether more substantial samples provided by Marsden and by Bryant in 1785, is that, for some southern Gypsies at least, the process of Anglicization was considerably further advanced than it had been in Boorde's day. The second, based on the *Discoveries of John Poulter* of 1753, is that, whilst a handful of Gypsy words may have filtered through into Cant, Romani itself had not at that time been pressed into service as a linguistic bridge between the Gypsies and the native English outlaws. 'The Gipseys', writes Poulter, 'are a People that talk Romney, a Cant that Nobody knows but Themselves' (*Discoveries*, second edn 36–7).

Having described their method of fortune-telling, Poulter, in a passage dealing with 'The Faws or Gipseys', goes on to say that 'they are great *Prigers* of *Caunes* and *Bucket-chats*, that is Sheep and Fowl'. *Prig* and *chat* are standard Cant and well represented in the literature. *Caunes* and *bucket*, on the other hand, although their meaning is apparently trans-posed, are suggestive of Romani English *kanni* and *bokro*, chicken and sheep. That *caunes* does, indeed, equal fowl rather than sheep is suggested elsewhere in the book where we find the phrase '*pyke* a *cauney prigging*; go a fowl stealing'. Elswhere, too, we find 'the Bus trap johns me; the Thiefcatcher knows me', where *john* seems to equate with the Romani English *jins*, knows.

35

If Poulter's samples are to be taken for Romani English, then this would not only suggest that his informants spoke a much reduced variety of the language, but that they spoke it with a far heavier admixture of Cant than is apparent in any other published sample. For a Gypsy to use the word *prig* (steal) would, for example, be most unusual; it is to be found in no other Romani vocabulary and even today, some 250 years on, there can hardly be a Gypsy in England who is not familiar with the conventional Romani equivalent, *chore*.

The notion that the form of language depicted by Poulter may represent that otherwise wholly elusive compromise said by Hancock to have been developed by the Gypsies in association with the English rogues may also be discounted for two further reasons. In the first place, Poulter makes it perfectly clear that his Gypsies spoke 'a Cant that Nobody knows but Themselves'; and, in the second, his Gypsy words (if so they be) occur in sentences said to be illustrative of the Canting Tongue, not of 'Romney'. Indeed, the three words mentioned above constitute the only possible examples of Romani in the entire work, the remaining items being drawn from conventional Cant. A more likely explanation of their inclusion is that Poulter or his rogues had simply picked up a few stray words of Romani or Scottish Tinkers' Cant – he was, after all, dealing in (or stealing) horses and, as Kenrick has pointed out, horse dealing is one of the principal routes by which Romani terms have found their way into English slang (Kenrick 1985).

That Poulter's informants were northern English or Scottish Tinkers might also be inferred both from his use of the term 'Faws' and from the form in which his Gypsy words are given. M'Cormick (1907, ix–xxiv) gives both *carey* and *kannie* for sheep, whilst *bucket chat* could conceivably be an onomatopoeic form, analogous to *meoutc[h]at* (mewing thing) = cat (Carmichael 1895), and signifying chicken. This would, at least, explain the apparent transposition of meaning in the Poulter text, although it would not account for the later, seemingly correct, use of *cauney*. *John* is altogether easier to place (cf. Groome 1880, 26; Winstedt 1911, 78–9).

By the 1780s, we are on surer ground in suggesting that the process of Anglicization was well under way, at least among some southern Gypsies. Thus, in Bryant's list (1785, 387–91), we find, among a number of other curious items later identified by Groome, the following which can only be described as *Poggadi Chib*: *bauro beval acochenos* = a storm (lit. a great wind a catchin' us); *jasia vallacai* = to command (lit. *jas* or *vel akai* = go or come here); and *redan* = yellow (lit. red one).

So also in Copsey (1818), *bilarrah* = kettle (Eng. boiler) and in Harriott (1830), *dein avai lova* = charity (lit. *dein'* away *lova* = givin' away money).

At the same time, however, all three offer examples, albeit unwittingly, of older inflected forms: thus, in Bryant, *adra peni paddee*, drowned (lit. in water they fell); in Copsey, *kannella*, bad food (lit. it stinks); and, in Harriott, *achipeleste*, bless (lit. rest on him).

On the basis of this, albeit slight, evidence, two conclusions are possible: that their informants, whilst speaking what might justly be called the *Poggadi Chib*, yet retained elements of the older inflected language which have since disappeared, or that, within the one group, different individuals spoke their Romani with varying degrees of purity. What is clear, however, is that, within the one community at the one time, the language had not yet reached a uniform low, but was still in a downward state of flux.

That the language was still in active decline some sixty years later may be deduced with some certainty from the altogether more substantial data available for the middle decades of the nineteenth century. Nowhere is this better illustrated than in the writings of Smart and Crofton, where the surviving elements of the *Puri Chib* are laid out side by side with their Turkish Romani equivalents as recorded by Alexander Paspati. The loss of entire tenses of the verb and the partial retention of others, the correct use of only a limited number of case endings and pronominal forms, and the imperfect grasp of idiom and syntax thus revealed are all indicative of a process of elimination as yet incomplete. Indeed, the picture presented is not so much one of a handful of fossilized remains but that of a living organism entering upon the final stages of a long and painful illness.

The question remains, however, why, following their separation some time during the latter part of the seventeenth or the early part of the eighteenth century, what we may now call the *Puri Chib* should have declined so dramatically compared with its Welsh analogue. Once again, we may look to the Welsh spoken in north Pembrokeshire for a possible clue for, whilst the latter has been subject to English influence since the thirteenth century, long before Romani was first spoken in these islands, there can be no doubt that it has proved infinitely more resilient.

Unlike those of their continental counterparts who continued to travel extensively in middle Europe, the first Gypsies to arrive in England would have had to contend with only the one dominant language – English (Cornish, it is true, was still spoken in parts of the far south-west but was itself already in terminal decline, and it is unlikely that the Gypsies would have encountered many speakers who had no knowledge whatsoever of the official language). Under such circumstances, there is every reason to suppose that, within a very short space of time, the new arrivals would have become at least commercially competent in the new language. Useful as this may have been, it is unlikely to have served the long-term interests of their native tongue. In a bilingual situation in which one of the two languages involved is manifestly weaker, not only numerically but in terms of its perceived value and economic status, it is almost inevitably placed at a severe disadvantage. As David Greene has pointed out,

> the situation of the speaker of a patois is well known; he will use his inherited words for the ordinary affairs of life but when faced with new objects or institutions, he will automatically take the word used by the socially dominant language . . . The dangers of this attitude are obvious, since it implies the cultural inferiority of the vernacular. (Greene 1972, 27)

The problem for Romani in the sixteenth century, as for many minority languages today, was that 'in a society in which all members know language "A" and a minority also know language "B", and in which "A" serves all purposes at least as well as "B", if not better, "B" will quickly come to be regarded as an outdated and pointless convention' (Price 1984, 124). Thus, as the Gypsies became increasingly confident in their use of English, and Romani became increasingly a language of the hearth, so their command over the full range of resources available to their native tongue would have been correspondingly diminished, leading eventually to a more or less complete breakdown. Although the situation in west Wales is by no means as acute, the same process is nevertheless clearly discernible in the inter-action between English and north Pembrokeshire Welsh; the significant factor in both cases being that it was not through the development of a reduced contact variety but among native speakers alone that their language was to be emasculated. In this context, T. Arwyn Watkins's observations on the effect of bilingualism on contemporary Welsh may be said to apply with equal force to the Romani spoken in sixteenth- and seventeenth-century England: 'This effect', he says,

> is less a question of a gradually shifting language frontier than of the linguistic penetration of a weaker language by a stronger one. It is as if the battle between Welsh and English has been transferred from the geographical field to the mind of each individual Welsh speaker. (Watkins 1962, 43)

Unlike north Pembrokeshire Welsh, however, English Romani lacked the support of a strong literary language which, whilst it may have had only a limited direct influence on everyday speech, was nevertheless accessible to the broad mass of the people through the medium of religious worship and other forms of cultural expression (James 1972, 24). More importantly, perhaps, wandering the country in small detached groups, the Gypsies also lacked the support of larger settled communities in which the language would have had the opportunity to thrive and develop across the full range of social and economic activity. In considering the likely future health of any minority language, the actual number of speakers may well be less significant than the number of speakers expressed as a percentage of the population as a whole – the so called 'intensity factor'. Thus, as Glanville Price points out, the long-term future of Faroese, which is spoken by virtually all of the islands' 30,000 inhabitants, may well be more secure than that of Welsh, whose 500,000 native speakers represent only 20 per cent of the total population.

Against this background it may be supposed that British Romani was, from the first, peculiarly susceptible to linguistic penetration by English, and that thereafter, as the process of Anglicization gathered momentum and the number of 'deep' speakers declined, both in terms of the population as a whole and of the Gypsy speech community in particular, the rot would have spread ever more quickly until the old language, at last unable to sustain itself, disappeared altogether.

Among the isolated Gypsy communities of Wales and the northern counties of England, however, the intensity factor may have been far higher than in the more densely populated south-east and, even though their overall numbers may have been low, the language would have stood a far better chance of surviving in a relatively pure form. Yet even Welsh Romani could not hope to hold out for ever and, as the overall number of fluent native speakers declined, we may suppose that here, too, the language would eventually begin to show signs of marked deterioration. Thus Sampson speaks of that 'hybrid vernacular peculiar to this Welsh branch of the Lees [which] cannot be considered as representative of the classical tongue of the Woods' (Sampson 1926, viii), whilst elsewhere (ibid., xi) he is quite unequivocal regarding his concern for the future of the language as a whole:

> But while I have been fortunate in happening upon Welsh Romani in its Augustan, or at least its Silver Age, I cannot disguise from myself that decay has already begun to set in, and that another generation or two may see the end of this ancient speech. The Woods, probably as the result of repeated consanguineous unions, are not a prolific race, while inter-marriages with the Welsh Gajé or of late years with the English Gypsy clans of Lee and Locke, have resulted in the deterioration of the language. A surprising number of Welsh Gypsy adults remain single; the Ingrams have long ceased to exist as a co-clan with the Woods; the young generation of the Roberts have almost lost the tongue of which the veteran harper was so proud; while not a few pure-bred Gypsies bearing the old patrician name (among them Edward himself), marrying aliens, have neglected to hand down Romnimus to their children.

That, despite Sampson's worst fears, the language was still alive in the early 1950s is evidenced both by Kennedy's unique recording of the brothers, Manfri and Hywel Wood, in conversation at Penybontfawr in 1954 (Folktracks 441 and texts 131–2), and Tipler's 'Specimens of Modern Welsh Romani', gathered on the Llŷn peninsula in 1950 (Tipler 1957).

Like the Woods of Bala, Tipler's Gypsies were clearly still capable of formulating complete sentences in inflected Romani and, although there is nothing in his account to compare with the conversation and song recorded by Kennedy some four years later, the 130 or so examples given are sufficiently diverse to suggest that the language was still more than a mere 'special register' with only a limited number of specific functions. On being asked the Romani for a 'match', for example, one of his informants was sufficiently confident to run out the following variant of an old and well-tried joke: *sosoiesko kari ta tu* (a rabbit's penis and you).

What is particularly interesting about Tipler's *Romanés*, however, is the degree of interference from *both* English and Welsh, although there can be no question that it could ever have served as a working compromise between Romani and either of these two languages. Indeed, from the limited sample at our disposal it would seem that his informants may have been equally comfortable in Welsh and English and would, therefore, have had no use for a pidgin. The same would also seem to be true of the Woods who provided Kennedy with examples of English, Welsh and macaronic song texts. That Tipler's informants were well acquainted with Welsh is not only apparent from their use of a number of loan-words, both modified and unmodified, for which suitable Romani equivalents are still in use among English Travellers and which were certainly available to the Woods some fifty years earlier, but from their use of the Welsh *wedi* in forming the past tense (Tipler 1957, 6, 19 etc.), in their apparently correct use of the nasal mutation in the phrase *len barí si ym Mhala*, there is a big lake in Bala (59),[5] and in the calques *madiben bakri*, wart (Welsh: dafaden wyllt) and *sala 're to sero*, he is laughing at you (Welsh: mae fe'n chwerthin ar dy ben) (65, 112). Their habit of pronouncing *pedol*, a horseshoe, as if *bedol* is also suggestive of their correct use of the soft mutation following the definite article.

Other examples of interference from Welsh include: the use of the prepositions *ger*, *o* and *efo*, near, from and with (15, 28, 130); the negative particle, *ni* (43); and the conjunction *na*, than (10, 53).

Apart from a number of loan-words, English influence is apparent in the use of the verb endings '-ed' (7, 17, 18) and '-ing' (86); of the auxiliary verb 'will' (44, 122); and of the indefinite article, unknown in Romani or Welsh (111, 113, 121 etc.).

Of particular interest, however, is Tipler's sentence 18 in that it includes a Romani verb, inflected as in English but with a Welsh pronoun:

18. Awa, raker'd ō = yes, he said.

As well as making use of a number of loan-words apparently unknown to Sampson, Tipler's informants also spoke their Romani with a far heavier admixture of English and Welsh forms than did the Woods, as recorded by Kennedy. Yet the language was clearly still capable of augmentation from within, by means of such in-coinings as *bavalesko verdo*, motor car (129) and *verdo pakyensa*, aeroplane (131), which respectively make wholly appropriate use of the old genitive and instrumental cases. The following represent the sum of English and Welsh loan-words in the sample.

(*Romani*	*Welsh*)	(*Romani*	*English*)
cwrw	cwrw	a	a
droba	twrfa	duneni	dunes
evo	efo	fep	faith
ger	ger	fino	fine
gluro	glowr	grino	green
Jesi	Iesi	hopasava	I hope
kadira	cadair	krodi	curds
melino	melyn	komora	chamber
na	na	madimen	mad
ni	ni	minasela	he means
o	o	nevo	new
o	o/fo	richava	I reach
oriau	oriau	tap	on (top)
sgabora	sgubor	tinkarus	tinker
sketana	scertan	vlija	village
wedi	wedi	Walshi	Welsh
		(wi)ll	
		wi(th)	

Three further items, *solduro*, *papiris* and *inka*, could either be from English (soldier, paper, ink) or Welsh (soldiwr, papur, inc) whilst a fourth, *grit*, sick, is presumably *Shelta* (MacAlister 1937, 276).

Important as such examples may be as evidence of its general state of health, of greater significance for the future well-being of the language is Tipler's observation that the adults in the group spoke their Romani more fluently than their children: 'The children . . . ', he says, '. . . were no credit to their parents as regards the language, speaking a much more debased type of Romani, but even so their speech would be much too "deep" for any English Gypsy I know, and even the Hearnes and Lees of south Wales would hardly have been able to hold their own with them.'

Whether or not there now remain any speakers of 'deep' Welsh Romani is a moot point. Hancock (1970, 43–4) and Kenrick, *inter alios*, suggest that this was the case in the 1970s and 1980s but neither offers any supporting evidence. Jarman and Jarman, on the other hand, take the view that 'Welsh Romani in its pure state has now disappeared' (1979, 147).

That the *Puri Chib* had reached a similar critical point in England some time during the period 1750–1850 seems fairly clear. Almost without exception, those mid-nineteenth-century informants of whom we have any knowledge were either middle-aged or elderly and may well, apart from a few later outliers, have represented the last generation to have acquired the old language at their mother's knee.

Leland (1873, ix–xii), for example, tells us that, although 'the grammar has well nigh disappeared . . . within the memory of man, the popular Romani of this country was really grammatical . . .', while two years later Smart and Crofton distinguished between 'the deep or old dialect known only to a few aged Gypsies' and the 'common widespread corrupt dialect' or 'vulgar tongue in everyday use by ordinary Gypsies' (1875, xi). Their principal informant, Wester Boswell, was quite clear on this point (ibid., 200):

Kánna sas mándi a Tíkno, sor o poóro *fólki* rókerdé tátcho poóro Rómani laváw. Kek naneí see jaw síklo konáw, see sas báshaw doósta palál. Konáw o tárno *fólki*, kek yon rókerénna tátcho konáw. Boot gaujékani *fólki* see-lé, konáw.

When I was a lad, all the old folk spoke good old Gypsy words. They are not so much used now as they were many years ago. Now the young folk do not talk deep. They are too gaujo-like now.

Norwood, too, in an entry in one of his notebooks dated 9 July 1858, speaks of an encounter with two 'pure' Gypsy boys at Elstone Hardwick – George and Frederick Lock – whose grandfather, Myrack Lock, he was told, spoke Romani so deep that not one word in twenty was English. His daughter, however, was unable to understand him whilst, from his two grandsons, Norwood succeeded in obtaining only eighteen words. It may also be observed that Edwin Buckland, whose Romani, though not as good as Wester Boswell's, was infinitely better than any he had previously encountered, was seventy-three when Norwood first met him in 1863.

Sampson's experience also seems to have led him to much the same conclusion as Leland and Smart and Crofton. 'For several decades before the period when my own Gypsy studies began', he wrote,

Anglo-Romani, through the gradual loss of most of its inflections and the greater part of its original vocabulary, had sunk to the level of a semi-jargon, with the so-called 'deep Gypsy', possessed by a few aged pundits of the tribe, exhibiting little more than the debris of a once stately and beautifully constructed language. (Sampson 1926, vii)

In other words, we may assume that some time during the latter part of the eighteenth or the early part of the nineteenth century, the number of 'deep' Romani speakers, expressed both in real terms and, more importantly, as a percentage of the Gypsy population as a whole, had declined to a critical low and was, thereafter, insufficient to sustain the language as a living speech. Again, the picture here presented of a language in retreat and increasingly the preserve of an older generation finds an echo elsewhere. In Wales, to return to our original analogy, a particularly noticeable feature of post-war census data is the extent to which Welsh has become the language of the middle-aged and elderly. Thus, in 1981, at which point it has been suggested that the decline in the language may have reached its nadir, whilst 19 per cent of the population as a whole described themselves as speaking Welsh, the number of Welsh-speakers aged sixty-five and over represented 40 per cent of the age group as compared with only 15 per cent of those aged sixteen to twenty-four and 13 per cent of those aged three to four (Price 1984, 111).

At the same time as the number of 'deep' Romani speakers had apparently reached the point of terminal decline, a change also seems to have taken place in the way in which the language was perceived by the Gypsies themselves and, more particularly, by those best placed to ensure its survival – women. As Dorian points out in her survey of the Gaelic-speaking fisher folk of east Sutherland,

the home is the last bastion of a subordinate language in competition with a dominant official language of wider currency. An impending shift has in effect arrived even though a fairly sizeable number of speakers may be left, if those speakers have failed to transmit the language to their children so that no replacement generation is available when the parents' generation dies away. (Dorian 1981, 105)

The evidence for this, it is true, is slight, but may nevertheless be significant, particularly when viewed in the light of such contemporary studies of language shift within minority speech-communities as Gal (1979) and Dorian (1981). Thus, in chapter 5 of *Romany Rye*, Jasper's wife has the following to say:

> For my own part, I am not fond of using Romany words unless I can hope to pass them off for French . . . I heartily wish that there was no such language and do my best to keep it away from my children lest the frequent use of it should altogether confirm them in vulgar habits.

So also Plato Lovell (Groome 1880, 52):

> . . . and I'll tell you another thing as makes me wild, and that is, to hear some of our people ashamed of their own tongue . . . It was me and my daddy went to Wolverhampton market with two ponies and a donkey, and we saw two swellish-looking women walking down among the horses, all covered with falderals . . . my daddy asked 'do you see those two ladies, Plato?' 'Devil's ladies', I says; and my daddy said, 'they're two monkey Gypsies, married to colliers. And if you spoke to them in Romanes, they'd turn their noses up, make as they didn't know such vulgar talk. Such women as them is never no good. They ought to be burnt.'[6]

Compare also Belle Stewart's observations on those contemporary Scottish Travellers who would abandon the Cant for its supposed want of gentility:

> Mind ye, there's a good lot of snobbish Travellers. Och, I've met them mysel', especially at the berry-time. There's some o' them livin' aroond here and when you talk the Cant, it's 'oh, my goodness, what're ye talkin' like that for? Ye surely dinnae speak like that tae your bairns, do ye?'
> Of course, they're above this type o' thing. They think it's an awfu' low thing to talk Cant.

(Cf. Dorian 1981, 67. 'Since Gaelic had become one of the behaviours which allowed the labelling of individuals as Fishers, there was a tendency to abandon Gaelic along with other Fisher behaviours. As the same woman said "I think myself, as the children . . . got older, they . . . were ashamed to speak the Gaelic in case they would be classed as a Fisher." ').

Where only one parent is bilingual, the chances of any children acquiring equal fluency in both languages is significantly reduced. Thus, a survey carried out in Flintshire in 1953 found that of over 3,500 children of linguistically mixed marriages, only 115 (just over 3 per cent) were bilingual (Jac L. Williams 1958, 257), whilst a national survey of schoolchildren aged between five and fifteen years showed that, whereas 73 per cent of children, both of whose parents spoke Welsh, recorded Welsh as their first language, this was true of only 12 per cent of those with a Welsh-speaking mother and 7 per cent of those with a Welsh-speaking father (WJEC 1961, 10). (In her study of German–Hungarian bilingualism in Austria, Gal found that where marriage occurred between a German monolingual and a German–Hungarian bilingual, the children would grow up monolingual in German, whichever parent spoke only German (1979, 107)).

The negative attitude displayed by some Gypsies towards their language seems to have become more widespread as the nineteenth century progressed, until, for Sampson, writing in the early 1890s, the situation had clearly become acute (1891, 89):

> If it was permissible in Charles Lamb to complain of the 'decline of beggars in the Metropolis', surely, with equal propriety, the *Romano Rai* may lament the decay of our English Gypsies. For the old race is dying out and leaving no successor. Closer contact with civilisation, changed conditions of life, misdirected and unscientific philanthropy are rapidly reducing their customs and traditions to a dead letter, and their language to an ungrammatical jargon. The modern generation, 'bitten by that mad puppy they calls gentility', takes little or no interest in itself as a race, and shows an artless contempt for those who do. 'Isn't it wonderful, sir', said Mr. Lazarus Smith to me, apropos of perhaps the most charming of all books on English Gypsies, 'Isn't it wonderful that a real gentleman like Mr. G. could have wrote such a thing – nothing but low language and povertiness, and not a word of grammar or high larned talk in it from beginning to end? He's a nice gentleman but he couldn't have known what people would think of him, demeaning hisself in that way.'

If Borrow, Groome and Sampson are to be taken at face value, the reason for this growing disenchantment seems fairly clear. Lacking both the status and the socio-economic muscle of the dominant language, Romani had, by some Gypsies at least, come to be regarded as a symbol of cultural weakness rather than one of strength – a feeling which may also have been exacerbated by a belief that Romani was so much fallen into decay as to have become a mere cant, better suited to the requirements of a criminal fraternity than a respectable, law-abiding community, a point to which we shall return at a later stage.

Although, in recent years, there has been a resurgence of interest and pride in the language, little or nothing now remains of the older inflected variety. Between the wars, examples of inflected *Romanés* were reported from time to time in the pages of the *Journal of the Gypsy Lore Society* ('Anglo-Romani Gleanings', *JGLS passim*), but these, for the most part, would seem to have been drawn from the sometimes confused memory of an older generation rather than from everyday speech. Archdeacon D. M. M. Bartlett, introducing the last in this occasional series of 'Gleanings' (*JGLS* 28 (1949) 83), summed up the situation thus:

It must be confessed that here in the north, just as he [E.O. Winstedt] tells me is happening in the south, the old *Romanes* – the *tacho puro jib* of our earlier friends among the Herons, Boswells, Youngs, Lees – is now moribund if not actually dead. Occasionally one comes across a Romani who can *roker* connectedly but the 'younger end', as we say up in Yorkshire, only know a few short everyday phrases, and have a smattering of words which they try on the visitor, most of which are already sadly distorted and often used in a wrong sense.

More recently, Kenrick, writing in 1985, notes that 'One still hears talk of people who know "deep" Romanes but on investigation this means they simply use more Romani lexis in their English speech' (Acton and Kenrick 1985, 82).

But what of the *Poggadi Chib* itself? If, as suggested, *Romanés* today is the product of a more or less prolonged period of attrition, it would seem reasonable to suppose that, like the *Puri Chib*, it too will continue to decline until it eventually disappears altogether. Yet this does not seem to be happening. Not only has 'Broken Romani' changed relatively little over the past 150 years but, as a number of writers from Borrow on have pointed out, it is still apparently capable of augmentation, largely by in-coining from its existing root-stock. Such additions are, however, relatively insignificant in terms of the register as a whole, and certainly insufficient to justify any equation with the expansion in vocabulary and other linguistic resources normally associated with an emerging creole as it begins to assume the various extended functions of a mother tongue. Nevertheless, the fact remains that Romani English is more than a mere linguistic fossil and, indeed, as the Gypsy community gains in confidence, shows clear signs of renewed vigour both as a vehicle for asserting the Gypsies' own cultural identity and as a means of literary expression.

Our concern here, however, lies not with the future but with the past. Although it may be true to say that the *Poggadi Chib* has changed relatively little over the past 150 years as regards its outward form, it may also be argued that it has, at the same time, undergone a far more significant change in terms of its use and mode of transmission, and that it is this rather than its inherent vitality as a living language that has been largely responsible for its survival. In short, what seems to have happened is that *Romanés* has ceased to be a mother tongue, acquired in infancy and functioning as the common medium of social exchange within the community it serves, becoming instead a slang or special register, learned from other young people in early adolescence and serving only a limited number of purposes.

Although it seems likely that in the eighteenth century Romani, whether in its high or low form, was still the preferred medium of exchange for most

Gypsies, by the middle years of the nineteenth, this situation had begun to change. As early as 1841, Borrow, speaking of the widespread confusion between Romani and Thieves' Cant, goes on to say:

> The two languages are at the present day used for the same purpose, namely, to enable habitual breakers of the law to carry on their consultations with more secrecy and privacy than by the ordinary means. Yet it must not be forgotten that Thieves' Jargon was invented for that purpose while the Romany, ordinarily the proper speech of a particular nation, has been preserved from falling into entire disuse and oblivion because adapted to that same end. (Borrow 1841, 352)

Although Borrow is certainly overstating the case in suggesting that Romani in his day served no other purpose than 'to enable habitual breakers of the law to carry on their consultations with more secrecy', it may be reasonably inferred from his remarks that, for some Gypsies at least, it was no longer principally the language of hearth and home but was assuming a much more specialized role.

Although it is impossible to date this process of change with any degree of precision – the more so as it almost certainly occupied a period of many years – what does seem likely is that it may have begun to gather additional momentum at about the same time that the *Puri Chib* itself was embarking upon its final phase of life, say between the years 1750 and 1850. At that time, it is easy to imagine a younger generation, increasingly sophisticated and out of sympathy with the past, struggling with what little remained to them of the older language whilst their fathers (if not their mothers) sought to convince them of its continuing relevance, if only as a means of confusing the eavesdropping *Gaujos*. Thus it is that we find one of Borrow's Gypsy sages attempting to justify his own attachment to the poor old *Romano jib* in the following terms (Borrow 1874, 80):

> The tawno fokey often putches so koskipen se drey the Romano Jib? Mandy pens ye are sore dinneles; bute, bute koskipen se adrey lis, ta dusta, dosta of moro fokey would have been bitcheno or or nash'd but for the puro, choveno Romano Jib. A lav in Romany, penn'd in cheeros to a tawnie rakli, and rigg'd to the tan, has kair'd a boro kisi of luvvo and wafor covars, which had been chor'd, to be chived tuley pov, so that when the muskerres well'd they could latch vanisho, and had kek drom, but to mang also his artapen.
>
> The young people often ask: what good is there in the Romany tongue? I answers: Ye are all fools! There is plenty, plenty of good in it, and plenty, plenty of our people would have been transported or hung, but for the old, poor Roman language. A word in Romany said in time to a little girl, and carried to the camp, has caused a great purse of money and other things,

which had been stolen, to be stowed underground; so that when the constables came they could find nothing and had not only to let the Gypsy they had taken up go his way, but also to beg his pardon.

So, too, Tom Taylor, writing in the 1850s, tells us:

> I found on her part no reluctance to give me the Romani words for the objects about; and I may remark, by the way, that I have never found any difficulty of this kind among the younger Gypsies. The older ones are occasionally more suspicious, and will often pretend that they have no word in their language if they think the knowledge of it likely to be turned against them.

Although, in the course of its long history, Romani may occasionally have been used as a secret language, it is undeniably the case that there has never been any shortage of informants willing to share its knowledge – a fact which would seem to suggest that it was never universally regarded as such. In Wales, Romani would certainly seem to have been used quite openly, English or Welsh taking its place only when non-Romani speakers were directly addressed. By contrast, *Shelta*, which has also been character-ized as a secret language, somehow contrived to remain hidden until its 'discovery' during the later decades of the nineteenth century and has, for the most part, proved infinitely more difficult to collect. If, therefore, Romani is now regarded as a 'secret' language, it would seem reasonable to suppose that this represents a relatively recent development, associated perhaps with its demise as a mother tongue (for the advantages and dis-advantages inherent in the public use of Romani as a 'secret' language, see notes accompanying texts 34–7 and 103–8).

If Borrow had exaggerated the extent to which *Romanés* had, by the 1840s, sunk to the level of a mere cant, there can be little doubt that by the end of the century the process had been greatly advanced. 'In England', wrote Sampson in 1901, 'Romani is only used on special occasions when the Gypsies wish to conceal their meaning. In Wales, Romani is the mother tongue of the Welsh Gypsy, habitually used by him unless when addressing an Englishman or a Welshman' (Sampson 1901).

Today, the process of transition from mother tongue to cant is complete – the significant factor being that Romani English is no longer transmitted as a living language from parent to child. Nowadays, writes Kenrick (1979, 114–19),

> the everyday language in use among Gypsies in England is that of the surrounding urban or rural community in which they live and work. In

addition, they possess a special lexis of between 100 and 1,000 words which they can use to replace the English equivalents when they want or need to . . . The average six year old hardly knows ten word of the lexis and his knowledge does not exceed fifty before puberty. At this point, the girls learn the language from the younger women and the boys from the younger men. During the long drives looking for work, a boy can learn as many as thirty or forty words in a day and as he learns them he gets into situations where he needs to use them and is allowed to do so.

According to Kenrick, the secretness of the language is one reason why it is not taught to young children. 'If they don't know it, they can't reveal its secrets.' This may well be so but it must surely represent a *post hoc* rationalization of circumstances already in place for other reasons. As a mother tongue, Romani must at one time have been learned by children in infancy, and the need for secrecy, if recognized at all, conveyed in some other way as part of the normal process of socializing the young. In reality, although Romani may, on occasion, have proved useful as a means of ensuring privacy of speech, the desire to keep even its existence hidden from the *gaujos* may well have far more to do with the intimate connection between language and identity and the Gypsies' pressing need to preserve something which is wholly their own.

As a register of English rather than a mother tongue, Romani appears to possess only a limited range of functions. Its principal uses have been identified as follows (see Kenrick 1985):

(a) as a means of identification – never sufficient in itself but used in association with a range of other factors including dress, personal appearance, knowledge of friends, relations and stopping places etc.;

(b) as a trade register – Romani English items are, for example, to be found in horse dealers', market traders' and showman's cant;

(c) in singing, oath taking, terms of endearment and tattoos;

(d) in word-play;

(e) in private communication in a hostile environment; and

(f) for the reinforcement of group identity, e.g. at wakes and other similar gatherings.

One further development in the language requires mention here. The fact that Romani English is now something of an open book has apparently led some groups to look for other ways of retaining control over its use. The Gilligoolie Smiths, for example, have devised their own code, using some of the techniques employed in the formation of *Shelta* (Kenrick 1985), whilst according to Brune, others have achieved the same effect by altering the meaning of certain words by prior agreement. Thus, 'you chopped the grai, mush?' (you exchanged the horse, mate) may be used to mean 'you stole the chicken?' (Brune 1975, 753). Kenrick also describes how the Wilsons (Boswells) have augmented their vocabulary by borrowing both from books and from other continental Gypsies with whom they have come in contact: e.g. *espiba yeref'd gry* (a chestnut-coloured horse), where the first two words are taken from Borrow's Spanish Gypsy word list (Kenrick 1985). That the use of such techniques is likely to prove significant in terms of the future development of the language as a whole seems doubtful, however, as they are confined to individual families or subgroups and are almost certainly intended to confuse other Gypsies as much as the *Gaujo*.

If anything of substance may be gleaned from the foregoing brief and, it must be said, largely speculative survey, it is that whilst British Romani may have commenced life as a single more or less homogeneous entity, the pace and extent of its subsequent decline across the country as a whole has been far from uniform. What is also clear is that there is no evidence to suggest that at any time in its history was it used as a contact language either between the Gypsies and the host community as a whole or between the Gypsies and any other subsection of British society. This is not to say that its formation and subsequent development were not in some sense analogous to those of a pidgin/creole. The vital contact between Romani and English, however, would seem to have occurred not in the linguistic no man's land between the two speech communities, but within the collective mind of the Gypsies themselves, forced to cope first with bilingualism and subsequently with diglossia – the possession of two languages whose use is differentiated in terms of function and status.

This being so, the process itself is likely to have been far more protracted than is normally the case with a conventional pidgin/creole. So it is that even as late as the middle of the nineteenth century, by which time the *Poggadi Chib* had already assumed a dominant role, it is still possible to distinguish between three broad divisions of Romani in Britain, each characterized by differing degrees of purity – although, in all probability, even these merely represent the three main points on a much broader scale or 'post-creole continuum'. Thus, at one end of the spectrum stands the Welsh Romani of the clan of Abram Wood and, at the other, the 'vulgar' or 'Broken Romany' familiar to us from the writings of Borrow, Leland and so on. Towards the upper end of this scale may then be located the *Puri Chib* of Wester Boswell, and, at various lower points, the 'deep' northern Romani of the Boswells and Hernes as represented by Sampson in his 'Romani Gilli', the inflected Romani of Edwin Buckland as recorded by Norwood, and the 'hybrid vernacular' of the Welsh Lees.

Even today, Romani English may be said to take a variety of forms but such differences which remain are essentially lexical rather than grammatical in character. It is true that one occasionally encounters the odd plural ending or even an entire phrase (for example, in Wood 1973) – but these would, for the most part, appear to be mere formulae, generally associated with songs, oaths or other folkloric material.

Following the loss of its original syntax and morphology, and much of its native lexis, the language would then seem to have undergone a further change, involving its redefinition as a functionally specific Cant as opposed to a mother tongue. This change, it is true, may well have been responsible for saving the language from ultimate annihilation, but it has also posed certain problems of its own. As noted above, whatever the reality, Romani English is still regarded by some Gypsies as a secret language whose very existence they would wish to keep hidden. Yet, leaving aside the difficulties involved in actually maintaining and using a code of this type, there is also a further contradiction here which may well have a bearing on the future health of the language itself. Possession of their own highly distinctive lexis not only links the Gypsies of Britain with their fellows across the world but with their remote Indian ancestry, and as well as serving to reinforce their own sense of community, undoubtedly underpins their claim to wider political/cultural recognition on the part of society as a whole. If, however, the fiction of secrecy is maintained, the Gypsies of Britain may well be denying themselves use of one of the most effective weapons in their armoury. For the past 150 years, British Gypsiographers have been confidently predicting the more or less imminent demise of the language but, despite their worst fears, it has continued to thrive. Whether or not it continues to do so may well depend on the extent to which the Gypsies themselves are able to reconcile the dubious short-term advantages of a poorly-kept secret with the potentially far greater strategic advantage to be gained from the proud and public acknowledgement of a mode of speech emblematic of their own ancient and distinctive culture.

2

The Gypsies, A Musical Race?
The Indian Connection

As professional musicians, we meet with the Gypsies in most European countries, generally in small bands, roving from place to place and entertaining the people with the national melodies of the country. Thus we find them everywhere – especially in Spain, in Russia, in Hungary, Transylvania, Wallachia and even in South America. In the northern part of Russia, they excel as vocal performers, in the Ukraine, in the Danubian principalities and in Hungary, they are almost exclusively instrumentalists. It cannot exactly be said that they have anywhere preserved a national music of their own. They have adopted in every country the music of the people among whom they live.

(L. A. Smith, 1889)

When the great Gypsy musician, Béla Radics, died in 1930, his funeral in Budapest was attended by upwards of 50,000 mourners, and he was accompanied to his publicly funded 'grave of honour' by some 500 of his fellow artists. Three months later, at an open-air memorial service for which special trains were laid on from all over Hungary, his life and achievements were celebrated by an orchestra of 1,000 Gypsy musicians, including more than two dozen cimbalomists – exponents of the Magyars' own national instrument.

For many of those late nineteenth-century musicologists, convinced of the seminal importance of the Abbé Liszt's extensive collection of Gypsy airs, gathered in the Slavonic and Magyar provinces of the old Austro-Hungarian Empire, anything short of so heartfelt a show of national mourning would have seemed less than just. Charles Laporte, for example, writing in the preface to his *Gypsy Melodies* of 1876, was in no doubt of their importance for the musical life of the area:

The natives dwelling on the Danube – Hungarians, Moldavians, Slovenians, Wallachians, and others – owe their music to the Gypsies . . . and many of their melodies have become the national airs of those countries. Their music has been principally developed on the hospitable soil of Hungary, and from thence it has spread all over the Danubian principalities. The Magyars have adopted them as their national musicians, and there is hardly a village without their minstrels called Lautars.

Yet despite their undoubted pre-eminence as executants of the nation's popular music, the idea that the Gypsies of Hungary were responsible for the music itself did not go long unchallenged, and even the cimbalom itself, that quintessentially Gypsy instrument, has been shown to be of *Gaujo* origin. (In its present form it was developed from the older dulcimer some time during the 1870s by a *Gaujo* instrument-maker, J. Schunda of Budapest. Originally it was much lighter and, when played, was either laid across the thighs or on a table or barrel-top. It was Schunda who enlarged it, adding a number of chromatic strings and a damper pedal and setting it on its own four feet, thus creating the distinctive concert instrument of today.)

Although it was Bartók who was principally responsible for demonstrating that the so-called Gypsy music of Hungary was really Hungarian music composed by Hungarians, he was by no means the first to cast doubt on Liszt's underlying thesis. In 1890, for example, Francis Korbay, writing in *The Critic* (22 February, p.86), had already dismissed as 'too absurd' the notion that 'the poor, despised, cowardly, immoral, horse-thieving, tinkering Gypsy should be supposed to be the father of our heroic and martial music and our elevated and beautiful moral poetry':

> Outside of the fact that they play only the national music of the country in which they happen to live and disfigure it with their trashy embellishments (sometimes to the extent that the original folk song can hardly be recognized), they are entirely devoid of the feelings which lie at the bottom of all folk music – patriotism and love.

Even their skill in performance failed to impress:

> ... the Gypsy is the performer who can catch by ear what the paper refuses to do. He is a clever monkey and, above all, a charlatan. What the bad virtuoso used to do in fooling his audiences with astounding bravura, caricaturing a simple and great air until it becomes glittering nonsense, the Gypsy imitates in overloading the great and simple songs with cheap laces and fringes until they become a noisy and senseless chaos. Not being able to understand the pathos and breadth of the doric-like airs, the Gypsy lends them narcotic drunkenness which pleases the tipsy peasant and arouses the curiosity of the enquiring

foreigner. Hear him play an Italian opera piece or perhaps the overture to *Tannhäuser* and you will recognize the truth of my statement.

Vekerdi, albeit an altogether more objective observer, is no less equivocal in his conclusions, pointing out that most of what we now regard as typical of the work of the *Tzigan* café musicians was, in fact, as regards both words and music, composed either by Hungarians or 'Hungarianized Gypsies' – the so-called *Ungarika Roma* or *Lavutara* (violinists) – who neither spoke Romani nor ever communicated with their more traditional counterparts, the *Vlasika Roma, Lovara* and *Khelderara* (Vekerdi 1967).

Yet in one sense, Gypsies the world over may rightly claim to have more than a passing interest in the performing arts; for, whether or not they have shown themselves to be musically innovative, music may almost certainly be said to be in their very name if not actually in their blood. What is meant here is not the common English epithet, which simply reflects the once widely held belief that those to whom it was applied came originally from Egypt; nor is it the widespread European usage, familiar to us in its German form, *Zigeuner* – although this, too, has been derived by de Goeje from an oriental root, *tsjengi*, signifying 'musicians' or 'dancers'. Rather, it is the native Gypsy *Rom* which, whilst limited in meaning in Welsh Romani to 'husband', is still used in most central European and eastern dialects to signify 'man' or 'Gypsy male'. (In the Welsh dialect 'no instances occur of *Rom* used either in the sense of "Gypsy" or of "man", although the adj. *Romano* shows that the former must have been one of the original meanings' (Sampson 1926, iv, 317)).

As Sampson has pointed out (ibid.), *Rom*, together with its various eastern equivalents, stands in direct phonetic correspondence with the Sanskrit *Doma* or *domba*, signifying 'a man of low caste who gains his livelihood by singing and dancing', from which we may safely infer that it was among such people that the Gypsies first originated.

'This identification of the Gypsy race with the Indian Dom musicians' has, however, as Sampson goes on to say,

> been disputed by Pischel upon the ground that the Doms are apparently not a true Aryan people, but later ethnographical researches point to the name being an occupational rather than a racial term, applied loosely to any wandering, low-caste tribe of minstrels and dancers. It seems clear, therefore, that the word *Rom* preserves for us the original caste and calling, if not perhaps the race, of the ancestors of the Asiatic and European Gypsies.

The Doms of modern India are to be found in the western and north-western provinces and, even now, would appear to have a number of characteristics in common with their distant European cousins. In Dardestan, for example, their principal means of subsistence are said to be smithcraft and music, whilst, according to one observer, they demonstrate a marked fondness for 'sleeping, dreaming, sitting, talking, gambling, smoking, drinking, fighting and, above all, singing' – a description which, if the popular press is to be believed, might equally well be applied to many or most contemporary British Gypsies.

That the gypsies have for long been associated with the performing arts is further suggested by the tradition, noted both by Hamza of Isfahan – an Arab historian writing in Persian about AD 950 – and, some fifty years later, by the poet Firdusi in his *Shanama* (Story of the Kings).

Both men tell how, about the year 420, Behram Gur, a wise and beneficent prince of the Sassanid dynasty, sent to his father-in-law, Shankal, king of Cambodia and maharaja of north India, for a host of minstrels in order to raise the flagging spirits of his poorer subjects. According to tradition, the principal actors in the drama are said to have been the ancestors of the present-day Gypsies, a belief recalled by Sampson in his poem 'O Janik Aré Ravnos' (The Apotheosis of Augustus John) (Sampson 1931, 14).

Lonely and bored, and convinced that more fun was to be had singing and dancing in 'the other place', God summons Peter and orders him to send for the artist and a company of Gypsies to liven things up a little:

> 'P'uka leski pesa te rigerél
> Peske pala ta raikane chaia,
> T'a dosta Kâle, mursh t'a juvél,
> T'a dosta Romane Raia.
>
> Keráva maia sar yekar kedás
> Bahram Gur, o bâro kralíshus;
> 'Jâ péndas Firdúsi, bersha gilé.
> 'Re tachano paramíshus.'

'Bid him bring with him his special friends and some pretty girls, and a band of Gypsies, men and women, and a few Romany Ryes. I mean to follow the good example of Bahram Gur, that mighty monarch, whose veracious history Firdusi related long ago in his epic *The Shah Námeh*.'

The following translation of Firdusi's account is taken from Harriott's 'Observations on the Oriental Origin of the Romnichal' (*Transactions of the Royal Asiatic Society of Great Britain* ii (1830), 527–8):

Reason of Bahram's Bringing the Luri from India

The King addressed letters to the priests of each province enquiring who was distressed, and where the poor were afflicted; demanding of them every information relative to the state of his empire, that the same might be communicated to the royal heart. Each mobed, noble, and sage replied that the face of the country was populous, and on every side thanksgivings were heard: the indigent alone complaining to His Majesty of the hardness of the times; that the opulent drank wine and ornamented their heads with chaplets of flowers, quaffing liquor to the sound of music, without reflecting on their poor fellow creatures. The King smiled at the complaint; and, to remedy the privation complained of, despatched an envoy, with the following message, to Shankal, King of Canauj. 'O Prince, attentive to justice; the indigent classes here drink wine without music, a circumstance of which the wealthier cannot approve. Therefore, of those Luri (of India) chuse [*sic*] for and send to me ten thousand male and female to play upon the lute.' The Luri were accordingly sent to the Persian King, who assigned them an appropriate residence, and gave to each individual a cow and an ass; he desired them to nominate a village chief and bestowed also a thousand load of wheat on such as were most deserving; to the end that, labouring with their kine and asses, they might reap, in due season, the seed of their wheat and thus enable his poor subjects to have their music gratuitously performed.

The Luri departed; and heedlessly consuming all their wheat as well as their cows, toward the end of the year were left shamelessly destitute. The King rebuked them for their lavish conduct in wasting corn, and neglecting to harvest and crop: and then dismissed them, with an order that, taking their asses, they should load them with their chattels, and support themselves by means of their songs, and the strumming of their silken bows: and that each year they should travel over the country, and sing for the amusement of the high and the low.

The Luri, agreeably [*sic*] to this mandate, now wander about the world, seeking employment, associating with dogs and wolves, and thieving on the road by day and by night.

In Firdusi's version of the tale, these wandering minstrels are described as *Zatts*, reflecting the Arabic pronunciation of *Jatt*, whilst Hamza not unnaturally favours the Persian *Luri*. Of the descendants of these latter, Sir Henry Pottinger, writing on p. 153 of his *Travels in Beloochistan and Sinde* (1816), has the following to say:

They bear a marked affinity to the Gypsies of Europe. They speak a dialect peculiar to themselves, have a king to each troop and are notorious for kidnapping and pilfering. Their principal pastimes are drinking, dancing and music . . . In each company there are always two or three members who profess modes of divining which procure them a ready admission into every society.

Hutton, too, writing in 1949, notes that 'among the tribes of Beluch-istan, it is fitting to mention the humble Luri, wandering tin-smiths, workers in jewels in gold and silver, minstrels, musicians, midwives and common labourers. They are, in fact, Gypsies' (see also Clébert 1964, 17).

The American Gypsiographer, Charles Godfrey Leland, rightly con-vinced of the Gypsies' Indian origin, also attempted, somewhat less successfully, to establish a direct link between the Gypsy players of his own day and their remote oriental ancestors. 'All of my readers', he says (1873, 113), 'have heard of the Nautch girls, the so-called Bayaderes dancing girls of India; but very few, I suspect, are aware that their generic name is remotely preserved in several English gypsy words.' *Nauter*, for example, he refers back to the *Nats*, 'a kind of Gypsies . . . generally jugglers, dancers and musicians', whilst *nobbet*, he suggests, is derived from *naubatt* which, in the language of these same *Nats*, means 'time, turn, and instruments of music sounding at the gate of a great man at certain intervals'. In their English setting, both words are said by Leland to mean 'going about with music', although the latter may also mean 'a time or go': 'you can shoon covvo at the wellgorras when yeck rakkers the waver: You jal and nobbet.'

Neither of these words is, however, to be found in any other English Gypsy vocabulary and it is, perhaps, as well to treat Leland's observations on Gypsy etymology with some caution, particularly those words which he himself acknowledges to be rare (see, for example, pp.109–33 of *The English Gypsies and Their Language*). He would undoubtedly have been on surer ground had he confined himself to the Romani English *gilli*, a song, *kel*, to dance, and *bosh*, a fiddle, all of which are of proven Indian ancestry.[7]

Yet whilst Leland's wholly unscientific use of his Hindustani dictionary as a field-aid undoubtedly led him greatly to exaggerate the true extent of the Romani English lexis (his own collection, he thought, amounted to some 4,000 words, as compared with Borrow's 1,400 and Kenrick and Wilson's estimated current working vocabulary of between 850 and 1,000), he was quite right in assigning pride of place to words of Indian origin. Indeed, although the Gypsies' oriental credentials had been well established long before he first encountered the language, to Leland, more so than to Borrow, belongs much of the credit for drawing this to the attention of the wider reading public.

Lt.-Col. Laing, in a letter to the *Journal of the Gypsy Lore Society* dated 30 June 1891, wrote

Whilst reading Mr Leland's most interesting work on Gypsy sorcery I was struck by the numerous words which are still extant in India – some of the verses being perfectly intelligible phonetically. I ought to have known that Romany originally came from India, but I was not prepared to find that I could translate some of their incantations without the least difficulty. If I had the work by me now, I would give a specimen which would be understood by any fairly intelligent inhabitant of the Dekhan. (See also notes accompanying text 116)

Smith, too, speaks of a

very charming Hindu air . . . I heard sung by an English Gypsy woman almost note for note as I found it in a valuable book on 'Hindu Music from Various Authors, compiled by Sourindro Mohun Tagore; for private circulation only. Calcutta. 1875'.

This song is so plaintive and so pretty that I could wish some of our gifted nineteenth century song makers would reset it in a more worthy shrine of harmony. I give the original words as they are to be found in the work before referred to.

> Kurna na päee bat
> Ab myn. Peea soo jeea ke bat
> Oodowjee! Tahreean, myn bulaeen leongi ho!
> Mohe le'chulo oonhen ke pas.

(Smith 1889, 213)

The opening quatrain of Smith's highly coloured sixteen-line metrical English paraphrase runs as follows:

> I could not speak with him those fondest words
> Which I had treasured up to tell;
> My streaming eyes were dim with weary tears,
> Which then, alas! unheeded fell.

More recently, Lal (1962, 74) speaks of a Mr Dave – a native of Gujarat, resident in the United States for some two decades – who believed that American Gypsies were still singing 'old songs of Gujarat' which he had no difficulty in understanding. At his suggestion, the director of the New York Public Library arranged for a number of these to be collected, of which the following are reproduced here by way of example (see also Brown 1929, 307).

1

Mar man, Devla, mar man,
Samo Na Mudara man.
Devla, Tu men mudarya,
Misto nai Keresa.

Strike me, God, strike me,
Only don't strike me dead.
God, if you kill me,
Then my blood is on your hands.

2

Te merava, te merava,
Nai so te kerava?
Kana me merava, Devla,
Kon man rovlariela?

I could wish that I were dying,
What will ever become of me?
When I lie a-dying, God,
Who will mourn me bitterly?

3

Borane Jone man tiré kalé takhá,
Savé gozo Jone dryvan lavé jore,
Ai myon, hasian,
Ai da miré kalo sero.

Your (dark) eyes devour my soul,
Devour my soul with care;
How beautiful they are!
Your dark eyes, how fair.

Although the foregoing translations clearly suffer from a degree of
poetic licence (surely *misto nai keresa* means no more than 'you do not do
well'?), they still have sufficient in common with their Gypsy originals to
justify the name. One wonders, however, how far Mr Dave was responsible
for them. Mrs I. R. Jani, herself a native of Gujarat, to whom I offered
these verses in their original form and without benefit of translation, had
the following to say (personal communication, June 1992):

I would like to say immediately that they clearly sound very much Indian
and, in particular, they sound very similar to present-day Gujarati, more

especially the Mutchi and Marwadi dialects . . . I found the first verse (apart from the last line) to be wholly intelligible in orthodox Gujarati and would render it as follows:

> Mar man, Devla, mar man,
> God is in my mind;
> Samo na mudara man
> God is in the opposite temple;
> Devla, tu men mundarya
> God in me.
> Misto nai keresa.
> . . .?

Given the very real discrepancy between Mrs Jani's rendering of this verse and the version offered by Lal, I asked her if she would turn the latter back into Gujarati in order that I might compare the result with the Romani original. Her response was as follows (personal communication, August 1992). The Romani line is here followed by the corresponding line in Mrs Jani's transliterated Gujarati.

> Mar man, Devla, mar man
> *Mane maro, Bhagwan, mane maro*
> Samo na mudara man
> *Fakta mane marsho nahe,*
> Devla, Tu men mudarya
> *Bhagwan, jo tame mane marsho to*
> Misto nai keresa
> *Tame yogya nathe karta.*

Mrs Jani found Lal's second and third verses far more difficult, although she was able to pick out a number of words: *Karna* Lord Krishna; *Devla* God; *nai* no; *tu* you; *lave jore* bring; *kon* who?; *man* mind; and *hasin*, beautiful (Urdu).

Mrs Jani also offered the following translation into Gujarati of the second of Lal's verses. Once again, the Romani line is followed immediately by its Gujarati equivalent:

> Te merava, te merava
> *Jiare mari antim ghadi hashe,*
> Nai so te kerava?
> *Teeare marun shun theshe?*

> Kana me merava, Devla,
> *Jiare marun maddoo padioo hashe*
> Kon man rovlariela?
> *Teeare kon pok mukene radshe?*

For a brief introduction to Romani and its relationship with other modern Indian languages, see Glanville Price 1984, 232ff. and Fraser 1992, 29–33.

Laing in the *Journal of the Gypsy Lore Society* (1891) in a reference to Indian nursery rhymes, also makes the following point, suggestive of a possible link with certain types of contemporary Gypsy verse: 'I must explain that, in India at the present day, they consist in the first place of some permanent jingling expression and in the second place of topical hits invented by the nurses and suited, more or less, to their ideas.' By way of example, he cites the following:

> Kookooroo kookooroo ka!
> Murgisola baida dya,
> Jaldi batcha paida yaya,
> Kookooroo kookooroo ka!

> The cock shouts kookooroo!
> The hen laid sixteen eggs
> And quickly hatched the chicks.
> The cock shouts kookooroo!

Yet, tempting as it may be to look for a continuous and well-defined thread linking the singing tradition of the Indian subcontinent with that of contemporary British Gypsies, it is highly unlikely that any such connection could ever be satisfactorily proved. The Gypsies have been on the road for upwards of 1,000 years and the earliest surviving Romani song texts can only be dated with any certainty to the first half of the nineteenth century. Gypsy song is, moreover, highly volatile in character and, whilst the underlying thought process may be wholly alien to our western European tradition, has also shown itself to be extremely susceptible to external influence. It may also be observed that short songs of a type similar to that quoted by Laing are well represented in both the Gaelic and Welsh repertoire and, indeed, exhibit many features in common with child-rhymes everywhere. This being so, it is difficult to escape the conclusion that any similarities which may exist between Laing's example and the English Gypsy 'short song' are, for the most part, purely fortuitous, the result of a common rather than a derivative approach.

The alternative view, that the Gypsies left India with a stock of traditional material which, despite centuries of contact with a multiplicity of other cultures, has not only remained relatively true to type but may even have influenced the folk repertoire of other nations, seems hardly tenable. Yet Groome, whilst he may have had little enough to say on the subject of Romani verse, was apparently persuaded that this was indeed the case as regards Gypsy folk tales; and if he is right, unlikely as this may be, there is no reason why the same argument should not apply to Gypsy song. In summary, Groome's argument runs as follows (see Groome 1888 and 1899 and Thompson 1910a):

> To recapitulate, my theory, then, is this: The Gypsies quitted India at an unknown date, probably taking with them scores of Indian folk-tales, as they certainly took with them hundreds of Indian words. By way of Persia and Armenia they arrived in the Greek speaking Balkan peninsula and tarried there for several centuries, probably disseminating their Indian folk-tales, and themselves probably picking up Greek folk-tales, as they certainly gave Greek the Romani word *bakht* (fortune), and borrowing from it *paramísi* (story), and about a hundred more terms. From the Balkan peninsula they have spread since 1417, or possibly earlier, to Siberia, Norway, Scotland, Wales, Spain, Brazil, and the countries between, everywhere probably disseminating the folk-tales they started with and those they picked up by the way, and everywhere probably adding to their stories.

Although the Gypsies' nomadic way of life undoubtedly brought them into contact with a variety of different cultures, there is no evidence whatsoever to suggest that their relationship with the settled population was ever sufficiently relaxed to include the exchange of fireside tales. Indeed, the early European chroniclers make no mention of the Gypsies as entertainers of any kind, formal or informal, concentrating solely on their role as thieves and purveyors of magic and other novelties to the gullible poor. In England, too, although we know that they were reckoned 'pleasant dancers', performing before both Henry VIII and the Scottish king, there is no instance in the literature of their engaging in public story-telling or street singing (other than to cry their wares).

~

> In these days, at any rate, they seem apt to take on the local colouring of the music native to the land in which they are found; German Gypsy tunes, for example, are absolutely different in scale, rhythm, and general character from Serbian Gypsy tunes and they again from the Hungarian Gypsy. The Gypsy element, as in the case of

Hungarian music, probably comes out in the manner of performance.

(A. Gilchrist, 1911)

As Thomas Acton rightly points out in his note accompanying the 1986 edition of the *Romano Drom Song Book*, Gypsy song is a mirror of Gypsy life and for Gypsy children, therefore, it is impossible to ignore it, especially in the new spirit of hope created by the World Romani Congress. It is thus particularly heartening to find a growing number of British Gypsies seeking to express themselves in their own language. Whether, like Zilla Roberts, they write their Romani unselfconsciously, employing the natural rhythms of the spoken language without reference to any formal literary tradition or, like Oddley and Lavengro, using English literary forms interlaced with Romani words and experience, is, as Acton elsewhere suggests, of little consequence. Both are equally valid, utilizing, as they do, the power of the vernacular and giving respect to those who use it (Acton and Kenrick 1985, 12). What is important, however, if this trend is to continue, is that the Gypsies and, more particularly, the young, should be given the opportunity to acquaint themselves with the oral literature of their own people, past and present. Whether or not they choose to discard its peculiar forms and features in favour of their own distinctive style is neither here nor there; what matters is the self-confidence which comes from the realization that they are the beneficiaries of an ancient and worthwhile tradition, moulded perhaps by centuries of exposure to a variety of external influences but sufficiently resilient to retain its own distinctive flavour and character.

Yet, attractive as it may be, the idea that, in their music and song, contemporary European Gypsies may have preserved something of the flavour of the ancient Luri minstrelsy, finds little support. Like Kounavine, Sampson, writing in his introduction to MacAlister's *Romany Versions* (1928, 3), is characteristically unequivocal:

Whilst we would fain believe that the oriental *Luri*, or imported Indian minstrels of Persia, brought with them their own songs, sung to the strains of the lute, it may safely be surmised that both words and melodies soon lost any native characteristics they possessed and, chameleon-like, took on the colour of their last environment.

This, at least in historical times, is what we everywhere discover, when Gypsy music or Gypsy song . . . have been investigated in the hope of detecting survivals of a remote past . . . Wherever Gypsy lyrics have been collected, we find the same indebtedness to local folk song, theme and air alike being derivative.

Even among the *Tchinghianés*, hundreds of whose songs have been preserved by Paspati in his *Études*, what might otherwise have been supposed to be native Gypsy productions have for the most part been found to be nothing more than translations of popular Greek lyrics composed in the simple *Khleptic* measure. Read metrically, they at once resolve themselves into verses or half verses consisting of fifteen-syllable lines divided into two hemistichs of four and three iambic feet respectively, the final foot ending with an additional weak or unstressed beat, for example,

Ta ká | bashén' | o tchír|iklé ‖ te tchú|tchiá | sheráv | man.

And when the birds sing, I think of thy breasts.

So too in the following couplet introduced into Paspati's fourth folk tale, although here, instead of a true amphibrach, there is prolongation of the final vowel in the last foot.

O rúf | kamkhál | e bák|ritchés ‖ kamkhál | e mís|irká.
I métch|ka í | ritch(i)ní | dinás ‖ tradál|a yék | gadjó.

The wolf will eat the little lamb and eat the turkey also,
The pussy cat, she beat the bear; the gentile shrinks in terror.

It is the same metre as used in the Greek New Year Hymn to Saint Basil:

Saint Basil, see, is coming out; from Caesaraea coming;
He carries incense in his hand, and candle, ink and paper.

In Hungary, too, the Gypsies have adopted local forms, employing the dodecasyllabic, octosyllabic and heptasyllabic line in exactly the same proportion as they occur in Hungarian folk poetry and popular song (Vekerdi 1967). However, as the accent in Hungarian invariably falls on the first syllable whilst, in the Vlax dialect it is the final or, occasionally, the penultimate syllable which carries the accent, the rhythm established in any given text may well be at variance with the natural rhythm of the spoken language. Thus, in its ideal form, the dodecasyllabic line is divided into two half lines, each of six syllables, both of which are further subdivided into two groups of four and two syllables respectively, for example,

Gelas tar i | iboj ‖ po zeleno | reto

Ibolya went out on the green meadow.

As the verse ictus, or metrical stress, invariably falls on the fifth syllable of each half line, in those cases where the half line ends on an oxytonant (a word stressed on the final syllable), the natural cadence of the spoken word is ignored and the penultimate syllable stressed in accordance with the established prosodic rule. This, however, only happens when reciting without melody.When singing, the rhythm of the melody cancels out the rhythm of the text. Thus, 'andá peské | jakhá' (in his eyes) becomes 'andá peské | jákha'.

The simpler the measure, the better suited it is to the purposes of Romani improvisation. The following, in the Wallachian dialect, is from the singing of Elizabeth Horváth of Ipoly-Szászd in the Comitat of Hont. The octosyllabic metre used will immediately be recognized as that employed by Longfellow in his *Hiawatha* and by Jerome when describing the upper reaches of the Thames. The same metre has also been noted both in Silesia, and in Russia. Mrs Horváth was recorded by Anton Herrmann in Nagy-Maros, on the slopes of the Weisser Berg, on 20 April 1890.

> Dsava mange andi kricma,
> Tina man jek funto brinza,
> Hej, de bari me khelahi!
> Nane oda lavutari,
> Ko mri dili basavahi;
> Basavel le o Chuhari,
> Bacakero lavutari.
>
> I go into the tavern,
> I buy myself a pound of cheese,
> Ah! how great is my longing for a dance!
> There is no fiddler there,
> Who my song will play,
> Cuhar plays it,
> The fiddler of Waitzen.

In the couplets and quatrains of the Gypsies of Spain a similar indebtedness to local forms has also long been apparent. Many of them, as Sampson has pointed out, although imbued with the true Gypsy spirit, are closely akin to the assonantic stanzas of the *Romanceros*, which, in the peninsula, have furnished the model for so much extempore verse. Strettell, too, writing in 1887, found that even the *Flamenco* was becoming '*Gachonales*' (*gaujo*-fied), as the Gypsies themselves put it. The following Spanish Gypsy *copla* is from the singing of Fabian de Castro, the noted *Gitaristo*, as recorded by Augustus John (John 1911) some time prior to the First World War. It was also subsequently retrieved by Irving Brown from the great *Gaujo* singer, *Mochuelo* (Brown 1929, 176). The few slight variations in Brown's text are indicated in square brackets. Brown's translation is here preferred, however, as coming closer to the sense of the original.

> Quando chiriclo gillaba [guiyaba],
> Scena [sena] que vieneel chivel [e chibé],
> Quinaores [quinaore] de los [lo] drones
> Ligueranse [liguerarse] à vuestro quer.

> When the cock is crowing,
> You know 'twill soon be day.
> Home, you highway robbers;
> 'Tis time you sped away.

In Britain, too, *Gaujo* influence is everywhere apparent, a fact which may owe as much to the circumstance that the Gypsies seem not to possess any of their own melodies, specifically formulated with a view to meeting the peculiar requirements of native Romani verse. Smart and Crofton certainly found 'no English tunes . . . which can be said to be peculiarly Gypsy' (1875, 198), whilst Gilchrist, in her review of Gillington's *Songs of the Open Road*, notes:

the music of these *gilia*, with its short repeated phrases, is as primitive in structure as the traditional game-tunes of English children, and, indeed, two of the tunes are recognisable as belonging to such games, 'Mandi Jal'd to Puv a Grai' being a variant of 'The Jolly Miller' and 'Ovva Tshavi', a combination of two other familiar scraps. (Gilchrist 1911, 60–5)

'Nor is there anything un-English', she continues,

in the tunes of the two other *gilia* or of the Gypsy dances, their rhythms and phrases being also familiar, though they may have to be sought elsewhere under other titles, e.g. the Gypsies' step-dance 'Fish and 'taters' is the old reel or hornpipe air 'Will ye Go and Marry Katie'.

So, too, in the present collection, Manfri Wood's 'Doi Sas Chai' (text 131), one of the few surviving texts in the older Welsh Romani, was sung to an air variously associated with a number of well-known Welsh songs including 'Cosher Bailey', 'Claddu'r Mochyn Du' and 'Cân y Patriarch-iaid'. Even that most popular of Romani English quatrains, 'Can You Rokker Romani' (texts 15–22), although now generally given in the form of a rhythmical recitative, was apparently originally associated with the tune 'Money Makes the Mare to Go', whilst other similar verses – e.g. texts 23–6 – may be heard to the air of 'Bobby Shafto'.

Yet the use of even the least sophisticated *Gaujo* melodies and systems of versification seems fraught with difficulty. The majority of Romani English song texts are accentual rather than strictly quantitative in character and whilst the establishment of a strong underlying rhythm is clearly important, even regular syllable counting, regardless of stress, is comparatively rare. Thus, in the short song (which may be said to represent the most stable element in the repertoire), whilst the heptasyllabic line would seem to predominate, the number of syllables per line is rarely fixed. In the present collection, it will be seen that it ranges from 3 (text 32, l.4) to 16 (text 56, l.3) and, within the one text, from 9 to 16 (text 56). Apocopation, too, other than that occurring naturally in the spoken language, is seldom used simply to regulate line length, the singer merely adjusting the rhythm in order to accommodate any excess. Supplementary syllables, common in Irish Tinker song, are also rarely used in order to make good any shortfall, and never simply in order to supply a rhyme – this in marked contrast with the frequent pleonasms characteristic of the regular metrical productions of the *Romané Raiá*.

Use of the heptasyllabic line suggests a connection with a deeper and once more widespread tradition. With its underlying sense of urgency, it is the measure of enchantment, used by the witches in Macbeth, by Puck and by the authors of the Norse sagas. It also links the Romani English short song with many of the magical incantations obtained by Wlislocki from the *gulé Romni* (sweet women) or *lacé Romni* (good women) of the Hungarian Gypsies. For example:

> Páni, páni, sikova,
> Dikh the upré, dikh télé!
> Buti páni sikovel
> Buti pál yákh the dikhel
> Te ákáná mudárel.

> Water, water, hasten here.
> Look thou high and look thou low.
> Water hasten without stint;
> May you flood the evil eye
> May it perish, and not I.

Although the use of rhyme is not unknown in English Gypsy verse – for example, the opening lines of texts 23–6 – it is by no means a prerequisite and is rarely sustained. This, however, would seem to be a matter of preference rather than merely the result of prosodic incompetence, as one occasionally finds quite sophisticated examples (both full and assonantal) introduced into otherwise largely unrhymed texts. The following example is from Minty Smith's lament for her brother Levi's horse, killed whilst crossing the A2 at Stone, Kent, in 1962 (Kennedy 1975, 778):

> And that's when the car 'it 'im
> And 'e was all me brother 'ad to make 'is livin'
> 'E was a smart 'orse, a real good cart 'orse
> Gord, I wish 'e 'adn't tried to cross the road.
> O, Dordi, dordi,
> Dick at the gavvers, dick at the gavvers.
>
> 'E was charged with causing an obstruction
> And when ol' gavver 'eard me brother's pleas
> 'E thought 'e was a-startin' orf a big eruption
> And then 'e charged 'im for a-breachin' o' the peace.

Elsewhere, however, rhyme would seem to be consciously avoided even though this may involve discarding an otherwise wholly appropriate word in favour of a less obvious alternative. In the third line of the following extract from Wally Fuller's rendering of Brian O'Linn, for example (A), a *Gaujo* singer would almost certainly have transposed 'thin' and 'cold' in order to complete the rhyme – as, indeed, is the case in Séamus Ennis's version (B) of the same song on 'Music at the Gate' (Folktracks 60–079):

> A
>
> Now old Briney O'Linn and his wife's mother
> They all went into bed together.
> The blankets was thin and the sheets they were cold;
> 'Lay close to the wall', says Briney O'Linn.
>
> B
>
> And Brian O'Linn and his wife and wife's mother
> All climbed into the bed together.
> The sheets they were old and the blankets were thin;
> 'Lie close to the wall', says Brian O'Linn.

Again, in Carolyne Hughes's 'Drowsy Thoughts' (Black Dog and Sheep Crook, Folktracks 60–43), where 'lie' (l.4) and 'nigh' (l.8) are preferred for 'lies' and 'near':

> Now, the cuckoo she's called a merry bird;
> Love, don't she sing as she flies.
> Why, she brings us good tidings
> And she tells us no lie.
> O, she sucks all tiny birds' eggs,
> For to keep her voice clear,
> And every time she hollers 'cuckoo',
> O, don't the summer draw nigh.

Assonance, too, is relatively rare, despite the fact that it features so strongly in the coining of new words and in the formation of Romani equivalents of personal and place names: for example, *Purum* (leek, garlic) = Lee and Gaelic; and *Meilesto Gav* (donkey's town) = Doncaster.

In general, the overall impression is of a prose text, conceived in isolation and following the natural rhythm of the spoken language, loosely allied with a more or less suitable melody or verse structure but with little or no attempt made to achieve a more formal union between the two. Thus, where the *Gaujo* may find it necessary to adjust both word order and line length in order to achieve a satisfactory match between form and content, the Gypsy singer simply says what he has to say, even if this means ignoring the particular requirements of his chosen vehicle. Compare, for example, the following pairs of lines from Lias Robinson's Romani English rendering of 'The Raggle-Taggle Gypsies' with their English originals, both of which were apparently sung to the same air (text 163).

> A puv poordo o' Romni chels, sor adré a drom,
> A band of Gypsies, all in a road
>
> Sor so kâlo and chiklo, oh!
> All so black and brawny, oh
>
> Talé wel'd a râni rividi adré parr'ni,
> Away come a lady all dressed in silk
>
> To jas with the nashin' Romni chelâ.
> To follow the roving Gypsies oh.

That the Gypsies attach relatively little importance to such structural devices as metre and rhyme may perhaps best be explained in terms of their understanding of the function of the song itself – a subject to which we shall return in greater detail at a later stage. For the moment it will be sufficient to observe that whilst the use of metre and, to a lesser extent, rhyme may once have enjoyed a ritual significance, their principal purpose seems originally to have been to assist in fixing in the mind material whose accurate retention was, for one reason or another, thought desirable. Among the Gypsies, however, the song seems not to be regarded simply as a means of accurately preserving and transmitting traditional lore or even conveying information in the form of entertainment, but as a means of externalizing and sharing feeling and experience within the group. Under such circumstances, the use of such artificial means of ensuring that a song is retained in precisely the same form as that in which it was originally conceived serves no real purpose. Indeed, allowing form to influence content in this way might well prove to be a distinct disadvantage as it would undoubtedly inhibit the singer's all-important freedom to alter his text in the light of his own experience.

In those more sophisticated societies where poetry has been elevated to the status of high art, there is a tendency for the observation of prosodic law to become an end in itself, and the resulting distortion of the language of poetry has tended to render it both unintelligible and hence inaccessible to a wider audience. This is not the case with mainstream folk song, of course, although it may well be argued that in England and, more par-ticularly, Wales, too much attention to form and style has led to the tradi-tion parting company with its roots and to its becoming the property of an affectionated and largely self-absorbed élite. Among the Gypsies, on the other hand, still largely unselfconscious and free of the constraining influ-ence of an overpowering literary heritage, the language of song is still very much the language of everyday life and any attempt to limit its free use merely in order to satisfy a set of predetermined prosodic conventions seems doomed to fail.

There is, of course, a distinction to be drawn between sets consciously contrived in imitation of a particular *Gaujo* model – as, for example, in Philip Murray's use of the double couplet and classic ballad quatrain in texts 136 and 115 – and those altogether freer productions whose apparent formlessness proved so irksome to the *Romané Raiá* (e.g. texts 114 and 126). Like the language in which they are composed, the former clearly represent a comparatively recent development, the product of prolonged exposure to external pressure. As regards their content, however, even songs of this type seldom satisfy the narrative or descriptive requirements of those *Gaujo* forms on which they are loosely modelled, and should not be regarded merely as poorly executed copies of essentially alien types.

The absence of a classical Romani model, apparent in the Gypsies' widespread if imperfect use of the prosodic conventions of the various cultures alongside which they happen to reside, might lead one to conclude that theirs is an essentially *ersatz* tradition, little more than a 'pick 'n' mix' of extraneous influences owing little or nothing to their own creative genius save in the manner of its performance. Yet, whilst centuries of external influence have undoubtedly left their mark, the difference between Gypsy and 'mainstream' song generally is sufficiently obvious to suggest that there exists among British and European Gypsies an approach to the production of folk verse which may still rightly be termed *Romani*.

3

The Romané Raiá *as Collectors and Poets (1840–1940)*

The Anglo Romani Muse is dead; if indeed she ever lived.

(F. H. Groome, 1880)

For Prideaux, writing in 1887, it was the relentless utilitarianism of the new movement for mass education which posed the principal threat to the survival of the oral tradition of the English Gypsies. Gather what is left while there is still time, he wrote, for 'a few years hence it will probably be too late. The School Board Inspectorate cares for none of these things, and a Gypsy camp will be known no more' (*NQ* 7th ser. 4, 288). Yet, for all the misguided philanthropy of those who, like George Smith of Coalville, would have improved out of existence those 'hedge-bottom heathens of Christendom', it was among the *Romané Raiá* themselves that the true enemies of Gypsy song were to be found.

In Europe, the dramatic upsurge of interest in Gypsy studies which characterized the middle decades of the nineteenth century had resulted in the formation of a number of anthologies of genuine Gypsy folk poetry: in Austria-Hungary, for example, by Reuss (edited by Pott in *Zeitschrift der Deutschen Morgen Gesellschaft*, 1849), Friedrich Müller (Vienna, 1869), Meltzl (Klausen, 1871), Miklosich (Vienna, 1874), and Wlislocki (1880); in Galicia, by Isadore Kopernicki (ninety unpublished pieces); and in Wallachia by Barbu Constantinescu (Bucharest, 1874).

In Germany, too, Liebich was to devote a chapter of his *Zigeuner in Ihrem Wesen* to the subject of Gypsy *poesie* (Liebich 1863, ch.9), whilst, despite certain reservations as regards their literary merit, Paspati included the *disiecta membra* of hundreds of Gypsy songs in his monumental study of the Gypsies of the Ottoman Empire.

The wandering musicians know a few songs . . . intermixed with a number of Turkish and Greek words. Some few of these . . . have always seemed to me frivolous and wanting in good taste but in studying the history of a people one ought to neglect nothing for even after much labour bestowed on it the materials for this work are very poor and often very insufficient and that which to us appears frivolous might be to others very precious information. (Paspati 1870)

If the materials available to the student of Romani in the Ottoman territories were 'very poor and often very insufficient', the situation in England was a good deal worse. Yet, as we shall see, few of his British contemporaries would seem to have adopted Paspati's wholly objective stance and comprehensive approach towards this aspect of his subject. That they did not, should not necessarily be taken as evidence of any failure on their part to recognize the folkloric significance, or even the aesthetic appeal, of such material. On the contrary, early issues of the *Journal of the Gypsy Lore Society* contain numerous examples of European Romani song gathered by both British and European collectors. Rather, at a relatively early date, the *Raiá* would seem to have taken the view that British, as opposed to continental, Romani song had fallen so far into decay that it no longer possessed any real value for the serious student of Gypsy culture. Thus Axon, who had already published a number of continental texts – in the *Manchester Quarterly* (July 1883), *The Academy* (3 August 1889) and elsewhere – includes only one English set in his 1891 anthology of twenty-six 'Romani Songs Englished' (1891). The remainder are from Transylvania, Russia, Spain and France, and had already appeared in their original forms in Meltzl, Wlislocki, Colocci and Smith. The last item in the collection is not even of Gypsy origin but is a translation of Henri Cazalis's 'L'Illusion', first published in Paris in 1885.

As early as 1753, some one hundred years before the publication of Borrow's *Romany Rye* – from which the gentleman Gypsiographers of the late Victorian period were to take their name – Fielding was to set the tone. In chapter 12 of part 12 of *Tom Jones*, Tom, Partridge and the post-boy, whilst on the road to Coventry, encounter a group of Gypsies celebrating a wedding. At first, they see only lights flickering in the distance, which Partridge believes to be of supernatural origin. On drawing nearer, however,

They heard a confused sound of human voices; of singing, laughing and hallooing, together with a strange noise that seemed to proceed from some instruments but could hardly be allowed the name of music. Indeed . . . it might very well be called music bewitched.

It was a description which was to find a ready echo in the later literature. C. G. Leland, who was later to become president of the Gypsy Lore

Society, was, for example, to liken the singing style of the English Gypsies
to that of the North American Indians. Gypsy song, he says in the preface
to his own collection of Romani lyrics, 'is without form and void, wanting
in metre and rhyme and chanted to what only a very impressible disciple of
Suggestive Art could recognise as a tune'. Chorley, too, a noted authority
on world music, took the view that 'Gypsy music is of very limited value if
disconnected from the Gypsy performance of it and from the impression
made by it on those who, for the sake of sensation, will endure and relish
anything, no matter how eccentric it may be'. In short, Gypsy music was 'a
weed of the strangest form, colour, and leafage – one hardly to be planted
in any orderly garden'.

Even where outright criticism was avoided, English Gypsy song was
generally thought to be of sufficiently meagre importance to deserve only
the briefest mention and nothing at all by way of example. Crabb's sole
reference concerns 'a woman of the name of B— who lived to the reputed
age of a hundred and twenty years and up to that age was accustomed to
sing her song very gaily' (Crabb 1832, 30). Morwood, too, having spoken in
glowing terms of the virtuosity of the continental Gypsies, says only of
their English cousins: '. . . we may remark that they seldom sing, having but
few songs of their own. When women attempt to sing, they never aspire to
anything beyond a simple ditty over the washing tub or a soft, slow lullaby
to their dark eyed infants' (1885, 121).

Even Crofton – co-author with Bath C. Smart of the first major study of
the English Gypsy dialect – appears to have had no difficulty with Leland's
assessment. In his review of the latter's *English Gypsy Songs*, he writes as
follows:

> There is a great deal of what, by courtesy, may be called singing in Romany
> but, as the authors say, these songs, or rather chants, want metre, rhyme and
> tune and, it may be added, are in general too erotic to be included in a
> collection such as this. (*Academy* 8 (1875), 385)

Hoyland, Brockie, Simson and Groome are equally brief, although
Groome, having summarily dismissed the existence of dialect song, does at
least have something to say on the subject of Gypsy singing in English and
Welsh (see below). Even as late as 1906, by which time the folk-song
movement had already taken root, M'Cormick quotes only four songs
actually sung by Scottish Travellers – 'The Tinkler's Wedding', 'The Grey
Mare', 'The Boatman' and a verse in Cant of the Dick Derby type (text
162). M'Cormick spent some twenty years collecting among the 'Tinkler
Gypsies' of Galloway and the borders, and it is difficult to believe that the
foregoing represents the sum total of his acquaintance with Traveller song.

What is even more frustrating, however, is that, whilst his informants may have been unwilling or unable to sing for him, he was only too happy to sing for them: 'as I squatted by the burnside, the children gathered around and I rhymed to them Gypsy songs, in Romanes, which I had learned from the book published by Leland' (M'Cormick 1906, 247).

Borrow, alone among the great amateur Gypsiographers of the nineteenth century, is disposed to take a more positive view. On p.14 of *Romano Lavo-Lil* (1874) he says of the broken Romani that it is 'clear sounding and melodious and well adapted to the purposes of poetry', offering, by way of example, the lines beginning 'Coin si deya coin se dado' (text 120). Again, on p.137 of the same work he suggests that the well-known quatrain, commencing 'Can you Rokra Romany' (text 15), is, 'for terseness and expressiveness . . . quite equal to anything in the whole circle of Gentile poetry' – praise indeed from one who from his youth had thrilled to the music of Ap Gwilym.

It may also be observed, however, that Borrow, like so many of his contemporaries, seems to have devoted more time and effort to the production of his own Gypsy lyrics than to the collection and publication of genuine song material from the oral tradition. The reason for this is not hard to determine: the Gypsy language, we are told, was 'well adapted to the purposes of poetry' and if the Gypsies themselves had failed to exploit this obvious strength, it was only natural that Borrow, a compulsive rhymester with a passion for what we would now call minority languages, should seek to make good the resulting shortfall. Groome, Palmer, Leland and Gillington, too, were no less captivated by the 'nameless charm' of that 'strangely softly flowing language which gives a sweeter sound to every foreign word which it adopts', and it is hardly surprising that, on first encountering English Romani's unquestionably more refined elder sister, the dialect of the Gypsies of Wales, Sampson should also have found it irresistibly sweet. Thus, in his introduction to *Romané Gilié* (1932), he tells us that his 'first impulse to write verse in Romani arose from the inspiration of the tongue itself', going on to say that:

Romani may be likened to the lute which Ariel, in the person of Shelley, bestowed upon Miranda, a perfect instrument artfully fashioned and impregnated with all the natural joys and beauties it had known as a living pine on the steep. We are not told what rapture shook Jane Williams when she received the guitar from Shelley, but her passion could not have surpassed mine when, from my Gypsy friends, I too received the gift of a musical instrument perfected long ago in every curve and inflection and mellowed by age and the touch of master players.

A fanciful metaphor, no doubt, but perhaps no more than might be expected from so exuberant a scholar as John Sampson. Yet more than half a century earlier, a similar thought seems to have occurred to the undeniably more sober Smart and Crofton in connection with the altogether less well endowed dialect of the English Gypsies. 'Like Paganini playing on one string', they wrote, 'the Gypsy elicits from his imperfect instrument notes and phrases which a Gorgio in vain attempts to extract' (Smart and Crofton 1875, xix).

Even as late as 1910, by which time the old inflected Romani of the English Gypsies was little more than a memory, Thompson still found it 'a beautiful musical language', remarking that the Gypsies themselves were wont to boast 'with considerable truth . . . our speech is as the song of birds' (Thompson 1910a).

Borrow was also right in another respect: contrary to the wisdom of the age, the Gypsies would, indeed, seem to have possessed a body of traditional song in their own language. Crofton knew this to be the case, and Sampson certainly believed it to be so. Crowy Herne, for example, from whom Borrow apparently acquired much of his knowledge of deep *Romanés*, was said by one of his informants to have had 'as many Gypsy songs as you have buttons on your coat', yet none have survived which can be directly attributed to her.

Commonly known as 'The Crow', Sinfai Herne (née Buckland) was the second wife of No Name (Edward) Herne, by whom she had three daughters. By her second husband, Aniabai Herne, she was the mother of Isaac Herne who, according to Crofton, steadfastly refused to speak *Romanés* with Borrow, but who later proved extremely helpful to Sampson in his researches (text 6). It was, perhaps, this same 'Crowy' whom Borrow had in mind when he wrote (1874, 175):

> How black and inanimate is the countenance of the Gypsy man even when trying to pass off a floundering donkey as a flying dromedary in comparison with that of the female Romany peering over the wall of a par-yard at a jolly hog:

> Sar shan, Sinfye?
> Koshto divvus, Romany chi!
> So shan tute kairing acai?

> How are you, Sinfy?
> Good day, Romani girl!
> What are you doing here?

Simson, too, tells us that, 'my father in his youth often heard them [Scottish Gypsies] singing songs in their own language' and speaks of one

76

of his informants translating two English pieces into broken Romani. He does not, however, offer anything by way of example, merely noting

> as far as I can judge from the few and short specimens which I have myself heard, and had reported to me, the subjects of the songs . . . (I mean those composed by themselves) are chiefly their plunderings, their robberies, and their sufferings. (Simson 1865, 306)

More specifically, Borrow, in chapter 7 of *Romany Rye*, makes passing reference to an old Gypsy song called 'Gudlo Pesham' (honeycomb), whilst Leland also gives us a tantalizing glimpse of another piece (Leland 1873, 47), the rest of which, according to his informant, 'wasn't fit to sing':

> Jal 'dree the ker, my honey,
> And I will be your rom.

In *The Gypsies*, too, Leland also published portions of two further songs, the first of which (1882, 46), if not actually his own composition, bears the clear imprint of the editor's hand. The meaning of the second line is obscure.

> Me shom akonyo, gildas yoi,
> Men buti ruzhior,
> Te sar i chiriclia adoi
> Pen mengy gilior.

> I am alone, she sang;
> Although there are many flowers.
> And all the birds there
> Sing songs to me.

The second (1882, 276) has more the appearance of a proverb and may well be complete in itself:

> O manus te lela sossi choredo,
> Wafodiro se te choramengro.

> The man who takes what is stolen,
> Is worse than a thief.

Even Sampson, whose contribution to our knowledge of nineteenth-century English Romani song more than outweighs that of all his fellow *Raiá* put together, as often as not leaves the reader wanting more. In an article entitled 'English Gypsy Songs and Rhymes' (1891), for example, he has the following to say regarding one lost masterpiece: 'Another remarkable Gypsy song was that sung by poor Sinfi Boswell when, crossed in love, her mind became hopelessly unhinged. I have no copy of it but its subject, like that of Ophelia's in like unhappy case, was her lost lover.' It is also perfectly clear from his subsequent remarks that he knew more about Borrow's Gypsy lyrics than he was then prepared to say but, despite his expressed intention to return to the subject at a later date, he failed to do so. On more than one occasion, too, he makes it clear that whilst he might have included further examples of the sort of material under consideration, he refrained from doing so for fear of offending the reader (Sampson 1891, 91; 1892, 75).

Elsewhere in the same article Sampson also refers to a number of other Gypsies whose relatives were apparently possessed of a range of song material in their own language. 'My eldest brother', said one old lady, 'could sing a Christmas carol all in *Romanés*, and my father had three whole different Romani *ghilis*', whilst another informant, Ben Taylor's grandfather, knew a 'longish Gypsy song'.

Whilst Sampson rightly strikes a note of caution in referring to this and other 'similar testimony . . . not infrequently given . . . by other Gypsies', it is perhaps significant that in every case his informants were speaking of older relatives, and it may well be the case that, as the old language had fallen increasingly into disuse, so much of the oral literature associated with it had also been lost. Yet the apparent paucity of material available for study should not necessarily be taken as evidence of loss or decay. Kovalcsik, writing of the Vlax Gypsies of Slovakia, has noted that 'at a given time a community sings relatively few songs' and that the number of different items she recorded on any one occasion 'never exceeded ten or fifteen, and the four or five favourites were repeated several times – on each occasion in a slightly different form' (Kovalcsik 1985, 28). Like Leland, both Kovalcsik and Vekerdi have also noticed a certain reluctance on the part of their informants to sing in Romani before strangers – a reluctance born not of secretiveness but of politeness, it being considered unmannerly to use a language only imperfectly understood by one's guests or to expect them to endure material thought unworthy of consideration by a wider audience. As Vekerdi's principal informant put it: 'I could tell a lot of other songs . . . but they are too short, not worth writing down'.

> Bârio ladjav tuke mansa te gilaves,
> Ke imme sym Rom, ande kai la baliaki,
> Delai tzala, ril baliaki . . .

> Tu devrais avoir grande honte de chanter avec moi,
> Car je ne suis qu'un Bohémien, dans une baraque,

Dessous une tente, dedans la baraque . . .
(Zacharie Demeter, Baku, Cherbourg. *c.*1890; Augustus John 1909, 197)

> You should be greatly ashamed to sing with me,
> I am only a Gypsy in a shack,
> Beneath a tent, in the shack.

In England today, where the Gypsies seem to be far more conscious of the value of possessing what some still fondly believe to be a secret language, the problem of assessing the true extent of the Romani English repertoire may be further compounded as children may even be discouraged from singing Romani songs to their teachers or other trusted outsiders (Kenrick, British Association for the Advancement of Science section H.3, September 1971). But leaving such difficulties aside, it is also unfortunately the case that the somewhat off-hand approach of the *Romané Raiá* would seem to have outlived their passing until well into the present century. Brown, for example, writing in the 1920s gives only the first line of an Anglo-American Gypsy song commencing 'Lel a chumer, del a chumer' (Take a kiss, give a kiss) (Brown 1924, 82),[8] whilst Webb, in a chapter entitled 'A Song and a Dance and a Story', manages to avoid including a single line of Gypsy verse by way of illustration (Webb 1960).

Reeve, too, despite his professed enthusiasm for his subject, includes only two or three song fragments, only one of which is in Broken Romani (text 67). 'Most Travellers', he writes, 'especially the older ones, know a large number of delightful old folk songs and ballads, some of entirely Romani origin, others being influenced by the sentimentality of the early music hall. Many of the songs sung in Romani are centuries old and have been handed down for generations, never being heard of outside the race . . .' (Reeve 1960 3.3). Although, as the following example shows, such pieces as he does include are not without interest, they in no way serve to enhance our knowledge of Gypsy song in the *Poggadi Chib*.

An' I courted that girl fer near seven years,
An' I sez to her: 'little gal,' I sez. 'Little gal, ain't you never bin kissed?'
An' her dear mother there she shouts at me: 'go away, you h'evil young man.'
O I courted that girl fer near seven years, an' still she never wuz kissed.
I gid her fine covels, an' dear dimint rings, an' still she never wuz kissed.
An' I courted that gal fer near seven years,
An' I sez to her: 'little gal', I sez. 'Little gal, ain't you never bin kissed?'

Yet, disappointing as the foregoing undoubtedly is, it would be wrong to assume that the early period (1840–90) is entirely devoid of interest.

Borrow, Smith and Groome have all left isolated examples of unedited native song material in the broken Romani, whilst Leland, for all his open disregard for the integrity of the oral tradition and less than scientific approach to the collection of Gypsy materials generally, includes in his various writings upwards of a half a dozen pieces apparently in more or less the same form in which they were first noted down. Taken together with the material advanced by Sampson in his 'English Gypsy Songs and Rhymes' (1891), they are at least sufficient to suggest that Romani song was not only still thriving towards the end of the nineteenth century but that, as regards form and subject matter, it has changed relatively little over the intervening years.

~

Trashóva Romané Raiá te foshkené ghilé.
I fear the Gypsy gentlemen with their spurious songs.

(John Sampson 1891)

According to George Borrow, writing in the introduction to *Romano Lavo-Lil* (1874), the first three lines of the verse beginning 'Coin si deya, coin se dado' (text 120) are 'perhaps the oldest specimen of English Gypsy at present extant and perhaps the purest. They are at least as old as the time of Elizabeth and can pass among the *Zigany* in the heart of Russia for Ziganskie.' Exactly what led Borrow to make so bold an assertion remains unclear, and, in the absence of any corroborative evidence, it is difficult to escape the conclusion that it was based on nothing more than mere conjecture. The lines themselves offer few clues as to their relative antiquity; for, whilst it would perhaps be a little surprising, at so early a date, to find the vocative, 'deya', used in place of the nominative, 'dai', and the dative, 'mande', and accusative, 'tute', serving precisely the same function in relation to the principal verb, such inconsistencies cannot of themselves be said to be significant.

What is interesting, however, is that, in making this claim, Borrow was apparently wholly unaware of Andrew Boorde's earlier sample of 'Egiptt Speche' of *c.*1547. Although Boorde's original text had received a limited facsimile reprint in 1814, and was subsequently edited for the Early English Texts Society by F. J. Furnivall in 1870, it was Dr Julius Zupitza of Vienna who first alerted Miklosich to the true nature of his Gypsy sentences and Miklosich who, in turn, reported his findings to the Imperial Academy of Knowledge on 8 July 1874 (see Furnivall 1874, 100–1). In the same year, Miklosich also offered his own reading of the relevant passage in the first part of his *Beiträge zur Kentiss der Zigeunermundarten*, whilst Smart and Crofton also reproduced the sentences and a portion of the accompanying text on pp.289–90 of their *Dialect of the English Gypsies* of 1875. Unfortunately Borrow seems not to have been aware of these new discoveries at the time of going to press with *Lavo-Lil*. It was the same ill luck that, twenty years earlier, had led him to take his ale in the front parlour of the inn at Bala rather than in the common-room, where he would almost certainly have encountered the Woods with their *Romani Chib*, deeper by far than anything he might have heard spoken even among the Hernes.

But before going on to look at Borrow and his fellow *Raiá* in a little more detail, it is necessary to cast a glance at the period prior to their emergence and to consider for a moment the possibility that Boorde was not the only sixteenth-century English writer to include elements of the Gypsy language in his work, and that Borrow was not the first Englishman to use it in song. Although the literature of the sixteenth, seventeenth and eighteenth centuries contains a number of references to the Gypsies as entertainers – we know from Boorde, for example, that they were 'plesaunt daunsers', performing before both Henry VIII at Canterbury and the Scottish king at Holyrood, and that they 'were, of old, accustomed to gather in the stanks of Roslin every year, where they acted several plays' – we are told nothing of them as singers and musicians save that they were wont to beguile their woes with 'music of the bladder and the bag'. A number of songs from this early period have, it is true, been attributed to the Gypsies but, without exception, they are cast in Thieves' Cant and deal exclusively with the native criminal underclass. In the *English Rogue* of 1660, for example, the hero joins a band of 'Gypsies' and is given a 'mort' of his own, the ensuing celebrations being brought to a close with the first few verses of one of Dekker's Canting songs, first published in 1608. Jonson's *Gypsies Metamorphosed*, who made their first appearance before the king in August 1621, also sing and speak only in Cant, whilst another of Dekker's songs is misleadingly described by Shirley in his *Triumph of Wit*, first published in 1688, as 'The King of the Gypsies' Song, made upon his Beloved Doley or Mistress'. In *Bacchus and Venus*, too, 'A select collection of near two hundred of the most witty and diverting songs and catches in love and gallantry' (1737), we find 'The Canters' Holiday, sung on the election of a new Dimber Damber or King of the Gypsies', which subsequently reappears in Goadby's 1749 edition of *Bamfylde Moore Carew* as the 'Oath of the Canting Crew'.

Before leaving this early period, one other writer requires particular mention – William Shakespeare. Although it is impossible to believe that any countryman turned metropolitan actor could have been unaware of their existence at a time when their presence in the country had given rise to so much repressive legislation, the fact remains that there are no Gypsies in Shakespeare. This is particularly surprising given the popularity of the various 'low-life' characters to be found in the plays and the public appetite for more exotic forms of villainy apparent in his and his contemporaries' treatment of the Spaniard, Italian and Jew. Yet despite this unfortunate omission, it should not be supposed that Shakespeare was entirely ignorant either of the Gypsies themselves or their principal characteristics – real or imagined. Falstaff's allusion to the 'minions of the moon' (*Henry IV*, Part 1, Act 1 Scene 1) may, for example, be explained in the light of Dekker's observations on the Gypsies as 'Moon Men' (Dekker, 1609, ch.8), whilst the Moor's reference to the fatal handkerchief (*Othello*, Act 3 Scene 4) requires no further explanation: 'That handkerchief did an Egyptian to my mother give. She was a charmer and could almost read the thoughts of men.'

It may also be argued that not only did Shakespeare know something of the Gypsies themselves but that he also had at least an inkling of their language, obtained from sources other than Boorde. Is it, for example, mere coincidence that the very name of Caliban – 'this thing of darkness' (*Tempest*, Act 5 Scene 1) – should resemble so closely the Romani *kaliben*, itself signifying 'blackness' or 'darkness'?

Again, in *Hamlet*, Act 4 Scene 5, the distracted Ophelia refers to the owl as the 'baker's daughter', calling to mind the Gypsy usage *morengro chai* (*JGLS* n.s. 1 (1907), 90). According to the story, Christ, whilst on earth, asked a baker's daughter for a drink of water but was refused. Angered by her churlishness, he turned her into an owl, spurned by men and birds alike.

More importantly, if Charles Strachey is correct in his analysis of certain textual obscurities in Act 2 Scene 5 of *As You Like It* (*JGLS* o.s. 3 (1892), 96–9), Jaques's somewhat jaundiced comment on the outdoor life may well represent the earliest extant example of a poetic utterance incorporating elements of the *Romani Chib*. Having listened while Amiens sings the much better known 'Under the Greenwood Tree', Jaques responds in kind with a song of his own devising:

Jaques: I'll give you a verse to this note that I made yesterday in despite of my invention.
Amiens: And I'll sing it.
Jaques: Thus it goes:

> If it do come to pass
> That any man turn ass,
> Leaving his wealth and ease,
> A stubborn will to please,
> Ducdame, ducdame, ducdame;
> Here shall he see
> Gross fools as he,
> An if he will come to me.

According to Strachey, if the final 'e' is sounded and the preceding 'a' obscured, 'ducdame' might easily pass for the Romani *dukdom me*, I did harm, *dikdom me*, I saw, or *dukkerdom me*, I told fortunes – the last of which would certainly accord well with Jaques's own explanation of the phrase:

Amiens: What's that 'ducdame'?
Jaques: 'Tis a Greek invocation to call fools into a circle. I'll go sleep, if I can; if I cannot, I'll rail against all the first-born of Egypt.

That Jaques calls 'ducdame' a 'Greek invocation' presents no problem. The word 'Greek', which has long been used to mean unintelligible speech or nonsense, was, at one time, specifically applied to Thieves' Cant in the form 'St Giles's Greek'. According to tradition, the French king was out hunting one day when he accidentally shot the hermit Giles in the knee with an arrow. The old man refused any assistance, preferring to carry his wound as a testament to the greater glory of God. Thereafter he shut himself away in a cave near the mouth of the Rhône where he was visited every morning by a hind with a gift of milk. Thus he became the patron saint of cripples and, by extension, of all beggars. His parish, as in London, was always to be found outside the city walls and was the traditional haunt of all those within his care who were forbidden the city proper.

Thus, at a time when the difference between Cant and Romani was only imperfectly understood, if at all, 'a Greek invocation to call fools into a circle' would seem to be an entirely appropriate description of a Gypsy showman's cry. It would, moreover, also tie in well with Jaques's subsequent reference to 'the first born of Egypt'. Dr Johnson's suggestion that this latter was merely a 'proverbial phrase for high born persons' is doubly unsatisfactory in that he is unable to offer any other example of its use or any reason why, at this particular point in the play, Jaques should suddenly decide to vent his spleen upon his betters. The good doctor should, perhaps, have consulted his biographer on the point, for if his namesake, Sylvester, is to be believed, James Boswell was himself 'one of our fraternity'.

One problem remains, however: why should any Gypsy showman wish to address his audience in the past tense? That he should commence his pitch with a word or two of *Romanés* is perfectly understandable as the odd phrase in a foreign language might well be expected both to attract attention and to convey a proper sense of mystery (cf. *Hey Presto* or *Abracadabra*). That he should begin by saying 'I *told* fortunes' rather than 'I *tell* fortunes' is, however, less easily explained. A possible answer is to be found in a later issue of the Gypsy Lore Society's *Journal* (*JGLS* o.s. 3,

182), where it is suggested that what Shakespeare actually heard was *dukda me* (I tell fortunes). In support of this contention, the anonymous correspondent points to the existence of the alternative forms *durik* and *dukker* (to tell fortunes) in which the medial 'r' and final 'k' of the first are reversed in the second. Might we not, he asks, assume a third variant, *duked*, formed in like manner from the noun *dudik(aben)*, fortune telling?

Certainly, it was by no means uncommon to find the final *-ova* or *-awva* of the first person singular present indicative shortened in rapid speech to *-aw* or *-o* (Smart and Crofton 1875, 34), and there are equally almost as many ways of pronouncing any Gypsy word as there are speakers of the language. Yet, it is something of a forlorn hope to seek, at this distance in time, to pinpoint the precise form intended here. All one can say is that Strachey's analysis, particularly when set alongside Jaques's own explanation of the phrase, would seem to be broadly correct and certainly more persuasive than the various interpretations advanced, among others, by Hanmer (*duc ad me*), Mackay (*duthaich*) and Aldis Wright, for whom it meant nothing at all.

Two further candidates for consideration as the earliest examples of Romani verse are offered by R. Hodgson in his article, 'Early Romani' (*JGLS* 52 (3/4) (1973)). In it, he draws attention to two spells included by Peter Haining in *The Warlock's Book* (Haining 1972) which he reproduces without attempting a translation. The first is said to be an incantation for ensuring fertility, and the second, a charm 'which ensures the holding of a man':

A

Dui rika him mire mine [*sic*]
Dui yara hin leskro kor,
Avnas dui yek jelo,
Keren akana yek jeles.

B

Kay o kam ariavel
Kiya mange lel beshel.

Haining gives as the source of the former the *Grimorum Verum*, said to have been published in Memphis in 1517, and of the latter, a sixteenth-century manuscript held by the British Museum. Were this so, then either or both might claim to be the oldest specimen of the Romani tongue now extant, the first pre-dating Boorde by some thirty years.

Despite his best endeavours, Hodgson was able to learn nothing further from Haining save that he had acquired his first example from a 'European scholar'. Further investigations carried out on Hodgson's behalf by Mr (now Sir) Angus Fraser served merely to show that the *Grimorum Verum*, which is not listed in the British Museum catalogue, is now generally thought by scholars to have originated in the eighteenth rather than the sixteenth century.

Hodgson concludes by urging a systematic search of sixteenth-century manuscripts dealing with witchcraft in the belief that this might well yield further examples of Romani words or even the existence of a hitherto unknown Gypsy scholar. This may well be so, but one need look no further than chapters 6 and 7 of C. G. Leland's *Gypsy Sorcery and Fortune Telling* of 1891 for the source of Haining's verses. Thus, on pp.100 and 111 respectively of the Dover edition (1971) we find the following:

A

> Dui riká hin mire minc,
> Dui yará hin leskro kor,
> Avnás dui yek jelo,
> Keren ákána yek geles.

B

> Kay o kám avriávela,
> Kiya mánge lele beshel!
> Kay o kám tel' ável,
> Kiya lelákri me beshav.

> Where the sun goes up
> Shall my love be by me;
> Where the sun goes down
> There by her I'll be.

The first of the above is a charm for the relief of barrenness, the rhyme being repeated whilst eating grass from a grave in which a pregnant woman has been buried. The second is a male love charm. The lover takes a blade of grass in his mouth and, turning to the east and west, repeats the rhyme. The grass is then cut up and mixed in food which the girl must eat. She has only to swallow the smallest piece and she will be 'moved to love and true-hearted'. Leland offers no English translation of his first example, presumably because he considered it indecent. It may be roughly rendered as follows: 'my vagina has two sides; his penis has two eggs; coming together as one, the two make one life.'

Leland gives no indication of the source of these rhymes, but he almost certainly had them from Wlislocki. In any event, it is safe to assume that had he discovered a specimen of Romani verse apparently dating from the sixteenth century, and certainly no later than the eighteenth, he would not have allowed the fact to pass unnoticed.

~

If publication date is any guide, and it is quite possible that it is not, the oldest example of native verse composition in the 'vulgar or broken Romany' now extant is to be found on p.432 of Borrow's *The Gypsies of Spain*, published in 1841 (text 123). That it was but one of a number of possible examples then in the author's possession may be inferred from his accompanying note:

> Many other specimens of the English Gypsy Muse might be here adduced; it is probable, however, that the above will have fully satisfied the curiosity of the reader. It has been inserted here for the purpose of showing that the Gypsies have songs in their own language, a fact which has been doubted.

Apart from the plural *chavé*, children, the form of language used exhibits none of the characteristics of the *Puri Chib* as described by Smart and Crofton in 1873 and, as regards its Romani vocabulary alone, would, indeed, appear to be more accessible to contemporary Travellers than many of those pieces collected around the turn of the twentieth century. With few exceptions, all the Romani words used are to be found in Kenrick and Wilson's list (Acton and Kenrick 1985, 14–39), and none are otherwise unknown.

The fact that it was composed in what Kenrick has defined as a register of English rather than in the deep Romani of Wester Boswell is, however, of no help in fixing its date of origin. Although much of the 'contemporary evidence' adduced by Hancock for the early formation of 'Angloromani' as a contact language is wholly unsatisfactory (see above), there can be little doubt that the *Poggadi Chib* had already begun to take shape long before Borrow first encountered it during the early decades of the nineteenth century, and one cannot, therefore, rule out the possibility that the song originated some time prior to its first appearance in print. On the other hand, it would be equally unwise to read too much into the presence in Borrow's text of certain English archaisms – 'methinks', 'forenigh', 'thou wilt'. They are entirely absent from the variant printed on p.104 of *Romano Lavo-Lil* (text 124) and are, moreover, to be found nowhere else in the repertoire.

The use of such outmoded forms is a particular feature of many of Borrow's translations from the original Romani and is especially noticeable in his Gypsy dialogue. A single example will here suffice, although readers familiar with Borrow's work will have no difficulty in identifying others:

> Dost bid me from the land begone,
> And thou with child by me?
> Each time I come, the little one
> I'll greet in Romany.
>
> (Borrow 1841, 296)

Language which, in this way, is distanced from everyday speech, creates the impression of a world removed from ordinary experience, and there can be little doubt that this was Borrow's intention in much of his writing. Whether this means that he was responsible for the song in its entirety or merely sought to embellish an existing text in order to make it more interesting to his readers is, however, difficult to say. In all other respects the song is broadly typical of a number of other undeniably genuine pieces of comparable length and content and, indeed, in its secondary form, has clear affinities with Leland's 'Rauney on the Tober' (text 126). All we can say for sure is that, apart from the title, which is almost certainly Borrow's own invention, there is enough of the genuine Gypsy about it in its revised form to pass for *tatcho* with most contemporary Gypsies. Indeed, it, or something very like it, was subsequently recovered in somewhat fragmentary form from the singing of a Blackpool Gypsy some forty or fifty years after it first appeared in print (text 125).

Borrow followed up this early example with a number of other pieces included, in passing, in *Lavengro* (1851) and *Romany Rye* (1857). Despite their failure – between them they sold less than 5,000 copies in twenty years, whilst *The Bible in Spain* sold 20,000 in twelve months and appeared in pirated editions in both New York and Philadelphia – Borrow remained loyal to the cause and, in 1874, produced the first published collection of English Gypsy songs as part of his *Romano Lavo-Lil*. Although dismissed as 'nothing more than a *rechauffé* of the materials collected by Mr. Borrow at an earlier stage of his investigations' (*Athenaeum*, 25 April 1874, pp. 556–7), *Romano Lavo-Lil* in fact contains over twenty English Gypsy songs and poems of which only one or two had been previously published. Indeed, for Groome (*Academy* 5 (1874), 667), 'by far the best portion of Mr. Borrow's book is his specimens of Gypsy songs' and even the anonymous critic of the *Athenaeum* was forced to concede that 'the book contains a few specimens of Romany poetry, not particularly happy specimens, but to a certain extent forcible and characteristic'. That they were, for the most part, either of his own devising or heavily reworked in order to satisfy a more conventional literary taste, may be true, but the fact remains that Borrow was not only the first British writer to acknowledge the existence of a body of folk song in the English Gypsy dialect, but the first to publish a complete and apparently unmodified text (text 15).

Although he undoubtedly exercised the same degree of artistic licence in his treatment of Gypsy song as he did in his two quasi-autobiographical novels, *Lavengro* and *Romany Rye*, the precise nature of the relationship between Borrow's published work and any traditional material he may have had to hand remains far from clear. On the one hand, he was undoubtedly capable of reproducing the genuine article with little or no alteration (texts 15 and 124) and, indeed, unlike his two near contemporaries, Leland and Groome, seems to have entertained a true regard for the subject. Elsewhere, however, he is somewhat less fastidious in his approach, working over his basic material in such a way as to render it virtually unrecognizable and publishing it with no hint of its true provenance.

Something of this process may be seen in his treatment of the following quatrain from *Wild Wales* (1862, ch.98), of which he himself claimed to be the subject. It was, he says, composed by the mother of one of his Gypsy acquaintances – Captain Bosvile – and had earned the author a black eye from Isopel Berners, the workhouse girl with whom he shared his camp in the Mumpers' Dingle (*Lavengro*, ch.86).

A

Ando berkho rye cano
Oteh pivo teh Khavo
Tu lerasque ando berkho piranee
Teh corbatcha por pico

In the mountain, a gentleman shot.
There he drank and ate.
You (were) for him, in the mountain, a sweetheart
And (his) basket on (your) back.

The song first appears, in translation, in Borrow's original draft of *Lavengro* as a 'song from the Hungarian Gypsy language' (text B), before reappearing in somewhat more homely guise in the first draft of the appendix to *Wild Wales* (text C):

B

To the mountain the fowler has taken his way.
There he doth eat and doth make himself gay,

From the basket he slingeth his shoulder upon.
Thou art the fowler so handsome of mien
Who often within the mountain art seen,
Roving about with thy basket and gun.

C

The knight to the greenwood has taken his way;
The squirrels he shoots and the birds on the spray.
And he eats and he drinks when he lays down his gun.
Thou art the young nobleman's leman, I wean,
And rovest with him in the forest so green,
Bearing the basket thy shoulder upon.

The greenwood motif also occurs, in fragmentary form, in one of Borrow's notebooks (text D) together with a number of other pieces, including 'Mandy shoon ye Romany chals', 'Penn'd the Romany chi ke laki di' (text 134) and 'As I was a jawing to the gav yeck divvus' (text 123–4), before emerging in its final Romani English form in *Romano Lavo-Lil* (text E):

D

Drey o baro wesh cano.
Odoy pivo ta khavo.
Tu shan odoy miry piranee,
. . . oprey dumo.

In the forest he shot.
There he drank and ate.
There, you are my sweetheart,
. . . on (your?) back.

E

The rye he mors adrey the wesh,
The kaun-engro and chiricklo;
You sovs with leste drey the wesh,
And rigs for leste the gono.

The gentleman, he kills in the wood
The hare and bird;
You sleep with him in the wood
And carry for him the bag.

That A above was composed by an English Gypsy is, in itself, most unlikely as it would seem to be in a form of Hungarian Romani and, as Groome rightly says, 'though fairly intelligible to anyone acquainted with continental Romany, would, I fancy, be Hebrew to the travellers of the English roads' (1875, 667). That a *Gaujo* workhouse orphan would have understood it, however well acquainted she may have been with the travelling community, is frankly beyond belief. A similar difficulty presents itself in chapter 25 of *Lavengro*. Borrow, having learned of the death of Petulengro's parents, asks him what his own views on death are. By way of answer, Petulengro tells him that they are 'much the same as in the old song of Pharoah I have heard my grandam sing'. He then sings the following lines:

> Canna marel o manus, chivios ande puv,
> Ta rovel pa leste o chavo ta romi . . .

> When a man dies, he is cast into the earth
> And his wife and child may weep for him.

According to Thompson, Ambrose Smith/Reynolds (the original of Borrow's Petulengro) was the son of Faden John Smith and Mirelli Smith. Faden's mother was Constance Boss, whilst Mirelli was the daughter of another Mirelli Smith (Thompson 1910b). Although Hungarian Gypsies are known to have visited England during the mid-nineteenth century, it is, perhaps, unlikely, though not impossible, that either Constance or Mirelli would have had any knowledge of continental Romani song.

This is not the only occasion on which Borrow places continental Romani on the lips of English Travellers. On p.53 of *Lavengro*, for example, we find *Hir mi Divlis* (by God), and, on p.230 of *Romany Rye*, *Hir mi Divlis* which is elsewhere written *Heri Devlis* at the foot of the Lord's Prayer in the Transylvanian dialect (Borrow 1874, 78).

Elsewhere again Borrow has Petulengro say *chal Devlehi* (go with God). According to Pott, in some continental dialects, the instrumental case is formed by adding the suffix *-eha* in place of the more usual *-esa* and the instrumental of *Dewel*, God, is, therefore, *Deweleha* (Pott 1844–5, i, 192).

Such obvious exoticisms would, of course, be unlikely to trouble the general reader of what were, after all, never intended to be works of serious scholarship. It is noticeable, however, in his treatment of the foregoing verses, that in *Lavo-Lil*, by substituting the wood for the mountain and the game-bag for the basket, and by introducing the hare, he immediately succeeds in striking a domestic note, much more in keeping with his principal subject, the English Gypsies.

Borrow's indebtedness to the oral tradition is also discernible in his use of what, for convenience, may be termed the 'fundamental particles' of Romani song. As we shall see, a characteristic feature of the Gypsy repertoire both in England and in eastern Europe is the introduction into longer, often improvised, texts of free-floating lines or phrases otherwise held in suspension within the tradition. Borrow seems to have recognized both their function and their potential and there is no doubt that their judicious use lends greater credibility to his own Gypsy lyrics. A couple of examples will be sufficient to illustrate the point:

F.1

I sov'd yeck rarde drey a gran
a choring mas and moro
Along with a bori lubeney,
And she has been the ruin of me . . .
(text 77)

F.2

Mandi suv'd yek rardi
In the granze avri
Along with the tawna rakli o!
(text 74 and accompanying notes)

F.3

Mangen mas y moro
(text 3)

G.1

Oprey the chongor in ratti I'd cour,
For my Rinkeny Yocky Shuri
(text 50)

G.2

I will care up to my chungs,
Up to my chungs in rat,
All for my happy rackler.
(text 63)

Although he was later to deny the very existence of Anglo-Romani song, Groome, in reviewing *Lavo-Lil*, also tells us that in text 77 (F.1), 'more properly tugno se mande', he recognized 'an old Rommany favourite' and, indeed, the barn motif forms a common element in both English and Scottish Traveller song.

It would be wrong to assume, however, that Borrow's relationship with the oral tradition was wholly one-sided. We know, for example, that on at least one occasion the Revd Norwood introduced one of his informants to both 'The Broken Chastity' (text 134) and 'Poisoning the Porker'. Having spoken of his meeting with Joseph Holland, a 'peerdu' chairbottomer, in a lane near Swindon, he goes on to say of a second meeting on 17 August 1857,

> I chanced in the same place on the same man, Holland, his wife and tschavvy and gry and masengro-jukal. He was but just come, having been absent near a month in several parts of Worcestershire. I had in my possession Borrow's two foregoing songs which were in my pocket; a ready subject of Romany talk. (Grosvenor 1910)

Some thirty years later, Sampson, a thoroughly reliable witness, tells us that he himself met with fragments of the same 'Bálo Song' from one of the Smiths (Sampson 1891, 93), whilst T. W. Thompson was to obtain the 'tattered remnant' of the 'Broken Chastity' from two Norfolk Gypsies – granddaughters of Ambrose Smith/Reynolds, the original of Borrow's Petulengro (text 123). From the same informants, Thompson also obtained a version of Petulengro's 'vulgar ditty' on the subject of the *Petulengré* (text 44), although, in both cases, he was of the opinion that they were sung without understanding.

Sampson also obtained from one of the Smiths an accurate rendering of the couplet commencing 'koshko grai, Romano grai', originally published on p.189 of *The Bible in Spain* (text 48) and in a somewhat enigmatic aside tells us that in the course of his acquaintance with Isaac Herne, the son of old Crowy Herne, from whom Borrow is said to have acquired his knowledge of deep Romani, he was 'fortunate enough to extract . . . some curious information with regard to the authenticity of some of Borrow's songs' which he hoped 'on some future occasion to verify and extend' – an intention he seems never to have realized.

For all his evident fondness for the language, Borrow, like many of his contemporaries, seems to have found the apparent formlessness and triviality of much English Gypsy song difficult to accept. Yet Borrow himself was no poet, and those 'inscrutable principles of prejudice' which formed the basis of his literary judgement are primarily of interest for the light they shed on his own character. His poetry, as H. S. Milford rightly says, is all in his prose, his translations and verse originals alike being little better than doggerel. So much so, indeed, that one critic, George Saintsbury, was inclined to doubt his 'wonderfully high estimate of certain Welsh poets mentioned in Wild Wales': '. . . if the originals are anything like his translations of them', he wrote, 'I do not think that Ap Gwilym and Lewis Glynn Cothi, Goronwy Owen and Huw Morus can have been quite such mighty bards as he makes out' (*Macmillan's Magazine*, January 1886).

It is only fair to say, however, that Borrow's verse translations were by no means universally despised. W. Bodham Donne, for example, thought that in language and rhythm his renderings of the old Danish poets were 'vastly superior to Macaulay's "The Lays of Ancient Rome"', whilst James Hooper believed his version of 'Ewald's National Song of Denmark' bore comparison with Longfellow's. Yet Borrow's estimation of his own talent, or so it would seem, was somewhat more realistic. On the title page of *Targum*, an anthology of metrical translations from thirty languages and dialects, published in St Petersburg in 1835, he includes the entirely appropriate observation: 'The raven has ascended to the nest of the nightingale.'

But if Borrow failed to do justice to the greatest of medieval Welsh lyricists, he was no less careless in his handling of the altogether humbler productions of the English Gypsies. Not only is he less than faithful to the wording of his original texts but, as often as not, entirely fails to capture their true flavour. The point is well illustrated in the following example (Borrow 1874, 105), here printed together with a literal English translation and Borrow's own metrical paraphrase:

Pawnie birks	White breasts
My Men-engri shall be	My pillow shall be;
Yackors my dudes	Eyes, my lights (stars?)
Like ruppeney shine:	Like silver shine:
Atch meery chi!	Stay, my girl!
Ma jal away,	Do not go away,
Perhaps I may not dick tute	Perhaps I may not see you
Kek komi.	Ever more.

> I'd choose as pillows for my head
> Those snow-white breasts of thine;
> I'd use as lamps to light my bed
> Those eyes of silver shine:
> O lovely maid, disdain me not,
> Nor leave me in my pain:
> Perhaps 'twill never be my lot
> To see thy face again.

Not only does Borrow include a number of new words – expanding, without justification, the ideas expressed in the original text – but he also introduces at least one entirely fresh metaphor, an innovation which led one anonymous reviewer to wonder, somewhat unkindly, what exactly Borrow had in mind unless he 'wished to suggest that his hero used the young lady's eyes for a bed-candle or, mindful of his "Traveller" habits, imagined that he slept in a gig'.

Oddly enough, Axon employs precisely the same metaphor in his albeit more subdued rendering of the same text (1891, xxiii):

> Thy white breasts
> My pillows shall be;
> Thy bright eyes
> The lamps for me!
> Ah! dearest girl,
> Do not disdain,
> I may not see
> Thy face again.

If Borrow was no poet, he was also not a folklorist – at least not in the modern scientific sense of the word – and whilst his books may be both entertaining and, at times, informative, it would be wholly inappropriate to subject them to the same rigorous scrutiny demanded of a contemporary anthropological field study. It is unfortunately the case, however, that even in his own lifetime his outmoded scholarship was more apparent to his critics than his equally obvious literary talents. *Romano Lavo-Lil*, wrote one anonymous contributor to the *Athenaeum*,

> does not by any means represent the present state of knowledge on the subject. But at the present day, when comparative philology has made such strides, and when want of accurate scholarship is as little tolerated in strange and remote languages as in classical literature, the 'Romano Lavo-Lil' is, to speak mildly, an anachronism.

There is also a sense in which Borrow himself is as much the hero of his own writings as his ostensible subject, a fact which many of his contemporaries found equally irritating: 'Mr. Borrow', writes another commentator,

> no doubt knows the Gypsies well and could describe them perfectly; but his love of effect leads him away. In his wish to impress his readers with a certain mysterious notion of himself he colours his Gypsy pictures (the form of

which is quite accurate) in a fantastic style which robs them altogether of the value they would have as studies from life. (Taylor 1851)

Although there is some truth in this assessment, it is also a little harsh. Whatever his scholastic shortcomings, Borrow's vigorous personality and infectious enthusiasm for his subject, be it good ale or the poems of Dafydd ap Gwilym, have left an indelible mark on English letters whilst, as a popularizer of Gypsy lore, his equal has yet to be found.

~

The 1870s also saw the publication of a curiously ill-conceived work, a collection of *English Gypsy Songs in Romany with Metrical English Translations* by C. G. Leland, E. H. Palmer and Janet Tuckey (Trübner, 1875).

Charles Godfrey Leland, who seems to have masterminded the project, was an expatriate American dilettante, best remembered today for his Gypsy writings but equally at home on a variety of topics, including South China pidgin, North American Indian lore and English slang. At the time the work was conceived, however, he was the reluctant victim of an earlier success with a series of comic pieces written, under the name of Hans Breitmann, in the mixed jargon of the Philadelphia German community. Such was their popularity that Groome, in a brief reference to *English Gypsy Songs*, names Breitmann as one of its authors, confident that his readers would know exactly who was meant. Indeed, Leland himself was to introduce his own contribution to the 1897 *Jubilee Book of the Philosophical Institution of Edinburgh* as 'A Greeting from Hans Breitmann'.

Ernest Henry Palmer (1840–82), on the other hand, was a university-based academic, Lord Almoner's professor of Arabic in Cambridge (1871) and already well known for his edition of the poems of Beha ed din Zoheir together with an English verse translation. He was, however, no chair-bound pundit. He had learned Italian and French, largely from café conversations whilst a junior clerk in London and, having made the acquaintance of a Cambridge teacher of Hindustani, had entered St John's College as a sizar in 1863, obtaining a fellowship four years later.

In 1869–70, he accompanied Henry Spencer Palmer and Sir Charles Wilson on their survey of Sinai, spending some time in Palestine improving his knowledge of Arab dialects and publishing an account of his travels in *Desert of the Exodus* (1871). In 1881 he became a leader writer on *The Standard*, and in the following year was sent on a secret mission by Gladstone's government, the purpose of which seems to have been to detach the Arab tribes from the Egyptian rebels. He was subsequently appointed interpreter-in-chief to the British forces in Egypt but was murdered by bandits at Wady Sudr in the same year. His body was returned to England for burial in St Paul's in 1883. (See also pp.177–83 of Walter Besant's *Life and Achievements of Henry Palmer* (Murray, 1883) for a note on Palmer's Romani studies.)

Of the three, Tuckey was certainly the least well known – at least in academic circles – her principal claim to fame being a handful of society verses published in *Chambers' Journal*.

The book itself is also something of a mixed bag. Of the fifty-six pieces represented, seventeen are by Leland, thirteen by Palmer (including an English Romani rendering of Tennyson's 'Home they Brought her Warrior Dead') and fifteen by Tuckey, who also provided the English translation of a number of Leland's verses. Of the remaining eleven, two are unascribed, although they have every appearance of being composed by one or other of the principal contributors, and one, a Romani version of 'John Brown's Ten Little Indians' (see notes accompanying text 165) is by Hubert Smith, the author of *Tent Life with English Gypsies in Norway*; three are from Matty Cooper (texts 66, 146 and 148); two by an unnamed Gypsy woman, a house-dweller living in Walton on Thames (texts 63 and 126); and one, an edited version of another variant of 'The Ten Little Indians', by one of the Lees (text 165). The book also includes an unattributed, but undeniably genuine piece on the subject of pig poisoning (text 119) and an anonymous English Gypsy's rendering of one of Liebich's German Romani verses first published in his *Die Zigeuner* of 1863 (text 166).

Dedicated to the poet laureate, the book was first announced in *Romanés* in *the Illustrated London News* for 31 October 1875, and later, in Russian, as *Pyesni Tyzgan v Anglii* in *Moskovikina Vyddomosti* 170 (Moscow, 1875). It was also reviewed, without much enthusiasm, both by Crofton in the *Academy* (8, 385–6) and by Bataillard in the *Revue Critique*, 9 September 1876, pp.167–73. Five of the poems were later translated into Hungarian by Szzas Bela and published in *Budapesti Sszemle* (17, 174–7).

Perhaps the book's most striking feature is the marked contrast in language and style between the few genuine pieces and those contributed by the authors themselves. Compare, for example, the following lines from Leland's 'I Chóvihani' (The Witch) (*English Gypsy Songs*, p.190) with the anonymous 'Gilli of a Rommany Juva' (text 63 (*EGS* 235)) .

> 'Dickadói! – avélla kennā
> O wáfro cóvva kéllin ajā!
> Midúvel! Síkker!' – Men díkkdom aláy,
> Adói pāsh o wūder, díkkin adré,
> Vás a bōro jómpa hóckerin án;
> Yói shélldas: 'Adóvo's mi chóvihān!'

'Sār-dívvus, sār-óra avélla akái
Te hátchel' apré, i bengéskri dyé.
Si mándy chívāva o cóvva avrī
T'véla hóckerin 'pópli díckinav mi;
Sā-rāti shūnāva lis pāli o tan,
An' sūtto sārjā o the chóvihān.'

'Look there! Look there! It is coming now;
The evil thing is dancing, I vow!
My God! Oh, help me!' – And peeping in
At the open door, with a wicked grin,
Came a great grey toad, with a hop and a hitch;
'See there!' cried the woman, 'See – *there's* my witch!

'Every day and every hour it is coming here –
The devilish creature is always near;
If I throw it away, the first thing I see,
It is jumping again and staring at me,
All night I hear it hissing by the ditch,
And all night long I dream of the witch!'

That Leland was here consciously striving for effect is all the more apparent when the foregoing is compared with such other verses of his own composition as 'The Gávengróes' (*EGS* 168) which, he says, 'was written one day while associating with Gypsies and was drawn from their own remarks':

'Oh, I've lélled adústa o' kóvvo tem,
With its ryes and ráshis an' sitch as them;
An' its párl the páni 'fore lángs I goes,
To a tem where there isn't no gávengróes . . .

The 'Mericanéskro tem, my pál:
Adóvo's the tem for a Rómmany chál.
For fon sār I shūn, an' fon sār I knows,
They don't késsur adói for no gávengróes.'

Such obvious inconsistency is all the more surprising given Leland's assurance in his introductory notes that every care had been taken by the authors to avoid creating a 'Lengua del Aficion' or 'sham Rommany'. The songs themselves he 'believed to be impressed with true Gypsy spirit and perfectly idiomatic', being composed 'in current modern Rommany but retaining as much of the old as could be done with truth and ease'.

The question is, to what extent were Leland and his two collaborators able to reconcile two such ostensibly incompatible aims and yet retain the essential integrity of the spoken language? Certainly, the form of language used in the first of the above examples would seem to have more in common with the carefully worked productions of Sylvester Boswell – as presented by Smart and Crofton – than it does with such apparently un-edited examples of Gypsy speech as have survived from the same period. It is, however, only fair to say that Groome, at least, seems to have found Leland's use of language perfectly acceptable. In a composite review of Leland's *The English Gypsies and Their Language* and Borrow's *Romano Lavo-Lil*, for example, he says of the latter that 'it is the Romany of the study rather than of the tents' and 'Let anyone compare Mr. Leland's version of the story of the Deluge with Mr. Borrow's account of his visit to Thomas Herne and he will see what I mean' (*Academy*, 5, 667).

That Leland was an inveterate enhancer of primary source material is, however, beyond question. Jesperson, in a footnote to chapter 12, book III of his *Language: Its Nature, Development and Origin* (1940), makes pre-cisely this point in connection with his treatment of South China pidgin, remarking that the songs and stories included by Leland in his *Pidgin English Sing-Song* were 'artificially made up to amuse the readers and contain a much larger proportion of Chinese words than the rest of my sources would warrant'. In the same way, it is perfectly clear that the Gypsy tales included in both *The Gypsies* and *The English Gypsies and Their Language* are similarly flawed. Indeed, in his introduction to the latter, Leland makes no attempt to mislead the reader on this point: 'The truth is', he says, 'it is a difficult matter to hear a story among English Gypsies which is not mangled or marred in the telling so that to print it, restitution and invention become inevitable.'

Whether or not Leland succeeded generally in capturing the true flavour of spoken *Romanés* in his more sophisticated verses, his use of vocabulary remains highly suspect. Indeed, for Sampson, his method of collection was 'assuredly the worst in the world'. This, in essence, consisted in reading aloud from a Hindustani dictionary and inviting his informant to suggest the appropriate English Gypsy equivalents (Leland 1873, 98–9, 110–15, 130). Yet even Leland was not entirely insensible of the problems inherent in this approach. 'If it was difficult in the beginning', he says,

for me to accustom the Gypsy mind to reply clearly and consistently to questions as to his language, the trouble was tenfold increased in that he began to see his way, as he thought, to my object and to take a real interest in aiding me.

Thus, on one occasion, having asked his old friend, Matty Cooper, to elaborate on his assertion that *punji*, the Hindustani for 'capital', made equally good sense in *Romanés*, he received the following reply: 'Suppose a man sells 'punge-cake, wouldn't that be his capital? 'Punge must be capital.'

Although Cooper's attempt to force a connection between *punji* and 'sponge-cake' is clearly absurd, it nevertheless serves to illustrate the sort of difficulties which may arise if insufficient care is taken over the collection and analysis of field data. Less obviously, on pp.254, 262 and 266 respectively of *English Gypsy Songs*, we find:

(a) *kuder* = to open. In reality, an aspirated form of the more usual *Woóder* = door (Smart and Crofton 1875, 153), as represented in Welsh Romani by *gudar/hudar/udar* (Sampson 1926, iv, 117). The English Romani word for 'to open' is *píriv*;

(b) *chamor* = cherries – properly 'cheeks' (Smart and Crofton 1875, 63); and

(c) *mun* = forehead – properly *chikat* (Sampson 1926, iv, 62); *mun*, is the Hindi equivalent of Romani *moói* = mouth or face (Smart and Crofton 1875, 109).

Leland's sometimes misplaced eagerness to reinforce the well-established link between English Gypsy and such modern Indian languages as Hindi and Bengali is also apparent in the following lines from 'I Shunali Rakli' (*EGS* 62):

> Jala laki purus; kéti utar,
> Boro-panni-tem – shímál améngy,
> Dúlla wafri rakli si améngy
> Puvdo, mullo si avri te dívvus.

On p.125 of *The English Gypsies* we are told that

Although the Gypsies have sadly confounded the Hindoo terms for the 'cardinal points', no one can deny that their own are of Indian origin. Utar is north in Hindoostani and utar is west in Rommany. Shimal is also north in Hindoo and . . . poorub is the east in Hindoostani; in Gypsy it is changed to poorus and means the west.

In the lines quoted above, however, *purus* is placed in clear opposition to *utar* so that the meaning ascribed to one or other of them must be incorrect. As for *shimal*, Crofton has dismissed any suggestion that it is Romani in origin (if, indeed, it was ever used by a Gypsy), referring it to *sziml/schimmel* which, in *Hantyrka* (Czech thieves' Cant) and German Cant respectively, signify 'snow' (Pott 1844, ii, 16).

Leland's own English rendering of the quatrain merely adds to the confusion as, for no apparent reason, he chooses to place the south in opposition to the west, and the east in opposition to the north, even though their correct alignment would be perfectly possible without affecting either metre or rhyme:

> And whether she walk the south or west,
> Or live by east or north,
> That wicked girl is in her grave
> To me from this day forth.

This confusion is all the more surprising as the vocabulary accompanying the songs was apparently compiled by Professor Palmer, from whom a greater degree of scholarly precision might reasonably have been expected. Yet the glossary not only contains a number of words not used in the songs whilst omitting others that are, but also includes a handful of unmarked English provincialisms and slang terms including, somewhat surprisingly, perhaps the best known example of a *Shelta* word formed by inversion of the original Irish, *tober* (from *bóthar* = road).

Together with various items recorded nowhere else for *English Gypsy* and others also apparently unknown to their continental brethren – for example *suder-apré* (hang up) and *chingaror* (sparks) – we also find a number of words either of Leland's own devising, or used by him in a wholly arbitrary way, such as *wast hanik* (lit. hand well) – anvil, a word which seems to have been a source of considerable difficulty for a number of nineteenth-century writers. In *Romany Rye*, Borrow introduces us to *covantza*, a word missing from the dictionary in *Romano Lavo-Lil*, whilst Wester Boswell favoured the altogether more cumbersome circumlocution *o kóva so kédas o ggreiésto chóxa opré*, the thing he made the horseshoes on. So, too, in the following lines (text 165; *EGS* 225), *chury* (climb), a word found in no other Gypsy word list, *truppo* (body) = trunk, and *shók* (cabbage) = bough.

> Yéck bítto Róm'ni chal churyin ap a rukk,
> Chury'd ap t' truppo an' béshed apré a shóck.

Yet Leland's habit, often tongue in cheek, of supplying any awkward gaps with words of his own invention should not lead us to suppose that all those words which are found nowhere else in the literature are necessarily suspect (see notes accompanying text 146). For Groome, writing in his tripartite review of *Lavo-Lil, The English Gypsies and Their Language* and Miklosich's *Über die Mundarten*, the situation was far from clear-cut:

> Many of Leland's words, not occurring in any previously published collection, were already familiar to me when I first read his book; others, whose genuineness I was then inclined to question, I have since verified. There still remains a large number on which I cannot speak with certainty. Such words as *seemor*, dolphin; *kismut*, destiny; *shaster*, the scriptures, etc., may exist in English Romany; all I can say is that I have never met with them.

A further problem for both the specialist and lay reader is the lack of any clear statement regarding spelling and pronunciation. As Crofton says in his review, the text 'is by no means uniform and bristles with random accents and diacritics' whilst Leland's explanatory note 'leaves the orthography more unintelligible than ever'. Even common English words are arbitrarily misspelt – e.g. *kosts*, costs (*EGS* 184); *fotografengro*, photographer (*EGS* 47); and *sindor*, cinder (*EGS* 272). In many cases, too, the English participle ending -ing is apparently gratuitously rendered -an, -en or -in. Even in the few extracts included in the present section, we find the following obvious inconsistencies: *dick*adói, *dick*inav and *díkk*dom; *'véla* and *avélla*; *wáfr*o and *wafr*i; *mándy* and *mandy*; *acai* and *akái*; and *sikk*ered and *síkk*ered.

Given that neither Crofton nor Sampson were able to make any sense of Leland's own remarks on the subject, it is all the more surprising to find the following in the introduction to Dyneley Prince's American Gypsy vocabulary: 'I have followed generally the system of pronunciation given by Leland as this is in use today among such few Romanies as write their idiom; viz, *a* as *ǫ* in *spot*; *ā* as *a* in *father*; *ai, au* and *ay* as in English; . . *o* as *au* in *taught* . . .' etc. (Dyneley Prince 1907, 272). As Sampson has pointed out, this would suggest that alone among the English Gypsies, or those of English descent, Prince/Leland's informants pronounced *lollo* as *lawlaw*, *lav* as *larv* and *gad* as *God* (Sampson 1908, 80).

Against this background, one is left wondering exactly what purpose the book was intended to serve. With its combination of literary and linguistic invention and confused orthography it is hardly likely to have been of much interest to other serious Gypsiographers and, indeed, neither Crofton nor Bataillard had anything much to say in its favour. If, however, as seems more likely, its purpose was merely to entertain a somewhat wider audience, this might have been better served by recasting the Romani texts in a more accessible form based wholly on standard English orthography.

That entertainment was indeed the authors' principal purpose seems fairly clear. The songs themselves, particularly those contributed by

Tuckey, are often sentimental in tone, wholly at odds with the generality of Romani song but entirely in keeping with the popular taste of the day – the funeral of a Gypsy child, buried in the wild lest she be frightened by the clamour of Judgement Day in the churchyard (EGS No.5); the suicide of a Gypsy woman, married to a *Gaujo* and terrified of exposure (EGS No.8); and a gift of alms from the queen, recalling, perhaps, an incident mentioned by the young Princess Victoria in her diary for Christmas Day 1836 (EGS No.2).

Others, however, are less obviously mawkish and, as Crofton says, 'are of interest as revealing Gypsy habits and traditions'; e.g. 'The Hanging Matter', in which an old Gypsy woman recalls the belief that speaking Romani was once a capital offence (EGS No.52), and 'The Night Walkers', recalling the oath sworn by the Romani, Hayraddin Maugrabin (EGS No.48).

Again, whilst the darker side of the Gypsy character is hinted at, the *Romani Chal* is portrayed, in the main, as the victim of *Gaujo* intolerance who, despite the many privations of the travelling life, has somehow contrived to retain all the noble simplicity and pride of his ancient race. Thus, when one of the patrons of showman Frank Cooper is robbed whilst engaged at his stall (EGS, 153):

> Pukkerdas rai o Romani Chal:
> 'Miro chukko si choredo, avali!
> An' tute a-hatchin just anerjal –
> Ta pennas tute o' dovali?
>
> 'If foki sos lodderin miro ker,
> Choredi foki or barveli,
> 'Fore I'd muk 'em be luredo I'd sigger mer,
> 'An tute's a Romani, avali!'
>
> Frank Cooper si pordo o' kalo rat,
> As sano as yek kekava-li,
> But well'd as pano as if he were skat,
> To shun o' the rai, avali!
>
> The lord he said: 'Why, this is too bad!
> My coat is stolen, I tell you true,
> And you were near it, my Gypsy lad,
> Where's the thief, and what shall I do?
>
> 'If I had a guest', the lord he said,
> 'Rich like myself or poor like you,
> 'Fore I'd see him robbed I'd sooner be dead –
> And you're a Gypsy, aye that is true!'

> Frank Cooper's blood is as dark as night,
> As black as the pot in which Gypsies stew;
> But you'd think he was shot, he grew so white
> When he heard the lord, I tell you true!

Without a word, he dashes off into the crowd, to return a little while later with two black eyes but the gentleman's money and possessions intact. Cooper was, however, too much the *Rom* to refuse the *panj bar* (five pounds) which the gentleman offered him for his trouble, 'as a lord should do!'

Further examples of Leland's poetic genius are also to be found scattered throughout his other works, such as *The English Gypsies and Their Language* (1873), *The Gypsies* (1882) and *The Ballads of Hans Breitmann* (1888) – a *Gili Romaneskro* commencing:

> Schunava ke baschno del a godla,
> Schunava Paschomàskro.
> Te del miro Dewel tumen
> Dschavena bachtallo

and translated, in true *Breitmannesque* style:

> I hear de gock a-growin'!
> I hear de musikant!
> Gott gife dee a happy shourney
> Vhen you go to a distand landt.

Of particular interest are three 'rough ballads' attributed to the Stanleys and published on pp.65–7 of Hood's *Comic Annual* for 1886. Although there is some doubt as to whether these were obtained in precisely the same form in which they were published, they are reproduced below as texts 141, 142 and 144. Something of the flavour of Palmer and Tuckey's contribution may be gleaned from the following examples. Palmer's poem, *I Kéréngri* (The House-dweller) is said to be 'true to life in every line, as it was expressed to the writer by a Gypsy woman who had left off wandering' (EGS No.4):

> 'Tu pendas mengy "Sārishan?"
> De wāver dívvus, pal, acai
> Adrè acóvva werry tan.
> Pens mándy "So's adóvo rye?"'

103

"So's sikkered lis to be sā flick,"
I pens, "at rākkerin Rommany?"
Kek búti chals does mandy dick
For mándy's a kéréngeri.

Ah, rye! a gávs a wáfro tan;
Shom Rómmani, *I* kāms ye drom!
Avo! Fon *tute* "sārishan?"
And gorgio's jib fon nóko rom!'

You passed me by this werry way,
An' "Sarishan" you said to me.
I've often wondered, since that day,
What sort of person you might be?

Says I, 'Them's Gypsy words he spoke,
But where could he ha' learnt, and how? –
I don't see much of Rommany folk,
I'm livin' in a house, sir, now.

I hate this sort o' life, I do?
I'm Rommany, and want to roam. –
Just fancy! *"sarishan?"* from *you,*
And only English talk at home!'

Tuckey, whose contribution includes such titles as 'Death for Love',
'Cheer Up!' and 'Gypsy Love-Making', also offers the following
exhortation to petty theft. It was subsequently translated into Welsh
Romani by Sir Donald MacAlister, the principal of Glasgow University
and appears on p.30 of his *Romany Versions* (1928). For ease of
comparison, the English and Welsh Romani texts are reproduced below in
parallel and are followed by Tuckey's English paraphrase.

Lél Tiro Kām!	*Tiró Miró*
Sī o Rómmani mūsh sī kinlo,	'Velas o Kâló kinó,
Sī a gry adré o stanya;	Ake grai aré stanyáti;
Te o Rómmani chávo's bóckalo,	Sas po tikno bokaló,
Si a káni adré o gránya;	Oke kani top granzáti;
Shan Rómmani chálor trúshilo,	Sas o Romnichel trushló,
Si lévinor 'dré o kitchema;	But lovína kirchumáti;
Léla Rómano chīchi 'dré léskro fém,	Na sas chi 're pe vastésti,
Shan bárveli Górgior 'dré sār o tem.	Barv'le Gôje 're temésti.

Help Yourself!

If the Gypsy man is weary,
There's a horse in the farmer's stall;
If the Gypsy child is hungry,
There's a hen near the granary wall;
If the Gypsy lads are thirsty,
There's beer enough for them all;
And if there's nought in the Gypsy's hand,
There are enough wealthy gorgios in all the land.

~

Apart from Leland's three 'rough ballads', the 1880s were to produce only two examples of genuine Gypsy song, both variants of the one well-known quatrain commencing in Groome's version 'Well Done My Gorgio' (texts 75 and 76). The first appeared in Groome's *In Gypsy Tents* (1880), described by Sampson as 'one of the most scholarly, and certainly the most idyllic, studies of the nomad people ever written'; the second, in L. A. Smith's *Through Romany Songland* (1889).

For the student of Romani song, both books are something of a disappointment, albeit for entirely different reasons. Groome was a scholar, much admired by the doyen of all British Gypsiographers, John Sampson. Yet, for all his evident grasp of his subject, he was convinced that the Anglo-Romani muse had long ceased to be productive if, indeed, she ever had been. Thus, whilst drawing our attention to upwards of a dozen English, Scottish and Welsh songs then current in the Gypsy repertoire (Groome 1880, 141–57), he confines himself to the one traditional quatrain in the *Poggadi Chib* and two 'Macaronic effects, made years ago to meet the literary want that Miss Janet Tuckey, "Hans Breitmann," and Professor E. H. Palmer have since arisen to supply' (ibid., 146–8).

The first is a translation of Göethe's *Der König in Thule* (The King of Thule):

There jiv'd a Rómano krállis,
And a tátcheno rei was he,
'Fore yoi múlli'd a kúrruv o' sónakei
Del'd lésti his pírini.

There was chíchi yuv kom'd so míshto,
Sórkon chaíros he haw'd he would pi
'Vri adúvel, and out o' yuv's yókas,
The páni nash'd avrí.

105

And when lésti vel'd to múllaïn',
Yuv pen'd as how sórkon gav
Yuv del'd to the krállis arter him,
But kek o' the kúrruv a lav.

Yuv besh'd by the krállisko hobben,
With his kístaméngros sor,
'Dré his dádus's bóro kamóra,
Odoí by the dóriove shore.

Kek-kómi the púro píamóngro
The jívoben's yog should pi,
For he wússer'd the kómelo kúrruv
Right alé dré the dóriov's zi.

Yuv dik'd lis pélin', pórderin',
Jal alé dré the páni loon,
And his yókas pánder'd their kókoré.
And yuv was a gíllo coon.

Der König in Thule

Es war ein König in Thule
Gar treu bis an das Grab,
Dem sterbend seine Buhle
Ein goldenen Becher gab.

Es ging ihm nichts darüber,
Er leert' ihn jeden Schmaus;
Die Augen gingen ihm über,
So oft er trank deraus.

Und also er kamm zu sterben,
Zählt' er seine Städt ihm Reich,
Gönnt' alles seinem Erben,
Den Becher nicht zugleich.

Er sass beim Königsmahle,
Die Ritter um ihn her,
Auf hohem Vätersaale,
Dort auf dem Schloss am Meer.

Dort stand der alte Zecher,
Trank letzte Lebensglut,

Und warf den heil'gen Becher
Hinunter in die Flut.

Er sah ihn stürzen, trinken
Und sinken tief ins Meer.
Die Augen täten ihm sinken;
Trank nie einen Tropfen mehr.

Groome's second piece is a paraphrase of the eighth and last stanza of Burns's cantata, 'The Jolly Beggars':

Dórdi the toóvin' tátto-páni,
Dórdi the tátcheno Rómani chals!
With the bóshoméngro kéllin'
Muk us giv our gílli, Pals.

Júkel's ful for prástaméngros,
Mas for Kaúlos on the drom;
Kóngeris was but kair'd for ráshis,
Stáribens 'cos dínlos kom.

What's a púknius, so si wóngar,
What's to be a bóro rei?
So as we lels kúshto jívoben,
Why should we késser sar or kei?

Adré the dívvus pénnin' húkabens
All about the tem we jas,
And adré the raáti in a gránzi
Choómer our ráklis opré the kas.

That the rei's várdo with its kístaméngros
Prásters féreder, who might pen?
Or that the wúdrus of the rómer'd raúni
Diks any féreder kómobén?

Jívoben's kair'd o' dósta kóvas,
Méndi'll kek késser how they av;
Muk them róker about decorum
Who are atrásh for their kúshto nav.

Then kúshto bokh to tan and sásta,
Kúshto bokh to Kaúlos sor,
And kúshto bokh to the nóngo chávis;
Muk's pen sor on us *Amusháw**.

*A literal rendering of English 'amen', with no regard for its true meaning. Smart and Crofton give *'jaw see ta 'jaw see*; and Borrow, *si covar ajaw. Avali.*

See the smoking bowl before us!
Mark our jovial, ragged ring!
Round and round take up the chorus,
And in raptures let us sing:

Chorus: A fig for those by law protected!
Liberty's a glorious feast,
Courts for cowards were erected,
Churches built to please the priest.

What is title, what is treasure,
What is reputation's care?
If we lead a life of pleasure,
'Tis no matter how or where!

With the ready trick and fable,
Round we wander all the day;
And at night in barn or stable
Hug our doxies on the hay.

Does the train-attended carriage
Thro' the country lighter rove?
Does the sober bed of marriage
Witness brighter scenes of love?

Life is all a variorium,
We regard not how it goes;
Let them prate about decorum,
Who have character to lose.

Here's to budgets, bags, and wallets!
Here's to all the wandering train!
Here's our ragged brats and callets!
One and all, cry out, amen!

Chorus: A fig for those by law protected . . .

Fortunately, however, Groome was too much the scholar to be anything other than scrupulously accurate even when treating of so undeserving a subject as Gypsy song. He is thus willing for a moment to suspend his critical judgement and faithfully reproduce what he regards as a 'corrupt text', despite its many 'lacunae deeply to be deplored'. The following, a variant of 'The Poacher's Lament' (*Laws*, L14), appears on p.35 and provides useful early support for the contention that the differences which exist between *Romani* and *Gaujo* song are not simply a function of the depleted nature of the *Poggadi Chib*.

> Three of us went poaching out;
> To kill some game was our intench:
> The lafty pheasant they did fall
> With powder, shot and gun.
> He cried out for help
> And still he was denied.
> No more locked up in a midnight cell,
> To hear the turnkay push the bell.
> In his breast a mortail vound,
> While crames of blood did flow.

Although marred by the absence of any native Romani material, the various song titles mentioned by Groome are of interest in that they represent the earliest substantive account of the singing repertoire of the Gypsies of Britain. As we have now come to expect from the work of more recent collectors, the list is surprisingly varied, including items from the standard English, Welsh and Scottish repertoire:

The Unquiet Grave	The Shepherd of Snowdon
The Butcher Boy	The Bells of Aberdovey
The Jolly Ploughboy	*Llwyn Onn* (The Ash Grove)
Babylon	The Rising of the Lark
Sir Hugh of Lincoln	March of the Men of Harlech
The Leather Bottél	The Three Sisters
The Poacher's Fate	

L. A. Smith's *Through Romany Songland* (1889) consists of a series of chapters covering Gypsy song in India and various parts of Europe, including both England and Scotland but with the notable exception of the Ottoman territories and Wales. The material thus presented is drawn from a variety of sources, not always scrupulously acknowledged and sometimes dubious, and on a number of occasions there is clear evidence of a complete want of understanding of her chosen subject. Despite the work's professed breadth, there is no attempt at a coherent overview and, as with so many of her contemporaries, where she does adopt a critical stance her judgement is inevitably flawed by her failure to grasp the very real differences which exist between Romani folk song and its western European equivalents.

Her chapter on the Gypsies of England draws for the most part on the previously published work of Leland, Borrow and Groome, its only points of interest being the quatrain already mentioned and two full English texts, 'On the Banks of the Beautiful Severn' and the earliest printed version of 'The Squire and the Gypsy'. The chapter on Scottish Gypsy song, on the other hand, contains nothing in the way of dialect material, although it does include a mangled rendering of the Irish 'Brigade Ballad', *Siubhal a Rúin*, erroneously described by Smith as a 'pretty little slang Romany song'. Smith's contribution is considered in greater detail in the notes accompanying texts 173 and 174.

~

> I would venture to suggest that the Anglo-American Romany Ryes should form themselves into a club or correspondence society for the purpose of compiling and publishing by subscription a vocabulary and collection of songs as may be obtainable at this date . . .
>
> (Ibbetson 1887)

For William Ibbetson, David MacRitchie and others, like them, concerned for the future health of the language and culture of the Gypsies of Britain, the formation, in 1888, of the Gypsy Lore Society was a natural enough step. Yet, whilst the society's journal undoubtedly provided a hitherto unrivalled forum for the collation and dissemination of a wide range of material, both anecdotal and of a more serious academic nature, its membership, with one or two notable exceptions, did little to address the more specific issue of the preservation of English Romani song. The reason for this is not entirely clear, but it is possible that, just as the early leaders of the folk-song movement were to become caught up in the quest for an idealized national peasant repertoire, there was perhaps a tendency on the part of many of the *Raiá* to regard the Gypsies as 'natural aristocrats' and hence to emphasize the higher aspects of Romani culture at the expense of the more mundane. Thus, whilst revelling in the joys of Gypsy musicianship, or the artless simplicity of an old Romani folk tale, they seem to have regarded the 'tattered remnants' of English Gypsy song as offering no more than a useful example of the language in which they were composed (Philip Murray's song of the 'great trick', for example (text 115), despite its obvious importance as a historical document, is to be found tucked away in a composite vocabulary under the general heading 'Romani Flotsam' (Sampson 1892, 78)).

Among the more prolific contributors to the society's *Journal* was John Sampson who, self-taught in phonetics, comparative philology and Sanskrit, was eventually to produce that 'massive and scholarly study of the dialect of the Gypsies of Wales' – described by Augustus John as 'the best bedside book in the world' and hailed by Sir Donald MacAlister as providing us with 'a sure philological foundation for the intensive study of their idiom and its wider historical and ethnical relations' (*JGLS* 3rd ser. 11 (1932), 38). It is to Sampson, too, that we owe the first of only two printed collections devoted entirely to genuine Gypsy verse in broken Romani (*JGLS* o.s. 2 (1891), 80–93). Published under the title *English Gypsy Songs and Rhymes*, it consists of nineteen texts, 'collected in recent years within a comparatively narrow field' and, more importantly, 'taken down in every case *Romengero mostar*, from the mouths of Gypsies, and . . . given un-altered and unadded to in the form in which I heard them'.

Although Sampson appears to have believed that he had done little more than scratch the surface, and that there was 'pretty strong presumptive evidence to show that . . . Gypsy song was at one time much more common in England than it is now', any present shortcomings were, he thought, no more than a symptom of a far more widespread cultural malaise which was 'rapidly reducing their [the English Gypsies'] customs and traditions to a dead letter and their language to an ungrammatical jargon'. This is somewhat surprising in one in whom the critical faculty was so well developed; yet, like so many of his contemporaries, it does not seem to have occurred to him to judge his material by anything other than the standards normally applied to main-stream song, or to consider the possibility that what might at first appear to be no more than a symptom of cultural decline was, in reality, evidence of a continuing attachment to a mode of thought linking the English *Romani Chals* with their more traditional European counterparts. In the event, it was Bob Skot, in a lecture given before the Clevedon Naturalists' Association on 14 January 1909, who was the first British commentator to suggest that there was something qualitatively different about Romani song, arising not so much from a want of poetic genius as from a radically different mental set. Their songs, he suggested, seemed often to be condensed to the point of obscurity, the connecting link being supplied by the audience by tradition or instinct, so that to the outsider they may frequently appear wholly un-intelligible. Lacking either the time or the inclination, however, Skot chose not to develop the point, although it seems likely, given both the substance of his opening remarks and the fact that no English or Welsh sets were included in the recital accompanying his lecture, that his observations were based solely upon a consideration of continental Romani song texts (Macfie 1909).

With the publication of *English Gypsy Songs and Rhymes*, Sampson's interest in English Romani song would seem to have been exhausted for, with the exception of a brief postscript published in the next issue of the *Journal* and five songs from the Tinker, Philip Murray, included in a composite vocabulary published as 'Romani Flotsam' (1892), he seems never to have returned to the subject. Again, although in the long series of Welsh Gypsy tales which appeared from time to time in the pages of the society's *Journal* over the years 1907–32, he may well have 'given to posterity what has aptly been called the "canon" of their literature', he seems, like Borrow and Leland before him, to have preferred to devote his time to the production of his own Gypsy lyrics. In his otherwise comprehensive *Dialect of the Gypsies of Wales* (1926), for example, he includes only five short examples of Gypsy verse (texts 13, 14, 53, 140 and 161), a disappointing tally when one recalls that even as late as the 1950s, Kennedy and Brune were still able to recover three somewhat more substantial sets from their Welsh Gypsy informants.

That a great deal more remained to be said on the subject of Welsh Gypsy music and song is apparent from a list of twenty titles included by Sampson in his Welsh Romani lexicon under the catch-word *Gili*, song (Sampson 1926, iv, 105). Of these, one, 'Madimen Gili', is particularly intriguing in that it is said to have been composed by Thomas, grandson of Abram Wood. The remainder are, for the most part, Romani renderings of Welsh originals (including the national anthem, 'Hen Wlad fy Nhadau'), although it is not made clear whether anything more than their titles had been translated into Romani. The complete list is reproduced below. Where appropriate, the original Welsh or English title is given in brackets:

Lubnīénī g, Song of the Harlots (Lasses of Caernarvon);[9]
Ī madimen Gili, The Mad Song;
Ī Mātī Gili, The Drunken Song (*Glan Meddwdod Mwyn*);
Pīr(av)imáskī Gili, Song of the Wooing (*Serch Hudol*);
Tonénī g, The Bell Song (*Y Clychau Aberdyfi*);
Ī Bak'réskī Melanī Postī, The Sheep's Yellow Fleece (*Croen y Ddafad Felyn*);
Ō Bavál p'urdél Ō Giv, The Wind Blows the Corn (*Gwynt yn Chwythu'r Haidd* [lit. barley]);
Ī Čai Ka Mukdóm Pǻlē, The Girl I Left behind Me;
Čeriklésko Oriiben, The Rising of the Bird (*Codiad yr Ehedydd*);[10]
Kerabén k'ō Romeribén, Haste to the Wedding;
Ī Melanī Lovína, Yellow Ale (*Hufen y Cwrw Melyn*);
Ī Muklī (Nasadī) Raklī, The Deserted Maiden (*Yr Eneth gadd ei Gwrthod*);

Ī Nēvī Rat, The New Night (*Nos Galan*);
Ō Pårnō Giv, The White Corn (*Gwenith Gwyn*);
Pårnī Pisténa, The White Dove (*Y Golomen Wên*);
Ī P'urē Dakō Kåšt, My Grandmother's Stick (*Pen Ffon fy Nain*);
Ī P'uriākī Čai, The Old Woman's Daughter (*Merch Megan*);
Ī P'uriākī Plašta, The Old Woman's Cloak (*Mantell Shani*);
P'urō Dadénō T'em, Old Land of My Fathers (*Hen Wlad Fy Nhadau*);
Talál i Kåłī P'ūrj, Under the Dark Bridge (Dark Arches).

Apart from a number of items which appeared sporadically in various publications or which were intended for his friends alone, Sampson's remaining Romani verse output consists of his own metrical rendering of twenty-two quatrains from Omar Khayyam (Sampson 1902) and a collection of translations and original pieces in Welsh Romani which, as he says himself, 'make no claim to be specifically Gypsy in thought and feeling' (Sampson 1931).

Sampson was not alone among the *Romané Raiá* in lighting upon Omar as a suitable subject for translation into Romani. Three years earlier, Axon and Crofton had published their own English Gypsy rendering of the poet's best-known quatrain (*Manchester Quarterly* 18 (1899), 209), given here in FitzGerald's version:

> A book of verses underneath the bough,
> A jug of wine, a loaf of bread – and thou
> Beside me singing in the wilderness –
> Oh, wilderness were paradise enow!

For ease of comparison, Axon and Crofton's preamble is followed by their own version of the quatrain in parallel with Sampson's.

Akova si o tankeromengro's ghili adré o tanfolki's jib. O Tankeromengro Homer kedás akova kómomus-ghili adré purikano waver-temeskro jib dosta-dosta besháw aglal. O Ghilimengro Chavo-Gerald-Asar chidás-les adré Gorjikanes jib. O lilengro Tobar-Chavo chidás-les adré Romanes, ta o rokermengro Puv-gav kedás-les tatcho.

This is the tent-maker's song in the tent-dwellers' language. The tent-maker, Omar, made this love song in an ancient foreign tongue many many years ago. The poet, FitzGerald, translated it into English. The author, Axon, translated it into Romanes and the lawyer [? Crofton was a historian], Crofton, corrected it.

Sar kóosi maur' akai, talé de rook,
Sar mul te pi, sar ghili-lil ta Too
Ghilessa 'kei adré bikonyo-tem,
Ta 'konyo-tem te vela tem-opral.

Sas mandi Giliéngo Lil akái
Veshtésti, Mâro, Mol – ta TÜYA, chai,
Te mangi gīavés talál o Rūk –
'Vela o Vesht Devlésko Tem ke mai.

Sampson's verses were generally well regarded by his fellow *Raiá*, receiving a second impression in 1928 alongside a further selection from the same work and a number of other ballad translations by Sir Donald MacAlister (MacAlister 1928, 60–7). The only exception was the American academic, John Dyneley Prince, who, wounded by Sampson's blistering critique of his *English Romany Jargon of the American Roads* (1907; Sampson 1908b), made the unfortunate mistake of issuing a public rejoinder in the pages of the *Journal of the Gypsy Lore Society* (Dyneley Prince 1908). According to Prince, his interest in Romani had begun in his early teens when he and a friend, Professor H. A. Sill of Cornell University, had devised their own 'dialect' based largely on the writings of Borrow and Leland and supplemented, where necessary, by Spanish Romani with 'continental endings'. It was, he continues, 'an idiom every bit as real as the extraordinary dialect invented by Mr. Sampson in which to write his Omar' – a dialect 'deodorised . . . into a quasi-poetical lingo for the utterance of ideas which would be unintelligible to almost every Rom on the roads'.

There can be little doubt that Prince's ill-considered reference to the 'quasi-poetical lingo' of Sampson's Omar was, at least in part, prompted by the latter's unkind Parthian shot in what he calls the dialect of the New Jersey Gypsies (Sampson 1908b, 84):

Envoi

Prince! Tute *serbers* the *Kil-malliko*!
Aky muk *janwars gurings, gugerings,* kair;
Bender the *barya,* tute's *lunterdo*
And the *kovaskaruk-shok's* teerro (*rare*).

The quatrain, by reference to Prince's vocabulary, might be rendered thus:

Prince! you take the cheese cake!
Here let animals growlings and bellowings make;

114

Across the sea you are boasted of,
And the laurel crown is thine (*rare*).

The point of the verse and, indeed, of the review as a whole, becomes clear in the light of Sampson's principal conclusion, supported by copious example, that Prince's vocabulary offered 'nothing but a list of words compiled from Leland's publications, among them words which do not and cannot exist, words which may be traced to Leland's mistakes, or words which in songs or literary compositions he obviously invented for the nonce or nonsense'. With the exception of *kovaskaruk*, all the italicized words in the song fall into this category. Even Prince's somewhat unusual spelling of *aky*, here, may be traced to Leland. *Kovaskaruk*, on the other hand, as Sampson points out, offers an altogether more illuminating example of Prince's doubtful scholarship. The word may be traced back to an error of Jacob Bryant, copied by Pott and first identified as such by Smart and Groome. In his notebook, Bryant gives *covaseorook* for 'laurel', suggesting that, in response to his request for the Gypsy word for a particular bush, he must have received the altogether less specific response : '*kovva sí a rukk*', that is a tree. The original error was further compounded by a misprint in *Archeologia*, where the phrase appears as *covascorook* (Bryant 1785), in which form it subsequently appears in Prince's vocabulary, recast in keeping with his own (or Leland's) revised orthography.

It is only fair to say, however, that a number of those words to which Sampson takes exception, whilst somewhat unusual in form, are not, as he suggests, unique to Leland. *Malliko*, in place of the more usual *márekli* (Smart and Crofton 1875, 90) or *marikli* (Kenrick and Wilson 1985, 28) is, for example, wholly consistent with the equally unusual *tschilloko*, obtained by Norwood from the Coopers in 1859–60 and represented by Leland as *chilloko* (Leland 1873, *passim*). Again, as regards *gurings*, we read on p.12 of Groome's *In Gypsy Tents*,

'When you see the *malúna*, you will hear the *gúriben*' (thunder, lit., lowing of oxen), said Wester Lee to me at Nottinghill; but most English Gypsies can express 'thunder' and 'lightning' only by such periphrases as 'the voice of God', 'God's light.' (see also notes following text 145)

Had Prince merely called in question Sampson's poetry, as opposed to his scholarship, he might have been on surer ground. For Oliver Elton (*DNB*, 780), Sampson's *Romané Giliá* may well appear to have been 'charged with his intense temperament and with the wild humour and fancy which are also rampant in the posthumous volume "In Lighter Moments" (1934)', but for the present writer they are little more than an embarrassing mixture of the mawkish, coy and downright ludicrous. The work consists of twenty-six poems and a dedication also in verse, most of which, as Sampson says in his introduction, 'were written during the years when I was collecting material for my monograph on the speech of the Welsh *Kalé*' and 'were composed for the pleasure of myself and my friends without thought of publication'. Three of them are translations (*RG*, 22, 24 and 25) whilst three others, 'O Romano Rai' (*RG*,18), 'Arnaldos' (*RG*, 22) and 'Gaudeamus' (*RG*, 23), 'may be regarded as adaptations from German, Spanish and Latin sources' – the last being one of those which 'our gay company used to sing round the campfire, when in earlier days I led Walter Raleigh and Kuno Meyer on a caravanning tour through Wales'.

Although Sampson himself warns the reader that his English translations 'can convey to the reader but little of the spirit and sound of the original verses', my own feeling is that, as an enthusiastic signer interprets the gestures of the congenitally deaf-mute, he is apt to embellish his original material in such a way as to convey their intent rather than their bare meaning. Even in the original Romani, however, despite its greater simplicity, they seldom rise above the level of mere doggerel. Yet, whatever their merits as verse, Sampson does at least acknowledge that his poems 'make no claim to be specifically Gypsy in thought and feeling'.

The following extracts are drawn respectively from *Talane Kola* (Nether Things) (*RG*, 8) and *Iv Opré o Tem* (Snow) (*RG*, 12) which, in Sampson's own English translation, begins with the words 'Lo! The snow! The countryside looks like a maiden's white chamber . . .'

A

Talál tē prekhtē biti chufi
Si frilimen rokhénya,
Laj'nē dūi, rig rigáti
'Jâ-sar dūi nogē p'enya . . .

Beneath thy dainty little petticoat are thy frilly pantalettes, a bashful pair, clinging each to each, like fond twin sisters.

B

Biti mūri sikavén pen
'Jâ-sar raik'nē tarnē chaia,
Ridē posh 'rē pârnē īza
'Sana lajvanés top tuti.

'Rol gadésti 'shish dikésa
Raik'ne chuchiéngi shēpa;
'Kai t'a 'koi aról t'avésti
Raik'nē kâlē biti ruk'a.

The little hillocks appear like beautiful young maidens, half-clad in white garments, bashfully smiling at me.

'Neath their white covering thou canst divine rounded forms; and here and there through the white tracery little dark tufts peep forth.

One cannot say whether Sampson, like Borrow, had read Dafydd ap Gwilym, but he certainly seems to have shared the Welshman's fondness for rustic love-making:

Pansh romniá si mandi,
Būt būt kamáva len; . . .

Yek' romerdóm 'rē kangeri,
'Parl i shuvél vavér,
Yek' posh' i len, yek' ar' o vesht,
T'a yek' 'rē p'usano k'ēr.

I have five wives . . .

One I wedded in church, another over
a branch of broom, one on the river-bank,
one in a woodland glade, and one in a straw-thatched hut.

Unlike Dafydd ap Gwilym, however, whose woodland union with his beloved Morfudd was solemnized by the bard Madoc Benfras, Sampson's sylvan nuptials required no celebrant other than the girl herself:

Bâri Masa

Tū shan o mâro t'a o mol,
Tūya o khoben t''o rashái:
Yov te lhatéla tut te khol
Junél kek vaver bok' akái.

Siknē sherésa 'vava mē
'Rē bita kangeri kai tū shan;
Per'na mē dinē 'k'ā talé,
Kūr 'la mo trushalo 'zi drován.

High Mass

Thou art the Bread and the Wine,
thyself the Sacrament and the Priest,
and he that once tasteth of thee
shall know no other hunger.

With bowed head I enter
the little shrine where thou art;
my eyes are cast down,
my heart panteth thirstily.

His use here of the language of the Mass is also reminiscent of Ap Gwilym (as, for example, in the poem commencing: 'Lle digrif y bum heddiw' and known in translation as 'The Woodland Mass'), but there the similarity ends; for, with the clumsy double meaning of the second verse, the lofty imagery of the opening lines slips abruptly into bathos.

However mawkish and insipid his public amatory verse may be, in his more private moments Sampson was clearly capable of a far more robust style. The following lines, which are taken from a file marked 'Miscellaneous Songs', held in the Sampson archive in Liverpool University, are addressed in his own hand to his faithful follower and fellow Romanophile, Dora Yates (A. Sampson 1997, 111–12). Not only do they satisfy the poet Enderby's requirement that, in order to be successful, Rabelaisian verse must be 'Augustan in its neatness', but, unlike the *Romané Giliá*, they may also rightly claim to be 'specifically Gypsy in thought and feeling' (see texts 6–8 and accompanying notes).

I think of you with your dear feet up
And minjie [vagina] an inviting feast
But now alas! you've got your street up
And kar [penis] must wait three days at least! . . .

As I'm a man and wear a Kari
As you're a girl and sport a Minj
May I be damned or dead or hoary
Ere I forget sweet Fanny's fringe.

That Miss Yates was in no way abashed by Sampson's forthright approach is apparent from the following lines from a notebook preserved in her own archive:

Always merry is the kari
Always doing funny things
Mutering [urinating], karying [pricking], cumering [kissing] minjes
Always doing funny things

Always cheerful is the minjie
Always doing funny things
Mutering, gaping, biting, coming
Always doing funny things.

There is also, however, a darker side to Sampson's writing, evident in such pieces as *Mule Chati* (To a Dead Lily) (*RG*, 10), and *O kokalengero* (The Skeleton) (*RG*, 16), but, even here, his use of language and imagery is, for the most part, banal and unimaginative:

Kâlí s'i rat, konyó s'o k'ēr,
Lish lela man p'ârés.
Dē dud, kan; p'uter khestiár;
Muiál dik'áva Les.

Okēk'óv! sâkon kokalo –
'Kerát te pârné si!
'Sana o danda bukhledér?
P'and la, t'a niser 'vri.

The night is come, the house is still;
Too heavy grows the pain.
Unlock the cupboard; strike a light;
And face It once again.

Still there, you see, each bone the same –
How white they look to-day!
A little broader – what – the grin?
Lock door, and steal away.

But Sampson is surely at his best when in humorous vein, as in *Kushko Nēviben* (Good Tidings) (*RG*, 15), in which he describes the appointment of a new God from the ranks of Welsh Nonconformity – an elder uncle of Lloyd George, with long red whiskers and very light-fingered:

'Rē kangri godli dela drovén.
Yek'ar sas-lo 'rē staribenásti,
Te sovekherdás yov foshanés
Trushal bita piravimásti.

Haiavéla kek i Jutnéngi chib,
Kek lav Latī́na ta Grī́ka,
Bita bita Angitráko si les;
Rakeréla sâr Wolshitíka.

P'enéna te kela kushko Devél,
Fededér 'vela 'mârē fokéndi;
Bâri laj sas lendi 'jâ dūr te 'chilé
Tala vaver-t'eménḡē devléndi.

P'uri p'árani stādi rivéla yov,
T'a loli katili bangri,
T'a 'rē ravnos jala sâkon kurké
K'i Wesleyanéngi Kangri.

Būt gozherdo krafniéngero si,
T'a sâkon 'sarla ta rāti
Piéla buklo sutlo t'ud,
T'a khola pigína putā́ti.

Si les yogéngeri te yek'ar liás,
P'uri pushka – t'a kek lil lesti!
T'a bakaréngo bâro jukél
Te k'ār'n o ēnjéli 'Testy'.

'Rē ravnos, sar vaver Devél p'endás,
'Vena kek romniá ta róma.
Te kushko 'kanā́ te lasa Devlés
Te haiavél 'mârē dróma!

Kaméla tarnē t'ulē chaién,
Shi-lē sâr top leski dori;
T'a 'kana-sig jala to romerél
P'uri barvali pivli gori.

He cuts a great figure in Chapel.
Only once has He been in gaol,
For departing slightly from the truth
In a sweethearting case.

He does not understand a word of Hebrew,
Nor of Latin or Greek;
He has a smattering of English,
But only speaks Welsh.

They say He will make a very good God,
And a much better one for our people;
Indeed it was a great pity they had to endure
    for so long
These alien gods.

He wears an old black silk top hat,
And a red knitted waistcoat,
And in heaven, every Sunday he attends
The Wesleyan Bethel.

He knows all there is to be known about turnips,
And every morning and evening of His life
He drinks a mug of buttermilk,
And eats a peck of potatoes.

He has an old gun that once he borrowed,
A rusty firelock – but no licence!
And a bad tempered sheep-dog,
Whom the angels name 'Testy'.

In heaven, so the old God decreed,
There is neither marrying nor giving in marriage;
How pleasant it is to have a God today
Who really understands our Welsh ways!

He has a fancy for plump young girls,
And has plenty of them on His string;
And soon, so they say, He is to marry
A wealthy widow.

Sampson's rendering of 'MacPherson's Rant' (*RG*, 24) is also reproduced in full in the notes accompanying text 137.

As well as writing in the Welsh Gypsy dialect, Sampson also tried his hand at composition in both the *Puri* and *Poggadi Chib*. The first of the following examples is in the 'deep' *Romanés* of the northern Boswells and Hernes and was first published in the *Eagle* (St John's College, Cambridge) in 1887.

SHUKER, mi faino rinkno bengi,
Jal sutto, miro diro chor,
Me puker 'kova rai yek godli
Avri o purro chirosor.

Hush, my pretty imp of Satan:
Go to sleep, my own dear son,
Let me tell this Rye a story
Of the times now long agone.

Beshor ta beshor ghilo, raia,
Adré akova tem akai,
Jivdas 'men laki nogi foki
Yek tacho-bini Romni chai.

Years and years gone by, my Rya,
Just hard by this very place,
Lived a true-born Gypsy maiden
'Mongst the people of her race.

Sas mui pensa lollo pobo,
Mui te chumer, prosser, sav,
Yoi pirdas pensa rat'ski grasni,
Ta vasheti sas laki nav.

Lips had she like apples rosy,
Lips for kiss or jest aflame.
Like a thorough-bred's her step was –
Vashti was the maiden's name.

A purro Gorgio piriv'd lati,
Boro pukinyus tai sas-lo,
Sas lesti keror, puvor, kottors,
Ta sorkon-kova barvalo.

An aged gentile wooed her,
Mighty magistrate was he,
He had houses, lands and guineas,
He was rich as rich could be.

Yo pesserd ghere puker laki
Sar lavyor Gorginez te pen,
Ta kunjonez te siker lati
O Gorgio's gozvero jinipen.

Tutors hired he, who could show her
How to use the gentile's speech,
And they taught her all the wisdom
That the gentiles had to teach.

122

Sig jindas yoi o chollo gono,
Dias apre pensa rashai,
Ta sor o Gorgio's dromyor hodas
Pens' bauri zimin dova chai.

Quick she learned, read books like parson,
Cleared the whole bagful at a scoop,
All their curious gentile customs
Swallowed down like good snail soup.

''Glal mandi romerova tuti
Yek bitti kova mandi del;
Muk mandi yekos dik apopli
A tacho purro Romni kel.'

'Ere our wedding', said the maiden,
'I would fain one boon implore;
'Tis a real old Gypsy dancing,
Let me see one, just once more.'

''Dre kavo dui beshor, raia,
Kek kalo mui me diktom;
Puch lendi sor akai te siker
Sar faini rani mandi shom.'

'Two long years have come and gone, sire,
Since I saw a swarthy brow,
Bid them all come here and show them,
What a lady I am now.'

Kek but o purro rai komdas-les,
Nastis yov pendas, 'Kek nanai;'
Ta dosta Romni chelar avde,
Kakrachkinez ke mulo grai.

Fain the old squire had objected,
But he could not say her nay,
Like the carrion crows the Gypsies
Flocked together to the prey.

Adoi, 'dre lesko boro biuros,
O Romni-chalé pi ta ha –
Mai mulo dad! Komova dosta –
Mandi shomas adoi kona.

There within the lofty chamber
Gypsies ate and drank amain.
By my father's corpse! I would that
Such a day might come again.

O rai dikt buino ta tullo;
Krallisaîkonez yoi sas.
Yon roker'd salin ketenendi
Trustal o foki jindas.

Stout and haughty looked the squire,
She was like a queen to view;
Laughing, chaffing, they all chattered
Of the folks that once they knew.

'Kon si aduva sikermengro
Adré o kelinwardo gad,
'Dre dui diklos, boro skranyor?'
Yoi savdas, 'miro diro dad.'

'Who is yonder motley [*sic*] dandy,
With a shirt of strange device,
Double kerchief, spreading boot-tops?'
'That's my father dear', she said.

O pais jald. Yo pucherd lati,
'Kon 'duva hola ja drovan?'
Yoi pend, 'mai koko, kuremengro;
Kek pendan nashtas yov a dan.'

Sped the fun, again he asked her
'Who's that gorging without ruth?'
'That's my uncle, sir, the bruiser,
Scarce you'd think he'd lost a tooth.'

'Ta kon si purri chovihani
So diks ja wafidez 'pre men?'
Yoi pendas, 'miri churri bibi,
Tu lias trustal dukeripen.'

'Who's that ancient beldame yonder,
Glowering so wickedly?' he said.
'That's my poor old aunt you locked up,
Telling fortunes is her trade.'

O pais jald. Yo pucherd lati,
'Kon si aduvo ruzlo rom,
Posh beng, posh duvelesto-ghero?'
Nai diktas pendas 'kek jinom.'

Still the fun sped on – 'Pray tell me
If that stalwart wight you know:
Half a fiend he looks, half god-like.'
Eyes downcast she answered, 'no.'

'Kon dikasar?' Yo dinilez pendas,
'Yove si a monushesto chal.'
Yoi acht apre, ta porno dosta
Kerd laki kokeri palal.

'Who is he?' he urged unwisely,
'Sure he seems a proper man.'
Quick she rose, and deathly pallid,
Turned the Gypsy youth to scan.

Yog hocherdas 'vri laki yokyor
Sar diktas yoi aduva rom.
'Rai, miro nogo pirino sillo [*sic*],
So penchdom mandi bisserdom.'

Flamed her eye like fire out-flashing,
As it met the man she sought –
'Sir, it is my own true lover,
He I deemed I had forgot –'

'Av komlo! Mandi jova tussa.'
Hokterd graiakonez o chal:
Ruzles shundan o Romni jolta
O boro kamoros adral.

'Come beloved! Take me with you!'
Like a battle steed he sprang,
And through all the banquet-chamber
Gypsies' cries of rallying.

O Romni-Chalé shelde benges,
Sor divio 'vri wafripen
Leld bonnek dost barv'lo kalli,
Ta nashd adre o tamlopen.

Yelled like demons mad with fury,
Surged like waves the Gypsy horde,
Seized the gentile's costly treasures,
Out into the darkness poured.

Ta posh sas lino 'pre ta stardo,
Ta posh sas nashkedo, mai rai,
Ta tugno dosta bicherd pardel –
Kekera 'duva chal ta chai.

Some were caught and long imprisoned,
Some hanged high on gallows tree,
Some were sent to woful [*sic*] exile –
But the lovers wandered free.

Ta 'duva chal ta chai, mai kari,
Mai boro dad ta dai sas-lé.
Tacho! Miduvel rinker mandi
Te pukerava hokané!

My grand-parents were those lovers,
And this tale I've told you –
May the good Lord strike me handsome
If I lie – the thing is true.

This last piece is one of three 'Vagrom Verses', Sampson's contribution to the 1897 *Jubilee Book of the Philosophical Institution of Edinburgh*.

Comparative Philology
Nomen et Numen

No, *Rye*, no matter where you goes,
Sarch high or low where'er you please,
You'll never find another talk
So good as our old *Romines*.

What do you call this here in French?
Cuttow! That's Cant or *Mumpish* quite.
In *Jarman*? *Messer*! Well it hain't
A messer if you use it right.

Or take a talk one onderstands
Like Henglish; Still it's all the same.
Knife! Now, *Rye*, I axes you,
What is that only just a name?

But *Churi*! There you has it straight,
Churi Is a *Churi, Rye.*
A *churi* is the thing hitself,
And not a name you calls it by.

When Sampson died in 1932, he was cremated and his ashes scattered on
the hills near Llangwm, Denbighshire, to the sound of Gypsy music and
the words of his own elegy on his fellow *Rai*, Francis Hindes Groome –
'Stanyakeréski' (Sampson 1931, no.21):

Romano Ráia, P'rala, Junimángro,
Konyo chūmeráva to chikát;
Shukar java mangi, t'a mukáva
Tut te 'jâ kamdóm mē – 'Kushki Rat!' . . .

Scholar Gypsy, Brother, Student,
peacefully I kiss thy forehead;
quietly I depart and leave thee whom I loved –
'Good night'.

~

The first time I really heard folk songs was in Surrey, years ago when I
was staying with some people one Christmas and, after dinner, they
told me that a very extraordinary Gypsy, living in the neighbourhood,
would come in, as he often did, and sing to the guests. He accordingly
came in with a stringed instrument and sang a rather wild tune which,
perhaps now, with more experience, I should look upon as traditional
or, perhaps, as Monsieur Jacques would say, modal. The people there,
however, said that it was exactly like Wagner.

(Kate Lee 1899)

Although, in the years following its formation in 1898, a number of
individual members were to obtain a handful of items from Gypsy informants, the English Folk Song Society as a whole was to prove no more active
in the collection and preservation of Romani English song than the Gypsy
Lore Society had been. Indeed, not only was it apparently indifferent to the
existence of native Gypsy song, but it would also seem to have largely
overlooked the Gypsies' importance as carriers of mainstream tradition.
Yet the evidence was there for those who cared to look. Broadwood (1843),
Dixon and Bell (1877), Groome (1880) and Smith (1889) had all obtained
excellent mainstream texts from the singing of Gypsy informants, and
further examples are to be found scattered throughout the literature.

Vaughan Williams, it is true, does seem to have entertained a high regard for the Gypsies as carriers of folk melody. Asked by a journalist for his most memorable musical experience of 1912, he replied that it was hearing a Gypsy song at Monklands, near Leominster in Herefordshire, where he had been taken by Ella Mary Leather, his companion on a number of similar visits to various Gypsies of her acquaintance. There they had encountered a number of Gypsies, including Alfred Price Jones, with whose 'beautiful tenor voice' they had been particularly impressed: 'While Dr. Vaughan Williams noted down the tune', wrote Mrs Leather,

> his wife and I noted down alternate lines of the words. It is difficult to convey to those who have never known it the joy of hearing folksongs as we heard that ballad; the difference between hearing it there and in a drawing-room or concert hall is just that between discovering a wild flower growing in its native habitat and admiring it when transplanted to a botanical garden.

Yet the composer's preference for a 'good' text undoubtedly coloured his attitude towards the songs themselves. Following his first meeting with Mr Price Jones, he made a number of further visits to the area, recovering both words and music, some of which he later incorporated in his published work. Two of the tunes in his *Fantasia on Christmas Carols*, for example, came from Herefordshire Gypsies, whilst, in 1920, together with Mrs Leather, he published twelve traditional Herefordshire carols, of which at least nine were taken from local Gypsy informants. Unfortunately, whilst their treatment of this material would almost certainly have accorded well with Leland's notions of what was required in the editing of Gypsy texts, their occasionally wanton disregard for accuracy would be unthinkable on the part of any serious contemporary collector. One set, from the singing of Angelina Whatton, contains the words:

> Christ made a trance one Sunday view,
> All with his own dear hands,
> He made the sun clear all off the moon,
> Like the water off dry land.

In its published form, however, it reads:

> God in the Holy Trinity,
> All with his mighty hand,
> Hath made the sun, the stars, the moon,
> The water and dry land.

That the *Romané Raiá* were at least partly responsible for the continuing neglect of the Romani English repertoire is beyond question; for, if the *Raiá* themselves were of the opinion that British Gypsy song was all but a dead letter, it is hardly surprising that those claiming no special knowledge of the Gypsy community should have accepted their judgement at face value.

Despite the obvious importance of his collection of native Romani songs and rhymes, Sampson's later apparent indifference towards this aspect of his subject seems to have proved more infectious than his earlier enthusiasm. Following the publication in 1892 of 'Romani Flotsam', nothing else in the way of Romani English song material was to be published for the next fifteen years although, to be fair to the *Raiá*, their society's *Journal* had itself been forced into temporary abeyance owing to lack of funds. When the silence was eventually broken, however, with the publication, in the first volume of the newly revived *Journal*, of the earliest printed version of the *grai puvving* theme (text 78. *JGLS* n.s. 1 (1907) 164), the dismissive attitude of the *Raiá* remained unchanged. In 1912, when the *Journal* also carried the first three printed variants of the *Kosh Choring* song (texts 88–90), they were said by the society's correspondent to display 'all the ugliness of the genuine article' and, although publishing them 'in the hope of aiding some future specialist to reconstruct them', the editor nevertheless felt moved to remark that 'what was precisely the charm which popularised these verses so widely among English Gypsies that tattered remnants are still treasured by almost every family is not apparent in any fragment yet recorded'.

For MacColl and Seeger, however, there were other less honourable reasons for the folk-song establishment's neglect of this potentially fruitful source of native song material. 'There can', they say (1977, 3), 'be little doubt that social prejudice has been, to a large extent, responsible for the neglect of the Travellers' repertoire of songs and ballads', and it may well be the case that the more fastidious of early collectors were indeed influenced by such considerations. Henderson and Collinson, writing of the late Geordie Robertson, from whom the School of Scottish Studies obtained, *inter alia*, 'Robin Hood and the Pedlar', lived for many years within easy walking distance of the noted collector, Gavin Grieg, and yet the latter never made any attempt to collect songs from him. The reason for this, they suggest, 'was, in all probability, a social one; Grieg got the bulk of his wonderful collection from the farming community, and Geordie Robertson was a Tinker – a settled Tinker, a crofter and a "made horseman", but still a Tinker. In Grieg's day this represented a real social barrier' (Henderson and Collinson, *Scottish Studies*, ii, 2, in MacColl and Seeger 1977, 2–3).

It would, however, be unfair to urge this point too strongly, for there were undoubtedly others who would have found such false sensibility wholly alien. The Revd Sabine Baring-Gould, for example, seems to have been regarded with genuine affection by those Gypsies with whom he came in contact – as, indeed, was his wife. By way of illustration, Rebecca Penfold, a Devon Traveller, tells how a young cousin of hers, Willie Penfold, was buried in the churchyard at Lew Trenchard and how Mrs Baring-Gould asked that if anything should happen to her she might be laid beside him 'because he was buried in a new piece of ground and she thought he was lonely' (Folktracks 42 B1).

For the present writer, a far more significant factor in the Folk Song Society's failure to recognize the Gypsies' importance as carriers of mainstream tradition was their single-minded attachment to the idea of an English national folk repertoire, comparable with that of Scotland and Ireland, and characterized by the near perfect productions of an idealized peasantry. As a result, not only were the Gypsies to be largely ignored, but even that rich vein of urban folk song, the legacy of the industrial revolution, was, during the early years, to remain largely untapped.

Although the society's rules said merely that it should 'have for its primary object the collection and preservation of folk-songs, ballads and tunes, and the publication of such of these as may be deemed advisable' (rule ii), and that 'the selection of the words and tunes to be published by the Society shall be decided upon by a sub-committee appointed by the Committee of Management' (rule xiii), there is no mistaking the underlying sense of mission in the following extract from Hubert Parry's inaugural address (*JFSS* 1, 1 (1899), 1–3):

I take it that we are engaged chiefly with the folk-songs of England, and England is poorly represented in collections so far. Other nations have been far more keen about the matter. Even Russia, which not so long ago began to emerge from a state far removed from our idea of civilisation, had more than a century ago a very fine collection of folk music . . . In the neighbouring countries of Ireland and Scotland folk music has attracted more attention; and moreover town civilisation is not so rife in them, and in out-of-the-way places old tunes survive much longer, and the marked characteristics which they possess make it in some respects more easy to collect them. English tunes are not marked by such characteristic traits of melody and rhythm and are rather more difficult to lay hold of. Still we have no need to be ashamed of them, for they are characteristic of the race, of the quiet reticence of our country folk, courageous and content, ready to meet what chance shall bring with a cheery heart. All the things that make the folk music of the race also betoken the qualities of the race and, as a faithful reflection of ourselves, we needs must cherish it. Moreover it is worth remembering that the great composers of other countries have concentrated upon their folk music much attention, since style is ultimately national. True style comes not from the individual but from the productions of crowds of fellow-workers, who sift, and try, and try again, till they have found the thing that suits their native taste; and the purest product of such efforts is folk-song, which, when it is found, outlasts the greatest works of art, and becomes an heritage to generations. And in that heritage may lie the ultimate solution to the problem of a characteristic national art.

I think also we may legitimately reflect that in these late days when we are beginning to realise how little money profit can bring, and how much joy there lies in the simple beauty of primitive thought, and the emotions which are common to all men alike, even to the sophisticated, it is a hopeful sign that a society like ours should be founded: to save something primitive and genuine from extinction; to put on record what lovable qualities there are in unsophisticated humanity; and to comfort ourselves by the hope that, at bottom, our puzzling friend, Democracy, has permanent qualities hidden away, somewhere, which may yet bring it out of the slough which the scramble after false ideals, the strife between the heads that organise and the workmen who execute, and the sordid vulgarity of our great city-populations, seem in our pessimistic moments to indicate as its destiny.

Against this background, it would indeed have been surprising had the society commenced its work of recovering the purest product of the English collective consciousness among so obviously unregenerate a race as the Gypsies. Yet there is more than a hint of irony in all this; for, as Parry himself was aware, 'in this country we have not, until recently, had any idea of concentrating our attention on the collecting of our folk songs' (ibid.). Indeed, despite the widespread use of a range of traditional material in the ballad operas of the eighteenth century – albeit modified or reworked in accordance with contemporary taste – the belief had grown up that England as a whole possessed nothing in the way of a national folk repertoire. Burney, for example, writing in or about the year 1805, was of the opinion that, 'though the natives of Scotland and Wales can boast of national tunes, both plaintive and spirited, that are characteristic, pleasing and distinct from each other, the English have not a melody which they can call their own except the hornpipe and the Cheshire round' (Rees 1805, s.v. 'Simplicity in Music').

Even as late as 1878, no more than twenty years before the formation of the Folk Song Society, Carl Engel, a noted authority on national music, resident in England for upwards of thirty years, was able to report that 'some musical enquirers have expressed the opinion that the country people of England are not in the habit of singing . . .' – a remark sadly reminiscent of Groome's summary dismissal of Anglo-Romani song.

Yet despite the apparent indifference of both the folk-song movement and the Gypsy Lore Society, the years leading up to the Great War are by no means devoid of interest. In 1909, there appeared the only other printed collection, apart from Sampson's, of Gypsy verse devoted entirely to material in the *Poggadi Chib* ('Anglo-Romani Songs', *JGLS* n.s. 3, 157–60), whilst two years later, Gillington was to publish the first and, until MacColl and Seeger's (1977), the only self-contained collection of traditional songs, with their accompanying melodies, obtained exclusively from British Travellers.

The first of these, 'Anglo-Romani Songs', consists of ten pieces drawn from a variety of sources, including two of Borrow's songs from the singing of two of Jasper Petulengro's granddaughters (texts 44 and 133). Opening with the somewhat inauspicious observation that 'English Gypsies do not as a rule possess Romani songs', the anonymous collator goes on to refer to the various texts under consideration as 'fragmentary' or 'corrupt', a perception which leads him to conclude, somewhat wryly, that 'the Gypsies would appear to have either singularly bad memories or else a faculty for improvisation which causes them to alter the words wilfully to suit their momentary thoughts'. It is unfortunately the case that neither the editor nor any of his readers appear to have thought it worthwhile pursuing this latter possibility.

Gillington's *Songs of the Open Road* (1911) contains a number of songs and dances, collected in Hampshire and, more particularly, the New Forest, of which only four are in the *Poggadi Chib* (texts 17, 74, 80 and 113). In her introduction, she says nothing of her informants, other than that the Lees were once regarded as the best fiddlers, and makes no attempt to refer her material to other printed variants, even though she herself had been responsible for publishing the first recorded version of one of them (text 74) in an earlier edition of the *Journal of the Gypsy Lore Society* (Gillington 1907, 64; text 78).

Her only reviewer also seems to have found the airs to which the songs were sung of greater interest than the words, observing merely that 'the four Romané gilia may, as far as the words are concerned, claim to be of Gypsy origin. Trivial in subject, they reflect the daily life of the Gypsy, his love of fiddling, rabbits and pretty raklis, his antipathy to constables and handiness with his fists' (Gilchrist 1911). Although she goes on to say that 'as a first attempt at a collection of Gypsy music, the volume deserves all the praise due to the pioneer, and for the general public forms an interesting and attractive selection of "songs of the road"', she nevertheless rightly concludes that 'its value to the student would have been greatly increased by some reference to existing tunes and words'. From her subsequent remarks, however, it is clear that Gilchrist's interest lay not in the

differences which exist between *Gaujo* and Romani song texts but in the
way in which words and music, originally unconnected, may impact upon
each other when brought together. 'The comparison of varying copies of
the same tune', she writes,

> is an important branch of folk song study of value in arriving at the normal or
> typical form of an air; by comparing variants, one may note how the licence of
> the individual singer may alter the rhythmic or melodic character of a tune . . .
> By comparison of both texts and tunes, it may be seen how the words have been
> arranged by one line of singers to fit a particular tune, and, on the other hand,
> how a tune has been pulled out or curtailed to fit a ballad to which it has not
> originally belonged, thus becoming in the process of time almost a new tune . . .

Little or nothing is known of Gillington other than what may be gleaned
from her published work. Even her dates are unknown, for she is mentioned in none of the standard reference works on the folk-song movement
or in any dictionary of biography, and, despite her not inconsiderable
contribution, her passing seems to have gone unnoticed by the *Journal of
the Gypsy Lore Society*.

Between 1905 and 1912, her Gypsy pieces appeared in a variety of period-
icals, including *Outlook, Country Life, Littel's Living Age* and the *Romanitshels, Didikois and Folk-Lore Gazette*. Popular rather than scholarly in tone
and content, and suffused with the soft romantic glow of mid-Victorian
sentimentality, they include such titles as 'House of the Open Door', 'The
Bushes Green' and 'Flowers of the Forest', the last published in the name of
the 'Romany Rauny'. Like many of her male contemporaries, she, too, was
unable to resist the temptation to compose her own Gypsy verses as, for
example, in 'The Gypsies' Pass' (Gillington 1910b, 741) and 'The Bushes
Green' (Gillington 1911b, 53–4). The following are from 'My Sweet Sister', a
wholly unremarkable description of two Gypsy children, first printed in the
short-lived *Romanitshels, Didikois and Folk-Lore Gazette* in 1912.

> The dove is Mi Duvel's chiriclo,
> The bird of God;
> She flutters o'er the lonely trees,
> The wet brown sod;
>
> And like a Rawni sor in pawni,
> Miri kushtipen,
> She comes and goes as the wild wind blows –
> My sweet sister.
>
> Miri kushtipen!
> She comes and goes as the wild wind blows –
> My sweet sister.

And sar a Rawni in shubó pawni,
Miri kushtipen,
She sovs akei where Romanys lie –
My sweet sister.

To sov adrey the rukis in the rarde!
Miri kushtipen!
To come and go as the wild wind blows –
My sweet sister.

(Gillington 1912, 4–6)

Although the inter-war years were to yield a rich harvest of Gypsy material, both linguistic and folkloric, both the folk-song establishment and the Gypsy Lore Society continued steadfastly to ignore the possibility that the Gypsies possessed anything of interest in the way of native or main-stream song. Sampson, it is true, included a number of items in his study of the Gypsies of Wales but, as these are confined to the lexicographical section of the work, it seems clear that they were intended to serve simply as illustrations of his informants' use of language rather than as evidence of their capacity for verse composition. Indeed, as has already been suggested, whilst his interest in Romani prose literature continued undiminished – forty-two Welsh Gypsy folk tales were published at intervals in the *JGLS* between the years 1907 and 1933, and a selection of fifty Romani riddles in 1912 – he seems to have abandoned the collection and publication of traditional song in favour of the production of his own Gypsy lyrics.

Sampson was, however, not the only *Gaujo* academic to find the Welsh Gypsy dialect a congenial vehicle for the exercise of his muse. Four years before the publication of *Romani Gilia*, Sir Donald MacAlister, then principal of Glasgow University, produced his own collection of *Romani Versions*, a number of which had already been published separately both in the *Journal of the Gypsy Lore Society* and elsewhere (MacAlister 1928). As with *Romani Gilia*, it makes no claim to be genuinely Gypsy in character. As the title suggests, it contains no original work but, with the exception of a rendering of portions of the *Rubaiyat of Omar Khayyam*, consists entirely of Welsh Romani versions of well-known pieces from the Anglo-Scottish repertoire – three from Burns, four from Stevenson, two from Kipling and one apiece from Murray, Calverley, Buchan, Cornford and Scott. There are, besides, a Welsh Romani translation of Janet Tuckey's 'Lél Tiro Kam', reproduced in an earlier section, and a reworking of both 'The Raggle-Taggle Gypsies' and 'The Ballad of Johnnie Faa' (see notes accompanying texts 163 and 164).

4

The Post-war Years

A Gypsy can get up and sing on a dry crust of bread.

(Gypsy saying)

Although Groome, Gillington and others had earlier pointed the way, it was only as the post-war folk revival gathered momentum during the 1950s and 1960s that the true extent of the Gypsies' contribution to the preservation of mainstream traditional song became fully apparent. Yet even this belated recognition would seem to have owed more to a growing eclecticism within the folk-song movement itself than to any new-found enthusiasm on the part of the successors of the *Romané Raiá*. Peter Kennedy, for example, whose pioneering work during the 1950s may be said to have set the tone, is a mainstream folk-song collector of impeccable antecedents – a nephew of Maud Karpales and a great-nephew of Marjorie Kennedy Fraser – whilst Ewan MacColl, joint editor with Peggy Seeger of *Travellers' Songs from England and Scotland*, will perhaps be best remembered as a singer, song-writer and performer, a co-founder of Theatre Workshop and the originator, with Seeger and Parker, of the highly innovative *Radio Ballads*.

For this reason, perhaps, when the first anthologies of British Traveller songs appeared in the 1970s, they were almost entirely given over either to mainstream material obtained from Gypsy/Tinker informants or to songs, originated within the Traveller community but composed in English rather than in their own language. Thus Yates, whilst rightly drawing attention to the depth and breadth of the Gypsy repertoire, includes in his published work only a tiny handful of songs in the *Poggadi Chib*. The Sussex Gypsy, Mary Ann Haynes, who, with others of her family, provided Yates with upwards of 100 songs is represented by only two Romani English texts (Yates 1975a), whilst Sharper's Joe (Joe Jones/Harris/Ridley), from whom he obtained a further forty, including the first contemporary text of 'The Pear Tree', seems not to have been in the habit of singing in *Romanés* at all.

Indeed, in a list of titles obtained from Mr Jones and published in the *Folk Music Journal* (Yates 1975a, 79), the only set of Gypsy origin is 'Hartlake Bridge', a song which 'he preferred not to sing . . . because it reminded him of a dead son who had likewise drowned'. This is all the more surprising as he was already in his nineties when Yates first met him and might have been expected to have been exposed to the more extensive *Poggadi Chib* repertoire current in his early youth before the turn of the century.

That Mr Jones, despite his preference for English texts, may have been in touch with an older and arguably more 'authentic' singing tradition may be inferred from the manner of his performance. Although, for some critics, Jones's style was more that of a 'country' than a 'Gypsy' singer, the fact that a similar 'non-Gypsy' caste is also discernible in the singing of a number of other elderly southern English Gypsies has led Yates to suppose that the 'nasal-crooning', now considered typical of the genuine Gypsy performer, may be nothing more than a later innovation which has overtaken an older and once more widespread style of singing, traces of which may also be heard in the singing of the late 'Pop' Maynard, a former poaching companion of Jones's, from whom the latter also apparently acquired a number of his songs (Yates 1975a, 79; 1976, 14).

Having spent some time collecting old fiddle and pipe tunes in the north-east of England, Kennedy was 'converted' to traditional song by the singing of an old shanty-man whom he met in Bristol some time during 1950. Armed with a research prototype of the first domestic magnetic tape recorder, he recorded a number of songs in which he succeeded in interesting both HMV and the BBC. Thereafter, throughout the 1950s, he travelled extensively in Britain and Ulster, gathering songs wherever he went, a number of which were featured in his long-running Sunday morning radio show, *As I Roved Out*. It is probably no exaggeration to say that this programme was in itself responsible for 'turning on' a whole new generation of listeners and singers to a world of traditional song of which they would otherwise have been wholly ignorant.

In terms of the printed word, Kennedy is perhaps best known for his *Folksongs of Britain and Ireland* (1975), a ground-breaking work in which, abandoning the regional emphasis of earlier collections, he includes, alongside a representative sample of the English folk repertoire, examples of the singing tradition, both native and Anglo, of Scotland, Ireland and Wales, Cornwall, the Channel Islands and the Isle of Man. The book is also worthy of note in that it contains the first published anthology of Traveller songs since Gillington's *Songs of the Open Road* of 1911, thus according Gypsies and other Travellers equal status with the settled community. Unlike Gillington, however, whose informants were drawn exclusively from the Gypsies of Hampshire and the New Forest, Kennedy and his collaborator, John Brune, include a variety of items representative of the four principal branches of the Traveller community, the Gypsies of England and Wales and the Tinkers of Ireland and Scotland.

Despite their evident importance as collectors and publishers of Gypsy song, Kennedy and Brune's work is nevertheless open to criticism on a number of counts: Kennedy's eagerness for the prey, for example, occasionally leads him to abandon the normal courtesies due to his informants; the notes accompanying his published recordings are unhelpful, poorly presented and at times wildly inaccurate; and there is every reason to suppose that both he and Brune were not always fully aware of the true significance of their material.

On more than one occasion Kennedy stops his informant when he or she has already begun to sing, either because they had failed to deliver what was expected of them (Wally Fuller, Folktracks 140, A11) or because he (Kennedy) was unhappy about some other aspect of the recording (Rebecca Penfold, Folktracks 42, A1). In the first example, Mr Fuller was clearly thrown by the interruption as, having abandoned his first offering, he begins again with a verse of that much travelled song, known to the British army in Dublin as 'The Lock Hospital' and to 'Western buffs' as 'The Streets of Laredo', before veering off into 'The Game of Cards' or 'The One, Two and Three':

WF: Now I loved you more than words can say . . .
PK: You said you were going to sing 'As I Walked Out'.
WF: Now as I was a walking one mid-summer's morning . . . (etc.)

In the case of Rebecca Penfold, Kennedy also seems to display more than a simple want of manners. On two occasions, Mrs Penfold specifically asks that he should stop recording yet, whilst leading her to believe that he had done so, Kennedy clearly leaves his machine running:

RP: As I was walking one morning in May . . . Wait a minute, don't you put me on that now.
PK: No, no, I won't put it on yet.
RP: . . .Travelling my way . . . One was a soldier, his . . . um . . . One was a soldier dressed in blue . . . (etc.)
    And then it goes on, you see. You haven't got me on that, have you?
PK: No, it's all right.
RP: Because I ain't saying the words right, you know.
PK: No, I just want to get a bit of the tune of it.

And again:

RP: . . . For a meeting of a pleasant place, O between my love and I . . . now I don't want you to get playing this on the wireless, television, 'cos I shan't . . .

Mr P: Not afore she gets it right. She'll think on the words first.

PK: No, no, she wants to record it when it's right . . .

RP: For a meeting of a pleasant place,
O between my love and I,
I'll go down in yon yon valley
O and there I will sit and sing . . . (etc.)

It has also been suggested that he was guilty of an altogether more serious lapse in his dealings with Phoebe Smith, whom he visited on a number of occasions between 1956 and 1962 at the Smiths' scrap metal business in Mowbray near Woodbridge in Suffolk (Folktracks 100).

The tape, which has been heavily and somewhat crudely edited, contains a number of songs and scraps of music interspersed with, or overlaid by, recollections of his informant's early life. Much of this latter material, which does little to enhance our understanding of the intervening texts, is of a somewhat personal nature and, according to Yates, 'upset Phoebe Smith who was unaware that this material would ever be made available to the public' (Yates 1977, 13).

The notes accompanying the recording also serve to illustrate Kennedy's occasionally careless approach to the question of documentation. With the exception of a fragment of 'Hopping down in Kent', 'I'm a Romani Rai' and a verse of 'The Riddle Song', all those items appearing on the tape had already been published on three long-playing records issued on the Topic label, yet no mention is made of this. Even where the same song is obtained from one singer on different occasions, the result may well be of interest for the light it sheds on the way in which the informant has chosen to develop his or her material, and the provision of background information of this type remains a basic requirement (see, for example, texts 82–3, 106–7 and 167–8). It is also worth mentioning that the last named, 'The Riddle Song', was not sung by Phoebe's husband, as stated, but by her son, Joe Boy.

Some of the material published in the Folktracks series has, it is true, been reproduced in Kennedy's *Folksongs of Britain and Ireland* where an attempt has been made to place it in its proper context. Even here, however, Kennedy's collaborator, John Brune, has, on occasion, been less than thorough in his research, or has failed to do justice to himself in print. 'If ever I Dae Gang a-Choring', for example (text 103), is mistakenly dismissed as a 'nonsense song' whilst, in discussing Frank Cooper's 'Mandi Went to Poov the Grys' (text 81), mention is made of only one other printed version when a dozen or more related variants are to be found scattered throughout the literature (texts 74–93).

It is in his treatment of texts in Welsh Romani, however, that this want of thoroughness is particularly apparent. Somewhat surprisingly, in their few brief excursions into the Principality, Kennedy and Brune succeeded in gathering three quite remarkable examples of Welsh Romani song, each more substantial in its way than anything previously published by John Sampson. More importantly, unlike Sampson, who was forced to rely on his own ear and his ability to make rapid notes which were both textually and phonetically accurate, they had at their disposal the relatively sophisticated recording apparatus of the 1950s. Against this background, the results of their labours are, it must be said, somewhat disappointing and would suggest that they were wholly unaware of the true significance of what they had found.

In *Folk Songs of Britain and Ireland*, Brune offers us two complete texts in Welsh Romani, of which the first, 'The Fiddle Maker's Song' (text 137), is said to refer to Lucas Petulengro, of whom his informants apparently knew nothing apart from his dates and the fact that he was the only Gypsy to make fiddles *Gaujo*-fashion. The second (text 139) is even more remarkable in that it consists of two elements, the first bearing a quite astonishing resemblance to a set recorded in Hungary by Donald Kenrick, and the second an extraordinarily close variant of a quatrain included by Sampson in his *Dialect of the Gypsies of Wales* of 1926.

Unfortunately, Brune's failure to give either the number, age range or names of his informants means that it is impossible to say if they belonged to one of those families – Lees, Woods, Griffithses, Joneses – already known from other sources to have preserved a knowledge of the older dialect, or if they represented a further extension of the speech community. We are told that his second set, 'Oko Vela O Chavo', was obtained from children and this in itself is of considerable interest as it would suggest that they possessed a far deeper knowledge of the language than those belonging to the group encountered by Tipler on the Llŷn peninsula in the summer of 1950. Even this, however, is mere conjecture, as in the absence of any further examples of their speech, we cannot be sure that the quatrains themselves were not simply ossified and imperfectly understood remnants. That his informants were willing to sing in their own language upon so brief an acquaintance suggests that they would have been willing to say more had they been asked, and the fact that they were not is much to be regretted.

Kennedy also succeeded in capturing on tape the only commercially available recording we have of a song in Welsh Romani, a vocabulary and a lengthy conversation in the dialect (Manfri and Hywel Wood, Folktracks

441 A11–14), of which the latter two are also to be found on Folktracks 53. Once again, whilst in no way wishing to underestimate the importance of this material, one is left with a certain sense of disappointment at Kennedy's apparent failure to make better use of the opportunity presented. As well as those items already mentioned, the Woods' tape contains a handful of songs in Welsh and English (including the well-known 'Merch o Blwy' Penderyn' and an unusual maceronic variant of 'Claddu'r Mochyn Du'); a set of harp tunes played by Nansi Richards who, whilst influenced stylistically by the playing of the older Woods, was not herself a Gypsy; a number of anecdotes of no Gypsy interest whatsoever; and a collection of riddles told by Manfri. Even these latter, however, whilst corresponding well with those of their Welsh Romani equivalents published by Petsch in 1912, are robbed of much of their interest by being told only in English.

Not only are the Woods the only native Welsh Romani speakers to have been captured on tape but the sample obtained is sufficiently large to admit of comparison with those written specimens of the language noted by Tipler. What is particularly striking is that whilst their conversation was obviously contrived and, at times, somewhat laboured, the form of language used by the Woods, although clearly in decay, shows little evidence of any marked interference from English (some half-dozen loan-words and one plural form) and none at all from Welsh. Tipler's informants, on the other hand, whilst retaining elements of Romani grammar and syntax, spoke their Romani with a much heavier admixture of both English and Welsh loan-words and grammatical forms. One can only guess at the wealth of additional material that was there for the gleaning had Kennedy only taken the time and trouble to justify the confidence placed in him by his two informants.

As with many other tapes in the Folktracks series, the notes accompanying the cassette are both unhelpful and poorly printed and presented, with badly inked characters and lines running off the page. Although providing us with a transcription and translation of both Manfri's song and his conversation with his brother – a welcome departure from his usual practice – Kennedy's confidence in his collaborator is, unfortunately, wholly misplaced. Not only would Brune seem to have experienced some difficulty in determining which of the brothers was speaking, but his attempts at transcription and translation are, at times, regrettably wide of the mark (e.g. 1(A): 13–16; and 2(A): 1–4 below) and, at others, merely careless (e.g. 1(A): 25, 29–30; and 2(A): 9–10 below). The two extracts given below will be sufficient to illustrate the point. For ease of comparison, I have numbered each item in Brune's transcription, conflating them in my own revised reading where the speaker remains unchanged. This apart, the two extracts taken from Brune's transcription (1(A) and 2 (A)) are given below exactly as they appear on the printed sheet accompanying the cassette. For a revised reading of Manfri's song, see text 132.

1(A)

1. Kai shanas ke dives? (kerivash) Where were you today?
2. Pre o paani On the water
3. So tildan? What did you catch?
4. Tildom kushi matchi I caught some fine fish
5. Bare eks? Big ones?
6. Awa Yes
7. Bikendan len? Did you sell them?
8. Bikendom len soar Sure I sold them
9. Gian are o kutshiima? Did you go to the pub?
10. Doi shomas yekar kerivas I was there once today
11. Yan le'ena doi? You drank beer didn't you?
12. Awa, dosta Yes, enough
13. Matu ovyan You got drunk
14. Sapinesa I was 'soaped/snaked' in
15. Matu ovyan You got drunk
16. Ka o matu thefs Where the drunk soaks
17. Matu shan tu You are drunk
18. Piyava ma kek lo'ena I don't drink beer
19. Kerikom tut (ke dikom tut) I saw you
20. Kai, kai dikan man? Where, where did you see me?
21. Dre o Paano Kutshiima In the White Lion
22. Baro chochona Big liar
23. Madegodli (maa panshi) dinilo shan Be quiet(?) you are a fool
24. Dikom tu dre o Paano Kutshiima I saw you in th [*sic*]
25. Te na shi chochaben! Isn't it a lie!
26. Doi shanas ta rakeresas ku rakli You were there talking to the girl
27. Minor runkeni rakli shas? Isn't she a nice girl?
28. Minasa ti pirana dinna? (minna) She is your sweetheart, isn't [*sic*]
29. Raker ko mandi, junava me Tell me, I know
30. O, kamava me O, I like her
31. Ja kiyai papalee Go there again
32. Renkernii ranee shi She's a nice lady
33. Dina av akai Fool come here
34. Ja ko beng Go to the devil
35. Awa, Pira ter mui Right. Fuck your face
36. Marava akana sig You can drop dead presently
37. Awa junava Yes, I know
38. Junava tumen I know you

141

39. Kushku shan tu You are nice
40. Awa shtu fisawa tumen kenna

1(B)

1. Manfri: Kai shannas ke-divés? Where were you, today?
2. Hywel: 'Pré o pani. On the water.
3. Manfri: So tildan? What did you catch?
4. Hywel: Tildom kooshi matché. I caught a few fish.
5. Manfri: Bauré eks? Big ones?
6. Hywel: Aawa. Yes.
7. Manfri: Bikindan len? Did you sell them?
8. Hywel: Bikindom len sor. I sold them all.
9. Manfri: Ghian aré o kítchéma? Did you go to the pub?
10. Hywel: 'Doi shomas yeka ke-divés. I was there once today.
11. Manfri: 'Yan luvina 'doi? Did you have beer there?
12. Hywel: Aawa, sosta (dosta?). Yes, plenty.
13. Manfri: Matto gián? You got drunk?
14. Hywel: So penessa? What are you saying?
15. Manfri: Matto gián? You got drunk?
16–18. Hywel: Kaah! Matto? *feth*! Matto shan tu! Piava me kek Luvina. Kaah! Drunk. Faith! You're drunk! I don't drink beer.
19. Manfri: Te dikom tut'! But I saw you!
20. Hywel: Kai? Kai dikan man'? Where? Where did you see me?
21. Manfri: 'Ré o Porno Kitchima. In the White Lion (lit. the White Inn).
22. Hywel: Bauro khokhono! (That's) a great lie!
23–4. Manfri: Maa dé godli! Maw pen chi! Dinilo shan! Dikom tut' 'ré O Porno Kitchima. Be quiet! Don't say anything! You're a fool! I saw you in the White Lion (Inn).
25. Hywel: Penessa khokhoben. You're telling a lie.
26. Manfri: Adoi shannas ta rokkeressa ko (ke) rakli. You were there talking to a woman.
27. Hywel: Minaw rankeni rakli sas? Wasn't she a pretty girl?
28–9. Manfri: Minaw. Ti pirani, minaw? Ma pooker mandi. Junava me. Wasn't she. Your sweetheart, isn't she? Don't tell me, I know.
30. Hywel: Ah! Kamela me. Ah! She loves me.
31. Manfri: Ja, ja ki yoi popoli. Go, go back to her.
32. Hywel: Rankeni raani si. She's a fine-looking woman.
33. Manfri: . . . ? . . . ? av akai . . .? Come here.
34. Hywel: Ja k'o beng! Go to the devil.
35. Manfri: Aawa! pira to mui. Right! Fuck your face.
36. Hywel: Marava tu kana sig! I'll kill you in a minute!
37–8. Manfri: Aawa, junava. Júnáva tumen. Yes, I know. I know you.
39. Hywel: Kooshko shan tu. Good (clever?) you are.
40. Manfri: Aáwa, *stuffis*ava túmen kénnaw. Right, stuff you then.[11]

2(A)

1. Push-ta i lodaben Ask about the lodgings
2. Ab u gorjo mang las Go and ask the gentleman
3. O dorde – putsh puri gaane O heck – ask for the old hen
4. Shi tu puri gaane? Have you an old hen?
5. Shi amen dosta pus? Have we got enough straw?
6. Nai les kek There isn't any
7. Nai les kek? There isn't any?
8. Nai les kek There isn't any
9. Na, so kerava? Well, what shall we do?
10. Ja ta suta are o puv kela tu kek? Go & sleep in the field & make do, can't you?

2(B)

1. Hywel: Putchdan o lodoben? Did you ask about the bedding (lodgings)?
2. Manfri: Avel' Gaujo, mang les. A Gaujo's coming, ask him.
3. Hywel: Dordi, putch puré goné? Dordi, ask (for) some old sacks?
4. Manfri: Si tu puré goné? Have you (any) old sacks?
5. Hywel: Si men dosta pus? Have we got enough straw?
6. Manfri: Nai les kek. There isn't any.
7. Hywel: Nai les kek? There isn't any?
8. Manfri: Nai les kek. There isn't any.
9. Hywel: So kerava? What shall I do?
10. Manfri: Ja te sutta 're o puv. Kela tuke. Go and sleep on the ground. That will do (be good enough for) you.

Despite these reservations, the Folktracks series, which is still available from Mr Kennedy by direct sale, remains an invaluable resource for students of Traveller song, and readers wishing to breathe life into the texts included in this book should not hesitate to make use of them.

~

My own academic research among the Travellers has disclosed a vivacious singing tradition richly interwoven with strands of musical diversity – including songs of Country and Western, Music Hall, Popular and contemporary Pop origin together with Romanes songs.
(Denise Stanley, 1985)

Just as the 1870s saw the publication of three major works on the English Gypsy language, so the 1970s may be said to have been the decade of the song. Thus, the publication in 1975 of Kennedy's *Folk Songs of Britain and*

Ireland and Yates's *English Gypsy Songs*, was to be followed, in 1977, by MacColl and Seeger's *Travellers' Songs from England and Scotland*.

MacColl and Seeger first gave public notice of their interest in the Traveller community when, in the early 1960s, they included the Gypsies in their highly innovative series of sound portraits, the *Radio Ballads* (now available on CD on the Topic label). Speaking of the series as a whole in a broadcast interview with Jim Lloyd (BBC Radio 2, 8.30 p.m., Wednesday, 6 July 1994), Seeger described how the programmes were put together using material provided by the subjects themselves:

> Radio Ballads, unless you've heard them, are hard to explain. You go out and you collect from somebody who knows about something. You come back and you listen to the actuality – what they've spoken. That can be anything up to three hundred hours of just talking to people, say, about fishing or about the railways or about being a teenager. The subject seeps into you. Ewan writes a script. We talk about it, talk about it, talk about it, all the time. He writes the songs and we talk about it, talk about it, all the time – choose the actuality that's going to fit in between the songs and the music. I do the instrumentation. Charles Parker – who has also collected and talked to the people – Charles Parker isolates out the pieces of actuality that are going to be used and it's like a tapestry – you weave the music into the songs, into the sound effects, into the actuality, and you get a picture of what a way of life has done to people – to certain people . . . The technicians came up with ideas; the musicians came up with ideas. The script that you went with was like the bare bones and everybody who worked on it contributed something. You always brought a railwayman or a fisher person into the studio to comment on how things were being done . . .

As Seeger says, rather than using existing material from the oral tradition, she and MacColl preferred to write their own songs, drawing on their informants' own observations and rhythms of speech. Although this is somewhat disappointing for the student of traditional song, the result was a number of memorable pieces, some of which have become contemporary folk standards in their own right, of which perhaps the best known are 'The Get Along Song' and 'The Travelling People'.

For present purposes, an altogether more satisfying outcome of this early encounter with the Gypsies was the publication, in 1977, of their *Travellers' Songs from England and Scotland*. Although heavily weighted in favour of mainstream song sung in English, what is surprising is the range of material recovered. Of the 158 items included in the anthology, eighty-seven were obtained from English and seventy-one from Scottish Travellers. Of the former, thirteen are Child ballads, sixty-eight are from the standard English song-repertoire and only five are songs sung exclusively by English

Gypsies. Of the seventy-one items obtained from Scottish Travellers, fifteen are Child ballads, fifty-four are from the standard Scottish repertoire and only two are in Cant. What is also quite remarkable is that the entire collection was obtained from only seven English (four men and three women) and eleven Scottish Travellers (seven women and four men).

A decade later, MacColl and Seeger followed up this earlier work with *Till Doomsday in the Afternoon* (MacColl and Seeger 1986), a portrait of a Scottish Traveller family, the Stewarts of Blairgowrie. Originally intended to be no more than an anthology of traditional songs and ballads, what eventually emerged was a comprehensive account of a traditional culture operating within a single extended family group. Yet, far from losing sight of their original objective, the authors, by placing their core material in its wider social context, have not only greatly enhanced our knowledge and understanding of the singing tradition of Scottish Travellers generally, but have provided a useful model for other similar studies which may yet be undertaken.

As is often the case with both English and Scottish Travellers of the traditional type, there seems to have been general agreement among the Stewarts as to who were the *singers* in the group, the leading role being taken by the oldest of the three women, Mrs Belle Stewart. Thus, of the eighty-six songs included in the collection, forty-eight were given by Mrs Stewart herself, and twenty-eight and ten respectively by her two daughters, Sheila MacGregor and Cathy Higgins. The way in which the available material had been divided up among the three women seems, however, to have had more to do with individual personality and preference than with their ability to project particular types of song. Yet whatever the underlying rationale, this division, once made, appears to have been strictly observed. Thus, Mrs Stewart, although she almost certainly knew the words, chose not to sing 'The Dawning of the Day' as this was one of Mrs Higgins's songs, whilst neither she nor Mrs Higgins would sing 'Tifty's Annie' as this belonged to Mrs MacGregor. To Mrs Stewart, on the other hand, undoubtedly a gifted exponent of the big ballad, was assigned 'The Twa Brithers', and so on, through the entire repertoire.

Although only a tiny proportion of this material is in Cant, the fact that MacColl and Seeger recorded almost the entire repertoire on at least two separate occasions, between 1961 and 1963, and between 1969 and 1972, provides a useful insight into the way in which their informants treated their material. As the authors say in their introductory note: 'A comparison of the two sets of recordings shows that, as far as the songs are concerned, scarcely any melodic changes had occurred and the few textual changes are limited to the occasional word.' Furthermore, as they go on to say, subsequent recordings made during the period 1972 to 1979 were to yield much the same result. Belle Stewart's 1975 telling of 'The Overgate', for example (MacColl and Seeger 1986, 260), differs in only one word from her 1962 recording, this in marked contrast with those few English Gypsy texts which have also been recovered from the same informant at different points in time.

A further feature of the Stewart repertoire, and one which also distinguishes it from that of most English Gypsies, is the almost entire absence of those onomatopoeic substitutions and other apparent textual defects characteristic of many Gypsy sets. Indeed, where these do occur, as in the second verse of 'The Overgate', they are repeated with the same attention to detail apparent in other unimpaired portions of the text, a fact which would seem to suggest that they are regarded as integral to the song as a whole and, as such, no less deserving of accurate retention.

No less striking than this strict attention to detail is the family's wholly conservative approach to the repertoire itself. Thus Mrs Stewart, although apparently capable of acquiring the air to a new song at only one hearing, and the words after only two or three more, added virtually nothing to her stock of songs during the entire recording programme, a period of almost twenty years, whilst the repertoire of the two younger women seems to have become more or less permanently fixed some time during their early twenties.

The 1970s also proved significant in another way with the publication in 1971 of the *Romano Drom Song Book*, a first attempt at establishing, through the medium of international Romani song, 'a brief cultural meeting point between Gypsy children and their teachers and between them and the wider Romani community of the world as a whole' (revised edition: Stanley and Burke 1986). Although it was 'intended to be used by the Gypsies themselves', the editors also expressed the hope that the book would 'be of interest both to ordinary Travellers and to teachers in school' and, with this in mind, the songs themselves, which are representative of the singing of both British and continental Gypsies, are intended not only to be sung but to serve both as a basis for discussion and as a stimulus to further creative work. It is not, therefore, a folk-song collection in the strict sense but a Gypsy song-book, carefully edited in order to further the editors' underlying aims. Thus we find included, on the one hand, a number of items illustrative of Gypsy life and experience and, on the other, *Le Vêtement Blanc*, the anthem of the World Romani Congress, and the following, 'specifically written' in order to help Gypsy children learn the names of the numerals in what the authors call 'international Romanes':

> Yek, dui, trin, stor,
> Kakka pen hokkapens, or chor!

146

Panch, shov, efta, okto,
Tatchipen dels a mush kushti bok.
Enya, desh . . . I'm pukkering you
Kushti chavvies jin their lils – I do!
                    (Stanley and Burke 1986, 12)

One, two, three, four,
Don't tell lies or steal!
Five, six, seven, eight,
Truth brings a man good luck.
Nine, ten . . . I'm telling you
Good children know their books – I do!

Although a number of the English Gypsy songs included in the collection have clearly been slightly altered, presumably in order to facilitate their use by (*Gaujo?*) teachers, they remain wholly true to the spirit of their Romani English originals, and may usefully be compared with other printed variants obtained from the same or other informants (for example, texts 70, 93 and 171).

One further work requires brief mention here. Jeremy Sandford's *Songs by the Roadside* (Sandford 1995) consists of some three dozen songs, both traditional and of known authorship, some of which were first collected in the early years of the present century. One, a Gypsy lament from the Nazi death-camps, is in inflected (European) Romani (see Stanley and Burke 1986, 31), and two are from the pen of the *Gaujo* song-writer, Ewan MacColl. Of the remainder, two from the singing of Irish Travellers, Mary Delaney's 'Fourteen Last Sunday' and 'Pops' Johnny Connors's 'Poor Old Man', and are to be found on Mackenzie and Carroll's 'Early in the Month of Spring' (VWML.001, 1986). The work also contains three pieces in Romani English, two of which are reproduced in the present volume as texts 86 and 96. The third, with a few minor differences in spelling, would also seem to have been taken from Stanley and Burke's *Romano Drom Song Book*, although this is not made clear in the accompanying prose commentary. Burke and Stanley's set is reproduced below as text 22.

5

Gypsy Song – Its Nature and Function

1. The Short Song

The songs are as a rule exceedingly brief, generally a couple of verses
. . . They are condensed to the point of obscurity and the crudely
expressed notions follow one another like the visions of a dream
without any apparent logical sequence.

(Bob Skot, 1909)

As suggested elsewhere, whilst Romani English, save in its limited vocabulary, now has little in common with those deeper dialects still in use in eastern and central Europe,[12] English Gypsy song has remained fundamentally loyal to its roots and, despite centuries of separate development, is still recognizably Romani. It is, therefore, somewhat ironical that this very 'otherness', evidence of a mode of thought entirely alien to our western tradition, should have been instrumental in determining the largely negative attitude of the *Romané Raiá* towards this aspect of their subject. Yet rather than treating such material as a potentially useful resource, to be judged on its own merits, the *Raiá* seem merely to have compared it with those other forms of folk song with which they were more familiar and, finding it wanting in most respects, dismissed it out of hand.

It is quite true, of course, that were we to take mainstream British folk song as constituting some sort of ideal, then Romani English song would be unlikely to fare well by comparison. The same, however, might also be said of the singing tradition of native Australians or of the Eskimos of Alaska, but no one would think of applying the same critical yardstick in their case. One has only to listen for a moment to know that they are of an entirely different order of creation. Romani English song, on the other hand, is a little more difficult to pin down; for, whilst it is unquestionably different, few of its more exotic features are entirely without parallel elsewhere, giving it the appearance of a poorly executed copy of a familiar

148

original. What gives it its own unique flavour is the way in which these characteristics have been combined and retained, and the mode of thought underlying their use.

One of the more striking features of the English Romani tradition is the widespread use, both in isolation and in combination, of short self-contained snatches of song, usually amounting to no more than four lines and sometimes confined to only one or two. Used independently, such pieces may be improvised and the melody advanced by mouth music, or 'tuning' as the Gypsies call it. Used in combination, they may either form the starting-point of an extended text (e.g. texts 1, 2 and 11) or be woven into the fabric of a longer song at the discretion of the individual singer (e.g. texts 23–6 and 75–6). Texts of both types, where they are not simply extemporized *vers d'occasion*, are often relatively stable in character – compare, for example, texts 15–22, 23–6 and 75–6 – although these are comparatively rare.

Although indistinguishable from one another as regards their outward form, short songs, taken in isolation, have, or seem to have had, a variety of uses.

A. as an accompaniment to the dance or children's play
(for example, texts 23–6, 38 and 140). Short unconnected verses of this type are essentially childlike in character and it is easy to understand their appeal for a relatively unsophisticated and largely conservative folk audience. Indeed, as suggested elsewhere, in form and character they differ little from the rhymes used by children in their play the world over.

Romani English songs of this type are similar in form and function to the *khelimaski djili*, dance song, or *xuttjadi djili*, jump song, of the Vlasika Roma of Hungary and Slovakia. Vlax Gypsies do not, as a rule, play any instruments (Kovalcsik 1985, 36); rather, they sing their dance tunes, embellishing them with sounds imitative of various instruments (Vig 1974; Martin 1977, i, 427). Thus, the older type of dance song consists for the most part of 'rolling' or humming, only occasionally interrupted by one or two lines or the odd stanza, for example,

> Gelas i Otilka
> Hodj te hulavelpe,
> Ci misto huladas pe . . .
> Me sim i Hella, le phure Tutaski séj,
> La Ribizlaki séj andaj Sombata.

> Otilka went
> To comb her hair,
> She did not even comb her hair well . . .

(humming) I am Hella, the old Tuta's daughter,
Ribizla's daughter from Szombat.

(Kovalcsik 1985, 139)

More recently, there is a marked tendency among Slovakian Vlax to replace these traditional Gypsy dance tunes with the now very popular Hungarian *Csardas* which are not infrequently performed without words, e.g. Kovalcsik 1985, no.46 (see also Martin and Pesovár 1958; Martin 1965).

Vekerdi, too, writing of the Hungarian Lovars, has also noted that words rarely form part of the accompaniment to the dance:

> They are able to extemporize from topical motives (stereotyped lines or half-lines . . .) short semi-coherent songs . . . which we may call, adopting the name proposed by Hajdú, *khelimaski d'ili*, 'dance songs' (cf. *Le Folklore Tsigane: Etudes Tsiganes* 8, 1–2 (1962), 1–33, the most competent study on this theme). NB: They accompany their dance mostly not by these *khelimaski d'ili* but by singing without any text. (Vekerdi 1967)

As regards printed/recorded texts, it is noticeable that the majority of British Gypsy dance songs pure and simple have been given in English rather than *Romanés*, and one is struck by a similar willingness on the part of the Vlax Gypsies to improvise such pieces in Slovakian:

> Robota, Robota,
> Nem születtem dologra, dologra.
> Lábam termett a táncra,
> Szemem a kacsintásra,
> Két kezem a lopásra.

> Robota, Robota,
> I am not born for work, for work
> My feet are made for dancing,
> My eyes are for ogling,
> My two hands are for filching.

(Kovalcsik 1985, 143).

B. as simple vers d'occasions *or snapshots of life*
(for example, texts 43, 49, and 57). The Gypsy, according to Sampson, delights in the dramatic delivery of his words. 'It is', he says, 'not an unusual thing for him to suddenly break into a kind of metrical recitative, especially if he thinks he has an appreciative audience' (1891, 90). Leland, too, comments on a number of occasions on the Gypsies' readiness to

150

break into verse entirely unannounced. Writing of text 101, for example, he says that 'it came forth one day from a Gypsy, in my presence, as an entirely voluntary utterance. He meant it for something like poetry – it certainly was suggested by nothing' (1873, 143). See also Reeve (1958, 3.3) and MacColl and Seeger (1977, 17–18).

Fred Wood, too, the author of *In the Life of a Romani Gypsy* (1973), tells how, in his family, the men would often improvise short scraps of song while waiting for the women to brew up after a poaching expedition. The women, too, would make up hawking songs, or songs telling of their frequent brushes with the law. Songs of this type, concerned as they are with some passing event of the day or hour, are, therefore, essentially ephemeral in character, although they may occasionally strike a particular chord with the listener and hence find their way into the common repertoire, albeit with no special attention to accuracy.

The similarity between British verses of this type and their European Romani equivalents is also readily apparent. The first of the following is from Brucey Boswell (*JGLS* o.s. 2 (1891), 90); the second from an unnamed informant recorded in eastern Rumelia (Colocci 1889, 280–1):

> Yek gurishi sas mandi,
> I del'd it to a rakli
> To dik if latti's bitto wudrus
> Would loder dui mendi.

> I had fourpence,
> I gave it to a woman
> To see if her little bed
> Would lodge the two of us.

> Kamalav tut m'angaliate
> Kasoav ani dakar.
> Kamalav te peravav tut
> Veschinde tu o sudre panende.

> I will take you in my arms,
> And I will make love like a king.
> I will take you for a walk
> Through the forest by the stream.

C. as spells or charms
(texts 6, 9 and 116). Although the idea that children's rhymes and other similar, apparently trivial, material may contain the forgotten remnants of older, deeper beliefs has not gone unchallenged, it should not be dismissed

out of hand. According to Wlislocki, there is an old Gypsy tradition which
holds that the first men were made of leaves – a belief which, he suggests,
may well have survived in the following children's song from Transylvania,
an area in which the verse-charm, or spell proper, has also survived intact
into modern times:

> Amaro dad jal andro bes
> Cingerel odoy caves
> Del dayakri andre pada
> Yek cavoro ada avla

> Our father goes into a wood
> There he cuts a boy
> Puts it in mother's bed
> So a boy comes.

If Wlislocki is right then there would seem to be no reason why similar
material should not have survived in a corrupt form in the British Gypsy
repertoire. The evidence for such survivals is, however, slight, although it is
quite true that British Gypsies still retain elements of traditional lore
linking them with their more conservative continental cousins, as in the
case of the various practices surrounding the disposal of the dead (see
notes following text 50). Yet, tempting as it is to read a deeper meaning
into such texts, it is as well to strike a note of caution. Wlislocki's set
might, for example, just as easily represent a Gypsy mother's attempt to
deflect her child from an awkward line of questioning, much as *Gaujo*
parents have been known to tell their offspring that they were found under
a gooseberry bush.

D. as a means of conveying a warning
(see texts 34–7 and accompanying notes).

~

Although they are undoubtedly an extremely important constituent of
both British and continental Romani song, Brune is quite wrong in
suggesting that 'such stanzas have absolutely no parallel in other British
song traditions' (Brune 1975, 747). Short self-contained lyrics are by no
means unknown in both the Gaelic and Hiberno-English traditions, and in
Wales, as represented by the trochaic tetrameter quatrain and the
somewhat more complex *triban*, form an extremely important part of the
national folk repertoire.

In the Highlands and Islands of Scotland, they were used, for the most part, to accompany the dance, although the use of words rather than meaningless vocables for this purpose may represent a later development – in other types of Gaelic song with a recurring refrain (e.g. the waulking song), nonsense syllables almost certainly preceded words. The following example, used to accompany a strathspey, is typical of the form:

> Dhiult am bodach fodar dhomh
> 'S gun dhiult am bodach feur dhomh,
> Gun dhiult am bodach fodar dhomh
> A' chuirinn fo mo shliasaid. (repeat verse)

> Dhiult am bodach fodar dhomh
> 'S gun dhiult am bodach feur dhomh, (repeat couplet)
> Dhiult am bodach fodar dhomh
> 'S gun dhiult am bodach feur dhomh;
> Gun dhiult am bodach luideach odhar
> As an t-sabhal feur dhomh.

> The old man has refused me straw
> The old man has refused me grass;
> The old man has refused me straw
> To put under my thigh (to make a bed). (repeat verse)

> The old man has refused me straw
> The old man has refused me grass, (repeat couplet)
> The old man has refused me straw
> The old man has refused me grass;
> The old dun-coloured ragged man
> In the barn has refused me grass.

Although constrained by the rhythm of the dance, its affinity with certain types of Romani song texts is clear. Indeed, the language apart, one cannot help remarking that, as regards both form and content, songs of this type would be wholly accessible to most contemporary British and continental Travellers. Its repeated use of the same basic motif, with certain minor alterations, is, in particular, reminiscent of those more primitive Gypsy sets exemplified by text 119 and the following, included, together with a German translation, by Alfred Graffunder in his *Ueber die Sprache der Zigeuner* of 1835. Like so many nineteenth-century British and American collectors, Graffunder, too, seems to have been particularly struck by the musicality of the Gypsy language, noting that 'die sprache ist wohlklingend, und dem gesange sehr günstig' (the speech is fair sounding and the singing most congenial).

Gader wela! Gader stela!
ab, Miro tschabo ste!
i tarni romni dschalu, Manggel;
i puri romni balo póp priesterwela,

i tarni romni har i rosa,
i puri romni har i dschamba;
i tarni romni weli tarno rom,
i puri romni wel i puro rom.

Woher kommt er, woher springt er,
Where does he come from, where does he spring to
Auf mein Sohn und spring!
Up you get, my son, and jump
Die junge Frau geht betteln (geht bettelt),
The young woman goes and begs,
Die alte Frau hinterm ofen riestert(?).
The old woman runs behind the stove.

Die junge Frau gleich einer Rose,
The young woman is like a rose
Die alte Frau gleich einer Kröte,
The old woman is like a toad
Die junge Frau krigt einen jungen Mann,
The young woman shall have a young man
Die alte Frau krigt einen alten Mann.
The old woman shall have an old man.

In Ireland, too, short (four-line) songs in both Irish and Hiberno-English are, in the main, associated with dance tunes. The following, again typical of its kind, was sung to the well-known reel, 'Miss Macleod's'. It was used by itinerant dancing masters to assist those of their pupils who had difficulty in telling their right from their left. A withy would be tied to one foot and a straw to the other and, thereafter, each foot would be referred to in terms of its particular adornment:

Sin amach cos an ghaid agus crap cos an tsugain,
Bain cnag as t-altaibh agus starrabh as do ghlúnaibh,
Sios go dti an dorus agus suas go dti an cuinne,
Is go mbris' an riabhach do chosa mara deacair tu do mhuineadh.

Stretch out the withy foot and withdraw the straw-rope foot,
Take a crack out of your joints and a stretch out of your knees,
Down to the door and up to the corner,
And may the grizzled one break your legs if you are not difficult to teach.

Parallel forms are also to be found in Hiberno-English. The following example is sung to the tune of the polka known variously as 'Maggie in the Wood' and 'Ar Bhfaca tú mo Shéamaisín' (Have you Seen my Jimmie?):

> If I had Maggie in the wood,
> I'd do her all the good I could.
> If I had Maggie in the wood,
> I'd keep her there till morning.

In the following, used by the urchins of Dublin to taunt the police, we also have an example of a two-line text. The words would be repeated until either the law gave chase or the game was abandoned for lack of action. It is reminiscent of the old Romani-influenced London chant '*Dicky*, boys, here comes a copper':

> Harvey Duff, don't take me,
> Take the fellow behind the tree.

Such examples are by no means rare and, indeed, along with the more common quatrains, are currently being collected by Raymond O'Sullivan of Newmarket, Co. Cork. Neither type, however, is ever used, as are Romani short songs, to build up extended texts.

It is in Wales, however, that the four-line song, both improvised and fixed, has attained a kind of perfection in the trochaic tetrameter quatrain and the *triban* or *mesur gwŷr Deheubarth*, measure of the men of the south. The former, as Kinney has pointed out, is particularly well represented – so much so that, in volumes 1–5 of the *Welsh Folk Song Journal*, it forms, in various guises, the largest single class of song apart from ballad/carol tunes. The quatrains themselves consist of four octosyllabic lines, sometimes with anacruses and always ending on a weak or feminine beat. As with those Gypsy dance songs mentioned earlier, the verse lines may also be interspersed with vocal or instrumental refrains known as 'symphonies', even though the songs themselves would not seem to have been used as an accompaniment for dancing. Thus:

> O mae 'nghariad wedi 'ngad'l,
> ho ho ho ho ho ho ho!
> Ni chaf eto fyth ei chystal,
> ho ho ho ho ho ho ho!
> Cwyd dy galon, peid a hito,
> ffol lol lal di di o!
> Ti gei gariad newydd eto.
>
> (Williams 1972, 13)

My love has left me,
I shall not find her like again.
Lift your heart, do not worry,
You'll find a new love again.

Although clearly far more regular in structure, such verses also exhibit certain features in common with their Romani equivalents in the way in which they were used. According to Thomas Pennant, writing in his *Journey to Snowdon* (1781), they were, for example, often sung extempore and might be strung together regardless of content. Again, as with Gypsy songs of a similar type, many of them were concerned with local person-alities or events of no consequence beyond their own sphere and would, therefore, have held little or no significance other than for the audience for whom they were originally intended (the same point is also made by Kovalcsik in connection with the Vlax Gypsy repertoire).

The origins of the trochaic tetrameter quatrain are, it must be said, somewhat obscure, but it is interesting to note Ifor Williams's suggestion that they may be traced back to the *clêr*, the wandering bards of medieval Wales (Williams 1913–14, 191–3). Kinney, too, has pointed to their use in the *Carmina Burana* of the itinerant *clerici vagantes* of the late thirteenth century; for example,

Lingua mendax et dolosa
Lingua procax venenosa
Lingua digna detruncari
Et in igne concremari.

The use of repetition as a means of linking lines – common to both the above and to such contemporary Welsh sets as those beginning 'ar lan y môr' or 'oer yw'r rhew, oer yw'r eira' – is, as suggested earlier, also typical of certain types of Gypsy song (e.g. texts 15–22, 28, 54 and 137). Vekerdi, too, speaking of the altogether more primitive (or purer) tradition of the Hungarian Lovari, tells us that, in many cases, the only connecting link between the various elements of the one song may be 'a certain similarity of the sentiments or the repetition of a particular word . . .' (Vekerdi 1967).

Clearly, we are here in the realms of speculation, but it is, perhaps, worth considering the possibility of a continuous thread linking the highly polished quatrains of the Welsh folk repertoire with the altogether less sophisticated productions of the English Romani Chals and their Hungarian counterparts. This is not to say, of course, that the Gypsies have been in any way influential in the formation of contemporary Welsh folk song, merely that the various types mentioned may represent different phases in the development of the same verse-form; a form which has lingered longer in those societies which, for different reasons, may have proved more amenable to the retention of an older, once common, Indo-European tradition.

2. Extended Texts

> It is characteristic of Gypsy folk singers that they often sing fragmented and incoherent words to beautiful tunes. Just why this should be is not altogether clear. Even today, many Gypsies are illiterate but then, so too were many of the singers who provided excellent song texts to collectors such as Cecil Sharp and Ralph Vaughan Williams.
>
> (Mike Yates 1975c)

We turn now to the Gypsies' treatment of the long song or, more accurately perhaps, the extended text, for there is little in the Romani repertoire to compare with either the ballad or lyric in mainstream British folk song. Once again, Vekerdi's essay on Lovari song provides a useful reference point. In it he says that the Gypsies of Hungary

> do not possess epic songs in their own language, let alone poems without melody . . . even the short poems (songs) evince much fewer epic features than the songs of the same length in the folklore of the peoples surrounding them . . . in the Gypsy song, simple snapshots of life or sentiments are arranged statically without any chronological sequence or (epic) action . . . beyond this, the most striking peculiarity of Gypsy songs is the astonishing lack of logical coherence between the single lines . . . the whole disintegrates into monostichic (occasionally distichic) units almost quite independent, the one from the other . . . besides, if requested, they are able to extemporize from topical motifs (stereotyped lines or half lines . . .) short semi-coherent songs on the Hungarian pattern (for the most part non-strophic, too) . . .
> (Vekerdi 1967)

That this is not simply a recent development – the inevitable consequence of accelerated linguistic and cultural decay – is readily apparent when Vekerdi's material is compared with texts obtained during the second half of the nineteenth century. Thus, the following set, noted by Anton Herrmann near the small market town of Nagy-Maros in April 1890, would seem to consist of four, possibly five, unrelated elements, lacking any obvious thematic or verbal link. Oddly enough, Herrmann's source, Elizabeth Horváth, bore the same family name as Vekerdi's principal informants.

Yag* de* cavo sinom,
Krajcariha* na birinav*
Mangav kecen*, taj na den man,
Ace dzanen, hod'* nane man.

Cilla phandom, hod'* kamav tut,
Taj na pat'as hod'* kamav tut.

Okoj tele mar* basaven,
Akaren man, cak* the Khelav.
Na dzanav me the khelav,
Cak* Romane the khelav.

Ravu, Ravu, Ravu, rakli!
Tu mre sukari pirani!

Phagerel tut i siladi,
Soske pires tu melali?
Mange has dsavo
Ande mre at'he.

*Magyar loan-words.

Alas, what a poor fellow am I!
Not a Kreutzer do I possess;
I pray you to lend, and not to give to me,
Well you know that I have nought.

Long have I said that I love thee,
And thou dost not believe that I love thee.

Yonder below not you are playing [on the fiddle],
Playing [lit. sighing or groaning] to me, only that I may dance.
I do not know how to dance,
Only Gypsy [capers?] to cut.

Ravu, Ravu, Ravu, lass!
Thou my beautiful sweetheart!

Shake off from thee the fever.
Wherefore goest thou unclean?
To me art thou a disgrace
In my eyes.

Although it is still possible to identify a number of free-floating stereotypical motifs of the type described by Vekerdi (e.g. texts 1–5, 11, 24,

75–6 and 109), such obvious examples of 'mix and match' as that afforded by Herrmann's text are now comparatively rare in the *Poggadi Chib* (see, for example, texts 16, 74, 81 and 83). Yet, despite their evident scarcity, and the clear signs of external influence to be found throughout the repertoire, Vekerdi's observations, taken as a whole, are still sufficiently apt to leave us in no doubt that the singing tradition of the Gypsies of Britain is still fundamentally Romani rather than a mere perversion of mainstream British folk song.

Broadly speaking, extended texts are of two types: those which make use of existing material from within the tradition (e.g. texts 74, 81, 83 and 105) and those which are, so to speak, created *de novo* from the singer's own stock of basic ideas (e.g. texts 95, 114, 118 and 130). Where existing material is used, it may either serve as the starting-point for a longer (often) improvised text, or it may be introduced at a later stage in the song's development, sometimes with little regard for logical continuity. Thus, in Gillington's first variant of the 'grai puvving' theme, the singer begins with a recognized opening gambit which he then follows up with a series of references to a range of motifs also found elsewhere in the repertoire, both in isolation and in combination with other material (see text 74 and the accompanying table). The anonymous originator of text 63, on the other hand, opens with a highly personal statement which she then goes on to reinforce with a stereotypical phrase drawn from the common stock.

For the *Gaujo*, accustomed to a strict narrative line, the clear expression of ideas and emotions and a battery of poetic effects designed to catch and hold the attention, the extended text may often appear unnaturally sparse and wanting in clarity at both the verbal and structural level. At the verbal level, individual words or phrases may appear meaningless or corrupt whilst, at the structural level, entire texts may seem hopelessly disjointed or even incomplete. We shall deal first with the Gypsies' use of language and, thereafter, with the way in which the texts themselves are organized.

Not only is Gypsy song entirely lacking in those lyrical flights – at best inspired, at worst overblown and conventionalized – which are so marked a feature of the British and Irish pastoral tradition, but even the use of simple descriptives is comparatively rare. This is particularly apparent when Gypsy texts are viewed alongside their mainstream equivalents. Compare, for example, text 126 with the well-known Hiberno-English love song, 'The Banks of the Bann'. Both songs deal with a first encounter between a man and a woman and with the former's response.

In the Gypsy song, which consists of only ten irregular unrhymed lines, all we are told of their first meeting and of the lady herself is that

> There's a rauney jessin on the tober,
> There's Rye jessin after her

> There's a lady going on the road,
> There's (a) gentleman going after her.

In the Irish song, on the other hand, which consists of five four-line stanzas with an albeit somewhat irregular A-B-A-B rhyme scheme and occasional internal rhyme, two complete verses are given over to the circumstances surrounding the meeting and to the impression made on the would-be suitor:

> When first to this country a stranger I came,
> I placed my affections on a handsome young dame,
> She being fair and tender, her waist small and slender,
> False nature had formed her for my overthrow.

> On the banks of the Bann, 'twas there I first met her,
> She appeared like an angel or even a queen;
> Her eyes like the diamonds or the stars brightly shining,
> I thought her the fairest in the world that I'd seen.

In order to add colour to the encounter, the author of the latter makes use of seven adjectives and one adverb – handsome, young, fair (in both the positive and superlative degree), small, slender, false and brightly – and four similes – the lady is said to resemble an angel or a queen and her eyes to shine like diamonds or stars. The Gypsy singer, on the other hand (other than in his final affirmation), uses not a single adjective or simile in the course of the entire song.

Again, in the Gypsy set, the suitor simply says that

> He would del all the louver
> In his putsey if the rauney
> Would beshtolay with him

> He would give all the money
> In his pocket if the lady
> Would sit down with him

telling her,

> You will have plenty of vonggar
> If you jess with mandy

160

> You will have plenty of money
> If you go with me.

In the Irish set, the young gallant is a good deal more forthcoming:

> If I had all the riches that there are in the Indies,
> I'd put rings on her fingers and gold in her ears;
> And there, on the banks of the lovely Bann river,
> In all kinds of splendour I'd live with my dear.

That this want of verbal colour is simply due to the depleted nature of the *Poggadi Chib* itself seems somewhat unlikely. A similar want of descriptive detail is also to be found in the singing tradition of the Lovari (Vekerdi 1967) and Vlasika Roma (Kovalcsik 1985), despite the fact that, for both groups, Romani remains the language of bed and board. Again, even where the original language is retained, songs borrowed by the Gypsies from the mainstream are, more often than not, stripped of all unnecessary ornamentation, leaving them virtually indistinguishable from native Romani texts.[13] So, too, texts composed by the Gypsies in English differ little in this respect from texts told in Romani English, all of which would seem to suggest that, whatever its deficiencies, the *Poggadi Chib* itself has not had a significant part to play in determining the peculiar character of those texts of which it is the sole medium of expression.

Disconcerting as this want of detail may be, it is unlikely to prove a bar to understanding. The same cannot always be said, however, of those curious verbal lapses characteristic of what we might call 'Romani as she is singed'. Lapses of this type may be said to fall into three broad categories: the use of apparently corrupt or meaningless words or phrases; the incorrect use of what the Gypsies themselves call 'little words'; and the use of otherwise wholly intelligible phrases in which the various elements would seem to have been unaccountably transposed.

Typical of the first category are 'chadders in their bottlers, they got to lel out' (text 72, 1.8) and 'I jin duva'll pogger me to zi' (text 33, 1.4). Lapses of this type are not confined to the *Poggadi Chib*, but are also by no means uncommon in sets originated in English by the Gypsies themselves or borrowed by them from the mainstream. Thus, in Levi Smith's telling of 'The Life of Georgie' (Topic 12T253) we have:

> 'Come saddle to me' said my lily white breast
> 'Come saddle to me' said my pony.
> With bright guns in his hand and his sword by his side,
> And I spare me the life of my Georgie.

The two Romani English examples given above may be explained by reference to alternative forms of the same words found elsewhere in the literature (*chavvies, potter, dzi*), whilst the meaning of the third, clear after a moment's thought, may be confirmed from other printed versions of the same song.

Apart from such obvious 'mistakes', it is sometimes the case that Travellers will assign meanings to words for which there is no lexicographical precedent – 'With regard to what they call "little words", the Gypsies are as resolute as Humpty-Dumpty in their determination to make words mean just what they choose them to mean' (Sampson 1891, 87). Thus, in line 4 of text 118, *keker* (never) is given for 'cannot' (*nastis*), and in l.5 *pencha* (like) for 'about' (*trustal*). So, too, in verse three of text 163, the informant uses the affirmative, *aawali*, to form the future tense and, in verse five, *yov's* (his) for 'your' (*tutti's*).

Yet, even where words are used 'correctly', further confusion may sometimes arise as a result of their unusual placement within a particular phrase or sentence – a practice which cannot be explained away by reference to the *ordo verborum* of the old inflected speech. In text 43, for example, the second line – *kek Mandi tacho dik'd him ker les* (never I true saw him do it) – might have been better expressed *tacho, Mandi kek dik'd him ker les* (true, I never saw him do it). Similarly, in text 76, the word 'again' ought perhaps to have been placed at the end of the second rather than in the middle of the third line.

Although this somewhat idiosyncratic use of language may sometimes be exacerbated by the informant's ignorance of the meaning of certain words and phrases which have been handed down intact by an older generation (e.g. texts 18, 44 and 133), this is hardly a significant factor when viewed in terms of the repertoire as a whole. Even though an informant may be uncertain as to their true meaning, texts may still be given in a form wholly consistent with the normal requirements of the language. Thus, in text 18 (Solomon Smith's 1960 telling of 'Can You Rokker Romani'), the words used, although imperfectly understood, accord very well with those employed in the earliest recorded version of the song in Borrow's *Romano Lavo-Lil* of 1874 (text 15).

The practice of singing songs whose meaning has been wholly or partially lost is, or was, apparently not confined to the Gypsies of England but has also been noted in Scandinavia where the form of language used has much in common with the *Poggadi Chib*. Thus Pischel: 'Norway is not the only country where Gypsies are found who sing old songs whose words, it is true, they will remember but whose meaning they can no longer clearly explain' (*JGLS* n.s. 3 (1909), 157).

It is not only in its somewhat unconventional use of language that English Gypsy song has been found wanting by its sterner critics. Leland, for example, in seeking to justify his own highly questionable attempts at Anglo-Romani verse composition, took the view that it was 'without form and void', whilst according to Yates, an altogether more sympathetic observer, 'it is characteristic of Gypsy folk singers that they often sing fragments of incoherent verse to beautiful tunes'.

That Romani song may sometimes appear to lack any obvious formal structure is perfectly true, but to suggest on that account that it is 'void' – that is, empty, ineffectual or useless – is surely absurd. Were this the case, it would almost certainly not have survived the redefinition of Romani English as a functionally specific Cant or would long since have shed those features which even yet proclaim its Gypsy ancestry. It has not, and this being so, one cannot escape the possibility that the apparent formlessness of much Romani English song is evidence not of degeneration but of a mode of thought entirely different from that underlying most mainstream song; a mode of thought which finds expression in a series of unadorned vignettes rather than in a succession of clear linked statements.

In our western tradition, we are accustomed to taking a strictly linear view of events, characterizing action in terms of cause and effect. Thus, a song or a story has a beginning, a middle and an end, with each succeeding episode determined by what has gone before. The Gypsy, on the other hand, does not appear to be bound by the same conventions. Thus, the action of a song may be joined at a point other than that which to us would seem to be its natural point of entry, and the focus of attention may be switched in what may appear to be a wholly arbitrary fashion. In text 16, for example, the first two lines would seem to make more sense if taken in reverse order, whilst the second couplet, which deals with the altogether more peaceful pursuits of music and courtship, might be better placed at the head of the quatrain.

As often as not, however, these apparent discrepancies are purely sub-jective in character. If the various elements of which a text is composed are viewed as a whole, rather than in strict sequence, there is generally sufficient information to construct at least the skeleton of a coherent narrative. In other words, rather than treating the song as a series of serially linked events, the Gypsy singer views his material as a *gestalt* – a patchwork quilt, the various panels of which may be stitched together in a number of different but equally valid ways, and which only make sense when taken as a whole.

In the following English rendering of text 91, for example, whilst the overall meaning is perfectly clear, a more satisfactory order of play for a *Gaujo* audience might be as follows (the bracketed numbers refer to the ordering of the lines in the original Romani):

> I am going across a field (5)
> The Policeman ran (3)
> I'll get taken (4)
> Hit him in the belly (6)
> So help me (7)
> I can fight well (8)
> I'm going to jail (1)
> For taking a bit of wood (2).

In some cases, what seems to have happened is that the principal idea has been brought to the head of the text – somewhat in the manner of a newspaper headline – to be revisited at a later stage, with or without amplification. Thus, in text 90, there can be little doubt that the action of the song actually commences at line 5, whilst the opening quatrain is nothing more than a preview of lines 8–12.

In this respect, texts of this type may be said to resemble the *Siguiryas Gitanas* or *seguidillas* of the Gypsies of Spain. Mentioned by Cervantes in *La Gitanilla* (1614) and described by Brown as the 'keystone' of the *Cante Jondo*, the *Siguirya* is perhaps the most typically Gypsy of all the many Flamenco 'styles'. Although, according to Strettell, writing in the mid-1880s, songs of this type were already 'becoming corrupt . . . becoming *Gachonales* as they express it', her subsequent remarks concerning their formal structure are of considerable interest here. Unlike its Spanish namesake, the *Siguirya*, she says,

> consists of four lines only, the first two and the last of which are short whilst the third is long, and the second and fourth lines rhyme. A prolonged guitar solo ushers in the song which commences with a long 'ay' wailed out upon a succession of 'fioriture' [cf. texts 55 and 56]. After this, the voice pauses, the guitar again plays several bars and then the seguidilla is sung. The second or third line, whichever is the most tragic or important to the verse being taken first and the song closing with the line upon which it began. (Strettell 1887)

Despite such apparent similarities, to suggest that the organization of Gypsy song texts may be governed by a set of unspoken rules would be greatly to overstate the case. Yet it is noticeable that whilst certain commonly occurring motifs are sometimes found in combination with other material, others never are. What is also apparent is that where such motifs are found in combination, their use is limited to texts of a particular type. In other words, for a song to be regarded as *tatcho*, or true to the tradition, it must first meet certain well-understood if imperfectly defined criteria: namely, that the various elements of which the song is composed are appropriate to songs of that type and that the song itself is organized in such a way as to satisfy the Gypsies' own understanding of the unities of time and action.

Exactly what is and what is not appropriate in this context, only a Gypsy could say, and it is likely that for most Travellers such questions will always remain a matter for feeling rather than definition. In much the same way, one of Vekerdi's informants, when asked to explain his use, in Romani song texts, of certain commonly occurring Hungarian loan-formulae, for which there existed perfectly adequate Gypsy alternatives, could only say: 'I cannot say it in Gypsy, this is *so* in the song.'

Kovalcsik, in her study of Vlax Gypsy song, makes much the same point, although, wisely perhaps, she does not attempt to define either the underlying thought process or the rules governing its operation:

> The extreme fragmentation of the events makes the understanding of Gypsy folk poetry rather difficult. There is, however, another reason too, which lies in the Gypsies' specific mode of thought, alien from the Western Bourgeois tradition. The form appears to organise the material loosely, but the ideas behind it, conveyed by particular formulas, which may remain unrecognised by us, are very strictly controlled by the tradition representing an archaic way of thinking. (1985, 34)

Something of the same mysterious process may perhaps be observed in the Gypsy practice of in-coining – a practice almost certainly born of a shortage of native root-stock but one long since regarded as something of a game. Commenting on this aspect of the language, Smart and Crofton took the view that it was carried on 'not in an altogether arbitrary fashion but according to established usage so that the fresh word sounds natural and conveys a meaning to the ears of his fellows hearing it perhaps for the first time'. They were, however, unable to shed any further light on the principles underlying successful word-building, noting simply that 'like Paganini on one string, the Gypsy elicits from his imperfect instrument notes and phrases which the *Górgio* in vain attempts to extract' (Smart and Crofton 1875, xviii–xix).

Even where texts are wholly intelligible at the verbal level and are organized in a manner broadly consistent with mainstream expectations, they may still appear marred by inexplicable gaps and omissions; e.g. texts 115 and 164. Thus, whilst the former presents none of those confusing features outlined above, its overall meaning remains far from clear. It may be translated as follows:

When I closed the handkerchief,
She fainted.
When the handkerchief was opened up,
She fainted.

But I, so clever,
Her money did get,
And came to my husband
The very same day.

We sat on our backsides,
Had a cup of tea,
And straightaway in the morning
We ran away.

In fact, there can be little doubt that the subject of the song is the *hokano Baro* (great trick), a species of fraud peculiar to the Gypsies whereby the victim is duped into believing that it is possible to increase his existing wealth by magical means, but which usually results in his losing everything he already has (see notes accompanying text 115). Yet, even if one happens to possess the information necessary to arrive at this conclusion, one is still left wondering why the singer should have chosen to approach his subject from such an oblique angle. One possibility is that the singer was anxious to avoid details of the trick becoming more generally known but, as the song was originally given in Romani English, it was presumably intended for use only within the Gypsy speech-community and, this being so, it is difficult to see what purpose would have been served by any additional obfuscation.

That the various classes of verbal and textual defects summarized above are simply a by-product of the process of oral transmission may almost certainly be dismissed out of hand. As a rule, one would expect any essentially non-literate people such as the Gypsies to exhibit a high degree of conservatism in their treatment of traditional material. Thus, O'Grady, commenting on the integrity of native story-telling in the Irish *Gaeltacht* during the early part of the nineteenth century, tells us that

tales used to be read aloud in farmers' houses on occasions when numbers were collected at some employment, such as wool-carding in the evening, but especially at wakes. Thus the people became familiar with all the tales. The writer has heard a man who never possessed a manuscript, nor heard of O'Flannagan's publication, recite at the fireside The Death of the Sons of Uisneach without omitting one adventure, and in great part retaining the very words of the written version. (S. H. O'Grady, 'Tóruigheacht

Dhiarmuda agus Gráinne', *Transactions of the Ossianic Society* iii (1857), 29)

So, too, in an article on the English Gypsies in *Tramp Magazine*, Thompson notes that 'The text of their folk tales is as fixed as if it were printed: they will repeat the same story again and again without changing a word or a syllable or even an accent' (Thompson 1910a, 52). That Leland should have found it 'a difficult matter to hear a story among English Gypsies which is not mangled or marred in the telling' (Leland 1873, viii), might, it is true, appear to rob Thompson's statement of much of its value; but, whilst Leland may well have been right according to his own limited understanding of what is and is not proper in the telling of tales, what is important here is not the quality, real or apparent, of such texts taken individually, but their *shared* characteristics. In other words, if all Gypsy tales (or songs) appear similarly flawed, yet continue to satisfy the particular requirements of the audience for whom they were originally intended, it would seem reasonable to conclude that any such apparent weaknesses are the result, not of a simple want of narrative skill, but of a more or less deliberate formative process. This does not mean that Gypsy singers and storytellers are any less careful of their material than the *seanchaí* of nineteenth-century rural Ireland, merely that they may approach the conservation issue from a different standpoint.

The apparently haphazard combination of a number of unconnected elements in the one song is not a uniquely Gypsy trait. A similar want of internal cohesion is also to be found in the Scottish Gaelic tradition, particularly in the *iorram* (rowing-song) or *oran luadhaidh* – a song once used to accompany the waulking or fulling of homespun cloth. It is also the case, as Thomson has pointed out, that individual lines, or even whole stanzas or verse paragraphs, are held, as it were, in a state of suspension within the tradition, and may attach themselves now to one song, now to another (Thomson 1977, 63).

Waulking songs are generally formed of single lines or couplets, preceded, separated or followed by a vocal refrain, consisting either of words or, in more primitive examples, of meaningless though functionally significant vocables. Indeed, these refrains, irrespective of type, would seem to represent the most archaic element in such songs and are generally far more stable in character than the intervening verse lines. The texts, too, may exhibit certain archaic features – drawing, for example, on the Ossianic Lays or medieval ballad tales of Fionn Mac Cumhail and the *Fianna*. Thus, in the following example, the third element, although fragmentary, is clearly Ossianic in origin, and may, perhaps, be explained by reference to Tolmie's note on 'The Lay of the Black Dog' in *JFSS* 16,

254. The song opens with a short lyrical keen of unknown origin, followed by a much reduced variant of a narrative ballad also found in Barra by J. L. Campbell (*Gaelic Folk Song from the Isle of Barra*, 1950) and noted elsewhere by Tolmie (*JFSS* 16, 253–4), Mac Donald (*The Gesto Collection and Appendix*, p.45) and Craig (*Orain Luaidh Mairi nighean Alasdair*, p.46). The version given here is from the singing of Mrs Mary Morrison (*Waulking Songs from Barra*, Tangent Records, TNGM333).

Leader: Ho ro hug o hug o
Chorus: Ho ro hug o hug o
Leader: mulad is lionn-dubh tha gruaim
Chorus: hug a ri a sir hug oro
Leader: mulad is lionn-dubh tha gruaim
Chorus: ho ro hug o hug o

Mulad mor a deoghaidh Ruairi
'S iomadh aite an dug mi cuairt leat
Bha mi 's taobh-deas is 's taobh-tuath leat
Bha mi'n Glasachu nam bua leat
Bha mi an Dun-Tuilm na stuadh leat
Bha mi 'sa Ros fada shuas leat
'S ann a sin a thug iad bhuam thu.
Latha bha Ridire 'g ol
San taigh-osd, e fhein 's a bhean
Ghearr a' Ridire 'mheur
An fheoil go'n d'rainig i 'n cnamh glas
Thug an fhuil 'na struth go lar
Air eagal 's nach bi e beo
Fios air a chinneadh gu luath
Fios air a chairdean gu leir
Gos an corp a thoirt go cill.
Thug ise na mionnan mor,
Nach dealaicheadh i beo ri'lic
Gos an cuairt i fhein sios
A's an talamh comhla ris.
Gorach liom thus, a bhean bhaoth
Saoil an tusa ceud bhean og
Air 'n do chuireadh fod a fear
B'fhearr a chuireadh 'shuil a seilg
B'fhearr a mharcaicheadh ri strein.
Thug an cu dubh leis a bheinn
Dh'eirich Conan labhairt Conn
Dh'eirich friogh is fraoch air Bran.

168

Great longing after Ruairi
Many a place I visited with you
I was in the south and the north with you
I was in Glasgow with its wonders
And in turreted Dun Tulm with you
I was in the Mull of Ross with you, far away;
That is where they took you from me.
One day the knight was drinking
In the tavern, himself and his wife
The knight cut his finger
Through the flesh to the grey bone
The blood came in a stream to the floor
For fear that he does not live
Let word be swiftly sent to his kinfolk
Let word be sent to all his friends
To carry his body to the church
She swore a great oath
That she would not leave his grave
Till she herself was buried
In the earth beside him.
Foolish I think you, silly woman,
Do you think you are the first young woman
To see her man put beneath the sod?
The best who ever hunted
The best who ever rode a bridled horse,
Took the black hound to the mountain;
Conan arose; Conn spoke;
Bran bristled and grew furious.

Although the immediate juxtaposition of such obviously disparate elements is no less apparent here than in text 74, the unrestrained expression
of personal grief in the opening lines, and the accompanying richness of
language, immediately distinguish such texts from their Romani counterparts, proceeding, as they do, from an entirely different understanding of
the nature and function of the song. Indeed, this very depth and breadth of
expression, coupled with a relentless beat and oft-repeated refrain, is
sufficient to invest the whole with a sense of unity often lacking in Gypsy
composites. Even so, songs of this type can never be said to be wholly
integrated, although, in much the same way as semi-permanent forms may,
on occasion, emerge from the shifting mass of Romani song, texts may,
from time to time, achieve a certain degree of stability. In both traditions,
however, the connecting link between members of the same song-group is
likely to be thematic rather than strictly verbal in character. Thus, within
the song-group represented by texts 74–92, the incident around which the

song is built may be the theft of hay or firewood or the illicit grazing of horses, the unifying factor being the commission of a petty offence, its discovery and the resulting clash with the farmer, the keeper or the police. So, too, as Thomson points out in chapter 2 of his *Introduction to Gaelic Poetry*:

> Occasionally in the folk songs we find specific themes and specific workings of themes that must at one time have been known from end to end of the Gaelic [Scottish and Irish] area . . . The homogeneity here is a thematic rather than a verbal one, though there are some very close verbal resemblances. (Thomson 1977, 62–3)

3. Gypsy Song: A Mirror of Gypsy Life

> Often it's only among ourselves, at family gatherings, that Gypsies play their own true music – the old Gypsy songs, heard again and again as we travelled, helping us to put up with our troubles, to tell out our hopes and emotions, to complain of the lack of understanding by the *Gajé*.
>
> (Jan Cibula in Acton 1981)

Given the various similarities which exist between certain types of Gaelic and Romani song, one is naturally bound to ask whether this is merely coincidental or the result of some as yet undisclosed factor common to both cultures. Writing of Highland and Island society during the period in which many of those Scottish Gaelic song texts under consideration here were first formulated, Thomson notes that it was 'close, kin-based, rural, independent and self-sufficient', and, whilst 'not cut off entirely from external contact . . . not . . . strongly attracted to external influences' (1977, 58). Although the picture thus presented suggests certain parallels with the Gypsy experience, it may be argued that such similarities are, in practice, more than outweighed by the many real differences which also exist between the two communities. Most importantly, perhaps, the Gypsies are (or were), in the main, a loosely organized, pre-literate nomadic people, operating within the limits imposed by, and at the very margins of, an essentially hostile society. The Gaels of early modern Scotland, on the other hand, were settled agriculturalists, fiercely independent and hierarchical, and with a strong and, at times, prescriptive literary tradition linking them with the richly varied culture of medieval Ireland.

Yet the question still remains: to what extent may environmental factors be said to have influenced the development of folk song within a given

170

culture such as the Gypsies', and hence to what extent may Gypsy song be said to mirror Gypsy life and thought, not simply in terms of its content but in its very structure? With this in mind, the Gypsies' treatment of the song might perhaps be more usefully compared, not with the Gaels of early modern Scotland, but with their more precise contemporary socio-economic counterparts, the Tinkers – the Travelling People of Scotland and Ireland.

The first thing that strikes one about the former is that, in their presentation of traditional song material, Scottish Travellers would seem to have rather more in common with the settled population than they do with the Gypsies. Scottish Traveller songs, for example, evince far fewer of those more confusing features normally associated with Gypsy song and are, for the most part, retained in a form wholly accessible to a non-Traveller audience. Indeed, it has become increasingly apparent over recent years – largely through the work of such contemporary collectors as Fullerton, Shepherd, Imlach, Henderson, Seeger and MacColl – that Scottish Travellers constitute an extremely valuable source of information on many aspects of Scottish traditional song. Hall, in particular (*FMJ* 3, 1 (1975), 41ff.) has rightly highlighted their importance as carriers of the so-called 'big ballads' and, more especially, those characterized by the extensive use of incremental repetition as a narrative device (e.g. Child and Kiltredge 1882–9, 11–14). The fact that songs of this type are now better represented among Travellers than among the settled population has also led him to consider the possibility that their selection and retention may well have been influenced by environmental factors peculiar to the Traveller community. In the article already referred to, he writes as follows:

> The narrative sequence of the songs cited does not conform to our modern stereotype of cause and effect relationship. Instead of a gradual unfolding of the story with logical connections between events, these pieces rely upon repetition of a basic situation suddenly and catastrophically overturned by an unexpected tragic revelation. In many ways, the view implicit in these songs mirrors the Travellers' experience in making the protagonist passive rather than active. Victim rather than hero. Tinkers are less insulated from natural disaster and must contend with social institutions they perceive as external and alien, which they have little or no possibility of manipulating. (Hall 1975, 43–4)

Persuasive as Hall's analysis undoubtedly is, it cannot be said to be wholly applicable to the Gypsies – at least, not in the form stated. This is not to say that such environmental factors have had no part to play in the evolution of Gypsy song, merely that the way in which they operate, even within two ostensibly similar cultures, cannot be assumed to be either uniform or predictable. Scottish Travellers, Hall suggests, are attracted by certain types of song which, in terms of their formal narrative structure, seem to mirror their own experience and which, once admitted to the repertoire, may be retained intact over long periods. The Gypsies, on the other hand, no less victims of circumstance than Scottish Travellers, appear to interpret the world somewhat differently, giving voice to the precariousness of their existence, not through the slow and inexorable accumulation of events over which they have no control, but through a series of shifting images devoid of any obvious plan or structure.

As might be expected, however, it is impossible to draw any absolute distinction between the two traditions. Just as there are Gypsy singers, like Phoebe Smith, who are perfectly capable of returning texts wholly consistent with mainstream expectations, so, among both Scottish and Irish Travellers, one may also encounter sets evincing certain of those characteristics normally associated with Gypsy song. Songs of this type, it is true, are far less common in the Scottish than the Irish repertoire and, indeed, are generally given in Cant rather than English (e.g. texts 31 and 110). Among Irish Travellers, however, who do not, as a rule, sing in their own language, they are by no means uncommon and are represented here by the following from the singing of 'Pops' Johnny Connors. The song itself is said to refer to an incident, involving the Connors and the Moorhouses, which took place in New Ross, Co. Wexford, some ninety years ago. According to the story, the Moorhouses, having fought the Connors through the town, eventually gained the upper hand when the latter barricaded themselves in an abandoned cottage. Having thus secured their prey, the Moorhouses brought the business to a swift and bloody conclusion by dropping in on them through a hole in the thatch and giving them a thorough beating. Although there is some confusion as to its precise date, the incident is well known among other Travellers; indeed, it was described, somewhat grandly, by one informant as 'the second Battle of Aughrim'. The song begins with three lines lilted.

'What brings you down from Kerry?' Says the poor old man.
'Sure it's the Connors's is the blame and don't the country know the same,
And look at them running down the lane', says the poor old man.

'Bad luck to you, young Gerry', says the poor old man,
'If you cook a stew, you don't cook it near ballaroo,
If you will, you're bound sure rue', says the poor old man.

(three lines lilted)

'Oh, they were coming through Ross town and they had ponies big and brown,
And at me they did lick', says the poor old man.

'Bad luck to you, young Gerry', says the poor old man,
'I run to take up my stick and I got orders to drop it quick;
I'll not, I'll roar and squeal', says the poor old man.

'Bad luck to you, young Gerry', says the poor old man,
'But wasn't I an unlucky whore, for to barricade my door?
Wasn't I an unlucky whore?', says the poor old man.

(Mackenzie and Carroll, *VWML* (1986), 8)

What is perfectly clear is that, underlying texts of this type, is a mode of thought quite different from that apparent in most mainstream song – a mode of thought which, as suggested earlier, finds expression in a series of brief, sometimes apparently opaque, word pictures or 'snapshots' rather than in a succession of clear, serially linked statements. It is as if, by means of a few simple cues, the Gypsy singer has merely to tap into the well of feeling and experience shared with his audience, leaving them to fill in the gaps heuristically – 'The song does not say it, but the story says it', as Ursula says of her 'Song of the Broken Chastity' (see notes accompanying texts 133–4).

This is particularly apparent when a Traveller sings for a *Gaujo*, whose understanding of what constitutes a song is clearly somewhat different. An example of this type of misunderstanding is provided by Carolyne Hughes's rendering of 'The Gypsy Laddie' or 'The Raggle-Taggle Gypsies' on Folktracks FSA 60–43. She does not sing the song as we would expect to hear it but confines herself to the principal point – the lord's request that his wife return home and her refusal. Out of politeness, however, she fills in the background beforehand and is clearly puzzled by Kennedy's request for more. At no time does Mrs Hughes suggest that it is her memory which is at fault. What is also particularly noticeable is Mrs Hughes's much fuller use of language in her spoken description of the Gypsy lover. As suggested earlier, this would be highly unusual in the case of sung texts.

CH: The Gypsies come to stay in the field on a farm.
PK: That's the one.
CH: This was a tall handsome dark curly-headed Gypsy – and this lady, this lord's wife, took to this 'ere man and she felled in love wi' 'im – and she walked over to 'im and saw 'im with the tent – and they fell and she 'ad 'im. And this lord bishop [lordship?] missed 'er and 'e went:

O, will you come 'ome to your new wedded lord
Or will you come 'ome to your babies o so small?
Or will you come 'ome to your 'ouses and land
And seek all the Gypsies in the field?
O no, o no, I won't come 'ome
I'll lie with the Gypsies in the field
While you walk high an' I'll walk low
An' I'll still be the draggle tail Gypsies o!

At this point, Mrs Hughes makes an aside to her daughter signalling her intention to begin another song and is encouraged to do so. Kennedy, however, continues unabashed:

PK: What's the chorus of that, Carolyne?
CH: Well, there were a Gypsy man – look, the Gypsies come to work for the lord – a lordship, you know what I mean – well, there were a tall handsome dark young man an' this lordship's wife took to this handsome young man and 'e 'ad a tent – a bender tent, with sticks and a cloth over it – she took to 'im and they falled in love and she left the lord and went to live with 'im – an' 'e asked 'er come 'ome to 'er 'ouse and land an' she wouldn't come 'ome – she foresaked 'im in the fields – an' when they say you go' igh an' I go low 'cos 'e was a lordship an' the Gypsy 'ad nothing.

This highly fragmented approach to the song, if not actually determined by, would at least appear to be wholly consistent with the Gypsies' deeply rooted sense of kinship. It is almost inevitable that, in a society exposed to centuries of rejection and isolation, there should emerge a degree of mutual understanding going far beyond mere fellow-feeling, and it is this community of thought and experience, which, perhaps more than anything else, allows the Gypsy singer to disregard what might otherwise be accounted the usual narrative conventions.

Once again, the point may be illustrated by comparing two songs of a similar type, one from the mainstream and one from the Gypsy repertoire. The first of the following examples, although originally from Scotland is also found in the north of Ireland. It recalls the loss of upwards of 200 miners following an explosion in one of the shafts of Dixon's colliery at High Blantyre, near Glasgow, on 22 October 1877. The second tells of the death, by drowning, of twenty-six adults and four children on their way home from the Kent hop-fields on 20 October 1853 when the horse-drawn brake in which they were travelling was swept away with the collapse of Hartlake bridge on the Medway at Hadlow. Among the party were three

174

members of the Herne family and Comfort, Charlotte, Alice and Selina Leatherhand. Of the remaining names mentioned on the memorial in Hadlow churchyard, eight are Irish and the rest English. Groome also mentions a certain Betsy Leatherlund, 'daughter of Thomas Horam (Heron), travailer', who was christened at Chinnor on 24 April 1763 and goes on to say that her eldest son, Samuel, was drowned at Hadlow on 20 October 1853. He does not, however, mention the disaster as such, despite its obvious importance to the Travelling community, nor does he refer to the song.

Although there are a number of discrepancies between the two sets printed below, they quite clearly belong to the one essentially stable text, which would suggest that the form adopted by the original author, however disjointed it may appear to us, was no mere aberration but wholly acceptable and accessible to his Gypsy audience. Yates mentions that he had been told by other older Travellers that there were more verses to the song but had never succeeded in capturing any. Text B(1) is from the singing of Nelson Ridley (MacColl and Seeger 1977, 343) and Text B(2) from Jasper Smith (Yates 1975a).

The Blantyre Explosion (text A) is from John Maguire of Roslea, Co. Fermanagh, who learned it, together with a number of other pieces, whilst working in Scotland during the 1920s (Morton 1970, 9).

(A) The Blantyre Explosion

1. On Clyde's bonny banks where I lately did wander,
   Near the village of Blantyre where I chanced to stray,
   I espied a young woman, she was dressed in deep mourning,
   So sadly lamenting the fate of her love.

2. I boldly stepped to her, said I 'My poor woman,
   Come tell me the cause of your trouble and woe,
   I do hear you lamenting the fate of some young man,
   His name and what happened him I'd like for to know'.

3. With sighing and sobbing she at length then made answer:
   'John Murphy, kind sir, was my true lover's name,
   Twenty-one years of age and a mild good behaviour,
   To work in the mines of High Blantyre he came.

4. 'And the day was appointed, her friends were invited,
   Oh, had he lived, my true love, husband he'd be,
   But woe to that disaster occurred in High Blantyre,
   He's gone and alas I will never more see him.

5. 'On the eleventh of December I long will remember,
   In health and in strength to his labour did go,
   But on that fatal morning without one moment's warning,
   Two hundred and ten in cold death did lie low.

6. 'There were fathers and mothers, there were widows and orphans,
   In Stonefield High Blantyre where hundreds did mourn,
   Ah, there were old aged parents, for their sons they loved dearly,
   By that sad explosion will never return.

7. 'But the spring it will come with flowers of summer
   That bloom through its wildness so lovely and fair,
   I will gather the snowdrops, primroses and daisies,
   Round my true lover's grave I will transplant them there.

8. 'For they say it's not right for the dead to be grieved,
   There's nothing but trouble bestowed on me,
   He is gone from this world but short time before me,
   I hope to rejoin him in sweet purity.'

B(1)

There was four-and-twenty strangers there, hopping they had been,
Replied to Mr. Coxes all near old Golden Green;
All in the parish of Addlehouse, all near old Tonbridge Town,
That little did those poor souls thought that they were going down.

Some was men and women and the others girls and boys,
They kept in contact to Larklake bridge till the horses they took shy;
They kept in contact to old Larklake Bridge till the horses they took shy,
That to hear the screams from those poor souls as they were going down.

B(2)

Now seven and thirty strangers, oh, a-hopping they had been;
They were 'plied by Mr. Cox's, oh, near old Golders Green.
It were in the parish of Hadlow, that's near old Tonbridge Town,
But to hear the screams from those poor souls as they were going down.

Now some were men and women, and the others girls and boys;
They kept in contract with the bridge till the horses they took shy.
They kept in contract with the bridge till the horses they took shy.
But to hear the screams from those poor souls as they were going down.

Now some were men and women, the others girls and boys.
They were 'plied by Mr. Cox's, oh, near old Golders Green.*
It was in the parish of Hadlow, that's near old Tonbridge Town,
But to hear the screams from those poor souls when they were going down.

*The victims were subsequently washed up at a spot called Golden Green. The fact that both informants are not always clear about the place-names mentioned in the song merely serves to emphasize the fact that what is important is their emotional response to the event not its precise detail.

From the outset, it is perfectly clear that Ridley/Smith and Maguire approach their common theme from two entirely different standpoints. The two Gypsies begin by plunging straight into the action with a direct statement of fact. Maguire, on the other hand, opens with two complete stanzas (eight lines) whose sole purpose seems to be to explain to the audience exactly where and how the information to be imparted was originally acquired. Of the remaining six stanzas, numbers three, four, seven and eight are concerned with the effect of the tragedy on a single individual, the stricken girl. We are told, by the girl herself, her lover's name, age and demeanour, and that their wedding plans had already been made. She then elaborates on her own grief, contrasting the young man's death with the new life that comes with the spring and concluding with the pious hope that she may shortly 'rejoin him in sweet purity'. Only six of the thirty-two lines of which the song is composed deal directly with the disaster and its aftermath.

It is as if we, the audience, require an *entrée* into the matter of the song, a hook on which to hang our emotional response. Thus, it is as outsiders that we are invited to view the events described, our perceptions filtered through the eyes of one person. However much we may feel for the girl, we are, in this way, spared the full horror of the tragedy, and its enormity thus becomes manageable.

The Gypsies' song, on the other hand, seems set to function at an altogether different and deeper level – an approach demanding far more by way of audience involvement. The clue is in the last line, '*to hear* the screams from those poor souls as they were going down'. It is as if the singer is asking his audience to experience what happened for themselves rather than presenting them with a series of explicit and, therefore, limited images which both define the event itself and determine the appropriate response. It is the difference between sympathy and empathy, the Gypsy audience feeling *with* rather than for the protagonists.

Viewed in this light, the song ceases to be simply a means of conveying information or emotion from one person to another and becomes, instead, a shared experience between singer and audience, an expression of community feeling. As Dr Jan Cibula, a Lovari Rom and past president of the World Gypsy Congress, has said,

> Often it's only among ourselves, at family gatherings, that Gypsies play their own true music – the old Gypsy songs, heard again and again as we travelled, helping us to put up with our troubles, to tell out our hopes and emotions, to complain of the lack of understanding by the *Gajé*. (Acton 1981)

Needless to say, few songs deal with events as shocking as those described in the 'Hop Pickers' Tragedy' but, even where the subject matter is much less dramatic, the same principle applies. A family member led off to gaol (text 63), a spot of poaching (text 113) or a camp, broken up by the police in the middle of the night (text 72) – such are the all too common occurrences of the travelling life, but, even here, there is the same assumption of understanding. In the case of text 63, for example, we are told nothing of the circumstances surrounding the arrest, the nature of the offence, when and where it was committed or what sort of sentence was handed down; nor are we told anything of the conditions of confinement, such as the type of diet or labour required of the prisoner. The singer confines herself to the central point: her husband has been taken from her; she feels herself surrounded by hostile *Gaujos*; and she will fight to the last to save him. There is no need to say more. There can be few Traveller families who have not shared this experience at one time or another and most would have no difficulty in casting themselves in the role of the anonymous protagonist. It has been suggested by some critics that Gypsy song lacks the emotional range of much mainstream song; but surely there is both dignity and genuine pathos in this brief cry from the heart.

Only when a song speaks directly to its audience in this way is it likely to find a permanent place in the repertoire; although, even then, because of their loose construction and the individual singer's freedom to relate the events described to his own experience or understanding, texts are rarely fixed:

> You see, I'll tell you what it is. We don't sing it proper. You never see two people sing a song alike, do you know? There's always some word different. One 'ould be singing this, another – Then they'll learn it and go on singing that and somebody else'll learn it and put another word in, you know. (Rebecca Penfold, Winkleigh near Hatherleigh, 1971. Folktracks 30–042)

Indeed, in one sense, the one song can never be sung twice, even by the same person (see texts 82–3 and 167–8).

To put it another way, for the Gypsy, the song is an idea rather than a finished artefact and, rather than being preserved and reproduced intact, may be expressed with equal validity in different ways at different times. Thus, whilst the *Gaujo* singer may learn and repeat a song word for word (subject perhaps to certain stylistic differences), to attempt to reproduce a Gypsy song in this way would be wholly meaningless.

Even when a singer gives the same text in quick succession it is unlikely to be repeated word for word. This is shown to good effect in Carolyne Hughes's telling of the old ballad, 'Hugh of Lincoln' or 'The Jew's Garden'. The two sets were delivered end-on, without pause, the first in the form of a rhythmical recitation. Both may also usefully be compared with Amy North's version as reproduced in an earlier section of the present work.

A.

Down, in merry, merry Scotlin,
Where the rain it did come down,
There was two little boys went out to play,
To have a game with the ball.

They pitched the ball so very very high,
They pitched him down so low,
Till he pitched all over the Jew's garden
Where the Jew lived down below.

Well, the Jew come out to this little boy
And asked him what he meant;
He took him in and he gave 'er sugar sweet.
He laid him on the table and he stuck him like a lamb
He said: 'Just before I drawn my last breath, sir,
Take this word to my tender hearted mother.'

B

There were two little boys went out one day
For to have a game with a ball.
They pitched the ball so very, very high,
And they tossed him down so low,
Till he pitched all over in the Jew's garden,
Where the Jew lived just down below.
Out come a one of those old Jews,
'How come you here, my pretty little boy?
Oh, you shall have your ball again.'
He 'ticed him in with sugar sweet,
He laid him on the table.

He said: 'Will you let me say one word,
Just before you stick me, sir?
You'll dig my grave so very, very wide;
Put a marble stone each end;
And if my tender mother now should come this way,
You pray tell her that I lays asleep.'

The idea of the song as common ground, occupied jointly by singer and audience alike, is further reinforced by the absence of any formal structure; for, in this way, neither the singer's freedom of expression nor the audience's ability to share in what is being said is, in any way, limited or frustrated by the peculiar requirements of the medium itself. In the language of literary criticism this apparently anarchic approach might best be described as free verse, a form given respectability in contemporary Anglo-American letters by Whitman and, somewhat ironically, brought to a kind of perfection by such ostensibly inaccessible writers as Eliot and Pound.

Just as in Hall's analysis of Scottish Tinker song, Travellers appear to select certain types of material which in some way mirror their own perception of themselves as victim rather than hero, so the uncertainty of the travelling life would seem to find an echo in the Gypsies' rejection of any formal structural constraints. In our western poetic tradition, poets have used metre and rhyme to impose order and harmony on what is perceived to be an increasingly fragmented world of thought and action. The Gypsy, on the other hand, sings out the chaos of existence as it is, allowing his audience to make what they can of it in the light of their own experience.

For the Gypsy, therefore, the song is not simply a closed unit, encompassing and defining a particular event or aspect of experience, but an open-ended and integral part of life itself. Thus, when Ursula tells Borrow that 'the song does not say it but the story says it', what she is really saying is that it is quite impossible to separate the two; they are indivisible. Unfortunately, for those of us who do not share that wider experience of which the song is only a part, understanding the song in isolation may well prove impossible.

In performance, the want of any formal boundary between the song and the generality of the singer's experience is evident at two levels. On the one hand, as suggested earlier, the action may be joined at a point other than that which, to an outsider, would seem to be the obvious starting-point, and the text itself may appear to lack coherence. On the other hand, the singer may make little or no distinction between ordinary utterance, rhythmical speech and what, for want of a better term, we may call the song proper. Thus, MacColl and Seeger, commenting on the singing style of certain of their informants, note that they would enhance a song by dropping into speech, swinging back into melody at will, not as an actor does (with histrionics and gestures) but in an almost conversational manner. The borderline between speech and song was often so tenuous that we did not realise that the transition had been made until the new form of expression was established. (MacColl and Seeger 1977, 17–18)

Reeve, too, tells us that 'it is not regarded as the least odd for anybody to break into song without any ostensible cause – sometimes even in the middle of a sentence – and then resume the conversation as if there had been no break in it' (Reeve 1958, 3.3). See also Leland (1873, 143 and *passim*) and Sampson (1891, 90).

Yet whilst English Gypsy song may well lack consistency as regards its form and structure, the same cannot be said of the principal images which it evokes. These, for the most part, are, as it were, frozen in time and as such would be wholly accessible to any English Gypsy living within the past 200 years; that is, since extensive records of their language and culture first became available. Indeed, given the various changes which have taken place in recent years due to increasing bureaucratic pressure, the displacement of many traditional trades and the advent of mechanized transport, many of the most popular songs heard today might at first glance appear less relevant now than they would have been in Borrow's time.

Given the essentially conservative nature of much mainstream folk song, this may not seem surprising, and yet we are bound to ask why the singer's freedom to manipulate his basic material should not be matched by a similar want of constraint in the use of language and imagery. Certainly, this would seem to be the case as regards the *loki dili* of the *Lovari Rom* where, as Vekerdi has pointed out, a very real distinction may be drawn between the genre as a whole and the actual wording/imagery of the texts themselves. 'The former', he suggests, 'seems to be archaic, at any rate pre-European. Nothing of the kind is to be found in Hungarian or Balkan folklore. The latter, however, is quite modern, and constantly *in statu nascendi*' (Vekerdi 1967).

'Linguistic data', he continues, 'serve as proof of the recent origin of the actual texts. They are full of recent Hungarian loan-words, loan-translations and even lines told in Hungarian which are integral parts of the recitation.' Whilst many of these forms may be referred to Hungarian popular songs of the late nineteenth century, evidence of more recent influence may also be detected in, for example, the oft-repeated usage *lole sela*, red one-hundreds. Here, as Vekerdi explains, the reference is to the restyled 100-forint note, known in Hungarian slang since the early 1950s as *lila* (lilac, mauve), and first introduced on 1 August 1946.

A similar openness to contemporary influence is also to be found in the repertoire of the Vlax Gypsies of Slovakia, where 'new lyrical motifs appear, tending to replace the older ones . . . the . . . young man sits into his car instead of getting on horseback or harnessing a wagon; he does not earn money in general but "makes lots of dollars". . .' (Kovalcsik 1985, 34). In other examples from Hungary and Slovakia, we find the song's protagonist threatening to take her own life by dousing herself with petrol and applying a match to it; a postman bearing a telegram; a woman carried away in an ambulance; and a Gypsy driving a Dacia or a Lada.

For Kovalcsik, 'these changes in the lyric indicate that Gypsy folk song is still alive, as it is still able to perform its original function, that of reflecting the changes of everyday life' (ibid.). One might also argue, however, that such developments rather serve to emphasize the *changeless* nature of the Gypsy predicament – the constant struggle for survival in the face of an unswervingly hostile world – and that the modernizing tendency of the Vlax and the apparent conservatism of the English Gypsy are thus complementary rather than contradictory. As suggested elsewhere, a key element in the Gypsies' ability to cope with centuries of external pressure has been that highly effective blend of conservatism and adaptability which has allowed them to absorb the many changes thrust upon them by the outside world whilst, at the same time, retaining their own sense of identity. Thus, the Vlax may sing of trading for dollars rather than gold and of riding in a Lada rather than in a horse-drawn trailer, not because he welcomes such developments but because he is a pragmatist; the English Traveller, on the other hand, may sing of stealing hay for the horses, rather than petrol for his lorry, not through any sentimental attachment to the past but because the situation itself and the feelings which it evokes are emblematic of his dealings with, and necessary contempt for, the *Gaujos*. The one tells how things are, the other tells how they have always been and ever will be.

4. Subject Matter

> The songs are as a rule exceedingly brief . . . little fragments chipped from Gypsy experience, scarce large enough to serve as samples; interjections and exclamations gathered from Gypsy conversation; footnote comments on current events in Gypsy life.
>
> (R. Scott Macfie)

As regards their subject matter, *Poggadi Chib* songs are, for the most part, wholly prosaic in character, dealing, in Gillington's words, with 'some passing event of the day or hour; such as travelling the road together, stopping at an alehouse for drink, leading the horses out to grass, sleeping in a barn, being taken up by the police or catching a rabbit' (Gillington 1911a, Introduction). Yet the fact that these simple 'Diddikei Ditties', as she calls them, have survived both the redefinition of *Romanés* as a functionally specific Cant, and the introduction of other more sophisticated forms of entertainment, and are still much valued, even though the events they describe may often appear to lack any obvious contemporary relevance, would suggest that they are of far greater significance than mere doggerel.

One reason for its continuing vitality may be that *Poggadi Chib* song represents one of a number of ways in which the *Poggadi Chib* itself, and the culture of which it is an integral part, is kept alive (see notes accompanying texts 15–22); another, as suggested in the foregoing section, is that it provides an opportunity for the community to sing out its troubles and hence to cope with the seemingly endless hostility of the settled population. In this connection, too, it has been suggested that, in its apparent formlessness, Gypsy song reflects both the uncertainty of the travelling life and the high degree of mutual understanding which exists between the Gypsies themselves. This being so, it would be surprising indeed if Gypsy song did not also take as its principal theme the Gypsies' own direct experience. This would certainly seem to have been the case in earlier times. 'As far as I can judge . . .', writes Simson in his *History*, a work which, he tells us on p.64, was already in preparation as early as 1817, 'the subjects of the songs of the Scottish Gypsies (I mean those composed by themselves) are chiefly their plunderings, their robberies, and their sufferings' (Simson 1865, 306).

Even in less troubled times, what, for Gillington, may be no more than 'some passing event of the day or hour' may, for the Gypsy, be of far greater significance. Apart from the catch-all, 'being taken up by the police', four of her remaining examples might well result in civil, if not criminal, proceedings whilst even calling in at a pub offers no guarantee of a friendly reception.

If prolonged exposure to institutionalized discrimination is not to result in complete demoralization, it is essential for any minority group such as the Gypsies to develop an unshakeable sense of its own self-worth, not to say cultural superiority. At worst, failure to do so may well result in its own unquestioning acceptance of the 'official' view: that is, that what in reality may be nothing more than the mindless persecution of the misunderstood outsider may be explained away in terms of the wholly justified reduction of an essentially dangerous and inferior subculture.

One way of reinforcing a positive self-image is to emphasize those characteristics in which the group is thought (and hence believes it desirable) to excel, or which distinguish it from others, and to denigrate those perceived as typical of society as a whole. At the same time, just as the dominant culture may seek to legitimize its actions by devaluing and depersonalizing the alienated minority, so the latter, if it is to retain its own sense of worth, must deny the possibility of any normal human feeling on the part of the dominant culture. For the Gypsies to acknowledge that those in authority may have a positive as well as a negative side would be tantamount to allowing for the possibility that they may have good reasons for acting as they do and, this being so, that they themselves must bear some responsibility for the consequences. Thus, just as the Gypsies have been variously depicted as 'locusts', 'lice' and 'dogs', so, in Romani song, the *Gaujo* ceases to be regarded as an individual and is represented instead by a series of one-dimensional stereotypes – the predatory 'spider' or unfeeling 'pig' (policeman), who haunts the town and breaks up the camp in the small hours (texts 14 and 72–3), the mean-minded farmer demanding payment for the return of the horses (texts 65–71), or the ever-vigilant keeper, standing between the Gypsy and his dinner (texts 112 and 167–71). Nowhere in the repertoire is there any attempt to understand, let alone sympathize with, the feelings of the other side. Although it may be perfectly proper for the Gypsy to feed his horses (text 23) and himself (text 111) at the *Gaujos'* expense, or even to steal their hard-earned cash (text 115), it is quite a different matter when those same horses are impounded (text 65) or the theft of poultry results in a stiff gaol sentence (text 108). This is not simply a piece of disingenuous 'double-think'; nor should it be taken as evidence of the Gypsies' innate amorality. It is how things are when two essentially incompatible cultures, labouring under the weight of centuries of mutual animosity and lacking either the will or the ability to understand each other, attempt to occupy the same ground. Although the following text shows clear signs of 'improvement', particularly in the last verse, there can be no doubt that, in spirit at least, it comes close to representing the Gypsies' point of view:

> The Romany chals
> Should jin so bute
> As the Puro Beng
> To scape of gueros
> And wafo gorgies
> The wafodupen.

> They lels our gryor,
> They lels our wardoes,
> And wusts us then
> Drey starripenes
> To mer of pishens
> And buklipen.

Cauna volélan
Muley pappins
Pawdle the len
Men artavàvam
Of gorgio foky
The wafodupen.

Ley teero sollohanloinus oprey lis!
(Borrow 1874, 116).

Sorrowful Years

The wit and the skill
Of the Father of ill,
Who's clever indeed,
If they would hope
With their foes to cope
The Romany need.

Our horses they take,
Our waggons they break,
And us they fling
Into horrid cells,
Where hunger dwells
And vermin sting.

When the dead swallow
The fly shall follow
Across the river,
O we'll forget
The wrongs we've met,
But till then o never:
Brother, of that be certain.

Yet, whilst in song the Gypsies may see themselves in terms of the distraught father of starving children (text 66), the grieving wife whose husband has been dragged off to prison (text 63) or the plucky bare-knuckle fighter ready to do battle for his beleaguered family (text 76), the situation is, in reality, somewhat more complex, for the overbearing and all-powerful *Gaujo* is also the legitimate and all too easy victim of superior Romani guile. Small game is taken (text 113), hen coops successfully raided, the intrepid thief escaping by the skin of his teeth (text 114), and avaricious fools relieved of their hard-earned cash (text 115). And thus, the balance is restored. The dominant *Gaujo* may seem to have the upper hand but the self-reliant Romani, living on his wits, knows that this is not altogether true.

> O dear me! o dear me!
> What dinnelies these Gorgies be.
> (Borrow 1874, 134)

Although both anger and despair are also apparent in a number of songs of the victim type (texts 63, 66 and 137), they are, for the most part, wholly matter-of-fact in tone and rarely if ever descend to the level of genuine self-pity. There is, moreover, nothing to compare with those stereotypical expressions of woe common in British and Gaelic folk song – 'it's oh and alas!', 'pity my sad plight', 'Ochón, ochón, 's mór mo mhulad mór!' The common Gypsy exclamative *dordi!* now seems broadly to equate with the English 'dear me!' although, as a corruption of *dadrus* (father), it may once have carried the same weight as such other oaths as *'pré mo mulo dad* (on my dead father) or *tatcho like my mullo dad* (true like my dead father), cf. German Gypsy: *ap i mulende* (by all the dead). Although such formulae may now have lost some of their original force, Sampson, writing in 1897, took the view that if Gypsies could be sworn this way in court they could be relied upon, with every confidence, to speak nothing but the truth ('The Gypsies', *Transactions, Warrington Literary and Philosophical Society*, 1897).

Even where the atmosphere is one of unrelieved gloom, as in 'O Boshkelomengro' (text 137), the overall effect is achieved without the use of a single adjective, adverb or exclamative, the singer relying on the cumulative force of the repeated phrase *nai man keck* (I have no . . .). Matty Cooper's 'Song of Starvation' (text 66) is something of an exception, but it is quite clear that the old man was consciously striving to impress his patron in the hope of financial gain: '. . . Mandi'd die if 'twasn't for miro kushto rye . . .' Needless to say, he was not to be disappointed, receiving for his pains the expected half-crown. This is not to say that sentimentality has no place in the Gypsy make-up – this is clearly not the case, judging by their marked preference for the more maudlin type of *Gaujo* popular song – it is simply that in dealing with their own private distress through the medium of song, the outward and obvious expression of *individual* emotion becomes unnecessary.

If, as suggested, *Poggadi Chib* song is primarily concerned with the release of shared emotion and the reinforcement of self-esteem, it is hardly surprising to find an almost complete want of material in the repertoire whose principal purpose is merely to inform or entertain. This is in marked contrast with much *Gaujo* folk song which, prior to the advent of more or less universal literacy, served not only as entertainment but as a means of publicizing and celebrating events of local or national importance, be it a particularly juicy murder or the outcome of a crucial naval engagement. There is thus a complete absence of *Poggadi Chib* song dealing with service life, industrial pay and conditions and the sort of stories for the dissemination of which the broadside ballad has now been superseded by the tabloid press.

Few Travellers would, in any case, have had any interest in such matters, although the absence of service songs is a little surprising given the various attempts at enforced enlistment to which the Gypsies have been periodically subjected. Even today, stories are still current among contemporary British Gypsies of young men dragged off to war by the police and their families settled in the new suburban housing estates of the inter-war years. This is not to say, however, that many Gypsies have not given gallant service in the armed forces both in Britain and abroad. Indeed, the Archduke Frederick, writing in the preface to his Gypsy grammar, tells us that he was 'considerably helped in this work by the circumstance that I served in Infantry Regiment 60 from 1853 to 1856 which recruited its personnel from among the Gypsies'. Closer to home, we know that a number of Gypsy musicians served with the British fleet in the Crimea, whilst another, the fiddler Adolphus Wood, was found frozen to death in a Belgian trench in 1917, his rifle in his hand. Sylvester Boswell's grandfather, Shadrak, was also a soldier, losing his life in Holland some time during the second half of the eighteenth century, whilst two of the Roberts, Jim and Harold, descendants of the great John Roberts, were among the many who perished in the war of 1914–18.

Yet during those years when many of our best soldier/sailor songs were first put together, economic necessity was generally a far more effective recruiting sergeant than loyalty to king and country, and the harshness of military discipline and the close confines of camp and shipboard life would have held little appeal for the free-moving Traveller – compare the following sayings, in Romani and *Shelta* respectively: *nanai kuripen Romani keripen* (war is not the Gypsies' business) and *sugu thoris, muilsha misli gliet thom to loban* (war is coming, I'll be off to my cabin in the mountains). Indeed, such was the Gypsies' aversion to the military life that some would go so far as self-mutilation in order to avoid enforced enlistment. Simson speaks of their willingness to sacrifice one or two fingers to this end or even an arm or a leg and of mothers meting out similar treatment to their children. Groome, too, tells of Gypsies donning women's clothes in order to avoid the press-gang, whilst one of Smart and Crofton's informants, Ike M—, refers to the practice of cutting and binding the fingers with string steeped in lime and soft soap in order to make them crooked and so incapable of handling a gun: 'Romani-chals used to chin alé lenghi wongushties then, so they wouldn't "press" them . . . and some used to pander lenghi wongushties with dori, and lime, and soft-soap, to kair them bongo, so they wouldn't lel them for the Kooromongri' (Smart and Crofton 1875, 276).

The practice of self-mutilation is also mentioned in a Russian Gypsy song quoted by Smith on p.101 of *Through Romany Songland*. It was translated for her by a Mr Vesseloffsky of the Russian Consulate General and she gives only the English words. The second and third verses run as follows:

> They chop off their fingers, they pull out their teeth,
> Not to enter military service,
> They do not wish to!
> White hazel tree; o, raspberry bush.
>
> John the Horse-radish is accepted as a recruit;
> The whole village began to grieve,
> They weep!
> White hazel . . .

The nomadic life itself, however, as the following verse suggests, might well have offered an equally effective and far less painful way of expressing one's contempt for the colours or of avoiding them altogether:

> My bonny lass, I work in brass,
> A Tinkler is my station;
> I've roamed around all Christian ground
> In search of occupation;
> I've ta'en the gold and been enroll'd
> In many's the noble squadron
> But in vain they searched when off I marched
> To go and clout the cauldron.

One Scottish Traveller who seems to have made something of a career of desertion was William Marshall, the 'Caird of Barullion' and 'King of the Gypsies of the Western Lowlands'. Marshall, in the course of his 120 years (1671–1792), is said to have been forcibly enlisted seven times and to have deserted on each occasion. He was, besides, three times press-ganged by the Navy but always managed to jump ship. According to Easton, writing in his *Human Longevity* (Salisbury 1799), the old man retained his senses almost to the last hour of his life, and remembered distinctly to have seen King William's fleet riding at anchor in the Solway Firth and the transports lying in the harbour. He was present at the siege of Derry, where, having lost his uncle, who commanded a King's frigate, he returned home, enlisted in to the Dutch service, went to Holland and soon after came back to his native country.

The absence of industrial folk song from the Gypsy repertoire is equally understandable as the way of life of which it speaks would also have been beyond the experience of most Travellers. For, despite the rapid growth in demand for urban labour in the wake of the Industrial Revolution, and the loss of so many traditional occupations through the mechanization of agriculture, the Gypsies have, in the main, remained loyal to the black economy and the free life of the wandering entrepreneur. Yet, for many Travellers, towns have always constituted an important source of employment, offering, as they do, a ready market for the various goods and services they are able to provide. Their pursuit of this market has left us with a range of trade cries, the best of which (such as 'Who Will Buy My Sweet Blooming Lavender') may rightly take their place in the folk-song repertoire. The following, whilst it may well lack the popular appeal of the 'Lavender Song', is fairly typical of its kind. It was noted by Cecil Sharp from the singing of a group of Gypsy 'van-sellers' whom he encountered in Adelaide Road on 16 May 1908, and was first published in the *Journal of the Folk Song Society* some two years later (*JFSS* 15 (1910), 99):

> All kinds of fancy chairs, easy armchairs,
> Will you buy a pretty basket?
> Clothes basket, cheap basket, flower basket.
> We've all kinds of chair.
> For I say, ladies, don't delay,
> Come and buy your chairs and baskets today.
> Buy 'em of the maker.
> For we are sons of the jolly basket-makers.
> We mean to sell 'em all and make no more.
> Come and buy your parlour rugs today.
> Buy 'em of the maker.

There can be no doubt that such cries are, for the most part, native British rather than Gypsy in origin. Musically, they are not infrequently modal in character, suggesting a link with early English folk song or even plain chant, whilst, from those Elizabethan/Jacobean settings which have come down to us, it seems clear that the tunes themselves were already well established in the popular tradition at a relatively early date. Thus, in

Weelkes (*c.*1575–1623), Gibbon (1583–1625) and Deering (1580–1630), wherever the same words are used, they are invariably associated with the same music.

That the crying of wares and services was common practice in these islands prior to the arrival of the first Gypsies, whilst it may be taken for granted, is also apparent from various literary sources as, for example, 'The London Lackpenny', a vivid description of metropolitan life and manners, usually ascribed to John Lydgate (1370–1450) but omitted by H. N. McCracken from his list of the poet's minor works.

> Then met I one cryed *Hot shepe's feete*;
> One cryde *mackerell*; *rushes grene* another gan grete;
> One bade me by a hood to cover my head;
> But for want of money, I might not be sped.

In his biography of the sculptor Nollekens, John Thomas Smith seems to have been so impressed by his subject's habit of imitating the cries of the street whilst measuring stone or 'improving the attitudes of his Venuses' that he devotes several pages to a more general discussion of the genre. Among a number of examples he includes a description of a pair of itinerant cork dealers, a trade which, according to Leland (1882, 304), formed part of the repertoire of the Marshall clan, on which account they were known in some quarters as the *Bungoror* or corkers.

Besides the musical cries mentioned above, about sixty years back (1770) there was also two others yet more singular which, however, were probably better known in the villages round London than in the metropolis itself. The first of these was used by an itinerant dealer in corks, some times called 'Old Corks', who rode upon an ass, and carried his wares in panniers on each side of him. He sat with much dignity and wore upon his head a velvet cap; and his attractive cry, which was partly spoken and partly sung, but all in metre, was something like the following fragment:

Spoken:	Corks for sack
	I have at my back;
Sung:	All handy, all handy;
	Some wine and some for brandy.
Spoken:	Corks for cholic-water,
	Cut 'em a little shorter;
	Corks for gin,
	Very thin;
	Corks for rum,
	As big as my thumb.

	Corks for ale,
	Long and pale.
Sung:	They're all handy, all handy.
	Some for wine and some for brandy.

Attractive as such cries may be, there is an alternative school of thought which holds that brevity and unintelligibility rather than clarity and charm hold the key to successful street trading. As Solomon Smith told John Brune when he recorded him in west Kent in 1960 (Brune 1975, 750):

I reckon myself the best street cry is the shortest yelp you can think of what nobody can understand – makes women curious and chase arter you an' you get a lot o' things for nothing. You get a bell, tinkle it an shout 'maheeeeup! maheeeeup!' Nother tinkle an' 'maheeeeup! maheeeeup!' . . .

Smith, however, also provided Brune with a totter's cry, running to forty-six lines, which must be one of the longest on record, a variant of which is also to be found in Reeve's *Smoke in the Lane*, first published in 1958. Both are clearly derived from the same (written?) source and, indeed, both Smith and Reeve mention Travellers of their acquaintance who had had it printed up on cards. On coming to a new area, they would first be distributed and then collected on the following day along with any trade goods. Reeve's set runs as follows:

I beg with most respectful feeling,
Leave to inform you what I deal in:
I have not come your purse to try,
Yourself shall sell and I will buy.
So please look up that useless lumber
Which long you may have left to slumber.
I'll buy old boots, old shoes, old socks,
Jackets, trousers and smock frocks.
Towels, cloths and cast-off linen,
Cords, cashmeres and worn-out women's
Old gowns, caps, bonnets torn to tatters,
If fine or coarse, it never matters.
Bed-ticking, fustian, velveteens,
Stuffs, worsted cord and bombazines;
Old worn-out handkerchiefs and shawls,
Umbrellas and parasols.
Sheep-netting, canvassing and carpeting,
Whatever else you have to bring:
And of the weight, I'll soon convince you,

For which I pay the utmost value.
I'll purchase dirty fat dusty bags,
Old roping, sacking and old rags:
Both bottles, horsehair and old glass,
Old copper, pewter and old brass:
Old saucepans, boilers, copper kettles,
Pewters, spoons and other metals.
Old coins (not silver), ancient buttons,
Ladies' and gentlemen's left-off clothing,
Skins whether worn by hare or rabbit,
However small your stock, I'll have it.
I'll buy old rags, however rotten,
If made of woollen, hemp or cotton.
I'll buy old iron, cast or wrought,
And pay the money when 'tis bought.
If you have any bones to sell,
Their value in a trice I'll tell.
So over your dwelling, give a glance,
You never will have a better chance.
My price is good, my weight is just,
And mind, I never ask for trust.
Just look up if but a handful,
And with the same I shall be thankful.

Perhaps the most surprising omission from the *Poggadi Chib* repertoire is the lullaby. Common sense would suggest that songs of this type must at one time have been current in Romani as in all other languages and, indeed, as mentioned elsewhere, Morwood, in a somewhat dismissive reference to the singing of English Gypsy women, speaks of their aspiring to no more than 'a simple ditty over the washing tub or a soft, low lullaby to their dark-eyed infants'.

Gypsy lullabies have certainly been noted elsewhere in Europe. Alecsandri includes a number in his *Ballades et chants populaires de la Roumanie* (1855), of which the following is fairly typical. The meaningless syllables, 'nani-nani', which occur elsewhere in the same context, would seem to be equivalent to the common English formula, 'hush-a-by'.

Nani-nani, little treasure,
Sleep, dear angel, near thy mother,
For mother will rock thee
And mother will clasp thee,
And mother will sing thee,
Nani-nani, nani-nani.

Xavier Petulengro, too, albeit a less than reliable witness, tells us in chapter 18 of *A Romany Life* that 'a Romany mother in her lullabies makes her child promise three things: to rokker Romany, to kil-i-bosh and nante della gorgio vek a kash' (speak Romani, play the fiddle and never hit a *Gaujo* with a stick). But this is clearly nothing more than a confused reference to the widespread quatrain 'Can You Rokker Romani' (texts 15–22), and nowhere else in the literature is it suggested that it was ever used in this way.

May Byron's 'Gypsy Mother Song' (Byron 1903) and the Gypsy lullaby in George Smith's *Gypsy Children* (Smith 1889) may also be discounted. The words of the latter are by Edward L. Wakerman and the sentiment of both wholly *Gaujo*.

Borrow also includes the following 'Romany Suttur Gillie' on p.108 of *Romano Lavo-Lil* but, although it was later reprinted by L. A. Smith with one or two minor amendments (Smith 1889, 115), these are so slight as to suggest that it was merely a poorly executed copy. Indeed, there can be little doubt that Borrow, if not the author, at least had a hand in its final form, despite Smith's accompanying note suggesting that it was once widely known among southern Gypsies: 'The wrinkled old beldame who never fails to form part of the household of a Gypsy camp may', she says, 'sometimes be heard crooning this little ditty as she rocks the Romany cradle beneath the leafy shade of some forest monarch.'

> Jaw to sutturs, my tiny chal;
> Your die to dukker has jall'd abri;
> At rarde she will wel palal
> And tute of her tud shall pie.
>
> Jaw to lutherum, tiny baw!
> I'm teerie deya's purie mam;
> As tute cams her tud canaw
> Thy deya meerie tud did cam.

The lack of *Poggadi Chib* lullaby may, almost certainly, be explained in terms of the way in which the language itself is now passed on from one generation to the next. The significant fact here is that Romani English is no longer transmitted from parent to child as languages generally are, but is acquired through contact with other young adults. As Kenrick has pointed out (Acton and Kenrick 1985), the average six-year-old hardly knows ten words of the lexis and is unlikely to have acquired more than fifty before puberty. At this point, girls learn the language from the younger women of the group and boys from the younger men. In this way, a youngster may learn as many as thirty or forty words in the course of a day's travelling, meeting, at the same time, the various situations in which they may be used.

As represented in print, Romani English song not only constitutes a relatively small part of the Gypsy repertoire, but also shows clear signs of external interference. Taken in isolation, too, certain of its salient features are not without parallel elsewhere. Taken as a whole, however, and, more particularly, viewed in association with other material for which Romani English is not the usual medium of expression, there can be little doubt that contemporary English Gypsy song is fundamentally different in thought and character from the dominant British folk repertoire. That this difference is not simply a function of linguistic and cultural decay, as has sometimes been suggested, but arises from the Gypsies' own peculiar understanding of the world, seems clear from the various similarities which exist between English Gypsy song and its European Romani equivalents. What remains to be seen, however, is whether the 'ad-men' and the TV moguls will prove more successful than the gallows and the branding-iron in breaking down the Gypsies' resistance to *Gaujo* influence, or whether the old language and culture are sufficiently resilient to withstand such new and infinitely more insidious pressures to conform. As with the language, whether or not Gypsy song survives in a recognizable form will depend to a great extent on the way in which it is perceived by the Gypsies themselves and, more particularly, by the younger generation. Whilst I hope that this book may go some way towards highlighting the peculiar flavour and importance of Gypsy song, it would be foolish indeed to suggest that it represents a definitive statement on the subject. Rather, I would like to think that it may encourage others better qualified than me, and preferably from within the Traveller community, to take a fresh look at the subject, to gather and disseminate the as yet unpublished remnants of the tradition, and thus ensure that it remains as productive as it undoubtedly once was.

Gypsy Song Texts

The boshom engro kils, he kils,
The tawnie juva gils, she gils
O puro Romano gillie,
Now shoon the Romano gillie.

The fellow with the fiddle plays, he plays;
The little lassie sings, she sings
An ancient Roman ditty;
Now hear the Roman ditty.

(George Borrow, 1874)

Index of First Lines and Sources

Short Songs

27. Finor Coachey innar Lundra. Anon. (Borrow 1874, 108).
28. As I Bung Through the Dodder's Wood. Cathy Higgins (MacColl and Seeger 1986, 148).
29. Hi, Bara Manishee, Will Ye Bing Wi' Me. Cathy Higgins (MacColl and Seeger 1977, 363; 1986, 281).
30. I've a Hurley and a Prag. Peter Mac Donald, Blairgowrie, July 1955 (Folktracks, 183).
31. It's Hi, Bara Gadjie, Will You Jas Avri. Jimmie McBeath. Banff, 18 November 1953 (Kennedy, Folktracks 441).
32. Hokka Tute Mande. Anon. (Borrow 1874, 104).
33. Del Mandi a Chūma, My Rinkeni Chai. Adolphus Smith (Sampson 1891, 90).
34. Mâ Kin Duva Grai. Johnny Gray (Sampson 1891, 87).
35. Shoon Thimble engro. Anon. (Borrow 1851, 280).
36. Gare Yourselves, Pralor (Borrow 1874, 109).
37. Bing Avree, Barry Gadgie. Jeanie Robertson, 1962 (Henderson, *JSS* 21 (1977), 97).
38. O Ballovas an' Yarrers. Gypsy children near Colney Heath, Herts. 1962 (Kennedy 1975, 748).
39. Bállovas an' Yóras. Anon., Walton on Thames (Leland 1875, 87).
40. We Shall Lel Some Luva. Liberty Buckland, Kingston Blount, 1909 (Wellstood, *JGLS* n.s. 3 (1909), 159).
41. Balowas and Porno. Poly Herne (Sampson 1891, 88).
42. Balêsto Nokyas and Bokochesto Peryas. Anon., Knotty Ash–Prescot road (Sampson 1891, 88).
43. The Beng Del'd Mandi 'dré the dumo. Kenza Smith (Sampson 1891, 90).
44. The Čovahānī and the Čovahāno. Norfolk (Thompson, *JGLS*. n.s. 3 (1909), 157).
45. There's a Chovahanee and a Chovahano. Ambrose Smith? (Borrow 1857, 33).
46. There's a Chovahanee and a Chovahano (Knapp, 387).
47. Koshko Grai, Romano Grai. Smith (Sampson 1891, 93).
48. The Rommany Chal to his Horse Did Say (Borrow 1842, 189).
49. Yek Gurishi Sas Mandi. Brucey Boswell (Sampson 1891, 90).
50. Tuley the Can I Kokkeney Cam. Ryley Bosvil? (Borrow 1874, 162).
51. Canna Marel o Manus. Anon. (Borrow 1851, 156).
52. Vov Sos Bichala dur Cherionos. Anon. (Petulengro, (1948) ch.8).
53. Kai Sī Romanī Grānza. Edward Wood (Sampson 1926, iv, 29).
54. Dâ, Dabla, Dâdi. Cornelius Buckland, alias Fenner or Fender (Winstedt, *JGLS* n.s. 3 (1909), 159).
55. Aai Dadi, Da Dublea Da–di. Alice Gray (Sampson 1892, 83).
56. When I First Chiv'd My Pīro 'Dré de Bōri Gav. Boss (Sampson 1891, 89).
57. Wafri Bak Kairs. Anon. (Leland 1873, 213).
58. Atchin' in the Pudden Ken. John Doran. Waterloo, July 1985 (Coughlan).
59. My Name is Barney Mucafee. Anon., Aberystwyth, 1877 (Leland 1882, 368).
60. I Mislayed to a Grippa and the Gloak He Got So Gammy. Bernie Reilly, King's Court, Co. Cavan, 5 September 1975 (Munnelly, Irish Folklore Commission, TM 446).

61. As I was a Krushing through the Town One Day (Acton and Connors 1974, 11–12. Reprinted in Trudgill 1984, 389).
62. As I Was A-walking Through the Gav One Day. Bill Cooper, 1970 (Acton 1971, 32).

Extended Texts

63. Dic at the Gargers. Anon., Walton on Thames (Leland 1873, 186; 1875, 235).
64. Dic at the Gargers. Job Lee (Smith 1889, 152).
65. When it is Raining, the First Thing in Mind. Charlie Scamp. Canterbury. (Kennedy. Folktracks. 60–441).
66. Mándy's Chávvis shan Bokelo. Matty Cooper (Leland 1875, 98).
67. When We Stops Travelling, the First Thing in Mind. Anon. (Reeve 1958).
68. We Pulls in by the Roadside. Frank Copper, Kent, 1960 (Brune 1975, 793).
69. When it Starts Raining, My First Thing in Mind. Mary Ann Haynes, Sussex, January 1973 (Yates 1975, 63).
70. When We Stops Travelling, the First Thing in Mind (Stanley and Burke 1986, 8).
71. When it's Raining, the First Thing in Mind. Nelson Ridley (MacColl and Seeger 1977, 361).
72. We Packed up Our Tent-Rods, Our Ridge-Poles, Our Pots and Kittles. Carolyne Hughes, Blandford, 1966 (MacColl and Seeger 1977, 362).
73. We Went Along the Drom 'Til We Did Stop. Anon. (Stanley and Burke 1986, 13)
74. Mandi Jall'd to Puv a Grai. Anon, New Forest (Gillington 1911, no.2).
75. Well Done, My Gorgio. Prices, Swansea (Groome 1880, 50).
76. Cush Dearie Romany Chile. Gypsy children, Upton Manor (Smith 1889, 139).
77. I'm Jalling across the Pani. Anon. (Borrow 1874, 106).
78. Mandy Welled to Puv the Grys. Anon. (Gillington, *JGLS* n.s. 1. (1907), 164).
79. Mandy Went to Puv Some Griys. Lucy Curtis (née Smith). Cowley, January 1908 (Wellstood and Winstedt, *JGLS* n.s. 3 (1909), 158).
80. Mandi Well'd to Puv the Grai. New Forest (Gillington 1911, no.4).
81. Mandi Went to Poove the Grys. Frank Copper, W. Kent, 1960 (Brune 1975, 777).
82. O 'Tis Mandi Went to Poov the Grais. Carolyne Hughes, Blandford, 1962 (MacColl and Seeger 1977, 359).
83. Mandi Went to Puv the Grais. Carolyne Hughes, Blandford, 1968 (Kennedy, Folktracks 60–441).
84. Mandi Jelled to Puv the Grai. Bill Kerswell (Traveller Education, no.2(5), 32).
85. Mandy Went to Pouv the Gries. Maggie Gratton (Coughlan, personal communication, April 1993).
86. Mandi Went to Poove the Grai. Amos Smith (Sandford, 1995, 38).
87. Jal Down to the Stágus. Esther Buckland (née Smith) (Atkinson, *JGLS* 3 (1909), 158).

88. Mandi Went in a Woš. Anon., Epsom races, June 1910 (Robert Phillimore, *JGLS* 6 (1912), 67).
89. All Through the Rakoli. Anon. Epsom races, June 1910 (Robert Phillimore *JGLS* 6 (1912), 67–8).
90. Well Done My Romani Tšavi. 'Egyptian rogues about Watford and Radlett'. (*JGLS* 6 (1912), 68).
91. Mandi's Jâin' to Stariben. Charlie Webb (Thompson, *JGLS* n.s. 3 (1909), 158).
92. Now, All Through Mi Rakli. Mary Ann Haynes, Sussex, January 1973 (Yates 1975, 71). Reproduced in Trudgill (Hancock 1984, 381).
93. Mandi Went to th' Wesh One Night. Mary Ann Haynes (Burke and Stanley 1986, 9).
94. O, a Beggin' I will Go. Carolyne Hughes, Blandford, 1966 (MacColl and Seeger 1977, 358).
95. I'm The Romani Rai. Anon. (Acton 1981, 33).
96. I'm a Romani Rai. Mark o'Gallaidhe (Sandford 1995, 27).
97. I'm a Romani Rye, a Dear Didikai. Anon. (Richardson 1976–7, 23).
98. I'm No Romany Rye. John Smith, Birmingham, 1962 (Brune 1975, 750).
99. I were Borned in an Old Gypsy's Wagon. Phoebe Smith (Kennedy. Folktracks).
100. Del Mandy the Romanichals Meriben. Anon. (Thompson 1910).
101. It's Kushto in Tattoben. Anon. (Leland 1874, 143).
102. Dui Hundred Besh a Hatchin'. Anon. (Leland 1875, 31).
103. If Ever I Dae Gang a-Chorin'. Travellers at Fillans, Loch Aern, Perthshire, 1956 (Brune 1975, 768).
104. When I Jâs a-Čoring. Esther Buckland (née Smith) (Atkinson, *JGLS* 3 (1909), 159).
105. O My Name it is Big Jimmie Drummond. Big Willie McPhee (MacColl and Seeger 1977, 296).
106. For Ma Name it is Young Jimmy Drummond. Jeanie Robertson (*JSS* 21 (1977), 96.
107. I Was Neatly Handcuffed and Shackled. Jeanie Robertson, Aberdeen, 10 November 1953 (Folktracks 60–441).
108. O My Name it is Young Jimmy Drummond. Jessie Mac Donald (Hall 1975, 57).
109. Last Night I Lay in a Gransee. John Mac Donald (Peter Shepherd. Hall 1975, 56)
110. O, Last Nicht I Was in the Granzi. Davey Stewart, Dundee, 3 June 1953 (Kennedy. Folktracks 60–441).
111. When Mandi Went a-Kannying. Jim Penfold (Stanley and Burke 1986, 19).
112. For There Was a Nasty Broom-Dasher. Levi Smith, Surrey, May 1974 (Yates 1975, 72).
113. We All Went on a Christmas Day. Anon., New Forest (Gillington 1911, no.3).
114. It's a Kušti Bright Rāti. Israel Smith, Stratford on Avon, 1909 (*JGLS* n.s. 3 (1909), 160).
115. When I Pandered the Pósinakás. Philip Murray (Sampson, 1892. *JGLS* o.s. JGLS, 3, 78).

116. Ekkery, Akkery, ukery An. Philadelphia (Leland 1891, 209). 116(a). Ek-keri (yekori) akai-ri, you Kair An (Leland 1891, 210).
117. Britannia is My Nav. Britannia Lovell (Borrow 1874, 133).
118. Mandi's Churri Purri Dai. Lias Robinson (Sampson 1891, 86).
119. Oh! I Jāssed to the Kér. Anon., Brighton, *c.*1870 (Leland, 1875, 131). See also Smith 1889, 121.
120. Coin si Deya, Coin se Dado. Anon. (Borrow 1874, 14).
121. Kâlo Kâlo Komlo. Manful — ? (Sampson 1891, 92).
122. Charlotta Is My Nav (Borrow 1874, 140).
123. As I Was a Jawing to the Gav Yeck Divvus. Anon. (Borrow 1841, 432).
124. As I Was a Jawing to the Gav Yeck Divvus (Borrow 1874, 104).
125. As Mandi Was a Jallin' to the Bōro Gav. Teni Mullenger (née Robinson). Blackpool. (Sampson, *JGLS.* o.s. 2. (1891), 191).
126. There's a Rauney Jessin on the Tober. Anon., Walton on Thames (Leland 1875, 233).
127. Av My Little Romany Chal. Anon. (Borrow 1874, 100).
128. Av, My Little Romany Chel. Anon. (Borrow 1874, 101).
129. If You're a Drūkerimongero. Philip Murray (Sampson 1892, 75).
130. Daisy's Chai Across y Dera. Manfri Wood, Penybont Fawr, November 1954 (Kennedy: Folktracks 60–441).
131. 'Doi Sas Chai 'Cross y Dor(i)a(v). Corrective to 130. Coughlan.
132. My Mush is Jal'd and the Beng may Lel Him. Florence Lovell? Liverpool (Sampson 1891, 89).
133. Romani Čai Bešing Adré the Tan. Lavinia and Esther Smith, Norfolk (Thompson, *JGLS* n.s. 3 (1909), 157).
134. Penn'd the Romany Chi Ké Laki Dye. Anon. (Borrow 1857, 44).
135. Casro Manishi-o. Davie Stewart, Dundee, Angus, 1960 (Brune 1975, 766).
136. For Sūvin' This Rokli They Lel'd Me Apré. Philip Murray (Sampson 1892, 79).
137. O Bosh-Kelomengero Beshtas. Anon., Llanrhaeadr-ym-Mochnant, *c.*1956. (Brune 1975, 796).
138. Romany Chalor. Anon. (Borrow 1874, 175).
139. Oko Vela o Chavo. Gypsy children, Rorrington, Shropshire, 1962 (Brune 1975, 780).
140. Ō bå̊rē-čōřéskerō'vela. Anon. (Sampson 1926, iv, 70).
141. Ki Did the Romanys Hatch the Tan. Vitruvius Stanley, Weybridge (Leland, *Hood's Comic Annual* 19 (1887), p.66).
142. O, Mandy Had a Gry. Sylvestros Stanley, Weybridge (Leland, *Hood's Comic Annual* 19 (1887), 65–7).
143. Keker mandi koms kek juvel (Sampson 1891, 91).
144. The Givengro Rye he Penned. Artaros Stanley, Weybridge (Leland, *Hood's Comic Annual* 19 (1887), 65–7.
145. My Dai's Cherikl Never Puker'd a Hukipen. Lee (Sampson 1891, 91).
146. Shūn the Húnnalo o' the Pánni. Matty Cooper (Leland 1875, 129).
147. Mi Deeri Duvvulesti, Kair Sig Shunessu Mandy. Mrs Cooper (née Eliza James?), Swindon, 1860 (Norwood).
148. O Bōro Divvúsko Dívvus. Matty Cooper (Leland 1875, 187).

Songs from the Mainstream

Short Songs

The following examples of one-line texts were collected by John Brune, along with other non-folkloric material, whilst gathering information for the first 'Memorandum of the Gypsy Council' to the Ministry of Housing and Local Government in 1967 and were first published eight years later in Kennedy's *Folksongs of Britain and Ireland* (Kennedy 1975, 748). They may well have come from Abraham Cooper or one of the Smiths or Scamps. As Brune points out, however, it is sometimes difficult to know if an informant has given his true name.

1. Ballovas an' yarrers.
2. Mandi jalled to poove the gry.
3. Mangen mas y moro.
4. Poove the groi, chav.
5. Purdilo baval.

Of the above, texts 1 and 2 have been recorded elsewhere on a number of occasions as forming part of a longer song (see texts 36–40 and 70). Whilst a slight variant of text 3 forms the refrain of Borrow's 'Tugnis Amande' (text 73):

> I'm jalling across the lpani –
> A choring mas and morro . . .

Text 4 would seem to be a variant of text 2 and was presumably used in much the same way. A further variant of the phrase was obtained by Arnold from an Irish Traveller, Lackey Costello, whom he met in up-state New York: 'Chiv the grais in the puv' (Arnold 1898, 220).

Text 5 is of particular interest, not least because it makes use of the inflected form of the verb, now no longer heard in spoken *Romanés*. It also occurs in the Revd Norwood's diary for 16 April 1863: 'baval purdelles'.

His informant was Edwin Buckland of Charlbury, Oxfordshire. Twelve years later, it reappears in Matty Cooper's 'Bokelo Gilli' as 'o shillo bavol purdella' (text 66). More importantly, however, it is also offered by Vekerdi as an example of one of those stereotypical motifs characteristic of much Hungarian (Lovari) Gypsy song: – 'phurdel, balval, phurdel' (Vekerdi 1967, 1).

~

Unlike the foregoing, all but one of the following two-line texts (text 11) stand complete in their own right. Two are in Welsh Romani (texts 13 and 14), whilst the form of language used in texts 6 and 9 is somewhat 'deeper' than that found in more modern songs: for example, the use of the false genitive *jukelesto*, 'of the dog' (text 9).

In content, too, texts 6 and 8 would seem to operate at a much deeper level than the generality of *Poggadi Chib* song, and these three factors – self-sufficiency, language and content – suggest that they may have originated some time prior to their collection.

Text 10 belongs to the same category as text 2, allowing the singer to develop his theme as he pleases. A variant of the first line of this couplet also introduces text 119 and should, perhaps, be taken in isolation.

> 6. Ach, mi kâri! ach, mi kâri!
> Kanna sig men lach minjâri!
> (Isaac Herne, Sampson 1891, 91)

> Arise, my penis! Arise, my penis!
> Soon we will find a vagina!

Isaac Herne, from whom Sampson obtained this couplet, was the son of Mrs Herne, from whom Borrow is thought to have acquired his knowledge of deep Romani. She is not to be confused with that other Mrs Herne – Jasper Petulengro's mother-in-law – whose attempt on Borrow's life forms the subject of chapter 71 of *Lavengro* (see notes accompanying text 119).

Although the termination -*ari* in the second line may have been added to complete the rhyme, it is also possible that it represents an affectionate diminutive. According to Paspati, the Turkish Gypsies form the majority of diminutives in -*oro*, in imitation of the Greeks and Turks (Paspati 1870, 45), and Smart and Crofton have suggested that -*arus* and -*ari* (possibly an old plural ending) may well recall this practice (Smart and Crofton 1875, 18).

The rhyme itself seems to carry within it something far more significant than mere vulgarity. Trigg, in his *Gypsy Demons and Divinities*, has pointed to the fact that, even today, as with devotees of the Hindu Shiva, veneration of the regenerative principle, as symbolized by the male organ, remains, for certain groups of Slavonic Gypsies, their most important form of religious expression. Among these people, particularly the Gypsies of the former Yugoslavia, *kar*, the penis, is held to be not only the primary source of virility and new life but of all good fortune on a more mundane level. So sacred is *kar* in their thinking, says Trigg, that the phrase *hav co kar*, I eat thy penis, may sometimes be heard with reference to God himself as a means of commencing a prayer of supplication. The notion becomes less strange, perhaps, if thought of in the same light as the Roman Catholic doctrine of transubstantiation and, indeed, such prayers are regarded as entirely proper, emphasizing, as they do, the supplicant's own humility and dependence upon his maker.

The phrase *hav co kar* may also be used in general conversation when the speaker wishes to emphasize his own integrity or the truth of what he is saying, a fact which has led Trigg to suppose that it may once have formed the basis of a sacred oath.

All this being so, the size of a man's *kar* assumes great importance and may, indeed, be common knowledge in the community in which he lives. Possession of a large *kar* is thought to bring prosperity and good fortune, not only to its owner but to all who are close to him. Thus the well-endowed youth becomes not only a source of pride and comfort to his family but a highly desirable catch in marriage.

If a man wishes to ensure success on a business trip, it is important that he first have sexual intercourse with his wife or some other woman. Similarly, if he finds a particular task going badly, he has only to touch his *kar* and everything will turn out right. But not only is a man's *kar* the source of good fortune; it, or its representation in wood, clay, bread or other material, also serves as a means of averting bad luck. Thus, if a man meets a priest, a symbol of bad luck for some Gypsies, he has only to touch his *kar* in order to avert any potential evil. Again, a phallus or likeness of *kar* may be placed above the door or windows of a house or van, both as an object of prayer and as a talisman.

Although there is nothing in the literature to suggest that the penis ever played a significant part in the spiritual life of the English Gypsies, there is equally no reason to suppose that it did not, given their common ancestry with the Gypsies of Yugoslavia and the importance of the phallus in the ancient religions of their Indian homeland. It seems likely, however, from the following quatrain, that, by the mid-nineteenth century, the 'descriptive appellation' *baúro-kauréngro-moosh* (Turkish Rom.: *baré kareskoro*), as recorded by Smart and Crofton (1875, 99), had lost any deeper significance it may once have had. In the following stanza, at least, there can be little doubt that physical pleasure is the principal consideration:

7. Come sŭv me. Come sŭv me.
   Come sŭv me for joy.
   You bâro kâréngero,
   You sŭv like a groi.
   (Philip Murray; Sampson 1892, 76)

Presented with material of this kind, it is hardly surprising that a number of Victorian commentators should have been moved to remark on what they took to be the indelicate nature of much English Gypsy verse. Bataillard, for example, knew

from good sources that the popular literature of the Gypsies, which is nowhere rich, except for the tales of a few countries in the east, is particularly poor in England – especially in poems; and that, as elsewhere, most of their poems contain obscene and coarse details which prevent their presentation to the general public. (Bataillard 1876, 167. See also Crofton 1875, 385; Sampson 1891, 91; 1892, 76)

Sampson, too, normally the least squeamish of observers, says only of the following quatrain that the song which it introduced was 'certainly too bold for these pages':

8. Oh av along with me,
   And you jukl you will see
   How boki you will be
   With your bold drukerimóngero.
   (Philip Murray; Sampson 1892, 75)

That the English Gypsies' taste for the Rabelaisian was, at least, shared by the Gypsies of Spain is apparent from the following verse, one of two similar pieces included by Salom in his *Gitanos: Llibre d'Amor i de Pietat*, published in Barcelona in 1911:

El minche de esa rumi*
Dicen no tenela bales;
Los he dicaito yo
Los tenela muy juncales.

That woman's quim –
They say it has no hairs.
I have seen them
She has them very bushy.

*J. Steuart Maclaren gives *yumi* = *mulier publica* – perhaps a more appropriate usage in the present context.

The following stanza on the same subject is somewhat more oblique in character, though the meaning is nonetheless clear. It belongs to a Vlax Gypsy dance song from Slovakia:

> Beslas i séj po hordovo,
> Taj ci jánava soj tela la.
> Kali mackaj tela late,
> Phurdel o beng ande late!
>
> There sat the girl on the barrel,
> And I don't know what is under her.
> There is a black cat under her,
> The devil should blow into her!
> (Kovalcsik 1985, 149)

A similar want of taste, if such it be, was also rightly thought to inform much of the Canting repertoire as it emerged in the late sixteenth and early seventeenth centuries. So much so, indeed, that in an age somewhat less noted for restraint than the late 1890s, the author of *The English Rogue* (1660) clearly thought discretion the better course: 'We then sing a catch or two in our own language, of which we had good store, which, for their bawdry, I omit.'

It would, however, be unwise to read too much into all this. Honest-to-goodness sex is, after all, as well represented in the folk repertoire of most nations as is romantic love – even in the green and pleasant heartland of the English pastoral tradition (see, for example, Richards and Stubbs 1979, 141–51). Indeed, disappointing as Sampson's occasional bouts of good taste may be, they are as nothing compared with the outright textual vandalism practised by the more squeamish of late Victorian and early Edwardian collectors on discovering for the first time that the arcadian vision they had created for themselves also had its darker side. Even Vaughan Williams was by no means blameless in this respect, although he was quick enough to recognize the fault in others:

> We have not hesitated to include words, verses or whole texts which earlier collectors prudishly modified or omitted as being objectionable. The old habit of cleaning up or even entirely rewriting the texts led to the false supposition that folk songs are always 'quite nice'. The folk singer has no objection to plain speech. He is likely to be forthright in his treatment of the pleasures and pains of love though he may class some songs as 'outway rude' which we think quite harmless.

It is also noticeable that among Travellers, whatever their attitude to female morality generally, ribaldry is by no means a purely masculine preserve. Although sung by a man, Murray's song (text 7) was clearly composed by or for a woman and there can be no doubting the authorship of the following celebration of *kari* in Belle Stewart's song of Jimmy Stewart, 'The Highland Chief', his wife 'Brockie' and his 'twa wheeled cart':

> Now his kari was twelve inches long,
> And the colour of it was yellow;
> And he bunged it into Brockie's cheet,
> At the back o' his wee barrow.
>
> Oh, Jimmy, that's an awfu' thing;
> I have never seen its marrow;
> An' gin another nine month's time,
> I'll be bigger than your barrow.
>
> (Folktracks 184, A6)

~

> 9. Jukelésto* põri
> Kel an de põri.
> (Tom Lee; Sampson 1891, 91)

*The use of the dative ending, *-esto*, instead of the genitive, *-esko*, was once widespread among such northern families as the Bosses and the Boswells and, to a lesser extent, the Grays, Herons and Lees; cf. *balesti camyas*, pig's cheeks; and *balesto varo*, pig meal (I. Heron and Dur. Lee, *JGLS* 3rd ser. 27 (1948), 102. It is a usage peculiar to the English dialect and would seem to be the result of a gradual confusion between the genitive masculine singular *-eskoro* and the first and second dative singular endings *-este* and *-eske* (Paspati 1870, 50–1), influenced, perhaps, by the idiomatic use of the latter in denoting possession; e.g. *doóva stáardi see lésti*, lit. that hat is to him (Smart and Crofton 1875, 14).

Tom Lee, from whom Sampson obtained this verse, told him that 'it used to be sung on certain occasions by Gypsy children when he was a lad'. Although we are not told what these occasions were, it seems reasonable to suppose that Lee was referring to the mating of dogs, for the couplet appears to revolve around a play on the word *pori*, tail. Presumably, what is meant is that the dog's tail (i.e. his penis) makes play at the tail-end of the bitch. Once again, however, as with text 6, one is tempted to suppose that there may be more to this than mere vulgarity.

In a chapter dealing with Gypsy love magic and owing much to the work of H. von Wlislocki, C. G. Leland (1891) offers the following love charm which, he says, 'belongs to ancient black witchcraft and is known far and wide'. When dogs are coupling, the young man suddenly covers them with a cloth, repeating the following words. The cloth is afterwards given to the girl he wishes to win.

> Me jiuklo, yoy jiukli,
> yoy tover, me pori,
> me kokosh, yoy catra,
> ada ada me kamav.

> I the dog, she the bitch,
> She the axe, I the helve,
> I the cock, she the hen,
> This, this (be as) I wish.

Another Hungarian Gypsy charm involving dogs is the following, also collected by Wlislocki and published by MacRitchie in the *JGLS* for June 1890. On New Year's Eve, the girls would gather round a tree and, shaking it by turns, repeat these words:

> Perde, perde, prajtina,
> varekaj hin, hasz kamav?
> basa paro dsziuklo,
> Pirano dzsal mai szygo.

> Scattered leaves, around I see.
> Where can my true love be?
> Ah, the white dog barks at last
> And my love comes running past.

If during the singing a dog is heard barking, then the girl will be married before the year is out.

One cannot leave the subject of dogs without mentioning the fact that, according to Wlislocki, the Kukaya clan of southern Hungary believed themselves to be of canine descent. In his paper on the genealogy and family relationships of the Transylvanian tent Gypsies, he tells how, according to the myth, there were in the world, many thousands of years ago, a small number of 'pchuvushi' – beings of human form, dwelling under the earth. And if the women of this race were unattractive, the men were even more so, being entirely covered in hair. Every now and again, they would visit the surface of the earth in order to steal mortal girls for wives.

Once, the story goes, a young *pchuvush* woman came up to the world and sat in a beautiful green forest. There she saw a handsome young man sleeping in the shade and thought aloud how wonderful it would be to have such a one for a husband. Her man, who had followed her, heard what she said but, far from being angry, thought to himself what a good idea it would be to lend his wife to the youth that she might give birth to a family of beautiful children which he could then sell to his rich friends. With this in mind, he said to his wife that she might live with the young man for ten years if she would promise to deliver up to him every girl or every boy she bore him. His wife agreed and when the youth awoke, the goblin offered him much gold and silver if he, too, would consent to the bargain.

So the fairy woman lived with her mortal man for ten years and every year brought forth a beautiful son. When the goblin came to collect his prize, the woman told him that she had decided to keep the sons and let him have the daughters but that, unfortunately, there were, as yet, none to give. On hearing this, the goblin turned sorrowfully away, uttering the following words:

> Kuku, Kukaya!
> Ada kin jiukla!
> Kuku, Kukaya!
>
> Kuku, Kukaya!
> These are dogs here!
> Kuku, Kukaya!

Then the ten boys laughed and said to their father: 'We shall call ourselves Kukaya', and so the race was born.

~

> 10. Kek man camov te jib bolli-mengreskoenes,
> Man camov te jib weshenjugalogonaes.
>
> I do not wish to live like a baptized person,
> I wish to live like a dog of the wood.
> (Borrow 1874, 14)

In introducing this couplet, Borrow has the following to say:

Though the English Gypsy is generally spoken with a considerable alloy of English words and grammatical forms, enough of its proper words and features remain to form genuine Gypsy sentences which shall be understood not only by the Gypsies of England, but by those of Russia, Hungary, Wallachia and even of Turkey.

Whether this particular couplet ever issued from the mouth of an English Gypsy or, indeed, any Gypsy, is, however, open to question. As regards *bolli-mengreskoenaes*, Smart and Crofton note that there would seem to have been a number of verbs in continental Romani which, although apparently once available in English Gypsy, had long since fallen out of use (Smart and Crofton 1875, 40). The roots of a number of such lost verbs were, however, they go on to say, remembered in such derivative formations as *posh-beenomus*, placenta (lit. half-birth), and *stariben*, prison, which may be referred respectively to the Turkish Gypsy *benava*, to lie in, and *astarava*, to seize.

A further example, mentioned by Smart and Crofton and also found elsewhere in the literature, is *bolesko-divvus*, Christmas Day (lit. christening day), from *bolava*, to dip, used in its figurative sense, to baptize. Leland, in one of his stories (1882, 326), uses it to develop his own word *nebollongri*, unchristians, and, in noting this, Sampson suggests that he may have had in mind one of the 'variations played upon it' by Borrow, from which we may infer that he, at least, had his doubts regarding the authenticity of the term.

Be that as it may, Borrow's assertion that enough of the old language remained in his day to allow the formation of sentences which might be understood by the Gypsies of eastern Europe and Asia Minor is not as fanciful as it might seem. On p.252 of *In Gypsy Tents*, Groome makes the same point in respect of Sylvanus Lovell, '. . . whole sentences of whose Romanes would be quite intelligible to Turkish *Tchinghianés* . . .'. See also Smart and Crofton (1875, 272) for a set of comparative sentences in English and Turkish Romani. In order to test the resemblance between the two dialects, they say, they 'asked in English the following Gypsy sentences taken at random from Dr. Paspati's book. Parallelism could be drawn much closer by carefully selecting corresponding English Gypsy words, but, on principle, we have preferred a Gypsy's own language, even when unnecessarily discordant.' Three examples will suffice here:

Turk. Gyp. Savo mas kamena? (plural)
Eng. Gyp.   Savo mas kamessa? (singular)
English   What meat do you like?

Turk. Gyp. Sosta utchardán i khaning?
Eng. Gyp.   Soske chordán too o hanik?
English   Why did you steal the sword?

Turk. Gyp. Dinómas toot, ta na linánas len.
Eng. Gyp.   Mándi diom lendi toot, ta kek nanei too lian len.
English   I gave them to you and you did not take them.

Short Songs

~

11. Mandi jilled to the rakli's ken
    To mang a pair o' chockers.
                    (Kennedy 1975, 748)

A typical example of an opening gambit used to introduce an improvised account of the events of the day, the foregoing is broadly coincident with the opening lines of Leland's song of *Mulo Balor* (text 119):

O, I jassed to the kér
An' I tried to mang the balor . . .

~

12. Mickie, Huwie and Larry,
    Trin indity-mengre fashionovangust-engre.
                    (Borrow 1874, 148)

This little verse is of interest as, in it, the Gypsies are said to celebrate a family of Tinkers, a set for which, in general, they seem to have had little liking. The couplet refers to three Kerry-born brothers of whom the eldest, Mickie, besides being a notable exponent of the art of false ring-making, was something of a scholar, carrying in his head considerable portions of the work of Tadhg o Sullibháin, an eighteenth-century writer of religious verse.

According to Borrow, the art of false ring-making would seem to have taken precedence over simple tinkering among certain of the London Irish as it was, presumably, a good deal more lucrative. In essence, it consisted in converting cheap brass buttons into rings of counterfeit gold – the buttons worn by Chelsea pensioners being considered particularly suitable for the work. Once made, the rings were either disposed of by direct sale or passed on to 'ring droppers'. These latter were gentrified villains who, having installed their wares in flash boxes with spurious price tags, would let one fall in the street, retrieving it as 'lost property' within sight of a prosperous-looking victim. The ring would then be offered for sale at a price substantially less than that shown on the tag, the 'dropper' explaining the discrepancy by saying that he needed the money and had no time to seek out a dealer.

In the right company, says Borrow, the *hindity-mengré* were quite happy to acknowledge themselves 'cairdean droich oir' (workers in false gold) – a curious usage as the form of language employed here is Scottish rather than Irish Gaelic. This is an elementary error for one who had spent some time in both countries and who claimed more than a nodding acquaintance

212

with the language and literature of both. His remark is also of interest on two further counts. First, contemporary Irish tinkers do not speak Irish; second, is it not strange that one who had won the confidence of the Gypsies, and who was no stranger to the Tinkers, should have failed to have noted the existence of the latter's own secret language – *Shelta*? That he was aware of it but preferred to remain silent seems doubtful for, whilst he may well have been capable of keeping a secret, 'his wish to impress his reader with a certain mysterious notion of himself' would normally have compelled him to make it perfectly clear that such a secret was in his possession. Thus, if we are to believe what he says in chapter 13 of *Lavengro*, he had, when in Ireland, acquired the trick of enraging and pacifying horses by whispering in their ears – a trick which he refuses to divulge but whose mastery he freely and gratuitously acknowledges. By denying the reader this information, Borrow robs the story of much of its point, except as a piece of self-advertisement.

~

The following verses, which are in Welsh Romani, first appeared in print in Sampson's *Dialect of the Gypsies of Wales* (1926). The second was improvised by Harry Wood.

> 13. Okē čakanē te pēr'na!
> Komónī mēr'na.
> (Sampson 1926, iv, 52).
>
> Lo! The shooting stars!
> Someone will die.

Commenting on a passage in the introduction to E. C. Grenville Murray's review of the *Doine* or 'The National Songs of Roumania', Smith includes the following parenthetical note (1889, 21):

The Zingari, who swarm in Moldo-Wallachia and form a class apart, are the same extraordinary people known to us as Gypsies, and who seem to have formed a wandering settlement in most every country in Europe. There was also, I learn, at one time a distinct race of the Zingari settled in Roumania. They called themselves Netoti, and wandered about the forests little better than petty robbers. They had their chiefs, however, and paid a regular tribute to the government. They adored the sun and stars, believing in a faith which they are said to have brought from India. (The popular superstition in Moldavia believes that when anyone dies his star falls from the heavens, as they believe it first appeared there at his birth and influenced his destiny through life.) In 1831 they were forcibly baptised, and became slaves of the Boyards . . .

~

14. Na ĵava mĕ arĕ gavéndī,
    Trašáva mē spīdréndē*,
    Te 'vā ĵukerdō moskeréndé.

I do not go into the towns,
I am afraid of the spiders' (webs)
And of being tracked by constables.
(Harry Wood; Sampson 1926, 127)

*British Romani has no word for spider. Among a number of other equally doubtful
items, Petulengro gives *aranyi* (presumably from the French araignée), whilst Leland,
never at a loss for a word of his own when the genuine article was not available, offers
puv-suver or earth-spinner (1882, 316). The same word also turns up in Dyneley Prince's
American Gypsy vocabulary but there can be little doubt, despite his protestations to
the contrary, that this was based almost entirely on a wholly uncritical reading of
Leland. The fact that Sampson's informant opts for the English 'spider' rather than the
Welsh 'copyn' would suggest that it entered the dialect some time prior to the Gypsies'
removal into Wales.

~

15. Can you rokra Romany?
    Can you play the bosh?
    Can you jal adrey the staripen?
    Can you chin the cost?
    (Wandsworth 1864; Borrow 1874, 137)

Borrow, speaking of the Wandsworth Gypsies, says:

> of the trades of the men,by far the most practised is 'chinning the cost' and
> as they sit at the doors of the tents, cutting and whittling away, they
> occasionally sweeten their toil by raising their voices and singing the
> Gypsy stanza in which the art is mentioned and which, for terseness and
> expressiveness, is quite equal to anything in the whole circle of gentile
> poetry.

Whatever its merits as poetry, 'Can You Rokker Romani' is certainly
one of the best-known of all songs in the *Poggadi Chib*. Indeed, Sampson
was of the opinion that it was 'probably the only song which, in one form
or another, has attained any degree of popular acceptance among our
English Gypsies' (Sampson 1891, 81). Although this is clearly not the case,
his observation is of interest in that it would seem to suggest that songs
such as 'Mandi Jall'd to Puv the Grai' and its various cognates (texts
74–93), 'Well done my Romani Chal' (texts 75–6), 'Dordi, Dordi Dik
Akai' (texts 23–6) and 'I'm The Romani Rai' (texts 95–9) were not widely

214

known at the time or at least not in the north, where the bulk of Sampson's material was collected.

Although 'Can You Rokker Romani' seems to occur in almost as many versions as there are singers, all retain the basic format of a series of questions relating to various activities in which it is apparently thought desirable to excel. From Borrow's account, it would seem to have been used to accompany the manufacture of wooden skewers and pegs and, indeed, the same text appears in L. A. Smith's *Through Romany Songland* as a 'Gypsies' Whittling Song' (Smith 1889, 120). Sampson's version of the song, however, suggests a somewhat different interpretation. It is from the singing of Lolly Lally (Alice Gray) whose family apparently originated in the north-east of England.

> 16. Can you jas to stariben?
>   Can you lel a kosht?
>   Can you besh und'r a bor?
>   Can you kel the bosh?
>   Mīstō, Romni chel,
>   Del les adré his mūi;
>   S'help me dīrī datchen,
>   You can kūr mīstō!
>   Said the Romnī chai to the Romnī Rai.
>   (Alice Gray; Sampson 1891, 81)

The connection between the first and second quatrain of Alice Gray's set is not immediately apparent. Sampson, however, has pointed out that 'lelling a kosh', as well as signifying 'gathering firewood' might also mean 'wielding a cudgel' and, if this is so, then lines 2 and 4 of stanza one might usefully be transposed. 'Beshing under the bor' may either mean 'sleeping out' or, as Borrow's Ursula knew only too well, the formal act of courtship – an interpretation to which the second couplet of the following set lends positive support (see also line 4 of text 126):

> 17. O! Can you rokka Romanes?
>   Can you play the bosh?
>   O! Can you kiss the pretty rawni
>   Underneath the kaush? [hedge]*
>   (New Forest; Gillington 1911, no.1)

*A somewhat unusual use of this word and one which is not to be found in the composite vocabulary from Holybourne and Lindhurst published fourteen years later in the *JGLS* but collected some time earlier (*JGLS* 3rd ser., 4 (1925), 115–39). The common term for hedge is *bor* (Smart and Crofton 1875, 175).

Against this background, it might be argued that the song was originally intended to capture something of the flavour of a Gypsy girl's interrogation of a prospective lover. Would he be willing to go to jail for her? Can he play the fiddle and can he handle himself in a fight? Although it may be tempting to suppose that, in Sampson's set, the girl goes on to choose between two lads who fight for her affections, we must be cautious of assuming that the two halves of Lolly Lally's song necessarily belong together. The second quatrain has been noted elsewhere on a number of occasions, both in isolation and in association with other unrelated material (see notes following text 74).

As evidence of the song's durability, Brune has rightly drawn attention to the striking similarity between Borrow's 1874 version (text 15) and that given by Solomon Smith in May 1960:

> 18. Can you rocker Romany
>   Can you kil the bosh?
>   Can you jall the sturraben?
>   An' can you chin the kosh?
>   (Solomon Smith; Brune 1975, 748)

Smith believed that his version had once been in general use although now everyone was putting it differently – a fact which, coupled with his inability to give the meaning of 'kil the bosh', would suggest that he had obtained the song from another, possibly older, Gypsy with a deeper knowledge of the language.

Given its longevity and broad appeal, Brune may also be right in wondering if the song's persistence is due to some hidden significance rather than mere fluke. Although he does not pursue the thought, it is certainly the case that the first question always asked – with the exception of Lolly Lally's set – would be of prime importance to a people whose language and culture were under threat; hence, the following saying of the Lovari Rom: *amari shib si amari zor*, our language is our strength. In Irish, too, we find a similar sentiment expressed in *gan teanga gan tír*, no language, no land, and *tír gan teanga tír gan anam*, a land without a language is a land without a soul, whilst precisely the same point is made in the following triplet given to Edward Lhuyd by the clerk of St Just's in 1700 whilst the former was collecting material for the Cornish section of his *Archeologica Britannica* (for the second of two surviving sets see Berresford Ellis 1974, 103):

> An lavar goth ewe lavar gwîr,
> Ne vedn nevera doas vâs a tavas re hîr,
> Bes den heb tavas a gollas e dîr.

The old saying is a true saying,
Never will come good from tongue too long,
But a man without a tongue shall lose his land.

On p.107 of *The English Gypsies and Their Language*, Leland also gives the following in the *Poggadi Chib*: 'we're lullero adoi we don't jin the jib' (We're done when we don't understand the language).

Although the mere speaking of Romani was never a capital offence in Britain, this is likely to have been of small comfort to even the most loquacious of Travellers when he or she might go to the gallows anyway, just for being a Gypsy. Under an Act of 1554, designed to curb 'their accustomed devilish and naughty Practices and Devices', any Gypsy transported or conveyed into the kingdom was obliged to leave within forty days on pain of death. Those indicted under the Act were, furthermore, denied the protection of any licence or passport previously issued and both the privileges of sanctuary and Benefit of Clergy (1 and 2 Ph. and M. cap. 54). It was eventually repealed in 1783, as 'a law of excessive severity' (23 George 3 cap. 51), by which time the belief had grown up among English Gypsies that 'rokkering Romani' was itself a capital offence. Thus, in Leland's poem, 'A Nasherin Covvaben' (a hanging matter), we find his interlocutor, Old Rosa, insisting:

> Mán'y shundom mi dádas pen lis:
> Tute man pénnis or chin;
> Te buti foki shán náshered
> Ajáfera rakkerin . . .
>
> (Leland 1975, 219)

> I heard my father say it:
> You mustn't speak or write [it];
> Many have been hanged
> just for speaking [it] . . .

In Scotland, too, many Gypsies were condemned simply for being 'callit, knawin, repute and holdin Egyptians', a formula which, as late as 1770, formed part of the indictment against Jameson and M'Donald, whose execution on Linlithgow bridge is described in chapter 4 of Simson's *History* of 1865. Indeed, among the proofs advanced against MacPherson and his comrades at their trial in Banff some seventy years earlier was that they spoke a language which the witnesses could not understand but which was not Irish and that they were suspected of being unable to 'rehearse the Lord's Prayer, the Belieff and the Ten Commands'.

The last time anyone was hanged in England simply for being a wandering Gypsy was when thirteen Travellers were so condemned by the assize court at Bury St Edmunds towards the end of the interregnum (Hoyland 1816, 86–7).

Yet, harsh as the anti-Gypsy legislation of the sixteenth and seventeenth centuries undoubtedly was, it would not, at first glance, appear to have been specifically racist in character but was rather directed against what was perceived as a far wider social evil. The Gypsies, it is true, were something of a novelty as regards their strange appearance and exotic ways, but vagrancy was already endemic and legislative action had clearly been found necessary long before their first appearance in these islands. In Leslie's *History of Scotland*, for example, published in Rome in 1575–8, mention is made of a sixth-century decree of Eugenie (Eoganan), the pupil of St Columba, forbidding certain undesirables the kingdom:

> When, from his childhood up, he was brought up by St. Columba and by him informed in the way of virtue, he took far more trouble to defend his own with weapons than to seek what did not pertain to him, or other men's goods. To wicked men he was ever molestful, all good men he embraced with great love and charity. Cairds and bards, gamesters, gluttons (mimos, bardos, histriones, parasitos) and such kind of men that delighted in nothing but idleness, he banished, for the most part, quite out of his country and compelled many of them to seek their living with all hardship and drudgery. (see Father James Dalrymple's translation of Leslie's Latin text, edited for the STS in 1887–8 by Father E. G. Cody OSB, part ii, p.225)

The same or a similar enactment is also mentioned by Boce, writing some fifty years before Leslie, although in his account the author is said to have been the ninth-century king, Kenneth. Simson, too, mentions that the 'away putting of sorners, fancied fools, vagabonds, outliers, masterful beggars, cairds and such like runners about' was more than once enforced by the Parliament of James II whilst a further Act of the Scottish Parliament of 1449 was directed against 'sorners, overliers and masterful beggars with horses, hounds or other goods' (sorners were a species of itinerant who lived by forcibly quartering themselves on their helpless victims).[14]

In England, too, Harman speaks of those 'lewd loiterers', known variously since Henry III and Edward I's time as '*faitours, roberdsmen, draw-latches* and *valiant beggars*', and against whom 'as short and as speedy a redress' was to be wished 'as hath been of late years for the wretched wily wandering vagabonds calling and naming themselves Egyptians' (Harman 1566–7).

The dissolution of the monasteries and the growing trend towards enclosure further served to swell the ranks of the rootless poor, whilst the attempt to rid the country of private armies in the wake of the Wars of the Roses also resulted in large numbers of household retainers taking to the roads and terrorizing a defenceless population. As an anonymous mid-fifteenth-century ballad puts it:

> Temporal lords be almost gone,
> Householders keep they few or none,
> Which causeth many a goodly man
> For to beg for bread.
> If he steal for necessity,
> There is none other remedy
> But the law will shortly
> Hang him all save the head.

Even as late as the reign of Edward VI, by which time the Gypsies were already the subject of specific legislative action, the English Parliament still found it necessary to target 'tinkers and pedlars' as a particular source of concern:

> For as much as it is evident that tinkers, pedlars and such like vagrant persons are more hurtful to the commonwealth of this realm, be it therefore ordained . . . that . . . no person or persons commonly called pedlars, tinkers, or petty chapmen shall wander or go from one town to another or from place to place out of the town, parish or village where such person shall dwell, and sell pins, points, laces, gloves, knives, glasses, tapes or any such kind of wares whatsoever, or gather coney skin or such like thing, or use or exercise the trade or occupation of a tinker.

So great was the fear and animosity aroused by these itinerants that, having, in its preamble, condemned all 'foolish pity and mercy', the Act of 1547 went on to provide for all able-bodied vagrants to be branded on the breast with a letter V and to be made slaves for two years to any master who might bend them to his will 'by beating, chaining or otherwise, in such work and labour (how vile so ever it be)'. Rooted in desperation rather than in a genuine spirit of reform, the Act was, however, subsequently found to be unworkable and was repealed two years later (Davies 1966).

It is also apparent that many of those laws which did deal specifically with the Gypsies were more concerned with their way of life than their real or imagined ethnicity. Under the Act of 1554, for example, not only were all those under the age of fourteen exempt, but also all those who were prepared to give up that 'naughty, idle and ungodly Life and Company, and be placed in the Service of some honest and able Inhabitant . . . or that shall honestly exercise himself in some Lawful Work or Occupation'.

Again, it might be supposed from the available evidence that these anti-Gypsy laws were not always enforced as vigorously as they might have been. When, for example, the first case under the 1554 Act was eventually brought to trial in Dorset in 1559, the Gypsies concerned were allowed to go free on a technicality despite the Privy Council's advice to the lord lieutenant that the queen considered it 'very convenient that some sharp example and execution should be made upon a number of them'. The Gypsies' defence hinged upon the fact that they had not been 'transported and conveyed' into the kingdom, as specified under the Act, but had made their way there by way of the overland route from Scotland. In the event, they were driven out of the area (an expedient revived under the terms of the 1968 Caravan Sites Act) only to be re-arrested in the neigbouring county of Gloucestershire where they were confined for a while in Gloucester Castle before being scourged through the town.

Many of these laws, too, were directed with equal force against those allying themselves with and pursuing a similar way of life to the Gypsies. Thus, under an Act for the 'further Punishment of Vagabonds calling themselves Egyptians' of 1562, the provisions of the earlier statute of 1554 were extended to cover all those aged fourteen and above who, for a month 'at a Time or at several Times' were found in any company called or calling themselves Egyptians 'or counterfeiting, transforming themselves by their Apparel, Speech or other Behaviour: like unto . . . Egyptians' (5 Eliz. cap.20, 1562).

Whether this law was enforced with uniform severity is, however, again open to question. The Manchester constables' accounts, for example, record a payment of *2s. 8d.* 'for whipping of eight counterfeit Gypsies that were taken with a private search', whilst at Aylesbury in 1577, Roland Gabriel and Katherine Deago were, together with six others, hanged for 'feloniously keeping company with other vagabonds vulgarly called and calling themselves Egyptians and counterfeiting, transforming and altering themselves in dress, language and behaviour'.

So great a nuisance were these 'counterfeit Egyptians' that, in the opinion of some commentators sympathetic to the Gypsy cause, it was they rather than the Gypsies themselves who were largely responsible for the Romanichals' widespread reputation for lawlessness. The Somerset JP Edward Hext was in no doubt. 'But upon peril of my life', he wrote to the lord treasurer in 1596, 'I avow that they [the Gypsies] were never so dangerous as the wandering soldiers and other stout rogues of England . . .' Samuel Roberts, too, writing in the 1830s, speaks of 'rogues and vagabonds of the worst description *personating* Gypsies and *often passing for them*, and it is not improbable but the most of those who have been convicted of the greatest crimes have been of that description of vagabond' (Roberts 1836, 75). Indeed, even as late as 1819, by which time the more severe Tudor legislation had been withdrawn, it was unanimously agreed by the Norfolk Quarter Sessions that 'all those persons wandering in the habits and form of Gypsies are punishable by imprisonment and whipping'. (See also Groome 1880, 230; Borrow 1874, 176; and Crabb *passim*.)

For Fraser, however, the emphasis placed upon 'counterfeit Egyptians' 'arose less from a need to deal with *Gadzé* who were joining Gypsy bands than from a concern to avoid defence quibbles that some one born in England or Wales (even of Gypsy parents) could not, by definition, be considered "an Egyptian"' (Fraser 1992, 133); and, indeed, as he goes on to say, of the ten cases of consorting with and counterfeiting Egyptians which can be traced in the 100 years following implementation of the 1562 Act, many of the defendants can reasonably be identified as Gypsies (see also Fraser 1990 and Thompson 1923).

It is also the case that, whilst much sixteenth- and seventeenth-century legislation was undoubtedly directed against vagrants and vagrancy in general, it is perfectly clear from its obviously capricious application and from the observations of various contemporary commentators that the Gypsies were regarded with particular distaste. To begin with, they were foreigners, easily identified by their clothing, language and appearance. More importantly, perhaps, for a society in which the Saracen, Turk and Jew had for centuries been represented as the principal threat to Christian civilization, the Gypsies, with their dark complexion and real or imagined occult powers, were an obvious target of suspicion. And – as is so often the case when a society feels itself threatened in this way – there is good evidence to suggest that early British commentators sought to justify their hostility through ridicule and abuse, depicting the Gypsies as racially inferior. Thus they are seen as that 'lying *tawny* crew' and as '*tan-faced* loons' only surpassed in ugliness by the demons of hell; as 'the Children of Evil', 'more scattered than Iewes [Jews] and more hated', and as 'Egiptian lice . . . grasshoppers who eate vp the fruits of the earth and the poore corne fields'. This last description from the early Jacobean, Thomas Dekker, also finds a disturbing echo in the writings of the noted nineteenth-century 'philanthropist', George Smith of Coalville. The following is an extract from his address to the Social Science Congress held in Manchester in October 1879:

Some few Gypsies who have arrived at what they consider the highest state of respectable and civilised life, reside in houses which, in ninety-nine cases out of a hundred are in the lowest and most degraded parts of the towns, among the scum and off-scourings of all nations, and, like locusts, they leave a blight behind them wherever they have been . . . lying, begging, thieving, cheating and every other abomination that low cunning craft, backed by ignorance and idleness, can devise, they practise. In some instances, these things are carried out to such a pitch as to render them more like imbeciles than human beings endowed with reasons . . . In many instances they live like pigs and die like dogs.

Almost inevitably, as ignorance bred suspicion and suspicion gave way to fear and hatred, to their obvious outward differences were added a range of unnatural practices which, once established as 'fact' in the popular mind, merely served to reinforce the initial irrational prejudice. Thus, according to Dekker, the barns in which they lay not only housed their 'cook-rooms' and 'supping parlours' but were 'beds of incest, whore-doms, adulteries, and all other black and deadly damned impieties, and here grows the cursed tree of bastardy which is so fruitful. Here are writ the books of all blasphemies, swearing and curses that are so dreadful to be read' (Dekker 1608).

Yet, worse was to follow, for to such commonplace sins were added those of abduction, cannibalism and, above all, complicity in the crucifix-ion (see notes accompanying texts 169, 119 and 139 respectively).

So deep was the contempt in which they were held by some writers, that even their appropriation of the epithet 'Gypsy' was thought to be an affront to those to whom it rightly belonged – the enslavers of Israel, the chosen of God.

Against this background, one cannot help comparing the many atrocities committed against the Gypsies with those earlier acts of violence directed against the Jews. In 1636, for example, the Sheriff of Haddington, in passing sentence on a party of Egyptian Travellers, ordered 'the men to be hangit and the weomen to be drowned; and suche of the weomen as hes children to be scourgit throw the burgh of Hadinton and brunt [burnt] in the cheeke'.

Thomas Pennant, too, speaks of eighteen Gypsies slaughtered at White-foot in Flintshire, adding, 'I cannot learn their crime, possibly there were none, for they might have been legally murdered by the cruel statute of the 1st and 2nd Philip and Mary' (*The History of the Parishes of Whiteford and Holywell* (1796), 35).

Like the Jews, the Gypsies, too, were to be led away in their hundreds of thousands to the death-camps of Nazi Germany and it is right that we should remember their suffering when we contemplate the fearful act of genocide perpetrated upon their fellow wanderers.

Vi man sas ek bari familija,
Murdadas la e kali legija

I had a big family,
The black legion murdered them
     (Jarko Jovanobich, in Sandford 1995, 66)

Yet, how many contemporary Travellers, one wonders, realize the significance of that old Gypsy favourite 'Hugh of Lincoln' or 'The Jew's Garden', given here from the singing of Amy North, as noted by Groome in Shepherds Bush in 1872. According to report, at Eastertide in the year 1255, the Jews of Lincoln abducted the boy, Hugh, and, having tortured him for ten days, crucified him. Eighteen of the *wealthiest* Jews in the city were subsequently hanged and the child buried in state. The story forms the subject of Chaucer's 'Prioress's Tale' (see also Rymer's *Foedera*).

Down in merry merry Scotland,
It rained both hard and small;
Two little boys went out one day,
All for to play with a ball.

They tossed it up so very high,
They tossed it down so low,
They tossed it into the Jew's garden,
Where the flowers all do blow.

Out came one of the Jew's daughters,
Dressed in green all,
'If you come here, my fair pretty lad,
You shall have your ball.'

She showed him an apple as green as grass,
The next thing was a fig,
The next thing a cherry as red as blood,
And that would 'tice him in.

She set him on a golden chair,
And gave him sugar sweet;
Laid him on some golden chest of drawers,
Stabbed him like a sheep.

'Seven foot Bible
At my head and my feet;
If my mother pass by me,
Pray tell her I'm asleep.'
     (Groome 1880, 145)

For the negative attitude of some Gypsies towards their language see 'British Romani and the *Poggadi Chib*' above.

~

Another element common to a number of variants of the 'Can You Rokker Romani' type is the fiddle – the only instrument mentioned in the *Poggadi Chib* repertoire. Its undoubted importance both as a source of income and entertainment is discussed in the notes following text 137.

The following variants are typical of the pattern established in Borrow's 1874 version of 'Can you Rokker Romani'. Texts 19, 20 and 21 are taken from p.749 of *Folk Songs of Britain and Ireland* (Kennedy 1975); and text 22 is a composite version drawn from Stanley and Burke's *Romano Drom Song Book* (1986, 6) and repeated, with a few minor differences in spelling, on p.40 of Sandford's *Songs by the Roadside* (1995). A prose version is also to be found in chapter 18 of Petulengro's *A Romany Life* – a work apparently owing as much to the author's powers of invention as to his powers of recall:

A Romany mother in her lullabies makes her child promise three things: to rokker Romany, to kil-i-bosh and nante della a gorgio vek a kash (to speak Romanes, to play the fiddle and never to hit a Gajo with a stick). Having mastered these three precepts, he then goes on to learn how to catch and cook his own food . . .

Nante and *vek* would seem to be drawn respectively from Italian (*niente*) and French (*avec*). They are found in no other English Romani vocabulary, although the former has been recorded both for *Polari* (Hancock 1984) and Showman's Slang (Norman, personal communication, 1993).

19. Can you pooker Romany?
Can you Didikai?
Can you chor a cannie
While the mush is jallin' by?
(Wally Fuller, Laughton, near Lewes, Sussex,
11 November 1952; Kennedy 1975, 749)

Mr Fuller's version also appears on 'Can you Pooker Romanes' (Folktracks 60–441), and is there accompanied by the following explanation:

It means in other words, it means that we went to pinch some chicken, like, and the mush was coming – that means the man was coming, the bloke was coming, like. I says 'look out, Joey, here jals a man' – that means the bloke, like – so we both walked out of the gate, like, and away we went.

224

20. Now can you rocker Romany?
    An' can you lel a mush?
    An' can you chor a cannie?
    And a bittie kosh?
      (John Smith, Birmingham, 1962; Brune 1975, 749)

21. Can you rocker Romany?
    Can you pook a kosh? (read a sign-post)
    Can you mor (hit) a gavmush?
    With a knobbly kosh?
      (Frank Smith, A2 trunk road,
      August 1963; Brune 1975, 749)

22. Can you rokker Romani?
    Can you fake the bosh?
    Can you dik the vesher,
    While mandi chins the kosh?

    Can you rokker Romani?
    Can you puv a grai?
    Can you chor a kanni,
    While the mush is jelling by?

    Can you rokker Romani?
    Can you dukker a rai?
    Can you rokker Romesa,*
    And pukker as good as I?

    The musgroes avved along one day,
    To atch us on the drom,
    But when they dikked how many we was,
    They turned around and ran.

    I can pukker Romani,
    I can fake the bosh.
    I can dik a gavver mush,
    While tutti chins the kosh.

*Either the old instrumental case: = with a Rom (Smart and Crofton 1875, 15) or *Rom* + *asa* – an emphatic but with the primary meaning 'too' or 'also'.

~

23. Dick akai, Didikai*
    Daddy's jalled to poove the gry
    Off the drom into the tan
    At five o'clock torarty.
                        (Brune 1975, 748)

*Generally taken to mean 'half-breed'; perhaps a corruption of *dik akai*, look here. According to one tradition, those of mixed blood were also compared with Royston rooks, a variety distinguished by their whitish-grey backs. One of their kind, it is said, went among the rooks and was asked where he got his white coat. 'Why', came the reply, 'from those blessed fools, the pigeons.' Later, he went to visit these same pigeons and was asked where he got his fine black trousers. 'Why', said he, 'I stole them from those infernal ruffians, the rooks!'

The above was taken from the singing of Gypsy children beside the A2 near Stone in Kent. It first appeared in print in 1909 as part of an extended text (text 83) noted by Robert Phillimore 'at the prastering of the grais at Epsom' and forwarded to the Gypsy Lore Society by the Revd C. L. Marson:

24. Ušitel,[?]* didikai,
    Your father's gone to puv the grai,
    Na[?near]* the tober skai,[?]*
    Six o'clock in the morning.
                        (*JGLS*, 6 (1912), 68)

*Phillimore (or Marson) queries 'usitel', 'na' and 'tober skai', suggesting merely that the second might be a corruption of the English 'near'.

Palmer, in the vocabulary accompanying Leland, Palmer and Tuckey's *English Gypsy Songs*, gives *hushti*, to rise, as a variant of the even more unusual *hunter* or *huter*, whilst Leland, himself, on p.102 of *The English Gypsies and Their Language*, includes the following: 'Hatch apré! Hushti! The prastramengro's wellin!' (Jump up! Wide awake there! The policeman's coming!). Cf. Welsh Rom.: *ustilo* (to arise, get up) which, used reflexively, may also mean 'to rouse oneself'; e.g. *ne ne, ba, uste tut*, now then, mate, rouse thyself! (Sampson 1926, 389).

'Tober skai', on the other hand, is good *Shelta* for 'river' – *tober* is a back-formation of Irish *bóthar* (road) and *skai* = Irish *uisge* (water). *Tober* also appears in Palmer's vocabulary but is not there identified as *Shelta*.

A version of the song also appears on p.27 of Webb's *Gypsies*, where it is described as 'a sort of Romani nursery rhyme, one of those meaningless pieces of jingle, not at all unlike the nursery rhymes of our own childhood, which small dark-skinned children still sing at their mother's knee beside the wood fires'. He remembers hearing it, he says, one evening in March, shortly after the war. Webb's book is otherwise remarkable for the inclusion of a chapter entitled 'A Song and a Dance and a Story' in which he offers not so much as a single line of Gypsy verse by way of illustration.

25. Dik akai, didakai,
   Dadrus gone to poov the groi,
   Off the drom and into the tan,
   Five o'clock o' the rarti.
   (Webb 1960, 27)

The rhyme is still widely known and well deserves its inclusion in Stanley and Burke's *Romano Drom Song Book*:

26. Dordi, dordi, dik akai,
   Dadrus' jelled to puv the grai.
   Off the drom into the tan
   At twelve o'clock to-rarti.
   (Stanley and Burke 1986, 28)

As mentioned in the introduction, lullabies and dandling songs apparently no longer feature in the *Poggadi Chib* repertoire. Borrow, however, does include the following in his *Romano Lavo-Lil* and, although he says nothing regarding its origin or use, it seems likely that it was intended to be sung either by or to a young child:

27. Finor coachey innar Lundra,
   Bonor coachey innar Lundra,
   Finor coachey, bonor coachey,
   Mande dick'd innar Lundra.

   Bonor, finor coachey
   Mande dick'd innar Lundra
   The divvus the Kralyissa jall'd
   To congri innar Lundra.
   (Borrow 1874, 108)

Lullabies are also by no means plentiful in Scottish Travellers' Cant. The following example is from Cathie Higgins, née Stewart (see also text 160):

28. As I bung through the dodder's baysh,
   Deekin' for a kinchen,
   There I found a kinchen,
   Its jurvil was a' ajeer.

227

> Hush-a-ba, babbie,
> Lang-legged kinchen,
> If it wasnae for your lang legs,
> I'd gie ye a suck o' my sucklers.
> > (Cathie Higgins; MacColl and Seeger 1986, 148)

Mrs Higgins also gave the following English version:

> As I went through the doctor's woods
> Lookin' for a peekie (baby),
> There I found a peekie
> It's airse was a' akakkie (dirty).
>
> Hush-a-ba babbie,
> Lang-legged laddie,
> If it wasnae for your long legs
> I'd gie ye a suck o' my pappy.

The following is another of Mrs Higgins's short songs, which she learned from her mother-in-law, Charlotte:

> 29. Hi, bara manishie, will ye bing wi' me?
> Hi, bara gadgie, I dinnae jan your fee;
> Will ye bing, will ye ja, will ye bing tae the wattle?
> If ye dinnae get habben, ye'll get some peeve.
> > (Cathie Higgins; MacColl and Seeger 1986, 281)

Mrs Higgins belongs to the Stewarts of Blair, a Scots Traveller family who have produced a number of fine singers and musicians. A cross-section of their work is to be found on *The Travelling Stewarts* (Topic Records 12T179) and *The Berry Fields of Blair* (Folktracks 183–5). See also MacColl and Seeger 1977 and 1986; and Munro 1977.

'Long before we reach the date of our first Scotto-Romani list', writes Russell in the introduction to his composite vocabulary of 1914,

> the Gypsies of Scotland – probably because they were too few in number to stand alone in a poor and troublous country – had amalgamated with the Tinkers, a nomad class whose ethnology is still a puzzle. Through this union, the Gypsy stream broadened out and became correspondingly shallow . . . The Romani tongue in like manner was debased by the Cant or secret jargon of the Tinkers, losing not only all its inflections but its roots as well. The few hundred Romani words that survive lend a dignity to Scottish

Tinker Cant that elevates it above the jargon of the English Tinker, and entitles it to a place of its own in the Anglo-Romani thesaurus.

Today, Scottish Travellers seem to use the word 'Cant' to refer to their own ethnic speech, whatever form it happens to take. The form of language in use among many border Travellers, such as the Marshalls, Hutchinsons, Wilsons and Stewarts, might more accurately be described as a form of deep northern English Romani, although the border Stewarts are, in fact, related to their central Scottish namesakes. The Romani dialect divide may be said to follow the line of hills south of Glasgow and Edinburgh.

Apart from its Romani element, which seems to include a number of words now lost to the English dialect – such as *kalshies*, britches, *klisti*, soldier, policeman, *musi*, porridge, and *puska*, gun – Scottish Cant also contains a range of other material from a variety of sources. Among these, we may mention in particular, *Shelta*, the original speech of the Tinkers of Ireland and the Gaelic-speaking regions of Scotland (see notes accompanying text 58), old English Thieves' Cant, and lowland Scots. Also to be met with are occasional items from French, German and Latin, and a range of onomatopoeic and echoic forms.

Writing elsewhere of text 29, MacColl and Seeger say that: 'Among Scots Travellers, canting songs appear to be limited to odd lines and stanzas interpolated into otherwise Scottish texts' (1977, 363). Whilst this may hold good as a generalization, it is also the case that some Scottish Travellers at least are capable of extensive improvisation in the Cant (e.g. texts 37 and 62). Occasionally, too, one encounters isolated texts in Cant which, like their Romani English equivalents, may either stand alone or be incorporated into longer improvised sets (e.g. text 109). Others, like the following, may perhaps represent the detritus of longer texts now lost:

> 30. I've a hurley* and a prag,
> And a kushti bit o' swag;
> Will ye jal along the tober, pretty pavio?**
>
> I've a horse and a cart*
> And a tidy bit of gear to sell;
> Will you come along with me along the road . . .
> (Peter Mac Donald, Blairgowrie, July 1955;
> *Ballad Singers in the Berryfields*, Folktracks 183)

*In a list obtained from Travellers in Galloway, M'Cormick gives *hurley* = cow (1907, ix–xxiv).

**According to the singer, 'pretty pavio' means Traveller. Perhaps intended for *Paddy* = tramp. cf. Welsh: *padi*, tramp.

229

MacColl and Seeger also note that a number of Travellers claim to have heard further verses of Mrs Higgins's song. The following is from the singing of Jimmie McBeath. Unfortunately, I cannot vouch for the accuracy of the transcription. The informant appears to have been a little confused and was clearly far from the top of his form (compare, for example, his spirited rendering of 'The Muckin' o' Geordie's Byre' on the *Scottish Studies* album CDTRAX 9001). In v.3, l.1, he transposes the initial letters of 'pudden ken', whilst in v.4, l.1 he gives 'jara' for 'bara'. Similarly, in v.1, l.3 he gives 'hoggins', and in v.2, l.3 'cloggins' for 'noggins'. The meaning of the first two lines of the second verse is unclear and, indeed, the entire piece lacks the clarity and vitality of the other Cant items included in the present collection. In an equally confused postscript (Folktracks 60–441), Mr McBeath explains that a change of lodgings is made necessary because the man of the house objects to the Travellers bringing whisky in with them. This is by no means clear from the text. Mr McBeath adds that he 'learned it up north; there amongst the travelling classes; amongst the real travelling classes. It's a kind of Romani Cant, that; the real Romani Cant . . . it's very very difficult to understand if you're speaking it right, really right . . .'

31. It's hi bara gadji, will you jas avri,
    To the next pudden ken an' your jas upon your fee?
    For the gadgie in the hoggins is na sweet upon your noggins
    An' we'll a' jas avri to the next pudden ken.

    O this in his gadji with his pin for a fee[?]
    And the gadji in this keer house is gonna jan your fee,
    For the gadji in the hcloggins is na sweet upon your noggins,
    And we all jas avri to the next pudden ken.

    O when we go to pudden ken, we didn' know what to dee
    With this gadji in this keer not sweet upon your noggins;
    For this gadji in this keer is not sweet upon your fee
    An' we'll jas avri to the next pudden ken.

    Hi bara gadji, will you jas avri
    Will you come along with me to the next pudden ken?
    For the gadji in the keer is not sweet upon your noggins,
    And we'l all jas avri to the next pudden ken.

    Well, will you, manishi, will you jas avri
    And come along with me (for I'm?) sweet upon your noggins,
    For the gadji in this keer is not sweet upon your noggins
    An' we'll all jas avri to the next pudden ken.
    (Jimmie McBeath, Banff, 18 November 1953; Folktracks 441 B8)

~

32. Hokka* tute mande
    Mande pukkra bebee
    Mande shauvo tute –
    Ava Chi

If to me you prove untrue,
Quickly I'll your auntie tell
I've been over-thick with you –
Yes, my girl, I will.
                    (Borrow 1874, 104)

*Although not found as a verb in Smart and Crofton, Black includes *huka*, to cheat, in his edition of Sinclaire's American Romani vocabulary, published in the *Gypsy Lore Society Journal* for October 1915.

Emotional blackmail also forms the basis of the following quatrain which Sampson obtained from a North Country Traveller named Adolphus Smith but which is, in fact, one of a number of imperfectly recalled 'decoys' devised by Smart and Crofton in an attempt to draw out examples of genuine Gypsy folk poetry.

33. Del mandi a chūma, my rinkeni chai;
    Mandi jins I'll be bitcher'd avrí;
    Tutti's rinkeni mūi mandi'll keker dik apopli,
    And I jin duva'll poger me to zi.*
                    (Adolphus Smith; Sampson 1891, 90).

*Perhaps a mishearing of *dizí*, a once common variant of *zi*, heart (*JGLS* o.s. 3, 246).

~

34. Mâ kin duva grai
    Delamengro – lesti'll mōr tūt:
    Gorjos bin delin' him
    Drab sor de divus.
                    (Johnnie Gray; Sampson 1891, 87)

An example of functional improvisation, regarding which the singer, Johnny Gray, 'The Good Old Company Mush', had the following to say:

Yek divus, bor, I was at Bury wagâros, and I was a jalin' to kin a grai adoi – a rinkeni bitti grai tai duva sas – when I dik'd my koko prambalating past with his wastas palál his dumo. And he never del'd me so much as a yokeripen, bor, but kep a dikin' down on de ground, and ghivin' a bit of a ghili to his kokero . . . You dik he dusn't pen chichi, bor, for he was a jin'd by sor de ryas and ghivengro gheros adoi.

One day, mate, I was at Bury fair, and I was just a-going to buy a horse there – a pretty little horse it was too – when I saw my uncle 'prambalating' past with his hands behind his back. And he never gave me so much as a glance, mate, but kept a-looking down on the ground and singing a bit of a song to himself . . . You see, he daren't say anything for he was known by all the gentleman and farmers in the place.

One might, perhaps, include in this category of functional improvisation, Borrow's distichous warning to the thimble rigger in chapter 54 of *Lavengro*:

> 35. Shoon thimble engro,
>   Avella gorgio!
>   (Borrow 1851, 280)

Likewise, the following verse, printed on p.109 of *Romano Lavo-Lil*:

> 36. Gare yourselves, pralor!
>   Ma pee kek-komi!
>   The guero's welling –
>   Plastra lesti!
>   (Borrow 1874, 109)

> Hide yourselves, brothers!
> Drink no more!*
> The man's coming –
> Run for it!

*One old Gypsy who seems to have ignored this advice with impunity is remembered in the following epitaph composed by Legh Richmond, the rector of Turvey and author of *The Annals of the Poor*:

> Here lies Jim, the wandering Gypsy
> Who was sometime sober, yet oftener tipsy;
> But with the world he seemed to thrive,
> For he lived to the age of a hundred and five.

The idea of disguising a warning in a song is also found in the following verses taken from the singing of Wisdom Smith, recorded in Cheltenham in January 1974, and published by Yates on p.75 of the *Folk Music Journal* (1975). According to his informant, it was a Gypsy woman singing that song. She sang it in her trailer. Her husband was out poaching, you see, and a policeman was waiting to catch him in the trailer when he returned. Now the woman heard her husband coming, so she warned him not to come in. She took her baby in her arms, because he wasn't sleeping, and sang that song. The policeman thought she was singing the baby to sleep, but she wasn't, she was warning her husband not to come into the trailer . . . That's true, that is.

> You go from my window, my love, go.
> The devil's in the west and we cannot understand.
> Please go from my window, my love, go.
> You go from my window, my love, go.
> The cuckoo's in the nest and we cannot take no rest.
> You go from my window, my love, go.
> You go from my window, my love, go.
> For the devil's in the man and he cannot understand.
> You go from my window, my love, go.

This is not a Gypsy song but may be traced back to Beaumont and Fletcher's *The Knight of the Burning Pestle* (1613) and beyond. For a note on its history and European parallels see pp.186–90 of A. L. Lloyd's *Folk Song in England* (1967).

Songs of warning are also to be found in the Cant repertoire of Scottish Travellers. The following is from Jeanie Robertson as recorded by Hamish Henderson in 1962:

> 37. Bing avree, barry gadgie,
>   Here's the hornies bingin up the glim,
>   For the grae it's eatin the grannin,
>   Bing avree, barry gadgie, O.
>
> Bing avree, barry gadgie,
> Here's the hornies bingin up the glim,
> For the ganny's on the glimmer,
> Bing avree, barry gadgie, O.
>   (Jeanie Robertson, 1962; *JSS* 21 (1977), 99)

An example of an unintentional sung warning is also given on p.38 of Groome's *In Gypsy Tents* where Plato explains how Pyramus and Belcher Lee went to buy some ponies from a group of *Langarians* (Hungarians) whom they met near London.

Well, Belcher was a-looking at this here pony, and all the while one of their women was walking round and round. She had got a baby in her arms and she kept rocking it and rocking it and singing away. What do you think she sang? 'Bángo grai, bángo grai,' broken like; but any fool might know she meant the horse was lame. Leastwise Belcher did, and all he said was, 'You can keep your bóngo grei, and I wish you a very good morning.'

See also text 164 and Wally Fuller's observations on 'Can you Rokker Romani' (text 19).

Much has been said about the value of Romani as a secret language and, indeed, there can be little doubt that it has, on occasion, proved extremely useful in this regard. Yet, whilst there are still many Gypsies who would prefer to remain silent regarding not only its content but its very existence, such reticence would, as matters now stand, appear to be both unrealistic and even counter-productive. In the first place, Romani has long since been thoroughly documented by *Gaujo* scholars assisted by their all too willing Gypsy informants; in the second, if the language is to remain completely hidden, it is difficult to see how it can ever function successfully as a means of private communication in the presence of outsiders without immediately alerting them both to the fact of its existence and to the possibility that it may be being used to their disadvantage. Thus, in the case of Regina *v.* Wilmont, Young and Harmsworth (Chelmsford, July 1975), by translating a letter containing the threat to *muller* the victim, a prison officer was instrumental in securing the defendants' conviction on a charge of premeditated murder.

On certain occasions, it is true, the judicious use of an unobtrusive word may still prove highly effective, as in the case, cited by Kenrick, in which the mother of a young lad, accused of theft and questioned as to his address, called out to him: 'don't forget you've got to 'ave a *kenner*' (house), meaning that he should give the address of a relative as, if the magistrate found out that he lived in a trailer, bail would almost certainly be refused (Kenrick 1971).

Use of the sung warning is, however, by no means confined to the Travelling People. According to tradition, Owain Glyndŵr was warned of Gray's treachery at Sycharth by a timely *englyn*, uttered by the poet Iolo Goch in good literary Welsh, whilst Daniel O'Connell is said to have been alerted to an attempt on his person at a London dinner by a young Irish speaker breaking into postprandial song. Mícheól O Chorduibh of Ros Dómhnach in Co. Mayo also recalls another instance, involving the attempted abduction of a young country girl who had apparently been left in charge of her brother and the baby when her parents had been called away for some reason. Some time toward dawn, a party of men had arrived with a view to carrying her off and forcing her into marriage. The girl persuaded them to allow her to rock the baby to sleep before they left and, by way of a lullaby, sang the following lines which immediately alerted her younger brother who was able to slip away and summon assistance:

> Éirigh a Aoidh agus gabh (go) 'na bhuaileadh,
> Aithris dóf go bhfuil an fuadach ann,
> Ceathar, cúigar, cú agus buachaill.
> > (Béal Oideas; *IML* xiv (1945), 269)

> Rise up Hugh and go to the *bulley*;
> Tell them there is abduction afoot –
> Four, five men, a hound and a boy.

See also notes accompanying text 103.

~

> 38. O ballovas an' yarrers,
> O ballovas an' yarrers,
> An' the rai an' the rawny
> Come jelling up the drom.
> > (Brune 1975, 748)

The foregoing was obtained in 1962 from a group of Gypsy children near Colney Heath in Hertfordshire. It is wholly consistent with the opening stanza of one of Leland's *English Gypsy Songs* of 1875, of which he writes:

A part of this trifling song is of Gypsy origin, and well known to most 'Travellers'. The remainder was composed one day in a tent on the banks of the Thames, with the help of several Gypsies, who greatly admired the rhymes, especially those contributed by themselves. Nothing can be said of it, except that it gives a tolerably accurate idea of the style of much Romany [*sic*] singing.

> 39. *Bállovas an yóras,*
> *Bállovas an yóras,*
> *An the rye an the rāni*
> *A pīrryin āp the drom.*
> If tūtes mándys pīrrynī,
> If tūte's mīri pirrynī,
> Te well tu mándy's pīrrynī,
> Then mándy'll be your Rom.

Mándy latched a hotchewítchi,
A bōro hotchewítchi;
A tūllo hotchewítchi,
A jāllin 'dré the wésh.
'Dói welldé rye te rāni,
O kūshto rye te rani,
An' adói, 'tūll the rūkkor;
Mándy dicked the dūi besh.

Yúl kékn'ai jíndé mándy,
Yúl kékn'ai pénd'te mándy,
Yúl násti shūndé mándy
Díkdom sār o léndy kaired:
If they jínned I dicked the chūmors,
The kūshti bitti chūmors
If they'd jínned I shūned the chūmors
Oh! – the rāni would a-méred.

Oh, hátchin ain't a-hóckerin,
An' gíllyin ain't rākkerin,
An' gíllyin ain't pūkkerin,
Penāva mán asā.
So leláv akóvo kūnjernes,
Rikkāva lis sār kūnjernes,
Rikkāv' akóvo kūnjernes –
Sā tu shūnéssa k'nā.

Oh! The eggs and bacon;
And oh! The eggs and bacon;
And the gentleman and lady
A walking up the way.
And if you will be my sweetheart,
And if you will be my sweetheart,
And if you will be my darling,
I will be your own, to-day.

Oh! I found a jolly hedgehog;
Oh! I found a good fat hedgehog;
Oh! I found a good big hedgehog,
In the wood beyond the town
And there came the lord and lady,
The handsome lord and lady,
And underneath the branches
I saw the two sit down.

236

They didn't know the Gypsy,
They didn't think the Gypsy,
They didn't hear the Gypsy
Was looking – or could hide.
If they knew I saw the kisses,
The pretty little kisses,
If they knew I heard the kisses,
Oh, the lady would ha' died!

Oh! sitting still's not springing,
And talking isn't singing,
So I tell you nothing, singing,
That's the way I make it square.
So I keep this thing a secret,
I keep it all a secret,
A very sacred secret,
As all of you can hear.

(Leland 1875, 87)

As suggested elsewhere, *Ballovas an' Yarras* seems to be one of those fundamental particles of Romani song on which the individual singer is free to improvise at his own discretion. It is to be found, for example, in the following 'rhythmic *vers d'occasion*' hummed by Liberty Buckland when Welstood visited him at Kingston Blount in the summer of 1909:

40. We shall lel some luva
    From the tarno rai,
    Balovas and yoris
    From the tarno rai.
    (Liberty Buckland, Kingston Blount;
    Wellstood, *JGLS* n.s. 3 (1909), 159)

Sampson, too, offers two variations on the same theme – the first from Poly Herne who had, apparently, spent much of his life among the 'old roots' in America. He was, we are told, extremely surprised to learn that Sampson had not come across it before: 'Why, that's an old, old little Gypsy song, *Mi Rai*. You won't find almost nothing that's older than that for real Gypsy.'

41. Balowas and porno,
    Mulomas and bâlo;
    Kek tu lel les adré the râti
    Lel les sig adré the sâlo.

237

Bacon and flour,
Carrion and pig;
If you don't get it at night,
Get it early in the morning.

(Poly Herne; Sampson 1891, 88)

Sampson's second example is from the singing of an unnamed Gypsy whom he met on the road between Knotty Ash and Prescot some time before June 1890:

42. Bâlesto* nokyas** and bokochesto* peryas**,
   Kushto hoben to chiv apré the chōryas**.

Pig's cheek and tripe,
Good food to put on the plates.
(Sampson 1891, 88)

*The dative ending, -*esto*, is here incorrectly used in place of the genitive, -*esko*. See note following text 9.
**A double form, combining both the Romani and English plural suffix. A practice apparently once widespread among such northern Gypsy families as the Lees, Herons, Boswells, Smiths and Grays (see *JGLS* 3rd ser. 27 (1948), 27).

The English Gypsies are not alone in their love of pork. Among Transylvanian Gypsies it was once customary for the bridegroom to do his own bidding, wandering about for a week before his wedding, soliciting gifts in song. In the following example, it is the gift of pork on which the singer's mind is set (Wlislocki 1890, 183):

Lune hin mir biyá,
Bicen mánge but' bálá.
Den máge but' bicápen,
Te ná den, te ná áven!

Monday is my wedding,
Send me many pigs.
Give me many gifts,
Those who don't give, let them not come!

Pig meat also features in the following couplet noted by Irving Brown (1924, 213). He was, he says, in Vienna in 1922 when he encountered a group of Gypsy musicians who were practically starving. Making a joke of it, they sang these words to the *Frishka* which would almost certainly have been understood by Sylvester Boswell or Sampson's North Country informants:

238

Nanai maro, nanai mas,
Nanai buko balovas.

No bread, no meat,
No liver (or) pork.

~

43. The beng del'd mandi 'dré the dumo:
    Kek mandi tacho dik'd him kēr les;
    But mandi jin'd his bongo pīro
    So del'd akóva dūka to mandi.
                    (Kenza Smith; Sampson 1891, 90)

'It is', says Sampson, 'not an unusual thing for him [the Gypsy] to suddenly break in to a kind of metrical recitative, especially if he thinks he has an appreciative audience.' The foregoing example was spoken by one Kenza Smith in answer to the *Rai*'s polite enquiry concerning his lumbago.

~

44. The čovahānī and the čovahāno
    The nav sī lendi* is Petulengro;
    Sâ the foki adré the tan,
    Every yek of lendi sī lubaniâ.
                    (Thompson, *JGLS* n.s. 3, 157)

The witch and the wizard,
The name they have is Petulengro;
All the people in the tent/place
Everyone of them is a whore.

*British Romani had no verb corresponding with the English 'to have'. Possession was originally conveyed by means of the third person singular of the verb 'to be' and the dative case of the relevant personal pronoun: *mandi si grai*, to me there is a horse. Cf. medieval Welsh: *a'm oes* to me there is; also Latin: *est mihi* and French: *c'est à moi*. As the language declined, the dative seems to have been abandoned in favour of the nominative or the accusative case: e.g. *too shánas trin greiáw*, you had three horses (Smart and Crofton 1875, 31); *si man kher*, I have a house (Lockwood 1975, 250).

Thompson obtained the foregoing from two Norfolk Gypsies, grand-daughters of Ambrose Smith/Reynolds, the original of Borrow's Jasper Petulengro. It is that same 'vulgar ditty' commenced by Jasper and interrupted by his wife on the occasion of their visit to Borrow in the 'Mumpers' Dingle' in chapter 6 of *Romany Rye*:

> 45. There's a chovahanee, and a chovahano,
> The nav se len is Petulengro.

On p.387 of his edition of *Romany Rye*, Knapp also gives the song in its entirety from one of Borrow's own manuscripts:

> 46. There's a chovahanee and a chovahano,
> The nav av se lende Petulengro!
> Sor the chaves 'dre their ten
> Are chories and lubbenies – Tatchipen.

The *Petulengré* is not the only one of Borrow's songs to have been recovered from the oral tradition. Sampson obtained fragments of 'Poisoning the Porker' from one of the Smiths and, from another Gypsy of the same name but no relation, the following couplet, first published in *The Bible in Spain* (see also text 133, a variant of Ursula's 'Song of the Broken Chastity'):

> 47. Koshko grai, Romano grai,
> Muk man kister tuti kenâ.
> (Sampson 1891, 93)

Borrow's original runs as follows:

> 48. The Rommany Chal to his horse did cry,
> As he placed the bit in his horse's jaw;
> Kosko gry! Rommany gry!
> Muk man kistur tute knaw.
> (Borrow 1842, 182)

> ~

> 49. Yek gurishi* sas mandi**,
> I del'd it to a rakli
> To dik if lati's bitto wudrus
> Would loder dui mendi.
> (Brucey Boswell; Sampson 1891, 90)

Gurishi, properly 'a groat', was often used in place of the more accurate *tringurishi*, 'three groats', to mean 'a shilling'.

**The third person singular of the past tense of the verb 'to be' combines with the dative case of the personal pronoun 'I', giving the meaning 'I had'. See note following text 44.

Sampson, in typically cautious vein, translates Brucey Boswell's verse as follows. A more accurate rendering of the last two lines would be: 'to see if her little bed would lodge the two of us'.

> I had one shilling;
> I gave it to a girl
> To see if her small home
> Could provide me with a night's lodging.

It is difficult to imagine that the girl was a *Romani Chai* as Gypsy women seem never to have engaged in prostitution (see notes accompanying text 133).

~

> 50. Tuley the Can I kokkeney cam
> Like my rinkeny Yocky Shuri;
> Oprey the chongor in ratti I'd cour
> For my rinkeny Yocki Shuri.
> (Ryley Bosvil; Borrow 1874, 162)

These lines are said to have been composed by Ryley Bosvil in celebration of his wife, 'Yocky' (clever) Shuri. The second line recalls the fifth line of text 63 and may perhaps be regarded as one of those stereotypical formulae which are to be found scattered throughout the repertoire.

Ryley was a Yorkshire Gypsy of the old school. According to Borrow, he had two wives (Thompson says five) – Lura, whom he loved for her beauty, and Shuri, for her skill at fortune-telling and cozening the simple-minded. For many years he lived in great style but eventually things got too hot for him in the North Country and he was forced to leave. For reasons of economy, perhaps, he decided to take only one of his wives and, although Lura loved him better, he chose Shuri for her wits. His decision seems to have suited her for she is said to have answered 'I'll jaw with you to heaven, I'll jaw with you to the Yaundors but not if Lura goes.' Ryley was somewhat less sanguine about the arrangement, however, and, turning on her, hit her a blow in the mouth which broke her jaw.

Lura, too, was far from happy, cursing Shuri and saying nothing of Ryley save that he would never thrive. He did not, dying in want in the Potteries, the old London Gypsery hard by Shepherds Bush. There he was given a traditional Gypsy funeral, his wife and daughter burning or smashing his few remaining goods and slaughtering his horse.

It should not be supposed that Shuri's destruction of her husband's possessions was merely the ill-considered outburst of a grief-crazed widow.

The Gypsy practice of destroying the possessions of the dead, with its obvious affinities with the Hindu *Suttee,* is well documented both in the literature and in the popular press. Indeed, as the following extract from the *Bristol Evening Post* for 16 February 1984 makes clear, it is still a living tradition. The humorous tone adopted by the author merely betrays an unfortunate want of understanding of a deeply held belief.

Mystery Chain of Events

Wansdyke District Council wants a roadside lavatory on the A37 to be removed but is unable to flush out the owner. The strange history of the lavatory was told to councillors at the district planning meeting last night. It was built by a Romany who lived in a caravan on the site at the side of the A37 between Pensford and Whitchurch. After he died, the Council had dealings with his son, Mr. John Jones, who, in Romany tradition, burned his dead father's caravan at the site. But Mr. Jones said that he would not demolish the lavatory for sentimental reasons. The construction of the concrete base had contributed to his father's heart attack.

Mr. Jones has disappeared, so the Committee agreed to post an enforcement notice at the lavatory calling for it to be removed.

Various suggestions have been made to account for the Gypsy practice of destroying the effects of the dead. For some commentators, it was done in order to avoid any argument on the part of the surviving relatives as to who should inherit the deceased's property (*JGLS* n.s. 2, 121–4) whilst, for others, it was simply intended as a mark of respect (*Yorkshire Post,* 24 August 1907). Others, again, have suggested that it served as a means of equipping the departed for the after-life, for which reason favoured possessions might also be buried along with them. According to the famous evangelist, Gypsy Smith, 'when an uncle of mine died, my aunt bought a coffin large enough for all his favourite possessions – including his fiddle, cup and saucer, plate, knife, etc. . . .' (Smith 1903, 7).

Although it is quite possible that individual Gypsies may, at various times, have acted from a variety of different motives, it is almost certainly the case that, taken in the round, Gypsy death and burial customs owe more to a superstitious dread of the power of the dead than to a simple concern for their future well-being (Wlislocki 1890a, 279; 1891, 97). For the Gypsy, death seems originally to have represented an unnatural and traumatic event, leaving the deceased both confused and resentful; and, if the proper steps were not taken, this resentment might well spill over into vengeful spite towards the living. It is fear of this anger and capacity for vengeance that seems to have coloured the Gypsies' response to the death even of those they loved. At worst, the dead person might return in the form of a vampire (Trigg 1975, *passim*). Thus, at Littlebury, it was said that the Gypsies kept watch over their dead in the period between death and burial in order to prevent this from happening as a result of someone jumping over the corpse (*NQ* 4th ser. 3 (1869), 461: Morwood 1885, 172).

The process of placating or containing the dead might begin with a death-bed vigil, during which family and friends would seek forgiveness of the dying for all transgressions, real or imagined. As soon as death occurred, however, many Gypsies would do all they could to avoid any further contact with the body, employing others to lay out the corpse. Mindful of their relatives' feelings in the matter, but reluctant to submit themselves to the attention of others, it was not uncommon, when *in extremis*, for the dying to make their own final preparations for the grave. Thus, according to Thompson, when Ambrose Smith/Reynolds's brother-in-law, Booey Brown, was dying, he managed to struggle into his best suit, asking that he be buried in it. His reason was that he did not wish his naked body to be touched, washed or seen by strangers (see Thompson 1910b; Groome 1880, ch.5).

The dead, however, were thought to be at their most dangerous during the period prior to decomposition and for this reason, among some groups, bodies were buried face down or at a great depth in order to make it more difficult for them to escape the grave. For this reason, too, heavy stones or concrete might be placed on top of the grave. Leitner mentions this practice in his study of the languages and races of Dardestan, noting that 'sometimes the grave is well cemented, and a kind of small vault is made over it with pieces of wood closely jammed together' (1880, ii, 37). Fear of vampirism may also lie behind the practice of burying the dead beneath the bed of a stream, temporarily diverted for the purpose (Smith 1889, 51) or of filling the grave with loose grain rather than earth, although, in England, it is quite possible that the older superstitious dread had become confused with more recent concern over the activities of the resurrectionists.

Not only was it necessary physically to restrain the dead, but a range of other precautions had also to be taken in order to avoid attracting their attention and hence their anger. Thus, not only had all physical traces of the deceased to be removed by the destruction or disposal of their goods, but their very name might become taboo, even if this meant renaming a living member of the family (Wlislocki 1891, 96). In some cases, too, the survivors might ever after avoid a particular food or activity of which the deceased was especially fond or with which they or the survivors had been associated at the time of death (*JGLS* n.s. 5 (1911), 146). In short, any thing or any action which was likely to arouse the interest of the dead had to be avoided at all costs even though, as in some cases, the surviving relatives might be reduced to abject poverty by the necessary destruction of the family's own living accommodation.

The destruction of livestock was and is still occasionally practised for the same reason, although in recent years it has generally been carried out under the supervision of the RSPCA or a qualified vet (*World*, 6 June 1888; *JGLS* o.s. 1 (1889), and n.s. 2 (1907), 121).

Rituals of this type are clearly primitive in character and may well represent the confused detritus of a set of beliefs common to many societies at a certain stage in their spiritual development. Among the Yanomani people of Brazil, for example, there is also a strong taboo against mentioning the dead by name, whilst any objects used by the dead person are immediately disposed of in such a way that no trace of their former owner remains. It would, however, be wrong to assume that all Gypsies respond to death in precisely the same way. Beliefs and practices clearly vary from time to time and place to place. Mr Jones of Bristol evidently felt quite safe in leaving his father's easance untouched whilst among certain Hungarian Gypsies the bereaved were known to engage in a game in which the dead person was apparently re-animated by means of cords attached to his arms and legs. In Britain, however, it is safe to say that, in recent years, and more particularly with the advent of motorized trailers and official sites, the wholesale destruction of property has fallen into decline for both economic and social reasons. Yet trailers may still be repainted in order to render them unrecognizable to the dead, or portable goods disposed of by sale, just as in earlier times matters might be arranged so that death occurred in a tent or wagon of less importance in order that the family home might be spared the flames.

Another aspect of Gypsy death and burial customs to which reference is made in the literature is the practice of burying the dead in ummarked graves far from human habitation. In *Lavo Lil*, Borrow speaks of the 'Tatchey Romany of the sacred black race who never slept in a house, never entered a church and who, on their deathbeds, used to threaten their children with a curse provided they buried them in a churchyard . . .' The two last of these, he goes on to say, rest some six feet deep beneath the moss of a wild hilly heath not far from Norwich. Myers, too, tells us that according to Noah Young, his maternal grandfather, John Chilcot, left the following death-bed injunction: 'bury me under a sod and plant briars over me. And don't bury me far down, and don't put no tombstone over me' (Yates, *JGLS* n.s. 4 (1911), 302). The truth of the matter is, however, that most English Gypsies seem to have preferred burial as close to the church as possible, if not actually under the porch itself, and to have been perfectly content with the rites of the establish church.

Leland (1873, 31), and Cussans (*NQ*, 15 May 1867) also speak of Gypsy burials in unconsecrated ground, but Groome is equally clear that this was never generally the case and, indeed, we know of a number of examples of Christian burial dating from the early years following the Gypsies' first appearance in western Europe. Crusius, for example, in his *Annales Suebici* (1594), mentions three: 'the high-born lord, Lord Panuel in Little Egypt and Lord Hirschhorn in the same land' (Steinbach, 1445); 'the noble Earl Peter of Kleinschild' (Bautma, 1453); and 'the high-born Lord Johann Earl of Little Egypt' (Pforzheim, 1598). It is only fair to say, however, that the individuals in question were all 'of royal blood' and anything other than Christian burial would have been difficult to justify given their claim to be on a pilgrimage ordained by the pope.

It is also possible that, in some parts of Europe, the tradition of isolated burial had its origin in the authorities' refusal to allow the Gypsies to lie in consecrated ground. In 1560, for example, the Swedish archbishop, Laurentius Petri Nericius, approved a series of articles forbidding his priests either to baptize Gypsy children or to bury their dead, a right only conceded to Montenegrin Travellers during the reign of Prince Danil (1851–60).

Although songs of mourning have been noted elsewhere in Europe – e.g. the *rovilyé* and *kaidávé* of the Transylvanian and south Hungarian tent-dwellers – they seem not to have survived among the Gypsies of Britain. Mention may be made, however, of two curious exceptions of equally doubtful provenance. The first is to be found in chapter 25 of *Lavengro*. Having learned of the loss of Petulengro's parents, Borrow asks him what he thinks about death. 'My opinion of death, brother', says Jasper, 'is much the same as in the old song of Pharaoh which I heard my grandam sing':

> 51. Canna marel o manus, chivios andé puv,
> Ta rovel pa leste o chavo ta romi . . .
>
> When a man dies, he is cast into the earth,
> And his wife and child sorrow over him . . .
> (Borrow 1851, 156)

He then concludes, somewhat wryly, that if a man has no wife and child, then his parents may mourn; and if he has no parents, then he is cast into the earth all the same. Perhaps he belonged to that class of Gypsy who, according to Trigg, preferred not to show any emotion in the presence of death lest it encourage the departed to take an unhealthy interest in the living. That he spoke the foregoing lines, or had them from either of his grandmothers is, however, somewhat unlikely. They are in continental Romani and, as mentioned elsewhere, both his maternal and paternal grandparents were native to these islands.

Somewhat ironically, Jasper himself, who died on 22 October 1878, was given a Christian burial, his friends erecting a stone to his memory during the summer of the following year. On it were carved the following verses, the original of which are to be found on pp.33–4 of the 1886 edition of *The Changed Cross* (first published in New York in 1865):

> Nearer my God's house
> Where the many mansions be;
> Nearer the great white throne,
> Nearer the jasper sea.
>
> Nearer the bound of life
> Where we lay our burdens down;
> Nearer leaving the cross,
> Nearer gaining the crown.
>
> Feel thee near me when my feet
> Are slipping over the brink;
> For it may be I'm nearer home,
> Nearer now than I think.

The second example of a British Gypsy death-song is to be found in the writings of one even less slavishly attached to the plain truth than Borrow – Xavier Petulengro. In chapter 8 of *A Romany Life*, he offers a description of a 'traditional' Gypsy funeral which is, to say the least, highly romanticized. Seven holes were drilled in the coffin lid, he tells us – one above the forehead to allow the soul free passage; two over the eyes, that the dead might see; two that they might hear the funeral music; and two, just below the heart, 'so as the body disseminates, it can pass through'. Why Petulengro's Gypsies should have taken so much trouble to ensure body and soul easy egress from the coffin when their fellows elsewhere were at such pains to ensure that they remained where they were, is hard to say. (Schwicker, it is true, mentions that the cloth placed over the dead Gypsy's mouth always had a hole in it in order to let the vampire in and out (1883, 150), and there are a number of examples of British Gypsies buried uncoffined – e.g. Mrs Herne (Borrow 1851, ch.81) and an unnamed Gypsy woman at Littlebury in 1829 (Winstedt 1909a, 361).)

Only when the coffin had been lowered into the grave, Petulengro continues, would the fiddles begin to play. Slowly at first, so that the music might convey to the dead 'what the hearts of the living felt and their eyes do not show'; then, with growing intensity, the listeners clapping softly in time. After a while, the dance would begin – 'The Death of the Spirit Dance', whose slow and reverential movements were intended to woo the soul from the body. At last, as the dance reached its climax, the soul would be 'wrenched' through the hole provided for it and the dance would cease. The box would then be covered with earth.

At this stage in the proceedings, says Petulengro, the soul was thought to have retired to a favourite tent or trailer and only then was it thought appropriate to begin the destruction by fire of the deceased's possessions by which it would be freed for its long journey to paradise. With this in mind a stout pair of boots would also be buried with the body in order to assist the soul in crossing the burning wastes that lay before it, its only other comfort being the words of the following *Mullah Gilli*:

> 52. Vov sos bichala dur cherionos t'a soli-pala andre
> dur boro-ceel lel soldo nanti coor, trustal odi dur
> kushti-duval rigs lekki mullah nanticoored
> kikavakiguglo-bashes san t'a kikavaki dur
> tarno-roy da bosh-avenos kils.
>
> He who guides the sun and stars on their ways so
> that two shall never meet among all the millions
> of these worlds, the good God shall take his
> spirit through unharmed to where a sweeter music is
> and where the prince of fiddlers plays.

Petulengro's song is as difficult to place as the rites in which it is said to have figured. The *Rovilyé*, or songs of weeping of the Transylvanian and south Hungarian tent-Gypsies, to which reference has already been made, take the form of 'an unstudied address to the dead', sung by the mourning women in a half-murmured, half-chanted monotone. They are non-strophic in character, resolving themselves into irregular units at the end of which, the woman who is then singing makes a longer or shorter pause according to the requirements of the leading idea (Wlislocki 1889, 161–3).

The following example is from Wlislocki's *Totenklagen*, as reprinted by Herrmann, together with an English translation, in *JGLS* 1 (1889), 294. Herrmann also offers the following brief guide to pronunciation: c = Germ tsch; x = Germ. ch; j = Germ. dsch; n as in Spanish; and sh and y as in English.

The Daughter to her Mother

1.

Gule dáy, gule, ná mán tu the kerdyelás, Inkáb yeká bár
tu the kerdyelás! E bár ná jánel, káná lákro dáy

247

merdyás, uvá me core pácirtá silyábáv pál bárvál,
silyábáv pálá kám meriben gule dáyákri.

Niko mán ákáná tátyárel, Káná me shilyáváv; Niko mán
usházin del, Káná me táte som! Te co mánge pádá kerel,
Káná sováles som! Bárvál ná hin mindig, O kám ná hin
mindig, uvá me Core rováv cák mindig.

Andro bes me jiáv, Káná hin bárválá, Te tut me ákáráv,
Oh gule dáy; Uvá tu ná áves, Mire álsá ná telikoses, M're
vodyi ná sáscáres. Cores me cák jiáv, Yeká core
Keshályi, beshávy me ákáná, upro epustá bár, Káy ciriklo
ná silyável, Káy cár ná bárvályel, Odoy me besháv te
rováv.

Sweet mother, sweet, would that thou hadst not borne me,
would rather that thou hadst born a stone! the stone
knows not when its mother is dead, but I, poor lark,
sing in the breeze, sing in the sunshine, the death of
my sweet mother.

No one now will warm me when I am cold; no one will
shade me when I am oppressed by heat! And who will
prepare my couch, when I am sleepy? The wind blows not
ever, the sun shines not ever, but I, poor one, shall
ever weep.

Into the wood will I go when the wind blows, and to thee
will I call, oh sweet mother; but thou comest not, thou
dost not wipe away my tears, my heart thou dost not
heal. Lonely shall I wander, a poor Keshályi*, henceforth will
I sit me down on barren rocks, where sings no bird,
where grows no grass, there will I sit in sorrow.

*A hill fairy who sits in the high mountain peaks and lets her mile-long hair blow
down through the valleys, thus causing the mist.

2.

Oh Dáy, tire muy hin pándles, T're luludyi ná cumides;
T're punrá ná já pro selene mál, T're vástá hin mules te
nikáná yon keren! Oh dá, T're yákhá ná diklen seleno bes,
T're káná ná áshunen ciriklen, Te tu ná jánes, Káná t're
luludyi merel!

E Ruká máyd meren, Te pále selinen, Uvá m're vodyi
somores hin, Te somores, mindig cák hin! E páni nácel,
Te pál vreme thávdel; M're ápsá mindig thárden, Te
nikáná nácen; Ciriklá hin blindes, Te ishmét silyáben;
Asáviben ná hin mánge, Te niko ishmét áshunel.

Bákrori ráciye kere jiál, Cirikli kere urál; Uvá me core,
káy the jiáv? Kánro beshel cores upro pro mál, Te cores
me besháv upro pro báv.

Oh Dáy, sostár mán corá tu muklyál? Juklyi me jiáv
jevende pál yiv, Te niláye pál brishind; Pxáres me
páshloyováv upro pro tro probos, Oh dáy! Asukáráv,
asukáráv Cin tu áves ándrál mulengre them.

Oh mother, thy mouth is closed, thou dost not kiss thy
little flower; thy feet go no more over the green heath,
thy hands are dead and work no more! Oh mother, thine
eyes see not the green wood, thy ears hear not the birds,
and thou knowest not that thy little flower is fading!

The trees fade quickly and grow green again, but my
heart is sad, and sad forever! The brook becomes dry and
in the springtime it flows again; my tears are ever
flowing, and they never dry; the birds cease their singing,
and then again they sing; gone is my laughter, and no
one hears the sound of my laughter any more.

At evening the little lamb returns to the fold, and home
flies the bird; but ah, poor me, whither shall I go? The
thistle stands solitary upon the field, and all alone upon
the heath am I.

Oh mother, why hast thou left poor me? As a poor
hound do I wander in winter through the snow, and in
summer through the rain; then I lay myself wearied upon
thy grave, oh mother! And I wait and wait, until thou
comest back from the country of the dead.

Akin to the *Rovilyé* are the songs of lamentation proper, the *Kaidavé*.
Unlike the *Rovilyé*, however, they are regular in construction and, in
common with other songs of the Transylvanian tent-Gypsies, consist of a
series of rhymed couplets. A further difference is that whilst the *Rovilyé* are
addressed to a particular individual, the *Kaidavé* are rather more general in

character, for which reason they are sung immediately before burial, whilst the *Rovilyé* commence with the laying of the body on the bier.

Wlislocki gives only his own German rendering of the *Kaidáve* mentioned in his original article. The following English paraphrase of the first of these is from Herrmann (*JGLS* o.s. 1 (1889)).

> Thou, my child, my only one,
> Ah! How soon from me thou'rt gone!
> Lovely rosebud, fair to see,
> Death, alas! has gathered thee!
> E'en the grave will treat thee kind,
> For indeed thou'rt gold refined.
> Purest gold, dear child, art thou,
> Rest in sweetest slumber now!

The following example of a weeping song in which reference is also made to the practice of destroying the possessions of the dead is taken from C. F. Keary's article on the Romanian peasants and their songs (*Nineteenth Century*, October 1882), where it appears in translation only. Unlike the *Rovilyé* of Wlislocki's Transylvanian tent-dwellers, it is formed of rhymed couplets (always assuming Keary has followed the original in the matter of prosody).

The wording of the fourth and eighth lines would suggest that the clothes of the dead woman were to be burned, not to prevent her return but in order that she might take them with her. Red (line 4) is a traditional colour of mourning.

> Swallows, swallows, little sisters;
> Sisters, seek my mother dear;
> Tell her from her daughter here
> That she send her kirtle red,
> For a raven she has wed;
> And a large thick veil for shroud.
> When the watch dogs bark aloud,
> Her brave dresses, that she take them,
> Into one rude bundle make them,
> Throw them in the street and burn them,
> Utterly to ashes turn them.

Although lacking formal structure like the *Rovilyé*, Petulengro's song resembles neither of Wlislocki's two types and, indeed, puts forward a somewhat idiosyncratic view of the after-life. The form of language used shows clear signs of interference from English, but is like nothing else in the literature. In all probability, as with so much else in his books, Petulengro has taken a grain of truth and worked it up in order to impress a wholly uncritical audience with a proper sense of mystery. Yet, exotic as his description of Gypsy funeral rites may be, Petulengro's repeated references to the fiddle are not without interest. At one point, for example, he tells us that music was also used after the funeral, 'not only to guide the spirit on its way but to injure any enemies who may be about'. A similar notion is recalled in the Revd Meredith Morris's account of the life of Aby Biddle, the last of the celebrated strolling fiddlers of Pembrokeshire (Morris 1907). At wakes, he says, Biddle would play 'weird and frenzied music to scare the ghouls who lurked near the chamber of the dead'.

Petulengro's reference to the fiddle used as a means of articulating the grief of the living also finds an echo in Smart and Crofton's description of Charlie Boswell's response to the death of a favourite child. Boswell, they say,

> refused to be comforted, abstained from food, becoming much emaciated in consequence, and spent all his time for several weeks after the child's death in playing on his fiddle. He seemed to find his only consolation in confiding his grief to his instrument and touching chords which responded in sympathy with his own sad mood. (Smart and Crofton 1875, 297)

Despite such apparent correspondences, there seems to be little or no evidence to suggest that the fiddle ever played a formal role in Gypsy funeral rites except among the Gypsies of Spain. There, a man might be buried with his fiddle beside him in order to test his willingness to forgive the sins of the living. If, following the act of contrition, the corpse remained silent, all was well. If, however, he began to play, the supplicant's prayers had been in vain and the music would eventually deafen him.

A further aspect of Petulengro's account requiring comment is the practice of burying the dead in a pair of stout boots. Although unsupported elsewhere in the literature, Leland, writing in 1891, believed that the practice had once been widespread among the Gypsies but had died out in Britain sometime during the middle years of the nineteenth century. He himself, he says, had heard an old Traveller speak of it some seventeen years before going to print, although he had been unable to say why it had been done. From Petulengro's account, however, it is clear that we are here dealing with a variant of the old Norse custom of the 'hell shoon', a practice given an additional twist in a sixteenth-century description of Cleveland quoted by Scott in his *Border Minstrelsy*:

> When any dieth, certain women sing a song to the dead bodie, reciting the journey that the party deceased must goe; and they are of beliefe that once in

their lives it is goode to give a pair of new shoes to a poor man for as much
as before this life they are to pass bare-foote through a great land full of
thorns and furzen – except by the meryte of the almes aforesaid they have
redeemed the forfeyt – for at the edge of the launde an oulde man shall meet
them with the same shoes that were given by the partie when he was living
and after he hath shode them, dismisseth them to go through thick and thin
without scratch or scalle.

~

53. Kai sī romanī grānza?
    Kai sī p'us t'ā k'as?
    Kai sī kamlī raklī
    Te delas 'men balovás?
    (Edward Wood; Sampson 1926, iv, 29)

'These simple lines', says Sampson, 'were composed by the harpist,
Edward Wood, to express the feelings of an old Gypsy woman on reaching
a barn where her family had always been hospitably received and finding it
deserted and in ruins.' He offers the following translation:

Where is the Gypsy barn?
Where is the straw and the hay?
Where is the friendly maid
Who used to give us bacon?

A Welsh version is also to be found on p.72 of *Y Sipsiwn Cymreig* (Jarman
and Jarman 1979):

P'le mae ysgubor y Sipsiwn?
P'le mae'r gwellt a'r gwair?
P'le mae'r forwyn gyfeillgar
A roddai gig moch i ni?

Edward Wood was the only son of Adam Wood and his second wife,
Winifred. He was born in 1838 and died, in Bala, in 1902. It was he who, in
the mid-1890s, first astonished and delighted Sampson with his knowledge of
pure Welsh *Romanés*. He also prided himself on his knowledge of Welsh and,
indeed, is said to have spoken the language 'like an old-fashioned gentleman'.

Wood, who, according to Sampson, was of a 'gentle, good and poetic
disposition', was twice married, to two daughters of John Roberts, New-
port, and between them they bore him ten children. Only one, however,
Winifred, was to inherit anything of his knowledge of deep *Romanés*.

Yet Wood's kinship with John Roberts went beyond the ties of marriage for, like his father-in-law, he was a gifted harpist, leaving behind a book of fine harp tunes (NLW, MS 3422). Indeed, as his obituary in the *Cambrian Journal* makes clear, his reputation went far beyond his native Wales:

The death of Mr. Edward Wood (Telynor Meirion), a well known Welsh Harpist, took place at Bala on Sunday week after an illness of only a few hours. Mr. Wood was well known as one of the ablest players of the Welsh triple harp and his services were in great demand. When the King and Queen (then Prince and Princess of Wales) visited Ruthin castle he had the honour of playing the harp before them. He also played at Pale Llandderfel when Queen Victoria visited North Wales in 1889.

~

> 54. Dâ, dabla,* dâdi!
> Tačikenâ lač stardi
> For činin' alé the rania košt
> And čorin mulo bâli.
> (Cornelius Buckland (alias Fenner/Fender);
> Winstedt, *JGLS* n.s. 3 (1909), 159)

Dabla is presumably the vocative of 'God', although Sampson also gives *Dubla*, God, and *Dublea ja lensa*, God go with them (Sampson 1892, 73–81). Cf. also *Dabla* (Groome 1880, 134).

Some nineteen years before Winstedt noted this song, Sampson published the following in his *English Gypsy Songs and Rhymes*. Given the degree of variation found in English Gypsy song texts, it is not unreasonable to suppose that they at least belong to the same family. As noted elsewhere, the singer goes straight to the heart of the action and, rather than recounting an incident removed in place and time, himself becomes part of the action, investing it with an immediacy seldom encountered in mainstream texts.

> 55. Aâi-dâdi, dâ dúbelâ, dâ-dí!
> Jal to kaséngri, ai-dâdi!
> Or tuti'll be lino apré;
> Mandi's been choring some ghiv,
> Now tuti'll be klisn'd apré.
> (Alice Gray; Sampson 1891, 83)

Alice Gray, from whom he also obtained a variant of 'Can you Rokker Romani' (text 16), told Sampson that she had learned this song from her 'puri Foki' when a child in Northumberland. The first line he believed to be very old, although the rest had apparently 'been subjected to the same process of bringing down to date which one observes in our English ballads and other traditional literature'. A few slight alterations would, he suggests, be sufficient to restore it to something like its original form. By way of example, he offers the following rewrite of the third line: 'O tu te vel lino apré'. Sampson's observations on this point should, however, be treated with considerable caution as there is no evidence to suggest that a Romani song has ever crossed the language divide between the *Puri* and *Poggadi Chib*.

~

56. When I first chiv'd my pīro 'dré de* bōri gav,
 I dik'd a ghēro jalin' talé de drom,
 And I puch'd kova ghēro sas a poshēro 'drē his pūtsi?
 Kek – De beng te poger lesti zī!
 Kek – De beng te poger lesti zī!
 (Boss; Sampson 1891, 89)

*A number of writers have noted the English Gypsies' mispronunciation of the definite article (see, for example, Smart and Crofton 1875, 10), and Korbay makes a similar point in connection with their treatment of his native Hungarian: 'I have never seen a Gypsy who could speak our language as it ought to be pronounced. The common Gypsy has a lisp very like the Negro lisp' (*Critic* 13 (1890), 86). MacRitchie, too, quotes the *Alonso* of Gerónimo de Alcalá on the lisping of Gypsies whilst Gil Vicente in his *Farsa das Ciganas* of 1521 seeks to imitate the lisping sound already regarded as typical of the Gypsies' use of Portuguese. Cervantes also mentions it both in his comedy, *Pedro de Urdemalas* (*c.*1611) and in his novella, *La Gitanilla* (1613). See also Pott (1844–5, ii, 216 and 236) and Sampson (*JGLS* n.s. 4, 174) where it is used to explain certain peculiarities in Bryant's vocabulary of 1785.

In England, the Romani article – *masc.* 'O' and *fem.* 'I' – seems to have fallen out of general use some time during the first half of the nineteenth century. Bryant (1785) and Bright (1818), app., p.lxxix) give a number of examples of its use but Smart and Crofton speak of its retention only in a few ossified phrases – e.g. *paúdel i paáni*, across the water (transportation) – their informants for the most part preferring the English form or omitting it altogether. There is no indefinite article in Romani.

Sampson says nothing of this verse other than that he had it from an Accrington Gypsy and that it was sung 'to a tune of no special merit, rather suggestive of a Negro minstrel ditty'.

~

57. Wafri bak kairs
 A choro mush ta jal alay
 But it muks a boro mush
 To chiv his kokero apre.

> Bad luck drives
> A poor man down
> But it allows a great man
> To pull himself up.
> (Anon.; Leland 1873, 213)

This verse forms the tailpiece to one of Leland's Gypsy tales concerning a hare and a cat. One day, the two were spotted by a huntsman. The hare ran off but the cat, seeking refuge in a tree, found a bird's nest.

According to Leland, the 'rhyme and metre, such as they are, are purely accidental . . . but as they occurred *verb. ad lit.* I set them down.'

~

> 58. Atchin' in the pudden ken [lodging-house],
> Along of all the navvy men,
> The Needies [Travellers] an' the Buffers [non-Travellers]
> They were rolling on the floor.
> (John Doran, Waterloo, July 1985)

John Doran, from whom I obtained these lines, was a Wexford Traveller who used to play the accordion outside the York Road entrance to Waterloo Station every Tuesday morning when the weather was not too cold. A cousin of the late Felix and John Doran, the noted pipers, he was in his mid-seventies when I first met him and had long since abandoned the travelling life. He had served his time in the army and was still most particular about his appearance. He had also been a boxer and carried a photograph of himself in boots and trunks.

John told me that, as a young man, he had often heard Irish Travellers singing in their own tongue, which he called the *Gammon*, a form of language which he firmly believed was originally derived from Italian. Yet, although he was happy to talk on the subject generally, he could give no specific examples of songs in which it featured, other than the above which, he said, was usually followed by a bit of lilting and dancing. My feeling was, however, that he may have got it from an English or Scottish Traveller and simply inserted the third line himself.

In his article, 'The Singing Tradition of Irish Travellers' (1975, 3–30), Tom Munnelly, a leading authority on the subject, notes that whilst 'one encounters the odd word or phrase in the occasional song . . . songs which contain sufficient Gammon, to the extent that even the most uninformed outsider would not be able to understand the song's content, just do not seem to exist.'

That this was always the case is, however, hard to believe. Music and song have always played an extremely important part in the cultural life of Irish Travellers and there is no obvious reason why they should choose not to express themselves through the medium of their own ethnic speech. The fact that *Gammon* may be an 'artificial language' presents no problem. If Dekker and Head are to be believed, this in no way precluded the emergence of a body of song in Thieves' Cant, itself a wholly artificial contrivance. More importantly, singing in Cant is also by no means un-known among Scottish Travellers.

The existence of a number of prose tales in *Shelta*, the ancient core-element of contemporary *Gammon* (e.g. *JGLS* o.s. 3 (1892), 22–6), would also suggest that it was, at one time, used for recreational purposes. Indeed, if it were no more than a secret code designed to exclude outsiders, it is hard to understand why so many informants should have been willing to reveal its content. As Munnelly goes on to say (ibid.),

> One could argue that, if songs of this sort do exist, because of their very nature Travellers would not wish to disclose them. But this for me does not hold water for, amongst those Travellers whom I know at all well, I have never met with any reluctance on their part to teach me their jargon. So amongst those with whom rapport is established, there is no great obstacle to acquiring a working knowledge of Gammon . . .

The assumptions underlying the foregoing are further reinforced by the fact that, in the course of their first encounter with the language on the beach at Aberystwyth, Leland and Palmer not only managed to secure a number of words and phrases but the following triplet which, although containing a heavy admixture of English, does at least satisfy Munnelly's test of unintelligibility:

> 59. My name is Barney Mucafee,
> With my borers and jumpers [tinkers' tools] down to my thee,
> An' its forty miles I've come to kerb yer pee [punch your face].
>
> My name is Barney Mac Fee,
> With my gimlets and cramps down to my thigh,
> And it's forty miles I've come to punch your face.
> (Leland 1882, 368)

Somewhat ironically, Munnelly, too, was to obtain a substantial song text in *Gammon* barely a month after his article appeared in the *Folk Music Journal* (text 60) and we may also point to another, a variant of 'The Little Beggar Man', included by Maher in his 'Road to God Knows Where' (text

171). The fact remains, however, that, as a rule, Irish Travellers sing neither in *Gammon* nor in Irish, but in Hiberno-English.

60. I mislayed to a grippa and the gloak he got so gammy
    I was solaking and lush as I seen;
    But the byore sent for the shadeog, she annoyed me, I got crazy,
    But I corribed in her grinjy as I leaved.
    But the shades they had a torry to me then
    And they says, – Sure the grineog you have corribed in!
    I corribed up his pee and the byore then says to me –
    You'll be mislayed to the nick.
    Now you're corribed, sublia, misli, leave the lurk behind you
    Or you go to rispon for the grineog that you corribed in the grippa
    Will you misli, sublia, now?
    I says, – Crawd ye, lackeen, just crawd ye as you misli,
    Crawd ye and don't trinnick my jeal
    Or the gloak could skeegs ye, who is your gloak?
    Don't miss my mideog, we're mislaying now.

    I went into a pub and the (bar)man got so abusive
    I was drinking and drunk as I saw;
    But the woman (owner's wife) sent for the police, she annoyed me,
        I got crazy,
    But I broke her window as I left.
    But the police had a talk with me then
    And they said, – Sure the window you have broken in.
    I hit him in the mouth and the woman said to me
    – You'll be taken to the jail.
    Now you're beaten, boy, go and leave the drink behind you
    Or you go to prison for the window you broke in the pub,
    Will you go, boy, now?
    I said, – Hush ye, girl, just hush as you go,
    Hush ye and don't tell my name
    Or the man could seize ye, who is your man?
    Don't leave(?) my shilling, we're going now.
    (Bernie Reilly, King's Court, Co. Cavan, 5 September 1975;
    IFC TM 446)

Reilly, who was born in Carrick-on-Shannon in Co. Leitrim, was camping at Navan when he was recorded by Tom Munnelly in Slowey's pub. He had the following to say regarding his song:

BR. – Me an' her was takin' a drink, ye see, an' I came into a shop, you know, an' I got drunk, ye see, an' the barmaid aggravated me, ye know. She wanted me out of the shop, d'ye see. The barmaid sent up then, ye see, for the Guards. When the Guards came on I told her not to tell my name, ye see, when I was goin'. But still I was that drunk I wasn't fit to go, ye know. But I was tellin' her I was goin': 'You go, an' don't tell the Guards my name as we're goin' just now' . . . I knew I was drunk but I knew I done wrong for breakin' the window. The guards wanted to find out who broke the windy and I didn't want tellin' them, 'cause, ye know, they'd send me up to the clink, ye know. I wouldn't tell them. I'd a wife an' a few children there, ye know, I didn't want gettin' up to the clink, you know.

TM – So it was yourself that made the song, was it?
BR – 'Twas meself made the song . . .
TM – When did you make it?
BR – I made it up in, ah . . . it'd be seventeen year ago now since.

(IFC TM 447)

In his spoken account of the incident which originally gave rise to the song, Reilly makes no mention of hitting the Guard or anyone else and it is possible that the phrase 'I corribed up his pee' is nothing more than mere bravado. A similar form of words occurs in Leland's triplet and is also popular among Gypsies – *Del'd him in the mui* (texts 16, 75, 76 etc.).

The last two lines are, perhaps, a little confused. The first half of the penultimate line might make more sense if 'me' were substituted for 'ye' after 'skeegs', as would the last line were it addressed to the informant's own wife.

Contemporary Scottish and Irish Travellers' Cant consists, in varying proportions, of a mix of *Shelta*, Romani, modified and unmodified Gaelic, old English Thieves' Cant and, more particularly in the mid-Scottish variety, a number of items from, *inter alia*, provincial and Scotto-English, French, German etc. As regards its grammar and syntax, it is now almost entirely English, its basic structure echoing that of the English used by speakers when not using Cant itself. Texts 60 and 172 are representative of the southern Irish variety and texts 27, 29–31, 37, and 62 are in the more heavily Romani-influenced mid-Scottish form. Apart from these, there also exist a south Welsh and a North American variety and a deeper, Gaelic-influenced dialect spoken in Ulster and the north of Scotland.

Although once apparently in common use, the term *Shelta* – variously, but unconvincingly, derived from *béarla* (Irish: language) or *Celtic* – now seems to have fallen out of use, the favoured usage among Irish Travellers being *Gammon* (possibly a back-formation of Ogam) whilst both Scottish and Irish Travellers more often than not refer to it simply as Cant (Irish: *caint*, speech?). Writing in the last decade of the nineteenth century, Sampson (1891, 204–21) distinguished between two types of *Shelta*, Gaelic and English, a distinction superficially analogous to that between the *Puri* and *Poggadi Chib*. The principal differences between the two forms were the use, in the former, of Gaelic grammar patterns and, in the latter, of a far greater number of non-English items borrowed from Romani and Thieves' Cant.

As with Romani, too, there is some evidence to suggest that Travellers' Cant today is the result of a more or less prolonged period of attrition. Harper and Hudson, for example, point to an 80 per cent loss of *Shelta* items in the North American variety of Travellers' Cant over a period of eighty years (Harper and Hudson 1971, 82), whilst in the British Isles, although one cannot rule out the possibility that the two forms existed side by side for some time before the period for which written records are available, the current widespread use of what, for convenience, we may still call English *Shelta* may also be the result of a relatively recent general movement away from a once more widely spoken Gaelic variety. Among a hundred *Shelta* sayings published by Sampson in 1908 are the following statements which, if taken at face value, might also suggest that, as had previously been the case with Romani English, the language was then, among some Travellers at least, in a state of transition involving its redefinition as a register of English rather than a mother tongue:

(a) Mwilsha bogg'd Sheldru swurth nadherum's miskon
   I learned Shelta on my mother's breast.

(b) A thari shirth gather to kam
   A speech came down from father to son.

(c) Mwilsha's kam granhes od luba
   My son knows (only) two words.

Any movement in this direction would, however, appear to have been limited in extent, for, as Binchey has pointed out, Irish Traveller 'children generally learn the language in infancy, as a joint first language . . . Children use it among themselves when they attend settled schools' (Binchey 1994, 134). O Baoill, too, is of the opinion that Irish Cant 'is obviously acquired as a speech system formed in childhood', arguing that

> much of the variation in the pronunciation of certain words (e.g. núspóg, múspóg, mústóg, from Irish *spúnóg* 'a spoon' . . .) can be shown to be the result of language learning processes as evidenced in the vast literature on first language acquisition . . . There are very strong arguments for claiming that núspóg is/was the original or basic form of the word in Cant and that

the other two variants are derived by normal sound substitutions during childhood language acquisition. These substitutions when left unchecked emerge as alternative pronunciations. (O Baoill 1994, 159)

Among some Scottish Travellers, too, the Cant may still be acquired in infancy in the conventional way and is used at home as well as among strangers (MacColl and Seeger 1986, 40). As Mrs Belle Stewart herself put it (ibid.), 'I'd never want to drop the Cant. Never! I've passed it on to all my family. Cathie and Sheila and Rena know it, so does John and Andy and they passed it on to their bairns' (see also texts 27 and 160).

The difference between Gaelic and English *Shelta* will be readily apparent from the following sentences. The first group are in Gaelic *Shelta*. The first pair, which are representative of the north Scottish variety, are from Tiree (Wilson 1891) and the second pair, in the Ulster dialect, are from Sampson's 'Hundred Shelta Sayings' (1908):

(a) S' guidh a bagail air mo ghil
It is raining (lit. water is giving on my head – the initial 's belongs to the following word);

(b) S' deis suim a meartsacha air a charan
We are going on the sea;

(c) Stimera dhi-ilsha, stimera aga
If you are a piper, have your own pipes (*aga* represents the Irish prepositional pronoun *agat*, denoting possession);

(d) Thom Blorne nijesh Nip glox
Every Protestant isn't an Orangeman.

The second set are in English *Shelta*. The first two sentences are drawn respectively from Findlater (1913) and MacColl and Seeger (1986) and are representative of the mid-Scottish variety; the second pair, which are in the southern Irish dialect, are from Maher (1932) and Binchey (1994):

(e) D'ye no jan it's morgan?
Do you not know it is morning?

(f) We've to bing avree to the vavver vile
We've got to go to the other town;

(g) The beor of the cena bucéads the ripsa
The woman of the house wears the trousers;

(h) Crush on, laicin, time to misli
   Come on, girl, time to go.

Compare also texts 60 and 172 with the following transcription of the
Lord's Prayer, dictated to Sampson by his informant, John Barlow, and
included in his article on *Shelta* in *Chambers's Encyclopaedia*. It was
subsequently reprinted from Sampson's original manuscript on pages
139–40 of MacAlister's *Secret Languages of Ireland* (1937), together with a
phonetic rendering and a word-for-word translation.

> Muilsha's gather, swurth a munniath,
> I's father, up in goodness,
> munni-graua-kradyi dhuilsha's munnik.
> Good-luck at stand(ing) thou's name.
> Gra be gredhi'd shedhi ladhu, as aswurth in munniath.
> Love be made upon earth as up in goodness.
> Bug muilsha thalosk-minurth goshta dhurra.
> Give I day-now enough bread.
> Gretul* our shaku, araik muilsha getyas nidyas gredhi
> gamiath muilsha.
> Forgiveness our sin like I forgive persons to do badness I.
> Nijesh solk mwi-il sturth gamiath, but bug muilsha achim
>   gamiath.
> Not take I into badness but take I out-of badness.
> Dhi-il the sridug, thardyurath, and munniath,
> Thou the kingdom, strength and goodness,
> gradhum a gradhum,
> life and life.

*Presumably a slip in pronunciation or writing for *getal*.

The following set, in the Southern Irish dialect, was not 'recorded in
London', as stated in Hancock's accompanying note (Trudgill 1984, 389).
Indeed, it is not an original *Gammon* text at all. It was derived by Connors
and Acton from a set in the *Poggadi Chib* (text 62), contributed by Mr Bill
Cooper to Dr Acton's *Mo Romano Lil* (1971a), and first appeared on
pp.11–12 of *Have You The Feen's Gread Nyocked* – a *Gammon* reader
issued by Romanestan Publications in 1974.

61. As I was a-krushing [going] through the town one day,
   A bold young Buffer [non-Traveller] boy passed by my way:
   I korbed [hit] him so hard, I broke his pi [jaw],
   And the next thing I knew, the shades [police] had took me.

Sing toorali-oorali-oorali-ay (twice),
I korbed him that hard, I broke his pi,
And the next thing I knew,
The shades had bogged [got] me.

Now I sit in the sherrig [cell]
By night and by day,
Eating mouldy potatoes
And rotten old feah [meat].

Now all you bold Travellers
Take warning hereto,
Don't you get to korbing [fighting]
Or the shades'll take you;
Whoa for that!

(Connors and Acton 1974, 11–12)

62. As I was a walking through the gav one day,
A saucy young Gaujo boy passed by my way;
I hit him so hard that I poggered his jaw
And the next thing I knew they had sent for the law.

Sing Toorali-oorali-oorali-ay,
Posh-mullered that Gaujo boy there on that day;
I hit him so hard that I poggered his jaw
And the next thing I knew they had sent for the law.

(Bill Cooper, *MRL*)

Extended Texts

When gorgio mushes meripen and Romany Chals' meripen wells
ettaney, kek kosko meripen see.

(Borrow 1874, 84)

63. Dic at the gargers (Gorgios),
    The gargers round mandy!
    Trying to lel my meripon,
    My meripon (meripen) away.

    I will care (kair) up to my chungs (chongs),
    Up to my chungs in Rat,
    All for my happy Racler (raklo).

    My mush is lelled to sturribon (staripen),
    To sturribon, to sturribon,
    My mush is lelled to sturribon,
    To the Tan where mandy gins (jins).
       (Anon., Walton on Thames; Leland 1873, 186; 1875, 235)

Originally obtained by Leland from a house-dweller, the foregoing 'Gilli
of a Rummany Juva' is repeated on p.152 of L. A. Smith's *Through
Romany Songland*, where it is described as a 'tent song'. It was sung to her,
she says, by Job Lee, a cousin of Jim Lee, 'King of the Paraffin Lees'. Her
set differs only slightly from Leland's and, as in a number of other cases,
one is left wondering whether she had in fact ever heard it sung herself or
was merely exercising a little dramatic licence. The only significant differences are her substitution of 'chump' for 'chungs' and 'ratcher' for 'racler'.
Her retention of the original spelling of 'dic', 'Gargers', 'care' and 'gin' are,
however, sufficient to betray her source. Leland, in his accompanying note,
explains that such oddities were the result of his leaving the text in the form
in which it had been taken down by his informant's *Gaujo* husband.

64. Dic at the Gargers,
    The Gargers round mandy!
    Trying to lel my meripon,
    My meripon (meriben) away.

    'I will care (kair)* up to my chump (chongs),
    Up to my chump in rat,
    All for my happy racher (raklo).
    My mush is lelled to sturribon staripen,
    To sturribon, to sturribon;
    My mush is lelled to sturribon,
    To the tan where mandy gins (jins).'
                                    (Smith 1889, 152)

*The word 'care' in the fifth line may, says Leland, be taken to mean 'go' or 'wade'. This is most unlikely. The phrase of which it forms a part would seem to be a variant of the third line of text 50 – 'oprey the chongor in ratti I'd cour' – and the word in question is surely an alternative form of *koor*, to fight, strike, beat, etc.

Unlike most other songs of *Romano–Gaujo* conflict, Leland's *gilli* is non-specific and lacks the burlesque quality typical of, for example, texts of the 'Mandi Jall'd to puv the grai' type. For this reason it seems to achieve genuine pathos.

~

A Caution

Maw mook teéro graiáw, chawóli, jal talé dóva drom, kei see dóva koóshto chor. Yon te vel pandadó.

Don't let your horses go down that road where the good grass is, mates. They'll be put in the pound.
                                    (Sylvester Boswell)

65. When it is raining, the first thing in mind
    Is tent rods and ridge poles and kettle-cranes to find.
    Up in the morning, the first thing to find,
    They find their old pony in pound for a pound.
    They pukker to the farmer and then they do find,
    They cob that old tit for a half a dollar.
    Up in the morning and then they do find,
    They cob that old tit for a half a dollar.
    Then they shab off on the drom the next day.
    The first thing they find is pannum and bread* for the chavvies.
        (Charlie Scamp, Chartham Hatch, 15 January 1954;
        Kennedy, Folktracks 60–441 A5)

*A needless repetition. *Pannum* is bread.

264

The 'Atchin' Tan Song' (or song of the stopping place) as it is sometimes called, is of particular interest in that, with the advent of motorized transport, the way of life which it describes is, for many Travellers, a thing of the past. It nevertheless remains a firm favourite, particularly among the Gypsies of southern England, being found in a number of versions with relatively little variation. Yet despite its subject matter, it does not appear to be of any great age – the earliest printed version dating from 1954 (text 65). That it is of relatively recent composition is further suggested by its limited use of *Romanés* and the fact that it is also sung wholly in English. Only one other piece in the present collection is similarly available in both forms (text 95).

Very few British Gypsies now live exclusively in tents and those who do are, perhaps, driven by economic/social necessity rather than by the desire to return to a more traditional way of life. The last group of whom I have any definite knowledge consisted of two or three Hertfordshire-based families who had abandoned a rake of extremely dilapidated caravans on an official site for the greater seclusion of the nearby woods. They were very poor and conservative in their habits and had clearly failed to adapt to motorized transport. Whether they genuinely preferred the greater simplicity of their more traditional way of life or had abandoned the official site in order to avoid the economic and legal consequences of poor social performance is difficult to say and one can only assume that their action was prompted by a range of interlocking considerations.

According to one report (Ivatts, personal communication, October 1984),

> Their tents were of modest construction and of traditional design – being semi-cylindrical in shape and some fourteen feet long and six feet wide. In height they were no more than four and a half feet, and were covered in old tarpaulins and carpets. The floors were covered in like manner. The framework was of yew or hazel. The centre panel of the roof could be removed so as to reveal the fire, allowing the smoke to escape whilst ensuring that the two closed ends retained most of the warmth. The principal furniture consisted of a number of upturned crates and a few others containing food, personal effects etc. Their sole means of transport appeared to be an old pram chassis and a couple of ramshackle bicycles.

Yet even this sorry picture assumes something of the character of luxury when compared with the wretched conditions described by Leland in chapter 9 of *The English Gypsies and their Language* (1873):

> One of the last Gypsy *tans* which I visited was merely a bit of ragged canvas, so small that it could only cover the upper portion of the bodies of the man

and his wife who slept in it. Where and how they packed their two children, I cannot understand.

Something of their plight may be guessed at from the *Bokelo Gilli* performed for Leland by Matty Cooper as they stood in the road outside the Oatlands Hotel, Weybridge, one evening in the early 1870s. It is, however, perfectly clear from the last two lines that Cooper's improvisation was first and foremost intended to touch the *Rai*'s heart and, more importantly, his pocket. We may assume that he was successful on both counts as Leland tells us that he slipped the *puro pirengro* the usual half-crown.

> 66. Mándy's chávvis shan bokelo – ókelo – kókelo.
> Shan mūllerin o' shíllaben – híllaben – íllaben.
> Yul lena lek (kek?) hābben – obbin – abobbin
> Shan pauveri, te chúvveni – púvveni – húvveny
> Man'y's bitto tan sī chíngerdo – híngerdo – bíngerdo
> Sī sār in cútter-éngerees – mingerees – fingerees.
> O shillo* bávol pūderla 'dré ye hévyor – shévyor,
> Sārráti mándy shūnova ye wāfo bávo bávela.
> Sārráti mendūi rúvv, mérin for mōro 'pré the púv.
> Man'ys chávvis got kek dye; high de dy, dy dy!
> Diddle dum dum.
> Mandy'd die if 'twasn't for mīro kūshto rye!
> Diddle dum dum, dum dum,
> Diddle, dim dam dum
> Mándy's a chúredo – húrredo – kúrredo.
> High diddle diddle!
>> (Matty Cooper, Weybridge; Leland 1873, 98)

*Sampson, in a discussion of Dyneley Prince's American Gypsy vocabulary (*JGLS* n.s. 2 (1909), 74–84), objects to this form of the adjective, preferring either *shilino* or, following Paspati, *shilalo*. Smart and Crofton give both *shilino* and *shírilo*, but also offer *shílo* in the compound *shilo-tem*, the north (Smart and Crofton 1875, 135). The phrase 'o bávol purdela' is one of those free-floating stereotypical formulae which lie at the heart of the Romani English repertoire. See text 5.

According to Borrow, writing a year before Leland, one might 'walk from London to Carlisle but neither by the roadside nor on the heath or common . . . see a single Gypsy tent' (Borrow 1874, 221). Yet, whilst police harassment and enclosures had undoubtedly forced many Travellers to abandon many of their traditional stopping-places, Borrow's remarks should not be read as implying that the tent itself had fallen out of favour. Nor should it be supposed that the image presented by Leland of the Gypsy *tan* and its occupants was altogether typical. Smart and Crofton, for example, speak of a general movement towards the coast, mentioning one Blackpool Gypsy in particular who, 'though living in a tent, has been so long a squatter on the same spot as to have been assessed for the Poor Rate, which he duly discharges' (1875, 192).

That the Gypsy tent, or 'old sticks and rags' as it came to be known, was often far from modest in construction is also apparent from the following account by Elias Boswell, included in chapter 3 of Groome's *In Gypsy Tents*:

> The tents are of rough blankets. They are nearly always made of brown ones because the white blankets are not so good for the rain. First of all, when they make up the tent, they measure the ground with a ridge pole. Then they take the kettle prop and make the holes exactly opposite each other. Then they take up the ridge pole and stick all the rods into the ridge pole. Then there is a blanket which goes on behind, that is pinned on with pinthorns. Next to that comes the large ones over the top of all, also pinned with the same pins. Now there are some very large and others much smaller; but, for my part, I like a middling size one quite as well, because the large ones are often cold.

By way of comment, Groome goes on to say that the largest tents were some twenty feet long, twelve feet wide and ten feet high, the cost ranging from £10 to £20, according to the materials used. Tilt-like in form, they were, he says, sheltered in winter by a 'balk' or 'barricade' – a kind of 'fore-tent' in which stood the hearth stone or charcoal burner and which might be used to connect two tents pitched front to front. The whole was then surrounded by a shallow trench in order to carry off the rain. Around the inner walls ran a kind of divan, made of straw and covered with rugs whilst, at the further end, was placed a dais of featherbeds and blankets. Among the wealthier Travellers, a carpet might then be laid upon the floor.

A more detailed description of the materials used is given by Sylvester Gordon Boswell. The favoured covering when he was a child in the early years of the twentieth century was, he says, the blankets used to wrap the pulping rollers in the paper mills, the colour varying in accordance with the type of paper produced. The skewers used to pin them together were made of hardwood – mahogany or 'dog wood' or, for preference, the long thorns pulled from the blackthorn or sloe. In order to preserve them, the bark would be scraped off before they had properly dried and the clean wood fried in mutton fat. Thus treated, they would last for years (Boswell 1970).

That such tents were, indeed, comfortable places in which to live is evident from a report in the *Birmingham Daily Post* of 7 June 1869: '. . . the interiors are warm and snug and, more often than not, there is an air of comfort about them which householders hardly believe could be had under

Gypsy conditions of life.' Chairs and tables were by no means a prerequisite, the article continues, but 'the Gypsies were supplied with an abundance of such fabrics and appointments as lent to their dwellings something of an eastern air.'

This likening of Gypsy interiors to those of the east is also to be found elsewhere. 'I wish', says the anonymous author of 'My Friend's Gypsy Journal' (*Good Words*, November–December 1868),

> I could give a vivid picture of the Gypsy tents as they presented themselves to me – two or three in succession. There was an agreeable contrast between the nomadic restlessness and comfortlessness without and the warmth, picturesqueness, almost luxury, of what has more the air of a Turkish divan than of an Arab tent within . . .

Although the tent has been called 'the proper and congenial home of the Gypsies', there is some doubt as to whether this has always been the case. In a letter to the lord treasurer of 1596, Sir Edward Hext, a Somerset JP, speaks of them lying in hay-houses, whilst Dekker, in his *Lanthorn and Candle Light* (1608), tells us that 'the cabins where these land pirates lodge in the night are the out-barns of farmers and husbandmen . . .' Even as late as 1700 we read in the account of the trial of the Browns and Mac Pherson at Banff that it was their habit to lie in kilns or to rent houses for the purpose (*Spalding Club Miscellany*, iii, 275–91).

Many of the early accounts of the Gypsies in Europe are similarly silent on the subject of tents. Kornel's statement, 'extra urbes in campis pernoctabant' and Rufus's 'Se legen in deme velde, vente me wolde se in den steden nicht lyden' are interpreted by Groome as meaning nothing more than that Gypsies of the first wave (*c.*1417) were not allowed to pass the night within the walls of the Hanseatic towns. Arnold von Harff, who visited them at Nauplia (*c.*1497), also makes no mention of their sleeping in tents.

Tents are mentioned, however, as early as 1540 by the German commentator, Agrippa of Nettesheim. The Gypsies, he says, 'lead a vagrant existence everywhere on earth. They camp outside towns, in the fields and at crossroads, and there set up their huts and tents, depending for a living on highway robbery, stealing, deceiving and bartering . . .'

Again, some two centuries earlier, in the *Itinerarium Simonis Simeonis et Hugonis Illuminator ad Terram Sanctam* – an account of the wanderings of two Franciscan friars who left Dublin for the Holy Land on 15 April 1322 – we read of an encounter with a group of tent-dwelling nomads, thought by some commentators to have been Gypsies. According to the author, these tents were of humble appearance, small, black and oblong, somewhat after the Arab fashion. Their occupants, however, were not identified in the original text and it was left to Bataillard, some 500 years later, to suggest that the meeting must have taken place in Crete rather than in Cyprus as originally supposed.

Exactly when the Gypsies of England adopted the tent as their common form of habitation is unclear. Groome thought that the change occurred some time during the second half of the eighteenth century – tents are not mentioned in the Canning papers of 1753 (see note following text 163) – whilst Thompson believed that 'a hundred and fifty years ago they travelled with panniered asses and lived in small tents. Then, good horses and tilted carts were substituted and tents increased in size' (Thompson 1910a, 46). Whatever the truth of the matter, what is perfectly clear from the following account in the *Annual Register* for 1797 is that, by the end of the eighteenth century, some Travellers at least had taken to the tent. The situation described has an ominously familiar ring about it:

> About five o'clock in the morning, twenty police officers came to Norwood in three hackney coaches, threw down all the Gypsy tents, and exposed about thirty men, women and children in the primitive state of man, whom they carried off to prison to be dealt with according to the Vagrant Act.

For a note on the coming of the tent into Wales, see notes accompanying text 137.

What also seems clear is that, as an essentially nomadic people, the Gypsies must always have made use of some form of temporary night-shelter. On exchanging the relatively mild climate of the Mediterranean for the altogether harsher conditions of eastern and central Europe, it also seems likely that some Gypsies may have found it expedient to abandon the tent in favour of something a little more substantial – either houses or agricultural outbuildings. That they were to be found in relatively large numbers in the cities of northern Europe is evident from the writings of the early chroniclers and, indeed, so great a nuisance were they to become that they were eventually forbidden the Hanseatic towns during the hours of darkness. In England, too, the presence in their midst of large numbers of Travellers also seems to have given rise to considerable concern on the part of the settled community. Thus, according to Dekker (*Lanthorn and Candle Light*), they were only allowed to lodge in barns and hay-houses because the latter 'dare not deny them for fear they, ere morning, have their thatched houses burning about their ears'.

Against this background, it is possible to envisage how, as their presence became more onerous and as the means of controlling their activities became more effective, Gypsies were once again forced to look to other less permanent forms of accommodation such as the tent, or more recently, the living wagon. (Somewhat ironically, the pendulum would now seem to have swung back in the opposite direction as the number of stopping-places are reduced and the right to make use of them curtailed by increasingly hostile legislation.)

The idea that the Gypsies may have temporarily abandoned the tent at some point on their westward march only to return to it some time after their arrival in England is further suggested by the fact that whilst Turkish Romani contains some twenty words referring to the tent and its various appurtenances, British Romani has only four. The first, *zigaira*, for which Sampson suggests a possible origin in the Latin *tegurium*, a hut, shed or lodge, is found only in Welsh Romani, whilst the second, *tshater*, apparently a Hindi derivative, appears in only one list, published in the Welsh-language periodical, *Seren Gomer*, for February 1823. The third, and the only one in use among English Gypsies, is *tan*, a transferred epithet which also retains its original meaning of 'place' (Sanskrit: *sthana*; Prakrit: *thana*; Turkish: Romani: *tan*, a place). To these may be added a fourth, *katun*, which has a variety of meanings, including altar cloth, linen and tarpaulin or covering. Like the first two, it is also confined to the Gypsies of Wales.

According to Groome, *tan*, used in its secondary sense of 'tent', is found in no other Gypsy dialect (Groome 1880, 59). Kogalnitchan (1837), it is true, has *tanya*, a tent, in his Romanian Gypsy vocabulary but, as with some 200 other items, including the undeniably British Romani *hotchawitcha*, hedgehog, this is clearly taken from Samuel Roberts (1836). It should also not be confused with the German Gypsy *than* (cloth) which, in common with our English word, 'tent', may be derived from Sanskrit, *tan*, to stretch.

In most versions of the 'Atchin' Tan' song, the horse, which has been allowed to stray on to the farmer's land, is impounded and is only released on payment of a fine. Although the Common Law remedy of Distress Damage Feasant in relation to animals was abolished by the Animals Act of 1971, section 7 of that Act confers a right to detain and sell trespassing livestock.

> 67. When we stops travelling, the first thing in mind
>   It's tent-rods and ridge-poles we now got to find.
>   We tied the old pony's legs and away he did go.
>   Where shall we find him? The Lord only knows.
>   We got up next morning, and searched all around.
>   Where did we find him? We found him in pound.
>   We jalled to the old rai and what did he say?
>   'Pack up your old trap, and clear right away.'
>
> (Reeve 1958)

68. We pulls in by the roadside
    An' first thing in mind
    Is tent rods and ridge poles
    We quickly must find

    We tie up the old pony's legs
    But away he will go
    And where shall we find him?
    The old mulla may know

    We get up next morning
    And search all around
    It's a hundred to one
    We will find him in pound

    We jall to the old mush
    And what will 'e say?
    Pay a bar and pack up
    And clear out right away
    (Frank Copper, Kent, 1960; Brune 1975, 793)

69. When it starts raining, my first thing in mind,
    Is my ridge-pole, my tent rods, my bedclothes to find.
    I put the straw down for my chavvs to lie on;
    I give 'em their supper and put 'em to bed.

    I feather me old pony's legs, there let him go.
    So where shall I find him, the Lord only knows.
    I got up next morning, I searched round and round,
    And when I found me old pony, he was in the pound.

    Oh, I goes to the house and I gives a bold knock;
    'My old pony you have-a-got here?'
    'Yes', said the farmer, 'there's one pound to pay.'
    'If you give me me pony and there let me go,
    I will 'sure you, my gentlemen, you've not seen me before.'

    He gave me m' pony and there I did go.
    I travelled all day till I found a sure spot,
    I unshipped me pony and unloaded me lot.
                    (Mary Ann Haynes, Sussex, January 1973,
                    Yates 1975, 64. Rec.: *Songs of the Open Road*,
                    Topic 12T253)

Mrs Haynes was in the habit of introducing her song with the following unconnected quatrain:

> I was born in an old Gypsies' wagon,
> In fields and by hedges so free;
> And down by that old Gypsies' wagon,
> Is the little tent I was christened in.

The song's evident popularity makes it an obvious choice for inclusion in Stanley and Burke's *Romano Drom Song Book*.

> 70. When we stop travelling, the first thing in mind
> Is moro and mas for the chavvies to find.
>
> Then when it's raining, the next thing in mind
> Is tent rods and ridge poles and kerapens to find.
>
> We tied our old grai's legs, but away he did jell,
> While we suttied all rarti, the truth for to tell.
>
> Up in the sarla the first thing we find,
> We find our old pony in pound for a bar.
>
> But we putch that old rai and after a while,
> We kur that old grai for just half-a-dollar.
>
> Then we shav on the drom the very next day,
> Take our old vardo, and jel right away.
> (Stanley and Burke 1986, 6; 1986, 8)

> 71. When it's raining the first thing in mind
> Is it's tent rods and ridge poles, hay for to find;
> The old pony to hobble I turned him on grass
> But where shall I find him, good Lord only knows.
> I hunted all round, no horse could I find
> I went to the farm door and gave a sound knock;
> Out came the farmer, what is it to pay?
> He said, 'Take your old pony and clear right away!'
> (Nelson Ridley; MacColl and Seeger 1977, 361)

~

When yeck's tardrad yeck's beti ten oprey, kair'd yeck's beti yag anglo the wuddur, ta nash'd yeck's kekauvi by the kekauviskey saster oprey lis, yeck kek cams that a diki-mengro or muskerro should wel and pen: 'so's tute kairing acai? Jaw oprey, Romano juggal.'

272

When one has pitched one's little tent, made one's little fire before the door and hung one's kettle over it on the kettle-crane, one doesn't care for a watchman or policeman to come up and say: 'What are you doing here? Move on, Gypsy dog!'

(Borrow 1874, 81)

The payment of a small fine for the retrieval of horses impounded for grazing without the landowner's consent would seem reasonable enough. The same cannot be said, however, of the distress and inconvenience caused by the unexpected arrival of the police, often long after the family has settled down for the night.

72. We packed up our tent rods, our ridge poles, our pots and kittles
    We went along the road so nice.
    We pulled off to camp, to have a cuppa tea.
    Long come the p'liceman, he said You gotta move.
    Where's your horses? In the poov, get 'em out!
    We have to shift at one o'clock in the morning to get on.
    Ridge poles and tent rods and all things like that
    Chadders in the bottlers* they got to lel out
    Broad day in the morning at four, O, p.m.
    Get the grais in their burdles (bridles) and jell straight away.
        (Carolyne Hughes, Blandford, 1966; MacColl and Seeger 1977)

*In their accompanying note, MacColl and Seeger say that they were unable to determine the meaning of this phrase. There can, however, be no doubt that the reading given in the following edition of the song – *chavvies in their potter* – is correct.

73. We went along the drom 'till we did stop
    With our tent rods and ridge poles, our kettles and a pot.
    To have a cup of tea.

    Along came the musgro, he said 'You gotta move'
    But where were our horses? They were in the puv.
    Get them horses out.

    It was one o'clock in the morning when we had to shift away
    Pack up our kovvels, he wouldn't let us stay.
    Shift along, shift along.

    Ridge poles and tent rods and everything like that,
    Chavvies in their potter, we had to lel them out.
    Lel them out, lel them out.

He wouldn't let us atch 'till four, 'till it were day,
We got the grais harnessed and jelled straight away.
Jelled straight away.

(Stanley and Burke 1986, 13)

~

The grais have taddered at the kas-stoggus – We must jal andurer –
The gorgio's dicked us! (The horses have been pulling at the hay-
stack – We must hurry away – The man has seen us!)

When Gypsies have remained over night on a farm, it sometimes
happens that their horses and asses – inadvertently, of course – find
their way to the hay-stacks or into a good field. *Humanum est errare*!

(Leland 1873, 102)

74.	Mandi jall'd to puv a grai,	1
	All around the stuggas avri;	2
	A mush olv'd to mandi	3
	To lel mi avri.	4
Chorus:	Mandi stripped off at him	5
	And dell'd him in the yak!	6
	And sap mi dira datchel!*	7
	Can't the mush kûr well!	8
	It was all through mi rakli	9
	A-making of the godli,	10
	It brought the mush to mandi	11
	To lel mi avri.	12
Chorus:	Mandi stripped . . .	
	Mandi suv'd yek rardi	13
	In the granze avri,	14
	All along with the tawna rakli, o!	15
	And the gavmush olv'd to mandi	16
	To lel mi avri.	17
Chorus:	Mandi stripped . . .	
	Ov along, miri mush fakker!	18
	Ov along of mandi!	19
	Mandi a mang a kushti cart	20
	From the kêr among the trees.	21
Chorus:	Mandi stripped . . .	

But when mandi mang'd the cart   22
And nisher'd it avri,   23
The gavmush olv'd to mandi   24
To lel mi meriben away!   25

Chorus: But what a kushti bit of fun 26
Mandi will lel   27
Along with my Romani rakli gel.   28
                    (New Forest, Gillington 1911a, no.2)

*See note accompanying text 16.

In considering texts characterized by variants of the opening line 'mandi went to puv the Grais', text 74 offers a convenient starting-point as it is by far the most comprehensive and, as such, best illustrates the way in which a number of free-floating elements may be brought together under the one head. The text itself consists of ten such elements, of which only the last (lines 26–8) would seem to be peculiar to Gillington's informants. In a number of cases, however, what may originally have been entirely unconnected stereotypical lines or phrases have, in the course of time, become inextricably linked and have taken their place in the repertoire alongside their component parts. Thus, although line 1 has been recorded independently (text 2), it is also commonly associated with line 2, and, in such cases, may form the starting-point of a longer set.

In tabular form, these elements, together with the texts in which they are also found elsewhere in the repertoire, may be expressed as follows.

Text 74		Incidence elsewhere in the repertoire
A	(l.1)	2 78 80 81 82 83 84 85 86 88
B	(ll.1–2)	78 79 80 81 82 83 84 85 86 87
C	(ll.1–4)	78 79 80 81 82 83 84 85 86 87
D	(ll.5–8)	16 75 76 78 79 82 85 86 87 88 90 91 92 93
E	(ll.9–10)	78 92 93
F	(ll.5–12)	78 92 93
*G	(ll.13–15)	77 105 109 110
H	(ll.18–25)	94
J	(ll.25)	63–4
K	(l.26–8)	–

*Lines 16–17 appear to be no more than a variant of the formula contained in lines 3–4, 11–12 and 24–5.

Although, as shown above, it is possible to identify almost a dozen individual lines or phrases which, at one time or another, would seem to have enjoyed an independent existence, text 74 may be said to consist broadly of four essentially separate elements – (C), (E), (G) and (J) – held together by an originally unconnected four-line chorus – (D).

From the outset, (C) seems to have formed a relatively stable alliance with (D), the chorus to Gillington's first set. Both are present in the song in its earliest printed version (text 75) but the fact that there would seem to be no established order of precedence would suggest that they were not originally connected. Indeed, (D) was recorded independently on three separate occasions some time prior to the publication of text 75, and in places as widely scattered as Swansea, London and Northumberland.

It first occurs in print in that 'most charming of all books on English Gypsies', F. H. Groome's *In Gypsy Tents*. According to the author, he was talking with one of the Lovells about how difficult it was to recognize some Gypsies for what they really were, and how not only had the language become known to many *Gaujos* but how many Gypsies, particularly the women, now thought it vulgar and beneath their notice. His informant agreed, saying how, on one occasion he was visiting a Swansea tavern, when he found himself in company with a group of quarrelsome Lees, 'a pretty Gorgio' and some 'mumply gorgiofied-looking fellows' who later turned out to be Prices. To look at them, he said, 'You'd never have thought they had one word of Romanes', but when the Lees began to fight, they had responded by singing out:

> 75. Well done, my Gorgio,
>   Del him adré the múi,
>   S'help mi deari Dúvel,
>   You can mill kushtó.
>   (Groome 1880, 50)

Nine years later, a variant of the same quatrain turns up in Smith's *Through Romany Songland*. On a visit to the Gypsies at Upton Manor, Smith tells us how her companion, Mr George Smith of Coalville, 'induced some of the more intelligent youngsters among them to repeat this one verse to him':

> 76. Cush dearie Romany chile,
>   Delli in the moi.
>   Sop me dearie again, Daddy,
>   If I can cawer well.
>   (Gypsy children at Upton Manor;
>   Smith 1889, 139)

The first line of Smith's verse is perhaps meant for *kushto, deari Romani Chal*; whilst 'Sop' in the third is a contracted form of 'so help'. Regarding the word 'cawer', Smith notes that 'the children of the Gypsy tribes invariably speak of singing in this fashion' – a misapprehension which would perhaps account for the otherwise unyieldingly fastidious Mr Smith's interest in the piece. *Cawer* = *koor*, to fight.

Finally, Sampson's informant, Alice Gray, attaches a variant of this quatrain to her set of 'Can you rokker Romani' (text 16), a fact which would seem to confirm its existence as an independent unit in that 'Can you rokker Romany' is nowhere else recorded in association with this or any other material.

The barn motif (G) has also been recorded both in isolation (text 109) and linked with other material (texts 105 and 110). In all three cases, the informants were Scottish Travellers. It first appears, however, in one of Borrow's songs, recognized by Groome as an 'old Romany favourite':

Tugnis Amande

77. I'm jalling across the pāni –
     A choring mas and morro,
     Along with a bori lubbeny,
     And she has been the ruin of me.

     I sov'd yeck rarde drey a gran,
     A choring mas and morro,
     Along with a bori lubbeny,
     And she has been the ruin of me.

     She pootch'd me on the collico,
     A choring mass and morro,
     To jaw with lasa to the show,
     For she would be the ruin of me.

     And when I jaw'd odoy with lasa,
     A choring mas and morro,
     Sig she chor'd a rawnie's kissi
     And so she was the ruin of me.

     They lell'd up lata, they lell'd up mande,
     A choring mas and morro,
     And bitch'd us dui pawdle pāni,
     So she has been the ruin of me.

I'm jalling across the pāni,
A choring mas and morro,
Along with a bori lubbeny,
And she has been the ruin of me.

Woe is Me

I'm sailing across the water,
A-stealing bread and meat so free,
Along with a precious harlot,
And she has been the ruin of me.

I slept one night within a barn,
A-stealing bread and meat so free,
Along with a precious harlot,
And she has been the ruin of me.

Next morning she would have me go,
A-stealing bread and meat so free,
To see with her the wild-beast show,
For she would be the ruin of me.

I went with her to see the show,
A-stealing bread and meat so free,
To steal a purse she was not slow,
And so she was the ruin of me.

They took us up, and with her I,
A-stealing bread and meat so free:
Am sailing now to Botany,
So she has been the ruin of me.

I'm sailing across the water,
A-stealing bread and meat so free,
Along with a precious harlot,
And she has been the ruin of me.
(Borrow 1874, 106)

Although texts 78–93 are here treated together with text 74, their relationship is thematic rather than strictly verbal. Thus, in texts 79, 84 and 86, the
incident takes place by the water rather than in a field, whilst in texts 88
and 92, the offence for which the Travellers are 'taken up' is said to be the
theft of wood rather than hay. In the latter case, this may be the result of
an earlier confusion of *kas* and *kast* (cf. text 74, line 20 where *mang* is given

for the more usual *mong*). If the forms given by Smart and Crofton and Kenrick and Wilson may be regarded as broadly representative of English Romani, and Romani English, it would seem that the medial 'a' typical of many 'purer' continental dialects and, indeed, of certain varieties of Scotto-Romani, has been broadened to an 'o'; e.g. *boro, bokro, kongri, nok* and *yog* (Kenrick and Wilson) as compared with *baro, bakrè, kangri, nak* and *yag* (Baird 1840, 32–6). Thus, Weir (1912a) gives *kasti* and Carmichael (1899–1901) *castis* for *kosht*.

A more likely explanation, however, is that as both actions were likely to result in the same outcome, the same stereotypical formulae would be seen as equally appropriate in both cases.

> 78. Mandy welled to puv the Grys
>   All around the stiggus oprey!
>   Here wels a mush to lel mi oprey!
>   Mandy stripped, ovved to him and delled him in the pur!
>   Sap mi diri tatcheko!* The mush coored well!
>   All thro' the raklos, a-kickin' up a goedli,
>   The mush lelled the Grys.
>   (Gillington, *JGLS* n.s. 1 (1907), 64)

*Presumably a variant of *datchel*, for which see Vocabulary, 109 and text 169. The line is clearly intended to represent the common formula 'so help me God'.

> 79. Mandy went to puv some griys
>   all round the pany side
>   up come the gabmush
>   to lel mandy griys
>   mandy deld him in the moiy
>   todi todi todi cant mandy cour.
>   (Lucy Curtis (née Smith), Cowley, January 1908;
>   *JGLS* n.s. 3 (1909), 158)

Although the foregoing set was apparently obtained from Mrs Curtis by F. C. Wellstood and E. O. Winstedt, it was 'printed as a specimen of Romany orthography from a copy which she, or one of her family, wrote down for another *Romani Rai*'.

> 80. Mandi well'd to puv the grai
>   All around the stiggus akai,
>   Ovva, here's a mush, mi dai,
>   Ovven up the drom!

Ovva, tshavi, mush akai,
Up the drom again!
Dawdi! Dawdi!
You'll get mor'd to-night!
        (New Forest; Gillington 1911a, no.4)

81. Mandi went to poove the grys
    In among the stuggers akai
    The gavvers are arter mandi
    To lel o' me oprey

    Ma, says the rakli
    Dickin at the gavvers
    'Tis like our dear ol' daddy say
    We can't jawl avree

    Up comes the farmer
    Wi' the titties in the pound
    If mandi doesn't want a charge
    I'll have to find three pounds

    Then all around the stuggers
    A tittie my beebee chased
    The gavver said: Now move along
    And don't atch 'ere again
        (Frank Copper, West Kent, 1960; Brune 1975, 777)

The third and fourth verse of Mr Copper's set appear to belong to that other well-known piece, 'At the Atchen Tan' (texts 65 and 67–71). They are also unusual in introducing a burlesque element into the proceedings in the form of the old woman's pursuit of one of the horses 'all round the stuggers'.

82. O, 'tis mandi went to poov the grais,
    All around the stiggers to kai,
    The gavver's arter mandi
    To lel me oprey.

    'Ma,' says the rakli
    Pickin' up a shovel,*
    ''Tis like your dear old daddy says
    You can't kor well.'

*The first time Mrs Hughes sang this line as 'kicking up the godli'.

Well, all around the stiggers
Stealin'** a bit o' kas,
The gavver said 'Whaddaya got?'
I had to put it down.
    (Carolyne Hughes, Blandford, 1962/6;
    MacColl and Seeger 1977, 359)

**An unusually frank admission. See texts 103–11.

83. Mandi went to puv the grais,
    All around the stoggers akai.
    O there ovved the gavver to lel mandi away.
    Jal, jal, chavi, as quick as ever you can,
    The gavver's off to lel you right away now.
    Where is the vonger, to pesser all the vonger?
    We haven't got a penny in the whole widey world.
    O mandi jall'd up the road;
    He dik'd a kanni in the bush;
    He lel'd a stone and mor'd the kanni
    And went and sold it there.
    I sold it to the butcher for five shillings the next day;
    Then the p'liceman come along and lel'd him away.
    Ma, said the gavver, a-picking up the godli,
    Praster through the yard and you won't find more.
        (Carolyne Hughes, Blandford, 1968; Folktracks 441–A10)

84. Mandi jelled to puv the grai,
    Down adre the pani side.
    Up jumped the gav-mush
    And chored my grai away.
    Mandi jelled to dik the rai,
    To lel the grai palé.
    The rai, he pukkered mandi,
    ' 'Twill cost you twenty bar!'
    Mandi delled the bitchering mush;
    The gav-mush lelled me there.
    Now mandi's locked in stiraben
    Until this time next year.
        (Bill Kerswell, *c.*1974; *Traveller Education*, 2 (5), p.32)

Like Frank Copper (text 81), Mr Kerswell would seem to have drawn on that body of material generally associated with songs of the 'Atchin Tan' type.

85. Mandy went to pouv the gries
    All around the didakois
    Here jals the gav mush to lowl mandy gries
    Kakker rukker Romany
    Del him in the porr
    Swop me Dorri ductions if you can't corr well
        (Maggie Gratton, April 1993)

Mrs Gratton, aged 69, explains that this is

a little song my grandfather used to sing to us . . . to my knowledge it's about a man who took his horses and turned them loose around some other Travellers and when the police came to lock them up, his mate said speak in Romany and hit him in the belly. When this was done his mate said God help us you can fight well. (personal communication, April 1993)

She has, however, reversed the meaning of the fourth line.

As noted elsewhere, not all Travellers (Gypsies or otherwise) are persuaded of the value of their language. When Mrs Gratton married, some fifty years ago, her sisters-in-law 'would say when I would start to rukker, oh don't start to talk that old Gypsy talk. But I knew you couldn't make a silk purse out of a sow's ear and anyhow I am what I am and nothing can change that' (ibid.).

86. Mandi went to poove the grai
    Down along the parni side
    Up jumped a gaero
    To low mandi's grai.
    Mandi made a putch at 'im,
    Hit him betwixt his snitch and chin,
    Dordi Dordi Dordi
    Can't mandi couer?
        (Amos Smith; Sandford 1995, 38)

87. Jal down to the stāgus
    To lel a bit o' kas.
    Up veled the gavengro
    To lel me opré.
    Keker be atraš, čavi,
    Keker prāster away.
    Del 'im in the mui, čavi,
    Del 'im in the pur.

282

And mi dīri duvel dačen
He can kūr well.

(Esther Buckland (née Smith);
Atkinson, *JGLS* n.s. 3 (1909), 158)

88. Mandi went in a woš
To tšin a bit of koš,
And mandi got prastered
Because he couldn't džel.

Up stepped the bala.
Kako puk of mandi;
Hit him in the pur.

When mandi dzel'd in the wos,
Muskro wanted to lal him
'Cause he'd tsin'd the kos.
Mandi wouldn't dzel.

(Epsom races, June 1910;
JGLS n.s. 6 (1912), 67)

89. All through the rakoli
Kicking up a gudali
'Long came a muskro.
Tell dad lel'd!

Up with my vastu,
Hit him a nobbalo.
S'up me dīri dad,
And he can't call (kur) well!

Ušitel[?] didikai,
Your father's gone to puv the grai,
Na [near?] the tober skai[?],
Six o'clock in the morning.

(Robert Phillimore, Epsom races, June 1910;
JGLS 6 (1912) 67–8)

The two foregoing sets were noted down by Robert Phillimore and forwarded to the *Journal* by the Revd C. L. Marson. It is not clear whether the editor or one or other of these gentlemen inserted the question marks in the final stanza. These last four lines have been noted separately on a number of occasions. See texts 23–6 and, more particularly, the notes accompanying text 24, where these apparent obscurities are explained.

90. Well done my Romani tsavi!
    Del him up the maisa*,
    Like my dear old dádus;
    Then he did kor well!

    Mandi went round to the stuges
    To tsor a bit of kost:
    Out come the veshengro.
    Well done, my Romani tsavi!

    Did him on the nob:
    That's the way to kor my Romani tsavi.
    If you're like my dear old dádus,
    Then you do kor well.

    Up came the gavengro
    To lel mandi apre.
    Prasti my Romani tsavi
    Like my dear old dad;
    Then you do dzel well!
    ('From the Egyptian rogues about Watford and
    Radlett', January 1912; *JGLS* n.s. 6 (1912), 68)

*Perhaps US boxing slang: *mush*, mouth (Simpson 1986, 603). Alternatively, a variant of *maisie*, a jug (M'Cormick 1907, x–xxiv), for which Russell suggests a possible etymon in the Shetland dialect, form *maishie*, an open basket. Cf. English. slang, *mug*, bread-basket.

91. Mandi's jâin' to stariben
    For lelin' a bit o' košt.
    The muskrâ's prâster'd,
    Mandi will get lel'd.
    Mandi's jâin' across a puv.
    Del him adōr his perinob
    And it's s'help mi dīri dačen
    I can kūr well.
    (Charlie Webb; *JGLS* n.s. 3 (1909), 158)

Charlie Webb is said to have 'derived his Romani from his mother, a Shaw'.

92. Now, all through mi rakli,
    Kicking up a goudli;
    Like my dear old dadus, boy,
    I'll leave her in the tan.

Mandi went to wesh one night
To chin a bit o' cosh;
'Long come a baulo,*
Lelled mandi opre.
Mandi's lifted up the mush
And delled him in the pur;
Says, 'like my dear old dadus, boys,
You can kor well.'
All through mi rakli,
Kicking up a goudli;
Like my dear old dadus, boy,
I'll leave her in the tan.
     (Mary Ann Haynes, Sussex, January 1973;
     Yates 1975a, 71)

*Apparently a rare example of English slang, borrowed by the Gypsies and turned into *Romanés*. In a reissue of Grose's *Classical Dictionary of the Vulgar Tongue* published in 1811, 'pig' is given for police officer and 'China Street Pig' for Bow Street Runner. According to Hotten (1864 edn), the term came to be applied more particularly to a detective or 'nose', which would seem to point to a possible origin in the notion that law officers were given to snouting out their prey as a pig snouts for roots. Cf. the alternative usage, 'grunter'.

Mrs Haynes's song also appears in a slightly modified form in Stanley and Burke's *Romano Drom Song Book*.

93. Mandi went to th'wesh one night
    To chin a bit o' kosh,
    Now all through mi rakli
    Kicking up a guddeli
    'Long came a balo
    Lelled mandi opre.

    Mandi lifted up the mush
    And delled him in the pur.
    Then says mi rakli
    Dordi you can kor well
    Now the balo's lelled mandi
    To stiraben akai.

    All through mi rakli
    Kicking up a guddeli
    Next time I go to th'wesh at night
    To chin a bit o' kosh
    Like me dear old dadrus says
    I'll leave her in the tan.
         (Mary Ann Haynes; Stanley and Burke 1986, 9)

In their note accompanying the following set, MacColl and Seeger say that they were 'unsuccessful in their attempts to trace this little song in any collection'. There can, however, be little doubt that, the first two lines apart, it represents an extended variant (or at least incorporates elements) of the antepenultimate and penultimate sections of text 74. For this reason, it is difficult to accept their suggestion that the phrase 'a kushti cant' (l.3) signifies 'a good house for food'. Rather, it would seem to be a corruption of Gillington's 'kushti cart' (text 74, l.20). If this is so, then 'among', in the third line of Mrs Hughes's song may be read as an attempt to make sense of Gillington's 'mang', to beg. It is, of course, quite possible that Mrs Hughes herself believed that 'cant' meant 'house'. Cf. Thieves' Cant: *ken* = house, a usage still current among some English Gypsies.

94. O, a-beggin' I will go, my love,
    And a-beggin' I will go;
    But a kushti cant among you
    At the farm all in the trees.

    Jal along, jal along, my kushti cant,
    Jal along, jal along, jal along;
    But if our matches ain't gilted
    I'm sure we're to get no scran.

    O, since we been to bed all night
    We been rolling in champagne,
    But there isn't a penny amongst us
    To buy a brimstone pot.

    Jal along, jal along, my ravvle of a nee,
    Jal along, jal along, jal along;
    But a kushti cant among you
    At the farm all in the trees.
            (Carolyne Hughes, Blandford, 1966;
            MacColl and Seeger 1977, 358)

Mrs Hughes explained her song as follows:

Well, years and years ago, hundreds of years ago, the people had a struggle to get their living. Well, they used to go and make match-sticks out of wood and buy the brimstone to gilt the matches to sell 'em. Well, they gilt all the matches and sold 'em and they bought champagne and they got drunk and they never had no money to get no bread with, nor matches the next day-morning. Well, in the trees there was a farm and they went to beg bread there.

In the fourth verse, 'ravvle of a nee' is, perhaps, as the editors suggest, a corruption of 'rakli' or 'romani', but compare *rovval*, wife (Kenrick and Wilson 1985, 36).

Returning to the opening lines of Mrs Hughes's set, it seems possible that these were borrowed, at some stage in the song's development, from the song now generally known as 'A Begging I Will Go', a ten-verse variant of which appears in Playford's *Choyce Ayres and Loyal Songs* (1684). Chappell also suggests that it was sung as 'a beggars' chorus' in Brome's comedy *The Jovial Crew* or *The Merry Beggars*, performed at The Cockpit, Drury Lane, in 1641. Here, however, he would seem to be mistaken. Although *A Beggars' Chorus* is certainly to be found in Act 4 Scene 2 of the play as represented in the first edition of Dodsley's *Old Plays* (Dodsley (1744), 6, 372), it is noticeably absent from the earliest published text, printed by J.Y. for E.D.N.E. and sold at The Gun in Ivy Lane in 1652. Dodsley's song, moreover, is a Canting ditty having no discernible connection with the song here under consideration.

The version given below, which seems to be fairly typical, is from John Holland, an expatriate Yorkshireman living in Worcester in the mid-1960s:

> Of all the trades in England,
> The begging is the best,
> For when a man is tired,
> He may sit him down and rest.
> *And a begging I will go*
> *And a begging I will go.*

> I make my bed where e'er I lie
> and I heed no master's bell;
> Yon man 'ud be daft to be a king
> When beggars live so well.
> *And a begging I will go,*
> *And a begging I will go.*

> I've a pocket for me oat meal
> And a pocket for me salt,
> A pair of lovely crutches –
> By, you ought to see me halt.
> *And a begging I will go,*
> *And a begging I will go.*

> I've a patch upon me fusty coat
> And a patch upon me e'e,
> But when it comes to tupenny ale,
> I can see as well as thee.

287

And a begging I will go,
And a begging I will go.

I've been a beggar all me life,
For I've a wooden leg;
And if a man is lame like me,
There's nowt to do but beg.
And a begging I will go,
And a begging I will go.

The second of the above verses is clearly a nineteenth-century 'rewrite' of Playford's final stanza, which runs as follows:

I fear no plots against me,
I live in open cell.
Then who would be a king,
When beggars live so well?

It has been suggested that this verse contains a veiled reference to the tradition that King James V of Scotland (1513–42) was in the habit of consorting with Travellers (see notes accompanying text 174). He was, it is said, obliged to abandon the practice when, having attempted to seduce one of their women, he was first felled with a bottle and then forced to act as a pack animal (Percy 1765).

What truth there is in this is hard to say but it is perhaps significant that a similar story is also told of the English King John (1199–1216). According to the story, which appeared in the *Lonsdale Magazine* (iii (1822), 312) and was later repeated in Hampson's *Medii Aevi Kalendarium* (i (1841), 224), the king, whilst resident at Alnwick Castle, decided to go incognito among the local peasantry in order to see what they thought of him. On St Mark's Day, 25 May, he fell in with three Tinkers who, having first mocked him, led him to a boggy bottom and caused him to flounder about until he was covered in mud.

On his release, he returned by way of Alnwick town where he was jeered by the people as he passed; but he answered them, saying that their posterity should tread in his footsteps. He then sent armed soldiers after the Tinkers, two of whom were subsequently hanged. The third, who had attempted to intervene with his fellows on the king's behalf, was allowed to go free with a gift of money. The king then made a law to the effect that if three Tinkers were found travelling together, two should be hanged and the third allowed to go free. A similar enactment is also mentioned in the Scottish version of the tale, the king decreeing that whenever three male

Tinkers or Gipsies were found going together, two of them should be hanged and the third set at liberty (Simson 1865, 104–5).

True to his word, the English King also decreed that no man should enjoy the freedom of Alnwick until he had been through the same bog as that into which the Tinkers had led him.

~

Ker si kushto keringrensa
A house is fine for a house-dweller.

(Gypsy proverb)

I leave it to those who have been accustomed to visit the habitations of the poor in the Metropolis, in great cities, in country towns, or in any but those arcadian cottages which exist only in the fancy of the poet, to draw a comparison between the activity, the free condition, and the pure air enjoyed by the Gypsy, and the idleness, debauchery, and the filth in which a large part of the poorer element are enveloped.

(Bright 1818, 530)

95 I'm the Romani rai
   I'm a true didikai,
   I build all my castles beneath the blue sky,
   I live in a tent, and I don't pay no rent,
   And that's why they call me – the Romani rai.

   Kakka chavvi, dick akai,
   Father's gone to sell a mush a kushti grai,
   And that's why they call him – the Romani rai.

   I'm the Romani rai,
   Just an old didikai,
   My home is a mansion beneath the blue sky,
   I was born in a ditch, that's why I'll never grow rich,
   And that's why they call me – the Romani rai.
                              (Anon.; Acton 1981, 33)

96. I'm a Romani Rai
    I'm a young didikai
    I travel the roads with me dog and me grai
    I don't pay no rent
    'Cos I live in a tent
    And that's why they call me
    The Romani Rai.

Dikka chavi, dik akai
Dikka chavi, dik akai
Daddy's trying to sell the mush a kushti grai
Kakka chavi, dik akai
Kakka chavi, dik akai
That's why they call me
The Romani Rai.

I'm a Romani Rom
I travel the drom
I hawk all the day and dance through the night
I'll never grow rich
I was born in a ditch
And that's why they call me
The Romani Rai.

I'm a Romani Rai
I'm a true didikai
I make willow creels, on the bosh play the reels
I'll sing you a song
'Fore the gavvers gell me on
And that's why they call me
The Romani Rai.

(Mark o'Gallaidhe; Sandford 1995, 27)

Although it has been suggested that the foregoing has something of the
appearance of a music-hall borrowing, it continues to enjoy considerable
popularity among English Gypsies and is clearly regarded by many of
them as their own. Thus, Wally Fuller in conversation with Peter Kennedy:

WF: This song's years old, you know – a hundred years – it is; well, before
         ever my father's time, i'n it? –
PK: And is it sort of well known among you people?
WF: Only just like us class of people, like, you know – that's right – no
         strangers, like, you know. No locals – no locals know this.

(Wally Fuller, Sussex, 1950; Kennedy, Folktracks 140)

Richards's Gypsy informants, however, appear to have viewed the
matter somewhat differently. 'You will not hear many Gypsies singing
songs like "The Romani Rye" ', he writes in his *Countryman* article, 'Songs
the Gypsies Saved' (1976–7, 23). 'It is not that they dislike such songs, but
they probably do not know them. One Gypsy in north Devon who did
happen to know one verse of the . . . song explained that he did not think it
was an old song, and certainly it was not made up by "real Travellers".'

290

Although, whatever its origins, the song now seems to be unknown outside the Gypsy community, it is as often as not heard only in English, with the exception of the key words *Romani rai* and *diddikai*. Richards includes the following fragment in his article and Brune offers two further variants (1975, 750), of which one is reproduced below as text 98:

97. I'm a Romany rye, a dear didikai
    I live in a palace beneath the blue sky
    I don't pay no rent and I live in a tent
    And that's why they call me the Romany rye.
                                    (Richards 1976–7, 33)

98. I'm no Romany Rye, I'm a real Didikai
    I bide in a bender beneath the blue sky
    In a van or a tent where I don't pay no rent
    That's why the locals calls me a Romany Rye

    And I'm thinking of getting married
    With a mort* or two of me own
    And move around all over England Like the ones fully blown.
              (John Smith, Birmingham, 1962; Brune 1975, 750)

*Originally Thieves' Cant and included in almost all Cant vocabularies since Harman; e.g. the *Dictionary of the Canting Crew* (*c*.1690): 'a woman, wife or wench'. Perhaps from old French *amorete*.

As might be expected, whilst the song's message remains the same, the link between variants is as often as not thematic rather than strictly verbal. The following set is from the singing of Phoebe Smith, as recorded by Peter Kennedy some time during the period 1956–62 (Folktracks 100). Mrs Smith recites the song before singing and one is immediately struck by the high degree of consistency between the two texts – the only significant difference between the two occurring in line 10, of which the spoken form is given in brackets. There are, however, clear signs of editing between the antepenultimate and penultimate lines of the spoken text and one cannot help but agree with Mike Yates's observation to the effect that, taken as a whole, the tape has something of the air of a poorly edited radio documentary (Yates 1977).

99. I were borned in an old Gypsy's wagon;
    I were brought from those commons you know.
    An' our troubles begin in the winter,
    That's when we've nowhere to go.

But I'm intermined to marry the girl that I love,
Take a wagon and tent on my own.

I'm a Romani rai, a poor diddikai,
Borned in a tent underneath the blue sky;
I want no gilted mansion,
That life will jist suit me
(I want no lovely 'ome).
You give to me the open sky
And the song of the lark as it flies so high.
Roamin' around the country,
That life will jist suit me.
For I am a Romani, everyone knows,
An' a Romani I shall be.

For Brune (1975, 750), 'The Romani Rai' is wholly romantic in tone; yet there is surely more than a hint of self-mockery in the idea that the Gypsy is a man of property and his mansion a tent or a ditch. The idealized notion of the simple open-air life serves merely to highlight the harsh realities of experience; for, even as outsiders, we are conscious of the gap which exists between the pleasant fiction advanced in the song and a way of life which, for much of the time, is characterized by hardship, un- certainty and conflict. In the following Gypsy *malaguena*, quoted by Brown and Lal, no attempt is made to conceal this underlying irony:

Me has despreciado por pobre
Y cuatro palacios tengo:
El asilio, el hospital,
La carcel y el cementierio.

I have riches, though I am poor;
Of palaces fine, I've four:
The mad-house and the hospital,
The cemetery and the jail.

Something of the same insouciance is also to be found in the third verse of Mrs Hughes's song 'A Beggin' I Will Go' (text 94):

O since we been to bed all night,
We been rolling in champagne,
But there isn't a penny amongst us
To buy a brimstone pot.

292

That the travelling life does have its compensations is, however, apparent from the following, taken from a letter written by a reluctant Gypsy house-dweller and published by Thompson in *Tramp Magazine* in 1910:

100. Del mandy the Romanichals' meriben to jal on the drom and shune the dear bitty cherikles gillying in the rookies and atch in a green puv and dick at the staris sore the rarty. Dordy, pal, mandy do hate to be clisend opray in a nasty ker.

The joys of the travelling life also find expression in the following expansion of text 98:

> I want no gilded mansions,
> I want no gilded hall.
> Oh, give me the open sky
> And the song of the lark that is flying high.
> I'm a Romani, everyone knows
> And that's good enough for me.
>
> I will travel all round this country
> With a heart that's ever willing
> And I will cry, why you can buy
> Three pots for a shilling.
> (Fred Wood, Boxhill; Brune 1975, 751).

According to Mrs Hughes, 'All our troubles begin in the winter. That's when we've nowhere to go'; but in the summer time, even the unwelcome attention of the *gaujos* may seem marginally less onerous. The following, says Leland, 'came forth one day, from a Gypsy in my presence, as an entirely voluntary utterance. He meant it for something like poetry – it certainly was suggested by nothing and, as fast as he spoke, I took it down.'

101. It's kushto in tattoben for the Rommany chals. Then they can jāl langs the drum, and hatch their tan acai and odoi pré the tem. We'll lel moro habben acai, and jāl andūrer by-an'-byus, an' then jāl by rātti, so's the Gorgios won't dick us. I jins a kūshti puv for the graias; we'll hatch 'pré in the sala, before they latcher we've been odoi, an' jāl ān the drum an' lel moro habben. (Leland 1873, 143)

Another of Leland's informants, asked if he knew anything of the *surelo rukk* or oak tree (lit. strong tree), replied: 'Only what I have often heard our people say about its life'; and, although these few lines of remembered lore cannot be called verse in the accepted sense, as with text 100, the picture they convey is surely suggestive of a poetic imagination.

102. Dui hundred besh a hatchin, dui hundred besh nasherin his chuckko,* dui hundred besh 'pré he mullers, and then he nashers s(r his ratt and he's kekoomi kushto.

> Two hundred (shel) years growing,
> Two hundred years losing his coat,
> Two hundred years before he dies,
> And then he loses all his blood
> And is no longer good.
>
> (Leland 1873, 31)

*Janet Tuckey, in one of her Gypsy lyrics, gives *kral-rukk* (the king's tree) for the oak.

But poetry and romance are essentially subjective and there is always the danger that we may read more into a text than was originally intended. This is all the more likely if the text has been composed in a language other than our own and by a people whose habits of thought may be entirely foreign to us. The following is a rendering of an original Gypsy lyric obtained from a group of 'so-called German Gypsies' camped near Penwortham Bridge on 31 July 1906 and published as such on p.31 of Macfie's *Romanichels, A Lucubration* (1909). Along with a number of other 'examples of genuine Gypsy melodies compiled by Bob Skot of Liverpool', it received a somewhat unlikely public airing at a *conversazione* of the Clevedon Naturalists' Association held on 14 January 1909, where it was performed by Messrs Hazell, Lockett and Winsor, accompanied, on the pianoforte, by Miss Margaret L. Lloyd of the Somerset Weavers.

> A thought came to my head,
> O Greto, sweetheart mine,
> To drink with thee the red,
> The ruddy blood-red wine.
> To sport with thee all day,
> And dance the whole night long:
> I'd gold enough to pay;
> 'Twould cost us but a song.
> Greto, it cannot be.
> The woods must make our home;
> The meadows by the sea,
> The dusty roads to roam;
> The melodies birds sing;
> To hearten us, the sun;

Our wine, the crystal spring,
For money have I none.

The original, together with MacRitchie's rather more literal and arguably more effective translation, runs as follows:

Sas man gindo, Greto,
Tusa te mulati,
Trin jes tai trin racya
Pe parni molori;
Ci kostal lil mai but
Valbar ek-selénzi (bis)
Aía! aía! aíaaa!

Kade si te nasas
Sar le sosoiora
Santzóne, le buréne,
Le bare droméne (bis)
Le bare baryéne
Ta l' bare veséne
Aía! aía! aíaaa!.

I had a thought, Greto,
(To be) with thee at the wine,
Three days and three nights
At the white light wine;
'Twould not cost (us) more
Than a bill for a hundred (marks).
So we must run away
Like the little hares
To the burrows, to the brushwood,
To the high roads,
To the parks,
And to the great woods.

(*JGLS* n.s. 2 (1907) 118–19)

~

. . . an old Gypsy man once gravely assured me that they had no word in their tongue for 'thief'. The old rogue, I may remark, was convicted of sheep stealing at the Bury assizes, after he had solemnly assured me that the name and the practice alike were unknown among the Romané.

(Tom Taylor, 1859)

Loud when they beg, dumb only when they steal.
(William Cowper, 1785)

> 103. If ever I dae gang a-chorin'
> By Heavens an' I chor by mysel'
> A-moolin' the ghahnees be dozens
> An' I'll hae nae-baddy wi' me to tell
> *An' if ever I dae gae to the stardie*
> *As I hope to the Lord I ne'er wull*
> *I'll meet a' my comrades an' 'lations*
> *For they've a' gat a twelve-month in jull*
>
> An' if ever I dae gae to the stardie
> As I hope to the Lord I ne'er wull
> I'll go back to my wife and my family
> As true as there's Erin's Green Isle.
> (Travellers at Fillans, Loch Aern, Perthshire, 1956;
> Brune 1975, 768)

Described elsewhere by MacColl and Seeger as 'this strange Cant ditty', the foregoing set is accompanied by the following brief editorial note: 'A nonsense song with a surprisingly wide distribution, having been noted all over the British Isles with only slight local alteration in the words . . .' (Brune 1975, 795). Strange it may be, but nonsense, no – even though, in its most comprehensive form, it would seem to represent something of a departure from the normal run of Traveller song, echoing those macaronic sets from the Irish tradition in which the conciliatory tone of the English words is turned on its head in the intervening Gaelic lines. That it has been noted all over the British Isles is also open to question. Indeed, for all his airy assurance, it is noticeable that, in a work otherwise copiously annotated, Brune refers to no other printed or recorded sets. It seems first to have been printed in 1909 in a much reduced form given by Esther Buckland:

> 104. When I jâs a-čoring,
> I'll jâ by my kukeri;
> Then there'll be no rumbling nor grumbling,
> And no one lel'd but my kukeri.
> (Esther Buckland née Smith;
> Atkinson, *JGLS* n.s. 3 (1909), 159)

In the following sets, obtained respectively from Willie MacFee and Jeanie Robertson, the hero of the song is introduced as Jimmy

296

Drummond. Indeed, according to Robertson (*JSS* 21, 96), the song was composed in gaol by this same Drummond, a distant relative of her granny. The jail in question has, however, never been satisfactorily identified. Oldham, Dublin and Arran have all been suggested without much conviction. The song should also not be confused with 'Durham Gaol', an entirely unrelated piece composed by Tommy Armstrong, 'the bard of the Durham coalfield', who died in 1914.

> 105. O, my name it is Big Jimmie Drummond,
>   My name I will never deny;
>   I will moolie the ghanies in dozens,
>   And there'll be naebody there for to tell.
>
>   O, last nicht I lay in a cauld granzie,
>   (Last nicht) I lay in the cauld gaol;
>   O, my mort and my kinshins are scattered,
>   And I dinna jan whaur they may be.
>
>   But if ever I dae gang a-chorin'
>   I'll be sure for to gang by mysel',
>   I will moolie these gahnies in dozens,
>   And there'll be naebody there for to tell.
>   (Big Willie MacFee; MacColl and Seeger 1977)

> 106. For ma name it is young Jimmy Drummond,
>   I'm a man that youse aa know quite well;
>   I was quickly handcuffed and shackled
>   An I was led to poor owl' Dan'l's jail.
>
>   For I quickly did alter my colours
>   When I heard one round twelve-month in jail;
>   For I quickly did alter my colours
>   When I was led to poor owl' Dan'l's jail.
>
>   For it's nae mair I'll bing a-chorin'
>   For I swear to my God 'at's above,
>   And whenever the hornies bings on me
>   They'll have no one to snatch but mysel.
>   (Jeanie Robertson, 1962; *JSS* 21 (1977), 96)

In an earlier recording, made in Aberdeen in 1953, Robertson omits the first two lines. It is, however, clearly the same song; the only other change of consequence being the use of the word *chavvies*, children, in the penultimate line in place of the more obvious *hornies*, police.

297

107. I was neatly handcuffed and shackled
     An' I was led to poor owl' Dan'l's jail.
     For I quickly did alter my colours
     When I heard one round twelve month in jail.
     For I quickly did alter my colours
     When I was led to poor owl' Dan'l's jail.

     But it's nae mair I'll bing a chorin'
     For I swear to my God it's above,
     An' whenever the chavvies bings on me,
     They'll have no one to snatch but mysel'.
          (Jeanie Robertson, Aberdeen, 10 November 1953;
          Folktracks 60–441)

Of the six sets reproduced here, the following, from the singing of Jessie MacDonald, is clearly the most comprehensive and for this reason, for the non-Traveller, the most satisfactory. More importantly, the change of language between the end of the third and the beginning of the fourth verse would seem to be particularly significant:

108. Oh, my name it is young Jimmy Drummond,
     Oh, a man that youse all know quite well;
     I was tooken and neatly got shackled,
     Aye and laid into old Arran jail.

     Oh, it's up spoke his aul' aged mother,
     She was standin' back by in despair;
     'Oh well, son, we will go broken hearted,
     If you be logged this day.'

     Oh, it's up spoke the Sheriff and jury;
     Oh, and him to poor Drummond did say,
     'Oh it's Drummond, oh Drummond, you're guilty,
     You're lookin' so white and so pale.'
     But he very soon altered his colours
     When he heard upon twelve months in jail.

     If ever I dae get oot o' this,
     I will swear to my great God above,
     I will decently work for a living
     And go home to the friends that I love.

     If ever I dae gang a-chorin',
     I'll be sure aye and chor by mysel,
     And if ever the gaffies comes on me,
     There'll be naebody there for to tell.

And I'll moully the gaffies (ghahnies) in dozens
And there'll be naebody there for tae tell.
(Jessie MacDonald; *JFSS*, Hall 1975, 57)

It will be noticed that both MacFee and Robertson also switch from English to Cant at some point in the narrative – MacFee limiting himself to two lines of English by way of introduction before 'crossing over', Robertson distinguishing between the arrest/imprisonment element (English) and Drummond's statement of intent (Cant). But what, if anything, is the significance of this change?

One possibility is that we are here dealing with two entirely separate songs, a view strengthened by the early appearance and subsequent retention in isolation of the Statement of Intent element – in *Romanés* rather than in Cant or English (texts 104 and 103). This, however, seems unlikely, for whilst it is by no means uncommon to find portions of two or more English or two or more Romani/Cant pieces brought together in this way, examples of cross-grafting are extremely rare. Indeed, there is only one other limited instance of this in the present collection (text 94).

The alternative is that 'Jimmy Drummond' is not a composite but a single item and that texts 103 and 104 were simply hived off from an original whole, just as text 159 has been extracted from the original ballad of 'Captain Grant the Highwayman'. If this is so, then we have the one song consisting of a public statement in English and a private statement in Cant, the reason for which becomes perfectly clear in Jessie MacDonald's set. In the first half we learn of Drummond's arrest, trial, imprisonment and, most importantly, his repentance; in the second part, however, we, or rather his fellow Travellers, are told an entirely different story. Far from leaving off the *choring*, it is his intention to redouble his efforts and to reduce the risk of betrayal by going solo – a clear vindication of the old German saying, 'Gypsy repentance for stolen hens is not worth much.'

Although by no means common, a similar device is also employed in certain macaronic texts from the Irish repertoire. In the following example (Royal Irish Academy, MS 23. a. 16), said to have been composed in Newfoundland by the Clare poet Donncha Ruadh Mac Conmara (1715–1810), it is the author's true feelings for the English king which are concealed in the Irish lines. In each case, I have inserted the meaning of the latter in brackets.

As I was walking one evening fair
Is mé go déanach i mBaile Sheáin,
(and I (out) late in Baile Sheáin)
I met a gang of English blades

Is iad á draochadh ag a namhaidh;
(And they getting a beating from their enemies)
I sang and drank so brisk and airy
With those courageous men of war –
Is gur bhinne liom Sasanaigh ag rith le foiréigean
(sweet to me to see the English running for their lives)
Is gurb iad clanna Gael bocht a bhuaigh an lá
(and the poor irish win the day).

I spent my money by being freakish,
Drinking, raking and playing cards –
Cé nach raibh airgead agam ná gnéithre
(Although I had neither money nor store)
Ná rud sa saol ach ní gan aird
(Nor anything in the world of any value);
Then I turned a jolly sailor,
By work and labour I lived abroad
Is bíodh ar m'fhalaingse gur mór an bhréag sin
(And by my cloak! T'is a great lie)
Is gur beag den tsaothar a thit lem' láimh
(It was little work that came my way.

Newfoundland is a wide plantation,
'Twill be my station before I die;
Mo chrá go mb'fhearr dom bheith in Éirinn
It is my torment that I would rather be in Ireland)
Ag díol gáirtéirí ná ag dul faoin gcoill
(Selling garters or wandering in the wood).
Here you may find a virtuous lady,
A smiling fair one to please the eye –
An paca straipeanna is measa tréithe
(A pack of whores of the worst sort),
Is go mbeiread féin ar bheith as a radharc
(Would that I were out of their sight).

Come drink a health, boys, to royal George,
Our chief commander – nár ordaigh Chríost
(Whom Christ has not ordained),
Is aitchimis ar Mhuire Mháthair
(Let us implore Mary, our Mother)
É féin is a ghardaí a leagadh síos
(To strike him down and his soldiers, too);
We'll fear no cannons or loud alarms
While noble George shall be our guide –
Is a Chríost go bhfeiceadas iad dá gcárnadh

(Christ grant we see them piled in heaps)
Ag an mac seo fán uainn ag dul Frainc
(By the lad who is leaving us, going to France).

That so effective a device is not employed more often in the English and Scottish Traveller repertoire is almost certainly due to the fact that dialect song is an essentially private affair. Indeed, as far as the Gypsies are concerned, even singing in English before strangers is far less common than among Scottish and Irish Travellers, for whom street singing has long represented a recognized source of income. Somewhat less unusual, however, is the related song type, the sung warning, whose successful use also depends upon the listener's ignorance of the chosen language (see texts 34–7).

Romani, it is true, has been described as a 'secret language', one of whose functions is the exchange of restricted information in the presence of outsiders. Yet, whilst on occasions it may also have been used merely to tease the curious *Gaujo*, it does not seem to have acquired the same agressively subversive edge as, for example, the *Lasson Acodesh*, the so-called Holy Dialect of the Piedmontese Jews which 'a few generations back . . . still numbered a few hundred words and locutions consisting, for the most part, of Hebrew roots with Piedmontese endings and inflections' (Levi 1989, 8).

'Even a hasty examination', as Levi goes on to say,

points to its dissimulative and underground function; a crafty language, meant to be used when talking about *Goyim* when in the presence of *Goyim*; or else to reply boldly with insults and curses, that are not to be understood, against the regime of restrictions and oppressions which they (the *Goyim*) had established.

Something similar to the linguistic shift evident in 'Jimmy Drummond' is, however, to be found in the following Vlax Gypsy *mesaljaki djili*, or 'table song', in which the prisoner, having thrown himself on the prosecutor's mercy in Slovakian (the official language of the court), goes on to curse him roundly in Romani when his request is denied. The effect is marred, however, as both the prosecutor's refusal and the prisoner's subsequent (public) blandishments are also spoken in Romani.

> . . . '*Jaj* Pane prokurator,
> Pustite ma domov,
> Lebo mám tri deti,
> Peknú mladoženu!'

'Naštig me mukhav tu,
Trestničina kerdan,
Trestničina kerdan,
Le Jeros murdardan.

'Le Jeros murdardan
Lesk o pistoji lan.'
'Je bebaszom, čořej,
Tjira dake Devles!'

T apal phendas
Jaj 'jano tuke, jano
Pa čeri čerhaja, jaj
De palpale, mo, hej,
Muři slovodija!' . . .

. . . *'Yoi, Mr Prosecutor,*
Let me go home,
I have got three children,
And a beautiful fiancée.'

'I cannot let you go,
You committed a sin,
You committed a sin,
You killed Jero.

You killed Jero,
You shot him with a pistol.'
'Fuck you, wretched,
Fuck your mother's God.'

Then he said

'I'll fetch you, I'll fetch you
Stars from the sky,
Just set me, heh,
At liberty.' . . .

(Kovalcsik 1985, 87)

As suggested elsewhere, apparent textual lacunae in sets drawn from the British Gypsy repertoire may, for the most part, be explained by reference to the Gypsies' radically different understanding of the nature and function of folk song generally. It has also been pointed out that the way in which the same or similar material is handled by Scottish Travellers has rather more in common with the approach adopted by the settled community. Yet, whilst this is undoubtedly the case as regards material

originated and retained in Scottish-English, the apparent corruption of
'Jimmie Drummond' and other similar texts (texts 31, 110 and 131) would
seem to suggest that something of the same reductive process typical of
much Romani song may also inform Scottish Travellers' treatment of texts
normally only associated with Cant.

The reduction of 'Jimmie Drummond' may be expressed in tabular form
as follows.

Text	Intro	Arrest	Trial	Sentence	Repentance	True intent
108	****	****	****	****	****	****
106	****	****	----	****	****	****
107	----	****	----	****	****	****
105	****	----	----	****	----	****
103	----	----	----	----	****?	****
104	----	----	----	----	----	****

Robertson, whose command of the Big Ballad is beyond dispute, seems to
have missed the point here as in both of her sets Drummond's intention to
reform is spoken in Cant. Her account of the trial/sentence is also
somewhat confused.

In all probability, the second verse of MacFee's set (text 105) had no
place in the original song as it has been recorded elsewhere both in
isolation (text 109) and in association with other material (texts 74, 77 and
110). In the last case, it is used as the starting-point for a piece of extended
improvisation for which the informant, Davey Stewart, is particularly well
known (see text 135). The barn motif itself may at one time also have
functioned independently as the quatrains which it introduces may vary in
content. It seems first to have been recorded by Borrow (1874, 106), who
used it to introduce the second verse of his 'Tugnis Amande' (text 77) – 'I
sov'd yeck rarde drey a gran'.

> 109. Last night I lay in a gransee,
> My mort and my kencheens vree (there),*
> But tonight I lie in ker stardee
> And I dare nae nash avree.
> (John MacDonald; Peter Shepherd ex L. A. Hall 1975)

*The note in the original printed version suggesting that 'vree' (l.2) means 'there' is,
perhaps, mistaken. So far as I am aware there is no other recorded instance of the word
being used in this way. Rather, its usual meaning, 'out of' or 'away', would seem to
accord better with 'scattered' in l.7 of MacFee's set. It may, however, be no more than a
mishearing of 'three' as in l.2 of text 110.

110. O last nicht I was in the granzi,
    Me an' my mort, my gethrin three.
    O the nicht I'm in caul' iron, geddie;
    How could I bing avri?

    O to bing avri fae the hornies,
    The thing I'll never do;
    To bing avri fae the stardi,
    I cannae get oot the noo.

    O me an' my manishi, laddie,
    We set out from Aberdeen to bonny Dundee,
    But we couldna get to stollich(?),
    We had to bing avri.

    O to bing avri in the winter, geddie,
    It's caul' weather you ken the noo,
    An' we took a wee bit campie
    Upon Blaire Gowrie, too.

    O next morning noo it was snawin',
    I didna ken what to dae
    I lifted my pipes into my hond
    An' started for to play.

    O the hornies come that darkie
    To lift my kenshins three;
    They binged me avri to the stardi,
    I got sixty days, you see.

    So last nicht I was in that granzi,
    Me an' my mort an' my gethrin three.
    O the nicht I'm in caul' iron, geddie;
    How could I bing avri?

    To bing avri fae the hornies,
    The thing I'll never do.
    To bing avri fae the stardi,
    I cannae get oot the noo.

    Now I'm singing this song from London town,
    It's great to hear my voice;
    An' people back in bonny Dundee
    Shall always now rejoice.

They'll think of Davey the singer,
Whereever he may be;
Ah, geddie, last nicht I was in the stardi,
But how could I get avri?
(Davey Stewart, Dundee, 3 June 1953; Folktracks 441)

Kanni choring also forms the subject of the following piece, taken from the singing of Jim Penfold for inclusion in Stanley and Burke's *Romano Drom Song Book*:

111. When mandi went a-kannying up by the raiko* ker,
The kannies they were jassing, they were jelling everywhere.
I kurred a kanny in a gonner and lelled it on my back
Prastering across the bori puv, 'twas mandi jelling back.

I diks a gav-mush on his bike and the gavver he diks me
So mandi started prastering as fast as I could be.
I atched down in a bori ditch the gavver couldn't dik
And bent down to me chokkers while the gavver dikked.

I kurred me chokkers in some khin cause khin laid everywhere
Couldn't atch opre the bori ditch the gav-mush was still there
I suttied there all the rarti, I was a pretty sight
Covered from sherro to chokkers with khinder all the night.
(Jim Penfold; Stanley and Burke 1986, 19)

*An extremely rare survival of the genitive of *rai*.

Despite Crabb's assertion that Gypsies seldom if ever steal from hen coops (Crabb 1832, 49), the practice does seem to be one with which they have long been associated. As early as *c*.1475, an anonymous Swiss play opens with a farmer telling his wife to fetch in the hens and make fast the barn because the *Heiden* are coming (Mone 1846, 2, 378ff.), whilst in Jonson's *Masque of the Gypsies Metamorphosed*, given before King James I in 1621, we find the following stage direction: 'Enter a Gypsy, leading a horse laden with five little children bound in a trace of scarves upon him; a second, leading another horse laden with stolen poultry.' In the Denham Tracts is also to be found the following quatrain, from which we may deduce that in Scotland, too, *kanni choring* was once as much a part of the Gypsies' stock-in-trade as fortune-telling:

For every Gypsy that comes to toon,
A hen will be a missing soon;

305

And for every Gypsy woman old,
A maiden's fortune will be told.

That the importance of *choring* was recognized by the Gypsies themselves is suggested by the following prayer, cited by Vaillant and translated from the Romanian Gypsy by Sampson in a paper given before the Warrington Literary and Philosophical Society in 1897:

Sweet little God, I beseech you to give me everything I demand because thou art lovely, great and strong. If thou permittest me to steal a loaf, if thou permittest me to steal a brandy, a hen, a goose, a sheep, a pig, a horse, I will give thee a grave candle; If I have stolen anything and the gentiles enter my tent to see what I have stolen, and find nothing, I will give thee two grave candles; if the officers of the law enter my tent in search of stolen property and, having searched and found nothing, depart in peace, I will give thee three grave candles because thou art my sweet little golden God.

For the Gypsy to invoke the aid of the Almighty in such matters might, at first glance, appear little short of blasphemous. Yet nothing could be further from the truth, for whilst if not actually a religious duty, theft from the *Gaujo* has its own morality and may, at least in part, be regarded as a wholly justified political act. Thus, be it poaching, the *hokano baro*, the provision of imperfect goods and services, or even, in rare cases, outright theft, a successful outcome, whatever the ostensible motive, involves the renewal of self-esteem and the affirmation of equality or even superiority. Even the mere attempt may be justified as a legitimate act in the continuing war of attrition between the two communities. As one unnamed Gypsy put it:

It's a rotten town . . . They *lel* you *opré* for *cici* (arrest you for nothing at all). It's ag'i'n the law to dope horses (*bik driz*), do any bootleggin', or *sima covas* as was *cord* (pawn stolen goods). In fact, it's gettin' so you can't make an honest livin'. (Brown 1924, 177)

Small wonder, perhaps, that such strait-laced Victorian commentators as George Smith of Coalville went so far as to impute an almost pathological lawlessness to certain Gypsies of their acquaintance:

lying, begging, thieving, cheating and every abomination that low cunning craft, backed by ignorance and idleness, can devise, they practice. In some instances, these things are carried out to such a pitch as to render them more like imbeciles than human beings endowed with reason. (Address to the Social Science Congress held in Manchester in October 1879)

Sampson, however, like Crabb, had found little evidence of the Gypsies engaging in gratuitous acts of straightforward larceny, 'being far too clever to need to have recourse to such barbarous methods for acquiring other people's property', and this assessment would certainly seem to be supported by the following testimonial to the good character of the New Forest Gypsies which appeared in *The Times* for 12 October 1842:

> Their conduct is well worthy of admiration . . . Not one single article of his [the farmer's] property is found missing whilst these vagrant supplicants remain on the outskirts of the premises. The farmers consider themselves, as to their homesteads and property, always safe when Gypsies are encamped near them . . . A farmer considers a Gypsy a good watch-dog against poachers, sheep stealers, and 'neighbours'.

In a second article, however, dated 14 November 1842 (p.5, col.6), these same New Forest Gypsies are shown in quite a different light. In it, we read how a rash of unexplained fatalities among the local sheep population was only brought to a close when a farmer, who also kept a kennels, had one of the carcasses quartered for his hounds. The Gypsies, it transpired, had been surreptitiously stuffing the unfortunate animals' mouths with their own wool, thus causing them to suffocate. They would then beg the bodies from the mystified owners who were only too happy to part with them, fearing the possibility of contagion.

Perhaps Moses Holland was right when he told Norwood that, in his opinion, the Gypsies' principal means of subsistence consisted in 'drabbing the bawlee, tschuring kas for the gry and tassering the maso' – poisoning pigs, stealing hay for the horse and choking the sheep (diaries, 24 July 1857). At any rate, a century earlier, a similar tale is told in the *Discoveries of John Poulter*, the horse thief, a work consisting of a confession of his own crimes and an account of those of his accomplices, a description of the principal branches of roguery common at the time and a few specimens of the Canting Tongue. In a section dealing with the 'Faws or Gipseys', he tells us that 'they are great *Prigers* of *Caunes* and *Bucket chats*, that is sheep and fowl', and 'great *Prigers* of *Lulley*, that is Linnen, and ought to be taken up and sent home as Vagrants' (Poulter 1753, 36–7).

As regards their method of stealing sheep, he has the following to say:

> . . . and the Way they steal Sheep and break his Neck, and they leave it there till the Morning, when the Shepherd or Owner comes in the Morning and skins it, then the Gypsies beg the Flesh for their Dogs, when at the same Time they intend it for their own eating.

307

This method of sheep stealing is also mentioned by Myers (*JGLS* o.s. 2 (1891), 201), whilst, as regards the theft of linen, at least one Gypsy would seem to have suffered death for the practice if we are to believe the tale of Gilderoy Scamp in *The Life of Bamfylde Moore Carew* (Carew 1802, 61–3).

~

Sure, who do wild things fly and run for, if not for them as is wild themselves?

(Gypsy saying)

In England they avoid poaching, knowing that the sporting gentlemen would be severe against them and that they would not be permitted to remain in the lanes and commons near villages . . .

(George Crabbe, 1832)

112. For there was a nasty broomdasher,
　　　Shabbin' through the cracks;
　　　With his vans and his under-potter,
　　　With his vans upon his back.

　　　For he met with a yogger,
　　　For he stamped and he swore:
　　　'You can believe me, Mr. Yogger,
　　　I've never been here before.'

　　　As the broomdasher rises up on his feet,
　　　He did pogger him nice and neat,
　　　And away went the broomdasher,
　　　Shabbin' for his life.

　　　He said* there was a farmer in the field,
　　　But he hollered to his wife.
　　　He said, 'There goes a stark naked broomdasher**
　　　Shabbin' for his life.'

　　　　　　　(Levi Smith, Surrey, May 1974; Yates 1975a, 72)

　　*The phrase 'he said' (l.13) seems not to refer to any of the characters in the song and may perhaps correspond with the form *apal pendas*, then he said, as used in the 'slow songs' of the *Vlasika Roma* to announce the introduction of a new motif (see Kovalcsik 1985, 35).
　　**At one time it was thought that a poacher would be invisible to the keeper if he went about his business stark naked – a belief which still lingers on in parts of the Balkans. In the Tyrol, the same result might be achieved by carrying in one's pocket the left eye of a bat.

Somewhat ironically, nakedness also forms part of a particularly power-ful Transylvanian Gypsy charm *against* theft, mentioned by Leland in chapter 5 of his *Gypsy Sorcery and Fortune Telling* (1891). In order to achieve the desired effect, the owner must run stark naked thrice round the beast or object to be protected, whilst repeating at every turn:

> O corena na prejia.
> Dureder na ava!
> T're vasta, t're punra
> Avena kiornodya
> Te ada peda laves.

> O thief, do not go.
> Further do not come!
> Thy hands, thy feet
> Shall decay
> If thou takest this animal.

Given the importance of poaching both as a means of obtaining food and of confirming the Gypsies' ability to outwit the *Gaujo*, poaching songs in Romani English are surprisingly rare. This is not the case, however, as regards poaching songs borrowed from the mainstream and sung in English, although only one, text 167, seems to have 'crossed the bridge' into *Romanés*. The following two sets, which both date from before the First World War, are clearly Gypsy in origin.

> 113. We all went on a Christmas day,
> There all we Didakais jal!
> Never mind the chavis!
> Never mind the puddens (puddings),
> Never mind the dinner!
> There all we Didakais jal!
> We'll all go home together,
> And we'll catch a Shushai* tomorrow!
> (New Forest; Gillington 1911a, no.3)

*For a discussion of this word, see notes accompanying text 167.

> 114. It's a kušti bright rāti,
> We'll sâ jal avrí,
> We'll lel out our jukels,
> And beš our raklis avrí.
> The rāti's very pīro;*
> Kušti rāti, mi rakli,

For we're jal-in' a hoči-in'**
I'll lel pâlé a few puvengris,
And I want you to lel avrí
And lel a drop o' pāni,
And košt I will bring;
Then while the yog is burning,
I'll lel adré wudrus,
And suv you again.

(Israel Smith, Stratford-on-Avon, 1909;
JGLS n.s. 3 (1909), 160)

*Mr Smith gave 'moonlight' as the meaning here.
**Rarely encountered as a verb in Romani English. See note following text 32.

Poaching has been the subject of statute law since 1389; yet, even for so eminent an authority as Blackstone, not only is the crime itself of a somewhat questionable nature, but the many and various Acts since dedicated to its suppression are 'not a little obscure and intricate'. One thing is clear, however, and that is that, contrary to popular belief, poaching was never the sole preserve of the dispossessed. For, under the 'Game Act' of 1671, it was forbidden for *anyone* to take game unless he held freehold property in the sum of £100 per annum, held a ninety-nine-year lease to the value of £150, or was the son and heir of a substantial land-owner. What this meant in practice was that whilst some might hunt and trap wherever they pleased, others were prevented from doing so even on their own land. It was not until 1883 that tenants were eventually allowed to take rabbits and hare on their own farms.

Although man-traps and spring-guns had been outlawed during the 1830s and hanging was a thing of the past, keepers continued to exact summary justice whilst those poachers unfortunate enough to fall into the hands of the authorities could expect a seven-year prison sentence or even transportation (fourteen years under an Act of 1819). Anticipating contemporary 'Sus' laws, anyone suspected of possessing poaching implements might also, under the 1862 Poaching Prevention Act, be stopped and subjected to a summary search. Yet, whilst the 'Romani Rai' (texts 95–9) is somewhat ambiguous in tone, there can be no doubting the mood struck by Israel Smith. Text 114 was collected by Messrs Wellstood, Winstedt and Thompson whilst 'on the *drom*' in their '*Romanical's vardo*' in the summer of 1909.

~

Great skill have they in palmistry, and more
To conjure clean away the gold they touch,
Conveying worthless dross into its place . . .
                                    (William Cowper, *The Task*, 1785)

115. When I pandered the pósinakás,
     She mēr'd right away(?);*
     When she dik'd it unklizn'd,
     She mēr'd right away;
     But mandi so yoki
     Her lōva did lē,
     And av'd to my romado
     The very same day;
     We besh'd on our buls,
     Had a korō of tay,
     And sig drē the sala
     We praster'd away.
                          (Philip Murray; Sampson, *JGLS* o.s. 3 (1892), 78)

*Presumably, the meaning here is 'fainted'. cf. *mándi shom náflo pensa jawin' to soótto*, I am sick like going to sleep (Smart and Crofton 1875, xix).

The foregoing is, I believe, the only recorded example of an English Gypsy song celebrating the *boro hokkano*, or great trick – a species of fraud whereby the victim was relieved of his or her valuables whilst under the impression that they were to be greatly increased by magical means. Although subject to some variation, the victim was generally persuaded to place his or her jewellery or money in a cloth or box and then told to look away whilst certain mystical rites were observed. He or she would then be instructed to place the bundle in a safe place and leave it undisturbed for a period of days or weeks. If he or she was tempted to look before the appointed time, the magic would surely fail. If an identical cloth was available, the bundle would be exchanged for another containing articles of little or no worth whilst the victim's back was turned; otherwise, the perpetrator would return at a later date, removing the loot at her leisure.

For the most part, both perpetrators and victims would seem to have been women. In the following account, however, one of two which appeared in the Welsh-language periodical *Seren Gomer* for May 1823 and August 1826, the latter is clearly male:

One credulous simpleton, son of a small farmer in the neighbourhood [Monmouth], through 'the accursed lust of gold', was persuaded to trust twenty guineas, the fruit of hard work and much thrift, to the prophetic powers of the cheating swarm. The treasure was put in a small heap with much fuss and ostentatious simplicity, with injunctions to the youth not to look at the magic cover for four days, when, as they informed him, he would find his treasure doubled. Before the appointed time, however, the children of evil had removed their tents and had disappeared from the place; and when the adventurer opened his heap, to his grief he saw that his money had vanished with them, and that he had bought a little wisdom at a pretty high price.

Perhaps the earliest surviving reference to the practice in Britain is to be found in the St Cuthbert's (Edinburgh) Kirk Sessions Register in an entry dated 23 July 1643, in which we read of two women

for having correspondence with ane Egyptiane quho deluded them and got moneyes from them, promising to restore the doubles and took the moneyes with hir and left nothing in their keistes [chests] bot cooles [coals] bund in ane napkin, they suffering hir to goe to their keistes, the Session thinking them to be diffident of God's providence and giving themselves over to believe delusiones, for example to others ordeaned them to stand publictlie before the congregatione in the midst of the church.

If Cowper, England's 'sweetest and most pious bard' (as Borrow calls him), was enough of a man of the world to know a swindle when he saw one, there were plenty who were not, and the popular press bears eloquent testimony to their folly. The following account is from the *Manchester Guardian* for 13 August 1874 and would certainly seem to give the lie to Groome's assertion that 'this species of *dukeriben*' was 'a lost art in England, where it died lamented twenty five years ago' (1880):

Extraordinary credulity

At the Ashton-Under-Lyne County Petty Sessions, yesterday, a Gypsy named Zuba B– was charged with fortune telling and obtaining goods under false pretences. Mary Ann Ellice, a domestic servant at Oldham, said that on Sunday night she went with her sister Hannah to a field at Fitton Hill, in which there was a Gypsy encampment. The prisoner asked them into a tent, and witness gave her a shilling to tell her fortune. The prisoner told her there was a young man who wore a pencil beside his ear who loved the ground she walked on. (laughter) Witness took off her glove, and prisoner, seeing a ring on her finger, asked to look at it. Prisoner tried it on her finger and then got her brooch and cuffs from witness. She touched the end of witness's finger with the brooch, the ring, and the shilling, and then rolled them up and put them in a cigar-box and said it would take till Wednesday to 'make the charm work'. She told witness to be sure to come for them on Wednesday night. She became uneasy on Monday and went to the field but the Gypsies had gone. (laughter) – Hannah Ellice said the prisoner also told her there was a young man who loved the ground she walked on. The prisoner got her watch and guard, and also wanted her brooch and skirt, but she would not leave them. Prisoner looked at her hand and said there was luck before her, and all that. (laughter) Prisoner told them to go home, and tell no one, not even their parents. Prisoner told them the tribe had taken the field for nine months. Mr. Mellor M.P. (one of the magistrates): Have you received any education? – Witness: No, sir, I have not. – Superintendent Ludlam: Perhaps you don't understand. Have you ever been to school? Can you read and write? – Witness: no, sir. – Sergeant Barnett proved that he had apprehended the prisoner at Bardsley on Tuesday night, and recovered the property. – Mr. Thomas Harrison, the presiding magistrate, dismissed the case, but counselled the prisoner to be cautious. Addressing the girls, he said it was most extraordinary that silly people should go to such places to have their fortunes told. It served them right if they lost their money.

That the practice survived elsewhere into the present century is suggested by an account in the *New York Staats-Zeitung* for July 1909 which speaks of a lady living near Moscow who was induced by a Gypsy woman to put some 1,000 dollars' worth of jewellery in a cloth, hand it to her and turn her back whilst her fortune was told. The bundle was then returned with the strict injunction that it was to be left undisturbed for three days. When eventually it was opened, it was found to be empty.

Nearer home, there is perhaps more than a hint of the Great Trick about an incident said to have taken place in Cardiff between the wars. According to the report (*JGLS* 3rd ser. 13, 130), a Greek Gypsy, entering a café in the town, struck up an acquaintance with a commercial traveller and

talked to him with lightning rapidity in a foreign language mixed with English until the victim fell into a stupor, lost his power of resistance and lent the Gypsy thirty six pounds that was in his wallet. The latter made some pretence of telling the bagman's fortune, returned the notes and went out, leaving his dinner uneaten.

When the victim had recovered himself sufficiently, he found, on counting his money, that twenty-seven pounds was missing.

Although we shall never know exactly what form of words was used to accompany the Great Trick, Leland, at least, was willing to speculate. Writing in chapter 14 of *Gypsy Sorcery and Fortune Telling* (1891, 211), he says of the following rhyme:

I should be justly regarded as one of the seekers for mystery in moonshine if I declared that I positively believed this to be Romany. But it certainly contains words which, without any stretching or fitting, are simply gypsy, and I think it not improbable that it was some sham charm used by some Romany fortune-teller to bewilder Gorgios. Let the reader imagine the burnt-sienna, wild-cat-eyed old sorceress performing before a credulous farm-wife and her children, the great ceremony of *hakkni panki* – which Mr. Borrow calls *hokkani baro*, but for which there is a far deeper name – that of 'the great secret' – which even my best Romany friends tried to conceal from me. This is to *lel dudikabin* – to 'take lightment'.

> 116. Ekkeri (or ickery), akkery, u-kéry an,
> Fillisi', follasy, Nicholas John,
> Queebee – quabee – Irishman (or, Irish Mary),
> Stingle 'em – stangle 'em – buck!
> (Leland 1891a, 209)

The rhyme occurs in a variety of forms and has been widely reported on both sides of the Atlantic. In the form given above, it is, says Leland, 'exactly word for word what I learned when a boy in Philadelphia' and, 'With a very little alteration in sound, and not more than children make of these verses in different places', may be read as follows:

> 116(a). Ek-keri (yekori) akairi, you kair an,
> Fillissin, follasy, Nákelas jān
> Kivi, kávi – Irishman,*
> Stini, stani – buck!
> (Leland 1891a, 210)

*In an earlier essay on the subject, Leland gives 'sarishan', which would certainly make more sense in the light of his subsequent explanation of the meaning of these lines.

'This is, of course, nonsense', he goes on to say, 'but it is Romany or gypsy nonsense, and it may be thus translated very accurately:

> First – here – you begin!
> Castle, gloves. You don't play! Go on!
> *Kivi* – a kettle. How are you?
> *Stáni*, buck.

. . . Word for word every person who understands Romany will admit the following:

ek, or *yek*, means one.
yekorus, ekorus, or *yeckori*, or *ekkeri*, once.

314

U-kair-an. You kair an, or begin.
Kair is to make or do, *ankair*, to begin. 'Do you begin?'
Fillissin is a castle, or gentleman's country seat (H. Smith).
Follasi, or *follasy*, is a lady's glove.
Nákelas. I learned this word from an old Gypsy. It is used as equivalent to
don't, but also means *ná (kélas)*, you don't play. From *kel-ava*, I play.
Ján, Ja-an, Go on. From *java*, I go. Hindu, *jána*, and *jáo.*
Kivi, or *keevy.* No meaning.
Kavi, a kettle, from *kekavi*, commonly given as *kavi* . . .
Stini. No meaning that I know.
Stáni, a buck.'

Leland's explanation has, however, not gone unchallenged. The Opies
(1992, 355–6), whilst acknowledging certain similarities between a number
of the words used and their supposed Gypsy equivalents, go on to say that

> the resemblances are probably fortuitous. It is more likely that Gypsies, who
> are notorious borrowers, picked it up from their English neighbours . . . The
> tradition in England was that counting-out rhymes were remnants of
> formulas used by the druids for choosing human sacrifices. Charles Taylor
> mentions it in the *Chatterings of the Pica* (1820) and, seventy years later,
> Gomme gives credence to it. Such rhymes usually allowed the user to count
> to twenty and, for this reason, were described by A. J. Ellis (1877) as the
> 'Anglo-Cymric scores'.

A somewhat different view of the origin of this type of rhyme, and one
broadly consistent with that advanced by Leland, is offered by H.
Carrington Bolton in his 'Counting Out Rhymes of Children', published in
the *American Journal of Folklore* in 1888. In it, he says that he regards 'the
doggerels themselves . . . as the survival of the spoken charms used by
sorcerers in ancient times in conjunction with their mystic incantations'.
That such rhymes did at one time have a ritualistic significance is, indeed,
borne out by the following 'remedium valde certum et utile faucium
doloribus' (sovereign remedy for affections of the jaws) from the writings
of the third-century Gaulish doctor, Marcellus Burdigalensis. Marcellus
also gives the necessary instructions for its proper use:

> Glandulas mane carminabis, si dies minuetur, si nox ad vesperam, et digito
> medicinali ac police continens eas dices

> You shall make verses about the acorns in the morning if the days are
> shortening, in the evening if the nights are shortening, and holding them
> between the medicinal finger and the thumb, say these words:

Novem glandulae sorores
Octo glandulae sorores
Septem glandulae sorores . . . and so on until
Una glandula soror.

Nine acorn sisters
Eight acorn sisters
Seven acorn sisters . . . and so on until
One acorn sister.

Glandulae, besides meaning 'acorns', also signifies 'tonsils' and according to Macrobius, a near contemporary of Marcellus, the medicinal finger is the third or ring finger. I am indebted to Mr Bernard Peatey for the English translation of Marcellus' instructions.

Although we know that Leland had read *The Chatterings of the Pica*, it is only fair to note that he was fully aware of the dangers inherent in the interpretation of children's rhymes. 'It may be observed', he says (1891a, 210),

> that while my first quotation abounds in what are unmistakably Romany words, I can find no trace of any in any other child-rhymes of the kind. I lay stress on this, for if I were a great Celtic scholar I should not have the least difficulty in proving that every word in every rhyme, down to 'Tommy, Make Room For Your Uncle', was all old Irish or Gaelic.

The idea that simple verses, cast in one language, may be adopted as nonsense songs by the speakers of another should not, however, be rejected out of hand. Henry Baerlein, for example, in his *Landfalls and Farewells* (1949), tells us that in Anholt, the Danish island in the Kattegat, the children may be heard singing what is to them a nonsense rhyme but what is apparently a relic of the British occupation during the Napoleonic Wars:

Jeck og jill
Vent op de hill
Og Jell kom tombling efter.

One further interpretation of the particular child-rhyme under consideration requires mention here. According to an unnamed correspondent (*JGLS* o.s. 3, 183), such rhymes are as widespread as the Roman Catholic church and reflect the wonder with which the Latin Mass was heard for the first time. 'Hickory Dickory Dock', he suggests, is

316

meant for 'hic, haec, hoc', whilst 'fillisi, follasin, Nicholas Jan' stand for 'Matthias, Marcus, Lucas and Johannes'. 'Queevi quavi Irish Mary (or Virgin Mary)', he equates with 'ave, ave, virgo Maria', and 'stinglem stanglem buck', or 'stink stank stock', as it is sometimes given, may well have been heard for 'hunc hanc hoc'.

Support for the oriental origin of, at least, the first line of rhymes of the 'Ekkeri Akkeri' type is, however, forthcoming from a somewhat unlikely quarter. The following is an account of the origin of the game of 'pots', printed in the *Girls' Own Paper* for December 1891:

> This game is, of course, a form of the 'hopscotch' (hophen) played by English children and which has a history reaching back for centuries. Indeed, I am told that the little Hindoo children have a game closely resembling it called *Khapollo* from the piece of tile with which it is played. Only seven spaces are used, however, and no double ones, the spaces being marked in turn *Ekaria, Dukaria, Tikaria, Kachkolan, Sastanawa, Chotka* and *Barka*.

In a letter to the *JGLS* dated 30 June 1891, Lt.-Col. W. Laing takes this idea one step further:

> whilst reading Mr. Leland's most interesting work on Gypsy sorcery, I was struck by the numerous words which are still extant in India, some of the verses being perfectly intelligible phonetically . . . but I was not prepared to find that I could translate some of their incantations without the least difficulty.

Having advanced both 'Ikeri Tikeri Dekk' and 'Ikeri Tikeri Dzo' as the Indian equivalent of 'Hickory Dickory Dock', Laing goes on to offer his own version of Leland's rhyme. 'I would', he says, 'put it as follows and challenge the opinion of anyone whose work has lain in the districts of Western India.'

> Ikeri Akeri Ukeri a
> Fillasi Foolasi Nigelas Jan
> Queeva Queeva Aissa Man
> Stingle Stangle Bakk.

Although Laing offers no translation, Mrs I. R. Jani, a native of Gujarat with a knowledge of Hindi and Sanskrit, thought that it seemed to contain a number of Kutchi or Urdu words; e.g. *foolasi*, like a flower; *nigelas*, delicate; *jan*, life; *queev*, why; *aissa*, like this; and *man*, mind. She was,

317

however, unable to shed any light either on the first line or the two variant forms given earlier (personal communication, July 1992).

Although there may be a common thread linking some of the items identified by Mrs Jani (like a flower, delicate, life, mind), the meaning they suggest for the rhyme as a whole is entirely at odds with that advanced by Leland. The middle two lines might, perhaps, be said to mean something like 'life is delicate as a flower.Why should this be so?' Mrs Jani, however, wisely declined to speculate.

In introducing the rhyme of which Leland's is but one of a host of variants, the Opies describe it as 'a counting out formula (15 counts) the origin of which should probably be sought in antiquity'. It has been noted on both sides of the Atlantic on numerous occasions over the past 150 years and, everything considered, the deviations from their text version (text A below), which they believed to be the basic form, are remarkably slight. Text B is taken from *Mother Goose's Quarto* of *c.*1825.

A

One-ery, two-ery, ickery, Ann,
Phillisy, phollisy, Nicholas John,
Quever, quaver, Irish Mary,
Stickeram, stackeram, buck!

B

One-ery, you-ery, ekery, Ann,
Phillisy, follysy, Nicholas, John,
Quee-bee, quaw-bee, Irish Mary,
Stinkle-em, stankle-em, buck.

Further accounts of the 'Great Trick' from Britain and America are to be found in *Seren Gomer*, May 1823 and August 1827; Crabb 1832, 38–45; Borrow 1841, ch.6 and 1874, 240–4; *The Times*, 17, 21 and 26 February, and 1 March 1862; Smart and Crofton 1873, 206–8; *A New Orleans Journal*, 15 April 1880; and the *Daily Picayune*, 8 April 1880.

~

Shortly there appeared twenty demons, like Scotsmen with packs across their shoulders which they cast down before the throne of despair and which turned out to be Gypsies. 'Ho, there!', cried Lucifer, 'How was it that ye knew the fortunes of others so well that you could not know that your own fortune was leading you hither?'
(Ellis Wynne, *Gweledigaetheu y Bardd Cwsc*
(Visions of the Sleeping Bard))

Borra dinala se Gaujea te patsen ta kerla kava koskaben langay!
Great fools are women to believe that this does them any good!
(John Roberts, in Groome 1880)

An integral part of the *hokano baro* was the telling of the victim's fortune; for, once convinced that great wealth was in the offing, he or she would be only too willing to follow any instructions, however absurd, as to how it might be realized.

Fortune-telling and, more particularly, palmistry, has been closely associated with the Gypsies since their first arrival in western Europe. Pasquier, in an extract from the journal of a contemporary doctor of theology (1596, lib. iv, cap. 17), mentions the arrival before the gates of Paris, on 27 August 1427, of twelve *penanciers* (doers of penance) together with upwards of 100 of their followers. Very quickly, it became clear that '. . . there were among them women who, by looking into people's hands, told their fortunes and, what was worse, they picked people's pockets of their money and got it into their own by telling these things through airy magic'. Such was his concern over these developments, that the bishop of Paris ordered a Friar, Le Petit Jacobin, to preach a sermon excom-municating all those who had recourse to them.

So powerful was the image of the Gypsy fortune-teller that, by the end of the fifteenth century it seems already to have become an established commonplace of stage and canvas. As early as 1475, a Gypsy fortune-teller is introduced into an anonymous Swiss play (Mone 1846) and again by the Portuguese dramatist, Jil Vicente, in his *Farsa das Ciganas* of 1521. In the latter piece, the four female characters begin by introducing themselves as Greeks and Christians and, having failed in their quest for alms, offer to read the audience's palms. So, too, we find the Gypsy palmist depicted both in Bosch's *Haywain* of *c.*1500, and in one of several tapestries of the *ateliers* of Tournai, in which one of the subject's companions is, at the same time, being relieved of her purse by a Gypsy boy (the theme of the fortune-teller and her attendant cut-purse is discussed and illustrated in Curzin 1977).

In England, too, the Gypsies are first mentioned by name in a passage linking them, albeit incidentally, with the art of divination. Thus, in *A Dyaloge of Syr Thomas More, Knt*, published in London in 1529, we are told that, some time during the year 1514, the king sent his lords to enquire into the death of Sir Richard Hunne in the Lollards' Tower, and that one of the witnesses mentioned an Egyptian woman who, until her recent departure overseas, had lived in Lambeth where she had shown great skill as a palmist (*Dyaloge*, book 3, ch.15). In the following year, 1530, the practice receives special mention in an Act (the first of the great Tudor vagrancy laws in which the Gypsies are mentioned by name) concerning those 'dyverse and many outlandysshe People callynge themselfes Egyptians' who,

> using no Crafte nor faicte of Merchaundyce, had comen into this Realme and gone from Shire to Shire and Place to Place in greate Company, and used greate subtyll and crafty means to deceyve the People, bearyng them in Hande that they by Palmestre coulde telle Menne and Womens Fortunes and so many tymes by crafte and subtyltie had deceyved the People of theyr money and also had Comytted many and haynous Felonyes and Robberies to the greate Hurte and Deceyte of the People that they had comen amonge.

In 1549, too, the young King Edward noted in his journal that 'there was a privy search made through Sussex for all vagabonds, Gypsies, conspirators, prophesiers, all players and such like', whilst, in 1569, the bishop of Worcester, Edwin Sandys, in a list of magical practices proscribed by the church, mentions, in particular: 'Charms to cure men or beasts; invocations of wicked spirits; telling where things lost or stolen are become by key, book, tables, shears, sieves; looking to crystals or other casting of figures . . .'

Harman (1567) also mentions the practice in connection with the Gypsies, as does Reginald Scot in his 1584 *Discovery of Witchcraft*, in a section entitled 'The Cozening Art of Sortilege or Lottery Practised Especially by Egyptian Vagabonds' (first edition (1584), pp.197–8; 1665 edition, p.110). Already, however, a note of scepticism is to be heard in the writings of the more urbane of contemporary commentators. Dekker, for example, writing in the early years of the seventeenth century, is under no illusion as to the true nature of the fortune-teller's art:

> Upon days of pastime and liberty, they spread themselves in small companies amongst the villages and when the young maids and bachelors – yea sometimes old doting fools that should be beaten through this world of villainies and fore-warn others – do flock about them, they then profess skill in palmistry and, forsooth, can tell fortunes which for the most part, are infallibly true by reason that they work upon rules which are grounded upon certainty. For one of them will tell you that you shall shortly have some evil luck fall upon you and within half an hour after you shall find your pockets picked or your purse cut.

Like Ellis Wynne's Egyptians, however, not all fortune-tellers had the necessary skill to profit by their own art, as in a late seventeenth-century pamphlet entitled *Strange and Certain News from Warwick* and purporting to be a true relation how a company of Gypsies in Warwickshire chose one Hern for their king, who being accused for deceiving a maid of ten shillings under pretence of telling her fortune, solemnly wished before a magistrate he might be burned if he had it.

According to the author, Hern (a Gypsy name) had been master of a good trade in London before taking to the road. Arriving in Warwickshire, he had taken part in the annual election of the Gypsy king and succeeded in gaining both the title and a broken arm, sustained in the course of the traditional wrestling bout held in order to determine who should wear the crown. Having taken himself a queen, he had then established his court in Bedford, where he was attended by an eager host of 'young wenches (that neither hope nor wish nor dream of anything but husbands)'.

When one of his clients realized that, under pretence of having her fortune told, she had been relieved of ten shillings to no real purpose, 'she began lamentable exclamations as loud as an Irish hubbub', as a result of which both king and queen were arraigned before the local magistrate. When the charge was read, Hern protested his innocence, desiring that 'he might be burned that night if directly or indirectly he had meddled with any of the girl's money or knew what was become of it'.

Remanded in custody, he refused the offer of a bed, preferring to lie on straw and covering himself with costly blankets from his own store. Unfortunately, the straw caught fire in the night and, although his wife survived, Hern himself was burned to death – 'a sad example that should warn all people from wishing such curses upon themselves, nor neglect nor forsake their honest employment to engage in such wicked courses and society, which ever terminates in bitterness and misery'.

That this story has any basis in truth seems most unlikely as there is no other contemporary record of the affair – a somewhat curious omission, given that, according to the writer, Warwick gaol was all but destroyed by the fire and it was found necessary to break through from the house of an alderman living next door in order to contain the blaze.

By the beginning of the eighteenth century, whilst many of the more credulous sort were still willing to risk their money, if not their souls, in their eagerness to learn something of their fate, that note of cynicism, already apparent in Harman and Dekker, had become more widespread. 'You are like a lawyer', complains a character in one of Twm o'r Nant's interludes of the Gypsy seer, Anti Sali, 'you will give no labour to your lips without getting your fee.' 'Have you not heard, Welshman', comes the prompt reply, 'working for nothing is worse than begging.'

Shirley (1708) and Poulter, the horse-thief (1753) are equally clear regarding the Gypsies' wholly scientific approach to their art, the latter writing as follows:

They always travel in Bodies, Men and Women . . . pretending themselves to be true Egyptians, and deceiving ignorant People by pretending to tell their Fortunes, and are often sent for by Persons of Fashion. When they are applied to, they pretend they must consult their Books first, and take that Opportunity to enquire into the Family, that they may be able to give Account about what is ask'd them, and in this Manner they deceive the World.

The subject of the following verse would surely have found favour with Anti Sali, if not with her interlocutor. She is said to have 'told the good luck' to the Prince Regent on Newmarket Heath and to have been rewarded with 'foive guineas and a great smack', receiving the former with infinitely better grace than the latter:

> 117. Britannia is my nav;
> I am a Kaulo Camlo;*
> The gorgios pen I be
> A bori chovahaunie;
> And tatchipen they pens,
> The dinneleskie gorgies,
> For mande chovahans
> The luvvu from their putsies.
> (Borrow 1874, 133)

*See notes accompanying text 121.

Dukkering also features in the following mildly ironic piece obtained by Sampson from a Lancashire Traveller, Lias Robinson. In a subsequent issue of the *Journal*, however, he says that it was originally composed by Smart and Crofton as a decoy intended to draw out the genuine article.

> 118. Mandi's churri purri dai
> Jaw'd adré kongri to shūn the rashai;
> The gâjos sor sal'd as yoi besh'd talé;
> Yoi dik'd dré the lil, but yoi keker* del apré;
> The rashai roker'd pencha* dukkerin' – Pen'd duva sas a laj,
> But keker yov jin'd mandi duker'd yov's chai,
> Puker'd yov'd romer a barvālo rai.
> (Lias Robinson; Sampson 1891, 86)

*The word *keker* (a negative exclamative) in l.4 seems to have been substituted for

322

nastis (cannot), whilst, in the fifth line, *pencha* (like) is used in place of *trustal* (about). Commenting on this idiosyncratic use of language, Sampson says: 'With regard to what they call "little words", Gypsies are as resolute as Humpty-Dumpty in their determination to make words 'mean just what they choose them to mean – neither more nor less.'

Lias Robinson was, Sampson tells us, 'a quiet, self-contained man, enlivening, yet independent of society. Happiest, perhaps, when prowling by himself in some "dear little wesh". 'He is possessed of a pleasing degree of modesty for one of the Gypsy race, and it is only casually that one becomes acquainted with his many accomplishments.'

He was unable to read a word but was apparently capable of writing a good letter. This he managed by asking someone to read over any letter he received and by memorizing the shape of every word and phrase, so that when the time came for him to write, he would simply consult his papers and construct a suitable composite from the material already available to him. If he wanted a word which had not been used by any of his cor- respondents, he would ask a literate acquaintance, 'innocent like', how he would make the word, were he writing a letter. The acquaintance, '"cos he's so proud of his writing', would be only to happy to oblige and, since 'once he's seen it, he never forgets it', Lias would return to his task, his problem solved (Sampson 1891, 86).

Although the priest in text 118 undoubtedly represents the official view on fortune-telling, Fontella Lovell offers a refreshing alternative in the following memoir of her uncle, a *Gaujo* minister whose elopement with his Gypsy sweetheart caused as much resentment among his wife's family as amongst his own congregation.

They were happy 'til he died, though he didn't like to have her *dukkerin'* . . . But he'd say, 'as long as you don't try to fool anyone, as long as you believe what you say, you can tell fortunes. The *rasai* is only *dukkerin'*, after all; and there's many a man in the Holy Book as used to go round foretellin' the future'. He'd say, too, 'Maybe us *Gaujos* has lived so long in four walls that we shut out the sound of God's voice, so long under roofs that we can't read the signs in the sky.' (Brown 1924, 168)

~

Other things that an ordinary Englishman would throw upon the dung-hill, some of the Gypsies will carry home to make soup of.
(Adam Smith)

If it only had wings, the pig would be the Gypsies' favourite bird.
(Hungarian Gypsy saying)

119. Oh! I jāssed to the kér,
     An' I tried to māng the bālor;
     Tried to māng the mūllo bālor,
     When I jāssed to the kér.
     But the rāni wouldn't del it,
     For she pénnas les 'os drábberd,
     For she pénnas les 'os drábberd,
     Penn's the Rómmany chál had drábbed the bālor.
     (Anon., Brighton; Leland 1875, 130.
     See also Smith 1889, 121)

     Oh! I went to the house,
     And I tried to beg the pig(s);
     Tried to beg the dead pig(s),
     When I went to the house.
     But the lady wouldn't give it,
     For she said it was poisoned,
     For she said it was poisoned,
     Said the Romani Chal had poisoned the pig(s).

This 'trifle', as Leland calls it, will, he suggests, 'recall to many readers the ballad in Mr. Borrow's Romany Rye' (see below) and testifies to the fact that

> a weakness for *mullo baulor*, or pork which died by 'the hand of God' (or by disease, as the Continental Gypsies say), is certainly not one of the lost tastes, as I doubt whether there is a real Gypsy, old or young, in England who has not eaten it.

He himself had not tried it, he says, but had been assured on a number of occasions that it was not unlike pheasant or hedgehog – an assertion wholly at variance with the view taken by Sampson, for whom 'the moral guilt of dining on *mulo balo* must have been amply atoned for by the gastronomical discomfort . . .'

A taste for carrion and other things which, as one of Tom Musto's nephews put it , 'stink aloud' (Norwood, Diaries, 21 January 1857), is one of the many less attractive half-truths with which the Gypsies have long had to contend in their dealings with the settled population. Cowper evidently had it in mind when, in Book I, of *The Task* (1785) he wrote:

> I see a column of slow rising smoke
> O'er-top the lofty wood that skirts the wild.
> A vagabond and useless tribe there eat
> Their miserable meal, a kettle swung

Between two poles upon a stick transverse
Receives the morsel – flesh obscene of dog,
Or vermin, or, at least, of cock purloined
From his accustomed perch . . .

For Ellis Wynne, however, writing in his *Visions of the Sleeping Bard* of 1703, the Gypsies' taste for exotic flesh was altogether more sinister in character:

The first thing I perceived close by was a dancing knoll and such a fantastic rout in blue petticoats and red, briskly footing a sprightly dance. I stood a while hesitating whether I should approach them or not; and in my confusion I feared they were a pack of hungry Gypsies and that the least they would do would be to kill me for their supper and devour me without salt. But gazing steadily upon them, I perceived that they were of better and fairer complexion than that lying tawny crew.

That Wynne was not simply indulging in a flight of poetic fancy of his own devising is suggested by the fact that, as late as 1874, the article on the Gypsies in *Chambers' Encyclopaedia* (p.172) included the startling revelation that the Gypsies 'were or are wont to eat their parents'.

Two other Gypsy dainties to which frequent reference is also made in the literature are *baúri zimmen* (snail soup) and *hotchi-witchi* (hedgehog), whilst in chapter 5 of *Romany Rye*, Borrow speaks of dining on squirrel, and this in itself would probably be enough to give the Gypsies a bad name among their more gastronomically conservative neighbours. Indeed, dining on hedgehog might, on occasion, prove more than merely socially hazardous, as suggested by the following extract from an account of the trial of Guilliers Heron at York in March 1859. Common sense would seem to have prevailed, however, as Heron was eventually acquitted.

One of the prisoner's brothers said that they were all at tea with the prisoner at five o'clock in their tent; and when asked what they had to eat, he said they had a *hodgun* cooked. His Lordship (Mr. Justice Byles) – 'what do you say you had, cooked urchin?' Gypsy – 'Yes, cooked *hodgun*. I'm very fond of cooked *hodgun*.' (with a grin). His Lordship's mind seemed to be filled with horrible misgivings . . . (*Times*, 10 March 1859)

Yet if the Gypsies' taste for 'obscene flesh' has been much exaggerated, there can be no doubting their use of *mullo balo* or the flesh of pigs which have met their end other than at the hands of the butcher. Indeed, it was for this reason that Aaron Jakes/Shaw christened the father and grandfather of the great Gypsy evangelist, Gypsy Smith, 'The Igg-Pig Smiths' (*JGLS* n.s. 3 (1909), 150). What is also clear from the literature is that the preferred method of obtaining this somewhat unusual delicacy was, on occasion, equally unconventional. As Borrow, the first to draw attention to the practice in England, was to put it in one of his songs,

> The Romany chi
> And the Romany chal
> Shall jaw tasaulor
> To drab the bawlor
> And dook the gry
> Of the farming Rye.
> (Borrow 1851, 350)

As might be expected, Borrow's English translation is somewhat more elaborate than the original Romani text. The meaning, however, is perfectly clear:

> The Romany churl
> And the Romany girl
> Tomorrow shall hie
> To poison the stye
> And bewitch on the mead
> The farmer's steed.
> (Borrow 1851, 362)

Although the precise nature of the substance used by Borrow's Gypsies was to remain a mystery until its eventual identification in 1909, the fact that the Gypsies had long possessed a knowledge of plant poisons had not gone unnoticed by contemporary toxicologists. A. Wynter Blyth, for example, writes as follows in his introductory preface on 'The Old Poison-Lore' in the 1906 edition of *Poisons: Their Effects and Detection*:

The Gypsies . . . have long possessed a knowledge of the properties of the curious 'Mucor Phycomyces' . . . The Gypsies are said to have administered the spores of this fungus in warm water. In this way they rapidly attach themselves to the mucus membrane of the throat, all the symptoms of a phthisis follow, and death takes place in from two to three weeks.

The Adams, too, in their *Criminal Investigations*, translated and adapted from Dr Hans Gross's *System der Kriminalistik* (1907, 372), refer to the Gypsies' use of poisonous fungi:

When the Gypsy wishes to poison someone he uses neither phosphorous nor arsenic nor the like; he uses his infallible *dry* (also called *dri* or *drei*) . . . a fine brown powder made with the spores of a mushroom (perhaps the *Asper Gillus Niger*). These spores grow in animal organisms, developing a greenish yellow shoot of about twelve to fifteen inches in length. This powder is dissolved in lukewarm liquid and the spores, becoming fixed in the mucus membrane, and rapidly developing there, bring on consumption, coughing, often spitting of blood and death finally ensues after two to three weeks. When the body becomes cold, the mushroom also soon dies and disappears so completely that after death no trace of it can be found.

The word *drei*, as used by Dr Gross, is in all probability no more than a variant of the English Romani *drab*, 'poison, medicine' (cf. *driz* (Brown 1924, 177)), and the original authority for its use may have been a letter to *The Times*, dated 21 February 1862, the relevant portion of which was reproduced by Groome on p.24 of his novel, *Kriegspiel*. The case to which the letter refers concerned a young Gypsy woman accused of obtaining money by false pretences from a London lady and her servants. Although charges were never brought, the true nature of the case against her would seem to have been that she had provided the latter with a bottle of poison or *drei* in order to dispose of her husband (*JGLS* n.s. 3 (1909), 150–3).

According to a number of commentators, another Gypsy favourite, altogether less exotic than Gross and Blyth's fungal toxins, was mustard. Rankin tells us that one of the Bucklands advised him it was best administered in an apple, whilst another informant of the same name, Cornelius, told Winstedt that he preferred to use a potato. The latter, too, seems to have been the chosen method of the Smiths of Westmorland. Whilst dining in their camp one night, Thompson was somewhat taken aback when one of the younger family members, a lad of seven named Lulu, seeing some mustard on the table, 'recited in a loud sing-song way, as if he was saying something he had learned by heart': 'If you wants to *mor* (kill) a *bokensi* (sheep?), make a hole in a *puvengri* (potato) and fill it with mustard, and put it into the pig's stye and the *balo* (pig) will eat it, and choke like that 'un!' He then rounded off his performance with 'a horrible gurgling noise in his throat' (*JGLS* n.s. 3 (1909), 150).

Although the Bucklands appear to have believed that the effect of the mustard was both immediate and terminal, Leland was surely right in suggesting that its action, whilst no less satisfactory, was somewhat less dramatic (1873, Gudlo xxxix, 248–50):

Now, Rya, you must jin if you del a baulor kris* adrée a pabo, he can't shel avree or kair a gudlo for his miraben, an' you can rikker him bissin', or chiv him apré a wardo, an' jal andurer an' kek jin it.

Now, sir, you must know that if you give a pig mustard* in an apple he can't cry out or squeal for his life, and you can carry him away, or throw him on the wagon and get away and nobody will know it.

Kris, a Romani word of Romanian origin signifying 'council', is apparently a corruption of English 'cress', used here as in the common pairing, 'mustard and cress'.

From another of Borrow's songs, however, it would seem that his Gypsies' *drab* was altogether different in character:

> We jaws to the drab-engro ker,
> Trin horsworth there of drab we lels,
> And when to the swety back we wels,
> We pens We'll drab the Baulo,
> We'll have a drab at a baulo.

> We go to the house of the poison monger,
> Where we buy three pennies' worth of bane,
> And when we return to our people,
> We say, we will poison the porker,
> We will try and poison the porker.

It was Myers, however, who first drew attention to the fact that the Gypsies not only knew of the existence of a range of metallic poisons but understood the use of a certain mineral which, if the correct procedure was followed, would prove fatal to the chosen animal but harmless to those who dined upon its flesh. (Groome's reference to 'natural arsenic' on p. xxiv of *Gypsy Folk Tales* was, he thought, no more than a 'loose substitute' for any 'deadly poison'. This, however, seems unlikely for, as Groome goes on to say, when a quantity of the substance was found on the person of a Gypsy of his acquaintance, following his sudden death, the survivors told the policeman who examined the body, 'He used it, you know, sir, in his tinkering.' This would seem to suggest that it was, at least, a metallic poison and possibly even lead-based.)

From one of his informants, Myers learned that this mysterious mineral was 'a dirty-whitish, "carroty" or rusty-looking stone' found at Ponsenbury (Pontesbury) lead mines in Shropshire. Before it could be used it had first to be heated – as a result of which its colour changed from yellow to grey – then crushed to the consistency of flour. A small amount might then be introduced into a baked potato or mixed with dough and administered, by hand, *at midnight*. The prescribed dose was apparently about twenty grams or a piece the size of a small walnut, and any pig so treated would infallibly be found dead in the morning.

Another Gypsy told Sampson much the same story, although in his account the stone was said to be 'heavy' and was found somewhere between Porthmadoc and Beddgelert.

These and other similar accounts led Myers to undertake a critical examination of a range of mineral poisons and 'for various sound reasons' he was able to rule out all but arsenic and barium carbonate. With this in mind, the honorary secretary of the Gypsy Lore Society was dispatched into rural Shropshire with a view to locating a possible source of supply. (Borrovians will recall that Mrs Herne's attempt on the author's life on Saturday 11 June 1825 (Borrow 1851, ch.70), must have taken place not far from the south Shropshire lead mines, which are to be found on a direct line between Willenhall and Borrow's 'dingle' and the nearest point on the Welsh border.)

Following a series of fortunate accidents, he at last managed to obtain, from the wife of the foreman of the Baryta mining company, at their workings near Minsterley, a small quantity of a 'wax-coloured crystaline substance' known locally as witherite or water-spar, which he was told made excellent rat poison. On analysis, it was found to be almost pure barium carbonate, containing 77.36 per cent BaO and 22.25 per cent CO_2. Recognition of the stone by Myers's Gypsy informants was all that was required to complete the identification process.

Myers's principal contact was eventually located and offered in turn a sample of the Minsterley witherite, a piece of lime spar (which greatly resembles barium in appearance though not in weight) and a specimen of galena encrusted with lime spar and ferric oxide. He was immediately able to point to the correct substance.

But was this the same poison used by Borrow's Gypsies when *drabbing* the *baulo*, and on the author himself by Mrs Herne? Professor Sherrington, an eminent physiologist whom Myers consulted regarding the suitability of barium carbonate as a means of obtaining meat for human consumption, offered a useful clue. In his opinion, the flesh of a pig killed by barium poisoning could be eaten with safety provided the entrails were rejected and the parts of the animal which had come in contact with them were thoroughly cleansed. So it is that in Borrow's song we find the following:

> And then we toves the wendror well,
> Till sore the wendror iuziou se,
> Till kekkeno drab's adrey lis,
> Till drab there's kek adrey lis.
>
> And then we washes the insides well,
> Till all the insides are clean,

> Till no poison's in it,
> Till of poison there's none in it.

More to the point, perhaps, allowing for the fact that he was writing a novel rather than a toxicological textbook, the symptoms described by Borrow in chapter 71 of *Lavengro* are for the most part broadly typical of barium poisoning, although one, salivation, is missing, being replaced by thirst. There is also no mention of acute diarrhoea – an understandable omission. Borrow's symptoms were as follows: intense thirst; abdominal pains and colic; nausea and vomiting; muscular weakness; unconsciousness; convulsions and paralysis; high blood pressure; catarrh of the conjunctivi; and rally and relapse. Of these, the number of apparent references to an increase in blood pressure is the least convincing as with barium poisoning the pulse would normally have been weak and the heart's action feeble.

In a spirit of true empiricism, John Myers was to subject Borrow's account to a further test by seeking to determine whether it would be possible to administer a lethal dose of barium in a cake, as Mrs Herne is said to have done, without arousing any suspicion on the part of the recipient. He writes as follows:

> In order to ascertain if a poisonous quantity of water-spar might be administered in a cake without detection by the palate, a cake weighing two ounces and containing six grams of the poison was made. With the exception of a very slight grittiness, nothing was noticed on subjecting a portion of the cake to mastication. To prove that the mass was fairly homogeneous, the barium in five grams was determined and showed a total content of 4.86 grams of pure barium carbonate. It has been placed on record that 3.8 grams proved fatal to an adult.

Borrow also refers to the practice of pig-poisoning in chapter 5, part 2, of *Zincali*, offering the following quatrain from the original Spanish Gypsy:

> By Gypsy drow the porker died;
> I saw him stiff at evening tide.
> But I saw him not when morning shone,
> For the Gypsies ate him flesh and bone.
> (Borrow 1841, 262)

That the art still survived in the peninsula at least into the early years of the present century is confirmed by J. Stuart MacLaren's encounter with a

Gypsy family in Martot, Jaen, as they were in the process of quartering a '*drab'd balo*'. Unfortunately, Maclaren 'did not consider it prudent to ask any questions', so we are none the wiser regarding the particular type of poison used. From an old Gypsy woman in Murcia, however, he learned a number of phrases differing from the usual Spanish Romani, including, for *drabbing* the *balo*, *chivar yákhis al balicho*, which might suggest that she was hoping to conceal the truth beneath a cloak of folk magic.

In another of Borrow's *Gitano* songs, rather than poisoning the pig, the Gypsies are said merely to have stolen a flitch of bacon.

> Un erajai
> Sinaba chibando un sermon;
> Y lle falta un balicho
> Al chidomar de aquel gao,
> Y los chanelaba que los Cales
> Lo abian nicabó;
> Y penela l'erajai, 'Chaboró!
> Guillata a tu quer
> Y nicabela la perí
> Que terela el balicho,
> Y chibela andro
> Una lima de tun chaborí,
> Chaborí,
> Una lima de tun chaborí.'

> A friar
> Was preaching once with zeal and with fire,
> And a butcher of the town
> Had lost a flitch of bacon;
> And well the friar knew
> That the Gypsies it had taken;
> So suddenly he shouted 'Gypsy, ho!
> Hie home, and from the pot
> Take the flitch of bacon out,
> The flitch good and fat,
> And in its place throw in a clout,
> A dingy clout of thy brat,
> Of thy brat, a clout,
> A dingy clout of thy brat.'
> (Borrow 1874, 111)

An early British reference to the theft of bacon by Gypsies is to be found in Crouch's verse pamphlet, *The Welch Traveller or The Misfortunate Welchman* (1671). In the course of the action, the hero, in order to hide his

331

nakedness, takes refuge in a barn near Guildford and is there surprised by a band of Gypsies. Taking him for a sprite, they are ready to do battle but, having heard his tale of woe,

> Kind friend, quoth they, you shall be one
> Of our fraternity;
> Our secrets to you shall be known,
> And we'll live happily.

After some further talk, in which the Gypsies, somewhat surprisingly, acknowledge that they have never suffered any injury at the hands of the *Gaujos*, 'Taffie' is told of his first assignment as a member of the group:

> The first design we'll set upon
> If you'll our secrets keep,
> Shall be, for ought we know, anon,
> When people are asleep.

> And what is that? Quoth Taffie then . . .
> What is it I must do?
> Nothing but rob a house, quoth they,
> Of bacon, we tell you.

'Taffie', however, has stolen a march on the Travellers, for

> Quoth he, I was in such a fray;
> Hur's some; I pray fall to.

> He pull'd a piece out of his poke;
> The bacon it was warm;
> Quoth he, this was in fire and smoke,
> But I had all the harm.

~

A Gypsy in a market or public house can often pick out another, by his facial features and clothes. It is then an easy matter to slip a Romani word into the conversation to make sure. On the other hand, a perfect command of the language will not ensure acceptance, unless the speaker can produce a knowledge of stopping-places and some relatives the interlocutor knows.

(Kenrick, British Association for the Advancement of Science/
Annual General Meeting, Section H, 1971)

The importance of family relationships within any close and closed community such as the Gypsies need hardly be emphasized. The first three lines of the following verse, which 'contains the questions which two strange Gypsies, who suddenly meet, put to each other' are, according to Borrow, 'perhaps the oldest specimen of English Gypsy at present extant and perhaps the purest. They are at least as old as the time of Elizabeth and can pass among the Zigany in the heart of Russia for *Ziganskie*. The other lines are not so ancient.'

Borrow's claim regarding the antiquity of these lines is impossible to prove or disprove. It would suggest, however, that the opening section, at least, was not of his own devising. That the same can be said of the remaining ten lines is less certain. What is clear, however, is that he was quite wrong in supposing that they represented the oldest specimen of English Gypsy then extant. As mentioned elsewhere, the oldest surviving sample, not only of British Romani but of Romani of any kind is to be found in Andrew Boorde's *Fyrst Boke of the Introduction of Knowledge*, published in London in 1542.

Although, in the appendix to the 1858 edition of *Romany Rye* (vol.2, app. c.3, pp.274–5), Borrow quotes Boorde's doggerel on the English phrase for foreign customs, dress and language, it is impossible to believe that, having the book before him, he could have failed to recognize the latter's 'Egipt Speche' for what it really was and we can only assume that he must have obtained this verse from another source. Thompson, is probably right in suggesting that Borrow may have encountered it on pp.86–7 of the 1738 edition of *The Muses Library*.

> 120. Coin si deya, coin se dado?
> Pukker mande drey Romanes,
> Ta mande pukkeravava tute.
> Rossar-mescri minri deya!
> Vardo-mescro minro dado!
> Coin se dado, coin si deya?
> Mande's pukker'd tute drey Romanes;
> Knau pukker tute mande.
> Petulengro minro dado!
> Purana minri deya!
> Tatchey Romany si men –
> Mande's pukker'd tute drey Romanes,
> Ta tute's pukker'd mande.
>
> Who's your mother, who's your father?
> Do thou answer me in Romany,
> And I will answer thee.

A Hearne I have for mother!
A Cooper for my father!
Who's your father, who's your mother?
I have answer'd thee in Romany,
Now do thou answer me.
A Smith I have for father!
A Lee I have for mother!
True Romans both are we –
For I've answer'd thee in Romany,
And thou hast answer'd me.

(Borrow 1874, 14, 99)

According to Sampson, the following 'interesting little proverb' is also 'very old'. His informant is given no other name but 'Manful':

> 121. Kâlo kâlo Komlo,
> Gozwerikno Macho,
> Bokhy Petaléngro;
> Trin Romnichélâ
> Kūr the purro beng, bâ!
>
> Black, [black] Lovell,
> Cunning Herne,
> Lucky Smith;
> Three Gypsies
> That beat Old Nick!

(Sampson 1891, 92)

It is somewhat reminiscent of the many proverbial references to the Highland clans to be found in the oral literature of Gaelic Scotland – the rapacity of the Campbells, the poverty of the MacNeils of Barra, the treachery of the Cummings, etc.

A number of other Gypsy families would also seem to have attained proverbial status. Groome, for example, mentions that the Lees had a reputation for carrying lice which earned them the nickname *Juvalo Guné*, but this epithet is more likely to have been derived through assonance of lice and Lees. In text 120, the name Lee is rendered *Purana*, properly 'garlic' or '*leek*'. In the same way, it was also used to mean 'Gaelic'. The formation, in this way, of town names, family names and even common nouns was once common practice among the Gypsies, throughout western Europe and the United States.

Leland, too, has suggested that the saying 'it's a winter morning', meaning 'a bad day or that matters look badly', refers not to the weather

334

but to a Gypsy family of that name who once had an unfortunate reputation for trouble-making (Leland 1891, 206).

Another Traveller family whose name is remembered in a number of sayings are the Faws or Faas – 'worse than the Faw gang' – 'Those nasty Scotch Faws, with only a thimbleful of Romani to a bucketful of Gorgio blood'. It is only fair to say, however, that the name of Faa, once prominent among Scottish Travellers, came to be used as a cognomen for the race as a whole. Thus, in the Jarrow register, is to be found the following entry: 'Francis Heron, king of ye Faws, buried 13 January, 1756.' In much the same way, it was once common in Cardiganshire to hear all Gypsies referred to as Ingrams – *Mae'r hen Ingrams yn dyfod*, the Ingrams (Gypsies) are coming – and, more commonly throughout the Principality, as *Teulu Abram Wd*, The Family of Abraham Wood.

As mentioned above, English Gypsy town and family names are not infrequently suggested by a fancied resemblance in the sound of two English words for only one of which there is an appropriate Romani equivalent. Thus, *Meilesto Gav*, Donkey's Town, for Doncaster. So it is with Komlo or Kamomeskro, the first syllable of Lovell suggesting the Romani *kam(ava)*, to love – a word which, as Borrow points out, is connected with the Sanskrit 'kama' which, apart from its more mundane meaning, was the name given to the Hindu god of love. Kama, we are told, was 'black, black though comely' and, says Borrow,

> The Lovell tribe is decidedly the most comely and, at the same time, the darkest of all the Anglo-Egyptian families. The faces of many of them, male and female, are perfect specimens of black beauty. They are generally called by the race the Kaulo Camloes . . . (Borrow 1874, 127)

The epithet *kaulo*, black, was also used to signify purity of blood and, in Wales, as a noun answering to the continental *Rom*, 'Gypsy male'.

Another method of choosing surnames favoured both by the Gypsies of England and by Irish Travellers was to light upon the name of some local magnate upon whose land they were perhaps in the habit of wandering and with whom they might claim kinship in order to impress a credulous peasantry. This is almost certainly true of the Stanleys and, perhaps, of the Hernes – 'formerly a handsome, clean, picturesque gang' who at one time would seem to have enjoyed considerable prestige in the northern counties.

Smart and Crofton give three forms of the name in Anglo-Romani: *Bauré-Kanengri-Moóshaw*, Big Hare Men; *Mátcho* (fish) and *Bálaw* (hairs). The second two forms would appear to be related in that *Balaw-Matcho* or *baleno-Matcho* (lit. hairy fish) were once used to mean 'herring'. Whether the reference here is to the fine hair-like bones with which the fish

335

is cursed or to the similarity in sound between Heron and hairy remains a mystery, but it is quite clear that, one way or another, the word was formed by assonance in the manner described above.

In the same way, the use of *Matcho* as a family name must have been formed via the fancied resemblance in sound between Herne and Herring. Borrow's suggestion that it was formed by assonance with the Anglo-Saxon 'haaren' (hairs) is less than convincing.

As well as *Balorengré*, hairy fellows, Borrow gives the alternative forms *Rossarmescro* and *Ratziemescro*, 'Duck People', which, he suggests, arose from the absence in the language of any word for heron. Smart and Crofton, however, say that they had never come across this form, a fact which they thought somewhat strange, given that the major part of their researches had been conducted in the northern counties where the Hernes were considered to be one of the two principal Gypsy families.

The Hernes always seem to have been regarded as particularly 'deep'. Borrow is said to have acquired his knowledge of deep *Romanés* from one of their number whilst according to Sylvester Boswell they had continued to make use of the 'double' or inflected forms long after they had fallen out of use among other families. For Norwood, too, the Hernes above all others were 'descended from King Pharaoh'.

Readers of Borrow will also need no reminding of that other Mrs Herne who 'carried so much devil's tinder about with her' and who, according to her son-in-law, Jasper, was 'always too fond of covert ways, drows and brimstones' (see notes following text 119).

Whether or not the following triplet from the Denham Tracts refers specifically to the Hernes or to the Gypsies in general, it requires little imagination to see in it something of old Mrs Herne in all her terrible hirsute glory:

> Gypsy hair and devil's eyes,
> Ever stealing, full of lies,
> Yet always poor and never wise.

Compare also the old Scots saying:

> A hairy man's a geary man,
> But a hairy wife's a witch.

According to Borrow, *Petulengro*, a common noun signifying a smith, is one of only two trade names in use among the English Gypsies, the other being *Wardomeskro* which, although properly signifying a carter or wheelwright, was used in this connection to mean cooper. Smart and Crofton, however, also list *Sivomengro*, tailor, for Taylor.

The alternative forms *sastermengro* (*saster* = iron) and *kálomengro* (*kálo* = black) do not seem to have been used as personal names, the only regular substitute for *Petulengro* being *Curraple*. It has also been suggested that Marshal may have served the same purpose on the grounds that the French *maréchal* originally meant a 'shoeing smith'. The usual Gypsy forms of this name were, however, *Mokado-tanengré*, marsh men; *Bungoraw*, corkers; and *Chikkenomengré*, china or clay-ware men – the first, a literal rendering of 'marsh' and the latter from their customary trades of cork cutting and peddling or mending crock-pots.

The *Curraples* are first mentioned by Gilbert White in his twenty-fifth letter to the Hon. Daines Barrington (1775):

We have two gangs or hordes of Gypsies which infest the south and west of England and come round in their circuit two or three times in the year. One of these tribes calls itself by the noble name of Stanley, of which I have nothing particular to say; but the other is distinguished by an appelative somewhat remarkable. As far as their harsh gibberish can be understood, they seem to say that the name of their clan is Cureople. Now the termination of this word is apparently Grecian and as Mezeray and the gravest historians all agree that these vagrants did certainly migrate from Egypt and the East two or three centuries ago and so spread by degrees over Europe, may not this family name, a little corrupted, be the very name they brought with them from the Levant?

Borrow, too, in the first edition of *Zincali* (vol.1. pp.27–8), writes as follows of the 'clan Smith or Curraple' whose members, he says, were still to be found in two eastern counties:

The name Curraple is a favourite one among the Gypsies. It excited the curiosity of the amiable White of Selbourne who, in one of his letters, mentions it as pertaining to the clan Stanley [*sic*]. He conceived it to be partly Greek . . . Curraple, however, means a smith, a name very appropriate to a Gypsy. The root is *curaw*, to strike, hammer etc. *Curraple* is likewise a legitimate word signifying a sword.

(Tom Taylor also describes an encounter with a Sinfi Curapple in a series of articles published in the *Illustrated London News* under the pseudonym 'Roumany Rei' (Taylor 1851). See also Pott 1844–5, i, 49 and ii, 115).

Why the Smiths were thought to have been especially lucky, Sampson was unable to say. That a Smith did, indeed, beat the Devil – and God, too, for that matter – is, however, suggested by a tale recorded by Smart and Crofton in both the *Puri* and *Poggadi Chib*, and called 'How Petulengro Went to Heaven' (Smart and Crofton 1875, 219). See also

Acton and Kenrick (1985, 61) where the story is reproduced in the *Poggadi Chib* alone.

In summary, it runs as follows. One day, God came to a small town where, for want of an inn, he spent the night in the house of a smith. By way of thanks, he told the smith that he would give him four things of his own choosing. The smith asked for the following: that anyone who climbed his apple tree would be unable to descend unless he gave the word; that anyone who sat on his anvil would be unable to rise without his express permission; that anyone who entered his little iron box would not be able to get out until he gave him leave; and that if he himself should sit on his own hat, no one should have the power to make him rise against his will.

Many years passed and the Angel of Death came for the smith. 'Just a minute', says the latter, 'for I must just say goodbye to my wife. In the meantime, why don't you climb that old tree and help yourself to an apple?' Finding himself unable to get down, Death was eventually forced to agree to allow the smith a further twenty years of life.

When next Death came to call, the smith told him that he looked tired and suggested that he sit a while on his anvil. The same thing happened as before and once again Death was forced to grant the smith a further twenty years.

On the third occasion, the Devil himself came to claim his own but, piqued by the smith's suggestion that he could not possibly squeeze himself into the latter's little iron box, accepted the bait and found himself locked in. Despite his pleading, the smith brought the box to red heat and began beating it savagely with his hammer. At length, the Devil, like his messenger before him, was obliged to allow the smith a further stay of execution in order to gain his release.

Many years passed until, at last, God sent one of his own angels to fetch the smith away to hell. But when the Devil saw whom he had with him he refused to open the door, leaving the angel no option but to bring the smith before his master. God, too, would have nothing to do with him but agreed to allow him a brief glimpse of paradise before sending him on his way. But, no sooner had he opened the door than the smith threw in his hat and, dashing in after it, sat down on it. 'And dova see sar o petulengro ghias to Mi-doovel's kair.'

Another of Borrow's songs in which Gypsy surnames are mentioned is the following, composed for Charlotta Lee, the wife of the lightweight prize-fighter, Jack Cooper. Cooper, who had 'knocked West Country Dick to pieces and killed Paddy O'Leary, the fighting pot-boy', was eventually brought low himself by a woman. Having fallen badly for this 'painted Jezebel', he first beggared his own wife in order to keep her sweet and was then transported for taking the blame for her theft of a lady's purse. His term of transportation over, he stayed on in the *Sonnakye Tem*, the 'Gold Country' of Australia, where he is said to have made a living passing on his knowledge of the fight game. His wife, however, remained loyal throughout, living in constant expectation of his imminent return.

> 122.   Charlotta is my nav,
>   I am a puro Purrun;
>   My romado was Jack,
>   The couring Vardomescro.
>   He muk'd me for a lubbeny,
>   Who chor'd a rawnie's kissi;
>   He penn'd 'twas he who lell'd it,
>   And so was bitched pawdel.
>   (Borrow 1874, 140)

~

Then Mi-dibble kair'd Manoo drey his dikkipen; drey Mi-dibble's dikkipen kair'd he leste; mush and mushi kair'd Dibble lende and he chiv'd his koshto rokrapen opreylen.
                     (Genesis 1:27) (Borrow 1874, 75)

> 123.   As I was a jawing to the gav yeck divvus,
>   I met on the drom miro Rommany chi;
>   I puch'd yoi whether she com sar mande;
>   And she penn'd tu si wafo Rommany.*
>
>   And I penn'd, I shall ker tu miro tacho Rommany
>   Fornigh tute but dui chavé;
>   Methinks I'll cam tute for miro merripen
>   If tu but pen, thou wilt commo sar mande.
>
>   One day as I was going to the village,
>   I met on the road my Rommany lass:
>   I ask'd her whether she would come with me,
>   And she said thou hast another wife.*
>
>   I said, I will make thee my lawful wife,
>   Because thou hast but two children;
>   Methinks I will love thee until my death,
>   If thou but say thou wilt come with me.
>   (Borrow 1841, 432)

*Correctly used, the idiom requires the dative case. See note accompanying text 44.

Borrow includes the foregoing 'specimen of a song in the vulgar or broken Romany' in the appendix to the *Gypsies in Spain*, in support of his by no means universally accepted assertion that the English Gypsies did, indeed, possess a body of song in their own language. 'Many other specimens of the English Gypsy muse might', he says, 'be here adduced; it is probable, however, that the above will have fully satisfied the curiosity of the reader. It has been inserted here for the purpose of showing that the Gypsies have songs in their own language, a fact which has been denied' (Borrow 1841, 432). It is the earliest surviving example of a song text in the *Poggadi Chib*.

The first two lines also occur in chapter 85 of *Romany Rye*, where his companion, Isopel Berners, objecting to Borrow's use of *Romanés* in her presence, prevents him from going any further. The only difference in wording lies in the correct use, in the latter, of the feminine form of the possessive pronoun 'my', *miri*.

A variant of the same song also appears on p.104 of *Romano Lavo-Lil* and was subsequently reproduced by Smith in *Through Romany Songland* (1889, 116) with the comment that it 'savours somewhat of Salt Lake City'.

> 124. As I was a jawing to the gav yeck divvus
> I met on the drom miro Romany chi;
> I pootch'd las whether she come sar mande,
> And she penn'd tu sar wafo rommadis;
> O mande there is kek wafo romady,
> So penn'd I to miro Romany chi,
> And I'll kair tute miro tatcho romadi
> If you but pen tu come sar mande.
> (Borrow 1874, 104)

Although it is quite true that all three sets make use of the same stereotypical opening line, Sampson's contention that text 125 is simply another variant of texts 123 and 124 is, perhaps, open to question.

> 125. As mandi was a jallin' to the bōro gav,
> Mandi dik'd a romano chai;
> I pūch'd her to chūmer mandi –
> 'Aawa, bâ. Mīsto tū tai.'
> (Teni Mullenger (née Robinson), Blackpool;
> Sampson 1891, 191)

Although the form of words used to introduce these sets is reminiscent of the standard British/Hiberno-English opening, 'As I was a walking; as I roved out', it is noticeable that, in the Gypsy repertoire, songs of this type

are usually given an urban rather than a rural setting. Compare, for
example, the opening line of text 56, 'When I first chiv'd my piro 'dré de
bori gav', and the following set from Silesia:

> Gelas Chaiko pe o foro
> Tai raklias le tsinores:
> 'Moto mangi kater aves,
> Spaniatar, Franzosostar?'

> Chaiko wandered in the city
> And he met a youthful stranger:
> 'Tell me truly whence thou comest,
> Spain or France hast thou for birthplace?'
>
> (MacAlister 1928, 4)

An encounter on the road also forms the theme of one of two pieces
obtained by Leland from an unnamed Gypsy woman living in the vicinity
of Walton on Thames. Her husband, a *gaujo*, wrote it out at her dictation
which, as Leland explains, accounts for any peculiarities in the spelling. It
has been reprinted by Acton in *Romani Rokkeripen To-Divvus* with certain
minor orthographical alterations (Acton and Kenrick 1985, 66).

> 126. There's a rauney jessin on the tober,*
>   There's rye jessin after her;
>   He would del all the louver
>   In his putsey if the rauney
>   Would beshtolay** with him.
>   He pens: 'My dear rauney,
>   You shall have plenty of vonggar***
>   If you will jess with mandy:
>   For in the sarlow we will get
>   Rumoured, for that will be tatchey.'
>
>   (Anon., Walton on Thames; Leland 1873, 233)

---

*Tober = Irish *bóthar*, road. Widely recorded for *Shelta* but not noted as such in
Palmer's glossary to *English Gypsy Songs*.
**Properly two words and given as such in Acton and Kenrick's reprint: *besh telé* = to
sit down. The phrase also carried the additional meaning, to court.
***'Several . . . words are now disused by Gipsies, as having become intelligible to those
by whom they would not wish to be understood. Thus *wóngar* (lit. coal) is now
universally substituted by metropolitan Gipsies for *lóvo*, which had crept into Cant as
early as 1567' (Groome 1880, 252).

As with texts 123–4, Borrow offers two versions of the following song which he calls 'Lelling Cappi' (making a fortune), printing them on consecutive pages of *Romano Lavo-Lil*.

Lelling Cappi No.1

127.   'Av, my little Romany chei!
       Av along with mansar!
       Av, my little Romany chel!
       Koshto si for mangue.'

       'I shall lel a curapen,
       If I jal aley;
       I shall lel a curapen
       From my dear bebee.'

       'I will jal on my chongor,
       Then I'll pootch your bebee.
       'O my dear bebee, dey me your chi,
       For koshto si for mangue.'

       ' "Since you pootch me for my chi,
       I will dey you lati." '
       Av, my little Romany chel!
       We will jal to the wafu tem:

       'I will chore a beti gry,
       And so we shall lel cappi.'
       'Kekko, meero mushipen,
       For so you would be stardo;

       'But I will jal a dukkering,
       And so we shall lel cappi.'
       'Koshto, my little Romany chel!
       Koshto si for mangue.'
       (Borrow 1874, 100)

As is so often the case, Borrow's metrical English version adds unnecessarily to the sense of his original Romani text, robbing it of its essential simplicity. His use of anachronistic forms also strikes a jarring note, particularly in line 8 where 'trow' is clearly used simply in order to force a reluctant rhyme.

Making a Fortune

'Come along, my little gypsy girl,
Come along, my little dear;
Come along, my little gypsy girl –
We'll wander far and near.'

'I should get a leathering
Should I with thee go;
I should get a leathering
From my dear aunt, I trow.'

'I'll go down on my two knees,
And I will beg your aunt.
"O auntie dear, give me your child;
She's just the girl I want!"

' "Since you ask me for my child,
I will not say thee no!"
Come along, my little gypsy girl!
To another land we'll go:

'I will steal a little horse,
And our fortunes make thereby.'
'Not so, my little gypsy boy,
For then you'd swing on high;

'But I'll a fortune-telling go,
And our fortunes make thereby.'
'Well said, my little gypsy girl,
You counsel famously.'

(Borrow 1874, 101)

Lelling Cappi No.2

128. 'Av, my little Rumni chel,
Av along with mansar;
We will jal a gry-choring
Pawdle across the chumba.

'I'll jaw tuley on my chongor
To your deya and your bebee;
And I'll pootch lende that they del
Tute to me for romadi.'

343

'I'll jaw with thee, my Rumni chal,
If my dye and bebee muk me;
But choring gristurs traishes me,
For it brings one to the rukie.

''Twere ferreder that you should ker,
Petuls and I should dukker,
For then adrey our tarney tan,
We kek atraish may sova.'

'Kusko, my little Rumni chel,
Your rokrapen is kusko;
We'll dukker and we'll petuls ker
Pawdle across the chumba.

'O kusko si to chore a gry
Adrey the kaulo rarde;
But 'tis not kosko to be nash'd
Oprey the nashing rukie.'

'Come along, my little gypsy girl,
Come along with me, I pray!
A-stealing horses we will go,
O'er the hills so far away.

'Before your mother and your aunt
I'll down upon my knee,
And beg they'll give me their little girl
To be my Romadie.'

'I'll go with you, my gypsy boy,
If my mother and aunt agree;
But a perilous thing is horse-stealing,
For it brings one to the tree.

''Twere better you should tinkering ply,
And I should fortunes tell;
For then within our little tent
In safety we might dwell.'

'Well said, my little gypsy girl,
I like well what you say;
We'll tinkering ply, and fortunes tell
O'er the hills so far away.

344

> "'Tis a pleasant thing in a dusky night
> A horse-stealing to go;
> But to swing in the wind on the gallows-tree,
> Is no pleasant thing, I trow.'
>
> (Borrow 1874, 101–2)

Given the difference in form between certain words common to both texts – *koshto/kusko, aley/tuley, Romany/Rumni* – it might be supposed that they were obtained from two different informants or that Borrow himself was simply experimenting with two alternative drafts of his own work. Cf. Norwood's comments on the various versions of Borrow's *Creed* and *Pater Noster* (Diaries, October 1858). Yet, whilst the cautious tone of the girl's response might well suggest that Borrow himself was, indeed, the author of the piece, this cannot be assumed with any degree of certainty as a similar reluctance to engage in *grai choring* is also evident on the part of the girl in Philip Murray's 'Song of the Drukerimongero' (text 129).

Koshto/kusko is one of a small number of adjectives virtually restricted to British Romani. Bohtlingk, it is true, gives *kansto* in his 'Mélanges Asiatiques' of 1854 (vol.ii, Book 2), but the word was apparently unknown to Paspati who, in a letter to Bath C. Smart (Smart and Crofton 1875, 26) points out that its place is taken in most continental dialects by *latscho/laczzo*, a word also occurring in the earliest example of connected British Romani – the sentences recorded by Andrew Boorde in his *Fyrste Boke of the Introduction of Knowledge*, published in London in 1547–8.

The interchangeability of 'k' and 't' (*kusko = koshto*) is particularly well represented in Scotto-Romani/Tinklers' Cant: e.g. *rakli/ratli*, woman; *akhom/autem*, church/marry; *brickle/brittle*, bowl; *municleer/muncri-clear*, the sea; *plank/plant*, lay, place, hide; etc. (see Russell 1914).

Grai choring as a means of earning a living is also unsuccessfully canvassed in the following piece from Philip Murray. Murray, a Tinker, who had spent most of his life among the Gypsies, had learned it from one of his wife's relations, Cassy Smith. It is a long rambling piece and Murray, who was in his eighties when Sampson met him, could only remember a few disconnected fragments. It takes the form of a dialogue between a man and a woman, the man apparently speaking first:

> 129. 'If you're a drūkerimongero,
> As I takes you for to be,
> Chiv your tikno on your dumo
> And av along with me.
> If we chance to meet a muskro
> Unhappy we shall be.'

The woman:
'And if we're merin' with the buk
When rati wels apré,
Then chiv your wast apré my burk,
And blessed we shall be.'

The man proposes stealing a mare from an adjacent field and selling her at the fair. The question is discussed at considerable length, and finally (influenced by some oblique motives) they decide in favour of the honester course. The man apparently goes on:

'And if we've got to sut avrí
We've chichi boχ at all.
And if we're lel'd to storiben
'Twill be the worst of all,
And if we jol andré the gov
To lodopen we'll jâ.
And chiv talé your posinakés
For chumoni to χâ.'

It concludes:

'And if you pī a kusi livena,
You'll always think of me!'
        (Philip Murray; Sampson 1892, 75)

                                        ~

130. Daisy's chai across y dera
     Tardi avel are komera
     Atch o rai avel adoi
     Puk y das, av akai
     Kana dikan tu
     Mankyu 'vel o baro dives.

     There is Daisy's girl across (with) the string (or thread)
     Drawing (or knitting?) coming through the room
     Comes where the gentleman is staying
     Says the old woman, come here,
     Did you ever see?
     Such consoling coming in broad daylight (?)
         (Manfri Wood, Penybont Fawr, November 1954;
         Kennedy, Folktracks 60–441;
         transcribed and translated by J. Brune, Folktracks)

In answer to Kennedy's enquiry as to the meaning of this song, Mr Wood had the following to say (the emphasis is mine):

It's a gentleman and he's got a lady. *This lady is living in a parlour and this gentleman comes in and he calls her: 'come here!'* and she goes to him and then *he tells her something* and she starts to cry. And he catches hold of her and he pats her, takes her round the chair and brought her around. She starts to sing that with him.

Against this background, Brune's transcription and hence his translation appear less than convincing. I offer the following by way of a possible alternative:

> 131. 'Doi sas chai 'cross(1) y(2) dor'a', (3)
> Ta jivéla(4) 'ré komora.
> Ako, rai 'vel' adoi.(5)
> Pukadas: 'av akoi,
> Kana dikan tu, kana dikan tu, kana dikan tu(6),
> Manghé avela boro dives.'(7)

> There was a girl across the sea
> And she lives in a chamber (parlour).
> Lo, a gentleman comes there.
> He said: 'come here!
> Now do you see, now do you see, now do you see?
> A great day is coming for me.'

1. Eng. across.
2. The Welsh definite article: 'y'.
3. *Doriav*, the sea (Sampson 1926, iv, 78).
4. The apparent mix of tenses presents no problem. Mr Wood makes a similar 'mistake' when explaining the song in English. It is possible, however, that the use of the present tense in the second line was intended to convey continuity.
5. Cf. *Okki, a rei wela 'kei*, look out, there is a gentleman coming (Smart and Crofton 1875, 294). Also l.1 of text 139.
6. In Welsh Romani, as in other dialects, the past tense is formed by bringing together the past participle with the appropriate person of the present tense of the verb to be – cf. medieval Welsh: *ath-wyf*, gone I am. Thus, in the fourth line we have *pukadas* from *pukadó*, said + *sí*, he/she/it is = he said. So, too, in the following line, despite the omission of the medial t/d, *dikan tu* would seem to be from *dikdo*, saw + *shan*, you are = you saw/did you see. A more likely explanation, however, is that *dikan* is simply a misrepresentation of the more usual *dikassa*, you see/will see. Cf. *Lián to váriso*, will you take something? (Groome 1880, 35). The correct form here would be *lassa* or *lessa*.
7. According to Sampson, *manke* means either 'before', 'prior' or 'earlier than' – *mar'la man mank'o divés*, he will put me to death before morning (Sampson 1926, iv, 211). This being so, the line might be rendered either 'before daylight comes' or 'before a great day comes'. Neither, however, would seem to make much sense in the present context, although the latter would work if *manke* could also mean 'soon'. In the alternative rendering, *manghe 'véla boro divés*, a great day is coming for me, *manghe* represents the second dative of the personal pronoun *me*, I, me (Sampson 1926, 159; Smart and Crofton 1875, 42); cf. *koshto si for mangue* (text 127, l.4).

347

Although the song is obviously primitive in character, the melody employed by Mr Wood has nothing of the Romani about it, being well known throughout Wales as the vehicle for such widely differing pieces as *Claddu'r Mochyn Du* and *Cân y Patriarchiaid*.

In another of Sampson's pieces, the outcome is somewhat less amicable, the woman being left to cope alone with her children following her husband's desertion. It was obtained from a Gypsy woman, known to him only as Florence but whom he took to be one of the Lovells. A solitary character, she lived by day in a house but spent her nights in a wagon drawn up on a piece of waste ground near Smithdown Lane in Liverpool.

She was, says Sampson, 'a savage, half insane character' which made interviewing her a by no means agreeable task. She was, moreover, 'extremely violent and subject to various delusions', taking him for a 'swell-mobsman' – a notion which, although enhancing his reputation in her eyes, led her on one occasion to threaten him with the police. It was only with some difficulty that Sampson managed to obtain the full text, 'fragments of which she would often scream when intoxicated or in one of her mad moods'.

> 132. My mush is jal'd and the beng may lel him,
> When mandi's chiv'd talé under* the chik,
> He's nash'dedo* with a vasavi grasni
> And muk'd his chavis to mer of bok.
> I'll mong on the drom for my diri chavis,
> And puker lenghi a vasavo lav,
> 'Tutti's dad was a hochedo jukel,
> To ker a lubni of tutti's dai.'
> (Florence Lovell? Sampson 1891, 89)

*According to Leland, 'a phrase in which the Gypsy word is immediately followed by its English equivalent is a common form of expression for the sake of clearness'; cf. 'the jivviben has jawed avree out of his gad', 'the life has gone out out of his shirt' (Leland 1873, 104). It may equally be, however, that it is simply the result of speaking in a mixed jargon. Thus, in l.3, *nash'dedo* combines both the English and Romani forms of the past participle.

The idea that a Gypsy woman would be left destitute by her husband's desertion is hard to swallow as, more often than not, it is the woman who is the principal provider. Charlotta Lee kept both her husband and his 'painted Jezebel' until he was eventually transported, and thereafter continued to support herself without recourse to any other man (text 122). For this reason, Sampson was disposed to question the song's Gypsy origin. It may also be observed that Gypsy women have seldom if ever been known to engage in prostitution and, for this reason, I take the last line to mean that the man, by deserting his wife, has treated her as if she were nothing more to him than a common whore.

~

Rom Romesa, Gajo Gajesa – A Gypsy with a Gypsy, a Gaujo with a Gaujo.

(Gypsy proverb)

Kel as you kom wi' the tarno Gajo rais, but kek wafedu.

(Luréna Hern)

133. Romani čai bešing adré the tan.
Pen'd lāki dai: 'Mīrī dīrī čai,
Mâ rŏmer the rai, the gâjo rai,
Kist'ring astut a pireno* grai.
You bâri wafadi lubanī,
Jal avré mīrī tan and be kâmbrī;
Šūn** the wafadi lubanī
With gâjesko rat to be kâmbrī.'
(Thompson, *JGLS* n.s. 3 (1909), 157)

*Said by the original informants to mean 'swift', presumably from *píro*, foot.
**The original editor suggests this may be a corruption of *shan*, you are.

The foregoing 'tattered remnant' of Ursula's 'Song of the Broken Chastity' (Borrow 1857, 44; text 134) was obtained by T. W. Thompson from two Norfolk Gypsies, granddaughters of Ambrose Smith/Reynolds, the original of Borrow's Jasper Petulengro. With regard to it, Thompson says only that 'it is rather typical that the Gypsies who dictated it had entirely lost its meaning although they knew what many of the words meant'. Although he does not offer his own translation, the meaning seems clear enough:

A Romani girl sitting in the tent,
Said her mother: 'My dear girl,
Don't marry the gentleman, the Gaujo gentleman,
Riding astride a swift horse.
You wicked whore,
Go away (from) my tent and be pregnant.
You are the wicked whore,
To be pregnant with Gaujo blood.'

Borrow's original text runs as follows:

> 134. Penn'd the Romany chi ké laki dye:
> 'Miry dearie dye, mi shom cambri!'
> 'And coin kerdo tute cambri,
> Miry dearie chi, miry Romany chi?'
> 'O miry dye, a boro rye,
> A bovalo rye, a gorgiko rye
> Sos kistur pré a pellengo grye,
> 'Twas yov sos kerdo man cambri.'
> Tu tawnie vassavie lubbeny,
> Tu chal from miry tan abri.
> Had a Romany chal kair'd tute cambri,
> Then I had penn'd ke tute chie,
> But tu shan a vassavie lubbeny
> With gorgikie rat to be cambri.'
>
> (Borrow 1857, 44)

In answer to Borrow's enquiry, Ursula says of this song:

> We sing the song now and then to be a warning to ourselves to have as little as possible in the way of acquaintance with the Gorgios; and a warning it is. You see how the young woman in the song was driven out of her tent by her mother with all kinds of disgrace and bad language. But you don't know that she was afterwards buried alive by her cocos (uncles) and pals (brothers), in an uninhabited place. The song does not say it, but the story says it; for there is a story about it; though, as I said before, it was a long time ago, and perhaps, after all, wasn't true.

It is to this incident, no doubt, that Thompson refers when he says:

> As regards their marriage relations, the English Gypsies have been, and still are, a highly moral race (using the word moral in its conventional sense) . . . Romanichals have ever been faithful to their husbands and the punishment for odd cases of unchastity always of the severest. Three East Anglian Gypsies who committed this crime in the early part of the last century were punished, one by being buried alive, another by having her ears cut off and the third by being compelled to run naked around a large field every morning. (Thompson 1910a, 46)

Elsewhere, in conversation with Urénia Hern, he happened to mention that foreign Gypsies were in the habit of cutting off the nose and ears of the unfaithful wife, to which the latter replied:

That's what our old people used to do – cut off their noses . . . My uncle Manful – my father's brother – cut off his wife's hair an' cut off all 'er clothes by 'ere (pointing to her hips) an' chased 'er like that round a field with a bulldog. (Thompson 1912, 312)

Colocci (1889, 228), Leibich (1863, 50) and Beister (*Berlinische Monatsschrift* (February 1793), 118) all speak of facial mutilation as the punishment for female adulterers among continental Gypsies, whilst Yates, in a reference to the Gypsies of Hungary in the *Gypsy Lore Society Journal* for October 1908, mentions expulsion from the group, flogging, gashing and a night spent tied naked to a tree. Only Cervantes, however, in *La Gitanella*, specifies death as the prescribed punishment for the unfaithful wife (see de Rochas 1876, 273).

The twin punishments of gashing and cutting the clothes are also recalled in the following quatrain noted by Herrmann and MacRitchie from the singing of a Gypsy woman, Julie Lakatos of Perbete in the Comitat of Komorn, on 12 April, 1891:

> Ma cinger man, ma mar man,
> Ma cinger mro sano gat,
> Mer man nane pirano,
> Ko man tyinel sano gat.
>
> Do not rend me, do not beat me,
> Do not rend my fine smock,
> For I have no lover,
> Who buys for me a fine smock.
> (*JGLS* o.s. 3 (1892), 105)

Apart from Borrow, Thompson's principal source for the burying-alive story seems to have been a somewhat vague letter from a Dr Ranking, the relevant portion of which is reproduced below (Thompson 1910b, 170):

I cannot remember from whom I had the story; but one of the old men told me that the ancient punishment for unchastity was burying alive. He also professed to have himself seen the punishment inflicted when he was a boy; and showed me the spot where he said the grave was. It was a few miles out of Ipswich, near a village the name of which I cannot remember; I only know that there was an inn there called The Angel. The spot itself was a place where three roads met. There was a good sized, triangular piece of grassy ground where they met, and this he said was at one time a favourite place; the burial place was, he assured me, in the middle of this plot.

Whilst there is no reason to doubt what was left of Ranking's memory, it does seem a little odd that the family should have chosen to bury the unfortunate victim in the middle of one of their favourite stopping-places, and one is tempted to ask what the 'going rate' may have been for guided tours of the spot. As Logan remarks on p.141 of his *Pedlar's Pack*, many Gypsies had at that time 'taken to starring it through the country, and exhibiting their encampment, to the curious, for a small fee payable at the entrance gate' (Logan 1869, 141).

The following metrical English version of Ursula's song is by the Revd Norwood and is dated 18 August 1857. For an alternative rendering by Sampson, see p.151 of Borrow's *Romany Rye* in the Methuen edition of 1903.

> The Gypsy girl to her mother said –
> 'My dearest mammy, I am betray'd.' –
> 'And who was he thy faith beguil'd,
> My dearest child, my Romany child?'
>
> 'Oh mammy o' mine, a Gentleman fine,
> Who came on his horse in the sweet moonshine,
> On his bonny good horse to the shadowy glade,
> 'Twas he thy Romany child betray'd.' –
>
> 'Away, thou little sot defil'd;
> Away from my tent, no more my child!
> Had a Gypsy man entic'd thy will,
> Then had I call'd thee daughter still;
>
> But now in thy shame and grief begone,
> And the white blood swell thy Gypsy zone.'

Just as Norwood sang 'The Broken Chastity' to a family of Gypsies he met on the 'Swindon Drom' during the late 1850s (see note accompanying text 146), so Leland, some twenty years later, was to sing it to the Gypsies of St Petersburg. As with his account of Borrow's 'Kettle-mender's Song' in *Gypsy Sorcery and Fortune Telling* (1891), however, either his memory was at fault or he had before him an alternative draft. The opening lines run as follows (Leland 1882, 45):

> Pen de Romany chai ke laki dye:
> 'Miri diri dye, mi shom kameli . . .'

'I never knew', he says, 'whether this was really an old Gypsy poem or one written by Mr Borrow. Once, when I repeated it to old Henry James as he sat making baskets, I was silenced by being told: "That ain't no real Gypsy *gilli*. That's one of the kind made up by gentlemen and ladies." However, as soon as I repeated it, the Russian Gypsy girl cried eagerly, "I know that song" and actually sang me a ballad which was essentially the same . . .'

He then concludes, 'Now, as many centuries must have passed since the English and Russian Gypsies parted from the parent stock, the preservation of this song is very remarkable, for its antiquity must be very great.' Were the same song to occur in more or less the same form at so great a remove in distance and time it would, indeed, be very remarkable; that similar themes should inform the singing of English and Russian Gypsies is, however, only to be expected. Unfortunately, Leland does not appear to have thought it necessary to include the original Russian Gypsy text.

With few exceptions, those nineteenth-century writers who have commented on this aspect of Gypsy morals are agreed that, however lax they may have been in other respects, Gypsy women have always been extremely jealous of their virtue. Roberts, for example (1836), tells us that 'the females . . . are rarely if ever found among those dreadful pests to society in large towns – common prostitutes', whilst according to Crabb (1832, 33),

> The mutual attachment which subsists between the nominal husband and wife is so truly sincere that instances of infidelity, on either side, occur but seldom and, when otherwise, the parties are deemed very wicked by the Gypsies. They are known strictly to avoid all conversation of an unchaste kind in their camps except among the most degraded of them and instances of young females having children before they pledge themselves to those they love are rare.

As regards the propriety of their conversation, it is perhaps worth noting Tom Taylor's observations on the same subject. 'I have not known many of the Romany cheis', he writes, in the first of a series of articles which appeared in the *Illustrated London News* in November and December 1851, 'who were agreeable company in two-handed talk. Either they are intolerably rapacious, asking for everything that pleased them, or grossly and tiresomely *soft-sawderish* or pruriently coarse.'

Both Borrow and Smart and Crofton also refer to the darker side of the female Gypsy character, the latter drawing on the observations of their principal informant, Sylvester Boswell. There can be little doubt, however, that, in both cases, the women in question were regarded as an unwelcome exception.

Borrow's subject is an unnamed high-class tease whose conduct apparently found little favour among her fellow Travellers. The description of her activities is apparently taken from another unnamed Gypsy and is included in an account of the 'Wandsworth Gypsyry' dated 1864.

> She is kek tatcho; and that's what I like least in her; There's no trusting her, neither Gorgio nor Romano can trust her: she sells her truppos to a rye-gorgio for five bars, and when she has got them, and the Gorgio, as he has a right to do, begins to kelna lasa, she laughs and asks him if he knows whom he has to deal with; then if he lels bonnek of lati, as he is quite justified in doing, she whips out her churi and swears if he doesn't leave off, she will stick it in his gorlo. She is a wafodu grasni. (Borrow 1874, 142)

> She is not straight and that's what I like least in her; there's no trusting her, neither Gorgio nor Gypsy can trust her: she sells her body to a Gorgio gentleman for five pounds and when she has got them and the Gorgio, as he has a right to do, begins to play with her, she laughs and asks him if he knows whom he has to deal with; then if he takes hold of her, as he is quite justified in doing, she whips out her knife and swears if he doesn't lay off she will stick it in his throat. She is an evil mare.

It is of this same 'wafodu grasni' that Borrow speaks in the following couplet:

> Rinkeno mui and wafodu zee,
> Kitzi's the cheeros we dicks cattané.
> (Borrow 1874, 142)

> A pretty face and an evil heart
> Many's the time we see together.

As might be expected, Smart and Crofton, like Borrow, preferred not to embarrass the reader by offering anything in the way of a translation of the following extract.

> O Rómani-chei kedás kóshto láti-kókeri tall' sor láti's loóberiben. Kek naneí yöï rínkeni. Wáfedo díkomusti chei sas yöï . . . Yöï sas chíchi féterdér te loóbni. Yöï sas yek. Yöï atchéla opré dromáw adré o Gav, pósha kítchemáw, te dick tálla o gairé te del yöï trin-górishi, te shau-háuri, te sov *wi'* láti. Bítta Gaujé, raklé, vart asár láti dósta chaíruse*s*, te jal adré wesháw, te mook wárdi-gairé te sov *wi'* láti, *and* dóva see tátcho. Gaujé penéla jaw troostál láti konáw. (Smart and Crofton 1875, 210)

> The Romani girl did well for herself after all her whoring. She wasn't pretty. An ill-looking girl she was . . . She was no better than a whore. She was one. She used to stand (stands) on the roads in the town, outside the alehouses

hoping the men would give her three and sixpence to lie with her. Young Gaujos, lads, used to see her often, going into the woods to lie with the watchmen. And that's true. Gaujos still say it about her now.

Unambiguous as such statements may be, they are in no way representative of the way in which women are portrayed either in the literature as a whole or in the British Gypsy song repertoire. Only rarely are they shown taking the lead in a sexual encounter (text 7), the initiative remaining firmly with the man (texts 8, 49, 123–5 etc.). In Hungarian Gypsy song, on the other hand, the woman as adulterer and drunk has emerged as something of a stock figure. Vekerdi, for example, in a brief discussion of certain common themes of Lovari song has the following to say, from which it is clear that, far from borrowing such notions from the folklore of the surrounding people, the Gypsies, in this respect, have determined their own agenda:

> At the same time, it must be pointed out that the Hungarian-influenced lingual formulas clearly conceal non-Hungarian thinking and style. Thus, the expression *muli mati* (dead drunk) is a calque on Hungarian *holtreszeg* but the topic of drunken wife current in Gypsy songs never occurs in Hungarian folk song . . . the same applies to the other main themes occurring in Gypsy songs. The central figure in them is the wife (*romni*), especially as adulteress (*kurva*), whilst in Hungarian folk songs the wife does not figure. (Vekerdi 1967)

Somewhat ironically, however, the disorderly Gypsy woman makes her first appearance not in song, but in an official document of the Hungarian empire, dated 1493. In it, the Emperor Sigismund, having enjoined his subjects to offer assistance to 'our faithful Ladislas, *Voivode* (leader) of the Gypsies, and others dependent on him', goes on to say:

> . . . If there should be found among them some drunken women, if any troublesome incident should occur among them, no matter what its nature, it is our will and formal command that the said *Voivode*, Ladislas, and he alone, shall then use the right to punish and to absolve them to the exclusion of all. (Clébert 1964, 32–3)

Although the drunken wife would seem to be entirely absent from British Gypsy song, a number of references are to be found in the literature to the Gypsies' aversion to *female* insobriety. e.g. 'If there is one thing scandal ashamed, it is', says Sylvanus Lovell (Groome 1880, 130), 'to see a beastly drunken female. Such cattle as they ought to be shot. They be a nuisance to the road.'

Extended Texts

As the 'gashing' song (above) would suggest, the figure of the unfaithful wife, sometimes brazen, sometimes cowed, is not confined to the Hungarian Gypsy repertoire. Compare, for example, the following sets from Sweden and Slovakia. The first is taken from an unpublished paper by Elisabeth Skarpe ('Kaksanger. En Analys av en Fangelsetradition'), and was recorded in prison some time during 1969–70. For this reason, no further information is given regarding Skarpe's informants save that they referred to themselves as *Resande*, a derivative of the Swedish verb, *resa*, to travel, and apparently corresponding more or less exactly with our English 'Traveller' as used by the Gypsies themselves.

B.38. Dinglar-Stigs Visa

Oh sjun pre miro chavoar, jag gia vill en sång
Om hur livet har förfarit med mig engång,
Sa att ni inte tradrar uti samma spår och drom
For då skolen ni få ångra det engång.

Det honkar när jag jadde pre mitt artonde bast
När jag ifrån stillopat kom ut,
Då mirom fick se hur hon lett en vaver dräng
Så ni kan sjunna hurudan jag blev.

Jag ledde då drängen för halsen och mante han ut
Att le upp för sin nyförvärvda vän.
Ty jag avlete att jag becknar ej min fromnia för tji
Utan teknot dobbepa det ska det bli.

Så jadde vi to budrum i den kaloa rat
För att pröva våra veistar av atål.
Och det dröjde ej så länge förrän buroratti ran
När min tjuro i drängen försvann.

Jag baschar nu i cellen, jag har fyst mig ett bast,
För jag försvarar det jag ansåg vara mitt.
Och jag puckar eder tjavoar innan ni ler veistar fram dicka
    (upp hur det gick för Dingalar-Stig).

Crazy Stig's Song

O listen to me, lads, I want to sing a song,
About how life has treated me once,
So that you will not drive in the same track and road.
Because then you will regret it once.

It was when I went on my eighteenth year,
When I from prison came out,
Then I got to see how she got another boy.
So you can hear how I turned out.

Then I took the boy by the throat and challenged him
To stand up for his new-found friend
Because I don't sell my Gypsy woman for nothing.
But a little beating there should be.

So we went to the door in the dark night,
To try our knives made of steel.
And it didn't take long till the peasant's (Gaujo's) blood ran
When my knife was lost in the boy.

Now I sit in the cell – I have got twelve months –
Because I defended what I meant to be mine.
And I tell you, lads, before you take out your knives,
Take heed what happened to Crazy Stig!

This second set was learned in Slovakia by an unnamed Gypsy woman,
recorded in Praha-Kyje in 1977 (Folktracks 608):

Kiss me behind the Minta,
Not on the road where my husband can see;
Otherwise, he'll cut off my hair.
Sigh of shame! He'll shoot once, twice,
And he may kill two women.

Whilst it is quite possible that the many favourable references to Gypsy
morals which are to be found in the literature do, indeed, represent their
own authentic public stance in response to *Gaujo* enquiry, it is as well to
remember that even Sampson, who was more successful than most in
winning the confidence of his Gypsy informants, was forced to admit that
the outsider 'never succeeds in surprising them in a state of mental or
moral deshabille . . . their best manners and loftiest sentiments are always
assumed at his approach'. In reality, there is no reason to suppose that the
Gypsies' private attitude towards such matters is or was any more or less
rigid than that of their socio-economic equivalents among the settled
population. There may, of course, be a valid distinction to be drawn
between their attitude towards mixed Romani–Gaujo relationships and
those not involving outsiders but this is no more than one would expect
from any close-knit social, religious or ethnic group.

Among British Travellers of the more traditional type, the general pattern now seems to be that sexual awareness is acquired well before puberty and that pre-marital intercourse is a by no means infrequent occurrence. New babies born of such relationships are usually cared for by the maternal grandmother. In many cases, marriage follows the birth of the first or second illegitimate child, unless it becomes necessary for the male partner to lose himself elsewhere within the kin-structure. Yet, whatever their private attitude, one would expect them to portray themselves publicly as highly conventional, knowing that to do otherwise would be simply to confirm the settled community in its worst prejudices.

That children born out of wedlock were not unknown, at least to Welsh Travellers, is suggested by the following charm mentioned by Jarman and Jarman on p.186 of *The Welsh Gypsies* (1991). It may be, however, that so useful a remedy would have been equally attractive to the *Gaujo* in like condition and one cannot necessarily assume that the Gypsies either used it themselves or, indeed, took it at all seriously other than as a means of extracting money from the gullible.

> If a girl has an illegitimate child, and her lover has left her, she must split a rowan sapling in two and pass the baby through the cleft, saying 'I pass my child through the tree, and if his father loves me, he will return to me.' This has to be done on nine successive days. Afterwards, the tree must be bound by her left garter. If the tree grows together, the man will return to her.

Much has also been made of the widespread belief that the only form of marriage recognized by British Gypsies and other traditional Travellers involved the couple jumping over a broomstick or some other article associated with their particular trade or craft, such as a pair of tongs or a budget (Lytton's reference to a form of marriage, valid for five years and involving the breaking of a clay tile, finds no support elsewhere in the literature (*Life, Letters and Literary Remains*, 1883, Letter 21)). Miln (1900, 381) and MacRitchie (*JGLS* o.s. 1 (1889) 351) mention the practice, whilst Morwood also claimed to have witnessed something of the kind (1885, 137). Winstedt, too, had heard something of it although, according to one of the Smiths whom he questioned on the subject, 'they mostly *lels* one another's *lavs*' (Winstedt 1909a, 339).

Crofton (*Manchester Literary Club*, iii, 40) and Groome (1880, 3) also refer to nothing more than a simple verbal agreement whilst, not surprisingly, the evangelist, Gypsy Smith, is adamant in his rejection of anything of a more colourful nature: 'They make a covenant with each other. Beyond this, there is no marriage ceremony. There is nothing of jumping over tongs or broomsticks or any of the tomfooleries that outsiders attribute to the Gypsies' (Smith 1903, 5).

Certainly, nothing more than a simple agreement and the consent of the girl's family is mentioned in texts 8 and 123–8, and it is perfectly clear from the following set that an apparently *ad hoc* arrangement of this kind was no bar to a long and happy association among Scottish Travellers.

> 135. 1. Casro, manishi-O
> As I rode oot in the darkie-O
> And I binged avree to the hellum
> One fine day
>
> Greetings, woman-O
> As I rode through the night-O
> I went away to the town
> One fine day
>
> 2. I dicked a geddie playin' steemers
> O my shannas how he binged avree
> I spied a young dillie bingen doon the hellum
> And some pourin' and nothing to eat
>
> I saw a lad playing bagpipes
> O my goodness
> I spied a young girl going down the town
> I had some water but nothing to eat
>
> 3. As I binged near this dillie
> She dicked and gloored at me
> I said: Shanish-shanish, manishi
> Can you bing avree wi' me?
>
> As I went near this girl
> She looked and glared (glowered) at me
> I said: O my God, woman
> Can you go away with me?
>
> 4. I took my steemers out o' my baren
> And me'n her binged avree
> So one dark nax we ginned a-campin'
> Noo I hae binged her avree
>
> I took my pipes out of the bag
> And I and she went away
> So one dark night we went a-camping
> Now I have taken her away

5. For us binged tae the fairm in the darkie
And puddin' we did slum
But three four years are over
And four bonny children she bring

We went to the farm in the night
And we bedded down in the barn
But three, four years are over
And four bonny children she bore me

6. So all ye travellers an' hawkies
And nackers ae dick at me
I binged avree wi' a manishi
O pottachs a avree

So all you travellers and hawkers
And tinkers all look at me
I went away with a woman
O men all away

7. I bing o'er hame to the hellum
And I played some tunes, you see
And I loved my bonny wee manishi
And a wee kenchin on her knee

I go home over to the town
And I played some tunes, you see
And I loved my bonny wee woman
And a small child on her knee

8. The culyach says to the pottach
Bing avree, gheddie, get some peeve
There's nackers in their own campin'
My shannas bing avree

The woman said to the man
Go away, lad, get some beer
There are tinkers in their own camping
O my God, get away.

9. Doon to the peeven'-ken I binged wi' him
Wi' my kenchin on my knee
I've 'ome rowdie from the pottach
Playin' the steemers, you see

Down to the public house I went with him
With my child on my knee
I've some money from the man
Playing the pipes, you see

10. So a' ye tramps an' hawkers
Come listen to fat ye have heard
I binged avree wi' a young manishi
And back wi' her I gaird

So all you tramps and hawkers
Come listen to what you have heard
I went away with a woman
And back with her I came

11. So a' ye tramps an' hawkers
Listen unto me
A bonny wee manishi
And three kenchins she bore to me

So all you tramps and hawkers
Listen unto me
A pretty wee woman
And three children she bore to me
    (Davey Stewart, Dundee, Angus, 1960;
    Brune 1975, 766)

Whilst a simple word-of-mouth agreement may have been enough in many cases, there is always the exception that proves the rule. According to the *Scottish Leader* for 10 August 1889, one of the Northumbrian Blythes, who had emigrated to California, died, leaving a substantial fortune to his daughter. His English relatives disputed the latter's claim on the grounds that the marriage had been conducted 'without legal or religious formalities', but lost their case (Barker 1899, 229). Crofton also mentions a parallel case in which a similar form of marriage was upheld by a Scottish court (*JGLS* n.s. 1 (1907), 368).

Although in some parts of Europe the bride's word might also be taken as sufficient evidence of pre-marital chastity, elsewhere, as among elements of the settled population, more tangible proofs were required in the form of a cloth or article of clothing stained with the virgin's blood. This does not seem to have been generally the case in England, however, although one of Sampson's informants, Philip Murray, does refer to the use of the *dikla* for this purpose among certain Travellers of his acquaintance.

In the Gypsy quarters of Constantinople, as elsewhere, the bridal cloth, *but ratvali* (much bloodied), was paraded through the streets, the people singing as they went:

> Ghias yoi andrál te andrál Constantinople, Galata te Pera,
> Righadás-yoi sar-var ladjipéna!

> (*JGLS* o.s. 2 (1890), 56)

If Gypsy women were expected to guard their virtue both before and after marriage, their menfolk seem not to have been similarly constrained. Wlislocki, who was intimately acquainted with at least one Gypsy divorcée, speaks of a secret tribunal – *Manlaslo* – in use among the wandering Gypsies of the Balkans, whose business was the punishment of moral laxity but which clearly differentiated between the sexes on questions of marital infidelity. Offenders, he says, were privately handed a circular wooden token with a peg driven through the middle and required to present themselves by night at the nearest stream to the east of the camp. There they were met by a man wearing an animal mask who led them to a lonely spot where two others sat beside a fire where they eventually learned their fate – banishment, temporary or permanent. Wlislocki makes it clear, however, that men were never summonsed for infidelity, only for theft, murder or treachery ('Vehmgerichte bei den Bosnischen und Bulgarischen Wanderzigeuner', in *Ethnologische Mittheilungen aus Ungarn*, iii (1893), 3, 173).

Bigamy, too, seems to have been permitted if not actively encouraged, although among some groups this was only possible with the consent of the first wife. Indeed, in the case of the settled Gypsies of Serbia, if the woman was unwilling, she was permitted a divorce. In Britain, too, wife-swapping is said to have been 'by no means uncommon' (Norwood, MS note) whilst, according to Brown, bigamy itself was 'sanctioned by Gypsy custom, but rare' (Brown 1924, 167). Groome mentions two cases, Riley Smith who had two wives and Charlie Pinfold who had three (Groome 1888, lxxiii), whilst Barker, in his 'Gypsy-Life of Northumberland', notes, with regret, that 'their views on monogamy have come, in the ages of the past, to be very lax' (1889, 229). A relative of Davy Boswell is also said to have had two wives but, as Brown goes on to say (ibid.), 'as *Romanicel* women are often the chief breadwinners, and frequently carry the bank roll, they are inclined to giving orders; and what man wants to be ruled by two women?'

Yet the erring male was not always let off quite so lightly. According to Winstedt, for example, in both Germany and Hungary a slighted wife had the right to decide whether her husband should be shot in the arm or the leg, whilst, in the following song, the protagonist, though unrepentant, is apparently given ample opportunity to reflect upon his shortcomings.

136. For sǔvin' this rokli they lel'd me aprě.
   And to storiben they chiv'd me the very next day;
   Now I besh weary drē my weary cell,
   And oftentimes wish duva rokli in hell.

   My churi monishni and tiknos alsó
   Avrī on the drom they were forced for to go,
   Kek tan to sut in, and chichi to xâ.
   May hell sǔv the lubni was the cause of it sâ!
                    (Philip Murray; Sampson 1892, 3, 79)

Philip Murray, from whom Sampson obtained this song, was 'an old Tinker' who, since early childhood, had lived among the Gypsies. Some sixty years earlier he had married Harriet, daughter of Gilbert Smith, and had travelled with her until her death.

That the Gypsies with whom he had travelled had been of very 'primitive' stock, Sampson thought apparent from the archaic form of many of his Romani words and from his once casually observing that 'the old Romani-chels "favoured" them Zulus what came here'. He also alluded to the unintelligibility of the older Gypsies and seemed not to have assimilated any of the finer inflections of the *Puri Chib*. His vocabulary of root words was, however, unusually rich and many of the idioms which came perfectly naturally to him were no longer in common use.

Sampson also collected a number of tales from him and 'much curious information' regarding the manners, dress and superstitions of the previous generation of English Gypsies.

With its neat four-line stanzas and close attention to metre and rhyme, Murray's song has every appearance of *Gaujo* influence. It is quite unlike the prison-house laments of the Hungarian Gypsies as noted by Herrmann which, he says, consisted of 'a series of unconnected sentences, extremely primitive alike in rhythm and in rhyme', and to the recital of which he eventually had to call a halt for sheer weariness. One example, from the singing of Mojsa Churar, in the prison of Brassó (Kronstadt) in the summer of 1886, contained over 100 lines. First published 'in the second number of our journal (p.101, no.7, *Burzenland*)', it was subsequently reproduced in the pages of the *Journal of the Gypsy Lore Society*, together with an English translation, using the system of notation employed by the Archduke Joseph in his Gypsy grammar (*JGLS* o.s. 1 (1889), 290ff.). It was taken down hurriedly, he says, and in many places is doubtful. I give here only the first few lines. An asterisk denotes a borrowing from Romanian.

Vaj* Devla-le, na maj* marme,
Ke man, Devla, d'ekin* mardas,
Cin miscto na kerd'as.
Vaj* Devlica, vaj* Devlica,
Ke man ci maj* mares!
Tai zatar, Devla, zatar,
Pala mandi ci maj* dikhau.
Devla, Devla, the avau
Tar zav the pala leste
Ci maj* akarav-le palpale,
Te zal, zikaj se lumi . . .

Ah God! Afflict me no more,
For, since thou, Oh God, hast afflicted me,
Nothing good hast thou done.
Ah, dear God! Ah, dear God,
That me no more thou strikest!
To others trouble hast thou made,
God, strike and burn,
But me no more strike!
And I will go, Oh God, I will go,
Behind me no more will I look.
Oh God, Oh God, I come
And follow after her,
No more call I her back again,
And go the length and breadth of the world . . .

~

With our English Gypsies, the favourite instrument is the
tambourine and the 'boshomengri' or fiddle, especially the
latter, and we know several good executants on the strings.

(Smart and Crofton 1875)

As soon as ever the country people saw the old Gypsies with
their fiddles, they would laugh and their feet would begin
to dance, and their hands to clap.

(Matthew Wood)

137. O Bosh-kelomengero beshtas
  Oprey o poov arey Ackerlo

  Kedas o bosh y balano kosht
  Adrey i kushti zigaira.(1)
  Nai man keck dicklo

364

Nai man gad
Nai man keck pushka(2)
Nai man staadi
Nai man keck rinkeni vongustrin
Y nai man bosh y balano kosht.(3)
                    (Anon., Llanrhaeadr-ym-Mochnant,
                    c.1956; Brune 1975)

The fiddle maker sat
Upon the field at Ackerlo
He made the fiddle and the bow
In his fine tent
I have no neck-scarf
I have no shirt
I have no gun
I have no hat
I have no pretty ring on my finger
And I have neither fiddle nor bow.

(1) Unknown in English Romani where the common word is *tan* (see Groome 1880, ch.3). Whilst noting its close affinity with the Buk. Gyp. *cygyry*, tent, Sampson suggests a possible etymon in the Latin *tegurium*, a hut, shed or lodge (Sampson 1926, iv, 407). In Bernhard von Breydenbach's *Itinerarium in Terram Sanctam* of 1486 the reed-covered huts of the Gypsies of Modon in the Morea are called *tuguria* (*JGLS* n.s. 3 (1909), 60). In a Welsh Gypsy word list published in the February 1823 edition of *Seren Gomer*, the anonymous contributor offers *tshater* = *pabell*, tent. Manfri Wood was unable to recall any of these three alternatives when questioned by Kennedy in Penybont Fawr in 1954 (Folktracks 441).
(2) Although fairly well represented in the literature (e.g. Simson, Borrow, M'Cormick, Smart and Crofton), *pushka* seems to have lost ground in England to *yogéngro/yogger* (Smart and Crofton 1875, 180).
(3) In a document dated 25 April 1553, there is a list of Gypsy names, a number of which appear to incorporate punning references to various Romani and German words. Among them is Bernard Beige, which Crofton refers to the German *biege*, a fiddle bow. If this was an occupational nickname, it is surely the earliest British reference linking the Gypsies with the fiddle (MacRitchie 1894, 43).

In his accompanying note, Brune says that the fiddle-maker referred to in the foregoing song was said to be Lucas Petulengro, thought to be the only Romani to have made fiddles *Gaujo*-fashion. Some years earlier, he says, he had come across the back of an old instrument (in a private collection near Lingfield) with the maker's name – Lucas Petulengro – burnt into it in a seventeenth-century 'secretary's hand'. Lucas, he says, is said to have flourished *c*.1660–1740. No complete fiddles of his manufacture have survived, however, owing perhaps to the Gypsy practice of burning or smashing the possessions of the dead (see note following text 50). Inquiries made of the proprietor of the collection to which Brune refers have failed to elicit any reply, whilst the relevant specialist department at Sotheby's have no record of Petulengro's existence or work.

In what way the Gypsy fiddles of Petulengro's day may have differed in form or manner of construction from those of *Gaujo* manufacture is impossible to say. A photograph from the David H. Smith collection, reproduced on the front cover of the Welsh Folk Museum's edition of portions of Meredith Morris's *De Fidiculis*, may, however, offer a clue. In it, the Wood brothers, Cornelius and Adolphus, are pictured holding home-made fiddles made from Fry's shilling chocolate boxes of the type produced between 1897 and 1914, examples of which are still to be seen in the Cadbury archives, Somerdale, Keynsham, Bristol. On p.30 of MacColl and Seeger's *Till Doomsday in the Afternoon*, mention is also made of a meeting between Alec Stewart and an unnamed Traveller at the head of the Fermoy river some time before 1949. Having agreed not to go to town at the same time lest they should queer each other's pitch, the unnamed one took out his instrument which turned out to be made of a tin cigar box. It was, according to Stewart, 'helluva nice, awfu' nice'. Whilst cigar tins and chocolate boxes may not have been available in Petulengro's day, he and his contemporaries were, no doubt, no less imaginative in their choice of materials. In much the same way, according to tradition, Bunyan, whilst in Bedford gaol, is said to have played upon a flute which he had carved from the leg of a prison stool, returning it to its proper place whenever the gaoler came to see where the music was coming from. (Despite Scott's contention to the contrary, Bunyan was almost certainly not a Gypsy, although he was a tinker by profession, if not by ethnicity.)

Not all Gypsies, however, were forced to rely on makeshift instruments of this kind. In one of Sylvester Boswell's notebooks, dated January 1841–47 (*sic*), is to be found what appears to be a draft will including the following bequest:

> I bought this fiddle at Colchester. This is an old one also but the age I do not know but I bought it in September 1861. It's a Amatis, I believe and a very valuable one. I hear say that I desire that this shall not go out of my children's care but be among these selves. This I crave of you . . .

Unfortunately, his wishes do not seem to have been followed but it is interesting to note his clear intention that his fiddle should survive his death.

That the fiddle-maker's song existed in its present form in Petulengro's day is open to question in that there would seem to be some doubt as to whether British Gypsies were in the habit of lying in tents at that time. Groome quotes as follows from a letter he received on the subject from the celebrated Welsh harper, John Roberts, dated 22 January 1880 (Groome 1880, 58):

> The Welsh Gypsies was not known to camp out in those days [the early years of the nineteenth century] but they always used to ask leave to lodge (mong lodybens) in barns and other buildings, and they were allowed to make fire in the buildings as well as outside it. I often heard father say that it was him that made the first tent that was made for them in Wales by the instruction of my grandmother. She was one of the Stanleys (English Gypsies) and she used to praise my father for picking it up so soon.

Saiforeela Wood, speaking in 1909 of her great-grandfather, Abram Wood, the eponymous ancestor of the Gypsies of Wales, would seem to confirm this when she says of him: 'He always rode on horseback, on a blood horse, and would not sleep in the open but in barns.'

Robert Roberts's great-grandmother is also quite specific regarding the type of accommodation favoured by the Wood family on their arrival in Tynyfownog (near Llangernyw in western Clwyd) some time during the middle years of the eighteenth century (*The Life and Opinions of Robert Roberts, a Scholar, as Told by Himself* (Roberts 1991), 32): 'Abram built himself a *ty tywyrch* (house of turf) on the common, the other side of the great peat bog, a lonely place out of reach of all roads' – a place known to the locals as *Llety'r Gwr Drwg* (the Devil's Lodging House). Although the Woods referred to here should not be confused with the family of that Abram Wood from whose descendants Sampson acquired his knowledge of Welsh Romani, there is no reason to question the old lady's description of the form of habitation preferred by them.

John Roberts's remarks on the introduction of the fiddle into Wales (as reported in the *Wrexham Advertiser* for September 1876) are also of interest here as he makes no mention of Petulengro even though he places the event some time during the second half of the seventeenth century:

> A short account of Egyptians who first came to Wales where some came to be very noted players upon the Welsh harp and continue to the present day: – 'About two hundred years ago came an old man of the name of Abraham Wood, his wife, three sons and a daughter. He brought with him a violin and he is supposed to be the first one that ever played upon one in Wales. The eldest of his three sons, Valentine Wood, did very early take to the harp but was not considered much of a player. The second son, William, was considered a sweet violin player. He was father to Archelaus Wood . . . who was the first pupil to the celebrated Mr. Roberts of Carnarvon. Third, Solomon Wood'.

Valentine also had three sons, of whom only one, Thomas, took to the fiddle, being considered 'a very fine player'.

Roberts's dates may be a little out. According to Sampson, Wood in all probability entered Wales some time around the year 1730 which would accord broadly with the view taken by Groome.

The catalogue of woe which lies at the heart of the fiddle-maker's song is typically Gypsy in tone. Something of the same abject note may, for example, be heard in Matty Cooper's 'Bokalo Gilli' (text 66) and, in prose, in Sylvester Boswell's 'Eheu Fugaces' (Smart and Crofton 1875, 201).

Verses of this type are also by no means confined to the Gypsies of Britain. The first of the two following examples was taken from the singing of a group of French Gypsy coppersmiths travelling in Mexico and was published by Irving Brown on p.103 of his *Deep Song*. According to Lal (1962, 75) it is reminiscent of the *Malkaunsa* – one of six prime *ragas* normally associated with tragedy and death.

> Nai tu dad, nai tu dei,
> Nai tu pral, nai tu pei,
> Nai tu konik kalar lendar
> Mukav tut Korkovó hai Strainó.
>
> You have no father, you have no mother,
> You have no brother, you have no sister,
> You have none of your own.

The second example is in the Kolosvarer dialect of Transylvania and was first published by Wlislocki in his *Haidebluten* of 1880). Unlike his Welsh counterpart, however, the Gypsy musician here is at least spared the loss of his fiddle.

> Na janav ke dad miro as
> Niko mallen mange as;
> Miro gule dai merdyas,
> Pirani ne preggelyas
> Uva tu o hegedive
> In sal mindik pash mange
>
> I have known no father since my birth,
> I have no friend alive on earth,
> My mother is dead since many days,
> The girl I loved has gone her way,
> Thou, violin, with music free,
> Alone art ever true to me.

This 'miserable little song', as she calls it, was later reprinted by L. A. Smith (1889, 11) with a note to the effect that it was said to have been 'discovered' by Leland. Later in the same chapter, however (ibid., 40), and apparently without connecting the two pieces, she includes a metrical English version of the same song among a number of hitherto unpublished translations from Wlislocki by W. E. A. Axon. Axon's text runs as follows:

> My dear father left this earth
> Ere my eyes began to see;
> Long ago my mother died,
> And my loved one left me.
> Few my joys in life would be
> But for my fiddle's company.

Although wholly secular in tone, the pattern established in songs of this kind is reminiscent of certain types of Hindu religious verse. The resemblance between the text commencing 'Nai tu dad, nai tu dei' and the first of the following examples is particularly striking. It is a *meera bahjan*, or song of praise by Meerabai, a lifelong devotee of the Lord Krishna. A princess of Mewar and married to Rana of Chittor (Rajestan), she was to give up everything in his service.

> Mere to Giridhar Gopal, dusro na koi.
> Tat, mat, bhrat, bandhu up no na koi.
>
> I belong to Lord Krishna only.
> No one is my own, including father, mother, brother and friend.

In the second example, a prayer in Sanskrit, the same idea is expressed by means of a series of positive statements.

> Twmev mata ch pita twmev.
> Twmev bandru ch sakha twmev.
> Twmev vidya, dravinam twmev.
> Twmev sarva mm dev dev.
>
> You are my mother, you are my father.
> You are my brother and you are my friend.
> You are my knowledge and you are my wealth.
> O God, you are everything to me.

Something of the same repetitive quality is also to be met with in the native Welsh tradition. A good example is the song known variously as *Y Cardotyn*, The Beggar (*JWFSS*, IV, 19) and *Cwd Cardotyn*, The Beggar's Pack (Llanover c59 (the Iolo Morganwg MSS)). Although there remains some doubt as to its authorship, Iolo maintains that it was composed by his 'intimate friend', Dafydd Nicholas (1705–69), who was, for many years, family bard to the house of Aberpergwm. The word 'cwd' here signifies the beggar's pouch (*monging gono*), used for the reception of alms in kind.

> Hen gardotyn wyf a thlawd,
> Heb dad, heb fam, na chwaer na brawd,
> Eto 'r'wy'n canu 'dili dwd',
> Heb gywilyddio cario cwd . . .

> An old beggar am I, and poor,
> Without father, without mother, neither brother nor sister,
> Yet still I sing 'dili dwd',
> Unashamed to carry the cwd . . .

The fiddle, far from being simply an object of pleasure, was also a source of income – a fact recalled in the old Gypsy riddle quoted by Groome on p.159 of *In Gypsy Tents*: 'It plays in the wood and sings in the wood and gets its master many a penny.' Thus Hoyland, in his *Historical Survey* (1816, 213), tells us that the Gypsies' 'principal means of subsistence' were 'tinkering and fiddling at feasts and fairs, by which some, I believe, make a good deal of money, which helps them out in the winter when there is less work and less dancing'. For Smart and Crofton, too, writing some sixty years later, the Gypsy was 'always foremost among the "feast-finding minstrels" which attend our English country fairs and wakes', and even as late as 1910, Thompson found that they could still 'play the fiddle well enough for a public house audience and could earn a little baccy and a few shillings'.

By the early years of the present century, however, the fiddle would seem to have lost ground to the accordion, at least among the Gypsies of the southern counties (Gillington 1911a), and today is relatively rare.

Among the more important dates in the Gypsy calendar was the annual gathering held at Fairlop in Epping Forest on the first Friday in July and, in seeking to convey its particular delights to Esther Faa Blythe, 'the Gypsy Queen of Kirk Yetholme', Borrow offered the following lines:

138. Romany Chalor
    Anglo the wuddur
    Mistos are boshing;
    Mande beshello
    Innar the wuddur
    Shooning the boshipen.

    Roman lads,
    Before the door
    Bravely fiddle;
    Here I sit*
    Within the door
    And hear them fiddle.
                    (Borrow 1874, 175)

*Borrow's original word – *beshello* – has all the appearance of the third person singular but the meaning is clear. Whether or not Queen Esther would have understood the song is, however, another matter. Groome, for one, was far from impressed by her knowledge of *Romanés*: '. . . her majesty', he writes (1880, 19), 'calls "sugar" *sweetnams*, "fire" *glimmer*, "tea" *slap* and 'a sixpence' *tanner*, while half of her few genuine Romani words are basely clipped or otherwise corrupted. She cannot follow the simplest sentence addressed to her in Anglo-Romanes . . .'

Lucas also visited Queen Esther (Lucas 1882, 34–53). Like Groome, however, he, too, only managed to secure a handful of genuine Romani words and a few broken phrases, e.g. *'jawing* on the *groy'*, riding; 'that *gowry* has a *barra sheery'*, that boy has a fine head of hair; and 'fine *dickin rockly'*, fine-looking girl – for which Borrow obtained the altogether more satisfactory *'rinkeni rackli'*.

Of particular interest among the various items noted by Lucas and Groome is *kliti*, soldier, policeman – a form otherwise unknown in British Romani but possibly a derivative of *klister*, to ride, as noted by Sampson (*JGLS* o.s. 3, (1892), 76) in place of the more usual *kister*; cf. *klito* (Von Sowa 1898) and *cleestie* (Brune 1975). For a possible alternative, compare *cleechie* (M'Cormick 1906) which Russell tentatively refers to Eng. cleach/cleech = clutch.

Yet the Gypsies were not always as welcome as Smart and Crofton's 'feast-finding minstrels', a fact suggested by a number of banning orders of the type issued by the mayor of Oxford in 1838 prohibiting their attendance at the annual fair of St Giles. That they also had their allies is, however, apparent from the following verses, originally published in the *Oxford Herald* and reproduced, with a prefatory note, by G. V. Cox in his *Recollections of Oxford* (Cox 1868, 287–8):

The first week in September is marked, at least by the citizens of Oxford, as the season of St. Giles' Fair. Falling, as it does, during the Long Vacation, it never possessed any interest for the University; but at Cambridge, even in Long Vacation, 'Stourbridge Fair' used to be (I know not whether it still is) a matter of great excitement, – the Vice-Chancellor, in full attendance, going to the Barnwell suburb to open the Fair by a solemn proclamation and other ceremonies, some of them connected with eating and drinking, and ending with theatricals! Before starting in procession, 'mulled wine and cakes were presented and partaken of in the Senate House'. At the Oxford fair, a striking and picturesque group had been always formed by a large body of Gypsies, men, women, and children, with their rough ponies and rougher donkeys; but this wild tribe was looked upon unfavourably by the City magnates, and the Mayor of this year (1838) issued an order for the positive exclusion of the Gypsies from St. Giles' Fair. Pity for them, and early '*recollections*' of their fiddling, tumbling, stick throwing,* etc., suggested the following lines . . .

The Gipsies' Humble Petition and Remonstrance
Addressed to the Worshipful Mayor of Oxford

O Mr. Mayor, o Mr. Mayor!
What have we Gipsies done or said,
That you should drive us from the fair
And rob us of our 'custom'd bread?

O had you seen, good Mr. Mayor,
Our wand'ring, weeping, wailing band,
And marked our looks of deep despair
When first we heard your stern command;

Could you have witness'd, Mr. Mayor,
How young and old, and weak and strong,
Excluded, branded, cold and bare,
We sat astounded all day long;

Your heart had ac'd good Mr. Mayor,
And felt that Gipsies, too, were men;
Then deign our losses to repair,
Nor drive us thus to try the pen.

Alas! 'Tis true, good Mr. Mayor,
Our friend, Sir Walter Scott, is dead;
But Heav'n that hears the Gipsies' pray'r,
May raise another in his stead.

Dread not the name, good Mr. Mayor,
No more the witch's pow'r we claim,
But still we are the Muses' care,
And Oxford Poets guard our fame.

What place then so unfit, good Mayor,
A war against our tribe to raise,
As that which lately filled the air
With Gipsy-lore and Gipsies' praise?**

As welcome Lions to the Fair,
Tigers and Monkeys, Punch and Fool;
Then suffer us another year
To hold there our gymnastic school.

Meanwhile farewell, good Mr. Mayor,
Your frowns dismiss, resume your smiles;
We'll leave off cheating, take to prayer,
And claim thy patronage, St. Giles!

*Coconut-shies originally made use of sticks rather than balls.
**Apparently a reference to 'The Gipsies', A. P. Stanley's Newdigate Prize poem of 1837.

The fiddle is the only instrument mentioned in *Poggadi Chib* song, although the Gypsies do and undoubtedly did make use of others. Smith, although she had little enough to say in favour of English Gypsy musicians generally, was prepared to acknowledge that they often made 'respectable performers on the violin, flute, Jews' harp etc.', whilst both Gillington and Smart and Crofton speak of their using the tambourine, the former going on to say: 'After the day's labour in strawberry field or hop field is over . . . you may see two Romani Juvals walking round each other, skirt in one hand and tambourine shaken in the other to the prelude of a country jig.' Yet, despite its evident popularity, there is nothing in the repertoire to compare with the following French tambourine song quoted by Smith:

Tamburiça, mon passe-temps;
Archet, ma douce joie;
Assez longtemps tu as nourri ma faim,
Désaltéré ma soif.
Tu as attiré les filles a la fenetre,
Tu as allumé d'amour leurs visages.
Tamburiça, mon passe-temps;
Archet, ma douce joie;
Hélas! J'ai perdu les jours et l'anné,

A chanter sous les fenetres de Meira;
Meira ne veut meme pas mi regarder.

Tambourine, my leisure;
Bow, my sweet joy;
For so long you have fed my hunger,
Quenched my thirst.
You have drawn the girls to the window,
You have lit their faces with love.
Tambourine, my leisure;
Bow, my sweet joy;
Alas! I have lost days and years,
Singing beneath Meira's windows.
Meira doesn't even want to look at me.

From Sampson's manuscript materials for a history and genealogy of the Wood family, published posthumously in the *Gypsy Lore Society Journal* (third and fourth series, 10–13 (1931–4, *passim*) we know that, between them, John and Eleanor Roberts's nine sons played a wide variety of instruments including the pedal harp, English harp, flagelot (*sic*), piccolo, 'double bass viol' and violin, and that all were also taught the triple harp, flute and fiddle. Indeed, the old man's letters are full of references to the Gypsy bands and concerts organized by them throughout Wales where they were known as the 'Cambrian Minstrels'.

Something of the noise and confusion generated during practice sessions can be guessed at from the postscript to one of John's letters dated 'xmasday, 1878' when, in search of 'a little quiateness in which to write', he had 'dispatched the three cubs (two fidles & tamoreen)' and is told by his wife: 'Now man, do dat Letter write to de peple and tell dem chirlen not to make such a horrible din. Bless me! one cant hear from the little imps' playing anything but the devil's do, da, do, da, as I call it.'

Lamentina Lovell seems also to have suffered in like manner, judging by her remarks on p.150 of *In Gypsy Tents*: 'It's a poor heart never rejoices, sir. But often I say there's too much singing and playing. Scrape, scrape, scraping from morning to blessed night till I can't hear my own ears sometimes. And after playing, weeping comes next, you know' (Groome 1880).

Phoebe Smith, however, a powerful singer herself but apparently no great admirer of her husband's gifts as a fiddler, would seem to have found one answer to the problem:

One day, I was doing some scrubbing and, course, I looked at the fiddle and I stuck it into the bucket of boiling water and I hung it back where it were in the case. So, a few days after, they all come round again and they got this fiddle out and he were going to play. Well, course, soon as he starts to tune it and the strings begin to come tight, of course, it all bust in pieces! (Folktracks 100)

Brockie, in his account of the Kirk Yethome Gypsies (1884, 77), says that 'the violin and the bagpipes were the instruments they commonly used' and this is still true of Scottish Travellers today. Yet, perhaps the best-known of Gypsy pipers were William Allen and his son James – sometime piper to the Duke of Northumberland – who died in Durham gaol on 28 August 1806, twelve months after an earlier reprieve for horse stealing. It was of Allen the elder that the Reedwater Minstrel wrote:

> A stalwart Tinkler wight was he
> An' weel could mend a pot or pan,
> An' deftly weel could thraw a flee,
> An' neatly weave the willow wan'.
> An' sweetly wild were Allen's strains,
> An' mony a jig an' reel he blew,
> Wi' merry lilt charmed the swains,
> Wi' barbed spear the otter slew.

The pipes the Allens played were, however, not the *steemers* or Highland pipes favoured by the Stewarts, but the altogether sweeter bellows-driven Northumbrian small pipes, and it is perhaps to these that the English poet Cowper refers when, in Book 1 of *The Task* (1785), he says:

> Yet even these, though feigning sickness oft
> They swathe the forehead, drag the lumping limb,
> And vex their flesh with artificial sores,
> Can change their whine into a mirthful noise,
> When safe occasion offers; and with dance,
> And music of the bladder and the bag,
> Beguile their woes and make the woods resound.

James Allen's musical career was brought to a premature end by an injury to his right hand which he sustained on leaping from a wall in order to avoid capture. On being taken, he is said to have cried out: 'Ye ha'e spoiled the best pipe hand in Britain!'

The pipes, however, were by no means universally admired. The poet Lewys Glyn Cothi, for example, was more than a little vexed when, commissioned to sing to the harp at a wedding in Flint, he was abandoned by his audience in favour of an itinerant piper named William Beisir. His observations on Beisir's playing leave us in no doubt as to the extent of his annoyance:

> For William Beisir's bag they bawl,
> Largess for him they loudly squall;
> Each roared with throat at widest stretch,
> For William the Piper – low born wretch!
> William forward steps as best he can,
> Unlike a free ennobled man;
> A pliant bag 'tween arm and chest,
> While limping on, he tightly prest.
> He stares – he stares the bag to sound;
> He swells his maw and ogles round,
> He twists and turns himself about,
> With fetid breath his cheeks swell out.
> What savage boors! His hideous claws
> And glutton's skin win their applause!
> With shuffling hand and clumsy mien
> To doff his cloak he next is seen.
> He snorted, brindled in his face,
> And bent it down with much grimace.
> Like to a kite, he seemed that day,
> A kite when feathering of his prey!
> The churl did blow a grating shriek.
> The bag did swell and harshly squeak,
> As does a goose from nightmare crying,
> Or dog, crushed by a chest, dying:
> This whistling box's changeless note
> Is forced from turgid veins and throat;
> Its sound is like a crane's harsh moan,
> Or like a gosling's latest groan;
> Just such a noise, a wounded goat
> Sends from her hoarse and gurgling throat . . .

Having cursed the townsfolk roundly for their philistinism, Lewys concludes by swearing never to visit the place again.

Somewhat surprisingly, the dulcimer seems also to have been the favoured instrument of a number of British Travellers. Watkin and Robert Ingram, two of Abram Wood's great-grandchildren through the old man's only daughter, Damaris, were said to have been respectable performers. Watkin, however, seems not to have profited by his skill, dying in Caersŵs workhouse on 3 November, 1873.

Lucy Broadwood, too, tells how, from a Northamptonshire woman 'of respectable farmer class', she had learned some years earlier that in her young days the farmers used to hire Gypsy musicians to play for them and sing at their dances and gatherings. The Gypsy women used to be dressed in white from head to foot even in winter for these occasions and the instruments included dulcimers . . . (*JGLS* n.s. 1 (1907), 287)

The use of white clothes for dancing is also mentioned by E. C. Grenville Murray in the introduction to his study of the national songs of Romania:

The Zingari are now chiefly employed as musicians, artisans, and miners. They are slaves and can be bought, sold, and punished with impunity. There are still, a company of them who preserve their ancient traditions in almost every village; and if the traveller chance to be benighted in some peasant's hut, it is there that he will hear the tender *Doine* sung, and see a pretty national dance called the *Ora*, which will often remind him of the figures on antique vases. Their dress is notable. They wear full white trousers, a white tunic, and a gay coloured sash. (Murray 1854)

That white may once have been the favoured colour of Iberian Gypsies is also suggested by the following reference in the fourth chapter of the *Relecan Verdadeira* of the Gentlemen of Elvas, published at Evora, Portugal, in 1587. After telling of the arrival of De Soto's company at Gomeira in the Canaries, the anonymous author goes on to say: 'The governor of the island was apparelled all in white – cloak, jerkin, hose, shoes and cap – so that he looked like a governor of Gypsies.'

But to return to the fiddle; according to Gillington, the best exponents were to be found among the Lees whilst, in Smart and Crofton's opinion, the most gifted and renowned of English Gypsy violinists was one 'Horsey' Gray. 'We have been told by a Romani Chal', they say, 'that when Horsey had heard a tune, he could play it off straightaway, putting in such "variations, grace-notes, shapes and runs", that none of his confreres could compare with him. He played entirely from ear and not from notes . . .' (Smart and Crofton 1875).

We cannot leave the subject of Gypsy fiddlers without mentioning perhaps the best-known of all, MacPherson. According to tradition, he was the son of a Gypsy mother and a Highland earl who, brought up by his father, was taken in hand by the local minister and taught to play the fiddle, for which he showed considerable aptitude. On learning, at the age of fifteen, that he was illegitimate, he turned to his mother's people, Jacobites all, and took to the road, living the life of a latter-day Robin Hood – 'And had not M'Pherson . . . been leader of twenty-seven men in arms and a piper playing at their head as befits the son of a Highland gentleman by a beautiful Gypsy mother?' (Groome 1880).

The following brief account of his life and exploits is taken from the *New Monthly Magazine*, 1 (1821), 142–3. As might be expected, it seems to contain a number of folkloric elements, linking it with the Robin Hood cycle and other similar hero legends – the beauty of his mother, the Herculean proportions of his principal henchman, his humanity and generosity to the poor. Even the burlesque element of the butcher's dog is not without parallel elsewhere.

James Macpherson . . . was born of a beautiful Gypsy, who, at a great Gypsy wedding, attracted the notice of a half-intoxicated Highland gentleman. He acknowledged the child, and had him reared in his house, until he lost his life in bravely pursuing a hostile clan, to recover a *spraith* of cattle taken from Badenoch. The Gypsy woman, hearing of this disaster in her rambles the following summer, came and took away her boy; but she often returned with him, to wait upon his relations and clansmen who never failed to clothe him well, besides giving money to his mother. He grew up in strength, stature and beauty, seldom equalled . . . and if, it must be owned, his prowess was debased by the exploits of a freebooter, it is certain no act of cruelty, no robbery of the widow, the fatherless or distressed, and no murder was ever perpetrated under his command. He often gave the spoils of the rich to relieve the poor; and all his tribe were restrained from many atrocities of rapine by their awe of his mighty arm. Indeed, it is said that a dispute with an aspiring and savage man of his tribe, who wished to rob a gentleman's house whilst his wife and two children lay on the bier for interment, was the cause of his being betrayed to the vengeance of the law. The magistrates of Aberdeen were exasperated at Macpherson's escapades when they bribed a girl in that city to allure and deliver him into their hands. There is a platform before the jail at the top of a stair, and a door below. When Macpherson's capture was made known to his comrades by the frantic girl who had been so credulous to believe the magistrates only wanted to hear the wonderful performer on the violin, his cousin, Donald Macpherson, a gentleman of Herculean powers, did not disdain to come from Badenoch, and to join a Gypsy, Peter Brown, in liberating the prisoner. On a market-day, they brought several assistants; and swift horses were stationed at a convenient distance. Donald Macpherson and Peter Brown forced the jail, and while Peter Brown went to help the heavily fettered James Macpherson in moving away, Donald Macpherson guarded the jail-door with drawn sword. Many persons, assembled at the market, had experienced James Macpherson's humanity, or had shared his bounty; and they crowded round the jail as in mere curiosity, but, in fact, to obstruct the civil authorities in preventing a rescue. A butcher, however, was resolved if possible to detain Macpherson, expecting a large recompense from the magistrates. He sprang up the stairs, and leaped from the platform upon Donald Macpherson, whom he dashed to the ground by the force and weight of his body. Donald Macpherson soon recovered to make a desperate resistance; and the combatants tore off each other's clothes. The butcher got a glimpse of his dog upon the platform, and called him to his aid; but Macpherson, with admirable presence of mind, snatched up his own plaid, which lay near, and threw it over the butcher, thus misleading the instinct of his canine adversary. The dog darted with fury upon the plaid and terribly lacerated his master's thigh. In the meantime, James Macpherson had been carried out by Peter Brown, and was soon joined by Donald Macpherson, who was quickly covered by some friendly spectator with a hat and greatcoat. The magistrates ordered webs from the shops to be drawn across the Gallowgate; but Donald Macpherson cut them asunder with his sword, and the late prisoner got off on horseback. He was some time after betrayed by a man of his own tribe; and was the last person executed at Banff, previous to the abolition of heritable jurisdiction. He was an admirable performer on the violin; and his talent for composition is still in evidence in 'Macpherson's Rant,' 'Macpherson's Pibroch,' and 'Macpherson's Farewell.' He performed those tunes at the foot of the fatal tree; and then asked if he had any friend in the crowd to whom a last gift of his instrument would be acceptable. No man had hardihood to claim friendship with a delinquent, in whose crimes the acknowledgement might implicate an avowed acquaintance. As no friend came forward, Macpherson said the companion of many gloomy hours should perish with him; and breaking the violin over his knee, he threw away the fragments. Donald Macpherson picked up the neck of the violin which to this day is preserved, as a valuable memento, by the family of Cluny, chieftain of the Macphersons.

Accounts of his eventual capture vary. In Davy Stewart's version of the old rant, 'it was by a lady's treacherous hand' that he was betrayed; elsewhere, however, it is reported that he was taken by a number of shepherds who pinned their plaids together to form a keep-net in order to prevent him from escaping. The following account of his execution, which agrees with that given in the *New Monthly Magazine*, is from Robert Ford's *Vagabond Songs of Scotland* of 1899:

After holding the counties of Aberdeen, Banff and Moray in fear for a number of years, MacPherson was seized by MacDuff of Braeco, an ancestor of the Earl of Fife* and, along with certain Gypsies who had been taken in his company, was tried before the Sheriff of Banffshire and convicted of being 'repute an Egyptian and vagabond and oppressor of his majesty's free lieges in Bangstr Manor'. Brought to the place of execution on the gallows hill of Banff on 16th November in the year named (1700), he played on his violin, says report, the stirring tune he had composed for these words in the condemned cell and then asked if any friend was present who would accept the instrument as a gift from his hands. No one coming forward, he indignantly broke the violin on his knee and threw away the fragments, after which he submitted to his fate.

*Others say it was on the orders of the Laird of Grant.

In some accounts, his wife or lover was successful in obtaining a reprieve and a messenger was sent to the town bearing the good news. The townspeople, however, got wind of what was intended and advanced the church clock so bringing forward the hour of his death.

What are said to be the remains of his fiddle are on display in the MacPherson clan museum at Newtonmore in Inverness whilst, according to Groome, 'his great two-hand sword (the relic of an earlier day) is shown at Duff house, the residence of the Earls of Fife'. But 'relics more precious than either sword or fiddle are his reckless rant and the beautiful air to which he set the same'.

Many versions of this song have been noted, including a number sung by Travellers. The absence of a genuine Romani or Cant text is much to be regretted but Sampson has left the following Welsh Romani translation of a set included by Burns.

1. Mishtóga, kâlo stariben,
   I chorodésko dukʻ!
   Na 'chela dūr o bâro lūr
   'Prē nashimásko ruk.

Chorus: 'Jâ lóshanes, 'jâ múrshknes,
   'Jâ rájvelas giás;
   Talál o merimásko rukʻ,
   Bosh'vélas tʻa kʻeldas.

2. O meribén so si mūrshén?
   'Prē ratvalē pʻuviá
   Mūierélas man, tʻʻrēʻkava tʻan
   Tromáva les 'kana!

3. Chin doriá 'vri mē vastá,
   Tʻa mandi dē khanró;
   Nanái o mūrsh 'rē sâr o tʻem
   Kai kelas man trashnó.

4. Būt būt lūrdóm tʻa būt kūrdóm;
   Foshnéstē mē mēráv:
   Khoch'rél' mo 'zi te jā avrí
   Tini 'dolés māráv.

380

5. Te vel o tam! Me jal o kan,
   Ta sâr te dūdyerel!
   Lajako lavé 'pré lēskó nav –
   O mūrsh n'a shish merel'!

1. Farewell, ye dungeons dark and strong,
   The wretch's destinie!
   MacPherson's time will not be long
   On yonder gallows-tree.

Chorus: Sae rantingly, sae wantonly,
        Sae dauntingly gaed he;
        He play'd a spring and danc'd it round,
        Below the gallows-tree.

2. O, what is death but parting breath?
   On many a bloody plain
   I've dared his face, and in this place
   I scorn him yet again.

3. Untie these bands from off my hands,
   And bring to me my sword;
   And there's no a man in all Scotland
   But I'll brave him at a word.

4. I've lived a life of sturt and strife,
   I die by treacherie:
   It burns my heart I must depart,
   And not avenged be.

5. Now farewell light, thou sunshine bright!
   And all beneath the sky!
   May coward shame disdain his name –
   The wretch that dare not die!
                              (Sampson, 1931, no. 24)

~

So many smiths, so many Gypsies.
                              (Hungarian Gypsy saying)

139. Oko vela o chavo*
     Kon chindilo petalo
     Chindyas shee miro chavlo
     Drey i barri kertsheema

381

O bawley choresko** vela
Top pes kosh tenengo gry
Lesk' doodah 'ree leski po-chee
Topler shero gooii sheelo

Oko vela a chavo*
Kon petalo chindilo
Chindyas shee miro chavlo
Drey i barri kertsheema.

*It is difficult to account for the alternative rendering of this line in Brune's translation.
**Literally, the man with the long beard.

Here comes the lad
Who cut the horse-shoe
My boy cut the horse-shoe
In the big inn.

Father Christmas is coming
On his wooden horse
With sweetmeats in his pocket
And a pudding on his head

The lad came by
Who cut the horse-shoe
My boy cut the horse-shoe
In the big inn.
> (Gypsy children, Rorrington, Shropshire, 1962;
> Brune 1975, 780)

This song would appear to be a typically Gypsy composite. The subject matter of the two elements is entirely unconnected and both have been recorded independently. The first (and last) verse is of particular interest in this respect as the only other recorded version was collected in Hungary by Donald Kenrick in 1967. His informant introduced and concluded her performance with mouth music, varying her words with each repetition. She then dictated them differently again:

1. Kodo avla o shavo (here comes the lad)
1a. Kodo al' lako shav' (here comes her lad)
1b. Kodo avelas o shav' (the lad came by)
2. Kon petalo chinela (who cuts the horseshoe);
3. Chineles muro shav' (my lad cut (it))

3a. Chinelas muro shavo (my lad cut (it))
4. Ande bari kirtshema (in the big inn).

The middle verse of Brune's text is to be found in Sampson's *Dialect of the Gypsies of Wales* and, so far as I am aware, remains the only other printed set:

> 140. Ō bå̄rē-čōréskerō 'vela
> Tap peskō kå̄štenénō grai;
> Leskē dūda arḗ leskī počī,
> Tåp leskō šērō ši les goi.
>
> Father Christmas is coming
> On his wooden horse;
> In his pocket toffee,
> On his head a pudding.
> (Sampson 1926, iv, 70)

So remarkable is the similarity between Brune's set and those recorded by Kenrick and Sampson that one is almost disposed to believe that Brune may have misheard his informants or himself adapted Kenrick's text for his own purposes. Had he succeeded in capturing his informants on tape, this would certainly have represented an extremely valuable addition to the existing stock of such material.

The reference in the first and third verse to a lad engaged in the manufacture of horseshoes is suggestive of an old tale, one of a number of variants on a common theme, linking the Gypsies with the crucifixion. In the version given by Manfri Wood (1973), there was once an inn-keeper who traded in horses, and for whom everything was going very well until the Romans came and built their roads. At that time horseshoes were unknown and the new paved surfaces caused them great suffering. One night, however, the inn-keeper's son had a dream in which the idea came to him that the problem might be solved by making clogs for them of cedar wood. But whilst these worked for a while, they soon wore out, leaving the horses no better off than before.

After a while, the young man had another dream in which it came to him that the answer was to make the horseshoes of iron; and so, he became the first smith.

One day, a Roman officer came to the forge and placed an order for twelve long nails and only when nine of them had already been handed over did the smith find out that they were intended for the crucifixion of Our Lord and the two thieves. He was so appalled at the prospect that he determined to withhold the remaining three nails, with the result that the crucifixion had eventually to be managed with only nine. Yet when the mob found out who had made the nails, they were bent on revenge and, although the smith and his family managed to evade capture, they have ever after been hounded through the world.

Involvement in the crucifixion is not the only crime laid at the Gypsies' door. Since their first arrival in Europe they have been credited with a number of hideous blasphemies, any one of which would have been sufficient to justify their exclusion from Christian society. Indeed, mindful perhaps of possible financial advantage in the form of alms, they themselves accounted for their nomadic way of life by claiming to be on a pilgrimage of penance ordained by the pope (Fraser 1992, ch.4).

According to one authority, Adventinus, '. . . they pretend for their vagabond course a judgment of God on their forefathers, who refused to entertain the Virgin Mary and Jesus when she fled to their country' (Sir T. Browne: *Vulgar Errors*, Book vi, ch.13). It is to this incident that Stanley refers in his Newdigate prize-winning poem of 1837, delivered by him in the Sheldonian Theatre on 7 June:

> They spake of lovely spots in Eastern lands,
> An isle of palms, amid a waste of sands –
> Of white tents pitched beside a chrystal well,
> Where in past days their fathers loved to dwell;
> To that sweet islet came at day's decline
> A Virgin Mother with her Babe divine;
> She asked for shelter from the chill night breeze,
> She prayed for rest beneath those stately trees;
> She asked in vain – what though was blended there
> A Maiden's meekness with a Mother's care;
> What though the light of hidden Godhead smiled
> In the bright features of that blessed Child
> She asked in vain – they heard and heeded not,
> And rudely drove her from the sheltering spot.
>
> Then fell the voice of Judgment from above;
> Then 'who shut Love out, shall be shut out from Love;
> Who drives the houseless wanderer from their door,
> Themselves shall wander houseless ever more.
> Till He, whom now they spurn, again shall come,
> Amid the clouds of Heaven to speak their final doom.'

In Spain they were thought guilty of an altogether more sordid offence, recalled in the following verse included by Fernan Caballero in his *Cuentos y Poesias Populares Andaluces*:

En el portal de Belen
Gitanitos han entrado,
Y al nino recien nacido
Los panales le han quitado.
Picaros Gitanos
Caras de aceitunas,
No han dejado al nino
Ropita Ninguna!

In the gate of Bethlehem
The little Gypsies have entered,
And the new-born child
Have robbed of his swaddling clothes.
Rascally Gypsies,
Faces of Olive,
They have not left the child
One little rag!

The Gypsies, however, are to be seen in a somewhat more favourable light in another variant of the crucifixion story noted by Dr G. Muhl in his 'Die Zigeuner in Elsass und in Deutschlothringen' (*Der Salon*, 1877):

There were, it seems, two Jewish brothers, Schmul and Romschmul, the first of whom gloried in Christ's suffering whilst the other would have spared him. Finding this to be impossible, he endeavoured to hold up the proceedings by making off with one of the four nails prepared for the occasion. For this reason, it was necessary to place Christ's feet, one on top of the other, in order that one nail might serve for both. As a result, Schmul remained a Jew whilst Romschmul turned Christian and became the father of the Romani race.

In his introduction to *The Legends of the Holy Rood* (1871), Dr R. Morris suggests that the transition from four to three nails in images of the crucifixion occurred some time during the twelfth or thirteenth century – the earliest example being a copper crucifix of (perhaps) Byzantine workmanship dating from the late 1200s – and, as Groome suggests, it is perhaps significant that this should have occurred at about the time the Gypsies must have entered eastern Europe.

The significance of the middle verse of text 139 is also somewhat obscure, although the image of a sweetmeat-bearing benefactor mounted on a hobby-horse is also to be found in the Spanish Gypsy repertoire. The following is one of a number of songs collected by Augustus John from the singing of Fabian de Castro, *el Gyptano*, the master *gitaristo*, born in Linares in Andalusia in *c*.1866. When last heard of, de Castro was lodged in the *estaripel* (prison) of Toledo, whither he had been forcibly conducted by the commander of the Civil Guard for painting a picture judged subversive of public order (*JGLS* n.s. 5 (1911), 135–8).

> Con mi caballo de cana
> Y mis estribos de papel,
> Me voy a correr la Espana
> Y de alli te voy a traer
> Un celemin de castanas.

> With my wooden horse (lit. horse of cane)
> And my paper stirrups,
> I am off over Spain
> And from yonder I will bring thee
> A full measure of chestnuts.

~

> There is a recognised set of criteria used among Travellers as to what makes a Singer as opposed to a singer. The music is still a fluid and malleable medium, can be well or badly interpreted, and in a society where it is still one of the most important forms of entertainment – and education – it is imperative that your Singer is a good one.
>
> (MacColl and Seeger 1977, 9)

The following three 'rough ballads', as Ibbetson calls them (*NQ* 7th ser. 4. (1887), 197), first appeared in *Hood's Comic Annual* for 1887 (19th issue, pp.65–6). They are reproduced here, 'gross errors' and all, although in each case the likely intended form is also given.

According to Leland, all three were obtained in the course of an encounter with a group of Stanleys camped near Weybridge in Surrey. Warned of their presence by a gentleman whom he met on the road, Leland tells us that he managed to gain their fire undetected and had already seated himself and lit his pipe before they realized he was there. On being threatened with summary eviction, he broke into the *Poggadi Chib*, telling them he was an American *Rom* with news of their transatlantic cousins. He was immediately made welcome and invited to supper, to which he himself contributed two pails of beer.

Their meal over, Leland began to sing some scraps of song in *Romanés* and, on being told that there were singers in the company, produced a clasp-knife which, he said, would go to whoever sang the best song. Three of the company took up the challenge: Vitruvius, who looked like a retired prize-fighter turned poacher; Sylvestros, 'who began with a grimace and gestures which indicated that he was accustomed to appear in public'; and Artaros, 'a tall youth with a face like an Apollo in meerschaum'. Unfortunately, before Leland had time to award the prize, the party was interrupted by the police and he was obliged to throw the knife into the ring, suggesting that they should toss for it. The three songs are reproduced below in the order in which they were sung.

> 141. Ki did the Romanys hatch the tan?
> Hatch the tan, chiv the tan?
> Ki did the Romanys hatch the tan?
> Alay by the rikk o' the pani.
> Sā did the Romany geeros haw? (repeat apopli)
> Sā did the Romany geeros haw?
> Alay by the rikk o' the pāni?
> Kilmāro an bàllovas (repeat, apopli)
> Hotchenitchi* and mūlls, (mullo) mass,
> Alay by the rikk o' the pāni.
> How did they lel the covvas they haw
> Alay by the rikk o' the pāni.
> By dūkkerin au (or) māageren (manging) ajā,
> On the drum that jaws to the pāni.
> Sa did the Romany geeros pee?
> Sa did the Romany geeros pee?
> Levinor, muttermen geree,
> Alay by the rikk o' the pāni.
> What did the Romany kister, apray,
> On the drum that jaws to the pāni?
> He kistered apray a rinkers gry,
> On the drum that jaws to the pāni.
> What did he pessur for the gry,
> That he kistered alay for the pāni?
> He pessured a besh adray staruben,
> A door for (from) the rikk o' the pāni.
> O the beng may tosser the gavengro!
> The gavengro, the hop-per-core**!
> Oh! bengis tasser, the gavengro!
> That lelled the Rom by the pāni.
> (Vitruvius Stanley, Weybridge; Leland 1887, 66)

*The hedgehog, or *Romano baulo* (Gypsy pig), as it was sometimes called, seems always to have been regarded with particular affection by the Gypsies of England. Ask any *Gaujo* what they know of English Gypsy cuisine and they will almost certainly tell you that their staple diet includes, among other things, roast hedgehog, whilst, among those Welsh Travellers whom Tipler encountered on the Llŷn peninsula late in the summer of 1950, the very name was used as a soubriquet for their English counterparts: 'rakerena hoci-wici Romimus?', they asked, meaning 'do English Gypsies speak Romani?' (Tipler 1957, 9–24, no.54).

Among the English Gypsies themselves, Sampson also noted the phrase *wutchi si kingo* (the hedgehog is wet), meaning 'the man is drunk' (*JGLS* o.s. 3 (1892), 246). This may be explained in the light of the old saying, mentioned by Groome and Smith, to the effect that 'a hedgehog will open when it is wet' – that is to say, a man, and more especially a Gypsy, will become garrulous when in drink.

**Leland also used this term in his poem 'The Gavéngroes' (1875, 168):

> If I lels a koshter fon a bar,
> There wells ta mengy a hoppercore.

> If I steal a stick from a hedge,
> A policeman comes [after] for me.

I can, however, find no record of it elsewhere. In nineteenth-century urban slang a 'hop-picker' signified a whore, a term of abuse which, by extension, might conceivably be applied to a policeman. Phillips, however, in his *Rhyming Slang: A Dictionary* (1932), gives 'John Hop', together with its Australian derivative, 'Johnny Hopper' = cop(per), but this does not account for the suffix *-core*.

142. Oh, Mandy had a gry,
    Aboro (a boro) kusleto (kushto) gry,
    And I poored it to a rye,
    For a grassni. *Tachipen.*

    Then Mandy had a grassni,
    And I poored it for a groovni,
    For a groovni and keksomi (kek-komi),
    And a drop o' leviner. *Tachipen.*

    Then I latched a rye and rāni,
    And I poored it for a Shāni,*
    For a pawno rinkno Shāni,
    And a drop more leviner. *Tachipen.*

    Then I poored avree the Shāni,
    For a mylar flick and tāni,
    And a fashiono fauny,
    And a drop o tatto pauni. *Tachipen.*

    Then I hatched for a while, oh,
    And poored away my myla,
    Mandy poored his (lis) for a juva,**
    A juva te kekoomi *Tachipen.*

And hek (kek) mush for laki'd,
Del a swägler of tobaki,
So you dikks that I can't poor her,
And the gilly can't jaw doorer. *Tachipen.*

(Sylvestros Stanley, Weybridge; Leland 1887, 67)

*Somewhat unusual, perhaps, but also favoured as first choice for 'donkey' by Willie Smith in conversation with Seán O Boyle in Belfast(?), 1952 (Folktracks FDS60–441). See also Smart and Crofton 1875, 134 for *sháni* = mule. The more common word is *myla* (Smart and Crofton 1875, 107) for which Pott (1844–5, ii, 454) suggests a Latin etymon, *mulus*.
**An unfortunate, if common, error. *Juva* means 'louse' (Smart and Crofton, *joóva*; Paspati, *djuv*). The correct form would seem to be *juvel/juval* (Smart and Crofton, *joóvel*; Paspati, *djuvél*).

Now it's brother had a lice, sister had a flea,
Brother had the bottle and uncle had the tea.
We had some scratches from the *jub*, some bites from the flea,
Some drink from the cup and he's gone and lost the tea.

(Jasper Smith, TOPIC 12TS304)

The idea of exchanging one's donkey for a woman calls to mind the countervailing notion of the 'donkey-wife'. A common Gypsy allusion, born perhaps, like Andersen's 'Stork-wife', of the great affection with which these beasts were once generally regarded, the *grasni* or *mailla romadi* ('mare- or donkey-wife') was, according to Sampson, the subject of a number of similar verses of which the following is the 'least exceptionable':

143. Keker mandi koms kek juvel;
      Mandi'll romer a tarni mailla;
      If yoi kērs wafedo to mandi,
      I'll bikin lati for a balanser.

(Sampson 1891, 91)

Leland's third song runs as follows:

144. The givengro rye he penned,
         'If tute'll kair booti for me,
         Mandy'll del panje cawlor the divons' (divvus),
         So men dooee did agree.

         The rye he had a rauny,
         An' she was kusliti (kushti) to see;

389

She pens, 'I'll del a korauni,
If tute'll kair boots (booti) for me.'

The rāni had a rākli,
And she didn't del mandy cheechee;
But Mandi kaired for the locki (for laki),
The koomi of sar the three.
(Artaros Stanley, Weybridge;
Leland 1887, 65–6)

Although these songs are introduced as genuine Gypsy compositions, there must be some doubt whether they were given in precisely the form in which they eventually appeared in print. Leland, as mentioned elsewhere, made no secret of his low opinion of his subjects' ability to produce original material in a form fit for publication and, as with 'The Three Little Injuns' (text 165), thought nothing of a little judicious editing in order to bring it up to scratch. Certainly, they are unusually well formed and the second set, in particular, shows a degree of sophistication seldom found in genuine Romani song: e.g. by rhyming 'while, o' with 'maila' and 'poor her' with 'doorer'. In the first of these examples, the use of the suffix -*o*, a common enough device in mainstream folk song where a strong or masculine ending is required, is particularly unusual in Gypsy song. The only other example in the present collection is in the Robinsons' rendering of the 'Raggle-Taggle Gypsies-o', itself a reworking of a traditional Anglo-Scottish piece.

On the other hand, the form of language employed is somewhat less complex than that usually favoured by Leland in his own compositions. There is, for example, a complete absence of Romani verb endings whilst, as regards vocabulary, there is little evidence of Leland's customary inventiveness. A number of words have clearly been misread by the original compositor, but, these apart, only a handful of items give pause for thought: e.g. *rikk, kilmaro, maageren* and *hop-per-cor*, but these are insufficient in themselves to justify dismissing all three verses out of hand.

~

A chirrico 'drée the wast is worth dui 'drée the bor
A bird in the hand is worth two in the bush
(Leland 1873, 103)

145. My dai's cherikl never puker'd a hukipen.
My dai's cherikl rokers pencha rashai;

390

It pend koliko divus mandi'd mēr adré stariben,
Mandi'll jal kēri, and tarder its men.

If I tasser lesti, my dad will kūr mandi;
If my dad kūrs mandi, mandi'll mōr my dad;
If I mōr my dad, I'll be lino to stariben
(And then the rokerin' cherikl's lav will wel tācho).*

(Lee; Sampson 1891, 91)

*Sampson adds a footnote to the effect that this last line is partly conjectural owing to the illegibility of his original notes.

This elegant nineteenth-century 'catch 22' was given to Sampson by one of the Lees. It is, he says, a good example of a 'modern' Romani composition, some of which 'though quite rhymeless and frequently unmetrical . . . are by no means devoid of form and show a certain undeveloped capacity for lyrical expression'.

The Gypsies' evident fondness for caged birds is, perhaps, a little surprising as they, of all people, might be expected to understand their need for free movement. Colonel John Harriott must have been shown one by one of his informants whilst collecting examples of Gypsy speech in north Hampshire in 1819–20, for we find in his vocabulary the word *chariklo* given for 'cage' (Harriott 1830). For 'bird-cage', Smart and Crofton give *chériklesto-kair*, 'bird's-house' (1875, 64).

That bird-catching may still be numbered among the Gypsy trades is suggested by an article in the *Spectator* for 7 April 1984, entitled 'In Sherwood Forest': 'The local Gypsies were great bird-catchers, I was told. They used a singing bullfinch in a cage as a decoy. When another bullfinch landed on the cage roof, a trap door tipped it in and it could be sold for £20.' As regards the keeping of parrots, or *híndi kákarátchies* (dirty or shitty magpies) as they were sometimes called (Smart and Crofton 1875, 82), a writer in the *Daily News* for 19 October 1872, tells us that, among the Gypsies of Epping Forest, a number of such birds were to be found which spoke only in Romani. Cf. the further usage reported by Smart and Crofton – *romani-rokerin-chériklo* (1875).

More generally, the *Poggadi Chib* seems to have been relatively poorly provided with words for the commoner type of British song-birds – the stock in trade of the fowler as opposed to the poacher. The blackbird and the nightingale are something of an exception here. The former, commonly referred to as the *kaulo chiriklo*, is also said by Groome to have been known as the *fulano chumba* or muck heap, whilst the latter was called variously *raátenghi-chei-chériklo*, night-girl-bird, and *rartigillichal*, night song fellow. Apart from these, the wren seems to have been known among some

Travellers as the *chovihan* or 'witch' bird, perhaps from its apparent ability to appear and disappear at will. Further examples are also to be found in the dialect of the Gypsies of Wales as recorded by Sampson and Tipler.

Barnyard fowls and game birds fare somewhat better, with speakers making use both of Romani proper nouns and circumlocutions; e.g. *kánni*, chicken, *kauli-rani*, turkey (black lady), *rutsa*, duck, *pappingo*, goose, *ridjil*, partridge, *reisko-chiriklo*, pheasant (gentleman's bird), *pookeringonyas* and *hatch-pauli-kanni*, guineafowl – the first of this last pair because, according to Norwood, they say 'put you in your bags' and the second, according to Smart and Crofton, because they are called 'come backs' by *gaujo* provincials on account of their cry. Among these, *pappingo*, goose, is of particular interest as it also occurs, with an entirely different meaning – 'peacock' – in a variant of 'The Twelve Days of Christmas' noted by Reeves (1972). Wood gives *barripóari* for peacock (Wood, 1973).

> The king sent his lady on the first yule day
> A papingo-aye.
> Who learns my carol and carries it away.

~

Kai men vena fon? My Durel jins, ta yov sí tai ratvalo buíno ta muk mendi jin.

Where do we come from? God knows, and he's too bloody clever to let us know.

(One of the Smiths)

> 146. Shūn the húnnalo o' the pánni,
>   The húnnalo bōro pánni,
>   Húnnalin sārasā,
>   'Cos it can't jāl andūro,
>   An' gūryin ajā.

> Hear the roar of the water,
> Of the great and raging sea,
> Raging ever on,
> Because it can get no further
> And roaring all alone!

(Matty Cooper; Leland 1873, 129)

Matty Cooper, Leland's principal informant, spoke these lines when asked by the latter for his word for 'roar'. There is a double meaning here

392

in that, if Leland is right, *hunnalo* also meant 'rage'. It may be observed, however, that *hunnalo* is somewhat unusual, the common form being *hoïno*, as given in Acton and Kenrick's modified reprint of the poem on p.67 of *Romani Rokkeripen to-Divvus* (1985).

Before dismissing Cooper/Leland's usage out of hand, however, it is perhaps worth noting that, among some 500 items (including duplicates) obtained by Norwood from a Gypsy couple whom he first met on the Swindon Drom on 22 October 1859, is the apparently related form *únlo* = vexed. Among a number of other examples normally only associated with Leland are *búgny*, smallpox (Leland 1873, 51, *bugni*); *dosh*, harm (Leland 1873, 51, 257, *dush*) and *tschílloko*, bird (Leland 1873, 19, 175, 203, *chilliko*) and the fact that the couple are identified by Norwood as Mr and Mrs Cooper inevitably raises the intriguing possibility that the husband may have been that same Matty Cooper who, some ten years later, was to initiate Leland himself into the mysteries of the *Romani Chib*. If this is so, then Mrs Cooper (née Eliza James), to whom Norwood made two further visits in March and November of the following year, must have died some time during 1863 (see Leland 1873, 49). According to Norwood, Mrs Cooper spoke better Romani than her husband, using correctly a number of inflected verbs and, with less success, a handful of prepositions. She also offered him the following night-prayer – her own composition:

> 147. Mi deeri Duvvulesti, kair sig shunessu mandi.
> Day mandi zee adray tuti's tem.
>
> My dear God, make haste to hear me.
> Give me life in heaven.
> (Mrs Cooper; Grosvenor 1910)

Her husband, if so he was, also provided Leland with an example of sacred verse in the *Poggadi Chib*, in answer to his question regarding the nature of the Day of Judgement. It shows every sign, however, of Leland's editorial hand.

> 148. O BORO divvúsko dívvus,
> Ko si adúvvel?
> Kún tu sovéss' aláy
> Kéti bōro Dúvvel.
>
> Tell me what is
> The Judgment Day?
> It is when unto God
> You dream away.
> (Matty Cooper; Leland 1875, 187 (trans. CGL)).

Gillington also includes the following example of religious verse in the
Poggadi Chib in a sequence subtitled *New Forest Tent Dwellers' Night
Prayers* (*JGLS* n.s. 5 (1911b), 53).

> 149. A-trash'd we be of the mush in the baw and the mulo
>   upon the heth;
> The tshovihan with her tshuries sharp and the bird
>   that cries for death;*
> So say your second prayer, my tshavis, if you've
>   a-washed you clean,
> Before we jals to sutars all, this night in
>   bushes green.

*The *múlo-chériklo*: the goat-sucker or nightjar – 'It cries *kek-kek* and someone will die'
(Smart and Crofton 1875, 112). In Wales, the *aderyn corff* or 'corpse-bird' was thought
by *Gaujos* and Gypsies alike to be the screech owl or some other night bird: 'Divés
manke muiás i merimásko cheriklo oriás parl o ker ta kedás godli – the day before he
died, the death bird flew shrieking over the house.' Among the Lees and Hernes,
however, it was the moorhen whose cry carried tidings of imminent death (James, *JGLS*
n.s. 5 (1911), 145–6, and Yates, *JGLS* n.s. 4 (1911), 301–2). Oddly enough, one of
James's informants also described the cry of the moorhen as 'kek kek kek', her
companion adding 'may the lord stop their breath'. See also Ferguson, *JGLS* n.s. 4
(1911), 160, and, more generally, Swainson's *Folklore of British Birds*.

Although Gillington has elsewhere shown herself capable of faithfully
reproducing the words of her Gypsy informants, it is difficult to believe
that the above issued unaided from the lips of those same Travellers from
whom she obtained the various other sets reproduced in the present work
as texts 17, 74, 78, 80 and 113. Compare also the following obtained by the
Revd C. L. Marson from 'a pure Romani woman', Mrs Patience Davis.
The Revd Marson, who kept the parsonage at Hambridge near Taunton,
was also an enthusiastic folk-song collector (see texts 87–9) and the author
of a historical guide to Glastonbury – *The English Jerusalem*. In submitting
the following prayers, taught by Mrs Davis to her grandson, Marson also
mentions a set of 'pre-Reformation invocations of saints which a Gypsy
boy repeated to a friend' but a copy of which he had been unable to secure.

> (a) Little children is so wise,
>   Speak the truth and tell no lies,
>   Liars' portion is to dwell
>   For ever in the like* of burnin' hell.

*Lake?

    (b) Little bird of sparidise,*
        Do the work of Jesu Chrise.
        Go by sea, go by lan',
        Go by Goddes holy han'.

*A conflation of sparrow and paradise?

    (c) God make me a branch and flower,
        May the Lord send us all a happy hour.

    (d) Lay me down upon my side,
        And if I die before I wake,
        I trust in God my soul to take.

    Smart and Crofton also obtained a handful of religious verses from Wester Boswell, of which the following appear on p.248 of the *Dialect of the English Gypsies*. It is much to be regretted that their published work contains nothing in the way of verses of a secular nature.

    150. Talla boot peeromus besháw,
          Te goodlo see te atch
          Adré Komomus, ta Kooshtoben,
          Te sor mendi dik.

          After many roming years,
          How sweet it is to be
          In love, peace, and kindness,
          With all you see.

    151. Jaw mook sorkon ti zee *o'* mandi,
          Te too'*ll* tatcheni dik,
          Te Komomus kater mi *dearo* Duvel,
             te koshtomus te sor moosháw.
          Dova and'a tooti kater tatcho poov,
          So let all injoy the mind of me,
          And that you will plainly see,
          That love to God, and peace with man
          Will bring you to a Happy Land.

    152. O tatcho drom te ker aglál té kom teero
          Duvelesko Chavo,
          Kom lesti ta lesti heveski lavaw,
          Talla too'*ll* latch te too'*ll* atch tatcho,
          Ta kerav teero drom tatcho

Opré, adré mi duvelesko Tem te jiv,
Besháw ta beshaw. Amen.

The rite way. First to love your Christ
First, and obey His Holy Word,
Then you will find that you will be rite
And make your road quite
Strat, in Heaven to dwell,
For ever and ever, Amen,

~

When John went off to his supper, the children fell to asking riddles;
not modern conundrums, but good old-fashioned 'sense-riddles', like
the *zigádki* of the Russian peasantry. Ancient they must be; for who,
without the leisure of Methuselah, could ever discover that 'a nettle'
is meant by 'in the hedge, and out of the hedge, and if you touch it, it
will bite you?'

(Groome 1880, 159)

153. Kōlō sār vanár, t'ā nai vanár kek;
Pōrnō sār īv, t'ā nai īv kek;
Oxtéla 'koi t'ā 'kai
'Jō-sār tārnō bita grai.
Kakaráčko.

(Sampson 1926, iv, 130)

Black as coal, yet it is not coal;
White as snow, yet it is not snow;
It jumps here and there,
Just like a young foal.
Magpie.

One of fifty such *Romané zumivabena* 'picked up *kai ta koi* from Gypsy
children and adults' and first published, with an editorial note by Professor
Petsch (*JGLS* n.s. 5 (1912), 241–55), there is nothing essentially Romani
about the magpie. The following variant, perhaps the earliest extant
version but nonetheless typical of its kind, is from the *Booke of Meery
Riddles*, first published in 1600. Whether this was the same 'Book of
Riddles' lent by Slender to Alice Shortcake in the opening scene of *The
Merry Wives of Windsor* remains unproven but there is no doubting its
popularity. Further editions are known to have been published in 1617 and
1629 and again, following the Restoration, in 1660, 1672 and 1685.

What is that: as white as milke, as soft as silke, as blacke as a coale, and hops in the street like a steed foale,

to which is given the answer:

It is a Pye that hoppeth in the street, for part of her feathers be white, and part be blacke.

It has also been recorded in both Germany and France, the following variant being taken from E. Rolland's *Devinettes aux Énigmes* of 1877:

Qui est-ce qui est noir et blanc, Qui sautille à travers champs Et qui ressemble à monsieur le curé, Quand il est en train de chanter?

What is black and white, that hops about the fields, and looks like the parish priest when he is singing?

The riddle, with its emphasis on lateral thought, seems particularly well suited to the Gypsy temperament and, even today, as Yates has pointed out, still fulfils an important social function within Gypsy society (Yates 1976, 14). The two following examples are taken from his account of the singer, Sharper's Joe (ibid.), whose repertoire was such that the old man was never known to repeat himself in the course of a session.

(a) What goes up but never goes down? *Your age.*

(b) What goes into a wood, out of a wood but never touches the wood? *A watch.*

A number of examples of European Gypsy riddles are to be found scattered throughout the literature, as, for example, Gjorgjevic (1906, ch.4) and Wittich (1912, 55–6). Wlislocki, too, gives three examples (Romani text and German translations) in the third of his four Transylvanian folk tales and a further fifty (in translation only) in his *Volksdichtungen der Siebenburgischen und Sudungarischen Zigeuner* (Wlislocki 1890, 161–8). The following, in Turkish Romani, is to be found on p.598 of Paspati's 'études' together with a French translation. No solution is offered:

I rakli penghias: pen to lav.
O Raklo penghias: me daia urydinom la, me dades uglistiniom les, me meribenastar pani paliom.
Diklias i rakli andre po lil. Nast' arklias.

397

La fille dit: Dis ton énigme.
Le garçon dit: J'ai endossé ma mère, j'ai monté mon père, et de ma mort,
j'ai bu de l'eau.
La fille regarda dans son livre, elle ne put pas (l')expliquer.

Riddles are essentially of two types. The first, known aptly in German as *Halslösungenratsel* or 'neck-freeing riddles', refer to the peculiar experience or knowledge of the teller and can only be solved inspirationally or through possession of the relevant information (cf. Samson in Judges 14; 'the riddle of the Sphinx'; and Bilbo's questioning of Gollum in *The Hobbit*: 'What have I got in my pocket?'). The following example of this first type is from Edith Lea, 'a young Gypsy girl belonging to Cardiff', as recorded by Eileen Lyster:

> Riddle me, riddle me, highty-tight;
> Where were I last Friday night?
> When the clock of heaven
> Struck eleven,
> When the bough did bend, my heart did ache
> To see what that old fox did make.
>
> (*JGLS*)

According to Lyster's informant, the riddle refers to a proposed late-night rendezvous between a young girl and her lover. Not wishing to keep him waiting, she turns up early and makes herself comfortable in a tree overlooking the trysting place. Who should then appear but the lover himself, also early and armed with a pick and shovel with which he begins to dig a hole – her grave.

Riddles of the second type describe an object or action in terms of one or more of its salient features. Questions of this sort may, however, be further complicated by the use of metaphor, anthropomorphism or obliquity. In such cases, the characteristics assigned to the object or action in question are rarely those by which it is usually identified and may be selected with a view to suggesting an entirely different line of thought.

There is nothing uniquely Romani about the following examples and, indeed, according to Petsch (1912), they are simply drawn from the common repertoire of those peoples with whom the Gypsies came in contact in the course of their wanderings.

154.'Doi sas bōrī p'ūv t'ā p'ārdī guruvá t'a yek' pelénerō.

Bōrī p'ūv s'ō ravnos, guruvá s'ō čakanīá,
t'ā pelenérō sī šōnus.

There was a great field full of cows and one bull.

The great field is the sky, the cows are stars,
and the bull is the moon.

Writing of the above, Petsch notes that he was unable to find any European analogues. The same image, however, forms the opening motif of the medieval Welsh prose tale of Niniaw and Pebiaw, the one claiming ownership of the flocks of heaven, the other, ownership of the celestial fields.

> 155. Hikī Pikī 'drē bōrriātī;
> Čalá tū ī, Hiki Pikī dandéla tut.
> *Basavī patrín.*
>
> Hiki piki in the hedge.
> Touch hiki piki and she will bite thee.
> *A nettle.*

In Welsh Romani, the nettle was called the 'wicked leaf'. Among English Gypsies it was known as *dándiméngri chor*, 'biting grass' (Smart and Crofton 1875, 180). Groome heard this same riddle in the shadow of Cader Idris some time prior to 1880, whilst Kennedy obtained a further version from Manfri Wood of Bala at Penybont Fawr near Oswestry in November 1954. It will be noticed that Wood's version closely resembles Sampson's, preserving, as it does, the same meaningless jingle in the first line. Unfortunately, it does not seem to have occurred to Kennedy to ask his informant to repeat his question in Romani.

> In the hedge and out of the hedge,
> and if you touch it, it will bite you.
> (Groome 1880)
>
> Hiki piki in the hedge, hiki piki out of the hedge;
> You touch hiki piki, hiki piki touch you.
> (Kennedy, Folktracks 60–053)

A mainstream version of this riddle is given on p.81 of W. Gregor's *Notes on Folklore of North East Scotland*:

Robbie-stobbie on this side o' the dyke,
Robbie-stobbie on that side o' the dyke,
And gehn ye touch robbie-stobbie,
Robbie-stobbie'll bite ye.

156. Ō mūrš te kedás les bikindás les;
　　　Ō mūrš te kindás les na wontsélas les kek;
　　　Ō mūrš te 'yas les junélas čī trušal lesti.
　　　Muléskō moxtō.

　　　The man who made it sold it;
　　　The man who bought it did not want it;
　　　The man who got it knew nothing about it.
　　　A coffin.

Once again, the same riddle formed part of Manfri Wood's repertoire as recorded by Kennedy in the early 1950s:

　　　The man as made it sold it;
　　　The man who bought it didn't want it;
　　　The man as had it knew nothing at all about it.
　　　　　　　　　(Manfri Wood; Kennedy, Folktracks 60–053)

The coffin riddle is widely known. The following variant is again from Gregor:

　　　The wiz a man bespoke a coat;
　　　When the maker it home did bring,
　　　The man who made it would not have it,
　　　The man who spoke for't cudna use it,
　　　And the man who wore it cudna tell
　　　Whether it suited him ill or well.

157. Sō sī andilō̒ kī misálī t'ā p'agerdō̒
　　　t'ā nai kek te xalē̒ les?
　　　Ō vērdē

　　　What is brought to the table and cut
　　　but none ate it?
　　　A pack of cards.

　　　What's first brought to the table, cut, but not eaten.
　　　　　　　　　　　　　　　　　(Manfri Wood, ibid.)

400

Although variants of text 157 have also been recorded on the Indian subcontinent, this should not necessarily be construed as lending support to Groome's thesis that the Gypsies have been instrumental in the worldwide dissemination of international folk motifs, to which reference has already been made in the introduction to the present work. The riddle is undoubtedly an important element in the oral tradition of cultures untouched by the Romani diaspora, and it is hardly surprising, therefore, to find the same or similar notions occuring entirely independently.

> 158. Sō jala 'koi t'ā 'kai arḗ ō k'ēr
> T'ā 'čela 'rē yek' kunsus?
> *Ī šuvél.*
>
> What goes here and there about the house
> And then stops in one corner?
> *A broom.*

The following two Asian analogues are drawn respectively, says Sampson, from a set of seven quoted by Leitner in his account of Dardestan (1880, 17) and from the sixty-four Kashmiri riddles of B. Hinton Knowles (*Journal of the Asiatic Society of Bengal*, lvi pt. i (1887), no. iii):

Mey szik heyn, sureo pereyn, bas darre pato.
Buja.

Now listen! my sister walks in the daytime, and at night sleeps behind the door.
A broom.

> Kurih hana asam;
> Duhas asam phirit thurit yiwan,
> Kalachan asam baras tal bihan.
> *Lur.*
>
> I have a little girl;
> By day she wanders hither and thither,
> At night she sits down by my door.
> *A staff.*

401

Songs from the Mainstream

The young man sang part of two Gypsy songs to me in English and then, at my request, he turned one of them into the Gypsy language, intermingled with English words, occasioned, perhaps, by the difficulty of translating it.

(W. Simson, 1865)

The movement away from the land in the wake of the agrarian and industrial revolutions, the introduction of compulsory education for all and, more recently, the development of the mass media, have all, in their several different ways, contributed towards the gradual erosion of that linguistic and cultural diversity once so marked a feature of our island society. For the Gypsies, such far-reaching changes have been further reinforced by the loss of many of their traditional trades and stopping-places and the growing effectiveness of official intervention. And yet, despite the almost inexorable pressure to conform to *Gaujo* expectations, they have somehow contrived to hold on to enough of their ancient culture and way of life to remain, both in their own eyes and those of the settled population, a distinct and recognizable community.

That this has been possible is due, in large measure, to the Gypsies' natural resilience, a quality rooted in oppression and nurtured by a highly effective blend of conservatism and adaptability. We have already seen how, despite its almost totemic significance, the Romani tongue has never been allowed to stagnate, but, by a process of sustained adaptation, has always contrived to keep pace with the changing communication needs of those it serves. So too, in their choice of song, this gift for compromise is immediately apparent. Thus, whilst at the heart of the English Gypsy repertoire there still exists a core of fixed and free-floating native composition in the *Poggadi Chib*, surrounding this nucleus is a mass of extraneous matter, drawn from a variety of sources and, in its original form and inspiration, wholly alien to the Romani tradition. Yet, whilst it is

402

undoubtedly true, if volume alone is any guide, that this imported matter now represents the principal constituent of English Gypsy song, it is equally apparent from the way in which it has been modified following its adoption that the mode of thought underlying the original core element continues to exercise a wholly disproportionate influence over the character of the repertoire as a whole.

For this reason, perhaps, it is only in recent years that the Gypsies have come to be recognized as important carriers of mainstream song; for, whilst something of the richness of their repertoire may be guessed at from the writings of various nineteenth-century commentators, their tendency to reduce texts to the point where they may no longer be thought viable by a *Gaujo* audience undoubtedly deterred the majority of early folk-song collectors whose principal aim would seem to have been the discovery of a 'pure' native English tradition comparable with that of Scotland and Ireland.

What seems to have tipped the balance in favour of recognition is the fact that Gypsies are the only numerically significant group to have brought the English folk repertoire into the age of sophisticated sound recording. As Richards has pointed out,

> An old singer, town or country, is likely to be viewed as a character, an exception these days. Not so with the Gypsies. They have preserved our precious heritage of folk songs far longer than any other section of the population. You can hear a modern Gypsy sing a medieval ballad as if it happened yesterday, unaware that the folklorists spend hours researching such songs . . . (Richards 1976–7, 23)

Whilst Richards is undoubtedly right as regards the general thrust of his remarks, his last observation is not entirely apt. Many Travellers know very well that many of the songs they sing are of considerable antiquity – 'This is one of the oldest ones in the world', said Mrs Hughes of 'The Flower of Servantmen'; and again, of 'The Sprig of Thyme', 'my mother's mother, my grandfather, grandfather again, great grandfather, you go back four hundred years, the song I'm going to sing you now' (Kennedy, Folktracks 60–032). So, too, Charlie Scamp:

> These songs that I am singing to you is true. They were handed down from my great grandfather to his children and right down to my father to us . . . These songs that I'm going to sing to you was made up before song books come about. That's for why we like singing these songs that was handed down from our grandfathers right down to my father down to us kiddies. (Folktracks 45–140)

Somewhat ironically, perhaps, the earliest examples of mainstream texts obtained from Travellers are far less obviously 'corrupt' than is now generally the case, though this is almost certainly because only the 'best' were selected, the remainder being discarded as worthless. The Revd John Broadwood, for example, offers a complete set of 'The Lost Lady Found' in his *Old English Songs* of 1843 (reproduced in the notes accompanying texts 163 and 164), and Bell, too, includes an excellent version of the ballad known as 'The Death of Queen Jane' from 'the singing of a young Gypsy' (Bell 1857, 13) – a song which preserves the tradition that Jane Seymour was delivered of a boy child by caesarean section (see Hume 1889, 73). In it, the queen herself calls for the surgeon, having been 'in travail for six weeks or more', but seems already to have given up the ghost before the operation could be performed:

> . . . He gave her rich caudle
> But the death sleep slept she
> Her right side was opened
> And the babe was set free.
> The babe it was christened
> And put out and nursed
> While the royal queen Jane
> She lay cold in the dust.

Groome, too, quotes extensively from a number of mainstream texts, noting that 'gatherers of old songs and melodies may go further afield than Little Egypt to come back emptier-handed than if they had loitered an hour beside the tents' (Groome 1880, 142). In the same work (pp.141–57), he mentions some thirteen songs (six from the standard Welsh repertoire and seven English or Scottish), sung either in English or 'Welsh be-sprinkled gibberish', and gives several in full, including this 'fragment of an old-world ballad', a variant of 'The Unquiet Grave' (Child and Kiltredge 1882–9, 78):

> ' "Cold blows the wind over my true love,
> Cold blow the drops of rain;
> I never, never had but one sweetheart,
> In the green wood he was slain.
>
> ' "But I'll do as much for my true love
> As any young girl can do;
> I'll sit and I'll weep by his grave side
> For a twelvemonth and one day."

'When the twelve month's end and one day was past,
This young man he arose,
"What makes you weep by my grave side
For twelve months and one day?"

' "Only one kiss from your lily cold lips,
One kiss is all I crave;
Only one kiss from your lily cold lips,
And return back to your grave."

' "My lip is cold as the clay, sweet heart,
My breath is earthy strong;
If you should have a kiss from my cold lips,
Your days will not be long."

' "Go fetch me a note from the dungeon dark,
Cold water from a stone;
There I'll sit and weep for my true love,
For a twelvemonth and one day.

' "Go dig me a grave both long, wide, and deep,
I will lie down in it and take one sleep,
For a twelvemonth and one day,
I will lie down in it and take a long sleep,
For a twelvemonth and a day." '

Further examples, both sacred and secular are to be found in the literature of the late nineteenth and early twentieth century, as, for example, White 1892; Smith 1889; Broadwood 1908, 774–7; Gillington 1910a; Gillington, 1911a; and a thorough review of this and other related material would no doubt shed further light on the more recent collections undertaken by Yeats, Kennedy, MacColl, Seeger and others.

Gypsy eclecticism, however, involves far more than the absorption of traditional material from the dominant British folk repertoires. Country and Western, the music hall and other forms of contemporary popular song are also much favoured sources of supply. Indeed, unlikely as this may be, it has been suggested that the Gypsies' own peculiar singing style, with its slow delivery, long-drawn-out lines and frequent use of portamento, is itself derived from such contemporary country singers as Jimmy Rogers. Typical American borrowings include 'May I Sleep in Your Barn Tonight, Mister?', 'The Cottage by the Sea' and Will B. Hay's 'Little Old Log Cabin', first recorded commercially by Fiddling John Carson in 1923 and recovered by Peter Kennedy from the singing of

Rebecca Penfold at Winkleigh, near Hatherleigh, Devon, in 1971
(Kennedy, Folktracks 60–41). The same influence is also clearly discernible
in such native British productions as Louise Fuller's version of 'Twenty-
one Years on Dartmoor'. Across the southern states during the 1920s,
American string bands popularized versions of a similar song centred on
Birmingham gaol, Alabama, and perhaps elements of these have travelled
and been incorporated in Mrs Fuller's set.

> The judge said 'stand up, boy, and dry up your tears.
> You're sentenced to Dartmoor for twenty one years.'
> So kiss me goodbye, babe, and say you'll be mine,
> For twenty one years, babe, is a mighty long time.
>
> Just look down that railroad, oh babe you can see
> My comrades are waving their farewell to me.
> The steam from the whistle, the smoke from the stack;
> I know you'll be true, babe, until I get back.
>
> Go back to the Governor, babe, on your sweet soul.
> He has sent me to Dartmoor, so get up that road.
> If I've got the Governor, then the Governor's got me,
> But before Tuesday morning, I guess I'll be free.
>
> It is hailing, it's raining, this moon gives no light;
> Baby, please tell me why you never write.
> I'm here in this jail-house, my heart's broken down.
> I had a letter from mother in old Kempton town.

In some cases, elements of such extraneous material may even find their
way into native Gypsy compositions. Thus, in the following dandling song
from Carolyne Hughes, the chorus is drawn from Veigh and Bastow's 'The
Galloping Major':

> There was two purty Gypsy girls
> And their names was Hat and Kate;
> They come from Wood-Green-Trees
> On the far side of Sal'sb'ry, Hants.
> They goes out a hawkin'
> With their bundles up their backs
> And bubbies in their arms,
> Suckin' cryin' all day long.

La de de la de de doodle della de de,
Bumpety bumpety bumpety bump!
Comes the Galloping major.
O he's a gay old stager.
O, boys, clear the road,
Here comes the galloping major.

Bumpety bumpety bumpty bumpety,
Straight away into me charger,
All the boys declare, I think you're a gay old stager,
O, boys, clear the road,
Here comes the drunken sailor!
(MacColl and Seeger 1977, 351)

At times, this taste for the exotic may prove somewhat vexing to the over-earnest student of Traveller song. An old friend, a Wexford *Nacker* by the name of John Doran, once asked if I would like a tape of his favourite music and, knowing him to be a cousin of the late Felix and Johnny Doran, the noted Irish pipers, I accepted with alacrity. The proffered mix of Frankie Vaughan, Mrs Mills and the pride of Nashville was, I must confess, something of a disappointment. But, as John was quick to point out, anything that helped the party go with a swing was all right by him.

Yet having demonstrated their readiness to accept a wide range of new material from the surrounding culture, the Gypsies' innate sense of conservatism rapidly reasserts itself. Thus, however congenial it may be as regards its subject matter, such material is not infrequently subjected to a process of attrition whereby the original character of the song may be entirely lost, leaving it virtually indistinguishable from material generated by the Gypsies themselves. In such cases, not only may the language of the song be simplified and any unnecessary poetic effects rejected, but even its formal structure may be abandoned and the narrative condensed to the point of obscurity. In other words, it is the underlying idea of the song rather than its outward expression which assumes the greater importance for the Gypsy singer. To take one example, the song known variously as 'The Game of Cards' or 'The Game of All Fours' seems to have made its first appearance on an 1839 broadside by George Walker of Durham and has since been noted on numerous occasions from the singing of both Gypsies and *Gaujos*. If the mainstream version obtained by Gardiner from William Randall of Hursley (Reeve) is compared with those given by the two Travellers, Wally Fuller (Kennedy, Folktracks 45–140) and Levi Smith (Yates, Topic 12T253) it will be seen that both the latter have not only contrived to lose much of the overt sexual symbolism forming the core of the original set, but that, at various points, the wording has become totally obscure. Mr Fuller's opening verse is also entirely out of place, belonging to that much travelled piece known to 'Western buffs' as 'The Streets of Laredo'.

This is not to say that Gypsies are incapable of returning sets conforming more or less to *Gaujo* expectations, as is the case with another variant of 'The Game of Cards' from the well-known Gypsy singer, Phoebe Smith of Woodbridge, Suffolk (Rod and Danny Stradling; Richards and Stubbs 1979, 107). Unaccountably, Mrs Smith gives the lady's place of birth as Glasgow but, as is often the case with her singing, her text is far more accessible to the *Gaujo* ear than is normally the case with most Gypsy singers. Indeed, not only does her command of her material set her apart from most other Travellers, but such is the unique quality of her delivery that it has been suggested that she may have been persuaded to alter her singing style in order to meet the expectations of certain collectors determined to 'discover' an English Jeanie Robertson. Thus Mike Yates, writing in *Traditional Music* (1977, 13):

> What fascinates me about Phoebe is not so much her repertoire – which is of great interest in itself and which is far larger than most collectors suspect – but her style and manner of singing. I have heard it suggested that when Hamish Henderson discovered Jeanie Robertson and played those first tapes to English and American collectors, some of those collectors then went out determined to find an English female singer of equal stature. The implication, of course, is that Phoebe Smith was that discovery and that she was asked, directly or indirectly, to alter her singing style, to slow down her pace, to emphasise certain notes in far greater detail etc. Some readers may dismiss this as rubbish; but it intrigues me that Phoebe is the only English singer that I have heard who sings in this manner. The other members of her family – sisters and brothers, including the Kent Gypsy, Charlie Scamp, who now lives in Faversham – that I have heard certainly sound no different from most other Gypsy singers.

Although the Gypsies' published repertoire is now heavily weighted in favour of borrowed material of one kind and another, code switching is still relatively rare. That is to say, only a tiny proportion of *published* sets have actually 'crossed the bridge' into the *Poggadi Chib*. 'In our Isles', wrote Sampson in 1928 (MacAlister 1928, 4–5),

> while one occasionally meets with attempts to supply Romani renderings to the original air of some popular song, such efforts are usually sporadic as they doubtless were also with Paspati's Tchinghianés. Only once, in the broken dialect of the Robinsons, have I heard from an English Gypsy the translation of an entire song . . . (text 163)

Kenrick, however, writing almost sixty years later, takes a somewhat different line:

> There are a few songs which seem to have been composed originally in Romani English – at least they are never sung in standard English. These include *I'm a Romani Rai* 'I'm a Romani Lord' and *Can You Rocker Romani* 'Can You Speak Romani'. The majority of songs in English Romani, however, are translations of common English folk-songs or music hall songs of the nineteenth century. (Acton and Kenrick 1985, 84)

This may well be so in Dr Kenrick's experience but, if the index to the present volume is any guide, is certainly not the case if published material alone is considered.

Although there is no direct evidence for this, there are also grounds for supposing that the conversion of mainstream material into Romani may be a relatively recent phenomenon, associated, perhaps, with the displacement of the older inflected language by the *Poggadi Chib*. It was Sapir, the great American linguist, who crystallized the notion that every language has its own particular flavour or 'cut', uniquely expressive of the culture which gave it birth, and, if this is so, then it would not seem unreasonable to suppose that the language and content of folk song, with their respective roots deep in the collective consciousness, are in some way inextricably linked. Thus Breandán Breathnach, commenting on the paucity of native Gaelic folk-song material to be found in the Hiberno-English repertoire, has suggested that, whilst national/linguistic barriers appear to offer no obstacle to the interchange of tunes, 'One may deduce a rule . . . that there is an innate relationship between folk song and language which inhibits adoption by way of translation.' In Ireland, he says, 'the decline of the language involved the rejection of the body of folk song which had its existence in it . . . Irish systems of versification scarcely surviving the first generations of speakers adopting the dominant culture' (Breathnach 1971, 33).

Even the often quite startling correspondences, both thematic and verbal, found in sets recovered in various parts of Europe have failed to convince students of that not inconsiderable body of oral literature, known in England as nursery rhymes, of the existence of a significant trade in such material between different speech communities. 'The Comparison of these collections with ours', says Lina Eckenstein in her comparative study of English, French and German texts (Eckenstein 1906), 'yields surprising results. Often the same thought is expressed in the same form of verse. Frequently the same proper names reappear in the same connection.' Yet, 'Judging from what we know of nursery rhymes and their appearance in print, the thought of a direct translation of rhyme in the bulk cannot be entertained.'

For James Orchard Halliwell, too, such correspondences could not be explained in terms of the free dissemination across linguistic boundaries of more or less established texts. Rather, it seemed to him that their origin must lie deep in the collective monolingual past of the various cultures in which they have been noted. Although 'we find the same trifles that erewhile lulled or amused the English infant are current in slightly varied forms throughout the North of Europe', he writes in his pioneering survey of 1849,

> we know that they have been sung in the northern countries for centuries, and there has been no modern outlet for their dissemination across the German Ocean. The most natural inference is to adopt the theory of a Teutonic origin and thus give to every child rhyme found in England and Sweden an immense antiquity.

For a song to find its way from one language into another would, therefore, seem almost inevitably to require a *conscious* act of translation. There are, it is true, certain notable exceptions to this rule – e.g. 'The Hunting of the Wren'[15] – but these are rare. For the most part, where songs have 'crossed the bridge' this has meant not only adopting the new language but acquiring, at the same time, the principal characteristics of the receiving tradition.

How much more difficult is the process of spontaneous translation likely to be when one of the two languages concerned is purely synthetic in character and the other analytic, as would have been the case with Romani and English. Sampson was to encounter this problem when working in prose. 'How often, in translating a Gypsy folk tale', he wrote, 'is one held up by the bald appearance of repetitions which, in the inflected original, seem proper and unobtrusive?' (Sampson 1928); and again,

> We have no word for the state or condition of being a cat . . . [whilst] in the Turkish Gypsy folk tale, the princess, who has been turned into a cat, complains 'miro zi kaliter kater matchkipé' – my heart darkened by this condition of being a cat. (Sampson 1897)

Sampson, it is true, does suggest that the song commencing 'Aai-dadi, da dublea, da-di!' (text 56) 'has apparently been subjected to the same process of bringing down to date which one observes in our English ballads and other traditional literature', adding that 'a few slight alterations would suffice to restore it to what was probably its original form'. By way of example, he goes on to say that the change of a few letters would be sufficient to convert the third line *or tuti'll be lino apré* into *o tu te vel lino apré*, and that the remainder of the song might be similarly treated. He is here, however, almost certainly in error. Mainstream oral literature is, in general, essentially stable in character and, whilst the same song may occur in a variety of forms, once these have become established, they are rarely subject to radical reform. This is particularly the case as regards language. Personal and place names may be changed and words, too, where these have been misunderstood or misheard, but the language itself is seldom 'brought down to date', except in those cases where a traditional song is used as a vehicle for the expression of a new thought.

The following cross-section of loan material includes items drawn both from the oral tradition and from literary sources. What is particularly noticeable is that, with the exception of 'The Hearty Poacher', none of the examples given have been recorded on more than one occasion or from more than one informant. Although it is perhaps unwise to generalize from so small a sample, it may be that, as the products of a more or less conscious act of creation on the part of a particular individual or group (as would certainly seem to be the case with texts 159, 161 and 165), they lack the feeling of common ownership attaching to other better represented texts.

> 159. If you diks up a funy'chel* that's bukalo and shilo
>   Lel lesti to a kitchema
>   Del les tatti-panni, levina
>   And when the loovo is saw jalled,
>   Go a-looring for bootidair.
>   (Anon; Merrick, *JFSS* 3 (1901), 110)

*A corruption of *Romani Chal*?

Merrick includes this English Gypsy paraphrase of the third verse of 'Captain Grant the Highwayman' in the course of a note on a mainstream version of the song which he had obtained from a Mr Hill some time during the first decade of the present century. He says nothing of its source other than that he had heard it sung by an old Gypsy woman some years earlier. Its appeal is obvious.

Captain Grant figures only in the one ballad and nothing seems to be known about him other than what the song itself has to tell. A number of sets have been recovered from the oral tradition though, somewhat surprisingly, given its subject matter, the great majority of these appear to date from around the turn of the twentieth century. Among other sources, we may mention Gilchrist, Carey, Williams, Gardiner, Hammond and Sharp – from the singing of Charles Benfield in September 1909:

My name is Captain Grant, I am bound for to say.
I'm one of those bold heroes all on the King's highway.
With my brace of loaded pistols and my steady broadsword,
Oh! Stand and deliver! It is always the word.

To do a dirty action, I always did scorn.
In robbing of the rich, I thought it was no harm.
With the gold and the jewels I always did secure,
One half I gave myself and the other gave the poor.

If I meets with a traveller that's hungry and dry,
I'll take him to some ale-house and his wants I will supply.
With good ale, wine and brandy, boys, till I spend all my store.
When my money is all gone, I'll boldly rob for more.

To Edinburgh jail they marched me along
And there I did remain till my trial it did come on.
For shooting at the King I was then condemned to die;
But I never had no hand in that same robbery.

Out of Edinburgh jail then I made my way out
And those who did oppose me, I put them to the rout.
With my bars and iron bolts I knocked the sentry down
And I made my escape out of Edinburgh town.

Out of Edinburgh jail then I made my way good
And I took up my lodgings in the centre of a wood.
Until some wicked woman, she did me betray
And she had me surrounded as sleeping I did lay.

I flew to my arms but my powder being wet
And to my sad misfortune, I found that I was beat.
And to my sad misfortune, I gave myself up
To that noted hero called Natty-Take-Up.

To Edinburgh jail then they marched me again
And there I did remain in sorrow, grief and pain.
God bless my wife and family and may they never want
And the Lord have mercy on my soul, cries the bold Captain Grant.

The song has also been recovered in a reduced form from the singing of an English Traveller, Nelson Ridley (MacColl and Seeger 1977, 282).

~

160. Grib to your naiskel, my beenship kinchen,
     Grib to your naiskel till the beerie bings anee;
     You'll feek a flattrin in a wee mahzie
     If you'll grib to your naiskel till the beerie bings anee.
         (Cathi Higgins (née Stewart);
         MacColl and Seeger 1986, 146)

This popular dandling song, given here by Cathi Higgins (née Stewart), seems first to have appeared in print in Fordyce's *Newcastle Song Book* of 1842, where it forms the refrain of a five-verse set by William Watson called 'The Little Fishy'. Watson's verses, which seem not to have attained the same degree of popularity as their chorus, begin:

Come here, my little Jackey,
Now I've smoked my backey,
Let's have a bit of crackey
Till the boat comes in.

Dance to thy daddy, sing to thy mammy,
Dance to thy daddy, to thy mammy sing.
Thou shalt have a fishy on a little dishy,
Thou shalt have a fishy when the boat comes in.

This refrain, however, seems to have been adapted from earlier material as, for example, 'Sing to your mammy, my little lammy' (*Vocal Harmony*, c.1806). Watson's verses, too, are not wholly his own but include a stanza borrowed from 'The Keel Road'. They are mostly concerned with the mother, her thoughts on drink and her husband. (For these and further variants see Opie 1992, 140–1.)

~

161. Kuškō divés 'kedivés tuménī!
     Den xåbén ī mulénī!
     'Yam kuškibén akái
     Bērš 'kedivés.
         (Sampson 1926, iv, 232)

The foregoing is a Welsh gypsy rendering of one of a number of similar verses attached to the celebration of Hallowe'en and, more properly, All Souls' Eve. In its original Welsh form it runs as follows:

Dydd da i chwi heddyw!
Bwyd cenad y meirw!
Da gês i yma
Blwyddyn i heddyw.

Good day to you this day!
(Give me the) food of the messenger of the dead!
I was well treated here
A year ago today.

According to the custom, known in north Wales as *Hel bwyd Cenad y meirw* (collecting the food of the messenger of the dead) – Jones (1930, 152) suggests 'the food of the letting loose of the dead' – groups of men, women and children would wander from house to house seeking alms in the form of nuts, fruit and, originally, flat cakes or bread.

Sampson makes no mention of the source of his verse, but for further examples of related Welsh texts see pp.133ff. of Owen's *Welsh Folk Customs* and *Bygones* for 18 November 1885 and 13 November 1895.

~

162. My manishi's rumpy and tumpy,
Raw-boned, farn-teckled* and tall,
And above all the skukr** dickin manishis e'er i saw,
She beats the old ruffie and all.
Wi' my twang, twang, twang, fal di di do,
Wi' my twang, twang, twang, fal dal de,
Wi' my hub di bubbi, fal di do,
Richt fal dal dal doodle dal de.
(M'Cormick 1906, 301)

*Fern-tickled = freckled. See Jameson's *Etymological Dictionary of the Scottish Language* (1808–25).
**In MacAlister's *Secret Languages of Ireland* (1976 edn., 265), we find *sukr, suka, skukar* = 'five'. This is surely a misprint or a mishearing of 'fine'. *Skukar* or *shukar* is the Romani *shukár* which, in the English dialect, as recorded by Smart and Crofton (1875, 135), seems latterly to have been used only adverbially. Other examples of its use in Scotto-Romani/Tinklers' Cant as an all-purpose positive epithet include *shukar davies*, a good or sunshiny day; *shukar mas* fat meat; *shukar castie*, a good stick (M'Cormick 1906); and *shuker shauchi*, a good coat (Carmichael). For 'fine', MacAlister gives the Romani *Buri/bura*.

M'Cormick obtained this version of the opening stanza of the song commonly known as 'Dick Darby the Cobbler' from a group of Travellers of the MacMillan family, then in Galloway. It is clear from what he says that it formed part of a sequence which was both sung and 'acted' by his young informant, although exactly what he meant by this is unclear. Kovalcsik, in her study of Vlax Gypsy song (1985), notes that 'a performer often acts out the words (of a song) or the part which is left out of it. At other times, the movement may be substituted for the actual words.' She does not, however, offer any explanation of this, and my own feeling is that we have here nothing more than an 'action song' of a type common enough in these islands and elsewhere.

The 'Strodgribber' belongs to a widely dispersed group of songs whose immediate progenitor, 'My God How the Money Rolls in', is said to be 'a descendant twice, thrice removed from an English Commonwealth song, "Old Hewson the Cobbler", sung about a Cromwellian officer who eventually sat in judgment at the trial of Charles the First' (Cray 1969, 222).

Although he was, indeed, made the subject of a number of contemporary satirical verses, in referring songs of the Dick Darby type to 'Old Hewson', both Cray (ibid.) and MacColl and Seeger (1977, 162) appear to rely entirely on a brief note in James Dick's *Songs of Robert Burns* of 1903 (Dick, 1962 edn, 415). According to the latter, the song makes its first appearance on p.338 of the *Vocal Miscellany*, published in Dublin in 1738. A thorough search of both the Dublin and London editions of this work has, however, drawn a complete blank.

Dick also notes that many such 'scurrilous and indecent verses' are to be found in various Restoration song books but, whilst the *indicia* 'to the tune of Old Hewson the Cobbler' are by no means rare, the song itself continues to elude capture.

In Chappell there is an air entitled 'My Name Is Old Hewson the Cobbler' with a note to the effect that it was included in *The Jovial Crew* and *The Grub Street Opera* as early as 1731 (Chappell 1858–9, 451), and it is interesting to note that there is a clear resemblance between it and the melody advanced by Tommy Makem in his version of 'Dick Darby' ('The Lark in the Morning', TRADITION 1004), as reproduced in *Sing Out* XI, 2 (April–May 1961). We should, however, be wary of reading too much into this. The fact that two songs share the same air cannot of itself be taken as evidence of kinship. Greig's version of the song is, for example, sung to the Scots air, 'The Muckin' o' Geordie's Byre', as, indeed, is the wholly unrelated 'Lizzie Lindsay' (Bronson 1959–72, iv, 365).

Although one cannot entirely discount the possibility that songs of the Dick Derby type may ultimately derive from a mid-seventeenth-century political satire, it is perhaps more likely that words specific to Hewson were simply grafted on to an existing stock of verses whose peculiarly flexible format readily lent itself to such usage. It is a process common enough with the cruder type of political satire and one which, judging by the range and durabilty of the Dick Darby model, has been significant in ensuring its continuing popularity. In more recent sets, for example, the dyke-delvers, sheep stealers, carders, spinners and cobblers of earlier variants are replaced, *inter alia*, by a lawyer, a laundry worker and a tram driver. That verses of a similar type were current at least as early as the Restoration is apparent from the following lines, in English Cant, from a black letter broadside in the Bagford Collection, printed in London for W. Thackeray, T. Passenger and W. Whitwood in *c.*1671, and called 'The Joviall Crew, or Beggars Bush':

> A Craver my Father,
> A Maunder my Mother,
> A Filer my Sister, a Filcher my Brother,
> A Canter my Unckle,
> That car'd not for Pelfe, [ill-gotten money]
> A Lifter my Aunt, a Begger myselfe.

Whatever the circumstances surrounding their early development, songs of the Dick Darby type were to become extremely popular in both Britain and America, and a number of sets have been recovered from the singing of Traveller informants (e.g. Margaret Mac Phee, MacColl and Seeger 1977, 162). Speaking of the song in its transatlantic form, Cray (1969, 127) takes the view that 'this urban ditty can ultimately be traced to an Irish and Scottish Tinkers' song the first stanza of which is:

> My father was hanged for sheep stealing,
> My mother was burnt for a witch,
> My sister's a bawdy-house keeper
> And I am a son-of-a-bitch.'

'The bawdy parent text', he goes on to say, 'seems to have reached American shores in its unexpurgated form, but has not flourished. "My Father", meanwhile, crops up everywhere, carolled to the innocent melody of "My Bonny Lies Over the Ocean".' For a detailed discussion of American sets and sources see Cray (1969, 222ff.).

~

> 163. A pūv pōrdō o' Romni chels, sor adré a drom,
> Sor so kâlo and chiklo, oh!
> Talé wel'd a râni, rividi adré or'ni,
> To jas with the nashin' Romni chelâ!

Songs from the Mainstream

Chorus: The Romni chelâ,
The Romni chelâ,
To jas with the nashin' Romni-chelâ!*

Yoi's rom wel'd keri dūi panj o' râti,
And puch'd for his romadi pōrno, oh!
The rakli puker'd a tachō lav:
Yoi'd jas'd with the nashin' Romni-chelâ! – etc. – etc.

'Saliwardo mandi, mandi's purro grai,
Saliwardo mandi's bitto yek;
Mandi aáwali** kister kai chōr ach apré,
To lach the nashin' Romni-chelâ'. – etc.

'The waver râti yoi suter'd adré
A koshko pōryo wudress, oh!
Kanna sig râti yoi'll jâ to sutta
Adré a shilini granzi, oh! – etc.

'So did lesti*** muk yov's kērs ānd pūvs?
So did lesti muk yov's chavis, oh?
So did lesti muk yov's romado mush
To jas with the nashin' Romni-chelâ?' – etc.

Sossi mandi kessers for my kērs and pūvs!
Sossi mandi kessers for my chavis, oh!
Sossi mandi kessers for my romado mush!
Mandi'll jas with the nashin' Romni-chelâ!' – etc.
(Lias Robinson; Sampson 1891, 84)

*Sampson also heard 'chels' given here instead of 'chelâ'.
**The Sampson-Robinsons, to whom Lias belonged, were in the habit of forming the future tense by means of the affirmative, aâwali, particularly when added emphasis was required.
***The family also invariably used lesti for tutti and lesti's or yov's for tutti's or tiro. The same usage is also noted by Black in his edition of Sinclair's American Romani vocabulary, published in the Gypsy Lore Society Journal for October 1915, e.g. lestes a keren a činemangero = you are writing a letter; kusto sarla, (how does) leste ker todivis = good morning, how do you do, today?

Sampson tells us that he knew of the existence of this song some time before he eventually obtained the full text. He had, he says, heard portions of it sung by various Gypsies – including the entire chorus from one 'Booey' Boswell – a fact which led him to suppose that he had, at last, stumbled upon 'an original Romani composition of some length'. Tracing it to its source, however, he found that it had been made by a Traveller named Lias

417

Robinson (see note accompanying text 118) from an English set heard in a country alehouse. Lias, together with his three brothers, had 'turned it into Romanes one Christmas for the amusement of the family circle' – 'A poor ignorant thing as we put to pieces ourselves', as his brother, Airos said.

'It is', says Sampson, 'extremely interesting as an example of spontaneous and unaided translation by an English Gypsy'; and, indeed, one cannot help remarking upon its closeness to the original English version which Robinson was also able to supply:

> A band of Gypsies, all in a road, (row?)
> All so black and brawny,* oh! (bonny, oh)
> Away come a lady, all dressed in silk,
> To follow the roving Gypsies, oh!
>
> Her husband came home at ten o'clock of night,
> And asked for his lady fair, oh!
> The servants informed him very soon,
> She had gone with the roving Gypsies, oh!
>
> 'Saddle to me my bonny grey mare,
> Saddle to me my pony, oh!
> I will go where the green grass grow
> To find out the roving Gypsies, oh!
>
> 'Last night she slept in a fine feather bed
> And blankets by 'bonnins',** oh!
> Tonight she sleeps in a cold shed barn
> Through following the roving Gypsies, oh!
>
> 'Why did you leave your houses and your lands?
> Why did you leave your babies, oh?
> Why did you leave your decent married man,
> To follow the roving Gypsies, oh?'
>
> 'What cares I for my houses and my lands?
> What cares I for my babies, oh!
> What cares I for my decent married man?
> I will go with the roving Gypsies, oh!

*The word 'brawny' here seems to be Lias's own rendering of the more usual 'bonny'; his brother, Airos, apparently favoured 'boney'.
**A Cant term signifying 'plenty' or 'abundance'.

Lias's song is, as Sampson was later to learn, simply a variant of the ubiquitous 'Gypsy Laddie' or 'Ballad of Johnnie Faa' (Child and Kiltredge

1882–9, 200), now inextricably linked with the supposed abduction/ elopement of Lady Cassilis by way of the Gypsy steps across the Doon at Maybole. Although it is almost certainly Scottish in origin, the earliest surviving text is an English broadside set (*Roxburghe Ballads* iii, 685) known as 'The Gypsie Loddy' and with a conjectural date of 1720.

The Scots ballad seems first to have appeared in print in the fourth volume of Ramsay's *Tea-Table Miscellany* in an edition now entirely lost (1740). Yet despite its later appearance, it was this set which took the lead, being repeated in a number of subsequent collections together with certain variations, in Child's words, both traditional and arbitrary. (For a detailed account of early English, Scottish and American sources and variants, see Child and Kiltredge 1965 edn., 61ff.).

Over the years, the song has gained wide currency on both sides of the Atlantic – the Vaughan Williams Memorial Library contains upwards of 120 listings – and is also known in a variety of other forms such as 'The Ploughboy Laddie', 'The Cobbler Laddie' and 'The Brewer Laddie' (see, for example, Ord's *Bothy Songs and Ballads*). Baring-Gould also includes a set from north Devon which forms the sequel to the related story of a reluctant Gypsy girl married to a wealthy nobleman (1889–91, no. 50). Hearing her people singing at the castle gate, she flies with them, is pursued and killed. It is the same theme, albeit with a less dramatic denouement, to which Sampson turns in his 'Gypsy Ballad' published in the *Eagle* (16 (1887), 28–33), and reproduced in the introduction to the present volume.

The song is also well represented in Ireland where it is known variously as 'The Brown Eyed Gypsies', 'Seven Yellow Gypsies', 'The Raggle-Taggle Gypsies' and, most commonly, 'The Dark Eyed Gypsy'. Although Child includes a set from County Meath, dated approximately 1860 (Child and Kiltredge 1965 edn, 71), the task of fixing its Irish provenance has, however, in recent years, become more difficult owing to the popularity of a modern rewrite by Leo Maguire called 'The Whistling Gypsy'. Even those older informants who, like Dennis Healey of Glendaloch, once preferred the older form now seem to opt for the new or mix the two together. It seems likely, however, that it came to Ireland on broadsheets and was certainly disseminated there in that form. It has been widely noted and the majority of sets obtained from the oral tradition accord well with printed originals.

Not unnaturally, it has become something of a favourite among Travellers. The following is one of two variants from the singing of John Reilly, a Roscommon Traveller who died in poverty some years ago (*The Bonny Green Tree: Songs of an Irish Traveller*).

There was three of the Gypsies came to our hall door,
They came brave an' bol-del-o
But there's one sung high and the other sung low
And the lady sung 'the Raggle-Taggle Gypsy-o'.

It was upstairs, downstairs, the lady ran.
She took off her silks so fine and put on a dress of leather-o
And it was the cry all around our door,
'She's away with the Raggle-Taggle Gypsy-o!'

It was late last night when the Lord came in,
Enquiring for his lady-o.
And the servin' girls took from hand to hand,
'She's away with the Raggle-Taggle Gypsy-o!'

'You come saddle for me my milk-white steed,
My bay one is not speedy-o
And sure I'll ride and I'll seek my bride
That's away with the Raggle-Taggle Gypsy-o.'

O, for he rode east and he rode west,
Half the south and the east also,
Until he rode to the wide open field
And there he spied, was his darling-o.

Saying: 'are you forseekin' your house or land?
Are you forseekin' your money-o?
Are you forseekin' your own wedded lord
An' your goin' with the Raggle-Taggle Gypsy-o?'

'What do I care for my house or land?
Neither for my money-o,
Or what do I care for my own wedded lord?
I am goin' with my Raggle-Taggle Gypsy-o!'

'It was e'er last (night) you'd a goose-feather bed
With the sheets pulled down so comely-o,
But tonight you'll lie in the cold open field
All along with the Raggle-Taggle Gypsy-o.'

'What do I care for my goose-feather bed
With the sheets pulled down so comely-o?
But tonight I'll lie on a cold barren floor
All along with my Raggle-Taggle Gypsy-o.'

Sayin': 'you rode high when I rode low,
You rode woods and valleys-o.
But I'd rather get a kiss of the yalla Gypsy's lips
O than all lor' cash's o' money-o!'

Two further versions from the singing of Irish Travellers are to be found on Folktracks 168. Listed respectively as 'The Dark Eyed Gypsies' and 'Seven Little Gypsies', they are sung by Christy Purcell and Paddy Doran and were recorded in Belfast in July 1952.

On the British side of the Irish Sea, Charlotte Burne heard 'The Gypsy Laddie' sung by Gypsy children (Whartons?) in Shropshire over 100 years ago, as did Walter Starkie (from the Coopers) whilst a student at Shrewsbury. Indeed, so taken was he with the song that it became what he liked to call his 'signature tune' and provided the title for perhaps his best-known work. Starkie also used to tell how, whilst wandering the fairs of Donegal and Cork with various Travellers of his acquaintance, he was cursed by one of the Coffeys. He was, he says, somewhat alarmed by the experience until he met with one of the rival family of Burns who gave him a tune by way of antidote; the tune in question being a close variant of that used by John Reilly for his setting of 'The Raggle-Taggle Gypsies'.

More recently, MacColl and Seeger have included a set from the singing of Belle Stewart in *Till Doomsday in the Afternoon* (1986, 177) – their account of the Scottish Traveller family, the Stewarts of Blair. It was also recorded in a somewhat attenuated form by Mrs Carolyne Hughes, the 'Queen of the Dorset Gypsies', at her home in Blandford in 1968 (Folktracks 043).

Of particular interest, however, is the following fragment which Thompson obtained from one of the granddaughters of Ambrose Smith/ Reynolds, the original of Borrow's Jasper.

> 164. So did you muk my curi old dai
> Jâ with the rasrai, sa adré the drum,
> Sa so kâlo and ciklo?
> Nas the cavis from the drum.
> Till the rasrai jâ's out of the drum.
> Garav the cavis so kâlo and misto.
> (Thompson 1909, 158)

In a brief note, the editor suggests that it might either refer to the un-welcome visit of a Crabb or Baird or to the parson's elopement, incognito (*sa kalo and ciklo*), with the old lady. Although the latter suggestion was no doubt made tongue in cheek, it nevertheless calls to mind an incident mentioned by Irving Brown in chapter 6 of his *Gypsy Fires in America* (Brown 1924, 168):

> Fontella Lovell related how an aunt of hers had fallen in love with a preacher man in the *Puro Tem* (the Old Country); and in spite of her father's threats to kill her if she married a *Gaujo*, and in spite of the determination of the *rasai*'s congregation to have him expelled from the church if he took a heathen to wed, they had run off together, the preacher himself performing his own ceremony when the one in the next town had turned them away.
>
> 'Well', concluded Fontella, 'it was good in the sight of my dearie *Duvel* (The Lord), as my dear aunt used to say. They were happy 'til he died, though he didn't like to have her *dukker* (tell fortunes), and the life on the roads was hard on him, he was so soft . . . But when she saw the rough life was killing him, she'd beg him to settle down, though a house would 'a' choked her; but he'd say, "didn't The Lord tell his followers to go their way without purse or shoes, to bless them as gave, and never think about food nor dress, for seein' my dearie *Duvel* feeds the birds and covers the good green earth with grass and flowers." But I'm thinkin' they'd 'a' died more 'n once if she hadn't *chord* a chicken now and then and told him the farmers had give' it to her.'

A more likely explanation, however, is that text 164 represents a fusion of two entirely separate elements. The first, comprising lines 1, 2 and 3 and possibly the second half of line 6, would appear to contain a confused reference to the first verse and the opening line of the fifth of Robinson's telling of 'The Gypsy Laddie', whilst the second, comprising lines 4, 5 and 6, seems to belong to that class of sung warning exemplified by texts 34–7.

Apart from Robinson's set, the foregoing fragment, if such it be, represents the only recorded version of the song in the *Poggadi Chib*. Sir Donald MacAlister, however, includes a metrical paraphrase among a number of Welsh *Romani Versions*, gathered together 'at the instance of certain colleagues who are pleased to think that they may afford entertainment to students of British Romani' (MacAlister 1928, 28). In the same publication, he also offers a Welsh Gypsy rendering of Buchan's 'The Gypsy's Song to the Lady Cassilis' (ibid., 22) and the anonymous 'Johnie Faa' (p.24). The material on which he based the first of these appears to have been drawn mainly from Cecil Sharp (MSS 2308/2103), but with elements of the 'Draggle Tail Gypsies' from MSS 264/373.

O Shanede Kâlé

Trin Kâlé 'chen 'lan i Resko hudár,
Gyavén godliása, gyavén shukár;

I Râni beshél komoryáti ratí,
Bilavél sar o iv Râniáko 'zi.

'Jâ gudlés, 'jâ ruchés, Kâlé gyavén,
Te sig lake swâi talé perén;
Pi kishani shuba chivél talé,
Pe vangushtriá, ta sâ pe prekhté.

Tardél chiokhá, ke azén la opré,
I sherne chaméste si kedé;
Jal pes 'pre dromésti sâ piranlí,
Avriál 'r'i bavál ta 'r'o shil si-lí.

Chiv beshto opré mo pârno grai,
And mangi mo besho khuro tai;
Kistá te rhodá miri biadí,
Naklí i shanede Kalénsa si.

Kistiás 'doi opré, kistiás 'koi talé,
Kistiás 'rol veshá ta taná rukané,
Poste 'vyas ki pire bukhle puvyá,
Akái dikás yov pe Râni á.

So kel tut te mukés tiro ker ta sâ,
Te sunakeiéske trominyá?
So kel tut te mukés to nevó biadó?
I shanede Kâlé palyerésa, ho?

So keserá me keréski ta sâ?
So keserá trominyéngi, hâ?
So keserá me roméski mai?
Java man i shanede Kâlénsa tai.

The Raggle-Taggle Gypsies O

Three Gypsies stood at the castle gate,
They sang so high, they sang so low;
The Lady sate in her chamber late,
Her heart it melted away like snow.

They sang so sweet, they sang so shrill,
That fast her tears began to flow,
And she laid down her silken gown,
Her golden rings and all her show.

She plucked off her high-heeled shoes,
A' made of Spanish leather, o.
She would in the street with her bare bare feet,
All out in the wind and weather, o.

O saddle to me my milk-white steed,
And go and fetch me my pony, o?
That I may ride and seek my bride,
Who is gone with the Raggle-Taggle Gypsies, o.

O he rode high, and he rode low,
He rode through woods and copses, o,
Until he came to an open field,
And there he espied his lady, o.

What makes you leave your house and land,
Your golden treasures to forego?
What makes you leave your new-wedded lord,
To follow the Raggle-Taggle Gypsies, o?

What care I for my house and my land?
What care I for my treasure, o?
What care I for my new-wedded lord?
I'm off with the Raggle-Taggle Gypsies, o!

It will be noticed that neither Robinson nor MacAlister mentions the errant wife by name, and this is also true of most of the earliest surviving texts of the song. The story identifying her with the wife of the sixth Earl of Cassilis seems to have originated in Ayrshire. Indeed, according to Child, it was Burns himself who first insisted on introducing the lady's name into a reprint of Ramsay's basic text (*Johnson's Museum*, 1785), together with a note that 'neighbouring tradition strongly vouches for the truth of this story'. Thereafter, the tale, for such it must be, was repeated, with variations, by, among others, Finlay (1911, ii, 35), *Scots Magazine* (lxxx, 306) and *The Musical Museum* (iv, 217, 1853) and seems later to have been accepted without question by Groome in 1880.

According to the story, the sixth Earl of Cassilis took to wife one Jean Hamilton, a lady whose name had previously been linked with that of a certain Sir John Faa of Dunbar. Some years later, the earl being absent, Sir John, disguised as a Gypsy and accompanied by others of that race, presented himself at the castle gate and persuaded or forced the lady to fly with him. The earl, returning in the nick of time, gave chase and, securing the entire party, hanged them from the 'Dule tree', 'a most umbrageous plane' which stood upon a mound before the castle. His wife he thereafter confined in a tower, built for the purpose at Maybole, 'denying her both his bed and board'.

In a number of accounts it is said that the abduction took place while Cassilis was attending the Assembly of Divines at Westminster. This, however, took place in September 1643, some nine months after his wife's death in December 1642. Again, at the time of her abduction she is said to have had two children whom she abandoned in her flight; yet, according to *The Historical Account of the Noble Family of Kennedy* (Edinburgh, 1849, p.44), their marriage produced four children. It is difficult to see how the second pair might have been conceived if, following her return, she was ever after denied her husband's bed.

More importantly, perhaps, in two letters, written immediately after her death, the earl speaks of his wife as a sober and religious woman, calling her his 'dear friend and beloved yoke-fellow' and his 'dear bed-fellow' (Patterson 1846–7, i, 13) – hardly the language of an estranged cuckold. See also John Mackay Wilson's *Historical, Traditionary and Imaginative Tales of the Borders* (1, 161–8; 2, 233–6, 312–16).

But how could this confusion have arisen? MacMath suggests that it is simply the result of a misreading of 'Cassilis' for 'Castle', as, for example, in the opening line 'The Gypsies came to the castle gate' (*SES*, ii, 346) and, indeed, there is evidence of a good deal of confusion on this point in those texts surviving from the eighteenth and early nineteenth centuries. In Ramsay's set the unfortunate husband is given no name at all, whilst in MacTaggart's *Scottish Gallovidian Encyclopaedia* (1824, 284) he is 'Cassle', and in Margaret Reburn's telling (Child and Kiltredge 1965 edn, 71) 'Cashan'. More to the point, perhaps, in the earliest of these – the Roxburghe broadside – he is portrayed as the 'Earl of Castle'. Even if assonance alone is insufficient to account for the laird's inclusion in later texts, it would almost certainly have been so when underpinned by a tailor-made tradition of the type then current in his native county. (For MacMath, see Child and Kiltredge 1882–9, no. 200).

As regards the Faa connection, it was again MacMath who first drew attention to the fact that the seventh earl, some time before the year 1700, took as his second wife Mary Foix, also pronounced Faux (see Crawford's *Peerage*, 1716, p.76). Given that his mother, the wife of the sixth earl, bore the name Jean, it is not difficult to see how in some versions of the song, the lady came to be known as Jeanie Faa. Thus, in Finlay:

> 'Come with me, my bonnie Jeanie Faa,
> Oh, come with me my dearie;
> For I do swear by the head o' my spear,
> Thy gude lord'll nae mair come near thee.'

From this point the involvement of the Gypsy Johnny Faa is but a short step. Indeed, it becomes almost inevitable when we recall that the name Faa or Faw was at one time so common among the Scottish Gypsies that it came to be used as a cognomen for the race as a whole.

Although a John and a Patrick Faw are mentioned in the Great Seal of Scotland as holding land in Lothian in 1507, there is no reference to their race or origin. The name is first used in connection with the Gypsies in the Council Register of Aberdeen for 22 January 1530, where we find the servants of one George Faw of that race indicted for theft. Thereafter, the family fortunes seem to have been somewhat mixed. In a document issued under the Privy Seal and dated February 1540, for example, James V seems to have entered into what amounts to a treaty *inter pares* whereby John Faa's right and title as Lord and Earl of Little Egypt were recognized in full. From this paper it is also clear that letters had earlier issued instructing the king's officers to assist him 'in execution of justice upon his company and folks, conform to the laws of Egypt, and in punishing of all them that rebels against him'. Yet, in the following year, by an Act of the Lords of Council, dated 6 June, all Egyptians were required to quit the kingdom within thirty days on pain of death 'notwithstanding any other letters or privileges granted them by the King, His Grace having discharged the same'. Thereafter, despite a second 'treaty' of 1553, neither the Gypsies in general nor the Faas themselves were ever to regain their once favoured status.

By an Act of 1609 they were once again banished *en masse*, and on 31 July 1611, one Johnny (alias Willie) Faa, together with three others of that name, was sentenced to hang for breaking this embargo. Again, on 25 January 1615, a man was delated for the 'harbouring of Egyptians' and especially one Johnny Fall, 'a notorious Egyptian and chieftain of that unhappy sort of people', whilst on 24 July 1616, Johnny Faa, 'Egyptian', his son and two others were condemned to hang for 'contemptuous repairing to the country and abiding there'.

There then followed a succession of similarly distressing actions culminating in the death sentence passed on 'Captain' Johnnie Faa and seven others on 24 January 1624. On the fifth day following, the 29th, his widow, Helen, and ten others were sentenced to be drowned, but being merely children, pregnant women and nursing mothers, their sentence was commuted to one of banishment (see Pitcairn's *Criminal Trials*, iii, 201 and *passim*; *Acts of the Parliaments of Scotland*, iv, 440; W. E. A. Axon, 'Laws Relating to the Gypsies' (in Andrews 1897, 165–78)); and MacRitchie 1894, *passim*).

There can be little doubt that the suppression of 'Captain' Faa and his followers in 1624 caused something of a stir, and it is perhaps significant

426

that it was around this time that, according to Child, the ballad of Johnnie Faa may have originated. It is certainly the case that, as with Dick Turpin in England, Twm Siôn Cati in Wales and other such popular heros, numerous exploits were attributed to him with little regard for factual accuracy. Scott, for example, had a version of Captain Carr in which the action was transferred to Ayrshire and the incendiarist's name changed to Johnnie Faa (Sharp's *Ballad Book*, ed. Lang (1850), 142–54). It is, however, most unlikely that he could have played any part in the abduction of Lady Cassilis – real or imagined – as she would have been but seventeen and childless at the time of his death.

The following Romani rendering of the ballad of Johnny Faa is by Sir Donald MacAlister of Tarbert (1928, 28). His source text appears to have been drawn from James Johnson's *Scots Musical Museum* of 1788 (2, 189):

Joni Faa

Ki me Resko hudár o Kâlé 'vilé,
Aua dordi! Gudlés giavénas;
'Jâ gudlí ta sherní lendi sas i gilí,
Te talé raikni Râni avélas.

Shukár yoi avéla o podos talé,
Sâ o rakia 'lan lati piréna;
Ojâ kekar o rúaikano mui dién
Râniá o Kâlé chovekh 'réna.

'Av tu mansa, Rânía,' penél Joni Faa,
'Av tu mansa, te 'ves miri romi;
Sovekh'ráva 'pre me khenliáko trushúl,
Te to Rai na 'vél tusa kekkómi.'

Givésko mâró del yoi len te khân,
Tato gudlo mâró den yon lati;
Del yoi pâple chomóni but-but fededer –
I vangúshtri te 'yas vangushtáte.

'Anjer mande mi parrani plashta avrí,
Bâro diklo and man rivimésti.
Ta, te sâ me siménsi mârní chidilé,
Jâs me pala me Kâlé chavésti.

'Vaver rat aré kovle vodrésti sovós,
Kai mo Rai poshe mandi sovélas;

Me sová 're gâjéske granzáti 'ke-rát,
Te- 'vel mangi so mangi avélas.'

'Me vodréski av tuya,' penél Joni Faa,
'Me vodréski av tuya, mi romi;
Sovekh'ráva 'pre me khenliáki trushúl,
Te to Rai na 'vel tusa kekkómi.'

'Java man, Joni Faa, poshe tut' te sováv,
Java mangi te 'va tiri romi;
Sovekh'rá 'pre bavyáki patrín 're mo vast
Te mo Rai na 'vel mansa kekkómi.

'Aré miri ganí tatyeráv Joni Faa.
Tatyeráva les, shom leski romi'
Me-lel yov varesó ka mi kishti pandél.
Miro Rai na 'vel mansa kekkómi.'

Ake rati, o Rai pe keréski 'viás,
Sig puchtás trushal peske Rânyáti;
Ta yek t'i vavér rakiénde lav dyas:
'Gyas i Kâlé chavésa 'ke-ráti.'

'Chiv o beshto 'p'o grai, 'pre mo kâlo tamló,
Chiv o beshto 'pre leste, kistáva;
Manke khâva me, manke sováva me tai,
Te rhodáva miri râni me java.'

'Shamas desh-ta-panch murshkane Romani-chél,
Kek na raikne-moskré shamas 'maia;
Oke 'mé trushal yek râniáti kurdé,
Trushal tus', raikni blajvani Chaia!'

The Gypsies cam to our gude lord's yett,
And wow but they sang sweetly;
They sang sae sweet and sae very complete,
That doun cam our fair lady.

And she cam tripping down the stair,
And all her maids before her;
As sune as they saw her weel-faured face
They wist the glamourye ower her.

'O come with me,' says Johnie Faa,
'O come with me, my dearie,
For I vow and I swear by the hilt o' my sword,
That your lord shall nae mair come near ye!'

Then she gied them the gude wheat bread,
And they ga'e her the ginger'
But she gied them a far better thing,
The goud ring off her finger.

'Gae tak frae me this gay mantill,
And bring tae me a plaidie;
For if kith and kin and a' had sworn,
I'll follow the Gypsy laddie.'

'Yestreen I lay in a weel-made bed,
Wi' my gude lord beside;
This night I'll lie in a tenant's barn,
Whatever shall betide.'

'Come to your bed,' says Johnie Faa,
'Come to your bed, my dearie;
For I vow and I swear by the hilt o' my sword,
That your lord shall nae mair come near ye.'

'I'll go to bed to my Johnie Faa,
I'll go to bed to my dearie;
For I vow and I swear by the fan in my hand,
That my lord shall nae mair come near.'

'I'll mak' a hap to my Johnie Faa,
I'll mak' a hap to my dearie;
But he's got a' the sash gaes round,
And my lord shall nae mair come near me.'

And when our lord cam' hame at e'en,
And speired for his fair lady,
The t'ane she cried, and the other replied:
'She's awa' wi' the Gypsy Laddie.'

'Gae saddle tae me the black black steed,
Gae saddle and mak' him ready;
Before that either eat or sleep,
I'll gae seek my fair lady.'

'And we were fifteen weel-made men,
Although we were nae bonnie;
And we were a' put down for ane,
A fair young wanton lady.'

Despite the evident popularity of the abduction motif, there is no evidence to suggest that British Gypsies ever engaged in this type of activity. The travelling life would seem to have been hard enough without the added burden of an unwilling or, at best, ill-equipped guest and, apart from ransom, which does not seem to have been a factor in the best-documented cases, one cannot see what possible gain there would be for the perpetrators (Hugh Davis, in Masefield's story of the same name, was apparently taken for his lock of red hair – according to Leland, a charm much favoured by women anxious to ensure a successful pregnancy – but a few shillings would surely have secured the prize with far less trouble). Yet the rumours persist. Robert Southwell, the poet and Jesuit martyr (1560–95), is said to have been among their first victims, whilst the Latin grammarian Thomas Ruddiman (1674–1757) claimed to have been 'plundered and stripped at a place called Starbrigs by a band of Gypsies' whilst on his way from Banffshire to Aberdeen University at the age of sixteen. Lord Chief Justice Popham (1531?–1607) is also said to have been stolen by the Gypsies as a child, but the story has been discounted and the cabalistic signs with which they are said to have marked him, 'as graziers brand the lamb they fatten for slaughter', dismissed as nothing but a tattoo. The political economist Adam Smith also claimed to have suffered a similar fate, but his story, too, has been discredited (Scott mentions this in a footnote to chapter 13 of *Guy Mannering* but suggests that Smith remained captive for no more than a few hours).

But perhaps the best known of all alleged abductions was that involving Elizabeth Canning, an eighteen-year-old domestic servant of Aldermanbury. Canning disappeared for four weeks between New Year's Day and 29 January 1753, claiming on her return that she had been abducted by the Gypsies. She had, she said, been held prisoner in a loft by a group of Travellers who, by keeping her short of food, had tried to force her into adopting an immoral way of life. On the strength of her testimony, Mrs Wells, Mary and George Squires, Fortune and Judith Natus and Virtue Hall were subsequently arrested and brought to trial. The committal proceedings were presided over by the novelist Henry Fielding and were conducted with what can only be described as appalling laxity. Nevertheless, despite a remarkable conflict of evidence, when the matter came to trial at the Old Bailey, Wells was sentenced to be burned in the hand and Mary Squires to be hanged.

Believing that there had been a miscarriage of justice, the then Lord Mayor of London, Sir Christopher Gascoyne, ordered further inquiries to be made on behalf of the accused on the basis of which Squires was given a free pardon. Canning herself was then prosecuted for perjury and later transported.

It must be said, however, that the alibis offered by the Travellers did provoke a certain amount of comment. Fortune and Judith, for example, were eventually to swear that they had slept every night in the loft where Canning alleged she had been held, but were unable to say why they had not made this known at the original hearing. Mary Squires, on the other hand, brought thirty-eight witnesses to say that she had been in Dorset at the time, whilst twenty-seven others swore she had been in Middlesex. According to contemporary report, she was so uncommonly ugly that it is difficult to see how there could have been any doubt in the matter of recognition.

Fielding gives his own account of the affair in a pamphlet entitled *Elizabeth Canning who hath Sworn that she was Robbed and almost Starved to Death by Gypsies* (A. Millar, London, 1753), a summary of which also appeared in the *London Magazine* (28 (1753), 142–4). See also Daniel Cox's *Appeal to the Public on Behalf of Elizabeth Canning, in Which the Material Facts in her Story are Fairly Stated, and Shown to be True on the Foundation of Evidence*, published by E. W. Meadows in 1753 and reviewed in the *Gentleman's Magazine* (23 (1753), 298–9.

Another case in which the accused were eventually discharged with a handsome compensation involved Elizabeth Kellan who claimed she had been forcibly abducted, clothed in rags and threatened with death if she attempted to escape. Her captors, she said, had forced her to witness certain criminal acts such as poultry stealing and the milking of cows by night, it being their intention eventually to initiate her into their fraternity. To this end, also, they intended dyeing her face with walnut juice in order that she might the more closely resemble them. She was pronounced by the magistrates 'a gross impostor' (*Annual Register*, 7 July 1802).

The widely held notion that the Gypsies used walnut juice or some other form of dye to colour both themselves and new recruits from the settled population seems to have originated with Dekker:

> A man that sees them would swear they all had yellow jaundice, or that they were tawny Moors' bastards, for no red-ochre man carries a face of a more filthy complexion; yet they are not born so, neither has the sun burnt them so, but they are painted so, yet they are not good painters neither, for they do not make faces but mar faces.

So, too, in Middleton and Rowley's *Spanish Gipsie* of 1653, Alvarez speaks of 'Gipsies, but no tanned ones; no red-ochre rascals umbered with soot and bacon as the English Gipsies are', whilst, some 100 years later, an anonymous contributor to the *Annual Register* (xii (1769), 128) tells of two gentlemen who, whilst riding over Hounslow Heath, came upon

> A gang of Gypsies, about twelve in number, who were boiling and roasting in the modern taste, Al Fresco, on account of a conversion as they called it, such conversion consisting of rubbing or dyeing a fine young girl with walnut shell, it being the first day of her entering into the society.

Morwood, too, speaks of young Gypsy children smeared with walnut juice and a concoction of herbs and laid by the fire or in the sun but appears unable to account for the practice.

Despite the absence of any evidence to suggest that the Gypsies ever engaged in the forcible abduction of young women either for ransom or simply in order to swell their ranks, the idea seems to have taken a firm hold. In one related family of songs – 'The Lost Lady Found' – the heroine is unquestionably the victim of a foiled kidnap attempt and only her lover's prompt action saves her from a fate worse than death, and her uncle from the gallows on a charge of murder. Recorded as far north as Cheshire and as far south as Somerset, the song appears in a number of printed collections including Mason (1877), Broadwood (1890), Barrett (1891) and Udal (1922). It has also been recovered among the Travelling community. Kennedy, for example, includes a complete set, recorded in 1953, from the singing of Harry Cox of Catfield, Norfolk (1975, 775). The following, however, is from the Revd John Broadwood's *Old English Songs* of 1843 – said to be 'The first collection of folk song airs for their own sake'.

> 'Tis of a young damsel, that was left all alone,
> For the sake of her parents she sadly did moan;
> She had but one Uncle, two trustees beside,
> That were left all alone for this young Lady's guide.

> As she was a walking in the meadows so low,
> Her Uncle was pleased that loved her so;
> As she was a walking in the meadows so gay,
> Three gipsies betrayed her, and stole her away.

> Long time she'd been missing, nowhere could be found.
> Her Uncle he searched all the country round;
> He went to the trustees, 'twixt hope and despair,
> But all was in vain, for she had not been there.

And when that her Uncle his tale he had told,
They swore he had slain her, for the sake of her gold;
It shall be death for death, then, the trustees did cry,
Shall be cast into prison, condemned to die.

'Tis of a young Squire that loved her so,
Many years to a school house they together did go;
No rest could he find or by night, or by day,
In search of his lady he wandered away.

He travelled thro' Scotland, thro' France, and thro' Spain,
He ventured his life o'er the watery main;
He went to an ale house, for to pass the night,
And in that same house was his joy and delight.

How came you in Flanders, in Flanders? says he,
How came you in Flanders, pray tell unto me.
O, as I was a walking in the meadows so gay,
Three gipsies betrayed me, and stole me away.

Your Uncle's in prison, in prison doth lie,
And for thy sweet sake is condemned to die;
Carry me to my Uncle, my Uncle, she cried,
I'll give you ten thousand, or I'll be your bride.

Says he, my dear jewel, we'll order it so,
Since love it brings danger, to the church let us go;
To the church let us go, love, and be married indeed,
Then home to old England we will hie with all speed.

And when that old England they came for to see,
The cart was drawn under the high gallows tree;
She down on her knees, and for pardon did crave,
You see I'm alive, sir, my Uncle to save.

My father he left me fifteen thousand pounds,
My Uncle and two trustees to pay me my bounds;
To pay me my bounds, sir, as long as I live,
So now I'll enjoy my young Squire so brave.

In another variant of the 'Gypsy Laddie' itself (from the singing of
Woodie Guthrie), the lady of the piece, although content to leave her
husband, is clearly in some distress at the thought of parting with her child.
But, as the man said, 'lust is a must' and, despite the shedding of many
tears, she elects to remain with her Gypsy lover:

433

Have you forsaken your house and home?
Have you forsaken your baby?
Have you forsaken your husband dear
For to go with the Gypsy Davey
And sing with the Gypsy Dave
That song of the Gypsy Dave?

Yes I've forsaken my husband dear
For to go with the Gypsy Davey
And I've forsaken my mansion high
But not my blue eyed baby,
Not my blue eyed baby.

She smiled to leave her husband dear
And go with the Gypsy Davey
But the tears come a-trickling down her cheeks
To think of the blue eyed baby,
Pretty little blue eyed baby.

Take off, take off your buckskin gloves
Made of Spanish leather;
Give to me your lily-white hand,
We'll go home together
And we'll ride home again.

No, I won't take off my buckskin gloves –
They're made of Spanish leather.
I'll go my way from day to day
And sing with the Gypsy Davey
That song of the Gypsy Dave,
That song of the Gypsy Davey,
That song of the Gypsy Dave . . .

But the elopement/abduction motif receives perhaps its most curious twist in a story connected with the following verse quoted by L. A. Smith (1889). It is said to have been sung by a handsome, dissolute Gypsy youth beneath the window of his *Gaujo* mistress prior to their departure. Her husband, a cautious lawyer of the Auvergne, rather than rushing off in hot pursuit, sold his practice and moved to another area for fear of the scandal should she decide to return. L. A. Smith is a far from reliable source but it is a pretty tale and worth including on that count alone.

Quand je vous dis que la nuit et le jour
Je meurs pour vous d'amour,

Vous ne me croyez pas,
Mademoiselle d'Angla,
Vous ne me croyez pas,
Mademoiselle d'Angla.
Votre esprit est quinteux comme une mule,
Et cependant je suis si ridicule
Que votre corps
Fait mes transports.

When I tell you that, night and day,
I die for love of you,
You won't believe me,
Mademoiselle d'Angla,
You won't believe me,
Mademoiselle d'Angla.
Your spirit is stubborn as a mule,
And yet I am foolish enough
To be delighted by your body.

The Gypsy lover at the window also features in one of Borrow's Spanish Gypsy *coplas*:

Abillelate á la dicani
Que io voy te penelár
Una buchi en Calo
Y despues te liguerár.

Come to the window, sweet love, do,
And I will whisper there
In Romani a word or two,
And thee far off will bear.

An altogether more primitive Hungarian Gypsy variant of the elopement/abduction motif (recorded in Nagykoros) is to be found in Vekerdi's essay on Hungarian Gypsy Song of 1967.

Gelas tar e Iboj, trin des kodolake,
De rodave la rodav la kati cavo kalo.
Arakhlem la mama maskar le luluda,
Kacej uravel pe taj makel ve avri,
Ne, taj makel pe avri te camel la savo.
Av tar khere, Iboj, ka tse trin savora.
Nastig te zav, Mamam, ke man tamadina.

435

Ke man tamadina le Pestake cave.
Av tar khere, Boja, ka tse trin savora.
Nastik zav me khere, but si le Romora,
But si le Romora te . . .
. . . Sero le bute Romenge.

Ebolya went out, three days, alone,
I seek her, I seek her, among the black boys (the Gypsies).
I found her, mother, among the flowers;
There she is, combing her hair and is rouging herself.
Nay, she is rouging herself but a young man shall love her.
Come home, Ebolya, to your three children.
I cannot go, mother, for I shall be assaulted.
I shall be assaulted by the boys from Budapest.
Come home, Ebolya, to your three children.
I cannot go home, the Gypsies are many,
The Gypsies are many and . . .

The remainder of the song consists of a jumble of stereotypical phrases apparently unconnected with the theme established in the opening section.

~

An interesting footnote to the abduction story is provided by Dekker. 'The Egiptian lice', as he calls them, were daily augmented by various classes of native rogue, including *Priggers*, *Anglers*, *Cheators*, *Morts*, and 'Yeomens Daughters (that haue taken some by blowes, and to auoid shame, falls into their sinnes'. Shirley, too, in a discussion of those sturdy beggars that 'for the most part . . . call themselves *Egyptians*' (1688; 1724 edn):

The *Mumper* is the general beggar, male and female, which lie in cross-ways or travel to and fro, carrying for the most part children with them which generally are by-blows and delivered to them with a sum of money almost as soon as born

A little over a century later, under the catch-word, 'Gypsies', the anonymous editor of the 1811 *Dictionary of Buckish Slang*, a work owing much to Grose, lends further credence to Shirley's remarks:

That by which they are said to get the most money is, when young gentlewomen of good families and reputation have happened to be with child before marriage, a round sum is often bestowed among the Gypsies for some one mort to take the child; and that is never heard of more by the true mother and family, so the disgrace is kept concealed from the world; and if the child lives, it never knows its parents.

That embarrassed mothers and unwanted children may have been accommodated in this way is quite possible, although whether the Gypsies were ever involved is a different matter. It is easy to see, however, how so crude a system of paid fosterage might become confused in the popular imagination with child abduction and how this in turn would serve to confirm the Gypsies in the role of scapegoat and bogey-man:

> Of Fairies, Witches, Gypsies,
> My nourrice sang to me,
> Sua Gypsies, Fairies, Witches,
> I alsua synge to thee.
> > (Denham Tract)

~

165. Yéck bítto Róm'ni chāl chūryin* āp a rūkk
  Chūry'd āp t' trūppo an' béshed apré a shóck.**

  Dūi bitti Rómmanis chūry'd āp t' rūkk
  Yéck slommerin t' wāver as béshed apré t' shóck.

  Trín bitti Róm'ni chāls chūryin āp a rūkk
  Slommerin yéck a wāver till they póggered 'vrī the shóck.

  Trín bitti Róm'ni chāls pélled mūllo 'lay the pūv
  Lénter dye wélled alángus (along) ānkaired to rúv.

  Wélled sīg ānpālī a bōro chóvihān
  As káired sār the chávvos apópli jívven án (on).

  Lénters dye hátched a rúvvin, lénters dye lélled a kósh
  An del 'em all a kurin for a kairin such a bosh (dúsh).

Chorus: Yéck bitto Rómmani,
  Dūi bitti Rómmani,
  Trín bitti Rommani chāls.
  > (Lee; Leland 1873, 225)

*This word does not occur in any of the principal Romani English vocabularies, nor do Smart and Crofton offer any equivalent for 'climb'.
**A somewhat curious choice of word. Sampson, in his review of John Dyneley Prince's 'English Rommany Jargon of the American Roads' (1908b, 74–84), puts it thus: 'One of Leland's collaborators, in a line which somewhat detracts from the pathos of the ballad where it occurs . . . uses *shock* (= cabbage) as a translation of 'bough'; the American Gypsies would appear to have the same perplexing usage. Forfend the day when Omar, in transatlantic disguise, desiderates "a book of verse underneath the cabbage".'

The foregoing is a variant of the children's rhyme known in America as 'Ten Little Indians' and, in England, altogether less agreeably, as 'Ten Little Niggers'. It was originally written by Septimus Winner for the American Minstrel shows popular in the States during the 1860s and was subsequently adapted by Frank Green for G. W. 'Pony' Moore, a 'broad-humoured' tenor with the Christy Minstrels, then playing at St James's Hall, Piccadilly. It was an immediate success, a number of 'pirate' versions appearing in quick succession, commissioned by various rival troupes. It was Green's version, however, which inspired Agatha Christie's highly succesful novel 'And Then There Were None', later adapted for the stage as 'Ten Little Indians'.

Leland's informant seems to have been remarkably quick off the mark. Winner's original set was published in London in July 1868, and was followed by Green's in February of the following year. Three further sets also appeared in 1869, including W. Shepherd's politically correct 'The Ten Youthful Africans' and two more in 1870, including a broadside version (no imprint). The only other set which predates Leland's was published by Julius Crow in December 1874. Winner's original text runs as follows:

> Ten little Injuns standin' in a line,
> One toddled home and then there were nine.
>
> Nine little Injuns standin' on a gate,
> One tumbled off and then there were eight.
>
> One little, two little, three little,
>   Four little, five little Injun boys,
>   Six little, seven little, eight little,
>   Nine little, ten little Injun boys.
>
> Eight little Injuns gazin' under heav'n,
> One went to sleep and then there were seven.
>
> Seven little Injuns cuttin' up their tricks,
> One broke his neck and then there were six.
>
> One little, two little . . .
>
> Six little Injuns kickin' all alive,
> One kick'd the bucket and then there were five.
>
> Five little Injuns on a cellar door,
> One tumbled in and then there were four.

One little, two little . . .

Four little Injuns up on a spree,
One he got fuddled and then there were three.

Three little Injuns out in a canoe,
One tumbled overboard and then there were two
One little, two little . . .

Two little Injuns foolin' with a gun,
One shot t'other and then there was one.

One little Injun livin' all alone,
He got married and then there were none.

One little, two little . . .

Although the 'Trin Bitti Romani Chals' is said to have been composed by a Lee, Leland tells us that he obtained it from one of the James, 'a half-blood'. It was given, he says, 'in a very imperfect form', but did not differ materially from the printed version. Also included by Leland is a second set from the pen of Hubert Smith, the author of *Tent Life with English Gypsies in Norway* (1873) and himself married to a Romani (the heroine of his book), from whom he was subsequently divorced.

Desh Tāni Chavis Dūriken

Desh tāni chávis, all adré a row;
What welled o' lénder, tūte shall know.

Yéck tāno chávo was chívved up a rūkk,
Pélled to the pūv an yúv's neck 'us broke.

Dūi tāno chávo hatched apré his head,
Wery sig ānpālī yúv was látchered dead.

Trin tāno chávo his lévinor drank,
An' wery sig ānpālī was tássered in a tank.

Yéck tāno chávo – dūi tāni chávis –
Trín tāni chávis they are gone!

Shtor tāno chávo kélled himself lame,
Pélled alay a coal-hév an' was never dicked again.

Pánj tāno chávo was díckin at the rain,
An' wery sīg ānpālī méred o' thought upon the brain.

Shov* tāno chávo tumbled 'pré a log,
Adói yuv was hotchered to sindor 'dré the yog.

Shtor tāno chávis – pánj tāni chavis –
Shov tāni chávis, we must mourn.

Áfta tāno chávo prástered from a dog,
An' wery sig ānpālī was náshered 'dré a fog.

Oitoo tāni chavi was always at war,
Yéck dívvus yoi was náshered 'dré the tav of her guitar.

Enneah tāno chavo was kellin' with a match,
An' wery sig ānpālī was mullered by a witch.

Desh tāno chávo, yuv was booti tall,
Playin' Punch and Judy was tássered with his call.

Áfta tāno chávo – oitoo tāno chávo –
Enneah te desh all are dead.

Then the Drabéngro kūred his wife,
An, shook the tāni chávis till sār wélled to life.

Desh, enneah, oitoo, áfta chávis, all glad;
Shov and pánj chávis, dancing like mad.
Shtor, trín chávis, standing on their heads;
Dūi, yéck chávis, growing like weeds.

Desh tāni chávis, all in a row;
What wélled o' lendy, kennā you know.
(Hubert Smith; Leland, Palmer and Tuckey 1875, 228)

*'The English Gypsies', says Borrow (1874, 13),

> can count up to six, and have the numerals for ten and twenty, but with those for seven, eight, and nine, perhaps not three Gypsies in England are acquainted. When they wish to express those numerals in their own language, they have recourse to very uncouth and roundabout methods, saying for 7, *dui trins ta yeck*, two threes and one; for eight, *dui stors*, or two fours; and for nine, *desh sore but yeck*, or ten all but one. Yet at one time the English Gypsies possessed all the numerals as their Transylvanian, Wallachian, and Russian brethren still do; even within the last fifty years there were Gypsies who could count up to a hundred. These were *tatchey Romany*, real Gypsies, of the old sacred black race ...

Black blood or no, neither Sylvester Boswell nor Edward Wood, from whom Smart, Crofton and Sampson obtained so much of the old inflected British Romani, had the numerals seven, eight and nine, favouring instead the sort of uncouth formulae mentioned by Borrow (Smart and Crofton 1875, 45–6, and Sampson 1926, 153–7). Towards the end of the eighteenth century, Bryant had retrieved all three missing numerals from his informants – *afta, oitoo, enneah* – but even then, Marsden, publishing in the same journal, found only the one – *heftan* (*Archeologica* (1784), 382–91).

Forty years later, the complete set from one to ten is to be found in a Welsh Gypsy word list appended to an anonymous letter printed in the Welsh-language periodical *Seren Gomer* for February 1823: *ec, dws, trin, star, pantsh, tshow, efta, ochto, henia, desh*. In every case, the forms used would seem to conform with the Greek Romani: *eftá, okhtó, enéa*, themselves borrowings from the Greek.

A similar system of counting to that in use among English Gypsies is also to be met with in *Polari*, a curious Italianate jargon commonly associated with the stage and the sea and, latterly, with male homosexuals – *say oney, say dooey, say tray*, seven, eight, nine – although the alternative forms, *setter, otter, nobber*, have also been recorded. Both sets are based on the original Italian which forms the basis of this highly specialized lexis.

The number seven (héfta) also occurs in another song which, according to Leland, represents an unnamed English Gypsy's rendering of one of a number of German Romani songs given by Liebich in his *Die Zigeuner* (Leipzig, 1863):

> 166. I rāni shākerella o rye sār péskri bállor,
>   'I górgior shan tárderin péller the wūder.
>   Kāmena ta díkk mándy.
>   Ko káiren mén kéttene?'
>   'Mi'll net (not?) mūkkav tūte
>   If it kosts* méngy mīro míraben.
>   Shan tūkey héfta prālor,
>   Te mīro zī kéllela,
>   Apré léngeris hārro,
>   Tu shán mīri te atcha mīris.'
>   (Anon.; Leland, Palmer and Tuckey 1875, 186)

*One of a number of wholly arbitrary misspellings of English words with which the work is liberally laced.

Liebich's original text runs as follows:

> Čakervela i rani rajes peskere balensa
> I Gadze pal o wudur tarde
> Kamena te dikena me.
> Ho gerena kettané
> Me mukkava tute nit
> Kostela es gleich miropen

Te hi tut' efta prála
Te kéllela miro dzi
Ap o lengero charo
Tu hal miri te atchaha miro.

Leland offers the following metrical English rendering:

The lady with her flowing hair
Has covered her lover o'er.
'There are men who wish to see me here
Are hiding behind the door.
What can we do together –
What canst thou do for me?'
'I will not let thee go, my love,
Though I lose my life for thee.
Thou hast seven brothers. Though my heart
Should leap upon their sword,
Whilst thou art mine and I am thine
I ever will keep my word.'
(Leland, Palmer and Tuckey 1875, 189)

The song was also translated into Latin by Miklosich in *Uber die Mundarten und die Wanderungen der Zigeuner Europas* (Vienna, 1873).

~

167. I have a juk, he's a very good juk;
Mandi kurs him for his pleasure.
For to muller some game in the middle of the rorti
While the yoggers lay sleeping.

Up jumps an old morg and away he shavs,
Right down through some plantation.
Mandi kurs him up, then poggers his little crown,
Then he puts him in his little putsi.

Then he says to his old juk,
'We are best to be jelling;
Yes, the yogger mush will know it.'

Mandi kurs this old man
To some seaport town,
To see what the morgs were fetching.
'Five joeys a brace', said my bonny, bonny chavi;
'That's if you can kur mandi plenty.'

Mandi walked into the old Half-Way house,
To get a half of gather.*
Mandi spent one crown, left the other one down,
While the old yogger lay sleeping.
(Jasper Smith)

*Although it has long been customary to distinguish poaching from other forms of theft, as a mere diversion or as a 'social crime' born of hunger, the prevailing view among the landed classes and their traditional allies, the parson and the magistrate, has always been that there is no proven link between poverty and the theft of game. Indeed, any profit which might accrue was, it was thought, more likely to be spent on drink than on food. Thus, according to the Revd H. Worsley, writing in his *Juvenile Depravity* of 1849, and quoted here ex Lee 1994, 39:

> Intemperance and poaching act and re-act, the one vile habit on the other. 'Poaching', says a witness examined by the late Select Committee of the Game Laws, 'induces men and boys to be out at night, and brings them into connexion with individuals of very bad character, and carries them into those abominably bad places, the beer-shops . . .' It is in the beer-shops that individuals of notorious character meet, it is here they concoct their plans . . . The beer retailer is very frequently associated with the poachers, and to him they dispose of their plunder in payment for liquor.

Gather = Beer: a much travelled word. Used for English Cant in William Maginn's metrical paraphrase of one of Vidocq's argotic songs in *Blackwoods Magazine* for July 1828:

> I pattered in Flash like a covey knowing,
> 'Ay, bub or grubby, I say?'
> 'Lots of gatter,' says she, 'is flowing' . . .

Also noted for *Shelta* (Barrère and Leland 1889, i, 376; and *JGLS* n.s. 3, 206), and for Scottish Cant by M'Cormick (1906, xiv). One of Norwood's informants, Tom Musto of Cheltenham, gave *gatter* = rain. Partridge suggests a possible origin in lingua franca: *agua*, water.

The Gypsies, says Borrow (1874, 11),

> have no definite word either for hare or rabbit; *shoshoi*, by which they generally designate a rabbit, signifies a hare as well, and *kaun-engro*, a word invented to distinguish a hare, and which signifies ear-fellow, is no more applicable to a hare than a rabbit, as both have long ears.

Manfri Wood (1973) points out that the adjectives 'big' and 'little' were often used in connection with *shoshoi* in order to make it clear which animal was intended.

The Gypsies' inability to differentiate between the two animals in their own language should not, however, be taken as further evidence of linguistic decline for, as Borrow goes on to say, it simply 'serves to show

443

how closely related are Sanskrit and Gypsy'. *Shoshoi*, he says, is 'nearly of the same sound as the Sanskrit *sasa* . . . and exactly of the same import; for as the Gypsy *shoshoi* signifies both hare and rabbit . . . so does the Sanskrit *sasa* . . .'

Borrow is wrong, however, in suggesting that *kaun-engro* signifies 'ear-fellow', a derivation based upon a misinterpretation of its last two syllables. The termination *-engoro* was originally used to form the genitive plural (Paspati 1870, 50–1) and, together with the masculine singular ending *-eskoro*, is frequently used by English Gypsies to form nouns (as often as not) of agency or possession (Smart and Crofton 1875, 13).

Although in common use, the word *morg* or *morgan* is not of Gypsy origin but probably derives from the obsolete English *malkin* or *mawkin* which, in its northern or Scottish form, was used to signify a hare:

> The sun had clos'd the winter day . . .
> An' hunger'd maukin ta'en her way
> To Kail-yards green.
> (Burns, 'Vision', 1.1, 1785)

Among Scottish Travellers, the corresponding form, as noted by M'Cormick in his *Tinkler-Gypsies*, is *baurie maccam*, *maccam* alone signifying rabbit.

The song itself occurs in a number of mainstream versions, of which one of the best is Cecil Sharp's 'The Hearty Poacher', obtained from Shepherd Haydon of Bampton, Oxfordshire, in 1909. Although the earliest printed version is from Yorkshire (Kidson's 'Hares in the Old Plantation'), it seems to have been particularly popular in the southern counties. Gardiner (MS 1907–8) has three versions from Hampshire; Sharp (MS 1909–11), two from Oxfordshire and one from Cambridgeshire; and Williams (1923), versions from Berkshire and Wiltshire. It has also been recorded in Suffolk, Sussex and Kent.

Its relatively late appearance in print, coupled with the use, in some variants, of the term 'joey', would suggest that the song may be dated with some confidence to the middle years of the nineteenth century. A 'joey', signifying 'a fourpenny piece' and, latterly, any small coin, takes its name from Joseph Hume, the radical politician and student of public finance (1770–1855) and is unknown before 1840. In other variants, however, the alternative, 'crown', would allow a much earlier date to be assumed.

The version given below is from the singing of New Forest Gypsies as recorded by Alice Gillington for her *Songs of the Open Road* (1911a, 20):

My master turned me out of doors!
Now, wasn't that provoking?
All for to catch the game by night,
While the gamekeeper was sleeping!

I have a dog, and a good dog, too!
I keep him for my sporting!
All for to catch the game by night,
While the gamekeeper lies sleeping.

Me and my dogs were out one night,
To view the habitation!
Out jumped an old hare and away she ran,
She ran through my plantation!

She squeaked, she hollaed, she made a noise,
As something stopped her running,
Says I to my dog, 'it's time we were gone,
For the gamekeepers are coming!'

I picked her up, I broke her neck,
I put her in my pocket;
'Lay still, lay still, my puss!', I cried,
For the gamekeepers are coming!'

I went down to my uncle's house,
To see what they were fetching;
'A crown a brace, my boy!', he said,
'If you will bring me fifty!'

I went down to the public house
And drank till I was mellow;
For I spent that crown and put another one down.
Ain't I a good-hearted fellow?

The hare, like the pig, seems to have produced little in the way of waste. Cooked and eaten it may be served with crab-apple jelly, agrimony, sorrel and other herbs, whilst the skin may be used for caps, belts and the lining of coats. In eastern Europe, according to Wlislocki, Gypsy children were annointed with hare's fat and goose grease as a charm against extremes of heat and cold (Wlislocki 1891, 75), and even the entrails were of use – for, if Xavier Petulengro is to be believed, cleaned and treated with formaldehyde they make the finest possible cat-gut for fiddle strings: 'Strings treated in this way, according to the Hungarian, Romanian and

Magyar Gypsies, make the notes sound sweet and resonant, giving to the music a quality not otherwise to be found.'

Four further sets of the song have been recorded in the *Poggadi Chib* – three partial and one complete. The first, again from the singing of Jasper Smith (text 168); the second, from an unnamed Gypsy girl from Barking in east London (text 169); and the third, also from an unnamed informant which follows Smith's opening stanza so closely that one is inclined to think that it may very well have been from Smith himself (text 170). The fourth set is also from the singing of Jasper Smith and was included, subject to certain minor modifications, in Stanley and Burke's *Romano Drom Song Book* (text 171).

Smith begins his second set in English, both in order to demonstrate how the *Poggadi Chib* works and his own fluency in both media.

> 168. I have a dog, he's a very good dog;
> I keep him for my pleasure;
> For to kill some game in the middle of the night,
> While the gamekeepers, they lay sleeping.
>
> Up jelled an old morg and away he did shav,
> Right down through some big crack.
> Mandi kur'd him up and cracked his little crown,
> And kur'd him in his putsi.
>
> And I said to my juk, 'we are best to be jallin'.
> Yes, the yog mushes will jin us.'
> (BBC Radio 2, 1 April 1987)

> 169. Mandy had a juk,
> And a kushti juk;
> He kept them in his keeping.
> One Sunday night, they went out walking,
> While the gavver mush was sleeping.
> (Kennedy 1975)

> 170. I have a juk and a very good juk
> Mandi curs him for his pleasure
> For to muller some game in the middle of the rorti
> While the yoggers lay sleeping.
> (Anon; Richards 1976–7, 26)

171. Mandi has a jukkel, and a kushti jukkel, too,
     Mandi kurs him for his pleasure.
     For to muller some game in the middle of the rarti,
     While the yoggers lay sleeping.

     Up jumps a kannengro and away he shavs,
     Right down through some plantation.
     Mandi kurs him up then poggers his crown,
     Then he puts him in his putsi.

     Then he says to his old juk, 'We are best to be jelling,
     Or the yogger mush will know it.'

     Mandi kurs this old man to some sea-port
     To see what kannengroes were fetching.
     'Five joes a brace,' said my bonny chavvi,
     'That's if you can kur mandi plenty.'

     Mandi walked into the old halfway house
     To get a half of gatter.
     Mandi spent one crown, let the other one down,
     While the old yogger laid sleeping.
     (Stanley and Burke 1986, 10)

~

172. I don't give a damn, for gaiging [begging] is the best,
     For when a feen [man] is corrped [weary], he has a little rest.
     Sure he's got a little molly [tent] and he's got a little beor
         [woman]
     And it's off on the tober [road] with his molly and his beor.

     By night round the glimmer [fire] when the gallias [children]
         are'n lee [bed],
     You can see him dance a merry step a' there for you'n me.
     He doesn't have to worry and he doesn't have to care,
     So long as he's got a sark [field] for his old grey mare.
                           (Maher 1972, 114–15)

Known variously as 'The Beggar Man's Song' and 'The Little Beggar Man', the Hiberno-English original of these verses is well known among Travellers and mainstream singers alike. Yet despite its evident popularity, printed sets are comparatively rare, the principal sources being O'Lochlainn (1965, no.26, p.512 (from a ballad sheet)) and Kennedy (1975). It has, however, been recorded on a number of occasions by such popular entertainers as The Dubliners and Tommy Makem. O'Lochlainn's original apart, it seems first to have been published by Sam Henry (16 April 1938) from the singing of W. J. Lyons, Ballygan, Macfin, Ballymoney, as one of a series of Songs of the People which appeared in the *Northern Constitution* over the years 1923–39 (republished in 1990 by the University of Georgia Press, Athens, Ga.). Lyons performed it at the Coleraine Musical Festival, under the title 'The Oul' Rigadoo', taking first prize in the folk-song section from a field of fourteen.

> I am a little beggar man, a-begging I have been
> For three score and more in this little isle of green;
> I am known from the Liffey down to Segue,
> Sure, I'm known by the name of 'oul Johnny Hugh.
> Of all the trades that's going, sure, begging is the best,
> For when a man is tired he can sit down and rest;
> He can beg for his dinner, he's got nothing else to do
> But cut around the corner with his 'oul rig-a-doo.
>
> I slept in a barn down in Carrabawn,
> A wet night in August, sure, I slept till the dawn,
> With holes in the roof and the rain comin' through,
> And the rats and the cats, they were playin' peek-a-boo;
> Now whom did I waken but the woman of the house,
> With her white spotted apron and her calico blouse;
> She began to frighten and I said 'ho,
> It's don't be afraid, ma'am, it's only Johnny Hugh.'
>
> I met a little flaxey-haired girl one day,
> 'Good morning, little flaxey-haired girl,' I did say;
> 'Good morning, little beggar man, and how do you do,
> With your rags and your tags and your oul' rig-a-doo?'
> 'I'll buy a pair o' leggings, a collar and a tie,
> And a nice young lady I'll marry by and by,
> I'll buy a pair o' goggles and colour them blue,
> And an old-fashioned lady I'll make her, too.'
>
> Over the road with my bag on my back,
> Over the fields with my great heavy sack,
> With holes in my shoes and my toes peeking through,
> Singing 'skilly my rink a doodle, with my oul' rig-a-doo.'
> I must be going to bed, it's getting late at night,
> The fire's all raked and out goes the light,
> So now you've heard the story of my oul' rig-a-doo,
> So goodbye and God be with you from oul' Johnny Hugh.

As has already been remarked, songs in *Gammon* are extremely rare. See the note accompanying texts 58–61.

~

Strictly speaking, the last two items in this section have no place in a work of this kind as neither has anything whatsoever to do with British Romani in either its high or low form or, indeed, with either Scottish or Irish Tinkers' Cant. They have been included here because both were at one time thought to belong to the British Gypsy repertoire and because it would seem that neither has as yet been satisfactorily explained.

They are to be found in a somewhat curious volume, published in 1889 under the title *Through Romany Songland*, and consisting of a series of chapters dealing respectively with Hungary, Spain, Russia, England, Scotland, France, Germany, and India. Also included are two songs, in Spanish, from the *Chinganeros* of South America (pp.218–20), and the following remarks on the subject of the Gypsies of Scandinavia (p.209): 'Today they are almost unknown, and, with the exception of two so-called Swedish Gypsy tunes, which I found in a very old volume of Norske melodies, I have never come across any mention of music pertaining to the wanderers in Scandinavia.'

In fact, something very like *Poggadi Chib* song is not only to be found on the Iberian peninsula and in parts of South America, but also in Scandinavia where, as in the United States, broken Romani continues to flourish alongside the older inflected Romani introduced by more recent arrivals (see notes accompanying text 134).

Of the author of *Through Romany Songland*, little or nothing is known other than that, whilst acquainted with the noted philanthropist, George Smith of Coalville, she was in no way related to him. She is also mentioned in none of the standard British or American dictionaries of biography, and Black carries only the one listing under her name (Black, 3703)). The only contemporary review of her work (*Critic* n.s. 13 (1890), 103) is, moreover, anodyne in the extreme and wholly uninformative.

Smith's qualifications for undertaking a world survey of Romani song are equally obscure. On p.110 she makes the by then unpardonable mistake of confusing English Romani with Thieves' Cant. The English Gypsies, she says, have an inexhaustible supply of proverbs, although 'many of them are utterly untranslatable, save to the initiated in what is known as the Romany tongue or Thieves' Latin'. Again, on p.151, she describes how, in the course of a visit with Jim Lee at his camp on Plaistow Marshes, she was asked by his cousin Job if she spoke *Romanés*. Having explained that she did not but that she understood it, she goes on to accept as 'a Romany ballad' four lines of corrupt Irish (text 173). On p.169, she makes exactly the same mistake, describing a second piece, part Irish, part gibberish, as 'this pretty little slang Romany song' (text 174).

Finally, on p.139, she says of the word *cawer* in the well-known quatrain commencing, in her version, 'Cush dearie Romany chile' (text 76): 'The children of the Gypsy tribes invariably speak of singing in this way.' Whether her young informants thought merely to make sport of her or whether, in the presence of her earnest guide, George Smith, they thought tactful dissimulation the wiser course, is impossible to say. What is perfectly clear, however, is that, in this context, *cawer* means 'fight' and to offer any other explanation argues a want of understanding of the entire song.

Unfortunately, her companion seems to have been no better informed for, in a letter to the *Standard*, dated 20 August 1879, he reprimands those inclined to romanticize the Gypsies, saying:

> I may not be able, nor do I profess, to understand the singular number of the masculine gender of dad, chavo, tieno, morsh, gongeo, racloo, raclay, pal, pala; the feminine gender dai, chai, tieny, jovel, gongell, raclee, racya, pen penya; or the plural of the masculine gender dada, chava and the feminine gender daia chaia . . .

Later in the same letter, as if to emphasize his ignorance, he bemoans the rapid increase in the number of 'idlers, loafers, rodneys, mongrels, *georgies*, and Gypsies' (emphasis added).

As regards the material selected for inclusion in her chapter on English Gypsy song, Smith relies almost entirely on Borrow, Leland and Groome. Although this is a little surprising in one who apparently enjoyed the confidence of her own informants, it is at least understandable, given their early pre-eminence in the popularization of Gypsy lore generally; what is not, is her failure scrupulously to acknowledge her sources in every case. On pp.120–1, for example, she reproduces Borrow's 'Can You Rokra Romany' (text 15) and 'Here the Gypsy Gemman See' with no hint as to their provenance, and describes Leonora's 'The Romany Chi and the Romany Chal' as 'a kettle mender's song' – recalling, no doubt, Borrow's essay in smithcraft in the course of his stay in the Mumpers' Dingle. Indeed, in introducing the first of these, she also makes unascribed use of Borrow's own evaluation, observing that for terseness and expressiveness it is quite the equal of anything in the entire circle of gentile poetry.

So, too, on p.122, Leland's 'Mulo Balo' (text 119) is reproduced without acknowledgement as are a number of Groome's proverbs on pp.110ff.

Even where she does acknowledge the existence of an earlier set, she makes it clear that she is no mere borrower but has herself heard the items in question at first hand. This, however, is hard to credit as not only are all these pieces reproduced word for word (apart from one or two minor amendments), but the original spelling is also retained. This is particularly apparent in her treatment of Leland's 'Gilli of a Romani Juva' (text 63) whose somewhat idiosyncratic spelling arose from the fact that it was printed exactly as written by his informant's *Gaujo* husband.

Again, on p.115, she says of Borrow's lullaby (reproduced in the introduction to the present work), 'The wrinkled old beldame who never fails to form part of the household of a Gypsy camp may sometimes be heard crooning this little ditty as she rocks the Romany cradle beneath the leafy shade of some forest monarch'.

On the credit side, Smith's version of 'Cush Dearie Romany Chile' (text 76) is undoubtedly 'tatcho' and provides a useful early comparator for Groome's set (text 75). She also includes two interesting sets in full English – 'On the Banks of the Beautiful Severn' and 'The Squire and the Gypsy' (p.146). The latter may be compared with the variant given in Kennedy's *Folksongs of Britain and Ireland* which, according to the editor, 'does not seem to appear in any collections' (Kennedy 1975, 801).

> One spring morning early, a squire was straying
> Over the beauteous lands that nature gave birth!
> The primrose bloomed forth and the young lambs were straying;
> He sighs, 'I am lonely on this beauteous earth.
>
> 'But what are those notes that echo the valley?
> Yon smoke that's ascending, it shall be my guide.
> Let her be what she may, both wealthy or lowly,
> I'll swear by the powers I'll make her my bride.'
>
> He had not strayed far when struck with such beauty,
> He'd scarcely trot far in the deep woody dell,
> By the side of the tent two eyes shone like diamonds,
> And there he beheld the dark Gypsy girl.
>
> 'Shall I tell you your fortune?' 'Oh, dearest, I know it –
> The fortune I crave for, is you for my bride.
> You shall live in a castle surrounded by servants,
> Silks and fine satins shall be your attire.
> My sweet Gypsy bride shall be looked on with envy
> As she rides in her carriage, the wife of a squire.'
>
> 'You promised to me a grand proposal,
> You promised to make me as rich as a queen;
> Throw them all to the dirt while I so light-hearted
> And ride on my neddy that stands on the green.'

'So fly with me now, in a few months we'll marry
As man and as wife together can dwell.
I am not of age, that's the reason I tarry,
But I am sure for to marry the dark Gypsy girl!'

'O you are a squire and I'm a poor Gypsy.
Both wealth and great beauty are at your command.
There's more honour and virtue in the poor and the lowly
Than in half your proud ladies that walk through the land.'

As regards the first of the two unexplained fragments mentioned above, Smith tells on p.149 how she visited Jim Lee in his van at the end of Dirty Lane by Plaistow Marshes and how 'the old man seemed quite pleased to give me all the information he could on the subject of the songs of the Romanies'. In the course of their interview, Lee, whom she describes as 'King of the famous Paraffin Lee tribe' and, according to report, 'the purest specimen of a Gypsy at the present time to be found', sent for his cousin, Job, who, he assured her, was a fine singer. Having regaled her with Borrow's version of 'Can You Rokra Romany', Job then sang the following 'Romany Ballad' which Smith also remembered seeing in Leland's *The Gypsies*:

> 173. Cosson kailyard corrum me morro sari,
> Me gul ogalyach mir;
> Rahet manent trasha moroch
> Me tu sosti mo díele.
>
> Coming from Galway, tired and weary,
> I met a woman;
> I'll go bail by this time tomorrow,
> You'll have enough of me.

Leland's original text and translation, which Smith faithfully reproduces in every detail, was obtained from a Tinker named Owen whom he met in Philadelphia some time during 1880 (Leland 1882, 370).

Owen told him it was in *Shelta*, a language 'independent of Irish, Welsh or Gaelic', and Leland appears to have accepted this without question. 'Me tu sosti', however, he took to be good Romani (for 'thou shalt be (of) me'), elements of which he believed to be 'freely used' in the jargon.

I was, myself, at first disposed to believe that 'mo díele' was simply an alternative form of *my jil* which, in contemporary Irish Cant, may signify 'me' or 'myself', but, having read the piece aloud in conjunction with

Owen's own English translation, it became immediately apparent that it was nothing more exotic than modern Irish, set down by someone unacquainted with the language and the rules of Gaelic orthography. Restored to its original form it may be read as follows:

> Casadh an cailleach dhom, is mé marbh saraithe,
> 'S mé ag dul ó Gaillimh aniar.
> Raghad i mbainní ort faoin tráth seo amárach
> (Go) mbeidh tú sásta nó is mór é a dhíol.

> I met the old woman and I dead weary,
> Going east from Galway.
> I'll go bail for you that by this time tomorrow
> You will be satisfied or there'll be a great deal to pay.

Rehabilitated in this way, the song is recognizable as a somewhat truncated variant of the first verse of 'An tSeanbhean Liath' (The Grey-haired Old Woman), of which the earliest printed version, apart from Leland's, is to be found in 'Siamsa an Gheimhridh', edited by Domhnal ó Foltharta and published in Dublin by Patrick O'Brien in 1892.

That the song was already current in written form some fifty years earlier is, however, suggested by a manuscript reference in the archives of the Department of Irish Folklore in University College Dublin (vol.561, 407–9). The manuscript itself contains material gathered from Seán ó Rúnú in 1938 when he was seventy years old. O Rúnú, who had lived all his life in Baile Chláir Móinteach, east of Galway City, had learned the song some fifty years earlier from a 'book' written by Tomáisín Bacach ó Dúgáin who kept school in Móinteach around the year 1838. The first verse of ó Rúnú's set runs as follows. Those lines corresponding with Owen's set are marked with an asterisk:

> *Casadh an chailleach dhom is mé marbh saraithe,
> An t-ochtú lá roimh an gcogadh a thíocht,
> D'fhiafridh sí dhomsa 'an marbh atá tú
> Nó an dtabharfá páirtíocht don tseanbhean liath?'
> Sheas mé ar mo chois, rinne mé gáirí,
> 'Má tá do 'phurse' láidir, tean aniar
> *Is go rachaidh mé i mbannaí ort faoin tráth seo amárach
> *Go mbeidh an tseanbhean sásta nó is mór é a díol.

> I met the old woman and I was dead weary,
> The eighth day before the coming of the war.

453

She asked me 'Are you dead
Or would you give a share to the old grey-haired woman?'
I stood and laughed,
'If your purse is full, draw near;
I'll go bail for you this time tomorrow,
The old woman will be satisfied or she will have to
pay a great deal.'

A further six variants are mentioned in 'Clár Amhrán Bhaile na hInse', a list of the songs of Baile na hInse prepared for the Department of Irish Folklore by Ríonach ní Fhlathartaigh. In a number of these, the encounter is clearly located in or near Galway, which ties in with the second line of Owen's set. In every case, however, Owen's second line and the second part of his first line are conflated. A single example will suffice. It is taken from the singing of Nóra ní Chadhain of Cluain d'Rá Abhainn as collected by Brian mac Lochlainn in 1936 when the singer was sixty-nine years old: 'Ag 'ul thrídh Ghaillimh dom, is mé marbh sáruighthe . . .' The following is a translation of the prize-winning version given by Michael Ua Coinnif at the Galway Feis in July 1918. Ua Coinnif was a native of Tawin which then consisted of fourteen families. He had learned it, he said, from a young fellow from Connemara who used to visit the place to help with the harvest (Bean Mhic Choisdalbha 1923, 128):

O casadh an tsean-bhean orm, ar (a) beul na bearnán,
An ceathramhradh lá tar éis an cogar a thigheacht.
An fear atá meathta tú, nó'n marbh attá tú,
Nó a dtiocfaidh tú a bpáirtigheacht leis an tsean-bhean liath?

Ní fear atá meathta mé 's ní marbh atá mé
'S ní rachaidh mé a bpáirteacht leis an tsean-bhean liath,
Ach d'iompuigheas tharm agus righneas-sa gáiridhe,
'S má tá an sparán lán agat teann aniar.

O chuir sí a lámh in a h-oscal gránda,
'S nárabh dheas an mhaise nó'n tsean-bhean é?
Seo dhuit-se an t-airgead 's ná cainntigh go bráth air,
Tá ríar na h-Eaglais' Uilig fós 'do dhiadh.

O! Casadh an Sagart dom agus míonuigheas an cás dó,
Go raibh ceathair páistí go lag i mo dhiaidh,
'S go raibh máthairín dona aca nach ndeanfadh cás dóibh
Dá luighidís ráithe nó tuilleadh 's bliadhain.

O! Fill abhaile adeir sé, a pheacaidh gránda,
'S measa atá tú ná an t-é bhraith Dia
Smaonuighim gur bhean do bhain an t-úbhall 'san ngáirdín,
'S cuir cúl do láimhe leis an t-sean-bhean liath.

O! Sgríobhfainn litir, adeir sí, agus léighinn mo Bhíobla
An lá bhuaileadh draoidheacht orm agus smut de'n cheó.
Bhíodh culaidh gheal orm de thoghadh an tsíoda
Agus ráca círe chomh dubh le gual,
Bhíodh buclaidhe airgid in mo bhrógaibh síoda,
'S ná dheas an mhían le mealladh mé.

Ní sean-bhean mise, adeir sí, acht cailín óg mé
Fuair sgoil agus fóghluim i d-tús mo shaoghail,
'S dá maireadh mo dheada dhom go lá mo phósta
Go mbéidhinn-se i gcóisdí le clainn na Ríogh;
Acht bliadhain 'sa taca seo, 'seadh righneadh faoi an bhfód é
'S 'sé liath go h-óg mé agus ní le haois.

Oh I met the old woman in front of the gap
On the fourth day after the war had begun.
'Are you a worthless coward or are you dead,
Or would you become a partner with the grey-haired old woman?'

'No coward am I, nor yet am I dead,
Still I'll not enter into partnership with the grey-haired old woman.'
Then I turned away and laughingly said:
'But if you have your purse full, come over to me.'

Then she put her hand under her ugly arm –
Did not that become the old woman well?
'Here's the money for you and never say a word about it,
But you have yet to reckon with the whole law of the church.'

I met the priest and explained the case to him,
That there were four weak children behind me,
And that they had a bad little mother who would not pity them,
If they lay up for a quarter or more than a year.

'Oh return home,' replied he, 'you heinous sinner,
You are worse than he whom God has judged.
I call to mind that it was a woman who took the apple in the garden,
So turn the back of your hand to the old grey woman.'

455

'Oh I used to write letters and read my Bible',
Said she, 'till the day I was bewitched and caught in a mist.
I used to wear a bright dress of the best silk,
And combs for my hair, black as coal.
And silver buckles on my silken shoes;
So was not I to be desired and wooed?

'No hag am I,' said she, 'but a young girl,
Well educated from my earliest youth,
And had my father lived to see me married,
I should be (riding) in coaches with royal families.
But a year ago he was buried,
And it is that and not old age that has caused my grey hairs.'

By now, the reader will have formed his own opinion as to the likelihood of Smith's Gypsy informant possessing precisely the same corrupt Irish text as an old Philadelphia-based Tinker and any further comment on this point would seem to be superfluous.

Smith's second piece, which she obtained from George Smith of Coalville, is described by her (1889, 169) as a 'pretty little slang Romany song'. As with text 173, however, there is nothing of the Gypsy about it and, indeed, Russell quite rightly found nothing in it worth including in his vocabulary of Scotto-Romani and Tinklers' Cant (*JGLS* n.s. 8 (1914)). It is, rather, a much reduced variant of the old Brigade Ballad, 'Siubhail a Rúin', which, telling of a young girl's determination to follow her soldier lover into exile at the time of the Williamite wars, was later to reappear in America during the civil war as 'Buttermilk Hill'. Smith's text is here followed by a 'standard' set as sung to me by Cathy Coady of the County Limerick in her London flat in the summer of 1975:

> 174. Shela, shela
> Shela gang a' rue,
> Shela gang a'
> Ricki dicki
> Shela gaggie o;
> Shela gang a';
> Lagghi dagghi.
> Sweet malori
> Sweet Jamie's the lad
> That I'll gang wi'.
>
> I'll due my petticoatie,
> I'll dye it red,
> And wi' my bonnie laddie

I'll bake my bread.
Sweet Jamie's the lad
That I'm gaen wi'.

Siubhail a Rúin

I wish I was on yon green hill,
It's there that I would cry my fill.
And every tear would turn a mill.
Is go dtéigh tú mo mhuirnín slán.

Chorus: Siubhail, siubhail, siubhail a rúin,
Siubhail go socair agus siubhail go ciúin,
Siubhail go dti an doras agus éalaigh liom,
Is go dtéigh tú mo mhuirnín slán.

I'll sell my rock, I'll sell my reel,
I will sell my only spinning wheel,
And buy my love a coat of steel
Is go dtéigh tú mo mhuirnín slán.

Chorus: Siubhail, siubhail, siubhail a rúin . . .

I'll dye my petticoats, I'll dye them red
And around the world I'll beg for bread,
Until my parents would wish me dead
Is go dtéigh tú mo mhuirnín slán.

Chorus: Siubhail, siubhail, siubhail a rúin . . .

And now my love is gone to France,
All for his fortunes to advance.
If he e'er come back, 'tis but a chance
Is go dtéigh tú mo mhuirnín slán.

Chorus: Siubhail, siubhail, siubhail a rúin . . .

This song belongs to the period of the Wild Geese (1691–1745) when, in the years following the treaty of Limerick, the flower of young Catholic manhood left Ireland to enlist in the Irish Brigades of Spain and France. As Duffy has rightly said, 'the inexpressible tenderness of the air and the deep feeling and simplicity of the words have made the ballad a popular favourite notwithstanding its meagreness and poverty'. Not surprisingly, it has found its way into many printed collections, including Forde (half a dozen sets), Duffy's *Ballad Poetry of Ireland* and Graves's *Irish Song Book*. A version of the song was also published with the air harmonized by the well-known Dublin musician, Joseph Robinson, and it also appears on various sheets issued by Hay, Printer, of North Main Street, Cork (see also Breathnach n.d., 214; Joyce 1909, 236; and Sparling 1887, 232).

Charlotte Burne obtained a version of the song from a Shropshire Travelling family, the Whartons, which Smith, apparently unaware of its connection with text 174 also reproduces on p. 136 of *Romany Songland*:

> I'll have my petticoat bound wi' red
> And the lad I love, I'll bake his bread
> And then my parents'll wish me dead.
>
> And I'll go down to Yanders mill,
> And I'll lie down and cry my fill,
> And every tear shall turn a mill.

Among children, it has been further reduced in both length and stature, providing the words for a follow-my-leader game. The following is one of three sets included by Reeves in his *One's None* (Reeves 1972):

> I sell my bat, I sell my ball,
> I sell my spinning wheel and all,
> And I'll do all that ever I can
> To follow the eyes of the drummer man.

In this latter form, the song is also almost certainly connected with the much older 'Gaberlunyie Man', said to have been composed by James V of Scotland *c.*1530–40. A Gaberlunyie or Gaberlunzie man was a 'blue-gown' – a beggar wearing the king's badge or carrying a wallet – and the verses themselves are said to draw on the Scottish king's experiences as an uninvited guest among the Travelling People (see notes accompanying text 94 and pp.591–2 of Ribton-Turner's *History of Vagrancy* of 1887).

Romani–English Vocabulary

The following list contains all those Romani–English items in the various forms in which they occur in those texts forming the major part of the present collection. Where an item appears in the list for the first time, it is numbered and, where possible, referred to the form given by Smart and Crofton in 1875 (SC) and by Kenrick and Wilson in 1985 (KW). Where an item subsequently appears in a different form, the same number is used to indicate the relevant key entry.

A

1 Aawali: yes. Aáva(li), Our, Oúwa, Oúrli (SC); Ava(li), Awa(li) (KW).
2 acai: here. Akéi (SC); Akai (KW).
3 Ach: wait, stand, stay, stop. Atch, Hatch (SC); Atch (KW).
4 Adoí, Odí, 'doi: there (SC). Adoi (KW).
5 Adoor: farther. Doórdair (SC); Dur(ed)er (KW).
6 Adré, 'Dré: in (SC); A(n)dré, 'Dré (KW).
7 Aja: so, thus. Ajáw, 'Jaw (SC); Ajaw (KW). Akai: here. 2.
8 Akóva, 'Kóva: this (SC); Akova, kovver: that (KW). Aky: here. 2.
9 Alay, Alé, Aley: under, down. Talé, Alé, 'Lé (SC); Alé: down; Telé: under (KW).
10 Anglo, Aglál, 'Glal, Agál, 'Gal: before, in front of (SC); Angla: in front of; A(n)glé, Anglo: before (KW).
11 Ankair: to begin. SC and KW offer no Romani equivalent. The corresponding form in Welsh Romani is *bignas*, an English loan-word. Cf. English Gypsy: *biggnómus o' liléi*, spring – lit. beginning of spring.
   André: in. 6.
   Anduro, Andurer: farther. 5.
12 Anpali: again. Apópli, Pópli: again (SC KW).
13 Apré: on, up. Apré, Opré, 'Pré (SC); Opré (KW).
   Aré: in. 6.
14 Astut: astride. Possibly a form of Trustal.
   Atch: to stop, wait, rise. 3.
15 Atraish: afraid, frightened. Tráshlo, *a*trásh, Tráshedo (SC); Trashed (KW).
   Atras: afraid, frightened. 15.
   Atrash: afraid, frightened. 15.
16 Av: to come (SC; KW).
   Ava: yes. 1.
17 Avélla: is coming, comes (SC).
18 Avree: away Avrí (SC). Avri: out (KW). Avri: out of, away. 18.
   Awa: yes. 1.

B

19 Ba: friend. Bor (SC KW).
20 Bak: luck. Bok (SC KW).
21 Bal: hair (SC KW).
22 Bálanser: one pound sterling (SC).
23 Balesto nokyas: pig's cheeks.
   Bállor: hair. 21.
24 Bali: pig, policeman. Baúlo: pig (SC) Ba(u)lo: pig, policeman (KW).
   Apparently a rare example of English slang, borrowed by the Gypsies and turned into *Romanés*. Grose has 'pig' = police officer and 'a China Street Pig' = a Bow Street Runner. According to Hotten (1873), the term came to be applied more particularly to a detective or 'nose', suggesting a possible origin in the idea of the law officer snouting out the criminal. The term 'grunter' was also used in much the same way.
   Balo: pig, policeman (24).
25 Bal(l)ovas: pig meat. Bálovás: bacon; Baúlesko-mas: pork (SC); Balomas, Balovas: bacon, pork, ham (KW). Balowas: bacon, pork. 25.
26 Bar: one pound sterling (SC KW).
27 Bari: big. Baúri, -o (SC); Bori (KW). Baro: big. 27.
28 Bárvalo: rich (SC); Barvali (KW).
29 Bavella: it blows.
30 Bávol: wind. Bával (SC); Balval (KW).
31 Baw: hedge. Bor (SC KW).
32 Bebee: aunt. Beébi (SC). Beebee (KW).
33 Bender: tent made of hooped rods with an improvised waterproof covering.
34 Beng, Bang: devil (SC KW). Bengis: devil. 34.

35 Berk: breast (SC); Birk (KW).
36 Bes: to sit. Besh (SC KW).
 Besh (i): to sit. 36.
37 Besh (ii): year (SC); Bersh (KW).
38 Beshello: is sitting, sits. Beshéla (SC).
 Beshtolay: to sit down. Besh + talé. 36, 9.
39 Beti: little. Bíti, -o (SC); Biti (KW).
 Bibi: aunt. 32.
40 Bíkin: to sell (SC KW).
41 Bítcher: to send (SC; KW).
42 Bitchering mush: magistrate. Lit.
 sending man – a reference to
 transportation. 42, 278.
 Bitty: little. 39.
43 Bok: hunger. Bokh (SC).
44 Bokelo: hungry. Bókalo (SC); Bokkoli
 (KW).
 Bokh: luck. 20.
45 Bokhy: lucky. Bóky (SC); Bokki:
 unlucky (KW).
 Boki: lucky. 45.
46 Bokochesto-Peryas: tripe. Bókochésto-
 pur (SC).
47 Bolli-mengreskoenes: in the manner of a
 Christian.
48 Bóngi, -o: left, wrong, crooked, lame
 (SC KW).
49 Bonor: good. Noted for *Shelta* but poss.
 Cant ex French *bon*.
50 Boót(s)i: to work (SC); Booti (KW).
51 Bootidair: more. Boótodair (SC);
 Bootoder (KW).
 Bori: big. 27.
52 Bori Pánni: big water, the sea. 27, 287.
 Boro: big. 27.
53 Bosh (i), Bóshoméngro: fiddle (SC);
 Bosh(am) (KW).
54 Bosh (ii): noise.
55 Boshing: fiddling. Bóshervénna: they
 are fiddling (SC).
56 Boshipen: fiddle playing.
57 Bóshoméngro: fiddler (SC).
 Bovalo: wealthy. 28.
58 Broom-dasher: one who kills rabbits by
 knocking them on the head with a stick.
59 Bul: posterior. Bool (SC); Bul (KW).
 Burk: breast. 35.

C

60 Cai: girl, daughter. Chei (SC); Chai
 (KW).
61 Cam: to love, like, desire, wish. Kom
 (SC KW).
62 Cambri: pregnant. Káfni – of animals;
 Baúri, Shoóbli – of women (SC); Kabni,
 Bori (KW).

63 Camlo: Lovell. Kómelo, Kómoméskro
 (SC).
64 Camov: I want, I like etc. Komóva
 (SC).
65 Can: sun. Kam, Tam, Sken (SC); Kam
 (SC).
66 Cappi: a fortune. Lelling cappi: making
 a fortune. Perhaps a variant of *kolli*,
 things. Cf. *wáfedi-kólli*, misfortunes
 (SC).
67 Care: to fight. Koor (SC); Kor (KW).
68 Cavi: child, girl child. Chávi, o: boy
 (SC); Chavvi: boy, son (KW).
 Cawer: to fight. 67.
69 Cawlor: things. Kóllaw, Kollé: things,
 shillings (SC); Kollies (KW).
 Chai: Girl, daughter. 60.
70 Chal: young fellow (SC KW). Romani-
 Chals, English Gypsies.
71 Chalor: young fellows. Chaláw,
 Chálaw, Chalé (SC).
 Chav(i): boy. 68.
72 Chavés: children. Chavé (SC). A form
 incorporating both the Romani and
 English plural endings.
73 Cheechee: nothing. Chi, Chíchi (SC);
 Chikachi (KW).
 Chel: young fellow. 70.
 Chela: fellows. 71.
74 Cherikles: birds. Chériklo (SC);
 Chiriklo (KW).
 Cherikl: bird. 74.
 Chi (i): girl. 60.
 Chi (ii): nothing. 73.
75 Chick: dirt (SC KW).
76 Chíklo: dirty (SC); Chikli (KW).
77 Chin: to cut (SC KW).
78 Chingerdo: torn. Chíngar: to tear (SC).
79 Chiv: to put (SC KW).
80 Chocker: boots. Chok, Chókker (SC);
 Chokker (KW).
 Chokker: boot, shoe. 80.
81 Chong, Choong: knee (SC KW).
82 Chongor: knees. Chóngaw (SC).
83 Chor (i): to steal (SC). Chore (KW).
84 Chor (ii): grass (SC); Chaw (KW).
85 Chories: thieves. Chor, Chóroméngro
 (SC); Chorer, Choramengro (KW).
86 Choryas: plates. Chóro (SC); Shoodalin
 (KW).
87 Chovihanee, -o: witch, wizard.
 Choófíhóni: witch (SC); Chuvni: witch;
 Chuvihano: wizard (KW).
 Chovihaunie: witch. 87.
88 Chucko: coat. Cháko, Choóka, Chúka,
 Chóxa, Choófa (SC); Choka (KW).
89 Chumba: hill (KW); Choómba,
 Dúmbo, Kúmbo (SC).

460

90 Chumer: (to) kiss. Chómer (SC);
Choomer (KW).
91 Chumoni: something. Choómoni,
Kúmeni (SC); Chommoni (KW).
Chungs: knees. 81, 82.
92 Churedo: poor. 92.
93 Churi, Churo: poor. Choóri -o (SC);
Chori (KW).
94 Churyin: climbing.
95 Chuveni: poor. Chúveni -o (SC).
Ciklo: dirty. 76.
96 Clisend: locked. Klísin: to lock (SC);
Klichi: bolt (KW).
97 Cnaw: now. Kenáw, Konáw, Kánna,
Kónna, Kon (SC); Akno, Kenaw.
98 Coin: who. Ko, Kon: who, what (SC);
Kon: who (KW).
99 Collico: tomorrow. Kóliko (SC);
Koliko-Divvus (KW).
100 Congri: church. Kóngri (SC); Kongeri
(KW).
101 Cop: get. Nineteenth-century racing
slang (1864). When a bookie won on a
race, he was said to have 'copped' and
his clerk would mark the book with a C.
102 Corauni: a crown, five shillings.
Koórona (SC).
Corr: to fight. 67.
103 Cost: stick. Kosh(t) (SC). Kosh (KW).
Cour: to fight. 67.
Covahani, -o: witch, wizard. 87.
104 Covvas: things. Kóva (SC); Kovva,
Kovvel, Kovver (KW).
105 Crack: a wood. From Crackmans,
Cragmans, a Canting term signifying 'a
hedge' (Rowlands 1610).
Curi: poor. 93.
106 Curapen: a beating. Koóroben (SC);
Koripen: fighting (KW).
107 Cush: good, well (done). Koóshko,
Koóshto, Kúshto, Kóshto (SC); Kushti
(KW).
108 Cútteri-éngerees: tatters. Kótorendri:
fragments (SC); Koster: piece (KW).

D

109 Dacen: father. Poss. *Shelta: datan*, little
father (Carmichael 1895), a diminutive of
dhatair, father (Wilson 1889), from Irish:
Athair, father, Recorded by Sampson for
Romani English, *JGLS* o.s. 3, 246.
110 Dad, Dádus: father (SC); Dad, Dadrus
(KW).
Dado: father. 110.
Dadrus: father. 110.
Dadus: father. 110.

111 Dai: mother (KW); Dei (SC).
Datchel: father. 109.
Datchen: father. 109.
112 Del: give, hit (SC KW). Del apré: read.
Delli: hit 'im, hit 'ee. Romani *del* + Eng.
pers. pron.
113 Delaméngro: a kicking horse.
Déloméngro (SC).
Deya: mother. Properly, the vocative
case. 111.
114 Dic: to look, see. Dik (SC KW).
Dick: to see, look. 114.
115 Didakai: half-breed Gypsy (SC);
Didikai: rough Traveller (KW).
Diddakai: half-breed, rough Traveller.
115.
Dik: to look, see. 114.
116 Dinneleskie: foolish.
117 Diri: dear. English: dear.
118 Dívvus, Divés: day (SC). Divvus (KW).
Doorer: farther. 5.
119 Dórdi: lo, behold, see! (SC); dear me!
(KW).
Dorri: dear. 117.
120 Drab: poison, drug, medicine (SC KW).
121 Drábbered: poisoned.
122 Drom: road (SC KW).
123 Drukerimongero: fortune-teller. 125.
Drum: road. 122.
Ductions: father. 109.
124 Dui: two (KW); Doóï (SC).
125 Duka: to harm. Doóka (SC).
126 Dukker: to tell fortunes (KW); Dúker,
Doórik (SC).
127 Dumo: the back. Doómo (SC);
Dummer (KW).
128 Duva: that. Adoóva, 'Doóva, Adúvel
(SC); Adovo, Duvver: that, those (KW).
129 Dúvel, Doóvel (SC); Duvvel (KW).
Duvvel: God. 129.
Dye: mother. 111.
130 Dzel: to go. Jal, Jaw, Jil, Jol (SC); Jas
Jaw, Jel (KW).

E

131 Eft, Afta (SC); Efta (KW).

F

132 Fake: to play an instrument (SC KW).
A nineteenth-century Canting term with
a wide range of meaning (see Vaux's
glossary of 1812).
133 Fashiono: false. Fashiono Vangust-
engre: makers of false (gold) rings.

Fóshono: false, counterfeit, imitation; Fóshono-Wóngushies (SC).

134 Fauny: ring. Forni (KW). Irish *Fáinne.*

135 Ferreder: better. Féterdaíro, Féradair: better (SC); Feder (KW).

136 Finor: pl. fine. *Fíne*-o (SC).

137 Flick: clever. Origin obscure. In late sixteenth- and early seventeenth-century Thieves' Cant, *flicker* = a pilferer; later abbreviated to *flick*, in which form it is misprinted in Rowland as *afflicke*. Alternatively, it may be connected with the quick, sharp movement of a whip.

138 Foki: people. *Folki* (SC); Foki (KW). English: folk.

139 Funy'chel: Traveller. Possibly a mishearing of *Romani Chal*. 69.

G

140 Gáiro: man (SC); Gero (KW).

141 Gajesko: adj. non-Gypsy. Originally a genitive form (SC 13).

142 Gájo, Gaujo: non-Gypsy, 'gentile'. Górjo, Górjer (SC); Gaujo (KW).

143 Gare: to hide. Gárer, Gárav (SC); Garrer (KW). Garger: non-Gypsy, 'gentile'. 142.

144 Gather: beer. Gatter (KW and M'Cormick 1906, xiv). Noted for *Shelta* by Barrère and Leland (1897, i, 376) and in *JGLS* n.s. iii, 206. Partridge (1937) suggests a possible origin in lingua franca, *agua*, water. See also Maginn's *Vidocq Versified* (1818) for *gatter*, beer, liquor. One of Norwood's informants, Tom Musto of Cheltenham, gave *gatter*, rain.

145 Gav: town (SC KW).

146 Gav-mush, Gavver: policeman (KW); Gavéngro, Gávo (SC). Literally, a town-man. 145, 275. Gavver: policeman. 146. Geero: man. 140.

147 Ghiv: wheat, corn (SC); Giv (KW).

148 Gilly: song. Ghíli, Ghíveli (SC); Gilli (KW).

149 Gin: to know. Jin (SC KW).

150 Givengro: farmer (KW); Ghivéngro (SC).

151 Givengro-Ker: farmhouse. 149, 196.

152 Gódli, Gúdli: noise (SC); Guddeli (make a) noise (KW).

153 Gonner: bag, sack (KW); Góno, Gúnno, Kányo (SC). Gorgio: *adj.* and *subst.* non-Gypsy, 'gentile'. 142. Gov: town. 145.

154 Gozwerikno: clever. Gózvero: artful, sly (SC); Gozali: cunning (KW).

155 Grai: horse (KW); Grei (SC).

156 Gran: barn. Gránza, Gráinsi (SC); Giv-Ken (KW). Granzi: barn. 156.

157 Grásni: mare (SC KW).

158 Gristur: horse. *Grasta* – poss. recorded for Scotto-Romani in 1540 (MacRitchie 1894, 37). Griys: horses. 155.

159 Groóven, Groóvni: cow (SC); Gruvni (KW). Groy: horse. 155. Gry: horse. 155. Gudali: row, noise. 152. guddeli: row, noise. 152. Guero: man. 140.

160 Gurishi: shilling. Górishi (SC)

161 Guryin: roaring.

H

162 Habben: food. Hóben, Hólben, Kóben (SC); Hobben (KW).

163 Harro: sword. Khaúro (SC). Hatch: stand, stay, stop. 3.

164 Haw, Hol, Kol: to eat (SC); Hal (KW). Hefta: seven. 131.

165 Hevyor: holes. Hévaw, Hévyaw, Hévyaws (SC).

166 Hindity-mengré: Irish(men). Híndi-teméngro: Irishman, Híndi-teméngri-Gairé: Irishmen (SC). An unflattering soubriquet – *hindo* signifying dirty, wretched, squalid, filthy, and *hínder*, to shit. Hobben: food. 162.

167 Hokka: to deceive. Hokker: tell lies, deceive (KW). SC offer no Romani equivalent for the verb to deceive, lie or trick but give *hoókaben*, deceit. Wear, however, gives *hoki*, lie (1912a) and *hockying*, to lie (1912b). See also Black's edition of Sinclair's American Romani vocabulary for *huka*, to cheat.

168 Hochedo: damned. Hotch, Hótcher, Kátchar: to burn (SC); Hotcher (KW).

169 Hotchenitchi: hedgehog. Hótchi-Wítchi (SC); Hotchi(-pig), Hotchi-Witchi (KW).

170 Hukipen: a lie. Hoókaben (SC); Hokkapen (KW).

171 Húnnalo: roar, rage. Hóïno, Hóno, Haúrino, Kórni: angry (SC); Hoïno (KW). Sampson disputes this word, but Norwood, who may have met Leland's

462

informant, gives *unlo*, vexed (diaries, 22 October 1859).

I

172 Innar: within, inside.

J

Ja: to go. 130.
Jal(l): to go. 130.
Jas: to go. 130.
Jaw: to go. 130.
Jel(l): to go. 130.
Jess: to go. 130.
173 Jib: to live. Jiv (SC KW).
Jil(l): to go. 130.
Jin: to know. 149.
Jiv: to live. 173.
174 Joe(y): any small coin (KW). A slang term, unknown before *c.*1840 and derived eponymously from Joseph Hume, the radical politician and student of public finance (1770–1855). Originally a groat (see Hawkins, *The Silver Coins of England*).
Jol: to go. 130.
175 Jov: oats. Job (SC).
176 Juk: dog. Joókel (SC); Juk(kel) (KW). Jukl: dog. 176.
Juk(k)el: dog. 176.
jukl: dog. 176.
177 Jukelesto: of the dog. Properly a dative form. 'Besides -éskro, etc., there are, in the English Gypsy dialect, the terminations -ésko and -ésto, in common use, both as genitive singular and adjectival terminations. These may have arisen from a gradual confusion of the inflections for the masculine (-éskoro), and first and second datives (-éste and -éske) in the singular . . . due to the influence of the idiom for possession . . .' (SC).
178 Juva: woman. Properly, louse (see note accompanying text 142). Joóvel: woman (SC); Juvvel (KW).

K

179 Kair: to do (SC). Ker (KW).
180 Kakka: don't, no! (KW); Kéker (SC). Kako: don't, no, not. 180.
181 Kalo: black. Kaúli, -o (SC KW). Kambri: pregnant. 62.

182 Kamena: they want, like, love etc. Koménna (SC). 61.
Kánna: now. 97.
183 Kannengro: hare (KW). Kanéngro (SC).
184 Kánni: hen (SC).
185 Kari: penis. Kóro (SC); Kóri (SC KW).
186 Kas: hay (SC).
187 Kasengri: hay stack. Kaséngro (SC). Kaulo: black. 181.
188 Kaush: hedge. An extremely unusual use of this word. See 31 and 103.
189 Ke: to (SC). Ke-Divvus: today.
190 Kek: not (SC); none, not, any (KW). Kek(k)er: don't, no! 180.
Kekko: don't, no! 180.
191 Kel: to do, act, play, dance, make cook (SC). Khel: to dance (KW).
192 Kéllela: it leaps (dances). 191.
193 Ken, kenner: house (KW) Originally a Canting term (Harman 1566–7) and noted for *Shelta* (*JGLS* o.s. ii, 209). Also in common use among Scottish Travellers (Thompson, MS list 1910–13; Wilson, *JGLS* o.s. 1899, 121–2). Kena: now. 97.
Ker (i): to do, to make. 179.
194 Ker (ii): house (KW); Kair (SC).
195 Kerapen, Keripen: action, thing (KW).
196 Kerdo: done (SC).
197 Keri: homewards, at home. Kerri (KW).
198 Kesser: to care (SC KW).
199 Kéti: to(wards). Káter, Kátar: unto (SC); Katar: from (KW).
200 Kéttane: together. Ketané, Ketanés, Katené, Káteni, Kátenes (SC); Kitané (KW).
201 Khin(der): excrement (KW). Kínder, Hínder: to defecate (SC).
202 Ki: where. Kei (SC); Kai (KW). Kil: to play a musical instrument. 191.
203 Kilmaro: bread and butter. Kíl Mauro (SC).
204 Kin: to buy (SC KW).
205 Kissi: purse (KW); Kísi (SC).
206 Kistur: to ride. Kester (SC); Kister (KW).
207 Kítchema: public house (SC KW). Klisn'd apré: locked up. 96, 13.
Knau: now. 97.
Ko: who, what. 98.
Kon: who, what. 98.
208 Kókero: self (SC); Kokkero: alone, own, self (KW).
209 Kokkeney: never. Kek-Kómi (SC KW). Kom: to love, want, desire, wish, like. 61.
Komlo: Lovell. 63.

Kosh: stick. 103.
Kosht: stick. 103.
Kos(h)ko: good. 107.
Kost: stick. 103.
'Kova: that. 8.
Kovvels: things. 104.
210 Krallyissa: queen. Kralísi(SC KW).
Kukeri: self. 208.
211 Kún: when. Kánna, Kónna, Vónka, wónka (SC); Karna, Kana (KW).
Kur (i): to fight. 67.
212 Kur (ii): to keep, take, get, put, pick (up). Put, take (KW).
Kus(h)ko: good. 107.
Kushti: good. 107.
213 Kusi: a bit, a little. Koósi (SC).

L

214 Lac: to find. Latch (SC); Latcher (KW).
Lach: find, will find. 214.
215 Laj: shame. Ladj (SC); Ladge (KW).
216 Laki, Laki's: hers. A misuse of the feminine form of the second dative of *yoi*. 438.
217 Lal: to get, take. Lel, Law (SC); Lel (KW).
218 Las: her. Possibly a confusion of the feminine forms of the accusative and instrumental cases of *yoi*. 438.
219 Lasa: with her. The feminine form of the instrumental case of *yoi*, noted by Harriot and Borrow but not found by Smart and Crofton. 438.
220 Later: her. Originally the feminine form of the ablative case of *yoi*. 438.
221 Lati: her. Originally, the feminine form of the first dative of *yoi*. Lati: she, her; Lati's: hers (KW). 438.
222 Lav: word (SC KW).
Le: take, get. 217.
Lel: take, get. 217.
223 Len: them.
224 Lena: they (will) have, take, get. Léna (SC).
225 Lende: them. Originally, the first dative of *yon*.
226 Lender: them. Originally, the ablative of *yon*.
Lendi: them. Lendi: they (KW). 225.
227 Lengheris: their. An apparent confusion of the genitive and second dative of *yon*.
228 Lenghi: them. Originally, the second dative of *yon*.
229 Lénter: their. Originally, the ablative of *yon*.
230 Les: it, him. Originally, the accusative of *yov* (SC KW). 440.

231 Lesti: he, him, it. For it (text 34). Originally, the masculine form of the first dative of *yov*. Lesti: he, him; Lesti's: his (KW). 440.
232 Levina: beer. Lívina, Lovína, 'Víni (SC); Livena, Lovena (KW).
Levinor: beer. 232.
233 Lil: book, paper (SC KW).
234 Lino: taken. Past part. of Law (SC). 217.
Lis: it. 230.
235 Loder: to lodge. Lod (SC).
236 Lodopen: lodging. Loódopen (SC); Lodipen (KW).
237 Looring: robbing, stealing. Loor: to steal (SC); Lor (KW).
238 Loovo: money. Lúva (SC); Lovva, Luvva (KW).
Louver: money. 238.
Lova: money. 238.
Lowl: to get, take. 217.
239 Lubania: whores. Loóbniaw (SC).
240 Lubni: whore (KW); Loóbni, Loódni, Lúbni (SC).
Lubbeny: whore. 240.
Lubbenies: whores. 239.
241 Lúndra, Lundro, Lónderi: London (SC).
Luvvu: money. 238.

M

242 Ma: the prohibitive part.: don't. Maa (SC); Ma(w) (KW).
243 Macho: Hearne, Herne, Heron. Mátcho, Baúro-Kanéngro; Baláws: Hearnes (SC).
244 Mailla: ass. Meíla, Moíla (SC); Moila (KW).
245 Maisa: belly? Perhaps a variant of *Maisie*, jug (M'Cormick 1907, x–xxiv), which Russell refers to Scots Gael. *meas*, basket. Cf. Eng.: bread basket.
246 Man: me. Accusative of *Me* (SC 41).
247 Mande: I, me. Mándi: I, me (SC KW). Originally, the second dative of *Me* (SC 42).
Mandi: I, me. 247.
Mandy: I, me. 247.
Mandy's: my (SC KW).
248 Mang(er): to beg. Mong (SC KW). Mang(er)en. begging. *Mang* + Eng.: -ing. 248.
249 Mangue: for me. The first dative of *Me*. to mánghi (SC 41).
250 Mansar: with me. Mánsa – the instrumental case of *Me* (SC 41).
251 Mas: meat (SC KW).

252 Meéri, -o, Meíri, -o: my (SC).
253 Men (i): we (SC); Mendi: we, us (KW).
254 Men (ii): neck (SC KW).
255 Mendui: we, us. We two. 253 (i), 124.
256 Méngy: my. Probably a corruption of the first dative of *Me*.
257 Mel, mer: to die (SC); Mer (KW). Mer: to die. 257.
258 Mer'd right away: fainted. 257.
259 Meriben: life. Méripen: life, death (SC); life, life-span, death (KW). 'Life is, to a Gypsy, an abstract idea or state, and death is a fact. It terminates life. The Gypsies have therefore taken the preceding state as part of the terminating fact, making death part of a man's life, and thus call life and death by the same name.'
Meripon: life. 259.
260 Mi: my (SC). Originally the feminine form of *mo*, but latterly used in such masculine compounds as *Mi-Duvvel*, my God (SC KW).
261 Mill: to beat, thrash, punch, pummel; to fight with. An early nineteenth-century Canting term (*Sporting Magazine*, 1812). Perhaps an extension of the older Mill Dolly, to beat hemp in prison (Smith's *Lives of the Highwaymen*, 1714).
262 Minjari: vagina. Mindj: vagina, woman (SC); Minj (KW).
263 Minri, -o: my (Borrow 1874, 13 and 174). Noted for Turkish Romani by Paspati but otherwise unknown in the English dialect. Mínno (SC).
Míraben: life. 259.
Miri, -o: my. 252.
264 Mishto: well, good (SC KW). Misto: well, good. 264.
265 Moi: mouth. Moói (SC); Mui (KW).
266 Mook: leave, let (SC); Muk (KW).
267 Mor: kill. Hit (KW); Maur (SC).
268 Morg(an): hare (KW). Northern English/Scots dial.: Malkin, Mawkin (1724).
269 Moro (i): bread (KW); Maúro, Mánro (SC).
270 Móro (ii): our (SC).
Mui: mouth. 265.
Muk(kav): to leave, let. 266.
271 Mulla(h): ghost, devil. Moólo, Múlo: ghost (SC); Mullo: ghost; Mullo-Mush: devil (KW). 273.
272 Muller: to kill (KW).
273 Mul(l)o: dead. Moólo, Múlo (SC).
274 Musgro: policeman (KW); Moóshkero (SC).
275 Mush: man (KW); Moosh, Mánoosh (SC).

276 Mush-faker: umbrella-maker. See Wear: 'A Short Account of the Travellers of Central Northumberland' (*GFLG* i, 99–104 (1912)). Also M'Cormick (1906, ix–xxiv). *Mush* = mushroom (Mayhew 1851). Also 132 above.
277 Mushipen: man. Paspati notes that abstract nouns in the Turkish dialect are very numerous and are formed indiscriminately by adding *-be* or *-pe* to verbs, adjectives and nouns. Although rarely inflected, it may be inferred from the instrumental case that they were originally formed in *-ben* and *-pen* (1870, 46–7). In the English dialect, abstract nouns are also formed in exactly the same way by the addition of these more primitive endings (Smart and Crofton 1875, 18). That the same method was also used in both dialects to form concrete nouns is suggested by the Turkish *astaribe* and the English *stariben*, prison, both of which may be referred to the Turkish Rom., *astarava*, I seize.
Muskra, -o: policeman. 274.
278 Mutter mengree: tea. Mooténgri, Múterimóngri: tea, urine (SC); Mutterimengri (KW).
Myler: ass, donkey. 244.

N

279 Nas: to flee, hang. Nash, Násher (SC); Nash: to run; Nasher: to lose, to hang (KW).
násh(er): to flee, hang.
280 Nashing Rukie: gallows. 279, 352.
281 Nav: name (SC KW).
Nisher: to flee. 279.
282 Nobbalo: head. Eng. nob + Romani suffix?
283 Nokyas: noses. A form which combines both the Romani and English plural endings. Nok: nose (SC KW).

O

Odoy: there. 4.
Opray: on, upon, up. 13.
Opré: on, upon, up. 13.
Oprey: on, upon, up. 13. Opré, Apré, 'Pré: on (SC). Opré: on, over (KW).
Ov: to come. 16.

P

284 Pal: brother, mate (SC); Pal, Pral (KW).
285 Palé: behind, after. Pálla, Pálal, Paúli (SC); Palé: back, again; Palla: after, behind (KW).
286 Pánder: to shut, close, bind (SC); to shut, tie (KW).
287 Páni, Paáni, Paúni: water (SC); Pani (KW).
Pánni: water. 287. Bori Pánni: the sea.
288 Panj: five. Pansh (SC); Panch (KW).
289 Pannum: bread. Originally a Canting term ex Latin *panis* (Harman 1566–7). Panum (KW).
290 Parni: white. Pórni, -o (SC); Pauni (KW).
291 Pauveri: poor ex French *pauvre*.
292 Pawdle: across. Párdel, Paúdel (SC); Paudel (KW). Pawno: white. 290.
293 Pee, Pióva: to drink (SC); Peeve, Pi (KW).
294 Peer, Píriv: to walk (SC).
295 Peéro, Píro, Peéri: foot (SC); Peeri (KW).
296 Pel, Peróva: to fall (SC); Per, Pel (KW). Pélled: fell. 296.
297 Pellengro Gry: stallion. Pélengro-grei (SC). Péller: behind. 285.
298 Pen: to say, tell (SC KW).
299 Pencha: like. Pénsa, Pénza (SC); Pensa (KW).
300 Pénnas: he/she told/said. Pendás (KW). 298.
301 Per: stomach, belly. Pur (SC); Per (KW).
302 Peryas: stomachs. A form combining both the Romani and English plural endings.
303 Péski: himself, his (SC). Pasp. gives *Po*, his, of which the dative would be *Peske*.
304 Péskri: her. The feminine form of the genitive case of *po*.
305 Pésser: to pay (SC); Pesser, Pester (KW).
306 Petul: horse-shoe. Pétal (SC); Petal(o) (KW).
307 Petulengro: Smith; a smith. Pétaléngro (SC KW). Pi: to drink. 293.
308 Pireno: swift (footed?). 295.
309 Pírini, -o: sweetheart (SC). Piramni (KW). Piro (i): foot. 295.
310 Piro (ii): moonlit. Pirryin: walking. 294.

311 Plaster: to run. Plaster, Práster (SC); Praster (KW).
312 Plasti!: run! 311. Plastra: to run. 311.
313 Póger, Pog: to break (SC); Pogger (KW). Pogger: to break. 313.
314 Pook: to speak. Poóker: to tell (SC); Pukker: say, tell (KW). Pooker: tell, say. 314.
315 Poor: to change. Pára, Púra (SC); Parrer (KW).
316 Pootch: to ask (SC); Putch (KW).
317 Poov: field, earth (SC); Puv (KW). To graze a horse (on private land without the owner's consent). Poove: to graze a horse (on private land without the owner's consent). 317. Por: stomach. 301.
318 Pórdo: full (SC); Pordi: full, heavy (KW).
319 Póri: tail, end (SC); Pori (KW). Porr: stomach. 301.
320 Poryo Wudres: feather bed. Pórongo-Wúdrus (SC).
321 Porno: flour. Váro, Vóro, Pórno (SC). 290.
322 Poshero: a halfpenny. Posh-Hóri (SC); Posh + Hori (KW).
323 Posinakas: handkerchief. Poshneckus (SC).
324 Potter: clothes (KW). Pouv: field. To graze a horse (on private land without the owner's consent). 317.
325 Pralor: brothers. 284. Praster: to run. 311.
326 Prásterméngro: policeman (SC KW). Lit. (Bow Street) Runner. Puch: to ask. 316. Puk: say, tell. 314. Puk(k)er: to say, tell. 314. Pukkra: say, tell. 314. Pukkerava: to say, tell. 314. Pur: stomach. 301.
327 Purana: Lee (lit.: leek).
328 Purdella: he, she or it blows. Poodéla (SC). Purdilo: he, she or it blows. 328.
329 Puri: old. Poóri, -o (SC); Puri, -o (KW). Putch: to ask. 316.
330 Putsey: pocket. Poótsi (SC); Putsi (KW). Putsi: pocket. 330. Puv: to graze a horse (on private land without the owner's consent). 317.
331 Puvengris: potatoes. Poov(y)éngri (SC); Puvengri (KW).

R

332 Racher: man. Ráklo: man, lad, boy (SC); Rakkelo: boy, youth (KW). Racler: man. 332.
333 Rai: gentleman (KW); Rei (SC).
334 Raiko: of the gentleman (KW). A form unknown to Smart and Crofton, the common genitive case-endings being -esko and -eskro.
335 Rákli: woman (SC); Rakli: girl (KW). Rakoli: woman. 335.
336 Rani: lady. Raúni, Rauní (SC KW).
337 Rania: rushes. Rányaw: rods, osiers, etc. (SC).
338 Rarde: night. Raáti (SC); Rarti, Rorti (KW).
   Rardi: night. 338.
   Rarti: night. 338.
   Rarty: night. 338.
339 Rasai: priest. Rash(r)ei (SC); Rashi, Rashenggro (KW).
   Rashai: priest. 339.
   Rasrai: priest. 339.
340 Rat: blood (KW) Ratt (SC).
   Ratti (i): blood. 340.
   Ratti (ii): night. 338.
   Rauney: lady. 336.
   Rawni: lady. 336.
341 Rik: side. Rig (SC KW).
342 Rínkeni, -o: pretty (SC); Rinkeni: beautiful (KW).
   Rinkers: pretty. 342.
   Rinkno: pretty. 342.
343 Rividi: dressed. Rído (SC); Rivdo (KW).
344 Rocker: to talk, speak. Róker (SC); Rokker (KW).
   Rokka: to talk, speak. 344.
   Rokker: to speak, talk. 344.
   Rokra: to speak, talk. 344.
345 Rokrapen: a saying, speech, conversation. Rókeropén (SC); Rokkeripen: language, speech (KW).
346 Romadi, -o: wife, husband; married. Rómedo: married (SC).
347 Rómanes: the Gypsy language (SC KW).
348 Rómani, -o: wife; *adj.* Gypsy (SC KW). Romany: the Gypsy language. A word given a wide variety of spellings.
349 Rómer: to marry (SC); Rommer (KW).
350 Romesa: Rom + -asa? An emphatic with the primary meaning 'too' or 'also' (SC). Alternatively, the instrumental case of *Rom* = with a Gypsy. Rommadis: wife, married woman. 346. Rommady: wife, married woman. 346. Rommany: wife. 348.

351 Romni-Chels, Romni Chela: English Gypsies. Romani Chal (KW). 348 + 70/71.
352 Rook: tree (SC); Rook(er) (KW). Rookies: trees. 352. Rorti: night. 338.
353 Rossar-mescri: Hearne. Noted by Borrow but not found by SC. 243.
354 Rov: to weep (SC); Rove (KW). Rukie: gallows. 352, 280. Rukk: tree. 352. Rukker: to talk, speak. 344. Rumni: *adj.* Gypsy. 348. Rumoured: married. 346, 349. Rúv: to weep. 354. Rye: gentleman, lord. 333.

S

355 Sa (i): what. So (SC) Sa, So (KW).
356 Sa (ii): all. Sor (SC KW).
357 Sal: to smile. Sal, Sárler, Sav: to laugh (SC); Sav (KW).
358 Sala: morning. Saála, Saúla (SC); Sarla (KW).
359 Saliwardo: saddle. Used as a verb in text 162. Sólovárdo: bridle (SC); Solivardo: bridle (KW). Salo: morning. 358.
360 Sar (i): with (SC); 'Sa (KW). Sar (ii): all. 356.
361 Sarasa: ever thus, like so. Saratti: all night. 356 + 338. Sarla: morning. 358.
362 Sas: he, she, it was (SC).
363 Sávo: who? what? (SC).
364 Scran: food. Skran (KW). Eng. slang: a reckoning at a tavern, broken victuals (1724).
365 Se: he she, it is. See (SC; Si: am are (KW)).
366 Shab: to run away (SC KW). According to SC, 'a Mumpers' word', but said by KW to be of Indian origin.
367 Shakerella: he, she, it covers.
368 Shan: you are (SC).
369 Sháni: mule (SC).
370 Shauvo: to touch, be intimate with. Chárvo: to touch, meddle, tease (SC); Charver: betray (KW). Shav: run off. 366.
371 Sher(r): head. Shéro (SC); Sherro (KW).
372 Shilliben: cold(ness). Shil (SC KW).
373 Shilni: *adj.* cold. Shílini, -o (SC); Shil(al)o (KW). Shilo: *adj.* cold. 373.
374 Shóck: bough. Shok: cabbage (SC); Shok(ker): cabbage, lettuce (KW).

375 Shom: I am (SC).
376 Shoon: to hear, listen (SC KW).
Shun(e): to hear, listen. 376.
377 Shunova: I hear, listen. Shoonóva (SC).
378 Shushai: rabbit. Shóshi (SC); Shoshoi, Shushi (KW).
Si: he, she, it is. 365.
379 Sig: soon, quick, early, just (SC); Sig(ger): fast, soon, quick(ly) (KW).
380 Slommer: to follow. Slom: to hunt (KW).
So: what. 355.
Sor(e): all. 356.
Sos: he, she, it was. 362.
Sossi: what? 355 + 365.
381 Sov: to sleep, have sexual intercourse with (SC); Suv (KW).
382 Sovéss': (will) you sleep. Sovésa (SC).
383 Staggus: stacks. Stághi (SC).
384 Stárdi, -o: prison (SC).
385 Staripen: prison. Stáriben, Stéripen, Stérimus, Stárdo, Staúri (SC); Stiraben, Stirapen (KW). KW derive *Stiraben* from *Star*, four (Walls), but Sampson (1926, iv, 338) and SC (1873, 141) refer it to a Romani verbal form of Sanskrit origin signifying to seize or take hold.
Pasp: Astaráva.
Stiggus: stacks. 383.
Stiraben: prison. 385.
Storiben: prison. 385.
Stuges: stacks. 383.
Stuggas: stacks. 383.
Stuggers: stacks. 383.
Stuggus: stacks. 383.
Sturiben: prison. 385.
386 Sut: (to) sleep. Soóti (SC); Sutti (KW).
Sutars: sleep. 386.
Suter: sleep. 386.
Sutta: sleep. 386.
Sutter(s): sleep. 386.
Sutti: sleep. 386.
Suv: to sleep, have sexual intercourse with. 381.
387 Swagler: a (tobacco) pipe. Swágler, Swégler (SC); Swiggler (KW).

T

388 Tacikena: truly.
389 Tacho: true. Tátch(en)i, -o (SC); Tatchi, -o (KW).
390 Tai: too, also (KW); Tei: indeed (SC).
391 Talé: under (SC); Telé (KW). 9.
392 Tan: tent, place (SC); place (KW).
393 Tárderin: hiding. A usage peculiar to Leland. Tárder: to pull (SC); Tarder: to pick, pull (KW). For 'hide' see 143 above.
394 Tarney: young. Tárni -o, Taúni -o (SC); Tauni (KW).
Tatchey: true. 389.
Tatcho: true. 389.
395 Tátchipen: (in) truth (SC KW).
396 Tatti-Panni: brandy, spirits. Tátto-Paáni, -Paúni (SC); Tatti Pani: whisky, spirits (KW).
Tatto-Pauni: brandy, spirits. 396.
397 Táttoben: summer (SC); Tattipen: heat (KW).
Tawna: young. 394.
Tawnie: young. 394.
398 Te (i): to, and, at, how, with, what, than, but etc. (SC); Te: if; Ta: but, and (KW).
399 Te (ii): the optative particle, used to form the subjunctive.
400 Ten: country (SC KW).
401 Thimble engro: a thimble rigger.
Thimble rigging involves placing a small object, such as a pea, beneath one of three thimbles which are then moved rapidly in an attempt to confuse the other player. The latter is then required to guess under which thimble the object is hidden. A variant of 'Find the Lady'.
402 Tíkni, -o: small (SC KW).
Tiknos: little ones, children. 402.
403 Tit: a (small) horse. A nineteenth-century Canting term (Ainsworth 1834) from an earlier dialect source.
404 Tober: road (KW). *Shelta*: a back-formation of Irish: bóthar = road.
405 Tober Skai: river. *Shelta*: from Irish: *bóthar*, road + *uisge*, water.
Todi: oh, dear! 119.
torarty: tonight. Eng. to + Rom. Rarty 338.
406 Tosser: choke. Tásser (SC).
407 Traishes: frightens. Trasher: to frighten (KW). 15.
408 Trin: three (SC KW).
409 Tringórishi: shilling – three groats (SC).
410 Truppo: trunk. Troópo: body (SC); Trupos (KW).
Tsavi: (girl) child. 68.
Tshavi: (girl) child. 68.
411 Tshuries: knives. Choóri (SC); Choori (KW).
Tsin: to cut. 77.
Tsor: to steal. 83.
Tsovihan: witch. 87.
412 Tu: you. Too (SC); Tutti (KW).
413 Tut: you. The accusative case of *Too*. 412.
414 Tute: you. Originally the first dative of *Too*. 412.

Tuti: you. Originally the first dative of *Too*. 412.
415 Tuke: to you. The second dative of *Too*. 412. Shan Tukey: you have.
Tuley: under, beneath. 9, 391.

U

Under-Potter: underclothes. 324.
Unklizn'd: unlocked. 96.
416 Usitel: arise.

V

417 Vans: things, gear. Perhaps a form of *vániso*: anything. 52 (SC).
418 Várdo: caravan, wagon (SC KW).
419 Vásavi, -o: bad, wicked (SC). Vassavie: wicked. 419.
420 Vastu: hands. Vástaw (SC); Vast(er), Wast: hand (KW).
421 Vel, Wel: come, become (SC KW).
422 Veshéngro: gamekeeper (SC); Vesh-Cove, Vesher (KW). Vesher: gamekeeper. 422. Vesengro: gamekeeper. 422.
423 Vonger: money. Vángar, Vóngar (SC); Vongar, Wongar (KW). A slang term, still heard in its true sense of 'coal'. 238.
424 Vóngus(ti), Vóngushi: ring (SC); Angushtri, Jangustri, Wangushter (KW).

W

425 Wafadi: bad. Wáfedi, -o (SC); Waffedi (KW). Wafo (i): bad. 425.
426 Wafo (ii): other. Wáver (SC); Vavver, Wavver (KW).

Wafu: other. 426.
Wafri: bad. 425.
427 Wardo-mescro: Cooper. Wardéngro (SC). Wav(v)er): other. 426.
Wel, 'vel: to come, become. 421.
428 Wesh: a wood. Vesh (SC); Vesh, Wesh (KW).
429 Weshen-jugalogonaes: in the manner of a fox.
430 Wudder, Wuddur: door. Woóda (SC); Voodar, Woodar (KW).
431 Wudrus: bed. Woódrus (SC); Woodrus (KW).

Y

432 Yak: eye. Yok (SC); Yak, Yok (KW).
433 Yarras: eggs. Yóri, Yóro: egg (SC); Youra (KW). Yarrers: eggs. 433.
434 Yeck: one. Yek (SC KW).
435 Yog: fire (SC KW).
436 Yogger: gamekeeper. Yogéngri-Gaújo (SC); Yogger: gun. Yog Mush: gamekeeper (KW).
437 Yog Moosh: gamekeeper (KW).
438 Yoi: she (SC).
439 Yoki: clever. Yoky: knowing, wide awake, sharp (SC); Yokki: clever, saucy (KW).
440 Yov: he (SC KW).
441 Yul: they.

Z

442 Zi: heart. Zee: heart (SC); Zee: heart, memory, will (KW).

Scotto-Romani and Tinklers' Cant

Scotto-Romani/Tinklers' Cant draws on a variety of sources, including old English Cant, *Shelta*, Scottish dialect forms and a range of other material, native and foreign. In the following list, words of Romani origin are referred to the forms in which they appear in Smart and Crofton, whilst words drawn from English Cant are referred to Harman's *Caveat* of 1566/67. With one or two exceptions, the derivations suggested for the remaining items are no more than tentative.

A

1   Ajeer: shitty. Rom.: *jeer*, rump. A transferred epithet.
2   Akakkie: shitty. Gael.: *Cach*, excrement.
3   Anee: in. Rom.: *a(n)dré*, in, into.
4   A-Trochtan: away, off.
5   Avree: away, out of. Rom.: *Avrí*, away, out of.
    Avri: away, out of. 5.
6   Awaft-Lo: away. Perhaps Eng. Cant: *Bynge a waste*, go you hence, explained by Barrère and Leland (1889, i, 11–12) as Romani, 'go to the devil'.

B

7   Bara: good, fine; an all-purpose positive epithet. Rom.: *Baúri, -o*, big.
8   Baren: bag. Gael.: *sparán*, purse
    Barry: good, fine. 7.
9   Baysh: wood. Rom.: *Vesh, Wesh*, wood, forest.
10 Beerie: ship. Rom.: *béro*, ship, boat.
11 Beneship: fine, good, great, grand. Cant: *benshyp*, very good.
12 Bing: come, go, take etc. Cant: *bynge*, to go.
13 Bung'd: went. 12.

C

14 Casro: greetings.
15 Chavvies: children. Rom.: *chávi, -o*, child.
16 Chor: to steal. Rom.: *chor*, to steal.
17 Chover: shop. Slang: *chovey* (Hotten 1859, 117).
18 Cowal: man. *Cull*, an abbreviated form of *cully*, a slang term of unknown origin signifying 'man, mate' (Head 1676).
19 Culyach: woman. Gael.: *cailleach*, an old woman.

D

20 Darkie: night. Cant: *darkemans*.
21 Deek: look, see. Rom.: *dik*, to see, look.
    Dick: look, see. 21.
22 Dillie: young lass. Cant: *dell*, young female virgin rogue.
23 Dodder: doctor. Eng.: doctor. Cf. *noder*, doctor (Gunn, MS list from Hugh Mac Fee, Falkirk, 1912).

F

24 Fee: face. *Shelta: pi*, mouth.
25 Feek: get, have. An all-purpose word recorded for bring, carry, come, do, fetch, give, kiss, make, steal, take, etc. Cant: *fake*.
26 Flattrin: fish. Eng: flat?

G

27 Gadgie: man, fellow. Rom.: *Górjo, Górjer*, non-Gypsy.
28 Gaffie: policeman. Rom.: *gávo*, policeman.
    Gahjee: man. 27.
29 Ganny: hen. Rom.: *Kánni*, hen.
    Ghahnee: hen. 29.
    Ghanies: chickens. 29.
30 Geddie: lad. Scots: Caddie, but cf. 27.
31 Gethrin: child. *Shelta: gatrin*.
32 Glim: fire. Cant: *glymmar*, fire.
    Glimmer: fire. 32.
33 Gowl: stomach.
34 Grae: horse. Rom.: *grei*, horse.
35 Gransee: barn. Rom: *Gránsa, Gráinsi*, barn.
    Granzi(e), barn. 35.
36 Grib: dance. An all-purpose word recorded variously for make, dig, hang, kiss, plough, shoot, throttle, write, etc. *Shelta: gruber*, job.

37 Grinnim: corn, oats. Cant: *grannam*, corn.

H

38 Habben: food. Rom.: *hóben*, food.
39 Hellum: town. Irish: *baile*, townland.
40 Hog: shilling. Eng. slang: shilling (1673).
41 Hornies: policemen. Horned like the devil?
42 Hurly: cart. Eng.: a porter's barrow, a hand-cart.

J

43 Ja: to go. Rom.: *jal, Jaw*, to go. Jal: to go. 43.
44 Jan: to know. Rom.: *jin*, to know. Jas: to go. 43.
45 Jurvil: arse. 1.

K

46 Kencheen: child. Germ.: *kindchen*. Also Cant: *kynchen*, child. Kenchin: child. 46.
47 Keer: house. Rom.: *ker*, a house. Kinchen: child. 46. Kinshin: child. 46.
48 Kushti: good. Rom.: *Kúshti, -o*, good.

L

49 Lowie: money. Cant: *Lowre* (Harman) ex Rom.: *lúva*, money.

M

50 Mahzie: dish. *Mazer*, a hardwood, properly maple, used in the manufacture of drinking bowls. The bowl itself.
51 Manishi: woman. Rom: *Mónooshi*.
52 Moolie: to kill. Rom: *muller*, to kill. Moolin': killing. 52.
53 Mort: woman, wife. Cant: *morte*. Moully: to kill. 52.
54 My Shannas: goodness me! Lit.: my badness. For *shan* = bad, see *JGLS* o.s. iii, 253.

N

55 Nackers: Travellers. Borrow suggests ex Rom.: *nok*, nose (1874, 264).
56 Naggis: self. Rom.: *Nágo*, own.
57 Naiskel: father. Eng.: nice? + Cant: *cowal*. 18.
58 Nash: flee, go, get away. Rom.: *nash, Násher*, to flee, hang.

59 Nax: night. Scots: *nicht*; Germ.: *Nacht*. Noggins: self. 56.

P

60 Peeve: drink. Rom.: *Pee*, to drink.
61 Peeven-Ken: public house. Rom.: *pee*, drink, + Cant: *ken*, house (Harman). Peevie: drink. 60.
62 Pottach: man. Gael.: *bodach*.
63 Pourin': water. Eng.: pouring.
64 Prokhans: shoes. Gael.: *bróg*?
65 Pudden-Ken: lodging house. Cant: *pad*, to travel on foot as a vagrant (ex stand. Eng.: to walk) + *ken*, a house. Brandon distinguishes between a *padden crib*, a boys' lodging house, and a *padden ken*, a tramps' lodging house.

R

Rowdie: money. 49.
66 Ruffie: devil. Cant: *ruffian*, the devil.

S

67 Shan: bad. 52.
68 Shanish-Shanish: my God! 52.
69 Skukr: fine. Rom.: *shukár*.
70 Slob: tea. Eng.: slop?
71 Slum (i): to hit. Eng.: slam?
72 Slum (ii): sleep. Scots: sloom = a gentle sleep, a light doze.
73 Sprachet: begged. Germ.: *sprechen*, speak.
74 Sprag: horse.
75 Stardee: prison. Rom.: *stárdi, -o*, prison. Stardi(e): prison. 75.
76 Steemers: bagpipes. *Shelta: stioma* (*JGLS* n.s. i, 276).
77 Strod-Gribber: shoe-maker. Eng.: stride + *Shelta: gruber*. 36.
78 Suckler: breast: Eng. suckle.
79 Swag: gear.

T

80 Tober: road. *Shelta* = Irish, bótha.
81 Toggery: clothes. *Shelta* ex Latin *toga*? See Sampson (M'Cormick 1906, xv). Cf. also Cant: *togmans*, clothes.
82 Trangle: to start a fight with. Cf. Eng.: *tangle*.

W

83 Wattle: camp, tent. A reference to the rods forming the framework of the traditional 'bender' tent.

Notes

1. A similar want of Romani influence is also apparent in other varieties of early western European Cant. There are, for example, no Gypsy words in the French Canting vocabulary *Le Jargon ou Langage d'Argot Reformé* of 1634, or in the Italian *Il Modo Novo da Intendere la Lingua Zerga Cioé parlar Furbesca* of 1549. The same may also be said of the German *Liber Vagatorum/Der Betelerorden* of *c.*1510, whilst of some 1,200 words included in the Spanish *Romances de Germania* of 1609, no more than a dozen would seem to be of Gypsy origin.
2. Among Anglo-American Gypsies, Washington was apparently known as the *Belunigav*, or Queen's Town (Gatschett 1897, 334–5).
3. Writing of the *Romanitchels* of central and northern France on page lii of his *Études de Philologie Comparé sur l'Argot*, Francisque Michel tells us that

   > These maurauders speak among themselves a particular language to which they alone have the key and they use it even in the presence of other thieves; but as they meet frequently with the latter, at least fleetingly, especially with the nocturnal thieves of the department (called *sorgueurs*), it is impossible that they do not understand *Argot*. Furthermore, if one can trust a police note, Romani, in their mouths, carries numerous traces of the invasion of *Argot* . . . Now these words can only be claimed by *Argot*, and it is thus established that our *Romanitchels* understand it.

   The salient point here is that whilst these Gypsies had apparently admitted a number of Cant words into their language, it nevertheless remained wholly their own, even though they may have used it in the presence of native rogues.
4. For some commentators, the term 'language death' may properly be used only in those cases where the language in question has altogether ceased to exist. Thus, were Basque to be entirely replaced by French or Spanish, then 'language death' might be said to have occurred, whereas, were Patagonian Welsh to be totally lost, this would have little or no bearing on the future of Welsh in Wales. Again, for Dorian (1978, 647), the term 'language death', when applied to a specific speech community, is only appropriate if the shift is from one language to another rather than between two varieties of the same language. Although the old Romani tongue may have died out in Britain, it is still spoken elsewhere and, as Hancock has shown, it is even possible to argue that the *Poggadi Chib* represents an albeit much reduced variety of that language. For these reasons, when describing the gradual substitution of English for Romani as the everyday language of the Gypsies of England, the term 'language shift' rather than 'language death' would seem preferable.
5. The correct form would be *Mala*, not *Mhala*, which would suggest an initial 'p' in the radical state. It is not clear whether this represents an error in pronunciation or transcription.
6. The Lovells represented by Groome in his book were, in reality, Locks or Boswells – English Gypsies who had settled in Wales, intermarrying with their Welsh cousins. When Groome knew them, they were apparently using *Romanes* in a domestic setting (Groome 1880, 16).
7. It is perhaps worth noting that, in Anglo-Indian slang, 'nautch' was once used to mean 'A kind of ballet dance performed by women; any kind of stage entertainment; an European ball' (Yule and Burnell 1886). It was also used in combination as in the deceptively Romani-sounding 'poggly-nautch', a fancy-dress ball. *Poggle*, however, is here derived from the Hindi *pudgal*, 'a madman' or 'idiot', as in the following macaronic rendering of the old English adage: 'pudgal et pecunia jaldè separantur'. For the misuse of *nautch* as a personal noun see Browning's 'Fifine at the Fair' of 1872.
8. 'I know of no American Romanichel (English Gypsy) songs, recorded or no, in that

language, and the Gypsies, in fact, deny there are any' (Salo, personal communication, April 1992).

9. Among the Gypsies of north Wales, Caernarfon was known as *Lubnieno Gav*, Whores' Town – *Sar lubnia si-le are akava gav, rakia ta rania ta romerde juvia tai*, they are all whores in this city, working girls, ladies and married women as well. Elsewhere the air is referred to as *I Lubniénig Gili*.

10. The Romani for lark is elsewhere given as *oriimásko ceriklo*.

11. I have suggested *stuffisava* by analogy with *hopesáva*, I hope (Tipler, *JGLS* v, 28), and *wántasóva*, I do want (Smart and Crofton 1875, 150). According to Partridge, the word had already acquired its low meaning before the end of the last century, so it cannot be discounted on chronological grounds (Beale 1991, 441). Manfri completes the phrase with an accusative plural pronoun, although he elsewhere uses the correct form, e.g. in 24.

12. 'In the USA, where Angloromani speakers come into contact, but don't as a rule socialise with, speakers of inflected dialects of the language, they are scarcely recognised as being even lexically related, and are sometimes referred to as "Rooshians", or "Roos" by American Romanichals' (Hancock 1985, 101).

13. A similar point is made by T. Potter Coffin in connection with the way in which printed texts are dealt with by mainstream folk singers. On pages 165–6 of *The British Ballad in North America* (1977 edn), he suggests that what is most important to the singer about any song is its 'emotional core' rather than the detail of the action described. Thus a printed text, having acquired oral status, may ultimately be transformed into a folk song by a gradual process involving the wearing away of literary frills and narrative detail until it becomes a traditional ballad of the kind collected by Child. In the same way, left to the vicissitudes of oral transmission, a narrative ballad may eventually assume the character of a lyric or even a nonsense song. Although this process would seem to have much in common with the way in which mainstream texts are dealt with by the Gypsy singer, one has only to compare such mainstream originals with their Gypsy equivalents to realize that it falls far short of the process of Romanization referred to here.

14. For the Acts 'anent beggaris' of James I and IV, see Balfour's *Practicks*. fol. edn. 1754; and for a more wide-ranging history of anti-vagrancy legislation, Ribton-Turner 1887.

15. First published in Horncastle's *Music of Ireland*, 'The Hunting of the Wren' is to be found all over the British Isles and in France. A number of Welsh variants are given in *JWFSS* 1, part 3 (1911), 99–113, and a version in English from Carmarthenshire – 'The Cutty Wren' – in Mason's *Nursery Rhymes and Country Songs* of 1908. A Breton set is included by M. Luzel in his *Chansons Populaires de la Basse Bretagne* (Paris, 1971) and a number in Manx Gaelic in *JFSS* 28 (1924). See also the Buchan MS 1, 116a–117b and Chambers (1926) for the song in its Scottish form.

Bibliography

Acton, T. 1971a. 'Current changes amongst British Gypsies and their place in international patterns of development', *Proceedings of the Research and Policy Conference of the National Gypsy Education Council*. 26–8 March.

——1971b. *Mo Romano Lil*. Romanestan Publications.

——1974. *Gypsy Politics and Social Change*. Routledge & Kegan Paul.

——1977. *Mo Romano Lil*. Romanestan Publications.

——1981. *Gypsies: Surviving Peoples*. Macdonald Educational.

Acton, T. and Kenrick, D. 1985. *Romani Rokkeripen To-Divvus*. Romanestan Publications.

Ainsworth, W. Harrison. 1834. *Rookwood*. Chapman Hall.

Alecsandri, Vasilie. 1855. *Ballades et chants populaires de la Roumanie*. Paris.

Andrews, W. 1889. *Bygone Northumberland*. London. Pp. 222–49.

Andrews, W. 1897. *Legal Lore: Curiosities of Law and Lawyers*. W. Andrews & Co.

'Anglo-Romani songs'. 1909. *JGLS*, n.s., 3, 157–60.

Anon. 1874. Review of Borrow's *Romano Lavo-Lil*, *Athenaeum*, April, 556–7.

Arnold, F. 1898. 'Our old poets and the Tinkers', *Journal of American Folklore*, 11, 210–20.

Ascoli, G. I. 1865. *Zigeunerisches. Besonders auch als Nachtrag zu dem Pott'schen Werke: Die Zigeuner in Europa und Asien*. Halle: E. Heynemann.

Atkinson, F. S. 1909. *JGLS*, n.s., 3, 158–9.

Axon, W. E. A. 1891. 'Romani songs Englished', *JGLS*, o.s. 2, 5–7.

——1897. 'Laws relating to the Gypsies', in Andrews 1897.

——1899. 'Homer Tankeromengro 'Dré, Rómanis', *Manchester Quarterly*, 18, 209.

BAAS AGM. British Association for the Advancement of Science. Annual General Meeting.

Baerlein, Henry. 1949. *Landfalls and Farewells*. London.

Baird, J. 1840. *First Report of the Committee for the Reformation of the Gypsies in Scotland*. Yetholm. Pp. 32–6. Word list reprinted in Baird, W., *Memoir of the Rev. John Baird, Minister of Yetholm, Roxburghshire*, J. Nisbet, 1862.

Baring-Gould, Revd S. and Fleetwood Sheppard, Revd H. 1889–91. *Songs and Ballads of the West*. Willis and Patey. Revised edition, Methuen, 1905.

Barker, J. Hudson. 1899. 'Gypsy-life of Northumberland', in Andrews 1889.

Barrère, A. and Leland, C. G. 1889. *A Dictionary of Slang, Jargon and Cant*. The Valentine Press.

Barrett, William A. 1891. *English Folk Songs*. Novello.

Bataillard, Paul. Review of Leland *et al*'s *English Gypsy Songs*, *Revue Critique* 9 (Sept.), 167–73.

Beale, P. (ed). 1991. *A Concise Dictionary of Slang and Unconventional English*. London: Routledge (ex E. Partridge (ed.), *A Dictionary of Slang and Unconventional English*, 1937).

Bell, R. 1857. *Ancient Poems, Ballads and Songs of the Peasantry of England*. London.

Bercovici, Konrad. 1928. *The Story of the Gypsies*. New York.

Berresford Ellis, P. 1974. *The Cornish Language and its Literature*. Routledge & Kegan Paul.

Besant, W. 1883. *Life and Achievements of E. H. Palmer*. J. Murray.

Binchy, Alice. 1994. 'Travellers' language: a sociolinguistic perspective', in *Irish Travellers – Culture and Ethnicity*. Belfast Institute of Irish Studies, 135–54.

Black, George, F., 1914. *A Gypsy Bibliography*. Bernard Quaritch.

Boorde, A. 1547–8. *Fyrst Boke of the Introduction of Knowledge*. Copland. Reproduced and edited by F. J. Furnivall for the Early English Texts Society. Trübner, 1870. See also Furnivall 1874 for an account of Zupitza's discovery and Miklosich's of Boorde's text, and Crofton 1907 for a full analysis.

Borrow, G. 1841. *Zincali: Gypsies of Spain*. J. Murray. One-volume reprint 1921, Valentine Press.

——1842. *The Bible in Spain*. J. Murray. Everyman Library edition.

——1851. *Lavengro*. J. Murray. Repr. Heron Books, 1969.

——1857. *Romany Rye*. J. Murray. Repr. Everyman Library edition.

——1862. *Wild Wales*. J. Murray. 1919 edn.

——1874. *Romano Lavo-Lil*. J. Murray. Repr. Alan Sutton Publishing, 1982.

Boswell, S. G. 1970. *The Book of Boswell*. Gollancz.

Breathnach, Breandán. 1971. *Folkmusic and Dances of Ireland*. Talbot Press.

Breathnach, An t-Athair (Father) Pádruig. N.d. *Songs of the Gael: A Collection of Anglo-Irish Songs and Ballads Wedded to Old Traditional Irish Airs*. Brown and Nolan.

Breydenbach, Bernhard von. 1486. *Itinerarium in Terram Sanctam. Moguntina*. E. Reüwich. See *JGLS*, n.s., 3 (1909), 60.

Broadwood, Revd J. 1843. *Old English Songs*. Balls & Co.

——1890. *Sussex Songs*. Stanley Lucas and Weber.

Broadwood, L. 1908. *English Traditional Songs and Carols*. Boosey & Co.

Brockie, W. 1884. *The Gypsies of Yetholm*. J. & J. H. Rutherfurd.

Bronson, B. H. 1959–72. *The Traditional Tunes of the Child Ballads with their Texts according to the Extant Records of Britain and America*. Princeton University Press.

Brown, I. 1924. *Gypsy Fires in America*. Harper & Bros. Reissued by Kennikat Press, 1972.

——1929. *Deep Song*. Harper & Bros.

Browne, J. P. 1990. Ewan MacColl (obituary). *Folk on Tap*, 42 (March 1990), 10–12.

Brune, J. 1975 'Songs of the Travelling People', in Kennedy 1975.

Bryant, J. 1785. 'Collection on the Zingara or Gypsey Language', *Archeologia*, 7, 387–94.

Buchan, N. 1962. *101 Scottish Songs*. William Collins & Sons Ltd.

Byron, M. 1903. 'Gypsy Mother Song', *Spectator*, 99, 861. Repr. in *Littell's Living Age*, 238 (1903), 192.

Carew, Bamfylde Moore. 1802. *Life of Bamfylde Moore Carew*. London. First published in 1745 and with over fifty entries in Black's *Gypsy Bibliography*.

Carew, Francis Wylde (pseudonym of Arthur E. G. Way). 1890. *No. 747. Being the Autobiography of a Gypsy*. Simpkin Marshall & Co. Review: *JGLS*, o.s., 2 (1890), 315.

Carmichael, A. 1899–1901. List of Scotto-Romani/Tinklers' Cant, collected in Arran in 1895 and published by MacRitchie in 'Shelta: the Cairds' language', *Transactions of the Gaelic Society of Inverness*, xxiv (1899–1901).

Carroll, J. 1975. 'Irish Travellers around London', *FMJ*, 3, 1, 31–40.

Chambers, R. 1826. *Popular Rhymes of Scotland*. Edinburgh.

Chappell, W. 1858–9. *Popular Music of the Olden Times*. Cramer, Beale & Chappell.

Charles, B. G. 1971. 'The English element in Pembrokeshire Welsh', *Studia Celtica*, VI, 103–37.

——1982. *The English Dialect of South Pembrokeshire*. Pembrokeshire Record Society.

Child, F. J. and Kiltredge, J. L. 1882–9. *English and Scottish Popular Ballads*. Boston, Mass. 1965 edn, Dover.

Chorley, H. F. 1911. *The National Music of the World*. Reeves.

Clébert, J. P. 1964. *The Gypsies*. Translation by Charles Duff of *Les Tziganes*, B. Arthaud. Vista Books, 1963. Penguin edn, 1967.

Clement, D. 1981. 'The secret languages of the Scottish Travelling People', *Grazer Linguistische Studien: Sprachliche Sonderformen*, xv, 17–25.

Colocci, Marquis Adriano. 1889. *Gli Zingari*. Turin.

Connors, M. and Acton, T. 1974. *Have You the Feen's Gread Nyocked?* Romanestan Publications.

Copsey, D. 1818. 'Dialect and manners of the Gypsies', *Monthly Magazine*, 46, 303–4.

Cowper, William. 1785, *The Task. Selections from Cowper*. National Library for the Blind, 1935. For Gypsies, see Book 1 *passim*.

Cox, D. 1753. *An Appeal to the Public on Behalf of Elizabeth Canning, in which the Material Facts in her Story are Fairly Stated, and Shown to be True on the Foundation of Evidence*. W. Meadows.

Cox, G. Valentine. 1868. *Recollections of Oxford*. Macmillan.

Crabb, J. 1832. *The Gypsies' Advocate: or Observations on the Origin, Character, Manners and Habits of the English Gypsies*. Seeley.

Cray, E. 1969. *The Erotic Muse. A Completely Uncensored Collection of the Songs Everyone Knows and No one has Written Down Before*. Oak Publications.

Crofton, H. T. 1875. Review of Leland *at al*'s *English Gypsy Songs, The Academy*, 8, 385–6.

Crofton, H. T. 1907. 'Borde's Egipt Speche', *JGLS*, n.s., 1, 156–68.

Crouch, H. 1671. *The Welch Traveller or The Unfortunate Welchman*. Printed for William Whitwood at the sign of The Bell in Duck-Lane in Smithfield. See also W. C. Hazlitt's *Early Popular Poetry of England* (1864–6), 4, 321–53.

Crystal, D. (ed.). 1992. *The Cambridge Encyclopaedia of Language*. Cambridge University Press.

Cunningham, J. 1835. *The Songs of England and Scotland*. London.

Curzin, J.-P. 1977. *Catalogue la Diseuse de Bonne Adventure de Caravage*. Paris.

Davies, C. S. L. 1966. 'Slavery and Protector Somerset: the Vagrancy Act of 1547', *Economic History Review*, 532–49.

Davies, J. Glyn. 1930. 'Welsh sources of Gypsy history', *JGLS*, 3rd ser., 9, 64–86.

Dekker, T. 1608. *The Belman of London Bringing to Light the Most Notorious Villainies that are now Practised in the Kingdom*.

——1608. *Lanthorn and Candle-Light or the Belman's Second Night Walk*. J. Busbie.

——1616. *Villainies Discovered by Lanthorne and Candle-Light and the help a New Crier Called O Per Se O being an Addition to the Belman's Second Night-Walk and a Laying Open to the World of those Abuses which the Belman Because he Went i'th Dark Could not See. With Canting songs Never Before Printed*. J. Busbie.

The Belman of London ran to three editions in 1608 and was followed, in the same year, by *Lanthorn and Candle-Light* which, in turn, received two further impressions in 1609. A fourth edition of the latter also appeared in 1612 under the title *O Per Se O, or A New Crier of Lanthorne and Candle-Light, Being an Addition or Lengthening of the Belman's Second Night-Walk*. In all, it ran to some eight or nine editions during the period 1608–48, all differing, more or less, the one from the other, including the 1616 *Villainies Discovered*.

Denham, M. 1892–7. *The Denham Tracts*. A collection of folklore edited by Dr James Hardy for the London Folklore Society.

Dick, J. C. 1962. *The Songs of Robert Burns*. Hatboro, Pa. First published in 1903.

Dixon, J. H. and Bell, R. 1877. *Ancient Poems, Ballads and Songs of the Peasantry of England*. Percy Society.

Dorian, N. 1981. *Language Death: The Life-Cycle of a Scottish Gaelic Dialect*. University of Pennsylvania Press.

Dyneley Prince, J. 1907. 'The English Rommany jargon of the American roads', *American Oriental Society Journal*, 28, 271–308.

——1908. 'Anglo-American Rommany: a reply', *JGLS*, n.s., 2, 180–1.

Eckenstein, Lina. 1906. *Comparative Studies in Nursery Rhymes*. London.

Egan, Pierce. 1821. *Life in London, or Tom and Jerry*. London.

Éigse (ed. G. Murphy; B. O. Cuív), Dublin, 1939–.

Fasold, R. 1984. *The Socio-Linguistics of Society*. Blackwell.

Fielding, H. 1753. *A Clear Statement of the Case of Elizabeth Canning Who Hath Sworn That She Was Robbed and Almost Starved to Death by Gypsies*. A. Millar.

Findlater, Jane H. 1913. 'The Little Tinker: or free will and adoption', *Cornhill Magazine* (August), 218–27.

Finlay, J. 1911. *Scottish Historical and Romantic Ballads*. Ballantyne.

FMJ. Folk Music Journal.

Folktracks (audio tapes).

——60–031 The Roving Journeyman: Folksong of the Travelling People.

——30–042 The Sweet Primroses: Songs and Stories of West Country Gypsies.

——60–43 Black Dog and Sheep Crook: Songs and Stories of West Country Gypsies.

——60–053 Harps and Hornpipes: Music and Memories of Welsh Gypsies.

——60–067 What a Voice: Jeanie Robertson (documentary).

——60–76 Music at the Gate: Séamus Ennis – Folksongs and Pipe Tunes.

——60–100 I am a Romany: Phoebe Smith and Family.

——60–106 Jeanie Robertson Sings the Big Ballads.

——45–140 O, What a Life: English Gypsy Singers, Sussex and Kent.

——60–166 Songs of Irish Tinkers vol. 1.

——60–167 Songs of Irish Tinkers vol. 2.

——60–168 Songs of Irish Tinkers vol. 3.

——60–175 John Reilly: Irish Tinker Ballads.

——60–183 Ballad Singers in the Berryfields vol. 1.

——60–184 Ballad Singers in the Berryfields vol. 2.

——60–185 Ballad Singers in the Berryfields vol. 3.

——60–441 Can You Pooker Romany?

——60–608 Vlaxi Rom: European Romany Gypsy Singers.

Folktracks Publications, 16 Brunswick Square, Gloucester G11 1UG.

Ford, R. 1899. *Vagabond Songs of Scotland*. Gardner.

Fordyces's *Newcastle Song Book* 1842. *The Newcastle Song Book, or Tyneside's Songster*. Newcastle upon Tyne.

Fraser, A. 1990. 'Counterfeit Egyptians', *Tsiganologische Studien*, 2, 43–69.

——1992. *The Gypsies*. Blackwell.

Furnivall, F. J. 1874. 'The earliest known specimen of the Gypsy language', *The Academy*, 25 July, 100. See Boorde.

Gal, S. 1979. *Language Shift: Social Determinants of Linguistic Change in Bilingual Austria*. New York Academic Press.

Gatschet, A. S. 1897. 'Gypsy town names', *Antiquarian and Oriental Journal*, 19, 334–5 (Chicago).

GFG. Gypsy and Folk-lore Gazette. The publication of the Gypsy and Folk-lore Club and The Gypsy and Curio Co. began in 1912 as *Romanitshels, Didikois and Folk-lore Gazette* and subsequently became *The Gypsy and Folk-lore Gazette*, and ended in 1916 as *The Gypsy*, published by the Gypsy and Curio Co. alone.

Gilchrist, A. 1911. Review of Gillington's *Songs of the Open Road*, *JGLS*, n.s., 5, 60–5.

Gillington, A. E. 1907. 'The river running by', *JGLS*, n.s., 1, 60–5.

——1910a. *Old Christmas Carols of the Southern Counties*. J. Curwen & Sons.

——1910b. 'The Gypsies pass', *Country Life*, 28, 741.

——1911a. *Songs of the Open Road: Didakei Ditties and Gypsy Dances*. Joseph Williams.

——1911b. 'The Bushes Green', *JGLS*, n.s., 5, 51–4.

——1912. 'My Sweet Sister', *Romanitshels, Didikois and Folklore Gazette*, 1, 1 (January), 4–6.

Gjorgjevic, T. R. 1906. *Die Zigeuner in Serbien*. Budapest: Buchdruckerie.

Gray, L. H. 1939. *Foundations of Language*. Macmillan.

Greene, D. 1972. *The Irish Language*. Mercier Press.

Groome, F. H. 1875. Review of Borrow's *Lavo-Lil*, *The Academy*, 5, 665–7.

——1880. *In Gypsy Tents*. W. P. Nimmo. New edn Wakefield: E.P. Publishing Ltd, 1973.

——1888. 'Gypsy folk tales', *National Review*, 11, 659–73.

——1899. *Gypsy Folk Tales*. Hurst & Blackett.

Grosvenor, Lady Arthur (Helen). 1910. 'A Pilgrim's Progress', *JGLS*, n.s., 3, 204–24 (for diaries of Revd T. W. Norwood).

GDM. Grove's Dictionary of Music. First edn 1878; second edn 1910.

Haining, P. 1972. *The Warlock's Book*. W. H. Allen & Co.

Hajdú, András. 1962. 'Folklore tsigane', *Etudes Tsiganes*, 8 (1–2), 1–33 (Paris).

Hall, L. A. 1975. 'Scottish Tinker songs', *FMJ*, 3, 1, 41–62.

Hanchant, W. L. 1932. *The Newgate or Flowers of Hemp*. Desmond Harmsworth.

Hancock, Ian. F. 1970. 'Is Anglo Romani a Creole?', *JGLS*, 49 (1/2), 41–4.

——1971. Rejoinder to Kenrick in Acton 1971b, 15–18.

——1979. *Romani Sociolinguistics*. The Hague.

——1984. 'Romani and Angloromani' and 'Shelta and Polari', in Trudgill 1984, iii, 367–403.

——1985. 'The social and linguistic development of Angloromani', in Acton and Kenrick 1985, 89–122.

Harman, T. 1566–7. *A Caueat or Warening for Common Cursetors Vulgarly called Vagabones*. Imprinted at London in Fleet Street at the Sign of the Falcon by William Griffith. Extracts cited ex Salgado 1972, 79–154.

Harper, J. V. and Hudson, C. 1971. 'Irish Traveller Cant: an historical, structural and sociolinguistic study of an argot', *English Linguistics*, v, 78–82.

Harriott, J. S. 1830. 'Observations on the oriental origin of the Romnichal', *Transactions of the Royal Asiatic Society of Great Britain*, 2, 518–88.

Hazlitt, W. C. 1864–6. *Remains of the Early Popular Poetry of England*. J. R. Smith.

Head, Richard. 1676. *The Canting Academy or The Devil's Cabinet Opened.* London.

Herd, D. 1973. *Ancient and Modern Scottish Songs.* Scottish Academic Press. First published in 1776.

Herrmann, A. 1889. 'Gypsy songs of mourning', *JGLS*, o.s., 1, 289–95. The second part of Herrmann's article is extracted from Wlislocki 1889.

Hodgson, R. 1973. 'Early Romani', *JGLS*, 52 (3/4), 87–9.

Hooper, J. 1912(?). 'Borrow's forgotten ballads', *Romanitshels, Didikois and Folklore Gazette*, 1 (4), 107–17. Undated.

Horsley, J. W. 1879. 'The autobiography of a thief in thieve's language', *MacMillan's Magazine* (October). Cited in Hanchant 1932, 111–29.

——1887. *Jottings from Jail.* T. Fisher Unwin.

Hotten, J. C. 1859. *Dictionary of Modern Slang, Cant and Vulgar Words.* London. Also 1864 edn.

Hoyland, J. 1816. *A Historical Survey of the Current Habits and Present State of the Gypsies.* York.

Hume, M. 1889. *Chronicle of King Henry VIII of England, being a Contemporary Record of some of the principal events of the reigns of King Henry VIII and Edward VI written in Spanish by an unknown hand.* London.

Ibbetson, W. J. 1887. 'Songs of the English Gypsies', NQ, 7 ser., 4, 397.

James, A. 1911. 'The Death-Bird', *JGLS*, n.s., 5, 145–6.

James, B. Ll. 1972. 'The Welsh language in the Vale of Glamorgan', *Morgannwg*, 16, 16–36.

Jarman, E. and A. O. H. 1979. *Y Sipsiwn Cymreig.* Cardiff: University of Wales Press.

——1991. *The Welsh Gypsies.* Cardiff, University of Wales Press.

Jenner, Henry. 1876. 'The Manx language: its grammar, literature and present state', *Transactions of the Philological Society*, 1875–6, 172–97.

JFSS. Journal of the Folk Song Society.

JGLS. Journal of the Gypsy Lore Society.

John, Augustus. 1909. 'Russian Gypsy songs', *JGLS*, n.s., 2, 197–9.

——1911. 'Songs of Fabian de Castro' *JGLS*, n.s., 5, 135–8.

Johnson, J. 1787. *The Scottish Musical Museum.* Edinburgh.

Jones, R. W. 1930. 'Gypsies in Wales', *JGLS*, 3rd ser., 9, 87–9.

Jones, T. G. 1930. *Welsh Folk Lore and Folk Customs.* Methuen.

Jonson, B. 1640. *The Masque of the Gypsies.* J. Okes.

——1816. *Works.* G. & W. Nicol, 7, 365–424.

Joyce, P. W. 1909. *Old Irish Folk Music and Songs: A Collection of 842 Irish Airs and Songs Hitherto Unpublished.* Edited with annotations for the Royal Society of Antiquarians of Ireland. Longmans, Green & Co.

JSS. Journal of Scottish Studies.

JWFSS. Journal of the Welsh Folk Song Society.

Kennedy, P. (ed.). 1975. *Folksongs of Britain and Ireland.* Cassell/Schirmer. 1984 edn Oak Publications.

Kenrick, D. 1971. 'Anglo-Romani today', in Acton 1971b, 5–14.

——1978. 'Romani English', in Hancock 1979, 367–83.

——1979. 'Romani English', *International Journal of the Sociology of Language*, 19 (Romani Socio-linguistics), 111–20.

——1985. 'Romani English', in Acton and Kenrick 1985, 79–88.

Kenrick, D. and Wilson, T. 1985. 'Romani vocabulary', in Acton and Kenrick 1985, 15–56.

Kinney, P. 1979. 'The tunes of *Yr Hen Benillion*', *Welsh Folksong Journal (Canu Gwerin).*

Knapp, W. I. (ed.). 1900. *Romany Rye.* J. Murray. See Borrow 1857.

Kogalnitchan, M. 1837. *Esquisse sur l'Histoire, les Moeurs et la Langue des Cigains, Connus en France sous le Nom de Bohemiens: Suivi d'un Recueil de Sept Cent Mots Cigains.* Berlin, B. Behr.

Kovalcsik, K. 1985. *Vlax Gypsy Folk Songs in Slovakia.* Institute for Musicology of the Hungarian Academy for Sciences.

Krantzius, Albertus (Krantz, Albert). 1580. *Rerum Germanicarum Historici Clariss. Saxonia.* Frankfurt. First published in Cologne in 1530. The passage dealing with the Gypsies is reprinted in Dyrlund, F., *Tatare og Natmands-Folk i Danmark Betratede med Hensyn til Samfundsforholdene i det Hele.* Copenhagen, 1872, 361.

Lal, C. 1962. *Gypsies: Forgotten Children of India.* Government of India Press.

478

Laporte, C. 1876. *Gypsy Melodies*. Augener and Co.

Lee, Kate. 1899. 'Some experiences of a folk-song collector', *JFSS*, 1 (1), 7–11.

Lee, Stephen. 1994. *Crime, Punishment and Protest: 1450 to the Present Day*. Longman.

Leibich, R. 1863. *Die Zigeuner in Ihrem Wesen und in Ihrer Sprache*. F. A. Brockhaus.

Leitner, G. 1880. *A Sketch of the Changars and of their Dialect*. Lahore.

Leland, C. G. 1873. *The English Gypsies and their Language*. Trübner. 1968 edition, Detroit: Gale Research.

——1882. *The Gypsies*. Houghton Mifflin & Co.

——1887. 'Three Gypsy songs', *Hood's Comic Annual*, 19, 65–7.

——1889. 'An Italian Gypsy song', *JGLS*, o.s., 1, 212–13.

——1891a. *Gypsy Sorcery and Fortune Telling*. T. Fisher Unwin. 1971 edition, Dover Publications Inc.

——1891b 'An Italian Gypsy song', *JGLS*, o.s., 2, 320.

Leland, C. G., Palmer, E. H. and Tuckey, J. 1875. *English Gypsy Songs*. Trübner.

Levi, P. 1989. *The Periodic Table*. Abacus–Sphere Ltd.

Lieberson, S. 1972. 'Bilingualism in Montreal: a demographic analysis', in Fishman, J. (ed), *Advances in the Sociology of Language*, vol. 2. The Hague.

Liszt, Abbé F. 1859. *Des Bohémiens et de Leur Musique en Hongarie*. Paris: Bourdilliat.

Lloyd, A. L. 1967. *Folk Song in England*. Laurence & Wishart/Workers' Music Association.

Lockwood, W. B. 1975. *Languages of the British Isles Past and Present*. Deutsch.

Logan, W. H. 1869. *The Pedlar's Pack of Songs and Ballads*. W. Patterson.

Lucas, J. 1882. *The Yetholm History of the Gypsies*. J. & J. H. Rutherfurd.

Lyster, R. 1907. 'Two Gypsy riddles', *JGLS*, n.s., 1, 92.

MacAlister, Sir D. 1928. *Romani Versions*. Edinburgh University Press.

MacAlister, R. A. S. 1937. *The Secret Languages of Ireland*. Cambridge University Press. 1976 edn, Amsterdam: Philo Press.

MacColl, E. and Seeger, P. 1977. *Travellers' Songs from England and Scotland*. Routledge & Kegan Paul.

——1986. *Till Doomsday in the Afternoon*. Manchester University Press.

Macfie, R. Scott. 1909. *Romanichels, a Lucubration: by Tringurushi Juvalomursh*. R. M'Gee. The cover reads: 'A brief account of Gypsy history, persecutions, character and customs, with examples of genuine Gypsy melodies compiled by Bob Skot of Liverpool. Reviews: *Globus* 95 (1909), 372; *Nature* 80 (1909), 318.

MacKenzie, P. and Carroll, J. 1986. *Early in the Month of Spring*. VWML 001. Cassette and leaflet published by the Vaughan Williams Memorial Library of the English Folk Dance and Song Society.

Maclaren, J. S. 1909. 'Drabbing the Balo', *JGLS*, n.s., 3, 95.

MacRitchie, D. 1894. *Scottish Gypsies under the Stewarts*. D. Douglas.

MacTaggart. 1824. *MacTaggart's Scottish Gallovidian Encyclopaedia*. Edinburgh.

Maher, S. 1932. *The Road to God Knows Where*: A *Memoir of a Travelling Boyhood*. Dublin. Reissued Veritas 1998.

Marsden, W. 1785. 'Observations on the language of the people commonly called Gypsies', *Archeologia*, 7, 382–6.

Marson, C. L. 1909. 'Gypsy prayers', *JGLS*, n.s., 3, 77.

Martin, G. 1965. 'East European relations of Hungarian dance types', *Europa et Hungaria*.

——1977. *Encyclopaedia of Hungarian Ethnography*, i (ed. Otutay, Gyula). Budapest.

Martin, G. and Pesovar, E. 1958. 'The accomplishments and methodological observations of the Monographic Dance Research in Szabolcs-Szatmár County', *Ethnographia*, 69, 424–36 (Budapest).

Mason, M. H. 1877. *Nursery Rhymes and Country Songs*. Metzler.

M'Cormick, A. 1906. *The Tinkler-Gypsies*. J. Maxwell & Son.

Mhic Choisdealbha, Bean E. 1924. *Traditional Songs of Galway and Mayo*. Talbot Press.

Michel, F. 1856. *Études de Philologie Comparée sur l'Argot*. Paris: Didot.

Miklosich, F. 1874. *Beiträge zur Kentniss der Zigeuner Mundarten*. Vienna: Karl Gerold's Sohn.

Milford, H. S. (ed). 1924. *Borrow: Introduction and Notes*. Clarendon Press.

Miln, L. J. 1900. *Wooings and Weddings in Many Climes*. C. A. Pearson. Ch. 28, pp.377–86, deals with marriage 'In Gypsy Land'.

Mone, F. J. (ed.). 1846. *Schauspiele des Mittelalters*. Karlsruhe.

Morris, M. 1907. *De Fidiculis*. See Saer 1983.

Morris, Richard. 1871. *Legends of the Holy Rood: Symbols of the Passion and Cross-Poems*. N. Trubner & Co. (for the Early English Text Society).

Morton, R. 1970. *Folk Songs Sung in Ulster*. Mercier Press.

Morwood, V. S. 1885. *Our Gypsies in City, Tent and Van*. Sampson Low.

Munnelly, T. 1975. 'The singing tradition of Irish Travellers', *FMJ*, 3, 1, 3–30.

Munro, A. 1977. 'Lizzie Higgins and Belle Stewart', *Traditional Music*, 6, 22.

Murray, E. C. Grenville. 1854. *Doine or the National Songs and Legends of Romania*. Smith Elder & Co.

Myers, J. 1909. 'Drab', *JGLS*, n.s., 2, 199–207.

Nicklin, J. A. 1912. 'The Tinker of Elstow: was Bunyan a Gypsy?', *Morning Leader*, 13 January.

Ní Fhlathartaigh, R. n.d. *Cláir Amhrán Bhaile na hInse*. Department of Irish Folklore, University College Dublin.

Norwood, Revd T. W. (diaries). See Grosvenor 1910.

NQ. Notes and Queries.

Ó' Baoill, D. P. 1994. 'Travellers' Cant: language or register', in *Irish Travellers –Culture and Ethnicity*. Belfast Institute of Irish Studies, 155–69.

OCCSC. 1910. *Old Christmas Carols of the Southern Counties*. J. Curwen & Sons Ltd. Six are described as 'Gypsy'.

O'Connor, P. 1971. *Walking Good: Travels with Music in Romania and Hungary*. Weidenfeld & Nicolson.

O'Duibhginn, S. 1960. *Dónall Og, Taighde ar an amhrán*. An Clóchomhar TTA.

O'Foltharta, D. (ed.). 1892. *Siamsa an Gheimhridh*. Patrick O'Brien.

O'Lochlainn, C. 1939. *Irish Street Ballads*. Dublin: Three Candles.

——1965. *More Irish Street Ballads*. Dublin.

O Muirithe, D. 1980. *The Maceronic Song*. An Clóchomhar TTA.

Opie, I. and P. (eds). 1992. *Oxford Dictionary of Nursery Rhymes*. Oxford University Press. First published 1951.

Ord, J. 1930. *The Bothy Songs and Ballads of Aberdeen, Banff and Moray, Angus and the Mearns*. Alexander Gardner.

OCM. Oxford Companion to Music.

Palmer, R. (ed.). 1974. *A Touch of the Times: Songs of Social Change 1789 to 1914*. Penguin Education.

Parker, D. C. 1913. *Aspects of Gypsy Music*. Reeve.

Parry-Williams, T. H. 1923. 'The English element in Welsh', *Cymmrodorion Record*, series X.

Paspati, A. G. 1870. *Études sur les Tchinghianés ou Bohémiens de l'Empire Ottoman*. Constantinople: A. Koroméla.

Pasquier, Étienne. 1596. *Les Recherches de la France*. Paris: J. Mettayer. See lib. iv, cap. 17.

Patterson, James. 1846–7. *The Ballads and Songs of Ayrshire*. Ayr.

Paul, Sir James (ed.). 1901–3. *Accounts of the Lord High Treasurer of Scotland*. Edinburgh.

Peel, F. 1895. *Risings of the Luddites, Chartists and Plug-drawers*. Reprinted Cass, 1968.

Percy, T. 1765. *Relics of Ancient English Poetry*. Reprinted Routledge/Thoemmes Press 1996.

Petsch, R. 1912. See Sampson 1912.

Petulengro, X. 1948. *A Romany Life*. Methuen.

Phillimore, R. 1912. See 'Songs of Luriben and Kuriben' 1912.

Phillips, J. 1932. *Rhyming Slang: A Dictionary*. London. In Bodleian Library Catalogue, the author is given as P. P.

Pott, A. F. 1844–5. *Die Zigeuner in Europa und Asien*. Halle.

Pottinger, Sir Henry, 1816. *Travels in Beloochistan and Sinde*. Longman.

Poulter, J. 1753. *Discoveries of John Poulter Alias Baxter*. 2nd edn, Sherborne.

Price, Glanville. 1984. *The Languages of Britain*. Edward Arnold.

Prideaux, W. F. 1887. 'Songs of the English Gypsies', *NQ*, 7th ser., 4, 288.

Purslow, F. 1965. *Marrow Bones*. EFDSS Publications.

——1968. *The Wanton Seed*. EFDSS Publications.

Ramsay, A. 1724. *The Tea-Table Miscellany*. Printed by Mr Thomas Ruddiman for Alan Ramsay.

Bibliography

Rees. 1805. *Rees's Cyclopaedia.* London.

Reeve, D. 1958. *Smoke in the Lane.* Constable.

——1960. *No Place Like Home.* Phoenix House.

Reeves, J. 1961. *The Everlasting Circle.* London.

——1972. *One's None: Old Rhymes for New Tongues.* Heinemann.

Ribton-Turner, C. J. 1887. *A History of Vagrants and Vagrancy.* London.

Richards, S. 1976–7. 'Songs the Gypsies saved', *The Countryman* (Winter), 23–6.

Richards, S. and Stubbs, T. 1979. *The English Folk Singer.* Collins.

Rid, S. 1612. *The Art of Jugling or Legerdemain.* Printed in London for T. B. and sold by S. Rand.

Roberts, R. 1991. *A Wandering Scholar: The Life and Opinions of Robert Roberts*, introduced by J. Burnett and H. G. Williams. Cardiff, University of Wales Press. First edn edited by J. H. Davies, 1923, as *The Life and Opinions of Robert Roberts, a Wandering Scholar, as Told by Himself.*

Roberts, S. 1836. *The Gypsies: Their Origin, Continuance and Destination, as Clearly Foretold in the Prophecies of Isaiah, Jeremiah and Ezekiel.* Longman.

Rochas, Victor de. 1876. *Les Parais de France et d'Espagne (Cagots et Bohémiens).* Paris: Hachette et Cie.

Rolland, E. 1877. *Devinettes aux Énigmes.* Paris.

Roumany Rei (Tom Taylor?). 1851. 'Gypsey experiences', *Illustrated London News*, 19 (November/December), 655–6, 715–16 and 777–9. Thought to be by Tom Taylor (see *NQ*, 6th ser. 2, 362).

Rowlands, S. 1610. *Martin Mark-all, Beadle of Bridewell; His Apologie to the Bel-man of London*: London: John Bridge and Richard Bonian. In the second part of this work, entitled *The Runnagate's Race*, there is a reference to the 'Aegyptians', their king, Giles Hather, and his queen, Kyt Calot, and to the formation of Thieves' Cant. Extracts cited ex the 'complete works', printed for the Hunterian Club, Glasgow, 1880. The reference to the Gypsies appears on pp. 57–60.

Runnagates Race. 1610. See Rowlands 1610.

Russell, A. 1914. 'Scotto-Romani and Tinklers' Cant', *JGLS*, n.s., 8, 10–80.

Saer, D. Roy (ed.). 1976. *Caneuon Llafar Gwlad 1.* St Fagans: Welsh Folk Museum.

——1983. *Famous Fiddlers* (an edited transcript of the first part of Morris 1907). Welsh Folk Museum.

Salgado, G. 1972. *Coney-Catchers and Bawdy Baskets.* Penguin English Library.

——1984. *The Elizabethan Underworld.* Alan Sutton Publishing.

Salom, Pere. 1911. *Gitanos. Llibre d'Amor i de Pietat.* Barcelona: Societat Anonima Neotipia.

Sampson, A. 1997. *The Scholar Gypsy.* John Murray.

Sampson, J. 1891. 'English Gypsy songs and rhymes', *JGLS*, o.s., 2, 80–93.

——1892. 'Romani flotsam', *JGLS*, o.s., 3, 73–81.

——1897. 'The Gypsies', *Transactions of the Warrington Literary and Philosophical Society.* Printed for the Society at the *Guardian* office.

——1901. 'The Welsh Gypsies', Lecture to the Liverpool Welsh National Society, 25 January.

——1902. *Bish ta dui giliá Chidé Aré Volshitika Romani Chib.* D. Nutt. See also MacAlister 1928.

——1908a. 'One hundred Shelta sayings (in the Ulster dialect)', *JGLS*, n.s., 1, 272–7.

——1908b. 'Anglo American Romani: a review', *JGLS*, n.s., 2, 74–84. See also Dyneley Prince 1908.

——1912. 'Welsh Gypsy riddles' (ed. Petsch), *JGLS*, n.s., 5, 241–55.

——1926. *Dialect of the Gypsies of Wales: The Older Forms of the British Romani Preserved in the Speech of the Clan of Abram Wood.* Cambridge University Press.

——1928. Intoduction to McAlister, Sir D. 1928, 3–6.

——1930. *The Wind on the Heath.* Chatto & Windus.

——1931. *Romané Giliá.* Cambridge University Press.

Sandford, J. 1995. *Songs by the Roadside.* Redlake Press.

Scharpe, Elisabeth. 1970. 'Kaksanger. En analysis av en Fangelsetradition'. Pedagogiska Institutionen, Stockholms Universitet (unpublished).

Scot, Reginald. 1584. *The Discovery of Witchcraft.* London.

Shirley, J. 1688. *The Triumph of Wit, or Ingenuity Display'd in its Perfecton.* London. 1724 edn.

Simpson, J. (ed.). 1986. *A Dictionary of Historical Slang.* Penguin. (ex *A Dictionary of Slang and Unconventional English,* Partridge, 1937. Entries limited to those items in use before 1914).

Simson, W. 1865. *A History of the Gypsies.* Sampson Low.

Skot, Bob. 1909. *Gypsy Songs.* See Macfie 1909, chapter 2.

Smart, B. C. and Crofton, H. T. 1875. *Dialect of the English Gypsies.* Asher. 1968 edn, Detroit: Gale Research.

Smith, G. 1889. *Gypsy Children, or a Stroll in Gypsydom with Songs and Stories.* Woodford Fawcett & Co.

Smith, H. 1873. *Tent Life with English Gypsies in Norway.* R. Cox & Co.

Smith, L. A. 1889. *Through Romany Songland.* Stott. Review: *Critic,* n.s., 13 (1890), 103.

Smith, Reed. 1928. *South Carolina Ballads.* Harvard University Press.

Smith, Rodney. 1903. *Gypsy Smith: His Life and Work. By Himself.* London.

'Songs of Luriben and Kuriben' 1912. *JGLS,* n.s., 6, 66–8.

Sparling, H. Halliday. 1887. *Irish Minstrelsy: A Selection of Irish Songs and Ballads, Original and Translated.* New York: Walter Scott Ltd.

Speaight, George. 1975. *Bawdy Songs of the Early Music Hall.* David & Charles.

Stanley, D. and Burke, R. 1986. *Romano Drom Song Book.* Romanestan Publications.

Strettell, A. 1887. *Spanish and Italian Folk Songs.* London.

Taylor, Tom. 1851. See Roumany Rei 1851.

Thompson, T.W. 1909. 'Anglo-Romani songs', *JGLS,* n.s., 3, 157–60.

——1910a. 'Gypsies: an account of their character, mode of life, folklore and language', *Tramp Magazine,* 2, 46–53.

——1910b. 'Borrow's Gypsies', *JGLS,* n.s., 3, 162–74.

——1912. 'Punishment of infidelity', *JGLS,* n.s., 12, 312.

——1923. 'Consorting with and counterfeiting Egyptians', *JGLS,* 3rd ser., 2, 81–93.

Thomson, D. 1977. *An Introduction to Gaelic Poetry.* Gollancz.

Thomson, W. 1725. *Orpheus Caledonius.* Edinburgh. Facsimile of 1733 edition. Hatboro, Pa., 1962.

Thrush (The). 1827. *A Choice Selection of the Most Admired Popular Songs.* London.

Thurmond, John. 1724. *Harlequin Sheppard. A Night Scene in Grotesque Characters.* London. (Song by John Harper).

Tipler, D. 1957. 'Specimens of modern Welsh Romani', *JGLS,* 3rd ser., 36, 9–24.

Topic (Records). 12T253 *Songs of the Open Road: Gypsies, Travellers and Country Singers.*

12TS304 *The Travelling Songster: An Anthology From Gypsy Singers.* Since work on this book was completed in December 1995, much of this material, together with a number of other items, has been reissued on a CD: TSCD661 *My Father's the King of the Gypsies: Music of English and Welsh Gypsies.* In particular, track 20 – Peter Ingram, as recorded by Mally and Nick Dow in the singer's home, Selbourne, 1991.

Trigg, E. B. 1975. *Gypsy Demons and Divinities: The Magical and Supernatural Practices of the Gypsies.* Sheldon.

Trudgill, P. 1984. *Language in the British Isles.* Cambridge University Press.

Udal, J. S. 1922. *Dorsetshire Folklore.* Stephen Austin.

Vekerdi, J. 1967. 'Hungarian Gypsy folk songs', *Acta Orientalia Academiae Scientiarium Hungaricae,* 20 (Budapest).

Vesey-Fitzgerald, B. S. 1944. *Gypsies of Britain.* Chapman and Hall. New enlarged edition, 1973, David & Charles.

Vig, Rudolf. 1974. 'Gypsy folk songs from the Béla Bartók and Zoltán Kodály Collection', *Studia Musicologica Academiae Scientiarum Hungaricae,* 16, 89–131 (Budapest).

Von Sowa, R. 1898. *Wörterbuch des Dialekts der deutschen Zigeuner.* F. A. Brockhaus.

VWML (Vaughan Williams Memorial Library). 1986. *Early in the Month of Spring: Songs and a Story from Irish Travellers in England.* Sponsored by the London Irish Commission for Culture and Education and published by the Vaughan Williams Memorial Library together with a cassette, VWML 001. The material was recorded in the years 1973–83 by Jim Carroll, Pat Mackenzie and Dennis Turner.

Watkins, T. Arwyn. 1962. 'Background to the Welsh Dialect Survey', *Lochlann,* 2, 38–49. See Price 1984, 94ff.

Webb, G. E. C. 1960. *Gypsies: The Secret People*. Herbert Jenkins.

Weir, J. 1912a. 'A short Tinker's vocabulary', *GFG*, 1, 20–1.

——1912b. 'A short account of the Travellers of central Northumberland', *GFG*, 1, 99–104.

Wellstood, F. C. 1909. *JGLS*, n.s., 3, 158–9.

White, C. A. 1892. 'A Gypsy carol', *NQ*, 8th ser., 2, 504–5.

White, Gilbert. 1775. *The Natural History of Selborne*. Everyman's Library edn 1976.

Williams, A. O. 1923. *Folk Songs of the Upper Thames*. London: Duckworth.

Williams, I. 1913–14. 'Y Glêr a phenillion telyn', *Transactions of the Honourable Society of Cymmrodorion*, 191–3.

Williams, Jac L. 1958. 'The national language in the social pattern in Wales', *Studies*, 47, 247–58. See Price 1984, 94ff.

Williams, S. Gwynn. 1972. *Caneuon Traddodiadol y Cymry*. Gwynn Publishing Co., Llangollen.

Wilson, G. A. 1891. '"Shelta", the Tinker's talk', *JGLS*, o.s., 2, 121–2. Collected in Tiree.

Wilson, John Mackay. 1835–6. *Historical, Traditionary and Imaginative Tales of the Borders*.

Winstedt, E. O. 1909a. 'Forms and ceremonies', *JGLS*, n.s., 2, 338–66.

——1909b. 'Petalengro and the Devil', *JGLS*, n.s., 2, 380–4.

——1911. 'An early mention of the language Romney', *JGLS*, n.s. 5, 78–9.

——1912. 'Counterfeit Egyptians', *JGLS*, n.s., 5, 237–8.

Wittich, E. 1912. 'Einige Zigeunerische Rätsel', *Schweitzerisches Arkiv für Volkskunde*, Jahrgang 16, 55–6 (Basle).

WJEC. 1961. Welsh Joint Education Committee. Welsh Language and Culture Sub-Committee minutes, 10 November, section 5. Language Enquiry. See Price 1984, 111.

Wlislocki, H. von. 1880. *Haideblüten. Volkslieder der Transsilvanischen Zigeuner. Inedita, originaltexte und verdeutschungen*. Wilhelm Friedrich. Forty songs without music, of which fifteen were 'Englished' by W. E. A. Axon in *JGLS*, o.s., 2 (1891), 5–6.

——1889. 'Totenklagen in der Volksdichtung der Siebenbürgischen und Südungarischen Zeltzigeuner', *Magazin für die Literatur des in- und Auslandes*, 2, 161–2 (Dresden). See Herrmann 1889.

——1890a. *Volksdichtungen der Siebenbürgischen und Südungarischen Zigeuner*. Vienna: C. Graeser.

——1890b. *Vom Wandernden Zigeunervolke*. Hamburg.

——1891. *Volksglaube und Religiöser Brauch der Zigeuner*. Münster.

Wood, M. F. 1973. *In the Life of a Romani Gypsy*. Routledge.

Woodcock, H. 1865. *The Gypsies*. William Lister.

Wright, J. (ed.). 1896–1905. *English Dialect Dictionary*. Oxford.

Yates, D. 1911. 'I Merimásko Ceriklo', *JGLS*, n.s., 4, 301–2.

Yates, M. 1975a. 'English Gypsy songs', *FMJ*, 3, 1, 63–80.

——1975b. 'Some Gypsy singers in south east England', *English Dance and Song*, 37, 1 (Spring), 14–15.

——1975c. 'Songs of the open road'. Leaflet accompanying Topic 12T253.

——1976. 'By an Other Name (the Gypsy singer known as Sharper's Joe)', *Folk Review*, 5, 7 (May), 14–15.

——1977. 'Gypsy singers and musicians', *Traditional Music*, 6, 13–15.

Yule, H. and Burnell, A. C. 1886. *Hobson-Jobson: The Anglo-Indian Dictionary*. Reissued by Wordsworth Reference Ltd, 1996.

Subscribers to this volume

The following have kindly associated themselves with the publication of this volume through subscription:

Jane Aaron, Pontypridd
T. A. Acton, London
Anders Ahlqvist, Helsingfors, Finland
Dr Gertrude Aub-Buscher, Hull
Gwenllian Awbery, Caerdydd
David Russell Barnes, Caerdydd
Deirdre Beddoe and Christine V. Lee, Penarth
Mr and Mrs S. Bednarczyk, Rugby
Dennis Binns, Castle Douglas
Anna Brychan, Caerdydd
Nicki Bullinga
Mary Burdett-Jones, Aberystwyth
T. M. Charles-Edwards, Oxford
Gertrude and Joseph Clancy, Aberystwyth
Mary-Ann Constantine, Aberystwyth
Betty Coughlan, Cardigan
C. S. Coughlan, Newbury
Nikolas Coupland, Cardiff
Cynog a Llinos Dafis, Llandysul
Ceri Davies, Abertawe
Gareth Alban Davies a Carys Davies, Aberystwyth
Glyn Davies, Pontyclun
Janet Davies, Caerdydd
Gwilym Prys Davies, Pontypridd
John Drew, Cambridge
Owen Dudley Edwards, Edinburgh
Bob English, Llanarmon-yn-Iâl
Lyn J. Evans, Caerdydd
Meredydd a Phyllis Evans, Aberystwyth
Neil Evans, Harlech
Sir Angus Fraser, Richmond
Jane Freeland, Southampton
P. Geraghty, London
Jon Gower, Caerdydd

Subscribers to this volume

Rhidian Griffiths, Aberystwyth
Geraint a Luned Gruffydd, Aberystwyth
Eleri a Robin Gwyndaf, Caerdydd
Ian Hancock, Buda, Texas
Marged Haycock, Aberystwyth
Michael Holroyd, London
David Howell, Swansea
Belinda Humfrey, Desborough
Emyr Humphreys, Llanfair Pwllgwyngyll
Daniel Huws, Aberystwyth
Rhiannon Ifans, Aberystwyth
Arthur Ivatts, Oldham
Eldra Jarman,† Cardiff
T. C. Jenkin, London
Dafydd Jenkins, Aberystwyth
Erick Johnson, Killeshandra, Co. Cavan
Allan Wynne Jones, Machynlleth
Huw Ceiriog Jones, Bow Street
Ieuan Gwynedd Jones, Aberystwyth
Lloyd a Casi Jones, Caerfyrddin
Donald Kenrick, London
Stephen Knight, Cardiff
Ginny Lapage, Bodmin
Ceridwen Lloyd-Morgan, Llanafan
Marion Löffler, Aberystwyth
Peter Lord and Lorena Schultz Lord, Aberystwyth
Gerald Morgan, Aberystwyth
Jan Morris, Llanystumdwy
Yr Esgob Daniel J. Mullins, Abertawe
Siân Newman, London
Mícheál Ó Flaithearta, Uppsala, Sweden
M. E. Owen, Llanfarian
Trefor M. Owen, Bangor
Brynach Parri, Aberhonddu
Iain Paterson, Penrith
Gerald Porter, Vaasa, Finland
Glanville Price, Aberystwyth
Delyth Prys, Bangor
John Rea, Caerdydd
Margaret ac Ioan Bowen Rees,† Llanllechid
Gwyneth Tyson Roberts, Aberystwyth
Anthony Sampson, London
Peter Syme, Edinburgh